Encyclopedia of
Major League Baseball Clubs

ENCYCLOPEDIA OF

Major League Baseball Clubs

VOLUME I | THE NATIONAL LEAGUE

Edited by Steven A. Riess

Greenwood Press
Westport, Connecticut • London

Library of Congress Cataloging-in-Publication Data

Encyclopedia of Major League Baseball clubs / edited by Steven A. Riess.
    p. cm.
  Includes bibliographical references and index.
  ISBN 0–313–32991–5 (set : alk. paper) – ISBN 0–313–32992–3 (v. I : alk. paper).
– ISBN 0–313–32993–1 (v. II : alk. paper).
    1. Baseball teams—United States—History—Encyclopedias. 2. Major League
Baseball (Organization)—History—Encyclopedias. I. Riess, Steven A.
GV875.A1E52   2006
796.357'640973—dc22   2006015368

British Library Cataloguing in Publication Data is available.

Library of Congress Catalog Card Number: 2006015368
ISBN: 0–313–32991–5 (set)
      0–313–32992–3 (vol. I)
      0–313–32993–1 (vol. II)

First published in 2006

Greenwood Press, 88 Post Road West, Westport, CT 06881
An imprint of Greenwood Publishing Group, Inc.
www.greenwood.com

Printed in the United States of America

The paper used in this book complies with the
Permanent Paper Standard issued by the
National Information Standards Organization (Z39.48–1984).

10 9 8 7 6 5 4 3 2 1

Contents

Introduction: A Brief History of Major League Baseball Teams ix
   Steven A. Riess

THE NATIONAL LEAGUE, VOLUME I

1. **Arizona Diamondbacks** 3
   Laura A. Purcell and John H. Jordan

2. **Atlanta Braves** 13
   David Stevens

3. **Chicago Cubs** 55
   John E. Findling

4. **Cincinnati Reds** 99
   Edward J. Rielly

5. **Colorado Rockies** 143
   Thomas L. Altherr

6. **Florida Marlins** 153
   Kevin B. Witherspoon

7. **Houston Astros** 163
   Benjamin D. Lisle

8. Los Angeles Dodgers   181
    Steven P. Gietschier

9. Milwaukee Brewers   225
    John McCarthy and Christopher Miller

10. New York Mets   239
    Maureen Smith

11. Philadelphia Phillies   257
    John P. Rossi

12. Pittsburgh Pirates   299
    Richard Peterson

13. San Diego Padres   339
    Sarah Trembanis

14. San Francisco Giants   355
    Andrew Goldblatt

15. St. Louis Cardinals   401
    Jon David Cash

16. Washington Nationals   447
    Michel Vigneault

THE AMERICAN LEAGUE, VOLUME II

17. Baltimore Orioles   465
    William A. Borst

18. Boston Red Sox   499
    Robert K. Barney and David E. Barney

19. Chicago White Sox   535
    Richard C. Lindberg

20. Cleveland Indians   571
    Philip C. Suchma

21. Detroit Tigers   605
    Steven A. Riess

22. Kansas City Royals   639
    Myles Schrag

23. Los Angeles Angels of Anaheim   655
    Joel S. Franks

24. Minnesota Twins   671
     Kristin M. Anderson and Christopher W. Kimball

25. New York Yankees   705
     Steven A. Riess

26. Oakland Athletics   757
     Robert F. Lewis II

27. Seattle Mariners   801
     Adam R. Hornbuckle

28. Tampa Bay Devil Rays   815
     Paul M. Pedersen

29. Texas Rangers   825
     Jarrod Schenewark

30. Toronto Blue Jays   843
     Russell Field

Appendix A: National League Season Standings, 1876–2005   861

Appendix B: American League Season Standings, 1901–2005   891

Appendix C: National League Team Total Attendance,
            2005–1890   915

Appendix D: National League Team Daily Average Attendance,
            2005–1890   923

Appendix E: National League Team Attendance Rankings,
            2005–1890   931

Appendix F: American League Team Total Attendance,
            2005–1901   939

Appendix G: American League Team Average Daily Attendance,
            2005–1901   947

Appendix H: American League Team Attendance Rankings,
            2005–1901   955

Appendix I: National League Team Consolidated Profit and
            Loss, 1920–56 (Dollars)   963

Appendix J: National League Team Dividends, 1920–56
            (Dollars)   965

Appendix K: American League Team Consolidated Profit and
            Loss, 1920–56 (Dollars)   967

Appendix L: American League Team Dividends, 1920–56
    (Dollars)   969

Appendix M: Major League Baseball Team Salaries, Selected
    Years   971

Appendix N: Estimated MLB Revenues/Income, Franchise
    Values (in Millions), and Salaries, 1990–2004   975

Appendix O: Major League Team Payrolls, 1987–1989,
    2005–2006   999

Appendix P: Major League Ballparks, 2006   1005

Appendix Q: Major League Ballparks used by Current Teams,
    with Name Changes   1009

Bibliography   1015

Index   1037

About the Editor and Contributors   1061

Introduction: A Brief History of Major League Baseball Teams

Steven A. Riess

The cornerstone of Major League Baseball has been the leagues and their teams. The majors are comprised of the National League, which dates back to 1876, and the American League, which became a major operation in 1901. The NL was itself predated by the National Association of Professional Base Ball Players (1871–75), which was arguably the first major league. The NL itself operated in conjunction with the American Association, a major league from 1882 to 1891, and was rivaled by the short-lived Union Association in 1884 and the Players' League in 1890. Since then the only other league to proclaim itself a major league was the Federal League (1914–15), which at its death merged into the established big leagues.

The major leagues currently have 30 members, some of which date back over 125 years to the start of the NL, while Arizona and Tampa Bay just began in 1998. The NL now consists of 16 teams; the AL consists of 14. They are part of the most stable professional sports league in perhaps the entire world. No franchise has gone out of business for over 100 years, and between 1903 and 1952, no franchise even moved from one city to another.

Baseball became the national pastime in the 1850s, and has long been the preeminent team sport in North America. However, the first team sports in the United States and Canada were Native American contests like lacrosse and shinny. The initial Euro-American team sport was cricket, brought to the colonies by the English before the Revolutionary War. It became very popular by the 1840s when a cricket fad emerged in the Northeast among English immigrants and middle-class Americans. By 1860 there were some 400 cricket clubs and 10,000 players.

Cricket was quickly surpassed by the new game of baseball, which had simpler rules, was easier to play, had more dramatic shifts between offense and defense, and required less time to complete. Baseball evolved from such English games as rounders and old cat and surpassed in popularity other ball games, most notably the Massachusetts Game, which had less offense and might take an entire day to play. The rules of baseball were established by Alexander Joy Cartwright of the New York Knickerbockers, a club of athletic white-collar workers who played intraclub games at the Elysian Fields in Hoboken in 1845. Their rules called for a diamond-shaped playing field with bases at each corner, 90 feet apart. Three infielders, except the "short" fielder, stationed themselves by a base. The pitcher, or "feeder," threw underhand from 45 feet, with a running start. There were no balls or strikes, so hitters ("strikers") waited until they got a pitch they liked. Batters were put out by striking at the ball three times without touching it, by being forced out at first base, or by having their batted ball caught on the fly or on the first bounce. Catchers positioned themselves a few feet behind the striker to catch foul tips, which put the batter out. Runners could be put out by being forced out or tagged with the ball when off a base. Teams played an equal number of innings, with the first team achieving 21 aces (runs) the winner. There was a single umpire, often dressed in a top hat and tails. He sat at a table by third base, and rarely interfered with a game unless there was a controversy. The Knickerbockers originally played intraclub games, but in 1846 lost to the New York Club, 23–1. This was their only game against an outside opponent until 1851. Very little is known about their opponent, although an item in the press a year before reported a ball game played in Brooklyn between the New York Club and a Brooklyn squad.

In the mid-1850s the sport gained a lot of popularity, mainly in metropolitan New York, where there were 10 clubs, 3 in New York and 7 in Brooklyn. In 1857 delegates from early New York–area clubs formed the first baseball league, the National Association of Base Ball Players (NABBP) to make up the rules (including limiting games to nine innings), regulate competition, and maintain the fraternal nature of the amateur sport. The game's popularity was promoted by journalists in the daily press and the sporting weeklies like the *Spirit of the Times* and the *Clipper,* and by such events as the 1858 All-Star Game between New York and Brooklyn players and the 1860 tours by the Brooklyn Excelsiors, who played in upstate New York, Philadelphia, and Baltimore. One year later, when the Civil War began, there were at least 200 junior and senior teams in Greater New York. Their members and members of clubs in cities as far west as Chicago and south as Baltimore became known as the ball-playing fraternity. The clubs were social organizations mainly of young white-collar workers like small shopkeepers, clerks, and college students, but were also organized by residents of particular neighborhoods, workers in a particular craft (especially butchers, firemen, printers, and shipwrights), and African American organizations. Players were typically single men living in boardinghouses, looking for a chance to socialize and display physical prowess. They used their participation and the wearing of uniforms that designated them as ballplayers to gain a sense of self-satisfaction and accomplishment that was missing from their increasingly routinized labor. In 1864 the game became manlier when the rules required a fly ball to be caught to register a putout.

The growing seriousness of play was reflected by the establishment of a championship system, which required the challenger to defeat the prior champion in a two-out-of-three series in the same year, involving riotous behavior among spectators and the recruiting of players. In 1860 James Creighton was engaged to pitch for the Brooklyn Excelsiors, a middle-class WASP squad, for some compensation, making him the first professional ballplayer. Their fiercest rivalry was with the Brooklyn Atlantics, comprised of working-class Irishmen. They played each other for the championship in 1860. In the third and deciding game, attended by over 15,000 spectators, several unpopular decisions by the umpire led to a riot by the Atlantics' Irish Catholic fans, and the game was halted. The two teams never played again. In 1862, William Cammeyer built an enclosure around his skating rink at a cost of $12,000. He made it available for free to the Brooklyn Atlantics and began charging for admission. This was a major step toward the commercialization and even greater competitiveness. The Civil War hindered play in New York because so many young men went off to war, but did help spread the game in military camps.

After the Civil War, several clubs, like the New York Mutuals and Brooklyn's Eckfords and Atlantics, employed various inducements, including government sinecures, to recruit top men. By 1868, about 13 clubs were covertly professional even though that was barred by the NABBP. Then in 1869, the Cincinnati Red Stockings became the first overtly professional team, with players signed to contracts that ranged from $600 to $1,400 a season. The team, which went 57–0–1, was financed by subscriptions from 350 local businessmen led by attorney Aaron B. Champion, who sought to bolster the Queen City's national reputation. The Red Stockings' success encouraged leaders in other midwestern cities like Chicago to finance professional teams for the same reason. The Chicago White Stockings were established in 1870 as a $20,000 corporation by such boosters as hotelier Potter Palmer and *Tribune* publisher Joseph Medill.

THE NATIONAL ASSOCIATION

In 1871 10 professional teams that were either joint stock companies or cooperatives organized by players themselves formed the National Association of Professional Baseball Players (NA), the first professional league. The association was neither based on sound business principles nor controlled by the players as its title suggested. The NA lasted five years and went through 25 teams. Only the Red Stockings, Mutuals, and Philadelphia Athletics played all five years. In 1875, Boston won its fourth straight pennant with a record of 71–8 and made a profit of $3,261 from gross receipts of $38,000. Manager Harry Wright did a great job recruiting players, promoting teamwork and scientific play on the field, and taking care of nearly all the business details. NA teams had many problems, especially the unequal competition, which hurt fan interest. Membership cost only $10, which enabled insufficiently financed teams to join the league. Players jumped from one team to another during the season (revolving). Salaries averaged $1,300 to $1,600, which was too high to make much profit, and teams dropped out midyear if they were losing money. The league was poorly administered, with no control of schedules. Furthermore, there were rumors of fixes.

THE NATIONAL LEAGUE

In 1876 the National League of Professional Base Ball Clubs was formed to supplant the NA. The association was, as its name suggested, a business-oriented venture. The main mover was Chicago businessman William Hulbert, president of the White Stockings, who had previously signed up several star NA players for the forthcoming season. The NL had franchises in Boston, Chicago, Cincinnati, Hartford, Louisville, New York, Philadelphia, and St. Louis owned by small merchants and politicians. The league required a minimum of 75,000 residents to keep out cities with insufficient population bases. Teams were given a territorial monopoly in their city. Visiting teams received 50 percent of the 50-cent base admission to offset hometown population disparities and promote competition. The league banned Sunday games, liquor, and gambling to keep out the riffraff and encourage middle-class audiences. Despite the best-laid plans, the league struggled at first. In 1876, only the champion Chicago squad made money, and the Philadelphia Athletics and New York Mutuals were expelled for not completing their final road trip. Then in 1877 four Louisville Grays were discovered to have fixed games and were banned for life. By 1880, the NL had been through 16 teams. Some left because of financial losses and others were expelled for selling liquor and playing on Sundays.

The NL did not monopolize top-flight baseball in the late 1870s. There were many strong independent clubs, who in 1877 established the loosely linked International Association. In 1879 the NL filled its vacancies with Syracuse and Troy, two of the stronger IA clubs, and in 1880 added Worcester, even though those cities did not have 75,000 residents.

A key early problem for the teams was how to keep down salaries, which comprised nearly two-thirds of their expenses. In 1879 management placed a reserve clause into players' contracts that bound them to their club in perpetuity, although players could be sold, traded, or expelled for violating team rules. The NL started with five reserved men, but by 1883 it was reserving nearly all its players, which caused salaries in the early 1880s to drop by 20 percent.

By 1882 the NL had gained enough success or the promise of a bright future to encourage the establishment of a new rival league, the American Association. Popularly known as the Beer and Whiskey League because of its owners' prior businesses, the AA sought a working-class audience in the prosperous

1880s by selling beer, playing on Sunday, and charging just 25 cents for tickets. The new league included teams from St. Louis and Cincinnati, which had both been pushed out of the NL because of the drinking issue and Sunday baseball, plus Pittsburgh, Philadelphia, Louisville, and Baltimore. These six cities had a larger population base than the eight-team NL. After one season of bitter competition, the rival leagues agreed to recognize each other, honor the contracts of reserved players, and establish exclusive territorial rights. They cooperated in 1884 to repel the threat of a rival league, the Union Association. The NL and AA teams played exhibition games after the regular season in 1883, and the pennant winners played an exhibition series after the 1884 season titled "the United States Championship." One year later Chicago (NL) played St. Louis (AA) for "the Championship of America." In 1886 those teams played for "the world's championship," with the winning St. Louis team taking all the gate receipts. The series was repeated through 1889.

Owners made good profits in the 1880s, when average attendance ranged from 2,500 to 3,500. The valuable Chicago White Stockings reported very substantial earnings, and by 1887, had reportedly accumulated a surplus of about $100,000. One year later, the team made $60,000. Even more lucrative were the New York Giants, whose profits from 1885 through 1887 supposedly averaged over $100,000. Teams tried to sustain their prosperity by creating a $2,500 maximum-salary classification system in 1888, but it was not fully adhered to. Owners also sought to control the social behavior of players on and off the field. Albert G. Spalding of the White Stockings fined dissipated players for diminishing their skills, and hired detectives to watch the most recalcitrant, like Mike "King" Kelly, who along with his outfield mates were all traded because of their drinking escapades.

THE PLAYERS' LEAGUE

The players fought back in 1885 with the Brotherhood of Professional Base Ball Players, professional sports' first union. Then, four years later, the union's leaders organized their own major league, the Players' League, with the financial backing of politicians, streetcar magnates, and other businessmen who were similar in background to owners of the AA and NL squads. Seven of the eight teams were placed in NL cities. The PL dropped the reserve clause and the blacklist, and appealed to middle-class fans by barring Sunday games and beer sales; the basic admission was 50 cents. Any profits over $10,000 were to be divided with the players.

The PL was a huge threat to the NL and AA, and received the support of sporting weeklies. It put an excellent product on the field, signing many major leaguers, including most of the stars, and helped push up salaries for players who did not jump to the league. The PL outdrew the NL, but only the Boston Reds, with Mike "King" Kelly, made a profit. All of the leagues lost heavily in 1890. The once profitable New York Giants nearly went bankrupt and Spalding's team suffered a $65,000 loss. The NL fought back vigorously, killing the PL by co-opting the "contributors" or financial angels of the PL franchises, allowing them to buy into NL teams.

THE CONSOLIDATED NATIONAL LEAGUE

The PL war did not lead to baseball peace. Conflict over the reentry of certain players back to the Philadelphia AA team resulted in a new association war with the NL that continued the upward spiral of salaries. The outcome was the National Agreement of 1892, in which the AA closed down and four of its teams joined the NL, now a 12-team league. The AA had had its ups and downs, and 19 different teams had played in the league. Rosters were cut from 15 to 12 and salaries were cut 30–40 percent in 1892, and further sliced in 1893. A new unofficial $2,400 salary maximum was set and strictly enforced.

Team strength in the late nineteenth century was very unbalanced. The White Stockings, with their roster of stars, dominated in the 1880s, winning five NL pennants (1880–82, 1885–86), while the St. Louis Browns won four straight AA titles (1885–88) and fared well in postseason matches with the NL. In the 1890s the most successful teams were the innovative Boston and Baltimore clubs, which won 8 of 10 pennants, emphasizing "inside baseball." The Baltimore Orioles were especially renowned for such tactics as "the Baltimore chop," daring baserunning, intimidation of opposing players, unsportsmanlike play (tripping and blocking base runners), rowdy behavior, and confronting umpires.

The unbalanced 12-team NL failed to maximize fan interest, and attendance dropped to an average range of 2,000 to 3,000. Mediocre squads in the largest cities, New York, Philadelphia, and Chicago, consistently finished out of the money, while Louisville and St. Louis finished in last place for five of eight years. The sorriest situation was in Cleveland, whose Spiders went 20–134 in 1899. They drew under 200 fans at home, and spent the last two months on the road as the "Exiles" or "Misfits." The team's poor showing was the result of syndicate ownership whereby one magnate controlled two different teams. Stanley Robison traded his best players to his brother's St. Louis club, which was a better draw. Syndicate ball also resulted in Louisville's best players being shunted to Pittsburgh, and Baltimore sending its stars to the Brooklyn Trolley Dodgers, which helped them take the pennant in 1899 and 1900. In 1900 the NL dropped Cleveland, Baltimore, Louisville—all weakened by syndicate ball—and Washington, returning to an eight-team league, further limiting the number of jobs in the major leagues.

Teams then played at flimsily constructed wooden ballparks that were fire hazards. In 1894 alone four burned down. Fields were in accessible locations in safe neighborhoods, near good mass transit, where land costs were not too high. Parks were almost never in the central business districts, but rather in outlying middle-class neighborhoods. Teams were sensitive to rising rents and declining neighborhoods, and often moved. The White Stockings played at six different sites between 1870 and 1894.

The NL teams lost money in 1892 but made money the next three years by holding the salary line. In 1894, despite the Depression, eleven of twelve teams were profitable, ranging from $5,000 to $40,000. However, business declined in the late 1890s because of the long-term effects of the Depression, a lack of competitiveness among the twelve teams, a weak franchise in New York, and fan disgust at syndicate ball.[1]

THE RISE OF THE AMERICAN LEAGUE

A new era in major-league baseball occurred with the emergence of the American League as a major league in 1901. It was the vision of former journalist and Western League president Byron Bancroft "Ban" Johnson, who saw that professional baseball had a lot of profit-making potential. Johnson reorganized the old Western League into the American League in 1900, moving into locations that the NL had vacated (Cleveland, Baltimore, and Washington), and shifting the St. Paul franchise, owned by Charles Comiskey, to his hometown of Chicago. The new league was heavily funded by coal merchant Charles A. Somers, who helped finance teams in Cleveland, Chicago, Philadelphia, and Boston. In 1901 the AL tried to secure major-league status by raiding the senior circuit, offering higher salaries that attracted at least 74 NL players to the new league. This infusion of stars helped the AL surpass the NL in attendance in 1902. The final part of the puzzle lay in securing a New York franchise, made possible in 1903 because of the political clout of the local franchise's owners.

The leagues came to an understanding in the National Agreement of 1903, which ratified the AL's major-league status. The leagues recognized each other's reserve clauses, established a three-man National Commission to run organized baseball, and set up a minor-league draft system. The season ended with a best-of-nine competition between each league's champion, known as the World Series.

Major-league teams then were owned by small businessmen and a number of former baseball players, all of whom were politicians or closely connected to professional politicians. They found the game a very profitable venture, with growing audiences that rose from about 3,400 in 1901 to 6,133 by 1910. Teams were proud of their fans like "Nuf Said" McGreevey and the Boston Royal Rooters, or the Irish who sat at the Kerry Patch in St. Louis. As the noted *Independent* pointed out in 1913: "The profits of baseball investment have proven so dazzling in the last ten years that many prominent businessmen, politicians, and capitalists have gone into the business with every promise of success."[2] The Cleveland Indians, originally purchased for $10,000, were worth $100,000 by then, which was below the league average. The team made an average of $55,000 a year from 1904 to 1912, while the Tigers made an $80,000 profit from 1907 to 1911 and $48,000 a year from 1914 to 1918. The Cubs were probably the most profitable, making $1.2 million between 1906 and 1915. Furthermore, each team president made a salary of about $25,000.

Owners presented themselves to their communities as public-spirited citizens who supported baseball because of their interest in their hometowns, but they were cold-blooded businessmen. They used their political connections to secure inside information and preferential treatment from the municipality to help them run their operation as efficiently as possible. Their political connections helped them secure Sunday baseball and police protection, minimize license fees and undue municipal interference, hinder rivals like the Federal League, and even suppress bad publicity and damaging evidence, as in the Black Sox scandal.

The most important single problem owners faced after the rise of the AL was the construction of modern ballparks that enabled them to increase seating capacity, raise ticket prices, fulfill new building codes that stressed safety, and cope with competition from other amusements like the glamorous new amusement parks and luxurious downtown vaudeville theaters. The owners no longer moved from one wooden structure to another, but built expensive and permanent fire-resistant ballparks. The necessary technology, employing steel and reinforced concrete, had previously been available, but owners did not want to commit to expensive structures until the costs of construction had declined and there was a sufficient demand by fans. They relied on their political connections to get them inside information about the best potential sites, which they either rented with very long-term leases or purchased outright. The first fully modern ballpark was Philadelphia's 23,000-seat, $300,000 Shibe Park, built in a French Renaissance style, and the $1 million (for land and construction) Forbes Field in Pittsburgh, which seated 25,000 fans. By 1915 every major-league city had a new modern ballpark, often with its own unique architecture and interior dimensions, and the older grounds were remodeled with fire-resistant material.

Certain teams dominated the dead-ball era on the field and at the box office. Between 1901 and 1910 the Pirates and Cubs each won four pennants. The Giants took two in that decade and four more in the 1910s. The Giants also dominated at the box office, drawing about 20 percent of NL attendance in the early 1900s, more than triple that of the lowly Boston Braves. The AL was more competitive in the early 1900s, when no teams won more than the Tigers (three). Then between 1910 and 1914 Connie Mack's A's won four pennants, and the Red Sox, who had won twice in the early 1900s, won four between 1911 and 1918. Three teams won no pennants at all before 1920, including the Washington Senators, who only drew about seven percent of AL attendance. The Chicago White Sox led with 17.6 percent, which reflected the quality of its play, Sunday ball, and the largest section of 25-cent seats in the major leagues.

Teams in the dead-ball era had a lot of individual identity, usually reflecting a dominant player like Ty Cobb of the Tigers or Walter Johnson of the Senators, but also powerful managers or owners like Connie Mack of the Athletics,

John McGraw of the Giants, and Charles Comiskey of the White Sox. Some of the clubs' identities reflected their play on the field, such as "the Hitless Wonders," the world champion Sox of 1906, or Mack's "$100,000 infield" of the early 1910s, or the large number of college men on certain teams like the Athletics and Giants. Teams either maintained traditional nicknames like Dodgers or Giants or developed modern nicknames, usually reflecting an aspect of the team's identity, like the Boston Braves (named for a Tammany Hall owner), the Chicago Cubs (for the team's youth), or the Washington Senators (for Capitol Hill).

TEAMS IN THE INTERWAR ERA

In the golden age of baseball during the 1920s, teams' average annual profit margin was 18.3 percent on annual gross incomes exceeding $10 million. The typical team drew 7,531 spectators per game, drawn by the new style of play that emphasized power hitting over pitching. The majors had averaged from 1909 through 1918 a .254 batting average, 7.9 runs per game, and 198 home runs per season. Then in 1920 the AL improved to a .283 batting average, 9.5 runs per game, and 370 home runs for the season. Much of the change was due to Babe Ruth, who hit 54 home runs in 1920, more than any team in the AL, and became an instant role model. The popularity of the slugging game was supported by changes in pitching rules that banned many of the deceptive pitches. Hence, from 1922 to 1941, the majors averaged a .280 batting average, nearly 9.5 runs per game, and over 600 home runs per season.

The era was marked by the rise of the New York Yankees, whose owner, Jacob Ruppert Jr., was willing to spend heavily to buy top players from Harry Frazee of the Boston Red Sox. The Yankees won six pennants in the 1920s, while their crosstown rivals, the Giants, won four (1921–24). A second dynasty in the making was the St. Louis Cardinals (nine pennants between 1926 and 1946), and briefly the Philadelphia Athletics, who won three straight championships (1929–31) with one of the greatest teams of all time, including four Hall of Famers. Other strong teams in the 1930s included the Cubs, who won four pennants from 1929 to 1938; the Giants, who won three; and the Cardinals, who also won three.

The Yankees were the most profitable major league team in the 1920s, earning $3,272,214, and the most profitable NL team were the Pittsburgh Pirates, a small market team who drew who made $2,308,148 and distributed $708,700 in dividends. They were a good draw and won the 1925 World Series and the 1927 pennant. However, over the long haul, the Cardinals were the most successful small city in the majors because of Branch Rickey's acumen in scouting players, and creation of the lucrative farm system. Teams had previously owned or had affiliations with minor-league clubs, who did most of the scouting and recruiting of young ballplayers. In the 1920s, however, the high minor leagues were outside the baseball draft, and held onto their prize players until they got top dollar. Rickey decided to build a system of minor-league clubs to develop talent. The Cardinals only controlled 5 clubs in 1929, but by 1936 controlled 28, and scouted the country nationally looking for prospects. The Cardinals brought up the best and sold the rest off. Their system became a model that was soon widely emulated, especially by the Yankees, whose great dynasty won four straight World Series (1936–39) and was stocked by several players from their own farm system. According to baseball historian Benjamin Rader, "The Yankees became the quintessential representatives of the big city, of urban America with its sophistication, cosmopolitanism, and ethnic and religious heterogeneity, whereas the Cardinals were the quintessential representatives of the small towns and the farms of rural American with its simplicity, rusticity, and old stock Protestant homogeneity. Even the clean, understated elegance of the pinstriped Yankee uniforms contrasted sharply with the images of the dust-covered, baggy uniforms of the Cardinals' Gas House Gang."[3]

When the Depression started, Major League Baseball was doing very well, and in 1930 set a record profit of $2,318,847. At a time when millions of people were losing their jobs, entertainment was one of the last things they gave up so they could have a momentary relief from the bad times. Owners struggled to make ends meet during the depression, when attendance averaged only 6,578. Major-league attendance dropped from 10.2 million in 1930 to 6.1 million by 1933. Gate receipts fell from $17 million in 1929 to $10.8 million in 1933. Average salaries declined to $4,500 from over $5,300 in 1929. The American League began losing money in 1931, and the National League in 1932. The game did not regain its profitability until 1935. Low attendance, abetted by no Sunday baseball, caused Connie Mack to sell off his stars. Management was slow to innovate and adjust to the conditions. The first All-Star Game was held in 1933, and two years later the Cincinnati Reds introduced night games to appeal to working-class fans. By the end of the decade, all the parks but Wrigley Field were equipped with artificial lighting, but each host team was limited to seven night games. Teams also began to charge radio stations for broadcasting games, which had started as a free service in the early 1920s. Teams were worried that broadcasts hurt attendance, but in 1934, when the Cardinals halted them, attendance still went down. New York's three teams barred local radio broadcasts from 1934 until 1939. By then the profit potential of charging stations became more apparent, and the New Yorkers lifted their ban, each securing $100,000 contracts for radio rights

BASEBALL DURING WORLD WAR II

During World War II, the major leagues struggled to survive, as millions of baseball fans went overseas to serve their country, joined over time by hundreds of major league ballplayers. Only 40 percent of starters in April 1941 were still starting three years later. Organized baseball was worried that the government would curtail the national pastime, as it did in World War I, but

President Franklin Roosevelt believed that would hurt morale and did not interfere with the game. Teams did cut costs by holding spring training near their home. Attendance declined from a record 5,4 million in 1940 to 3.7 million in 1943, the first season since 1934 that the major leagues did not make money. Their teams had to rely on players who were too old, too young, or physically unfit for the draft. Performance levels declined to the point that in 1944, AL batting champion George "Stuffy Stirnweiss hit only .309, and homer leader Nick Ettan had just 22 homers. Cubs owner P.K. Wrigley was so concerned about the state of baseball that he organized the All American Girls' Professional Baseball League to sustain interest. Nonetheless, interest in the game remained strong, and there were limited entertainment options on the home front. Attendance revived in 1944 to a record 4.8 million and rose to nearly 5.6 million in 1945.

BASEBALL AFTER WORLD WAR II

Professional baseball was extremely popular after World War II. Profits in 1946 rose from $1.2 million the year before to nearly $4.9 million, and were replicated the next season. Major-league attendance doubled to an average of 16,027, and the minor leagues had their greatest boom ever, with 52 different leagues. With the business flourishing, the next great challenge after the war was the integration of baseball. Virtually all owners opposed it for fear of fomenting racial antagonisms among players and spectators, and because they did not want to lose revenue from renting their parks to local Negro League clubs. The Brooklyn Dodgers alone challenged the status quo. President Branch Rickey had a long history of thinking outside the box. Rickey was motivated by a desire to do the right thing and make a place for himself in history, but he also wanted to build up the Dodgers' roster with quality players available for little or no expenditure, and expected black players would make the turnstiles click. Baseball's Great Experiment did not go smoothly, and several racist teams vigorously challenged Jackie Robinson in 1947, with no success. Eleven weeks into the season Cleveland Indians' maverick owner Bill Veeck hired Larry Doby, the first African American in the AL. However, the pace of integration was very slow, and as late as 1953, only six teams had black players, despite their domination of such NL honors as Rookie of the Year and Most Valuable Player. The pace of integration was especially slow in the AL, which in the 1950s often had less than half as many blacks as the New York Giants alone. The last team to integrate was the Red Sox, who signed Pumpsie Green in 1959.

A second great challenge was the relocation of franchises, beginning with teams that were the least popular in two-team cities. This was connected to a decline in the baseball business in 1950, when MLB made just $689,000 compared to $3.3 million the year before. By 1952, ten of the sixteen teams were losing money. Baseball was having a hard time competing with other leisure options, and was surpassed in attendance by horse racing. The game was losing spectators to television, which at the same time, was a growing source of income for teams in big media markets that sought to maximize profits.

The long-term stability of the major leagues ended in 1953 when the Boston Braves, a struggling club that was the second-most-popular team in its city, moved to Milwaukee, abetted by local boosters who wanted to use baseball to promote their city and build up the local economy. The move was supported by the county government, which increased the capacity of County Stadium and leased it to the Braves for a nominal sum. The venture was an enormous short-term success at the box office and on the field, encouraging other teams to copy the Braves, who led the major leagues in profits for three of the next four years. In 1954 the hapless St. Louis Browns moved to Baltimore, where they played at publicly owned Memorial Stadium, and in 1955 the cellar-dwelling Philadelphia Athletics moved to Kansas City to play at Municipal Stadium. Then in 1958 the Dodgers and Giants left New York City for the West Coast. The Dodgers had failed to get New York City to support the team's quest for a larger, more accessible ballpark site, but Los Angeles was champing at the bit. Walter O'Malley traded the local Wrigley Field for Chavez Ravine, the last vacant sector in the vicinity of downtown. The county subsidized O'Malley by providing him with 300 acres of free land worth nearly $6 million, $4.7 million in new roads, a 99-year agreement on parking rights, and other concessions, although he had to build his own stadium. Further north, the Giants moved into San Francisco, where the city built Candlestick Park.

Three years later, MLB expanded for the first time. The lords of baseball were concerned about the protection of the antitrust exemption, especially after the Washington Senators were permitted to move to Minneapolis in 1960, and also the rise of a rival Continental League. The AL added two new teams in 1961 with a new Washington Senators and the Los Angeles Angels. One year later the Mets were established to fill the void in New York City, along with the Houston Colt .45s, the first franchise in the rapidly growing state of Texas. The new clubs had to pay a $1.8 million initiation fee and were staffed through a draft of fringe major leaguers who cost $75,000 apiece. The new teams were awful—the Mets went 40–122 in 1962—and for several years they were mired in and around last place in a 10-team league.

Attendance growth in the 1960s was just five percent over the 1950s, and did not justify further expansion. However, lawsuits and pressure from Congress following the Braves' removal to Atlanta in 1965 and the Athletics' move to Oakland in 1967, the presence of cities seeking franchises, and interleague power struggles resulted in adding Kansas City, Seattle, San Diego, and Montreal in 1968. The AL charged the new owners $5.15 million to join, while the NL doubled the fee to $10 million. In addition, each team paid $175,000 for players selected from a pool. MLB created two 12-team leagues and a new divisional playoff format.

Television became a major factor in franchise profitability. TV revenues were largely locally based and very uneven. Local TV revenues in 1950 amounted to $2.3 million for the 16 clubs, rising to $12.5 million in 1960 (in 1959 the Yankees were getting about $1 million from broadcast revenue, compared to $150,000 for the Senators) and $20.7 million in 1969. In the 1950s national networks had agreements only with particular teams, mainly in large-market cities, leaving teams in small cities without national televised games. Starting in 1953 each team set up its own local broadcast policy. League-wide packages were only permitted in 1961 following the passage of the Sports Broadcasting Act.

Several multipurpose cookie-cutter municipal stadiums were built in the period 1964–70, including downtown ballparks in Atlanta, St. Louis, Philadelphia, Pittsburgh, and Cincinnati. The latter four were constructed in declining rust-belt cities near major highway interchanges to promote central business districts and build confidence in the future. The parks in the mid-1960s in Atlanta, St. Louis, Anaheim, and San Diego cost $19–25 million, far less than the $45 million Astrodome, the first enclosed ballpark, completed in 1964. Costs for open-air parks nearly doubled within a few years because of higher construction expenses, to about $50 million for Cincinnati's Riverfront Stadium, Philadelphia's Veterans Stadium, and Pittsburgh's Three Rivers Stadium. In 1971, New York City took over Yankee Stadium and spent $106 million to rebuild it. There was also a boom in publicly built suburban sports complexes in sites like Bloomington, Minnesota, and Arlington, Texas, close to the homes of baseball's main fan base, as their communities also sought to promote economic development.

The quality of teams in the postwar era was as unequal as ever. The Yankees from 1947 to 1964 won every AL pennant except for three years, including five straight World Series between 1949 and 1953 and five straight pennants from 1959 to 1964. This was probably the most significant period of one-team domination in professional sports history. There was more balance in the NL, yet the Dodgers dominated the period from 1946 to 1968 with 10 pennants, followed by St. Louis with 4 and 3 each for the Giants and Braves. The Yankees' success was based on excellent scouting and a well-stocked farm system that produced great players and prospects for trade bait. The Dodgers entered the postwar era without a winning tradition, but made smart trades, spent money wisely, brought in black players, and had very stable managerial leadership. A team originally built on power for Ebbets Field retooled in Los Angeles for a larger ballpark with a team that stressed pitching and speed.

TEAMS IN THE MULTIDIVISIONAL ERA

The last teams to relocate were expansion clubs: the Seattle Pilots, who moved to Milwaukee in 1970 and became the Brewers, and the Washington

Senators, who moved to Arlington in 1972 and became the Texas Rangers. The AL expanded in 1976 with new teams in Seattle and Toronto, but there was no more expansion until 1993, when the NL added teams in Denver and Miami. In 1998 the AL added a team in Tampa Bay and the NL added one in Phoenix. That year Milwaukee moved from the AL to the NL, the first league switch since the American Association went out of business in 1891. The leagues divided themselves into three divisions in 1994, setting up a four-team playoff format with a wild card. Then, in 1997, interleague play was initiated to increase fan interest.

There was more parity in the 1970s and 1980s, in part because the new format enabled more opportunities to win at least a divisional title, and the long playoffs made it easier for favorites to stumble. In the 1980s, only five teams did not win a pennant. City size was less important than in previous eras. In the NL St. Louis and Cincinnati won as many as New York, Los Angeles, and Chicago combined, while in the AL, Oakland and Baltimore also won more than those three cities. Teams could less readily stockpile talent compared to the past because of 40-man roster limits and the introduction of the amateur free-agent draft in 1965, with teams selecting in reverse order of finish.

However, parity went out the door in the 1990s with the return of dynasties. The Indians and Yankees each won five straight divisional titles (1995–99), with the Yankees winning four of five World Series. The Braves' domination of the NL was even greater, winning their division every year from 1991 through 2005, including one string of eight straight appearance in the NL Championship Series.

The end of the reserve system provided a great opportunity for the cash-rich Yankees, who cornered the best free agents to win four times between 1976 and 1981, but then failed to return to the World Series until the mid-1990s. Free agency severely hurt other clubs, and led to the breakup of Cincinnati's Big Red Machine and the Oakland A's. Rader argues that small cities were able to win if they had excellent players, stable rosters, and unwavering strong leadership. Baltimore's success was tied to having the same manager, Earl Weaver, for 18 years. Yet managerial stability was not necessarily a hallmark of strong teams, since the Athletics had 12 managers in this era.

In the late 1990s free-agency era there was a heavy correlation between salaries and success. Baltimore was the only one of the four highest-paid teams in 1995–99 not to make every playoff. The gap between rich and poor widened. In 1995 the top seven teams spent 2.6 times as much as the seven cheapest teams, but in 1999 the margin had increased to 3.9:1. The Yankees were the most generous, paying players $88.1 million in 1999, compared to $15.1 million for the Florida Marlins. Teams with the lowest average payrolls rarely or never made playoffs, and did not win a single playoff game between 1995 and 1999. The poorest teams won only about 40 percent of their games.

Rader found that there were different routes for success. Certain teams emphasized building a core from within the organization through the amateur draft rather than trying for quick results through free agency. Some teams believed in drafting experienced collegians rather than high-school seniors, while others began to invest heavily in less expensive Latin players. The Dodgers heavily emphasized stability throughout their organization. Walt Alston managed for 23 years, and upon retirement was replaced by Tommy Lasorda, who spent 47 years with the organization. The Dodgers built a specially constructed village in Vero Beach for spring training, where they brought in their old heroes to instill a team tradition, and tried to sign players to long-term contacts rather than recruit free agents. On the other hand, teams in turmoil also won, like the individualistic Athletics of the 1970s with their unkempt hair and mustaches, although they were united in their hatred of owner Charles Finley. And of course there was the constant turmoil that beset the Yankees under George Steinbrenner and his revolving corps of managers—19 from 1969 through 1991.

Owners were fabulously wealthy men or corporate executives who treated their teams as hobbies for self-gratification and self-advertisement. The only owners in the 1990s who did not have independent wealth were the O'Malleys and Griffiths, scions of baseball families. The new owners were not baseball experts, but meddlers like Gene Autry, Ray Kroc, George Steinbrenner, Charles Finley, and Ted Turner, who enjoyed seeing their names in the papers. Owners used the team to make money, not necessarily by winning pennants, but by using tax advantages like depreciation of players and creating synergy, like the *Chicago Tribune* and its purchase of the Chicago Cubs, who appear on its TV station WGN; Ted Turner's cable network, which was heavily reliant on Braves ball games; and Disney, which purchased the Angels from Autry.

In the 1990s, a new style of ballpark emerged with the 1992 construction of Camden Yards in Baltimore, the first retro park. These parks are smaller in capacity (averaging about 45,000 seats). They combine the intimacy of the early modern ballparks with the ambience of Disney World, plus upscale dining and the comforts of expensive luxury suites that cater to corporate America. Only 8 of 30 ballparks in use today are privately owned.

Until recently the names of ballparks were readily identifiable because they were named for the team (Yankee Stadium), owner (Comiskey Park), or location (Three Rivers Stadium in Pittsburgh), or for an important contributor to the sport (Shea Stadium, in honor of the man who brought the National League back to New York). A few parks maintain this tradition, like Oriole Park at Camden Yards, and Turner Field in Atlanta. However, a new trend emerged with recent ballpark constructions, as the structures are now being named for businesses, usually with a local base, that are spending millions of dollars to secure the naming rights to advertise themselves. The average deal is for about $75 million over 25 years. Local corporations who have purchased naming rights include Petco in San Diego and Comerica in Detroit. Their management believes this investment enhances their visibility and displays hometown boosterism. This support is particularly keen among financial institutions like Citizens' Bank in Philadelphia, Chase in Arizona, Great American Insurance

Company in Cincinnati, and PNC Bank in Pittsburgh, as well as beer companies like Milwaukee's Miller Park, Denver's Coors Field, and St. Louis's Busch Stadium. Some name changes are often coming very swiftly, as in the case with the San Francisco ballpark that opened in 2000 as Pacific Bell Park, became SBC Park, and now is AT&T Park because of corporate mergers. Another reason for change has been the naming company's financial distress, notably Enron, whose name no longer graces Houston's major league ballpark.

Team profitability varied substantially based on several factors, including attendance, ticket prices, and media revenue, as well as concessions and parking. Overall teams averaged about 21,367 spectators a game in 1980, which appreciated significantly to 26,115 in 1990. The rise was due to the quality of the product, which was comprised of the team on the field and the ballpark (which includes accessibility, nature of the neighborhood, park ambience, ticket prices, and condition of the facility). When the Blue Jays moved into SkyDome in 1989, they set major-league attendance records for three straight years. The Orioles at the new Camden Yards in the late 1990s averaged 45,034 in their first five years, a 50 percent increase over their past four years at the old Memorial Stadium. Attendance still varies a lot among different teams. In 1989, for instance, the Chicago White Sox and Atlanta Braves were outdrawn by the minor-league Buffalo Bisons. In 2001, 7 teams drew over 3 million, led by Seattle with 3.7 million, while 10 drew under 2 million, with a low of 642,000 for Montreal.

Teams have widely different pricing strategies, which heavily impinges on profits; this was not the case in the past, when average prices were uniform. Ticket pricing reflects supply and demand and the introduction of skyboxes. Average ticket prices rose from $8.64 in 1991 to $14.91 in 1999. The average ticket in 2001 cost $19.70, ranging from tiny Fenway Park, where the Red Sox charged $36.08, down to $9.55 for Minnesota. Boston's cheapest bleacher tickets cost more than a field box seat at Dodger Stadium. The Dodgers outdrew the Red Sox by 400,000 fans, but earned $39 million less at the box office.

Ticket-price differentials have helped shape the social composition of audiences, which along with crowd behavior varies from team to team. Kansas City is well known for drawing a regional audience, while about 30 percent of Baltimore's crowds are from out of town. The Chicago White Sox traditionally drew white ethnic and black working-class fans from the South Side, its geographic home base. For several years these fans had a reputation for being pretty rowdy. However, more recently, its audiences are increasingly middle-class suburbanites. The Cubs always drew most of their fans from the North Side; for the last 30 years, it has drawn a fun-loving yuppie audience who come for the ambience and sunshine of Wrigley Field and the nightlife of the gentrified neighborhood more than for the Cubs. Similarly, the Dodgers' fans are considered the most easygoing, coming late and leaving early. On the other hand, the Phillies were known for having a mean-spirited crowd. Fan loyalty, always based on hometown pride, may have weakened with free agency, as star players no longer play their entire career with one club, but come and go for the dollars.

Besides ticket sales, the other big income maker for teams is media fees. Unlike professional football, this source of revenue is still very unbalanced. In 1987 baseball teams averaged about $6 million from the local media. The widest variance is naturally in the largest and smallest media markets. In the early 1990s the Yankees got about $41 million a year, compared to $3 million for Milwaukee. In 2001, the Yankees made $56.7 million from local media, compared to just under $6 million for Milwaukee and $600,000 for Montreal. The teams also share in the network contracts, which in 1983 reached $4 million per team. The 1990–93 package with CBS and cable TV went up to $14.4 million, and the latest contract with Fox reached $16.7 million in 2001 (comprising $2.5 billion over six years).

Most teams' main expense is player compensation, which ranged in 2001 from $118 million for the Red Sox to $30.4 million for the Twins. Half of the teams paid over $70 million in salaries.[4] Teams also vary widely vary in their nonsalary expenses. The average team spent about $54,646,300 on nonplayer expenses, which was around 46.2 percent of their operating revenue (average of $118,262,533). Most teams were near the norm, but Seattle spent over $84 million, while Montreal spent just $34 million. According to MLB, the average team in 2001 had a negative operating expense of $7,741,367.[5] Astonishingly, the most profitable team (after revenue sharing) was the Milwaukee Brewers, a small-market team, which made $16.1 million, closely followed by Seattle and the New York Yankees. The largest loser was the Dodgers, who lost over $54 million.

Despite the negative assessments of Commissioner Bud Selig on the financial health of baseball, *Forbes* estimated the average team to be worth $286 million, ranging from a high of $730 million for the Yankees (worth 66% more than the next closest team, the Mets, worth $482 million) to Montreal at $108 million. Yet even if teams did lose money, the value of the investment continues to appreciate.

By 2005, the Yankees were valued at $950 million, with revenues of $264 million, compared to the lowly Tampa Bay Devil Rays, worth just $176 million, with revenues of $110 million. Overall, the average team had a value of $332 million, with revenues of $142 million. The average operating revenues per team was $4.4 million, ranging from $30 million for Baltimore to a loss of $37.1 million for the Yankees.[6]

Major-league baseball teams, and professional sports teams in general, have a unique relationship. Teams in baseball compete with each other, as do rivals in other businesses. In baseball the contest is not to control as much of the market as possible, but to win the most games against other members of the monopoly, the only ball game in town. Even the Big Three car companies historically contended with other rivals, first at home and more recently from abroad. In the case of baseball, the competition to win means striving to secure the best ballplayers possible so you win and your opponent loses. However, it is not a zero-sum game. The goal is not to put the competition out of business. If certain teams win too often, and others lose too often, it is not good business. If Ford kills a competitor like Studebaker, that is good for Ford. But if the Yankees always win, that may not be good for the Yankees. Major-league members must cooperate with one another, since without each other there is no pennant race, no league, and no business. While teams don't actually try to improve the rosters of weaker teams to promote competition on the field, they have historically cooperated in many ways out of mutual self-interest, such as keeping down player wages and other expenses, and adjusting rules to promote fan interest.

NOTES

1. Financial date for the 19th century, especially press reports, must be dealt with cautiously. For example, the *New York Herald* reported that six teams had lost money, and the NL had broken even. The *New York World*, on the other hand, reported no team lost money, and they collectively made $352,000, which was unrealistic. If the NL had made so much money, they would not have dropped four teams after the season. The *Chicago Times Herald* reported that only the Cleveland Spiders and New York Giants had lost an undetermined amount, and the rest had made money, but only had numbers for six teams. See Steven A. Riess, *Touching Base: Professional Baseball and American Culture in the Progressive Era,* rev. ed. (Urbana: University of Illinois Press, 1999), 63.

2. George Ethelbert Walsh, "The Gilt-Edged Diamond." *Independent* 75 (31 July 1913), 263.

3. Benjamin G. Rader, *Baseball: A History of America's Game,* 2nd ed. (Urbana: University of Illinois Press, 2002), 138.

4. In 2005 the Yankees' payroll at the start of the season was $208,306,817, compared to $29,679,067 for Tampa Bay.

5. *Forbes* estimates that actually the average team *made* $2.57 million in 2001. Kurt Badenhausen, Cecily Fluke, Leslie Kump, and Michael K. Ozanian, "Double Play," *Forbes,* April 12, 2002, 92–95. The biggest discrepancy was with the Dodgers, who the magazine estimates lost $29.6 million, or half the report by MLB. Doug Pappas, "The Numbers (Part Eight): MLB vs. *Forbes,*" *Baseball Prospectus,* http://www.baseballprospectus.com/news/20020403pappas.shtml.

6. Kurt Badenhausen, Jack Gape, Lesley Kump, Michael K. Ozanian, and Maya Roney, "Baseball Team Evaluations," *Forbes,* April 25, 2005, 91–95.

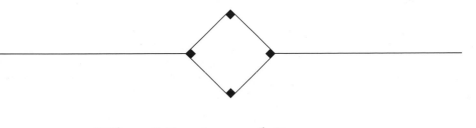

The National League

Arizona Diamondbacks

Laura A. Purcell and John H. Jordan

The Arizona Diamondbacks' short existence has been a roller-coaster ride. The franchise won a World Series in 2001, yet lost 111 games in 2004. The team has drawn millions of fans, but lost money every year. The franchise can be characterized best as a big spender, a big winner, and a big debtor.

Phoenix voters in a 1989 referendum rejected a tax to build a new professional baseball stadium, but one year later the state legislature easily passed Bill 1314 to allow the Maricopa County Board of Supervisors to levy a sales tax for the express purpose of building a new baseball-only stadium without a public referendum, and Governor Rose Mofford signed the bill into law. The Maricopa County Board of Supervisors voted three to one with one abstention to enact a one-quarter-cent sales tax. The contingent sales tax, capped at $238 million, only went into effect after MLB granted Phoenix a franchise in 1995. Some residents criticized the enactment of a sales tax without a public vote, and one outraged citizen shot and wounded a county supervisor who had voted for the tax.

In 1993, County Supervisor Jim Bruner and local attorney Joe Garagiola Jr. approached Jerry Colangelo, general managing partner of the NBA Phoenix Suns, about spearheading an effort to acquire an MLB expansion team. By 1994, Colangelo had assembled a syndicate comprised of local corporations, Arizona business leaders, and national celebrities. On March 9, 1995, MLB awarded Colangelo a baseball franchise for $130 million. Colangelo owned only a small percentage of the team, yet became managing partner and the public face of the Diamondbacks. Garagiola Jr., son of the former major-league catcher and broadcaster, became general manager. On November 15 he hired

Buck Showalter to a seven-year, $7 million contract to manage the club. Show-alter, a noted perfectionist and micromanager, eventually molded many aspects of the young franchise.

The team's new ballpark cost over $354 million, with $238 million funded by the county's sales tax and the remainder by the Diamondbacks. The site was a 22-acre lot in downtown Phoenix, less than two blocks from America West Arena, home of the Suns, the WNBA Phoenix Mercury, and the Arena Foot-ball League Arizona Rattlers, all partially owned by Colangelo. The new field was named Bank One Ballpark after the company bought the naming rights for 30 years at an annual cost of over $2 million. It is owned by Maricopa County and features a five-acre, 9-million-pound retractable roof, yet utilizes natural grass. The ballpark has an 8,000-ton air-conditioning unit that keeps the sta-dium cool even in Phoenix's brutal heat. The field features a dirt path from home plate to the pitcher's mound, reminiscent of nineteenth-century ballparks, and the first swimming pool in a major-league ballpark, located behind right center field.

Unlike most expansion franchises, the Diamondbacks spent heavily on players from the outset. Colangelo and his advisors believed that the Diamond-backs' location was a decided advantage over other MLB teams because a vastly disproportionate number of major leaguers had their permanent resi-dences in Arizona, and even more were familiar with the area due to Cactus League spring training. The management reasoned that if the Diamondbacks offered competitive salaries, players would welcome the chance to live in Phoe-nix year-round.

Even before the team was established, the Diamondbacks in October 1996 signed two recently drafted players whom the commissioner had declared free agents because of a technicality. The Diamondbacks gave a $6 million signing bonus to pitcher John Patterson and a record $10 million signing bonus to first baseman Travis Lee, neither of who ever fulfilled expectations.

In November 1997 the Diamondbacks selected 35 players in the MLB ex-pansion draft, which allowed the expansion Diamondbacks and Tampa Bay Devil Rays to fill their rosters with unprotected players. Five draftees remained with the team for at least three seasons: pitchers Brian Anderson and Omar Daal, outfielder David Dellucci, and catchers Damian Miller and Kelly Stinnett. The Diamondbacks used some of their new players in trades: they traded two players and $3 million in cash to Cleveland for All-Star third baseman Matt Williams, who wanted to be closer to his children, who were Phoenix resi-dents. Management's belief in the advantage of the Diamondbacks' location was proving correct. Wilson facilitated the trade by lowering his 1998 salary from $7 million to $4.5 million, but he was ultimately well compensated when the team signed him to a six-year contract worth $49.5 million.

In November 1997 the Diamondbacks signed veteran infielder Jay Bell to a five-year, $34 million contract with a no-trade clause, out of line for a player with a career .268 batting average. Rival teams feared the trend the contract heralded. The Diamondbacks felt their free-spending ways netted an underval-ued player and put them on the map as a legitimate destination for established major-league players.

The Diamondbacks participated in their first full spring training in 1998 in Tucson, home of their Triple-A minor-league affiliate Tucson Sidewinders. Having their spring-training facility and Triple-A club less than two hours from Phoenix gives Arizona residents an attachment to the club they might not oth-erwise have had.

The Diamondbacks aggressively market to Mexican Americans living in Ari-zona as well as the residents of northern Mexico, playing up the presence of their Mexican-born players. The team broadcasts every game in Spanish on radio, along with many in Spanish on television. Special promotions are held in honor of Hispanic Heritage Month in September, and the Diamondbacks also fly to Mexico for a spring-training game each March.

The Diamondbacks opened their first season on March 31, 1998, at Bank One Ballpark before 50,179 fans, the first of several sellout games in their in-augural season. The Diamondbacks finished the 1998 season with a 65–97 record, last in the NL Western Division, yet drew more than 3.6 million. The squad had a modest $30 million payroll, seventh lowest in the majors, yet re-portedly lost money and had to make cash calls to partners amounting to $29 million.

Colangelo believed that for the long term he had to create fans enamored with the Diamondbacks. The surest way to do this was to win. He developed an ambitious four-year plan to immediately become a contender and made sev-eral key off-season acquisitions, signing six free agents to multimillion-dollar contracts. The most important signings were Cy Young Award–winning pitcher Randy Johnson for four years at $52.4 million and center fielder Steve Finley for four years for $21.5 million. The team also traded for outfielder Luis Gonza-lez, who dramatically opened his batting stance and, at age 31, blossomed as an offensive player. "Gonzo," with his warm and friendly personality, quickly became a fan favorite and the public face of the Diamondbacks' players.

The revamped Diamondbacks dominated the NL West in 1999, winning 100 games. This was an extraordinary achievement for a second-year expansion team. Randy Johnson won the Cy Young Award. He accumulated a major-league-leading 364 strikeouts and led the NL in complete games and innings pitched. Steve Finley won the first of two consecutive Gold Gloves, while Jay Bell hit a career-high 38 home runs. The Diamondbacks met the New York Mets in the 1999 NL Divisional Series but were eliminated three games to one. Despite the success-es on the field, the team lost money. Attendance dropped more than 16 percent while the payroll more than doubled to $66 million. The Diamondbacks reportedly lost $30 million in 1999 and had to make another cash call to the 29 limited part-ners. Only 24 partners participated, raising $24 million for the franchise.

In 2000 a late-season swoon caused the Diamondbacks to finish in third place in the NL West with an 85–77 record. The starting pitching got a big boost in July, however, with the acquisition of pitching ace Curt Schilling, who had attended high school and college in Arizona. He and Johnson formed one of the most formidable starting duos in recent MLB history, with Johnson winning his second consecutive Cy Young Award. The disappointed front office made manager Showalter the fall guy, firing him and hiring Bob Brenly in his place. Attendance continued to drop in 2000, to 2.8 million, while the Diamondbacks' payroll rose to more than $80 million, seventh highest in the major leagues. The Diamondbacks continued to lose money and borrowed more than $10 million. Then bank considered the team such a high risk that MLB had to cosign the loan. The team cut costs by laying off 15 front-office employees, and in the off-season asked 10 highly compensated players to defer a portion of their salaries. They agreed to defer more than $100 million, enabling the team to sign several free agents, including first baseman Mark Grace.

The 2001 season started with a bang as left fielder Luis Gonzalez hit 13 homers in April, tying the major-league record. He continued to swing a hot bat for the entire season, finishing with a .325 batting average, 142 RBIs, and 57 home runs. The Diamondbacks won the NL West with a record of 92–70. Johnson struck out 20 on May 8, 2001 against Cincinnati, the fourth major leaguer to achieve that feat. He finished with 372 strikeouts, the third-highest season total in history, and his 13.4 strikeouts per nine innings was the best ever. Johnson won 21 games with a 2.49 ERA and won his third consecutive Cy Young Award. Schilling had a career year and finished second in the Cy Young voting, the first time since 1956 that teammates were first and second. He won 22 games with 293 strikeouts, second in the majors, and a 2.98 ERA, third lowest in the NL. Johnson and Schilling combined for 665 strikeouts, a new major-league record for teammates. But despite winning on the field and phenomenal seasons by Gonzalez, Johnson, and Schilling, attendance dropped to 2.7 million while the team's payroll rose to $85 million.

Schilling and Johnson continued their domination during the 2001 postseason, which started late because of the repercussions of the terrorist attacks on September 11 of that year. The Diamondbacks beat the St. Louis Cardinals three games to two to take the NLDS, and then quickly beat Atlanta four games to one in the NL Championship Series. The team advanced to what would be a memorable World Series against the New York Yankees. On October 27 in Phoenix the Diamondbacks demolished the Yankees 9–1, and then Johnson pitched a complete-game shutout and struck out 11 in a 4–0 victory. The series moved to New York and the Yankees won game three, 2–1. The Yankees also won games four and five, with both games going into extra innings due to dramatic ninth-inning game-tying home runs. Upon returning to Arizona, on Saturday, November 3, the Diamondbacks destroyed the Yankees 15–2. Johnson gave up only two runs in seven innings. The series was again tied at three games apiece.

Schilling started game seven for the Diamondbacks on only three days' rest and allowed only one run until the seventh inning. Johnson entered the game in relief less than 24 hours after he pitched in game six. Johnson faced one batter in the eighth inning and then retired the side in the ninth. With the game tied 2–2 with one out and the bases loaded, Luis Gonzalez drove in Jay Bell with a bloop single off reliever Mariano Rivera to win game seven and the World Series. This was the first major professional championship for Arizona in any sport and the quickest championship for any MLB expansion franchise. Appropriately, Randy Johnson and Curt Schilling were Series co-MVPs.

Despite winning the World Series, the Diamondbacks lost money in 2001. The beleaguered franchise courted four new investors to join the ownership group. They agreed to infuse at least $160 million into the franchise, diluting the ownership shares of the existing partners.

In the following season, with many of the players returning from the championship team, the Diamondbacks cruised to a 98–64 record, winning the NL West for the third time in their five-year existence. The team payroll

Luis Gonzalez celebrates the Diamondbacks victory over the New York Yankees in Game 7 of the World Series, 2001. © AP / Wide World Photos

climbed to more than $103 million and attendance increased to 3.2 million. Curt Schilling had a 23–7 record, 316 strikeouts, and a 3.23 ERA. His strikeout total was second to Randy Johnson, who had 334 strikeouts, a 24–5 record, and a 2.32 ERA. Johnson led the NL in wins, ERA, and strikeouts, taking the first pitching triple crown in the majors since 1985. Johnson won his fourth consecutive Cy Young Award, with Schilling finishing second for the second consecutive year. However, the injury-weakened Diamondbacks were defeated by the Cardinals in the NLDS in three straight games.

The Diamondbacks were plagued with injuries throughout the 2003 season. Sixteen Diamondbacks spent time on the disabled list, including Johnson and Schilling. In June the Diamondbacks released third baseman Matt Williams. Williams retired from playing after 17 seasons, but he became an investor in the team in 2005. The Diamondbacks finished the season with a record of 84–78, third in the NL West. The Diamondbacks' payroll in 2003 decreased

Randy Johnson, left, and Curt Schilling, right, hold the World Series MVP trophy they will share after being named co-receipiants of the World Series Most Valuable Player, 2001. © AP / Wide World Photos

to $82 million and attendance decreased to 2.8 million. In an off-season cost-cutting measure, the Diamondbacks traded pitching ace Curt Schilling to Boston for four prospects.

In March 2004 Colangelo quietly sold his general partnership interest for a reported $4 million to the four investors the team had brought in after the 2001 season. The new owners, led by Ken Kendricks, kept Colangelo as CEO and the fifth member of the ownership group, even though he no longer had any financial investment in the team, which was worth an estimated $285 million. He resigned as CEO on August 6. The team selected sports agent Jeff Moorad, who had represented some of the Diamondbacks' players, to become the new CEO. The same four investors whom Colangelo had courted in 2001 and who had bought Colangelo's general partnership in effect forced him out. The *Arizona Republic* newspaper estimated that the Diamondbacks had approximately $300 million in debt, almost $180 million of which was needed for deferred salary payments to players. Colangelo's free-spending ways finally had caught up with him, as his ouster reportedly was due to conflicts with the new ownership group over finances. The Diamondbacks' 2004 season was wracked with injuries, including season-ending surgery for Luis Gonzalez. After several horrendous losing streaks, the Diamondbacks fired manager Bob

Brenly in July. The Diamondbacks appointed third-base coach Al Pedrique as interim manager. In November, the Diamondbacks hired Bob Melvin as the new manager.

The demoralized and inexperienced team continued to lose. The Diamondbacks finished the 2004 season with a 51–111 record, the eighth-most losses in a major-league single season. Despite having one of the worst seasons in major-league history, the Diamondbacks drew more than 2.5 million in attendance. Johnson had several memorable games during the 2004 season, including a perfect game on May 18, only the 15th perfect game since 1900. On June 29 he became the fourth major-league pitcher to hurl 4,000 strikeouts. On September 15 Johnson surpassed Steve Carlton's strikeout total for the most strikeouts by a left-handed pitcher in major-league history. Johnson finished the season with a 2.60 ERA but a disappointing 16–14 record. He recorded 290 strikeouts for the season, and placed second in Cy Young voting.

Despite reports about the Diamondbacks' heavy debt, the team signed several free agents in the off-season, including pitcher Russ Ortiz to a four-year, $33 million contract and third baseman Troy Glaus to a four-year, $45 million deal. In January 2005 the Diamondbacks traded Randy Johnson, after six stellar seasons and four Cy Young Awards, to the New York Yankees for pitcher Javier Vasquez (with an $11 million salary), a prospect, and $9 million in cash. The Diamondbacks then traded four prospects to Los Angeles and received outfielder Shawn Green and $10 million in cash. The ouster of Jerry Colangelo, the trade of Randy Johnson, and a payroll reduced by 25 percent from $80 million symbolized the start of a new era for the Arizona Diamondbacks. In 2005 the team improved markedly to 77–85 and second place in the weak NL West, led by five men with 20 or more homers.

NOTABLE ACHIEVEMENTS

Cy Young Winners

Year	Name	Position
1999	Randy Johnson	LHP
2000	Randy Johnson	LHP
2001	Randy Johnson	LHP
2002	Randy Johnson	LHP

ERA Champions

Year	Name	#
1999	Randy Johnson	2.48
2001	Randy Johnson	2.49
2002	Randy Johnson	2.32

Strikeout Champions

Year	Name	#
1999	Randy Johnson	364
2000	Randy Johnson	347
2001	Randy Johnson	372
2002	Randy Johnson	334
2004	Randy Johnson	290

No-Hitters (Italics = Perfect Game)

Name	Date
Randy Johnson	05/18/2004

POSTSEASON APPEARANCES

NL West Division Titles

Year	Record	Manager
1999	100–62	Buck Showalter
2001	92–70	Bob Brenly
2002	98–64	Bob Brenly

NL Pennants

Year	Record	Manager
2001	92–70	Bob Brenly

World Championships

Year	Opponent	MVP
2001	New York	Randy Johnson Curt Schilling

MANAGERS

2005–	Bob Melvin
2004	Al Pedrique
2001–2004	Bob Brenly
1998–2000	Buck Showalter

Team Records by Individual Players

Batting Leaders

| | Single Season | | | Career | | |
	Name		Year	Name		Plate Appearances
Batting average	Carlos Baerga	.343	2003	Luis Gonzalez	.302	4,578
On-base %	Luis Gonzalez	.429	2001	Luis Gonzalez	.396	4,578
Slugging %	Luis Gonzalez	.688	2001	Luis Gonzalez	.542	4,578
OPS	Luis Gonzalez	1.017	2001	Luis Gonzalez	.938	4,578
Games	Luis Gonzalez	162	2000	Luis Gonzalez	1041	4,578
At bats	Matt Williams	627	1999	Luis Gonzalez	3902	4,578
Runs	Jay Bell	132	1999	Luis Gonzalez	687	4,578
Hits	Luis Gonzalez	206	1999	Luis Gonzalez	1178	4,578
Total bases	Luis Gonzalez	419	2001	Luis Gonzalez	2113	4,578
Doubles	Luis Gonzalez	47	2000	Luis Gonzalez	258	4,578
Triples	Tony Womack	14	2000	Tony Womack	.32	2,744
Home runs	Luis Gonzalez	57	2001	Luis Gonzalez	209	4,578
RBI	Luis Gonzalez	142	2001	Luis Gonzalez	701	4,578
Walks	Luis Gonzalez	100	1999	Luis Gonzalez	581	4,578
Strikeouts	T Glaus	145	2005	Luis Gonzalez	522	4,578
Stolen bases	Tony Womack	72	1999	Tony Womack	182	2,744
Extra-base hits	Luis Gonzalez	100	2001	Luis Gonzalez	492	4,578
Times on base	Luis Gonzalez	312	2001	Luis Gonzalez	1708	4,578

Pitching Leaders

| | Single Season | | | Career | | |
	Name		Year	Name		Innings Pitched
ERA	Randy Johnson	2.32	2002	Randy Johnson	2.65	1,389.7
Wins	Randy Johnson	24	2002	Randy Johnson	103	1,389.7
Won-Loss %	Randy Johnson	.828	2002	Randy Johnson	.678	1,389.7
Hits/9 IP	Randy Johnson	6.48	2004	Randy Johnson	7.05	1,389.7
Walks/9 IP	Brian Anderson	1.04	1998	Curt Schilling	1.35	781.7
Strikeouts	Randy Johnson	372	2001	Randy Johnson	1832	1,389.7
Strikeouts/9 IP	Randy Johnson	13.41	2001	Randy Johnson	11.86	1,389.7
Games	Oscar Villarreal	86	2003	Byung-Hyun Kim	243	323
Saves	Byung-Hyun Kim	36	2002	Matt Mantei	74	173.7
Innings	Randy Johnson	271.7	1999	Randy Johnson	1389.7	1,389.7
Starts	Randy Johnson	35	1999	Randy Johnson	192	1,389.7

(Continued)

Pitching Leaders (Continued)

	Single Season			Career		
	Name		Year	Name		Innings Pitched
Complete games	Randy Johnson	12	1999	Randy Johnson	36	1,389.7
Shutouts	Randy Johnson	4		Randy Johnson	14	1,389.7

Source: Drawn from data in "Arizona Diamondbacks Batting Leaders (seasonal and career)." http://baseball-reference. com/teams/ARI/leaders_bat.shtml; "Arizona Diamondbacks Pitching Leaders (seasonal and career)." http://baseball-reference.com/teams/ARI/leaders_pitch.shtml.

BIBLIOGRAPHY

Arizona Diamondbacks Media Guide. Phoenix: Arizona Diamondbacks, 1998–2004.

The Arizona Republic (Phoenix, AZ) 1995–2005.

Colangelo, Jerry, and Len Sherman. *How You Play the Game: Lessons for Life from the Billion-Dollar Business of Sports.* New York: American Management Association, 1999.

Olney, Buster. *The Last Night of the Yankee Dynasty: The Game, the Team, and the Cost of Greatness.* New York: Ecco, 2004.

Sherman, Len. *Big League, Big Time: The Birth of the Arizona Diamondbacks, the Billion-Dollar Business of Sports, and the Power of the Media in America.* New York: Pocket Books, 1998.

Atlanta Braves

David Stevens

A TALE OF THREE CITIES, 1871–2005

By migrating from Boston to Milwaukee to Atlanta in search of a bigger fan base, the Braves (along with the Chicago Cubs) can be considered the oldest continually operating sports franchise in the United States. The franchise's long history is indicated by the fact that more than one-fifth of Baseball Hall of Fame members were once Braves. Since the 1950s the team has set several major trends in American baseball. Its migration from Boston to Milwaukee in 1953 set off the first era of franchise shifts since the turn of the century. Then, in 1965, by deserting Milwaukee for Atlanta after 13 seasons, all winning, the Braves unleashed the modern era of frequent franchise moves to the West and South. After arriving in Atlanta, the Braves developed many followers nationally, via heavy marketing on cable TV, as "America's Team." The present-day Atlanta Braves, owned by Time Warner, are trendsetters as the first sports franchise that is merely a game piece in a powerful multinational media empire. Such corporate imitation is the sincerest form of flattery, and since 1991 the Atlanta organization has indeed been a paragon of stability and success, including capturing 14 straight National League divisional championships (1991–2005).

The Braves had dynasties in the nineteenth century and the late 1950s too. However, for much of its history, from 1903 to 1945 in Boston and 1972 to 1990 in Atlanta, the club suffered through long stretches of dreadful performances and unshakable public apathy, sometimes under blundering, conniving owners. In the roughest stretches, even some of baseball's brightest stars (including

Cy Young), shrewdest managers (including Casey Stengel and Joe Torre), and revolutionary owners (such as Ted Turner) couldn't present winning records to the Braves' fans. Nonetheless, the Braves' Hank Aaron provided what several national fan polls voted the greatest moment in baseball history, when on April 8, 1974, he belted homer 715 to break the legendary home-run record of Babe Ruth, set when Ruth was briefly a Boston Brave.

BOSTON, 1871–1900: THE FIRST MAJOR-LEAGUE DYNASTY—IRISH NEED APPLY

The Atlanta Braves can be traced back to before the rise of the National League. In 1871 Harry Wright, former manager of the pioneering Cincinnati Red Stockings, moved to Boston with brother George Wright, the club's short-stop, and other Cincinnati players, where they debuted as the Boston Red Stockings in the new National Association of Professional Base Ball Clubs, the first professional baseball league. Their team dominated, winning four straight pennants from 1872 to 1875, culminating in a 71–8 record in 1875, the highest major-league winning percentage ever. That domination hurt the NA, which lacked competitive balance. In the 1874 off-season, Harry Wright led the Boston and Philadelphia teams on the first international baseball tour. When the National League was formed to make professional baseball more businesslike, the Red Stockings provided the core for the Boston franchise in the new league. The NL wanted the Wright-led team because of their skill and honest reputation, significant in an era when throwing of games was widely suspected. One of their stars was future Hall of Famer Jim O'Rourke, who caught more no-hitters than any other catcher. Team owner Nathan Appolonio wanted him to change his name to disguise his Gaelic heritage, which he refused to do.

The Boston club was known as the Red Stockings or Red Caps until 1882. The name "Beaneaters" gradually came into use, to avoid confusion when Cincinnati joined the major leagues, also as the Red Stockings, to emphasize its own link to Harry Wright's legendary 1869 club. The name "Beaneaters" derived from Bostonians' love of baked beans, and the Boston club remained the Beaneaters until 1907, finally becoming the Braves in 1912.

The team played at the South End Grounds and came in fourth in 1876 with a record of 39–31. In 1877, Nathan Appolonio sold the Boston NL club to three shrewd Beantown businessmen (Arthur Soden, James Billings, and Bill Conant) known as "the Triumvirs," after the ruling trios of ancient Rome. The team took the pennant in 1877 (42–18) behind pitcher Tommy Bond, who went 40–17, starting and finishing every game, and repeated in 1878 (41–19) with Bond going 40–19.

In 1879, the Triumvirs fumed after George Wright, star catcher and third baseman Deacon White (a two-time batting champ), and O'Rourke (at the time, a Yale law student nicknamed "Orator" for his eloquence), all left the club for better salaries and off-season opportunities. Players then were free to change teams when their contracts expired, without any compensation to the club. Consequently, following that 1879 season, Boston president Soden, a roofing contractor, was inspired to draw up baseball's reserve clause, to restrict player freedom and drive down salaries. Defiant athletes were blackballed. Wielding the reserve rule, Boston reloaded and took the NL pennant in 1883. Soden became the second-most-powerful man in nineteenth-century baseball, after sporting-goods magnate Albert G. Spalding, who had a record of 253–65 as a pitcher for the Red Stockings and Cubs.

In 1887, the Triumvirs boosted the club by purchasing *the* national fan favorite of the century, colorful catcher and right fielder Mike "King" Kelly. The charismatic Kelly was hailed as "the $10,000 Beauty" because of the unprecedented sum Boston paid Chicago to acquire him. The amount was so astounding that the Triumvirs displayed the check in a storefront window, to quell skepticism while drumming up ticket sales. Boston fans, thrilled to have the exciting Irishman, even bought Kelly a fine house.

The year after acquiring Kelly, the Triumvirs shelled out $10,000 more to land another future Hall of Famer, the cunning pitcher John Clarkson, a handsome Cambridge native, who also drew Boston fans in droves. Image-obsessed Cubs proprietor Spalding unloaded the brainy Kelly-Clarkson pair, partly due to their wild off-field antics.

The Triumvirs expected to return to domination via their big acquisitions, but Clarkson's loss on the last day of the 1889 season cost the Beaneaters the NL pennant by one game. The overworked Clarkson pitched 620 innings that season, the most of anyone by an incredible 200 innings. The angry Triumvirs then fired rookie manager Jim Hart, who had paid two Cleveland players a $1,000 "incentive" to beat the world champion New York Giants in the season's last series in an effort to capture the pennant.

Such bribes and the Kelly-Clarkson purchases revealed the massive profits the big-market owners made, so to appease the struggling small-market clubs, the NL slashed players' salaries and rights, setting a $2,500 salary maximum (equal to about $60,000 in 2004). For a year, the NL refused even to discuss the unilateral cuts with the Brotherhood of Professional Base Ball Players, the players' union. As a result, all the players in the NL secretly signed written pledges to leave their owners, and en masse formed the Players' League. The union members did not sign their 1890 contracts, in effect declaring themselves free agents.

Boston was a major battleground in the 1890 players' revolt, with a team in both the PL and the NL. As part of an all-out war to destroy the PL, the NL tried to entice back King Kelly, offering a three-year contract at any salary the star catcher desired. However, Kelly declined, explaining he "couldn't go back on the boys" of the union. His club won the PL pennant. The Triumvirs did lure Clarkson back via a three-year contract at $7,500 each year, plus a huge bonus.

In response to the losses on the playing field, the Beaneaters added new manager Frank Selee, who brought with him, from minor-league Omaha, rookie fireballer Kid Nichols, who won 297 games over the next decade, the most wins ever by a pitcher in a 10-year period, and 361 for his career. In 1891 the Boston American Association team led by King Kelly captured its championship race. When the AA and NL consolidated one year later, the two local teams were merged, creating an enduring powerhouse. The demise of the PL and the AA left the NL as a monopoly from 1892 to 1900, which dropped wages dramatically. The consolidated 1892 Boston club lorded over "the Big League" with a 102–48 record. The 1893 Beaneaters averaged 7.7 runs a game, 101 more total than the powerful 2003 Braves, despite hitting 170 fewer home runs than the 2003 Braves.

Selee, who emphasized high batting averages and speed, piloted the NL Boston club superbly from 1890 through 1901, winning NL pennants in 1891–93 and 1897–98, for a total of eight since 1876. Selee's last championship team went 102–47. The three straight championships in the early 1890s garnered the Beaneaters permanent possession of the Dauvray Cup, named after New York Giants player-manager John Montgomery Ward's wife, the famous actress Helen Dauvray. Years later, Ward, the leader of the 1890 players' revolt, bought the Beaneaters.

Besides Selee and Nichols, Boston Hall of Famers in the 1890s included pitcher Vic Willis and three speedy, slap-hitting outfielders: Sliding Billy Hamilton, who held the career stolen-base mark prior to Ty Cobb; hit-and-run innovator Tommy McCarthy; and Hugh Duffy, who holds the record for the highest season batting average—an unbeatable .440 in 1894. Duffy amazed Boston fans in one game that year by taking two bases on a sacrifice fly. The tiny Duffy and McCarthy, known as "the Celestial Twins," were native Boston Irish, which helped attract many local Irish fans. Baseball was one of the few well-paid trades open to the Irish. That season second baseman Bobby Lowe hit a record four homers in one game. Boston fans tossed $160 in coins on the field for the 155-pound fan favorite.

The 1892–1900 monopoly era was characterized by dirty play and intimidation, primarily by Baltimore and Cleveland, but the dignified Selee took the opposite approach, in the tradition of genteel former Boston manager Harry Wright. The low-key Selee's philosophy included "If I make things pleasant for the players, they reciprocate." The Gay Nineties Beaneaters succeeded with inside baseball (then termed *scientific play*), such as originating the hit-and-run, plus perfecting signaling and place hitting. While "Dirty" Ned Hanlon's rowdy Orioles of the Gay Nineties, who captured three pennants, have the big reputation, the clean Boston Beaneaters, who won five, were the best team of the decade. Nonetheless, the club could not avoid the combative baseball tactics of the monopoly era. In 1894 there was a fierce and prolonged fistfight between Boston's Tommy "Foghorn" Tucker and Baltimore Orioles third baseman John "Muggsy" McGraw, and two months later, first baseman Tucker was twice beaten up by Philadelphia fans.

While Tucker and McGraw brawled, the wooden double-decked South End Grounds II burned down because of a rubbish fire started by boys under the right-field bleachers. The blaze ruined the park and damaged or destroyed 170 nearby buildings. The exterior of the third South End Grounds was designed like a castle, but the structure was much smaller because the old park was underinsured. The Roxbury Fire was the second in a series of tragedies that forced a long decline of the Beaneaters in the next century. The year before, Charlie Bennett lost both legs when he accidentally fell under a train after the 1893 season, as his best friend, pitcher John Clarkson, helplessly gazed in horror. Bennett was replaced by Marty Bergen, who sadly lost a son in 1898. Initially his teammates sympathized, and understood his frequent, sudden absences. But following two seasons of tolerating the catcher's increasingly hostile behavior, his teammates asked the owners to trade him. A few months later, in January 1900, before a trade could be arranged, the mentally ill Bergen killed his entire family. The Beaneaters, who had come in second the previous season, soon spiraled downward, to fourth (66–72) in 1900 and fifth (69–68) in 1901.

BOSTON, 1901–21:
THE RED SOX TAKE OVER THE TOWN

Another big factor in the downfall of the Boston NL franchise was the founding of the American League. The Boston AL franchise revived the discarded Red Stockings name (shortened to Red Sox), which reminded older fans of Boston's proud baseball heritage. In 1901 three Beaneaters stars signed with the Red Sox, including future Hall of Fame third baseman Jimmy Collins, who served as player-manager. Selee was then fired, and ace pitcher Kid Nichols quit for two years following a salary dispute, coming back in 1904 with the Cardinals. The underappreciated Selee immediately moved to Chicago, and assembled the great "Tinker to Evers to Chance" Cubs teams. He managed 17 years with a .598 winning percentage.

The club made a comeback in 1902 under manager Al Buckenberger, coming in third, and then the depleted Beaneaters nose-dived, going through 10 straight losing seasons. Soden, facing aggressive, renewed competition for Boston fans, grew fussier about penny-pinching than wins, even charging his own players' wives to attend Boston home games. In 1906 Soden saved a lot of pennies by hiring manager and first baseman Fred Tenney, who was required to wrench foul balls away from patrons. The owners told Tenney, "We don't care where you finish, as long as you don't lose us money." Tenney received a bonus each year the team posted a profit. Making a profit was difficult because in the 1900s the team was the worst draw in the NL, pulling in just 6.2 percent of the league's audiences.

The Triumvirs also cut costs by replacing the ornate South End Grounds, which burned down in 1894, with a small, plain, wooden structure. The rival AL club directly challenged the Beaneaters when they built their field across the street. In 1912 they built the new Fenway Park, which far outshone the

South End Grounds. The new league offered cheaper bleacher tickets and beer. This drew in the famous local fan club, the Royal Rooters, led by Mayor John "Honey Fitz" Fitzgerald, the grandfather of President John F. Kennedy. The Royal Rooters' defection from the NL helped the Red Sox gain primacy in Boston. The Rooters led the majority of Boston's upwardly mobile Irish away from the NL to the Red Sox, who put an excellent product on the field.

In 1906, Soden, after 30 years as owner, sold his failing Boston NL club, which finished last for the first time, 66 1/2 games out of first place. He sold the team to George and John Dovey for $75,000, and they renamed the team the Doves. In 1910 the club was sold to William Russell and renamed the Rustlers. He died after the season, during which the club went 44–97, the third of four straight eighth-place finishes. Ninety-five percent of the team's stock was sold for $187,000 to a New York syndicate headed by attorney John Montgomery Ward, a former major-league shortstop and pitcher and president of the Brotherhood, who knew Russell because both were active in New York politics as antimachine reformers. To allay Boston fans' fears of yet another futile out-of-town ownership, Ward moved from New York to Boston.

One way President Ward tried to revive the Boston club was giving them a new nickname. He called them the Braves, proclaiming that he wanted the club to sport an identity with spirit and pride, to inspire the players to a better effort. Ward redesigned the club's drab uniforms to feature a colorful Native American profile, similar to the long-popular Indian-head penny. The new name was also in honor of the majority owner, James Gaffney, a leader of the powerful New York City Democratic machine, Tammany Hall. The society, created during the American Revolution by working-class men, identified strongly with oppressed Native Americans rather than aristocratic British Americans. The group was named for Delaware chief Tammanend, renowned for his honesty and wisdom. Tammany leaders were dubbed "Chieftains" and their followers were "Braves." The society evolved into a powerful, and corrupt, Democratic political machine. The name "Braves" itself became associated with success when the 1914 "Miracle Braves" pulled off the most shocking World Series upset ever. Ironically, Ward, who named the club, had fought a lonely battle in the late nineteenth century to bring blacks, Hispanics, and Native Americans into the major leagues.

The Braves were the first major professional team to carry a Native American name. Following the club's stunning 1914 turnaround as the Boston Braves, Native American team names increased significantly. For example, the Boston professional football club was named the Braves, and later became the Washington Redskins. Team nicknames, which had previously been unofficial and shifted frequently, first became fixed in the 1920s. Such Native American sports mascots came under heavy fire from activists in the 1970s.

Ward tried to rebuild the Braves with Hispanic talent. Ward, who spoke Spanish and had played winter baseball in 1870s Cuba, brought in Miguel

Gonzalez of Cuba, one of the first Latino players in the major leagues. Gonzalez later became the majors' first Hispanic manager.

In 1913, veteran manager George Stallings, infamous for his bluntness and explosive temper, raged, "This club is a horror show . . . I've been stuck with some terrible teams, but this one beats them all." The 1914 Braves were dismissed as "a band of misfits" by the combative John McGraw, manager of the New York Giants, who had won the three previous NL pennants. Just before the season, starting pitcher Buster Brown died of heart disease. Stallings tried to make up for the young Braves' weak hitting by becoming the first manager to platoon many positions over a long period. The team started out very poorly at 4–18, yet in May 1914 Stallings predicted, "Give me a month, and we'll be in first place." The team was mired in last place as late as July 18. However, only 35 days later, the Braves climbed over all seven other NL teams to take first place. Giants-Braves matches were especially hotly contended. In one game, the Giants' Fred Snodgrass and Braves pitcher Lefty Tyler exchanged gestures and shouts over a pitch at Snodgrass's head, leading some Braves fans to pelt center fielder Snodgrass with bottles. Boston Mayor James Curley strode on the field to urge the umpires to eject Snodgrass, to avert a riot. To avoid being an additional target, manager McGraw, who usually coached third base, hid in the dugout. Then on October 1 all of the Giants on the bench were thrown out of the game except acting skipper Mike Donlin.

Sportswriters credited Stallings's leadership and the new nickname with inspiring the Braves to one of the most amazing makeovers in sports history. The Miracle Braves won the pennant by 10 1/2 games with a record of 94–59, leading the NL in attendance with 382,913. It was as big a surprise as the Braves' 1991 worst-to-first season, when another Native American element, "the Tomahawk Chop," was associated with a Braves turnaround.

The Philadelphia Athletics were heavily favored in the World Series, having won four of the last five AL pennants. Two days before the series, Stallings, dubbed "the Miracle Man," phoned the Athletics' dignified manager Connie Mack before a pack of reporters. To embarrass Mack, Stallings picked a bogus argument over practice times, told Mack the Braves would beat the A's anyway, and then hung up. Stallings assured the stunned media, "We'll beat them in four straight," although in the last game of the season, slick-fielding third baseman Red Smith, who hit a team-high .314 for the Braves, broke his ankle. A's veteran Chief Bender was dispatched to scout the Braves late in the season, but didn't bother, assuring Mack they were bush leaguers.

Hall of Famer Bender was 6–3 in prior World Series, but was belted in game one, the first time the Native American had failed to complete a World Series contest. When Mack walked to the mound to yank Bender, he asked, "Not too bad, for bush leaguers, huh?" After winning game two in Philadelphia, Stallings shipped the Braves' road uniforms back to Boston, explaining, "We won't be coming back here." After winning game three, Stallings canceled the Braves' Philadelphia hotel reservations for game five. The Braves then swept the defending champion Athletics. The Braves' pitching and airtight defense limited the Athletics to just six runs, besting their three Hall of Fame starting pitchers. In the first World Series sweep, Braves catcher Hank Gowdy hit .545, the second-highest series average ever, and "Seattle" Bill James pitched 11 scoreless innings. Gowdy, the first major leaguer to enlist for World War I, caught for the Braves for 12 seasons.

The Miracle Braves' spitballers Bill James and Dick Rudolph combined for 52 wins in 1914, with James winning 19 of his last 20 decisions in the Braves' incredible stretch drive. The Braves' emotional leaders were their double-play odd couple of Hall of Famers, NL MVP Johnny Evers and the MVP runner-up, young, big-eared Rabbit Maranville. In personality, the 125-pound Evers, nicknamed "the Crab," was the polar opposite of the effervescent Maranville, the Braves' cleanup hitter. Maranville, discovered by Ward in Springfield, Massachusetts, beat out Stallings's nephew for the shortstop job, assuring Stallings, "I know I haven't much chance going up against your family, but if you put me in there, you'll never take me out." Twenty-two years later Maranville was still playing for the Braves. Maranville originated the basket catch, later made more famous by Willie Mays. The acrobatic five-foot five-inch Maranville delighted fans with his backflips and pranks, such as crawling to the batter's box through a home-plate umpire's legs. Recalling the unique magic of Evers and Maranville, Chief Bender mused about the nature of team spirit, "You don't know where it comes from when you have it, and you don't know where it went when it's gone." Hoping to replicate the Braves' rapid turnaround, the Cleveland Naps latched onto the name "Indians" three months after the series.

In 1915, the year after the Braves' miracle season, a new 40,000-seat stadium, Braves Field, the last of the original concrete and steel ballparks and the largest in the United States, was opened to rival the Red Sox's Fenway Park. From the Braves Field stands on Commonwealth Avenue, fans could cheer Harvard rowers racing on the Charles River. Owner James Gaffney built a wide-open ballpark (402 feet to left and right, 550 feet to center) conducive to inside-the-park home runs. But in the 1920s, when homers over the fence became more popular, the long distances to the wall and winds coming in from center field hindered homers—no ball cleared the left-field fence until 1925—so in 1928 the fences were moved in, but that failed to improve team performance or raise attendance. The field included a covered single-deck grandstand seating 18,000 and two uncovered pavilions that each seated 10,000. Another 2,000 sat in the bleachers in right field. It was known as "the jury box," after a sportswriter one day noticed only 12 people sitting there.

The dimensions of spacious Braves Field helped make it the site for numerous pitching duels, including the longest one, the 1–1, 26-inning marathon between the Braves' Joe Oeschger and the Brooklyn Dodgers' Leon Cadore, who each pitched the entire May 1, 1920, contest. Only three balls were used in the game, typical of the penny-pinching NL prior to the lively-ball era. Braves Field is now part of Boston University's athletic facilities.

Stallings's club remained competitive, finishing second and third following the miracle season. A big factor in the Miracle Braves' fall was that 22-year-old Bill James, who went 26–7 in 1914 with an ERA of 1.90, ruined his arm, and won only five more games in his career. In 1916, Gaffney sold the team (but not the ballpark) for $500,000 to Harvard's renowned coach Percy Haughton and a banker associate. Haughton failed in his crusade to persuade his Braves to exclaim "Good!" instead of spouting four-letter words. In 1919, Haughton sold out to New Yorker George W. Grant, who used capital advanced by New York Giants owner Charles Stoneham. At this time, Giants manager and co-owner John McGraw and Grant were bidding on a Havana, Cuba, racetrack! The Braves-Giants symbiosis dated back to 1890, because Arthur Soden also owned part of the Giants. During the Grant era, allegations surfaced that the club secretly aided the Giants, which included certain sweetheart trades. One suspicious deal was trading 26-year-old lefty Art Nehf in 1919 just after he pitched the entire 21 innings of a 2–0 loss. Nehf won 60 games for McGraw over the next three years, and pitched in four straight World Series.

In 1917 the club fell to sixth, the first of four straight losing seasons. Stallings quit in 1920, claiming the Braves were underfinanced. The team's cheap travel arrangements during a 20-game exhibition trip inspired spectacular shortstop Maranville to lead a clownish team rebellion, which included growing beards and wearing the loudest clothes possible. Maranville's wild alcohol-fueled antics increasingly plagued the Braves' ever-changing owners, who, after Stallings quit, dealt Maranville away in 1921 to retain their sanity.

BOSTON, 1922–44: A GREAT DEPRESSION

The Braves sunk to their all-time low point in the years 1922–24, when the club dropped over 100 games each season. In 1923 Grant sold out for $300,000 to another New Yorker, Judge Emil Fuchs, who headed the club from 1923 to 1935. Fuchs had been the Giants' lawyer and once represented gambling czar Arnold Rothstein. The Braves lost money in six years during the 1920s, when MLB prospered, earning a total of $38,578. Then, during the depression, the team averaged an *annual* loss of $37,000.

The Braves suffered some tragedy off the field as well. In 1924 star third baseman Tony Boeckel was hit by a car and killed. In 1923, Fuchs brought in former Giants pitching great Christy Mathewson, a man of impeccable integrity, as club president. However, Mathewson was suffering from tuberculosis, and died in 1925. The Braves continued to dwell at the bottom of the NL standings.

In 1928 Fuchs secured the legendarily abrasive Rogers Hornsby to play second and manage. The great Rajah hit a league-leading .387 with 107 walks, but the team went 50–103, and he was a disruptive force. Fuchs sold him the next season for quick cash. With the self-centered Hornsby gone, team player Rabbit Maranville returned to the Braves. Fuchs hoped Maranville would lure in his faithful fans and advise Fuchs, who saved money by serving as manager, on game strategy. Playing for the 1933 Braves, the 41-year-old Maranville broke his leg severely trying to score by crashing into a catcher blocking home plate. The 155-pound Rabbit was in such pain as he lay on the field that he had his 240-pound teammate Shanty Hogan knock him out with a punch. He tried another comeback in 1935, but hit only .149. When Fuchs was asked if as manager he would use the squeeze play, he sniffed, "No, let us score in an honorable way." One reason Fuchs was strapped for cash that year was discovered by historian Steven Riess: to increase attendance, Fuchs had to spend $200,000 lobbying and paying bribes to get Sunday baseball approved in Boston. In 1930, Fuchs brought in veteran manager Bill McKechnie, who had three winning seasons during his eight-year tenure, very good by Braves standards. However, he also suffered through a miserable 1935 season when the team lost 115 games, then a major-league record.

That year, Fuchs, financially reeling from the Great Depression, acquired the washed-up 40-year-old Babe Ruth to counter the more successful Red Sox, with whom the Babe had launched his incredible major-league career. After the Yankees rebuffed Ruth's request to manage, the slugger was lured with a Braves' vice presidency, plus the promise that he would pilot the Braves after he retired. Ruth homered in his first at bat as a Brave, off future Hall of Famer Carl Hubbell, and smashed three mammoth homers in one of his final games. However, Ruth averaged only .181 for the Braves and retired in disgust in June 1935 when he realized that Fuchs wanted him only as yet another temporary gate attraction. Despite Ruth, that season the Braves' record was 38–115, one of the worst in baseball history. At one Braves home game the attendance was reported as 95. Fuchs then begged the Red Sox to allow the Braves to play at Fenway Park so he could convert underutilized Braves Field into a roller rink.

After this fiasco the NL wanted Fuchs out. In 1936, longtime baseball executive Bob Quinn, Red Sox president from 1923 to 1932, when they won only 35 percent of their games, took over the club. He was financed by $200,000 from majority stockholder Charles Adams, owner of the Boston Bruins. Adams always tried to keep a low profile with MLB due to his ownership of Suffolk Downs Race Track. To transform the Braves franchise's bad luck, Quinn asked fans to submit new names for the team. Suggested names included the Boston Blues, the Bankrupts, and the Basements. These nicknames were rejected by a group of sportswriters, who selected "Bees" as the new name. The club remained the Bees from 1936 to 1941. Braves Field temporarily became the Beehive, or National League Field.

In 1938 Quinn brought in another wild character that had played in Boston, Casey Stengel, who like Babe Ruth later gained greater fame and glory with the Yankees. Stengel had ended his on-field career with the 1924–25 Braves. The Braves had a winning record in 1938, finishing fifth, but thereafter averaged only about 64 wins per season. Manager Stengel missed part of 1943, which was his last season, after a Boston cabbie ran him down. Pittsburgh manager

Frankie Frisch dropped Stengel a sympathy note: "Your attempt at suicide fully understood."

Quinn's moves flopped, as the team seldom outdrew or outperformed its better-financed AL counterpart. This was especially true after Tom Yawkey bought the Red Sox in 1933 and upgraded Fenway Park. While America had recovered from the Great Depression by the late 1930s, the Braves continued their own Great Depression into the World War II years, when most major-league stars joined the military and were replaced by minor leaguers. The club lost money each year from 1941 to 1945. In 1944 the underfinanced Quinn sold the Braves to a well-off local trio of minority investors, much to the pleasure of his fellow NL owners.

BOSTON, 1945–52: "SPAHN, SAIN, AND PRAY FOR TWO DAYS OF RAIN"

The new owners, Lou Perini, Joe Marey, and Guido Rugo, had much deeper pockets than Fuchs or Quinn, having amassed fortunes in World War II construction. The trio became known as "the Three Little Steam Shovels." The 1940s Braves Field stands featured Hy Brenner's band and "the Three Little Earaches," who serenaded their team with tunes such as "Has Anybody Here Seen Kelly?" and razzed Braves' opponents. Both trios' ethnicity reflect the twentieth-century makeup of Boston Braves fans: primarily non-Irish, with working-class origins. Opening Day 1946 was a comical low point for the significant upgrading efforts of the Steam Shovels and provided fresh material for the Earaches, because the paint was still wet on Braves Field's seats, ruining about 5,000 fans' clothing. While the paint dried, Tom Yawkey let the Braves play in Fenway Park, and Braves team president Perini paid all fans' cleaning bills. The park really needed the paint due to the heavy soot from a nearby railroad. All other NL clubs except the Chicago Cubs had installed park lighting, so the Steam Shovels did so at Braves Field. Perini attracted highly accomplished manager Billy Southworth from the St. Louis Cardinals with an incentive-packed contract. General Manager "Trader" John Quinn, son of the former owner, set to work making up for the sins of his father by bringing in talented veterans for Southworth, who returned the club to respectability. That season a tomahawk first appeared on the Braves' jerseys. The club had a creditable winning mark of 81–71, good for fourth place, and actually made money. However, the $40,000 profit only surpassed one team that year, the Giants, who lost heavily. The Braves moved up to third in 1947 (86–68), and the excitement brought over a million spectators for the first time, and a return of $229,000, which was duplicated the following year.

The star of the team was left-hander Warren Spahn, who won 21 games and had an ERA of 2.33. Spahn's 363 career wins are the most of any left-hander, all but the last seven of them for the Braves, despite his missing three seasons fighting in World War II, including seeing action in the Battle of the Bulge.

Warren Spahn, 1953. Courtesy of the Baseball Hall of Fame Library

Spahn led the NL nine times in complete games. Spahn was a good hitter who sometimes pinch-hit, and slugged home runs in 17 consecutive seasons, a record for pitchers. On the mound he was famous for his high leg kick and mystifying screwball. For players, including Spahn, Lou Perini's construction business provided off-season employment in the Boston area.

Star hurlers Warren Spahn and Johnny Sain led the Braves in 1948 when Boston fans moaned, "Spahn, Sain, and pray for two days of rain," hoping the Braves' other, lesser, starters wouldn't need to pitch. The chant became famous when the Braves captured the NL pennant (91–62), as Spahn (15 wins) and Sain (24), a control specialist, combined for 39 wins. It was a veteran team that averaged 29.6 years old and had solid offense, batting .275, which led the league. The top hitters were outfielder Tommy Holmes (.325) and shortstop Alvin Dark (.322). Third baseman Bob Elliott, who hit .317 and had 22 homers, was NL MVP. The Braves' gate soared to 1.45 million. In their first World Series in 34 years, the Braves faced the powerful Cleveland Indians. Sain beat flamethrower Bob Feller 1–0 in the opener, but the Braves lost the next three, with little offense. The Fall Classic went six games, with the Braves losing the deciding game 4–3. Sain led the Boston effort with a sparkling 1.06 ERA.

A self-inflicted blow came when the Braves' fine double-play combo, veteran Eddie Stanky and 1948 Rookie of the Year Alvin Dark, were swapped to (surprise!) the New York Giants after confronting the fiery Southworth about his heavy drinking. That disastrous trade and the club's age, combined with Southworth's illnesses and demanding ways, brought the club down quickly. In that post–World War II era the major leagues finally slowly reopened their doors to black athletes, and the Braves were one of the earlier teams to recruit blacks. To replace the aged veterans of the 1948 World Series club, the Braves improved considerably by acquiring the excellent Negro League center fielder Sam Jethroe, who won the 1950 NL Rookie of the Year Award and twice led the NL in steals.

Despite the Braves' pennant-winning season, they struggled terribly in the Boston market. Even in 1948 they could not outdraw the Red Sox. The city's population only grew by 200,000 in the first half of the century and was not large enough to support two teams. In addition, the Braves' falling attendance has been linked to suburbanization and the breakup of many Boston ethnic neighborhoods after World War II, the advent of television, and poor play on the field. The decline of Southworth's Braves was typified by a game on May 13, 1952, in which Spahn lost in 15 innings despite homering for the Braves' only run and tying the NL record by striking out 18. In 1952, only 272,000 chilled fans came to the windy, outmoded Braves Field to see a 64–89 team, an 80 percent attendance drop since 1948.

MILWAUKEE, 1953–65: BUILD IT AND THEY WILL COME

In the early 1950s Milwaukee sought a major-league franchise, led by boosters including the chamber of commerce, the *Journal,* and especially brewer Frederick Miller. Political leaders made available County Stadium, which had originally been built for a minor-league club, and expanded it to meet the needs of a major-league team. The politicians saw a team as a means to gain prestige for Milwaukee and promote economic development. The local minor-league club was owned by the Braves, who hit bottom in 1952. Bill Veeck wanted to move his struggling St. Louis Browns to Milwaukee, where he once ran the minor-league club. But Braves president Lou Perini, who bought out his partners, invoked organized baseball's territorial privilege, claiming that Veeck had not offered the Braves enough step-aside money to supplant the Milwaukee farm club. Wisconsin attacked the Braves for blocking them from getting a major-league club. Perini planned to test the waters in Milwaukee's new stadium, but his timetable was speeded up when Wisconsin offered to take the St. Louis Cardinals instead. Though the Cardinals had 14 straight winning seasons, owner Fred Saigh was desperately seeking money to fight tax-evasion charges. Faced with losing his top minor-league club, Perini acted. Without any warning to Boston fans, he petitioned the NL a month before the opening of the 1953 season to shift his franchise. The NL approved the proposal just five days after receiving the formal application. Thus, after a 50-year period of no major-league team moves, the Braves' transfer unleashed an era of franchise shifts away from the economically declining industrial East toward the growing opportunities in the thriving West. Journalist Leonard Koppett cited the Braves' move as "the crossroads event of 20th century baseball."

So, in 1953, Milwaukee returned to the majors for the first time since 1901, and became just the second major-league franchise west of Chicago. A new winning era began for the Braves, and fans flocked to see popular Braves manager "Jolly Cholly" Charlie Grimm and his stars, whom they had followed when Grimm and his youngsters prepped with the Milwaukee Brewers of the American Association. In the Braves' first game in Milwaukee, center fielder

Billy Bruton had a triple, a walk-off home run, and a game-saving catch of a rocket shot by the Cardinals' Stan Musial. The team made a huge improvement to 92–62 and second place. They were average offensively, led by 21-year-old Eddie Mathews, who had a sensational year, hitting .302 with 47 homers and 135 RBIs. His combination of power, high on-base percentage, and fine fielding helped establish a new standard for third basemen, previously expected to excel only with the glove. The team's speed and defense were enhanced by former Negro Leaguer Billy Bruton, who led the league in steals his first three seasons. According to three-time Gold Glover Hank Aaron, "Watching Billy Bruton play the outfield gives me an inferiority complex." The Braves' greatest strength was the best pitching staff in the NL, led by Spahn, with his league-topping 2.10 ERA.

Attendance in the first season was an NL record 1,826,397, compared to 281,278 the year before in Boston. Local folk were energized by the presence of major-league baseball and a contending ball club. Furthermore, in their first season the Braves reportedly attracted $5 million in new business to the city. They brought an electric vitality that seemed to affect all local business and bolster the city's second-rate self-image. Fans were enticed by the ballpark itself, with its vast parking lots. It was the first facility in the majors constructed with lights, and one of the first to be situated adjacent to a major interstate highway to draw newly affluent suburbanites, and fans from other states. Local fans could not follow the Braves on TV because Perini believed television had hurt attendance in Boston, so he banned broadcasting of Braves games. After 50 years in the Red Sox's long shadow, the Braves seemed to have found their home in Milwaukee. For the next few years, the Braves were the most profitable team in baseball, drawing 2 million each year from 1954 to 1957.

In 1954, rookie Hank Aaron, a converted second baseman, got his big break when star right fielder Bobby Thomson shattered his ankle. Aaron was bought in 1952 for a mere $7,500 from the Indianapolis Clowns of the Negro National League. The scouting report on him from Dewey Griggs was that "[he] is one of the finest hitters God ever put on this earth." He and teammate Bruton needed a thick skin to withstand racist barbs such as Warren Spahn's frequent joke "What is black and catches flies? The Braves outfield." The Braves came in third in the NL with an attendance of 2.1 million and second in 1955. They drew over 2 million every year until 1959, when attendance fell to 1.97 million. After 46 games in 1956, "Jolly Cholly" Grimm was replaced by the strict Fred Haney. Haney led the Braves to a 92–62 record. They lost the pennant on the last day of the season when Warren Spahn was beaten in 12 innings.

The 1957 season belonged to the Braves. They had a terrific lineup, with four-time Gold Glove catcher Del Crandall; infielders Frank Torre, Red Schoendienst, Johnny Logan, and Mathews; an outfield of Aaron, Bruton, and Wes Covington; and a strong bench, including flash-in-the-pan rookie Bob "Hurricane" Hazle, who hit .403 as a sub when injuries crippled the Braves' outfield. The team led the NL in batting and was second in pitching with

Spahn, Lew Burdette, and Bob Buhl. They built up a commanding lead in August but struggled in early September. They clinched the pennant on September 23 on an Aaron home run. Spahn was the 1957 Cy Young winner and Aaron was the NL MVP, batting .322 with 132 RBIs. The newly famous Aaron became known as "Hammerin' Hank" and "the Hammer," while opposing pitchers dubbed him "Bad Henry." The friendly, small-town, midwestern atmosphere that fans bestowed on Milwaukee County Stadium, including bringing home-cooked meals to beloved players, paid off big. The team drew an NL record 2,215,404 fans.

The Braves then faced the New York Yankees in the 1957 World Series. During the series the Milwaukee fans turned a Yankee employee's dismissal of their enthusiastic welcome of the Yankees to Milwaukee as midwestern "bush" into a rallying cry. The slur was mistakenly attributed to Yankees manager Casey Stengel, which was unlikely because he had previously managed

Undated photo of the legendary Hank Aaron in action. Courtesy of the Baseball Hall of Fame Library

in Milwaukee and was proud of having been raised in Kansas City. To counter the Yankees' cool response to them, many Braves faithful sported signs proudly proclaiming Milwaukee as "Bushville." At the peak of Braves fans' boos in game three, Stengel graciously blew a kiss to the crowd. The exciting and competitive series went seven games. In game four a classic moment occurred with the Braves down two games to one and losing 5–4 in the bottom of the 10th inning. The Braves' Nippy Jones was awarded first base after convincing umpire Augie Donatelli that he had been plunked, by showing him the baseball had Jones's shoe polish on it. Two batters later Eddie Mathews smashed a game-winning home run. Then, in the next game, Covington preserved a 1–0 shutout when he crashed into the fence to take away a home run. The star of the series was pitcher Lew Burdette, who won three games with a 0.67 ERA, including the decisive game seven, 5–0, on two days' rest. He was the first pitcher in 52 years to throw two series shutouts. Burdette was acquired from the Yankees for Johnny Sain in 1951, and Burdette's remarkable World Series performance satisfied his long-held grudge against Stengel, his former manager in New York. All during 1957 opposing managers accused Burdette of pulling a spitter out of his deep trick bag, which included talking to the ball, fiddling with his uniform, and constant, distracting facial grimaces.

The Braves repeated in 1958 (92–62), sparked by league-leading pitching and defense. Burdette and Spahn combined for 42 victories. In the 1958 World Series rematch with the Yankees, Milwaukee took a 3–1 lead. However, for the first time in history, a team came back from that margin to take the Series.

The Braves in 1959, led by Aaron, who took his second batting title (.355), and Spahn and Burdette, who each won 21, tied for the 1959 NL pennant with 86 victories. The team was weakened by the loss of Schoendienst, who contracted tuberculosis. In the two-out-of-three playoff against the Los Angeles Dodgers, the Braves lost the first by one run, and then lost the second at home in 12 innings. Only 18,297 fans came to the rainy playoff contest, a portent of the attendance decline that would encourage the Braves' next owner to abandon Milwaukee.

A historic game was played at County Stadium on May 26, 1959, when the Pittsburgh Pirates' Harvey Haddix crafted a perfect game for 12 innings. A runner got on base in the 13th inning on an error and Aaron was intentionally walked. Joe Adcock then homered, but in the rain Aaron mistakenly ran off the base paths, assuming the game was over, allowing Adcock to lumber past him. Aaron and Adcock were called out, but Haddix still lost the game and his no-hitter, 1–0. The winning pitcher was Burdette, who shut out the Pirates while giving up 12 hits. Later, asking for a $10,000 raise, Burdette joked, "The greatest game that was ever pitched in baseball wasn't good enough to beat me, so I've got to be the greatest pitcher!" Haddix's masterpiece loomed even larger when it was revealed in 1993 that the Braves were stealing Pirates catcher Smoky Burgess's signs because he was unable to squat all the way down.

Five days after the playoffs Fred Haney quit even though he had come within three games of leading the Braves to four straight World Series. Haney was under heavy criticism for managing too conservatively and overusing Spahn and Burdette. In addition, ace general manager John Quinn, architect of the club's last three pennant winners, moved on to the Philadelphia Phillies.

Veteran manager Charley Dressen took over and led the team to another second-place finish in 1960, but fell to fourth in 1961, and was replaced by Birdie Tebbetts. Burdette and Spahn each pitched a no-hitter in 1960, and the 40-year-old Spahn pitched another in 1961, all at Milwaukee County Stadium. The boyish-looking Spahn even won 23 games at age 42. But the love affair between the Braves and the beer-and-bratwurst-adoring fans who journeyed hundreds of miles from four states to tailgate in Milwaukee County Stadium's big parking lot was coming to a bitter end for a variety of reasons. The declining attendance reflected the fall out of the first division, with the team placing fifth (86–76) in 1962 and sixth (84–78) in 1963; trades of popular players; and weak efforts at promotion. The Braves' fan base was cut after the Washington Senators moved to Minnesota in 1961. As TV revenue began to play a bigger role in sports, Milwaukee offered a small audience, with two Chicago teams also looming just across the Cheddar Curtain. Lou Perini's policy of not allowing patrons to bring beer into the stadium was heavily criticized. Despite the two World Series appearances, Perini, who remained in Boston, never gained the full trust of Milwaukee fans. In 1962 Perini sold the Braves to a consortium headed by Chicago insurance executive Bill Bartholomay. Milwaukeeans viewed Bartholomay's young group as carpetbaggers. They had little loyalty to the city and almost immediately began considering moving the club.

In April 1964 an Atlanta group courting a major-league club announced that an unnamed franchise had committed to move there. The Braves and Charles Finley's Kansas City A's were both looking to shift to the Sunbelt to take full advantage of booming populations and economic growth. The usually mild-mannered Warren Spahn accused Braves manager Bobby Bragan, a southerner, of intentionally trying to lose games so the team could be moved to the South. The declining Spahn was sold to the lowly New York Mets in November 1964.

In 1965 the new owners announced plans to move to Atlanta, primarily for better media opportunities, even though Milwaukee had the second-best major-league attendance between 1953 and 1965. Fans responded by staying away in droves. Attendance was just 555,584. Taxpayers were furious because County Stadium was the first major-league ballpark built entirely with public funds, was expanded specifically for the Braves' transfer from Boston, and was rented to the Braves at a very nominal fee. MLB temporarily blocked the move due to pressure from Milwaukee interests looking for a local buyer and because the stadium lease had a year to go. Wisconsin attorney general Bronson La Follette hit the team with an antitrust suit, claiming the NL had conspired to restrain trade and harm Wisconsin's economy by approving the transfer without offering another team. This was the first time a state had sued a major-league team in state court for violating an antitrust law. However, the case was ultimately lost because of baseball's exemption from the antitrust laws.

In Atlanta the key figure behind expansion was booster Mayor Ivan Allen Jr., who got the city to build $42.4 million Atlanta–Fulton County Stadium in 1964. He and other local politicians saw baseball as a way for Atlanta to prove it was a first-class city. Atlanta made the Braves an offer they could not refuse, which included paying to defend the antitrust case. The Braves got a radio-TV package of $2.5 million, compared to the meager $400,000 they got in Milwaukee. Thus, though the team posted a winning record every season in Milwaukee, Bartholomay gained league approval for 1966 to move the franchise to Atlanta.

ATLANTA, 1966–75: THE SOUTH SHALL RISE AGAIN, BUT WHEN?

The team was managed in Atlanta by southerner Bobby Bragan, the skipper since 1963. At the outset many of the black and Latin players struggled with the racial situation in the South, as opposed to that in liberal Wisconsin. This injured the club as it tried to maintain its winning tradition. The team ended in fifth place (85–77), its 14th straight winning season. During the Braves' first season in Atlanta a major link between the Boston, Milwaukee, and Atlanta incarnations of the Braves was rudely severed when Eddie Mathews, the only Brave to play in all three home cities, found out from a reporter that he'd been traded after 16 seasons. Mathews combined with Aaron to hit 863 homers as teammates, the most of any duo all time. A future Hall of Famer, Mathews later coached for the Braves and eventually managed them, with little success, from 1972 to 1974.

After seventh- and fifth-place finishes Bartholomay revived the Braves' old attendance ploy used with Babe Ruth and Cy Young by carting in a folksy, elderly gate attraction for 1968. This was actually a humanitarian gesture, since the new player was ageless pitching legend Satchel Paige, who at age 62 or so qualified for a major-league pension by spending an additional 158 days on a big-league roster. He never actually got into a game and later served as a coach.

MLB expanded to 24 teams in 1969 and created a playoff system. The Braves under manager Lum Harris won the first NL Western Division championship (93–69), a big improvement from the .500 season the year before. Hank Aaron, who wore uniform number 44, hit 44 home runs for the fourth time in his career. The Braves bolted from fifth place on August 19 to win the division in a wild race, only to be swept by New York's pumped-up "Miracle Mets" in the NL Championship Series, despite Aaron homering in all three games.

In 1970 Braves left fielder Rico "the Big Man" Carty won the NL batting title with a .366 average, but the Braves instantly slid back into mediocrity. Carty starred with the Braves from 1963 to 1972, but missed the entire 1968 and 1971 campaigns and was frequently beset by serious injuries and illness. Another factor in the Braves' decline was the May 1971 release of superb-fielding third baseman Clete Boyer following his bitter dispute with management and Boyer's being fined for betting on football. Boyer had 14 RBIs in his last nine games for Atlanta, but was blackballed and never played in the majors again.

Regardless of the Atlanta Braves' initial so-so performance, playing in a new stadium in a fresh town provided a temporary boost to attendance. The Braves' maiden year in Atlanta attracted 1.5 million fans, about three times as many as their bitter, lame-duck season in Milwaukee. Atlanta–Fulton County Stadium, across from the Georgia State Capitol, was shared with the NFL Atlanta Falcons. But the attendance bump was short-lived. From 1970 through 1981 the Braves were one of the worst draws in the NL, barely surpassing a million in 1970 and 1971, and then dropping all the way down to 534,672 in 1975.

Atlanta–Fulton County was one of the first multipurpose cookie-cutter stadiums situated downtown to promote urban redevelopment. It was considered the worst playing surface in the majors and did not have a full-time groundskeeper until 1989, when Bobby Cox became the manager. Atlanta–Fulton County Stadium was nicknamed "the Launching Pad" because its elevation (1,057 feet), the highest in the majors until the Colorado Rockies joined in

1993, helped make it extremely homer friendly. While Milwaukee County Stadium was a slight pitcher's park, the Launching Pad helped home-run hitters. In 1973 three Braves hit 40 or more homers. Aaron's amazing consistency, seemingly effortless style, and his being out of the national media glare during most of his 13 years in Milwaukee enabled the long-underrated right fielder to sneak up on many of baseball's career records. Flashier stars Mickey Mantle and Willie Mays had drawn far more national attention than Aaron, who had excelled in his few postseason opportunities. But the quick-wristed Aaron's superb effort in the 1969 playoffs threw him in the media spotlight to stay as he approached Babe Ruth's home-run record.

The closer Hammerin' Hank drew to the Babe's 714 round-trippers, the more pressure he confronted from racists, who sent Aaron hundreds of death threats for menacing a "white man's record." Most letters were postmarked from northern cities. On road trips he had to register under aliases at hotels. "As the hate mail piled up," Aaron reminisced, "I became more and more intent on breaking the record and shoving it into the ugly faces of those bigots."

Though people throughout North America followed Aaron's every move as he approached Ruth's record in 1973, only 1,362 fans in Atlanta saw Aaron hit number 711. Aaron hit his 713th in the next-to-last game of 1973. When he failed to hit 714 the next day, he graciously thanked the 40,000 Atlanta fans in attendance, saying, "I'm sorry I couldn't hit one for them, sitting in the rain like that . . . that applause was the biggest moment I've had in baseball."

The stress on Aaron was especially severe during the off-season. Aaron understated when he said that to break the record "all I've got to do this winter is stay alive." The Atlanta police assigned Aaron a bodyguard to protect him and his new wife, Billye Williams, an Atlanta civil rights activist and TV-show host, while the FBI uncovered a plot to kidnap his daughter Gaile from Fiske University in Nashville and sent undercover agents to protect her. He had to temporarily move out of his home. Twenty years later Aaron recalled that 1973 "should have been the happiest time of my life . . . but it was the worst year."

Aaron and Bartholomay agreed that Aaron would sit out the 1974 season-opening series in Cincinnati, not so much because of the mounting death threats but to reserve the big thrill, and biggest crowds, for Atlanta's home opening series. However, MLB commissioner Bowie Kuhn ordered the Braves to play Aaron. Kuhn had previously represented the NL against Wisconsin's lawsuit to keep the Braves in Milwaukee. Angry at Kuhn over being forced to play, Aaron crushed the long-anticipated 714 in the first inning of Opening Day.

On the April 8, 1974, Braves' home opener an Atlanta–Fulton County Stadium record crowd of 53,775 enjoyed a 45-minute pregame ceremony that featured Pearl Bailey belting out the national anthem. Present that cold, miserable night was Georgia governor and future U.S. president Jimmy Carter, a passionate Braves fan, who walked across the street from the state capitol.

Los Angeles Dodgers' pitcher Al Downing drew vigorous boos when he walked Aaron on five pitches in the first inning. When Aaron scored a few batters later, he broke Willie Mays's NL record for career runs. In the fourth inning, on Aaron's first swing of the game, his fabled wrists rocketed a Downing pitch 390 feet into the Atlanta bullpen to shatter Ruth's record with the long-anticipated number 715. Braves relief pitcher Tom House rejoiced as he caught the specially marked ball at 9:07 P.M. Two young white men leaped from the stands and joyously ran with Aaron between second and third base. Security guards, who had been alerted to the many threats that Aaron would be gunned down on the field, escorted the beaming college students away. Amazingly, the first person to reach Aaron at home plate was his tiny 62-year-old mother, who jumped out of the stands running and rushed ahead of the excited Braves waiting for Aaron at home plate. She explained, "If they were going to kill my son, they were going to have to kill me too."

Three months after Aaron broke the record, manager Eddie Mathews was fired and replaced by Clyde King. The team, surprisingly, finished in third, led by good pitching and defense and the hitting of speedy center fielder Ralph "Road Runner" Garr, who kept his Atlanta teammates loose with his Hank Aaron imitations and led the NL with a .353 average. Aaron had announced (like Babe Ruth) that he wanted the Braves job, which would have made him baseball's first black manager, but that was ridiculed by general manager Eddie Robinson. The fading 40-year-old Aaron saw that his days in Atlanta were numbered. So, again tracing Ruth's giant footsteps, the unflappable, graceful Aaron returned to Milwaukee in 1975 to finish out his career as a designated hitter for the Brewers. He retired with 755 homers and the records for career RBIs, extra-base hits, and total bases.

ATLANTA, 1976–90: CAPTAIN OUTRAGEOUS TAKES THE WHEEL OF AMERICA'S TEAM

Losing is simply learning how to win.

—Ted Turner

In January 1976 Ted Turner acquired majority ownership in the team from Bill Bartholomay's Atlanta-LaSalle Corporation for $10 million, though Bartholomay continued with the club as an active board member. When Turner acquired the Braves, his local WTCG UHF station, which started broadcasting Braves games in 1975, stood last in the Atlanta market, and its programming consisted primarily of old movies and 1950s TV shows. In 1977 he acquired the Atlanta Hawks basketball team. Two years later, Turner's channel 17 went national via cable to become "Super Station" WTBS. In 1979 he promoted the Braves as "America's Team," after the Dallas Cowboys were effectively marketed under the same nickname. For media-savvy Ted Turner, co-opting the designation also made a nice fit with the America's Cup, the international yacht race Turner participated in at the time. In 1980 he founded CNN, the first 24-

hour cable news network. Thus, the hyperactive, visionary Turner became the first of a new breed of fabulously wealthy, publicity-hungry sports magnates who wield their teams as marketing tools within a media empire.

Turner immediately jumped into baseball ownership hands-on by vaulting out of the stands in the first inning of Opening Day 1976 to shake the hand of Atlanta outfielder Ken Henderson, who had just homered. The enthusiastic young mogul's actions charmed numerous Atlanta fans but rubbed baseball's conservative old guard many wrong ways. Turner garnered praise from minority activists for hiring the highest-ranking black executive in major-league history to that point, general manager Bill Lucas, formerly head of the Braves' farm system. Lucas died in 1979 and is commemorated by Lucas Boulevard, the street on the first-base side of Turner Field.

Under the Braves' new owner Aaron returned to Atlanta triumphantly as director of player development. There the usually quiet Aaron escalated his criticism of the racist policies prevalent in baseball's omnipresent old boys' club, which keep minorities from front-office and managerial opportunities. "Old boy" general manager Eddie Robinson was gone when Aaron returned, replaced by Aaron's former brother-in-law Lucas. It was an early sign of how the Braves' new owner, Ted Turner, would totally transform the landscape of the team while revolutionizing broadcasting. Under Aaron the Braves became one of the first organizations to heavily recruit talented, inexpensive Latin American teenagers. In addition to Aaron, another Braves legend, Johnny Sain, returned to the Braves under Ted Turner. Sain, who'd become an esteemed pitching coach but often clashed with his managers, served with Atlanta in 1977 and 1985–86, all losing years.

Three months into the 1976 season, Commissioner Kuhn fined Turner for cozying up to soon-to-be-free-agent Gary "Sarge" Matthews Sr. while the hustling outfielder was still playing for the San Francisco Giants. Turner persisted in rabidly pursuing Matthews, so in January 1977, Turner got seriously burned when Kuhn suspended him for one year for tampering, though the Braves were allowed to keep Matthews. Turner's successful courtship of Matthews included Turner's own family billboard company erecting a huge "Welcome to Atlanta, Gary!" sign near the Atlanta airport.

While vigorously appealing his suspension in May 1977, Turner even managed the team for one losing game, trying to break a 16-game losing streak, defy MLB, and drive up TV ratings—all at the same time. Champion yachtsman Turner, who had no baseball experience at all, gave his manager Dave Bristol the day off. "Captain Outrageous" was the first manager without professional playing experience since Judge Fuchs in 1929. NL president Chub Feeney immediately removed Turner as manager due to a rule prohibiting a manager from holding a financial interest in a major-league club. Turner sued Commissioner Kuhn but lost, and Turner's detractors branded him "the Mouth of the South."

Turner also took a personal crack at boosting attendance by joining the team's ground crew and staging on-field ostrich races, with Turner and his baseball broadcasters as jockeys—silks and all. In the second race Turner's ostrich bolted straight at the visitors' dugout—causing giggling Los Angeles Dodgers to duck and hide. One jockey, Braves announcer Ernie Johnson, had pitched for the 1950–58 Braves. In the Great Baseball Nose Push, the only two contestants willing to scrunch down on all fours to nudge a baseball 90 feet down the baselines were the Philadelphia Phillies' flaky reliever Tug McGraw—and Turner himself. Turner won, his grinning face, cleft chin, and scraggly mustache dripping with blood. For years, the ultracompetitive Turner proudly displayed the bloody ball on his desk.

Turner was open to any idea from Bob Hope, the Braves' inventive public-relations director from 1966 to 1979. In 1976 70-year-old Karl Wallenda amazed Atlanta fans by walking a 300-foot wire without a net across the top of the stadium despite high winds. A 1985 Braves stunt backfired, infuriating people in the area, when the Atlanta management set off fireworks at 4:01 A.M. The rockets were launched to placate 10,000 faithful fans, who were understandably disappointed over losing a surreal 19-inning, 16–13 game, plus waiting 6 hours, 57 minutes to enjoy the traditional Fourth of July fireworks. With no Braves pinch hitters available in the 18th inning, longtime Atlanta pitcher Rick Camp hit his only career homer to keep the Braves alive, then lost the game in the 19th. The contest, before an initial crowd of 44,000, included two rain delays and ended at 3:55 A.M. when a two-run 19th-inning rally by the Braves fell short.

Turner quickly became active in the free-agent market after pitchers Andy Messersmith and Dave McNally sat out the 1975 season to challenge baseball's reserve rule. Turner signed Messersmith to a $1.8 million contract, more than most stars had earned in an entire career. By quickly signing Messersmith, Turner also broke ranks with fellow owners, who mulled blacklisting Messersmith for defying them. In 1976 Turner explained, "I bought the Braves because I'm tired of seeing them kicked around. I'm the little guy's hero." Like fellow showman and maverick owner Bill Veeck, "Terrible Ted" Turner quickly became a prime nemesis of the baseball establishment.

Turner drew fire and laughs when he inked flamboyant relief pitcher Al "the Mad Hungarian" Hrabosky to a 30-year contract, including the guarantee of a Braves broadcasting job. Hrabosky lasted only three mediocre seasons as a Brave and never made it into the Atlanta broadcast booth. The Turner regime's wild antics and expensive personnel gaffes at the dawn of the free-agent era, such as signing pitching busts Messersmith and Bruce Sutter, made the club the butt of jokes. But Turner and the Braves were the happy recipients of mega-publicity, new fans, and healthy TV ratings, if not wins.

The team struggled in the late 1970s, landing in last place four straight years and losing 101 games in 1977. Third baseman Bob Horner won the 1978 NL Rookie of the Year Award but thereafter seemed to constantly get injured. He had frequent contract troubles that drew as many headlines from 1978 to 1986 as his prodigious homers. Horner, from Arizona State, was the number-one pick in baseball's 1978 amateur draft and went directly to the Braves without playing in the minors. In 1986 Horner became the third Brave to hit four homers in a game (albeit a losing effort), following Bobby Lowe in 1894 and Joe Adcock in 1954.

Turner's teams did not have a winning record until 1980, when they went 81–80 under third-year manager Bobby Cox, but fell off to 50–56 in the strike-shortened 1981 season. The club made a big turnaround in 1982 under manager Joe Torre, a former Braves star (1960–68), winning the NL West with a record of 89–73, only to be swept by the Cards in the NLCS three games to none. A bizarre, pivotal event occurred on August 19 when young Braves pitcher Pascual Perez missed his first start because he literally ran out of gas after futilely driving around Atlanta freeways for three hours, unable to find the ballpark. The suddenly loose Braves, who had lost 19 of their prior 21 games, then won 14 of 16 to take first place back and capture the division championship. The star of the team was fan favorite Dale Murphy. He was converted from catcher to center fielder to overcome a mysterious block that affected his tossing the ball back to the pitcher. Murphy was the NL MVP in 1982 and 1983, a two-time home-run champ, and the winner of five straight Gold Gloves.

One of the Braves' few standouts in this period was portly Hall of Fame knuckleballer Phil Niekro. The converted reliever pitched until age 48 and won 318 games, all but the last 20 for the Braves. His 1973 no-hitter was the franchise's only no-hitter in the 30-year stretch between the dynasties in Milwaukee and Atlanta. "Knucksie" Niekro was also a fine fielder, winning five Gold Gloves. Niekro's brother Joe, himself a 221-game winner, pitched in Atlanta with Phil from 1973 to 1975. At age 43, Niekro wept openly when the Braves won the 1982 NL West championship. His 24 seasons without a single World Series appearance, including his 19 years with the Braves from 1965 to 1983, is a very unwanted record. Niekro's loyalty to the Atlanta fans and franchise, especially in the free-agent era when millionaire players annually chase greater fortunes from town to town, was reciprocated by both Bartholomay and Turner. Niekro is commemorated by a statue outside the Atlanta stadium. Dale Murphy and Warren Spahn are also honored with Turner Field statues.

Following the 1982 division championship WTBS viewership rocketed and Atlanta attendance peaked at 2.1 million. The gate then nose-dived as Atlanta fans' expectations of the Braves increased while the team began to lose ugly. One of the ugliest exhibitions on the Atlanta ball field occurred on August 12, 1984. Starting pitcher Pascual Perez initiated one of the most brawl-filled games in major-league history when he drilled the San Diego Padres' rail-thin Alan Wiggins in the back with the first pitch of the game. Nineteen participants were ejected, and Padres pitchers threw at the skinny Perez all four times he came to the plate. Unlike back in 1982, when "Highway Patrol" Perez could not find the stadium, this contest had the opposite effect on the NL pennant race, as the Padres easily beat out the third-place Braves and went to the World Series. Torre was fired even though he was Turner's personal choice for Braves manager, in part because the media-savvy Torre's likability played perfectly on WTBS.

The next six years were a disaster. After the team went 66–96, Chuck Tanner was brought in to manage, and in four years never surpassed 72 wins. The Braves released Perez on April Fool's Day 1986, along with fellow veteran pitchers Rick Camp, Terry Forster, and Len Barker. Perez had been jailed for drugs in 1983 and went AWOL from the team in 1985. Perez's legal weaponry included a high-arcing "eephus" pitch and an imaginary gun he fired at batters after striking them out. Forster had a career 3.23 ERA and .397 batting average, but is often remembered for being dubbed "a big, fat tub of goo" by David Letterman. Barker flopped in Atlanta after being acquired for tiny, speedy center fielder Brett Butler, a local favorite for his hustle and the similarity of his name to *Gone with the Wind*'s Rhett Butler.

The April Fool's Day massacre certainly did not produce instant success, but under new general manager Bobby Cox the Braves were steadily building a fine farm system that paid off in the 1990s, though in 1988 the club hit bottom, losing 106 games to finish 39 1/2 games out of first. The team's payroll was the 17th highest in the majors ($9,967,167). That miserable season led to another Braves low point the following season when the club was outdrawn by the minor-league Buffalo Bisons. Atlanta's attendance was 980,129. *Financial World* estimated that in 1990 only one major-league franchise was worth less than the Braves.

ATLANTA, 1991–2005: THE TOMAHAWK DYNASTY— "THEY'LL PROBABLY BURN OUR HOUSES DOWN!"

The worst sin, the ultimate sin for me, in anything, is to be bored.

—Ted Turner

The next big change in the Braves' history came in the late 1980s when Ted Turner ceased his sometimes counterproductive hands-on approach to baseball ownership. "Everything Ted Turner has been involved with has been a success, except us," observed infielder Jerry Royster, an Atlanta Brave for Turner's first nine seasons. At the end of their first 25 years as the Atlanta Braves, Turner's franchise had the ignominy of being the only existing team never to have won a playoff game. Advertisers and new Braves converts nationwide on TBS pressed Turner to deliver a winning product for their increasing cable rates. Consequently, Braves president Stan Kasten assembled a cadre of professional, proven baseball executives, whom Turner allowed to run the Braves ring of his big show.

Mobilizing the massive revenues generated by Turner's burgeoning empire, the team returned to prominence in 1991 (albeit with the 20th-lowest team salary) under manager Bobby Cox and new general manager John Schuerholz. Cox, a former Yankees third baseman and Toronto manager, had previously piloted the Braves from 1978 to 1981 and then served as Braves general manager from 1985 to 1990. Schuerholz, a former Baltimore schoolteacher, rose to the executive ranks in the Baltimore Orioles and Kansas City Royals organizations during their glory eras in the 1970s and 1980s. Cox had successfully built for the future as general manager. In 1990, to make room in the outfield for Rookie of the Year first baseman David Justice, Cox outraged Atlanta fans by trading declining fan favorite Dale Murphy to Philadelphia. Then, on becoming manager again, Cox directed his youngsters to victory. The easygoing Cox did not view his job change as a demotion, explaining, "I've always been most comfortable as a manager."

Before the 1991 season the Braves signed showy former Florida State cornerback Deion Sanders to platoon in the outfield with the weak-hitting Otis Nixon. A few Braves followers at spring training employed the Florida State Seminoles football fans' "Tomahawk Chop" rallying gesture whenever "Neon Deion" strutted up to bat. During the regular season the gesture, with raucous accompaniment by the stadium's organ, became a popular ritual to rally the Atlanta club. "The Chop" grew closely associated with the Braves' amazing turnaround, as the name "Braves" had been similarly linked to the 1914 miracle season. But the constant TBS close-ups of owner Turner and his then fiancée, actress Jane Fonda, beaming while leading Atlanta crowds en masse in the Chop to a Native American war chant, spurred further vigorous protests by Native American activists against the Braves' ownership. Another irritant was that the organization still employed a feathered and war-painted "Chief Noc-a-Homa" to lead cheers from a mock tepee in the outfield stands.

In the early 1980s the club had removed all Native American elements from the Braves' uniforms. But in 1987 a tomahawk reappeared on Braves jerseys after being off for 24 years. Ironically, in Ted Turner's frantic early years as Braves owner, he considered switching the club's moniker to the Eagles, after the name of his America's Cup yacht. But following a storm of national criticism Turner backed off the name, which dovetailed perfectly with the Falcons, the mascot of the NFL's Atlanta franchise, and the Hawks, the Turner-owned Atlanta NBA franchise.

Because merchandise prominently featuring such team nicknames and symbols had become extremely lucrative big business by the late 1980s, owners grew adamant about maintaining their patented logos as untouchable traditions, as long as they remained profitable, regardless of how outdated or offensive to a minority of consumers they might become. The Braves' logo became a tightly guarded trademark in a huge multinational media and merchandising realm, when Turner merged his business empire, including the Braves and the Hawks, with the Time Magazine–Warner Brothers conglomerate in 1995. By then, with Turner's America's Cup victory long behind him and the Braves going to another World Series, his idea of switching the club's name to the Eagles could be deemed unprofitable.

In 1991 the young Braves stood at the .500 mark at midseason and then began to accelerate. In August, with the Los Angeles Dodgers in first place just ahead of the Braves, Dodgers star Darryl Strawberry, who had bested the Braves for many years as a New York Met, commented that he had "never been concerned about Atlanta." Many observers took the 1991 Braves too lightly, but

Strawberry's crack fueled a late-season Braves run, beating out the Dodgers. Such July and August spurts became a trademark of Atlanta's 1990s clubs.

In late 1991, when Atlanta closer Juan Berenguer went down with a serious injury, Schuerholz acquired Alejandro Pena from the Mets. Pena saved 11 games in just a five-week stretch and combined with starter Kent Mercker and reliever Mark Wohlers to pitch a no-hitter on September 11. On September 21 the Dodgers regained first with a 2–1 victory over Atlanta, but the Braves rallied the last two weeks of the season. A dramatic high point came on October 1 when the Braves, down 6–0 after three innings, came from behind in the ninth to beat the defending world champion Cincinnati Reds' "Nasty Boys," spurred by a David Justice home run. The Braves finished first in their division at 94–68. The exciting season resulted in attendance more than doubling to 2.1 million.

The young 1991 Braves were led by 25-year-old 20-game winner Tom Glavine, who took the Cy Young Award, and third baseman Terry Pendleton, a free agent, was the MVP and batting champ. Twenty-six-year-old Ron Gant was a big help with 32 homers and 34 steals, his second straight 30-30 season.

The Braves took the 1991 NLCS from the Pittsburgh Pirates four games to three despite the absence of center fielder Otis Nixon, who had tested positive for cocaine. The fleet Nixon had tied a record when he stole six bases in a game in 1991. His replacement, Ron Gant, stepped up big in Nixon's absence in the playoffs, setting another mark by stealing seven bases in the Pirates' series. The series included two 1–0 games and two extra-inning contests. After six straight losing seasons, the Braves were going to the World Series for the first time in 32 years.

The 1991 Braves–Minnesota Twins series matched up two resurgent clubs. The Twins had finished seventh the prior season. That Fall Classic was one of the most exciting World Series ever, as four games were determined on the final pitch, five were decided by just one run, and three went into extra innings. In a memorable game seven the Twins' Jack Morris bested the Braves with a 1–0, 10-inning shutout, the first extra-innings World Series seventh game since 1924.

The 1991 Cox-Schuerholz Braves were the first team in NL history to go to the World Series after finishing with the worst record in baseball the previous season. For leading the turnaround Bobby Cox became the first to win the Manager of the Year Award in both major leagues.

Schuerholz assured Braves fans after the season, "We never dreamed it would happen this quickly, but since it has, it's my job to make sure we stay on top." To prevent a slide backward such as those experienced by the 1914 and 1948 Braves, Schuerholz obtained free agent Greg Maddux, who signed for the 1993 season for $6 million less than the Yankees offered him. His addition gave the Braves a big four "Young Guns": righties Maddux and John Smoltz, matched by hard-firing lefties Steve Avery and Glavine.

Glavine, Maddux, and Smoltz won seven Cy Young Awards with Atlanta. In the tradition of Burdette and Spahn, the trio excelled as hitters and fielders. Maddux won 13 straight Gold Gloves, 1990–2002. Smoltz was acquired from the Detroit Tigers as a minor leaguer, while Avery and Glavine (plus Justice and Gant) came up through the Braves' productive farm system. Massachusetts native Glavine had also been a hockey star, drafted by the NHL's Los Angeles Kings. In the 1990s Atlanta's Leo Mazzone succeeded Johnny Sain as the dean of pitching coaches, both for developing young talents like starters Kevin Millwood, Glavine, and Smoltz, and for mining the maximum out of journeymen acquisitions such as Denny Neagle.

Another part of the Braves' winning formula was that Cox supported his pitchers with stellar fielders, such as Terry Pendleton, second baseman Glenn Hubbard, and center fielder Andruw Jones, winner of eight straight Gold Gloves. Hubbard became Cox's first-base coach in 1999 and Pendleton his hitting coach in 2002. Another key to the Braves' success is that Schuerholz has cannily reaped the prime career years from much-traveled veterans, like first baseman Fred McGriff, who was obtained from the San Diego Padres in mid-1993 for three prospects who never panned out. In the following season, McGriff was the 1994 All-Star Game MVP.

The 1992 club started shakily and was in last place on May 27. But then it won 21 of 24. Atlanta proved 1991 was not a fluke by returning to the World Series again after shutting down Barry Bonds to win the NLCS over the Pirates in seven games. The Braves came from behind dramatically to take game seven with two out in the ninth inning when Francisco Cabrera's ninth-inning, two-run pinch-hit single scored Sid Bream in a photo finish at home plate. However, Atlanta fell to the Toronto Blue Jays in the first international World Series, losing a heartbreaking game six 4–3 in 11 innings when Joe Carter hit a walk-off homer.

In that World Series Braves center fielder and Atlanta Falcons cornerback Deion Sanders hit .533 with five steals after incurring the wrath of manager Bobby Cox when Sanders played a Falcons game in the afternoon, then led a national TV camera crew into the Braves locker room as he showed up late for an evening NLCS game. But under Cox, who loves to platoon, Sanders was more "Part Time" than "Prime Time" anyway. Sanders alienated Braves fans by refusing to provide autographs for them while signing for Falcons supporters. Sanders was a great football star but a limited baseball player, and his craving for maximum publicity over performance soon wore out its welcome in the major leagues, even with the media-driven Braves.

Following two straight World Series appearances, Atlanta set a franchise record in 1993 with a 3.9 million attendance. By then the team was up to seventh in player salaries ($38.1 million), and from 1994 to 2000 was no lower than the fourth. The Braves were 10 games out of first place on July 22, two days after acquiring first baseman Fred "Crime Dog" McGriff. He homered in his first day with the Braves to help them recover from a 5–0 deficit, and the team went on a 51–17 tear. The Braves won 104 games to take the NL West on the last day of the season, led by their "Fab Four" starting pitchers. The Braves went on to the NLCS to face the worst-to-first Philadelphia Phillies, who beat them in six games.

In 1994 the Braves moved to the NL Eastern Division. Kent Mercker pitched his second no-hitter, and Greg Maddux recorded a phenomenal 1.56 ERA. The Braves stood second to the Montreal Expos, managed by former Braves outfielder Felipe Alou, when labor strife aborted the 1994 season early and delayed the start of the 1995 season. The 1994 Braves missed Ron Gant, who broke his leg riding a dirt bike in the off-season and was released.

In 1995, for the first time, eight teams qualified for the major-league play-offs. The Braves started out sluggishly at 23–20, but came on strong with 18 last-at-bat wins after July 3 to win the NL East by 21 games with a 90–54 record. The strength of the team was still on the mound. Atlanta led the majors with a 3.44 ERA and 31 one-run wins. That season Greg Maddux had his best year, winning his record fourth straight Cy Young Award with a 19–2 record and a 1.63 ERA, and ended the season with a major-league record 18 straight road wins. The Braves bolted through the extended format to get to the World Series, taking three of four from the Colorado Rockies and then sweeping the Cincinnati Reds in four straight in the NLCS.

The World Series against the Cleveland Indians was marked by three unrelated controversies. First, because the Braves faced another team using a Native American mascot, the Indians' Chief Wahoo, pressure to abolish such names reached a peak. Next, Cleveland slugger Albert Belle was fined for shouting obscenities at reporter Hannah Storm before game three. The third controversy reared after game five with the Braves holding a three-games-to-two lead over the Indians when outspoken Braves right fielder David Justice blasted Atlanta fans as fickle and spiritless, predicting, "If we don't win . . . they'll probably burn our houses down." In game six Tom Glavine and closer Mark Wohlers shut out Cleveland on one hit and Justice turned Atlanta fans' boos to cheers when he homered in the sixth inning for the only run, giving Atlanta its only world championship in any professional team sport (and preventing a second burning of Atlanta). Five games were decided by one run. Glavine was the Series MVP, with two wins and a 1.29 ERA. The Braves hit a record 19 homers in those 1995 playoffs. The Braves were the first franchise to win the Fall Classic in three different cities. With that World Series win Atlanta's John Schuerholz became the only general manager to craft champions in both major leagues, and *Financial World* rated the Braves as the third-most-valuable baseball franchise.

The next year Atlanta went 96–66, led by its excellent starting pitching. John Smoltz led the NL with 276 strikeouts and 24 wins, including 14 straight, and the pitching staff set a major-league record with 1,245 strikeouts. He was rewarded with a $7 million salary for 1997. The powerful lineup contributed with 197 homers, second in the league. Atlanta swept the Dodgers 3–0 in the division series and came back from a three-games-to-one deficit to win the NLCS over the St. Louis Cardinals. The Braves went to their fourth World Series in five years. Atlanta seemed close to repeating as world champs in 1996 when they captured the first two games in hostile Yankee Stadium by a total score of 16–1. However, Atlanta then dropped four straight to Joe Torre's Yankees, including all three at home, culminating in a 4–3 defeat in game six.

Two Braves stalwarts were cut loose after missing much of that 1996 season with injuries. David Justice, newly divorced from actress Halle Berry, was traded to her hometown Cleveland, while starting pitcher Steve Avery was allowed to sign with the Boston Red Sox as a free agent. Avery had been 11–8 in the postseason for the Braves. Though only 26 at the time, Avery never had a decent season after leaving Atlanta.

A bigger change for the Braves took place in 1997 when hitter-friendly Atlanta–Fulton County Stadium was replaced by pitcher-friendly Turner Field, named after owner Ted Turner. Hitting is probably more difficult in the new park due to its deep power alleys, generous foul ground, and the fact that the playing surface is at a slightly lower altitude than its predecessor's.

The new 50,000-seat park was converted from the stadium erected for the 1996 Summer Olympics. Turner Field was built next to Atlanta–Fulton County Stadium, which was later demolished to provide parking for the new field. The Atlanta Committee for the Olympics raised $209 million for the Olympic stadium, while the Braves paid $26 million to convert the facility for baseball use. The throwback exterior look of Turner Field and many other new baseball stadiums was inspired by the huge success of the first retro park, Baltimore's Oriole Park at Camden Yards. Attendance in the first year was 3.46 million. Turner Field's address is 755 Aaron Drive, in tribute to Hank Aaron and his home-run record. Even today, many fan letters to Aaron begin "Dear Home Run King."

Turner Field can also be categorized as one of the new, downtown, state-of-the-art entertainment complexes and ballparks. Its features include a 27-foot neon tomahawk, luxurious skyboxes, fine dining, and an elaborate high-tech educational-recreational plaza. There is also a Braves museum and hall of fame. However, the park is surrounded by highways, and almost everyone arrives by bus or car. It has few retail neighbors, so the Braves provide almost all of the visitors' pre- and postgame entertainment.

Unlike many other teams, the Braves had no initial difficulty adjusting to such a different ballpark, winning 12 of their first 13 games at Turner Field in 1997. The Braves won 101 games and set a major-league mark by hitting 12 grand slams. Seven Braves made the All-Star team, including three pitchers. Their hurlers were by far the finest in the majors, and compiled a sparkling 3.14 ERA. Greg Maddux went 19–4 with only 20 walks, and Denny Neagle went 20–5. The Braves swept the Astros in the division championship but were upset in the NLCS by the eventual world champion Florida Marlins in six games.

The Braves were strong the next season and won a franchise record 106 games. Maddux won his fourth ERA title while first baseman Andres Galarraga hit 44 home runs and was one of three players with over 100 RBIs. Galarraga contracted cancer and had to miss the 1999 season, but came back in 2000 with 28 home runs. Five starters combined for 88 wins as the hurlers led the NL in virtually every statistical category except saves. The club swept the Cubs 3–0 in the divisional series but were stunned by the San Diego Padres, who won the NLCS in six games.

In 1999 the Braves won over 100 games for the third straight year (103–59) and finally made it back to the World Series. The team led the NL in defense and pitching, abetted by John Rocker's 38 saves. But he began to be seen as a hothead. Rocker's juvenile taunting antics targeting rowdy New York Mets fans, such as faking throwing the ball into the Shea Stadium stands, seemed the frat-boy pranks of a 24-year-old overnight sensation basking in the national spotlight. After winning the divisional series 3–1 over Houston, the Braves captured the NLCS over the Mets 4–2 after nearly blowing a three-game lead. However, they were swept by the Yankees in the World Series. Mets fans rooted for the rival Yankees because of their loathing for Rocker.

John Rocker became a very controversial figure after the season. A diatribe reported in a December 1999 *Sports Illustrated* slamming New Yorkers en masse and his teammates for their ethnic diversity made him public enemy number one in the Big Apple and persona non grata nationwide. Under heavy public and media pressure, MLB suspended Rocker for two weeks at the start of the 2000 season. The slurs puzzled his longtime teammates and embarrassed his parents, a liberal attorney and an educational consultant, because in the minors Rocker often brought his less fortunate black, Asian, and Hispanic teammates to stay at his parents' home in Macon, Georgia, a town famous for music pioneers Otis Redding, James Brown, and Little Richard.

In 2000 the Braves fell off their torrid pace and won just 95 games, again good enough to capture the East. The pitching staff led the NL in ERA with 4.05, reflecting the growing dominance of batting, with five teams hitting 200 or more homers. The club ended the season ignominiously, getting swept by the Cards in the NLDS, ending the Braves' streak of eight consecutive NLCS appearances. The defiant Rocker's sudden alienation from his Atlanta teammates may have factored in the outcome. The lack of a dominant stopper like Rocker had handicapped Atlanta throughout the 1990s. The Braves' management desperately tried damage control to salvage Rocker, who as an inexpensive flamethrowing young lefty closer was one of the most valuable commodities in baseball. Finally, in June 2001, after Rocker made obscene references to the New York media, the semirepentant pitcher, who has never surrendered a run in postseason play, was traded to the Cleveland Indians. Like Steve Avery, Rocker's pitching tanked without the guidance of coach Leo Mazzone.

Though John Rocker is gone, Atlantans can be reminded of a hotter-tempered, truly racist baseball star when they stroll to home games, because Georgia native and longtime resident Ty Cobb is honored with a statue, near Hank Aaron's, outside Turner Field. Aaron has kept hundreds of the hate letters he received during his march to the home-run crown and rereads them occasionally, "because they remind me of what people are really like." One writer promised Aaron, "My gun is watching your every black move" during Aaron's advance to the home-run record.

While the Rocker fiasco dragged on, Ted Turner lost control of the Braves due to corporate mergers with AOL Time Warner, but remains on the Braves' board of directors. Despite Turner's ouster and such controversies as the one Rocker put the Braves through, the club remains on top by retuning expertly each season while occasionally dumping players viewed as troublemakers. For example, in 2001 the Braves replaced Rocker by a unique readjustment. When John Smoltz was having difficulty returning as a starter after undergoing major elbow surgery that kept him out in 2000, Bobby Cox and pitching guru Mazzone converted Smoltz to a closer. Mazzone, who joined the Atlanta organization in 1979, guided Smoltz, Glavine, and Avery from minor leaguers to stars. The nervous Mazzone's constant bobble-head-doll motion in the dugout lures numerous TV close-ups every postseason as he constantly rocks on the bench next to the often grim-looking Bobby Cox. After the 2002 season Mazzone prize pupil and longtime Braves star hurler Tom Glavine turned free agent and signed with the New York Mets. The eloquent Glavine had often drawn fire from Atlanta corporate executives for his effective, high-profile leadership in baseball's powerful union.

In 2001 the Braves fell to 88–74 as the pitching, which still led the NL in ERA with 3.59, struggled to carry the team. Switch-hitting Chipper Jones, the 1999 MVP (who was paid $10.3 million), led the team with a .330 average and 38 home runs. Atlanta swept the Houston Astros in the 2001 NLDS but lost in the NLCS four games to one to the Arizona Diamondbacks, who went on to win the World Series, as the Braves hit a meek .207. MLB that year reported the team lost $25 million, but *Forbes* estimated the team actually made $9.5 million. The payroll was nearly $92 million and other expenses were about $57.5 million. On the other side of the ledger, *Forbes* estimated total revenues of $160 million, including $66 million from gate receipts; $20 million in local media revenue, 11th highest in MLB; and $37.7 million from local operating revenue, which includes concessions, parking, stadium advertising, and especially luxury boxes and club seats, plus money from national TV and postseason appearances.

In 2002 the team was average in batting, with enthusiastic Andruw Jones pacing the Braves with 35 home runs. As usual, the team led in defense and pitching. The hurlers amassed a brilliant 3.13 ERA. The strong starting pitching was backed up by John Smoltz and his nasty slider. Smoltz had an NL record 55 saves in 2002, and earned the Rolaids Relief Award as the best closer of the year. The team won 101 games yet was knocked out in the NLDS three games to two by the San Francisco Giants. Braves catcher Javy Lopez hit .333 with two homers in the series, but Glavine was clobbered and lost two games.

In 2003 Atlanta again won 101 games. The Braves let Glavine leave for the Mets, but new acquisition Russ Ortiz went 21–7, making John Schuerholz look like a genius once again. Schuerholz's productive big trades include acquiring former batting champ Gary Sheffield for oft-injured Brian Jordan, who was a star Atlanta Falcons defensive back. This was a very different team for Braves fans because the pitching was only average, but the offense led the NL, batting .284 and hitting 235 homers, 39 more than the next-best team. Four men, led by Gary Sheffield with 132, had over 100 RBIs. Catcher Javy Lopez hit 43 homers to go with a .328 batting average. The team had seven All-Stars and 12 players earning over $1 million. Yet the Braves lost the divisional playoffs to the Chicago Cubs, who had worst record of any playoff team. Cubs' fireballers Kerry Wood and Mark Prior shut down Atlanta's powerful, record-setting offense, which scored 907 runs in 2003. In those 2003 playoff contests there were almost as many victory-starved Cubs fanatics in the Turner Field stands as jaded and frustrated Braves supporters. Both the 2002 Giants and the 2003 Cubs who upset the Braves were managed by Dusty Baker, an Atlanta outfielder from 1968 to 1975, when Bartholomay owned the Braves.

The 2003 Braves payroll was led by Maddux ($14.7 million), Lopez, and Sheffield. The payroll was second only to the Yankees, but Atlanta ranked just 10th in attendance. Two months after the Braves' embarrassing playoff loss to the Cubs, the Braves declined contract arbitration to all but one of the Braves' 12 free agents. The only one re-signed was the ageless Julio Franco. Thus ended the Atlanta careers of longtime Braves stars Greg Maddux and Javy Lopez. Maddux left Atlanta with 284 wins. His 17 straight years with 15 or more wins is the longest such streak ever. The *Atlanta Journal-Constitution* praised the unflappable Maddux, the master of changing speeds: "We won't behold his likes again." A rebuilding project was the result, with Smoltz the only remaining player from all the Braves' consecutive division winners. The 2004 Braves had the 12th-largest payroll and ranked 17th in attendance at 2.4 million.

Just before the 11 free agents were cut loose, Stan Kasten, Braves president since 1986, resigned. Kasten also headed the Turner/Time Warner–owned Atlanta Hawks and Atlanta Thrashers hockey team—the only executive to simultaneously head franchises in three different sports. His resignation coincided with bad times for the struggling Hawks and the four-year-old Thrashers being up for sale. To reduce its huge debt, Time Warner unloaded the less successful Hawks and Thrashers as a package to a group of investors that included Turner's son Beau and Turner Broadcasting. *Forbes* ranked the 2003 Braves as baseball's sixth-most-valuable franchise, the team's lowest ranking since 1994. In 2004 the value dipped again to $374 million after being estimated by *Forbes* at $424 million in 2002.

There were no grand expectations for the 2004 season, although the team entered the season with a $90,182,500 payroll, eighth highest in the majors.

Schuerholz pointed out, somewhat derisively, "The longest active streak in baseball is our 12 divisional championships, the second longest is the number of years we've been predicted to fall apart." The Braves met the media's low expectations early on but suddenly caught fire after coming back from a 7–0 deficit versus the Orioles, and won the division by 10 games with a record of 96–66. One spark was Chipper Jones, who reversed a first-half slump after his father was brought in to consult on Chipper's hitting and Chipper was shifted back to third base. Several rookies provided low-budget sparks, especially catcher Johnny Estrada, who led all regulars with a .314 batting average. Pitching coach Leo Mazzone reversed the midcareer blues of pitchers Mike Hampton, Jaret Wright, and John Thomson. Despite the loss of their famous stars, the Braves still led the NL in ERA (3.74). J. D. Drew replaced right fielder Sheffield and finally stayed healthy enough to put up the monster numbers so long predicted for him (.305 batting average and 35 homers). Julio Franco was a revelation, hitting .309 at the age of 45. But in the playoffs the Braves were again knocked out in the first round, this time three games to two by Houston. Shortstop Rafael Furcal hit .480 and Andruw Jones .571, each with two homers, but Braves pitchers surrendered 11 homers. The early exit enabled Furcal to gain an early entry to jail to serve sentences for two DUI convictions.

The Braves have won 14 straight divisional titles (discounting the strike-shortened 1994 season). Yet despite the Braves' 1991–2005 in-season NL supremacy, often achieved by blowing away the competition via a long, white-hot streak in the second half of a season, the club has won only one World Series since 1957, and several times recently have been ousted early from the postseason by underdogs. In the expanded playoff format initiated in 1994, seasoned favorites such as the Braves have often fallen to inspired, small-market underdogs with minimal playoff experience. Atlanta's increased postseason problems also coincide with the 1997 move to Turner Field. Maddux, Glavine, and Smoltz have pitched well in championship play, but the team's offense, with the notable exceptions of Chipper Jones and Javy Lopez, has occasionally let them down. Furthermore, the 64-year-old Bobby Cox's big-game postseason strategy, such as relying on his veteran aces on three days' rest instead of using rested younger starters such as Horacio Ramirez in 2003, has also drawn media and public fire. Under Cox the Braves have an excellent 24–14 record in the NLDS, are 27–27 in the NLCS, but are only 11–18 in the World Series. Cox ranks ninth in wins (2,002) among major-league managers. According to the low-key Maddux, "He's head and shoulders above the rest. He always has been, always will be." Cox first won the AL Manager of the Year Award in 1985 with Toronto, then won in the NL in the Braves' 1991 worst-to-first season and for overachieving in 2004.

The Braves continued to terrorize the NL in the new century because Cox and Schuerholz are the longest-tenured manager and general manager in baseball. Schuerholz has also been in the same job longer than any general manager in the four major pro sports. He has also maintained continuity on the field by re-signing many Braves stars who came up through their farm system to long-term contracts. In the 2004 off-season the highly respected John Smoltz successfully went public with his own plan to win the Braves another World Series—put him back in the starting rotation. Further budget tightening for 2005 resulted in the loss of Russ Ortiz and J. D. Drew. The Braves, beset by injuries, rebuilt on the run in 2005, with 18 rookies being called up. The "Baby Braves," especially local boy Jeff Francoeur, surprised those who annually predict the club's downfall by spurring the Braves to their 14th straight Eastern Division crown. Andruw Jones led the majors with 51 home runs and played a pivotal role in the team's success. But the club was knocked out in the first round of the playoffs for the fourth straight year, losing to Houston in four games. Game four took 18 tense innings over 5 hours, 50 minutes. The Braves led by five in the eighth, but reliever Kyle Farnsworth and poor infield defense blew the lead, while Braves hitters stranded 18 runners.

The twenty-first-century Braves are powered by the multitalented, exuberant Chipper Jones (the number-one pick in baseball's 1990 amateur draft), Andruw Jones (from Curaçao), and the rocket-armed Rafael Furcal (from the Dominican Republic, the 2000 Rookie of the Year), all developed by the Braves' farm system. Thus the Braves' pioneering recruitment from the Caribbean has continued to pay strong dividends.

In the TV broadcast booth Braves fan have also been treated to enduring excellence and occasional controversy, beginning in 1976, the year Ted Turner bought the club and hired announcers Pete Van Wieren and Skip Caray (son of the legendary Harry Caray). Joe Simpson and Hall of Fame pitcher Don Sutton joined the crew in 1992 and 1989, respectively. In 2000 the Braves temporarily kicked their own announcers off the team plane when the broadcast crew aired allegations that the Braves widened the catcher's box in Turner Field and had their receivers set up outside the box to establish a broader strike zone for their already razor-sharp pitchers. The rhubarb featured an unusual balk call against Braves catcher Fernando Lunar for positioning himself outside the box. Another controversy blew up in 2003 when Caray and Van Wieren were confined to regional telecasts for a while in an attempt by Time Warner to give the Braves' national broadcasts a more neutral spin. However, Atlanta fans' strong protests brought the popular duo back. Beginning in 2005 Skip's son, the ex-Cubs broadcaster Chip Caray, joined his father in Atlanta to continue a great family tradition.

Despite the recent dispersion of Ted Turner, Stan Kasten, Atlanta's veteran stars, and many local fans, this low-key modern version (Schuerholz, Cox, and Mazzone) of the organization's nineteenth-century Triumvirs remains to power the media-friendly Braves on. While the many firsts pioneered by the Braves are partly due to longevity, the current organization's formula of flexibility, innovation, and stability is endemic of the methods of the great Braves organizations of the past. Unlike many other sports franchises that have relocated, the Atlanta Braves acknowledge and embrace their past triumphs and follies. If crusader John Montgomery Ward had the chance, he might wish to change the name he gave them, in deference to the now-empowered minorities he fought for, but these current multinational Braves have exceeded even his hopes and dreams for them.

NOTABLE ACHIEVEMENTS

Most Valuable Players

Year	Name	Position
1947	Bob Elliott	3B
1957	Hank Aaron	OF
1982	Dale Murphy	OF
1983	Dale Murphy	OF
1991	Terry Pendleton	3B
1999	Chipper Jones	3B

Cy Young Winners

Year	Name	Position
1957	Warren Spahn	LHP
1991	Tom Glavine	LHP
1993	Greg Maddux	RHP
1994	Greg Maddux	RHP
1995	Greg Maddux	RHP
1996	John Smoltz	RHP
1998	Tom Glavine	LHP

Rookies of the Year

Year	Name	Position
1948	Alvin Dark	SS
1950	Sam Jethroe	OF
1971	Earl Williams	C
1978	Bob Horner	3B
1990	David Justice	OF
2000	Rafael Furcal	SS

Batting Champions

Year	Name	#
1877	Deacon White	.387
1889	Dan Brouthers	.373
1893	Hugh Duffy	.363
1894	Hugh Duffy	.440
1928	Rogers Hornsby	.387
1942	Ernie Lombardi	.330
1956	Hank Aaron	.328
1959	Hank Aaron	.355
1970	Rico Carty	.366
1974	Ralph Garr	.353
1991	Terry Pendleton	.319

Home-Run Champions

Year	Name	#
1879	Charley Jones	9
1880	John O'Rourke	6
1891	Harry Stovey	16
1894	Hugh Duffy	18
1897	Hugh Duffy	11
1898	Jimmy Collins	15
1900	Herman Long	12
1907	Dave Brain	10
1910	Fred Beck	10
1935	Wally Berger	34
1945	Tommy Holmes	28
1953	Eddie Mathews	47
1957	Hank Aaron	44
1959	Eddie Mathews	46
1963	Hank Aaron	44
1966	Hank Aaron	44
1967	Hank Aaron	39
1984	Dale Murphy	36
1985	Dale Murphy	37
2005	Andruw Jones	51

ERA Champions

Year	Name	#
1937	Jim Turner	2.38

1947	Warren Spahn	2.33
1951	Chet Nichols	2.88
1953	Warren Spahn	2.10
1956	Lew Burdette	2.70
1961	Warren Spahn	3.02
1967	Phil Niekro	1.87
1974	Buzz Capra	2.29
1993	Greg Maddux	2.36
1994	Greg Maddux	1.56
1995	Greg Maddux	1.63
1997	Greg Maddux	2.22

Strikeout Champions

Year	Name	#
1877	Tommy Bond	170
1878	Tommy Bond	182
1883	Jim Whitney	345
1889	John Clarkson	284
1902	Vic Willis	225
1949	Warren Spahn	151
1950	Warren Spahn	191
1951	Warren Spahn	164
1952	Warren Spahn	183
1977	Phil Niekro	262
1992	John Smoltz	215
1996	John Smoltz	276

No-Hitters

Name	Date
Jack Stivetts	08/06/1892
Frank Pfeffer	05/08/1907
George Davis	09/09/1914
Tom Hughes	06/16/1916
Jim Tobin	04/27/1944
Vern Bickford	08/11/1950
Jim Wilson	06/12/1954
Lew Burdette	08/08/1960
Warren Spahn	09/16/1960
Warren Spahn	04/28/1961
Phil Niekro	08/05/1973
Kent Mercker	04/08/1994

POSTSEASON APPEARANCES

NL West Division Titles

Year	Record	Manager
1969	93–69	Lum Harris
1982	89–73	Joe Torre
1991	94–68	Bobby Cox
1992	98–64	Bobby Cox
1993	104–58	Bobby Cox

NL East Division Titles

Year	Record	Manager
1995	90–54	Bobby Cox
1996	96–66	Bobby Cox
1997	101–61	Bobby Cox
1998	106–56	Bobby Cox
1999	103–59	Bobby Cox
2000	95–67	Bobby Cox
2001	88–74	Bobby Cox
2002	101–59	Bobby Cox
2003	101–61	Bobby Cox
2004	96–66	Bobby Cox
2005	90–72	Bobby Cox

NL Pennants

Year	Record	Manager
1877	39–31	Harry Wright
1878	41–19	Harry Wright
1883	63–35	John Morrill
		Jack Burdock
1891	87–51	Frank Selee
1892	102–48	Frank Selee
1893	86–43	Frank Selee
1897	93–39	Frank Selee
1898	102–47	Frank Selee
1914	94–59	George Stallings
1948	91–62	Billy Southworth
1957	95–59	Fred Haney
1958	92–62	Fred Haney
1991	94–68	Bobby Cox

1992	98–64	Bobby Cox
1995	90–54	Bobby Cox
1996	96–66	Bobby Cox
1999	103–59	Bobby Cox

World Championships

Year	Opponent	MVP
1914	Philadelphia	
1957	New York	Lew Burdette
1995	Cleveland	Tom Glavine

MANAGERS

1990–	Bobby Cox
1988–1990	Russ Nixon
1986–1988	Chuck Tanner
1985	Bobby Wine
1985	Eddie Haas
1982–1984	Joe Torre
1978–1981	Bobby Cox
1977	Vern Benson
1977	Ted Turner
1976–1977	Dave Bristol
1975	Connie Ryan
1974–1975	Clyde King
1973–1974	Eddie Mathews
1968–1972	Lum Harris
1967	Ken Silvestri
1966–1967	Billy Hitchcock
1963–1966	Bobby Bragan
1961–1962	Birdie Tebbetts
1960–1961	Charlie Dressen
1956–1959	Fred Haney
1952–1956	Charlie Grimm
1951–1952	Tommy Holmes
1950–1951	Billy Southworth
1949	Johnny Cooney
1946–1949	Billy Southworth
1945	Del Bissonette
1943–1945	Bob Coleman
1938–1943	Casey Stengel

1930–1937	Bill McKechnie
1929	Emil Fuchs
1928	Rogers Hornsby
1928	Jack Slattery
1924–1927	Dave Bancroft
1921–1924	Fred Mitchell
1913–1920	George Stallings
1912	Johnny Kling
1911	Fred Tenney
1910	Fred Lake
1909	Harry Smith
1909	Frank Bowerman
1908	Joe Kelley
1905–1907	Frank Tenney
1902–1904	Al Buckenberger
1890–1901	Frank Selee
1889	Jim Hart
1887–1888	John Morrill
1887	King Kelly
1884–1886	John Morrill
1883	Jack Burdock
1882–1883	John Morrill
1876–1881	Harry Wright

Team Records by Individual Players

Batting Leaders

	Single Season			Career		
	Name		Year	Name		Plate Appearances
Batting average	Hugh Duffy	.440	1894	Billy Hamilton	.338	3,206
On-base %	Hugh Duffy	.502	1894	Billy Hamilton	.456	3,206
Slugging %	Hugh Duffy	.694	1894	Hank Aaron	.567	13,089
OPS	Hugh Duffy	1.196	1894	Hank Aaron	.944	13,089
Games	Felix Millan	162	1969	Hank Aaron	3,076	13,089
At bats	Marquis Grissom	671	1996	Hank Aaron	11,628	13,089
Runs	Hugh Duffy	160	1894	Hank Aaron	2107	13,089
Hits	Hugh Duffy	237	1894	Hank Aaron	3600	13,089
Total bases	Hank Aaron	400	1959	Hank Aaron	6591	13,089
Doubles	Hugh Duffy	51	1894	Hank Aaron	600	13,089
Triples	Dick Johnston	20	1887	Rabbit Maranville	103	7,537
Home runs	Andruw Jones	51	2005	Hank Aaron	733	13,089

(Continued)

Batting Leaders   (Continued)

	Single Season			Career		
	Name		**Year**	**Name**		**Plate Appearances**
Walks	Bob Elliott	131	1948	Eddie Mathews	1,376	95,313
Strikeouts	Andruw Jones	147	2004	Dale Murphy	1,581	8,094
Stolen bases	Mike Kelly	84	1887	Herman Long	431	7,497
Extra-base hits	Hank Aaron	92	1959	Hank Aaron	1,429	13,089
Times on base	Chipper Jones	309	1999	Hank Aaron	4,928	13,089

Pitching Leaders

	Single Season			Career		
	Name		**Year**	**Name**		**Innings Pitched**
ERA	Greg Maddux	1.56	1994	Tommy Bond	2.21	2,127.3
Wins	John Clarkson	49	1889	Warren Spahn	356	5,046
Won-loss %	Greg Maddux	.905	1995	Greg Maddux	.688	2,526.7
Hits/9 IP	Greg Maddux	6.31	1995	Tom Hughes	6.77	550.7
Walks/9 IP	Tommy Bond	.39	1879	Tommy Bond	.59	2,127.3
Strikeouts	Charlie Buffington	417	1884	Phil Niekro	2,912	4,622.7
Strikeouts/ 9 IP	John Smoltz	9.79	1996	John Smoltz	7.89	2,929.3
Games	Chris Reitsma	84	2004	Phil Niekro	740	4,622.7
Saves	John Smoltz	55	2002	John Smoltz	154	2,929.3
Innings	John Clarkson	620	1889	Warren Spahn	5,046	5,046
Starts	John Clarkson	72	1889	Warren Spahn	635	5,046
Complete games	John Clarkson	68	1889	Kid Nichols	475	4,538
Shutouts	Tommy Bond	11	1879	Warren Spahn	63	5,046

Source: Drawn from data in "Atlanta Braves Batting Leaders (seasonal and career)." http://baseball-reference.com/ teams/ATL/leaders_bat.shtml; "Atlanta Braves Pitching Leaders (seasonal and career)." http://baseball-reference. com/teams/ATL/leaders_pitch.shtml.

BIBLIOGRAPHY

"The Atlanta Braves." http://atlanta.braves.mlb.com/.

Biesel, David. *Can You Name That Team?* Lanham, MD: Scarecrow Press, 1991.

"The Braves Beat." http://www.bravesbeat.com/.

The Business of Baseball. http://businessofbaseball.com/.

Buege, Bob. *Milwaukee Braves: A Baseball Eulogy.* Milwaukee, WI: Douglas American Sports Publications, 1988.

Caruso, Gary. *The Braves Encyclopedia.* Philadelphia: Temple University Press, 1995.

————. *Turner Field: Rarest of Diamonds*. Marietta, GA: Longstreet Press, 2001.

Dewey, Donald, and Nicholas Acocella. *Total Ballclubs: The Ultimate Book of Baseball Teams*. New York: Sport Classic Books, 2005.

Kaese, Harold. *The Boston Braves, 1871–1953*. Boston: Northeastern University Press, 2004.

Klapisch, Bob, and Pete Van Wieren. *The Braves: An Illustrated History of America's Team*. Atlanta: Turner Publications, 1995.

Rader, Benjamin G. *Baseball: A History of America's Game*. 2nd ed. Urbana: University of Illinois Press, 2005.

Riess, Steven A. *Touching Base: Professional Baseball and American Culture in the Progressive Era*. Rev. ed. Urbana: University of Illinois Press, 1999.

Stevens, David. *Baseball's Radical for All Seasons*. Lanham, MD: Scarecrow Press, 1998.

Thorn, John, et al., eds. *Total Baseball: The Ultimate Baseball Encyclopedia*. Wilmington: Sport Media Pub, 2004.

Thorn, John, Pete Palmer, Michael Gershman, David Pietrusza, and Dan Schlossberg, eds. *Total Braves*. New York: Penguin USA, 1996.

Voigt, David Quentin. *American Baseball*. 3 vols. University Park: Pennsylvania State Press, 1983.

Ward, Geoffrey, and Kenneth Burns. *Baseball: An Illustrated History*. New York: Knopf, 1994.

Chicago Cubs

John E. Findling

As the 2005 baseball season drew to a close in the first days of October, Chicago Cubs fans had to face the dismal reality that, for the 97th consecutive year, the team would not become the world champions of baseball. While there are now probably just a handful of people who can remember the championship team of 1908, and a diminishing number of people who can recall the Cubs' last National League pennant in 1945, civic and indeed national support for the team has perhaps never been more enthusiastic. The perpetual mystique of the Cubs and their seemingly eternal attraction for their fans remains one of the great sports legends. The history of the Cubs' organization, a charter member of the NL when it was founded in 1876, may offer some helpful reasons for that attraction.

THE ERA OF A. G. SPALDING AND
CAP ANSON, 1876–1901

The direct ancestor of the Chicago White Stockings (as the club was known until the end of the nineteenth century) was the Excelsior Base Ball Club, formed in 1865 in the wake of the Civil War and part of the North-Western Association of Base-Ball Players. During the mid-1860s, the Excelsiors were the best team in the association, challenged only by the Forest City club of Rockford, which featured a teenage pitching star named Albert Goodwill Spalding. In 1868 the Excelsiors played badly and suffered economically, and they merged with another team for the 1869 season under the name of the Amateur Base Ball Club. The Amateurs played no better in 1869. The team was an embarrassment to the city and to sportswriter Lewis Meacham of the *Chicago Tribune*, who initiated a newspaper campaign to raise money to develop a better local baseball team.

In October 1869, a group of prominent business leaders met and created the Chicago Base Ball Club, headed by the well-known retail merchant and future hotelier Potter Palmer. Other civic dignitaries involved with the club included former Union general Philip H. Sheridan and *Tribune* owner Joseph Medill. They enlisted Tom Foley, a noted billiards player, gambler, and local celebrity, to build a winning team.

Foley's first acquisition was Jimmy Wood, a second baseman who had played for the Brooklyn Eckfords. Little more, however, had been done by January, and impatient stockholders called a meeting at which Foley was elevated to the board of directors and new officers were elected. Within a month, Foley had filled the club roster, and when the season opened, the players were resplendent in their blue caps, white flannel shirts trimmed in blue with a large C on the front, blue flannel pants, stockings of "pure white British thread," and spiked shoes of white goatskin. The *Tribune* thought they were the "showiest and handsomest uniforms ever." Because of the white stockings, the team became known as the White Stockings, or, from time to time, the Whites, White Legs, White Socks, or White Sox. The team played at Dexter Park, a horse-racing track five miles from the city center. It was inconvenient, since there was no streetcar service, but plans were in the works for a new field to be called the Union Grounds to be located between downtown Chicago and the lakefront. In their handsome uniforms, the White Stockings demonstrated the success of Foley's recruiting efforts by finishing the 1870 season with a 47–8 record, the best in the league.

Early in 1871, the White Stockings traveled to New Orleans for spring training, the first professional team to do so, although other teams had gone south to play exhibition games against local clubs. In March 1871, the National Association of Professional Base Ball Players was created, consisting of nine clubs including the White Stockings, now playing in the recently constructed Union Grounds, located at a downtown site originally donated to the city by the federal government. However, in October of that year, the Great Chicago Fire cost the club its new park, clubhouse, financial records, uniforms, and equipment, and every player on the team lost most of his personal possessions. The team finished the season on the road, demoralized from the fire and by a *Tribune* article stating that management was bringing in seven new players for the 1872 season.

However, because of the fire, Chicago did not field a team in 1872 or 1873. In the latter year, the club reorganized itself as the Chicago Base Ball Association and began to develop a new team starting with Jimmy Wood, lured away from Philadelphia to be player-manager. In January 1874, Wood severely injured his leg in a fall at his home and was confined to bed for several weeks.

Without his leadership, the White Stockings foundered amid allegations of ties with professional gamblers, injuries to key players, and retirements of others. Wood finally recovered sufficiently to get out of bed, only to fall again and re-injure his leg so badly that it had to be amputated. Eventually, Wood returned to the club, becoming the first nonplaying team manager. In July, the White Stockings' home field at 23rd and State Streets burned in a fire that spread over 19 square blocks. The team continued its home season at Ogden Park.

In August 1874, the Chicago Base Ball Association elected William A. Hulbert secretary. As secretary, Hulbert ran the team on a day-to-day basis, and one of his first tasks was to deal with the Davy Force matter. In September, Force, an infielder, signed a contract to play the 1875 season with the White Stockings. Two months later, he signed another contract, backdated to September, after it was realized that the first contract was invalid because he had still been under contract to another team, and league rules forbade a player from signing a contract while they were employed by another team. All player contracts expired at the end of the season, at which time players were free to sign with whomever they chose. In December, however, Force decided that he would rather play with Philadelphia and signed a contract with that team, based on the understanding that his backdated contract with Chicago was invalid. The association's judiciary committee met in December to decide which team owned Force. It ruled for Chicago on the grounds that the second contract, dated in September, had actually been signed in November. However, after the annual league meeting, another judiciary committee was appointed early in 1875 and reopened the Force case. The decision was reversed, and the committee awarded Force to Philadelphia. Hulbert and the White Stockings were outraged, but league rules provided no avenue of appeal.

William A. Hulbert was born in Oswego County in upper New York State in 1832, moved with his family to Chicago as a boy, and graduated from Beloit College in Wisconsin. He was hired as a clerk for a coal merchant in Chicago, married his employer's daughter, and eventually came to own the business. He earned a prestigious position on the Chicago Board of Trade and became a shareholder in the Chicago White Stockings in 1870 in order to enhance his civic image and because he saw the potential to make money from baseball. His affluence made him fat in the 1870s, but he was an ambitious, hardworking, forceful, and self-reliant individual with a strong sense of the virtues of capitalism.

Perhaps it was the Davy Force affair, or perhaps it was the pervasive influence of professional gamblers in the game, but sometime in 1875, Hulbert concluded that baseball, especially Chicago baseball, needed a sea change. He acquired Albert Spalding from the Boston Red Stockings for $2,000 and 25 percent of Chicago's gate receipts to be the new player-manager, and began working with Spalding and sportswriter Lewis Meacham to raid the best players from other teams. Spalding contributed his baseball knowledge and Meacham his public-relations skills. All of this was done in secret, since association rules forbade tampering with contracted players before the expiration of their contracts at the end of the season. At the same time, Hulbert announced that corruption in baseball necessitated a new organization of fiscally sound teams that would play only each other on a fixed schedule.

Most of Hulbert's raiding centered on the Boston team, and was so successful that the Red Stockings nearly disbanded. He also lured Adrian "Cap" Anson, a talented first baseman, from Philadelphia. The demoralized Chicago players reacted badly. Two players were found to have thrown games; one quit, and the other was expelled. Hulbert used Meacham and the press to his best advantage, and newspaper accounts of corruption threw the rest of the association into turmoil. Newspaper reports said that Chicago, St. Louis, and Cincinnati had formed a "western clique" to wrest control of professional baseball away from Philadelphia and end the practice of eastern teams refusing to make required road trips to the West.

On September 24, 1875, President George Gage of the White Stockings died. The former city treasurer, Gage was a popular executive who appeared to have led the club to victory in 1875, but he was merely a figurehead while Hulbert ran the organization from his post as secretary. Gage's widow gave Hulbert a proxy for her husband's shares, and that gave Hulbert majority control of the White Stockings. He was duly elected president; one of his first actions was to convince the other board members to add Spalding to the board and make him secretary. This put Hulbert in a much stronger position to bring about the creation of a new baseball league.

The *Tribune* reported on October 24 that Hulbert wanted the six existing stable clubs, and Cincinnati and Louisville as new clubs, to form an exclusive league or association. The new rules of this league would bear on a club's financial solvency, provide for a minimum size of member cities, allow only one club to represent each city, and require a $1,000–$1,500 deposit from each team. Many people scorned the proposal as too radical, but the White Stockings leadership believed that strong measures were necessary to save the game from becoming a "circus sideshow."

In November, the *Tribune* suggested that perhaps a western league should be formed, and that the eastern teams should be excluded altogether. Hulbert, a consummate businessman who certainly understood the financial benefits of large markets like New York and Philadelphia, insisted only on elimination of the game's bad elements: gamblers and drinkers, as well as the badly managed teams and those that would not meet their travel obligations. He also saw in Henry Chadwick, the game's earliest chronicler and statistician, a rival for leadership in the national game and an advocate for the owners from the East Coast, and he wanted to form a new league without Chadwick's involvement.

For Hulbert, the keys to the new league's success would be a monopoly of the best home markets and complete control over the players. He wanted

Chicago to be the centerpiece of the new league, and late in 1875, he secured commitments from St. Louis, Louisville, and Cincinnati. In December, he met with executives from Hartford, Boston, New York, and Philadelphia in order to create an eight-team league. Details were worked out in January, and the new league, known as the National League, was officially announced on February 2, 1876. The *Tribune* was pleased, explaining two months later,

> The game had grown, the West had grown, and both had outgrown Chadwick and all allied friends. The necessity for the League had arisen, and it was formed without the knowledge, consent, privity, counsel, or presence of the "Father of the Game" . . . he was a fraud in the business, he always depended on other brains than his own for his ideas . . . he is a played-out, passed-by man who never did care for the National Game further than as he could draw money out of it.

Hulbert's efforts in acquiring Spalding and other superior players during the 1875 season paid off. The White Stockings dominated league play in 1876, winning the championship with a record of 52–14, with an offensive machine, led by Ross Barnes and Cap Anson, that outscored the opponents by nearly three runs a game. Spalding won 47 games. Chicago's financial profitability was guaranteed by Spalding's off-field enterprises, such as a monopoly on producing the official baseballs for the league and publishing the annual postseason record book that Henry Chadwick edited after 1881.

Early in the 1876 season, the White Stockings attracted considerable attention when they acquired a house at 1030 Wabash Street for a clubhouse. The *Tribune* thought it "perhaps the most elegant location" in the city for its purpose. The house was only a block from the ballpark, and the club announced plans to convert the basement into a billiards room and to furnish the parlors elegantly.

Hulbert was elected president of the NL in December 1876 and soon put his mark on the game. He insisted that managers not sit on the bench during games, resisted a move to lower ticket prices, and staunchly opposed Sunday games and the sale of beer at ballparks. These measures were designed to limit the attendance of the working class at ball games and thus reduce the chance for rowdy behavior that was commonly associated with the poor during the Gilded Age. Hulbert also ensured that owner control over players was very strict. An owner determined a player's fitness to play and docked injured players their pay on days they could not take the field. Hulbert set the tone when he docked injured White Stockings player Ross Barnes half his 1877 salary when was out for three months because of an injury.

The White Stockings inaugurated the new Lake Front Park in 1878, built on the same public site as the field that had been destroyed in the 1871 park. In 1883, Spalding spent $10,000 remodeling the facility, which had a capacity of 10,000, making it the finest in the land. The park was notable for its short 196-foot right-field fence and its 180-foot left-field fence. The original ground rules made balls hit over the fences doubles, but in 1884, the rules were changed so that these became home runs. The White Stockings, led by third baseman Ed Williamson with 27, hammered 142 homers that year. The team was forced to move the following season, because it was a private enterprise that was not supposed to use city-owned space, to the $30,000 Congress Street Grounds on the city's west side. Its foul lines were 216 feet from home plate.

In 1879, only Chicago made a profit, even after competition from rival leagues had diminished. Owners were encouraged to cut player salaries, and they adopted the reserve clause in 1879, practically eliminating bargaining for better pay or conditions on the part of the players. The reserve clause bound ballplayers to their team and took away the principal leverage they might have used against the owner—the threat to sign with another team. Under the reserve clause, each team designated five players deemed essential for the following season. These players were "reserved," and no other team could sign them, or even contact them. All other players became free agents at the end of each season.

Following Hulbert's election as NL president in 1876, Spalding, the club secretary, manager, and captain, took on much more responsibility for White Stockings operations. He retained Anson and George Bradley, who had both signed to play in 1877 for Philadelphia, but the franchise had folded. Spalding's business activities were taking more of his time. He and his brother Walter had become partners in the sporting-goods business in early 1876, opening a store in downtown Chicago at 118 Randolph Street. As the business grew, Spalding had to spend more time at the store than he had anticipated. Later in 1876, his company received a contract to publish what became known as *Spalding's Official Base Ball Guide,* a yearly publication that included the league constitution and rules as well as the previous year's statistics.

As Spalding's business interests came to occupy the better part of his time, Anson became more important to the White Stockings. Born in Marshalltown, Iowa, in 1852, Anson broke into organized baseball with the Forest City club of Rockford, Illinois, in 1871, joining that team a year after Spalding had left it. Anson played for Philadelphia from 1872 through 1875, when Hulbert acquired him for the White Stockings. He played in Chicago from 1876 until the end of the 1897 season, starting at first base and batting .333 with 3,418 hits over his 27-year career. When Spalding retired from baseball after the 1878 season, Anson replaced him as manager, remaining in that position until the end of his playing career. Known as "Cap" early in his career, when he was team captain, he picked up the nickname "Pop" as he grew older. In his 19-year managerial career, the White Stockings won five NL championships. A strict manager who did not allow his players to drink or smoke, Anson was also an innovator, developing signals to the pitcher, encouraging base stealing and the hit-and-run play, and making good use of spring training, which for the White Stockings was often in Hot Springs, Arkansas. In 1880, Anson "rotated" his two-man pitching staff by having them pitch on alternate days, another innovative idea for the time and one that was very successful.

Apart from his skill as a player and field manager, Anson was a determined racist and was credited with a big role in forcing out black players from organized baseball. His intolerance was well known and dated back to at least 1883 when, as manager, he originally refused to allow his team to play an exhibition game with Toledo because it had a black catcher, Moses Fleetwood Walker. Anson's White Stockings finally played the game rather than forfeit their share of the gate receipts. Anson was not happy, and told the *Toledo Blade*, "We'll play this here game but won't play never no more with the nigger in." Anson was as good as his word; the White Stockings never played another exhibition game in Anson's time with a team having black players unless those players sat out the game. This practice soon became common in the entire NL.

Anson's (and baseball's) racism is well illustrated by the story of Clarence Duval, whom Anson hired as a team mascot. Duval, an African American of small stature, sang, danced, and twirled a baton to entertain the fans. To Anson, he was "the little coon," or "the little darkey," and he was often the butt of teasing and cruel practical jokes. In Anson's defense, most of white America would have described Duval in similar terms, given the prevailing racial bigotry.

Anson's White Stockings were enormously successful, and won league championships five times in seven years (1880–82, 1885–86), playing before large crowds. In Chicago amateur clubs and boys who marked out baselines on city streets were ubiquitous, and Mike "King" Kelly, acquired in the early 1880s, may have been the city's most popular celebrity. Kelly, notorious for his off-field rowdiness, was, however, a fine hitter and fielder and a great base stealer, and was instrumental in the team's championship seasons. A Hall of Famer, he led the NL in batting in 1884 and 1886. The White Stockings acquired a reputation for "greed," stealing bases and stretching singles into doubles and doubles into triples with remarkable regularity. When the team returned from its round-the-world trip in early 1889, hundreds of fans met the players at Union Station, and from there, a thousand cyclists led a parade to the Palmer House, where a homecoming celebration was held.

The White Stockings were closely linked to the growth of Chicago as a great city. Both were dependant on the railroad and the telephone, through which the local newspapers received the news to keep fans abreast of the team's exploits. The White Stockings were run by elite businessmen, the same sort who ran city government, and club leaders closely identified the White Stockings with Chicago. Spalding said that Hulbert was "a typical Chicago man. He never spoke of what *he* would do, or what his club would do, but it was always what *Chicago* would do." As Hulbert once told Spalding, "I would rather be a lamp-post in Chicago than a millionaire in any other city."

Like George Pullman and his company town, the White Stockings, under Hulbert and Spalding, were intended to help bring respectability to baseball by setting "honorable" and "morally elevating" examples. Spalding hired detectives to follow his players and report any bad behavior. "In fighting the encroachments of drink upon the efficiency of individual players, we are simply striving to give our patrons the full measure of entertainment and satisfaction to which they are entitled," he said. Team members had to sign a temperance pledge, and those who balked at this or any other club rule were fined, traded, or, worst, released and blacklisted. In these policies, the White Stockings were in line with the rest of the league, which in 1880 had established officially the imposition of fines on players for offenses such as profanity, and more serious penalties for misbehavior such as "drunkenness, insubordination, and dishonorable or disreputable conduct." Owners could and did fine players for errors made in the field, since it "reflected badly on their conduct."

The journalist Peter Finely Dunne played an important role in the citywide popularity of the White Stockings. Just 20 years old in 1877, Dunne was sent to cover the White Stockings for the *Chicago Daily News*. His stories went far beyond the dry box scores of the day, and readers learned about the highlights of games, the personalities of the players, and much more, all delivered in Dunne's characteristic pseudo-Irish slang and innuendo. Dunne did much to make Anson a sport hero and is credited with inventing the word *southpaw* to designate a left-handed pitcher—in the west-side stadium, a left-hander threw from the south side of the mound. Dunne's sportswriting also served as a model for writers at many other newspapers, which now began to create separate sports departments with an editor and a small staff of reporters.

Although Dunne and other journalists made the White Stockings popular in town, admission to games was still not easy for the working class. Chicago during the Gilded Age was divided between wealthy and xenophobic Republicans and a largely Irish and Democratic working class, many of whom had been Confederate sympathizers. Hulbert, while he ran the White Stockings, empathized with the respectable classes, opposing beer sales at the park, Sunday games, and low admission prices as devices to keep the poorer classes from attending games.

William A. Hulbert died after a lengthy bout with heart trouble on April 10, 1882. Spalding and John L. Walsh, another board member, took control of the club by buying Hulbert's shares from his widow, and Spalding was elected club president on April 26. Hulbert's death was particularly hard on Anson, who had relied on Hulbert as a kind of mentor, and the fortunes of the White Stockings declined after Hulbert's death, although the team did repeat as league champions in 1882.

The 1882 season saw the most spirited competition yet in the NL, further heightening public interest in baseball. Chicago's attendance reached 130,000, a record, and the success of the White Stockings probably helped some of the weaker teams in the league survive. The team failed to repeat as league champions in 1883, and after a poor start in 1884 imposed an 11 P.M. curfew on players during road trips, a move aimed at Kelly and several other players who caroused until very late at night. The curfew angered the players but did not bring about any significant improvement in the team's won-lost record. The team took the pennant in 1885 with a fabulous 77–25 record (.777), led by John Clarkson, who won 53 games and completed 68 of 70 starting assignments.

Spalding was a young capitalist caught up in the industrial revolution of the late nineteenth century. He made a lot of money from the Sox, with profits as high as $80,000 in 1887. He believed in the emerging theory of scientific management that asserted, among other things, that business must be divided into a management class that has to "have absolute control over the enterprise," and a worker class, under the control of management, that would perform the "actual work" of production. With that in mind, Spalding (and Anson) asserted even more control over their players. Anson fined two players $50 each for "dissipation" in 1885, and Spalding said that one-third of the clubs that failed in 1884 did so because of players' excessive drinking.

In 1886, the team captured the pennant, led by Kelly's .388 batting average. But the team lost the postseason championship series with St. Louis of the American Association. Spalding blamed the defeat on drunken players, especially Kelly, whom he then sold to Boston for $10,000. Spalding never worried about losing a star player. His White Stockings pioneered in using scouts to identify talented players in other parts of the country and in selling off aging veteran players to other teams. He also urged other teams to emulate his practice of hiring detectives to watch players' behavior. Even Anson occasionally got into trouble; in 1886, Spalding fined him $110 for arguing too vehemently with an umpire.

Between the 1888 and 1889 seasons, the White Stockings and a group of All-Stars from other teams took a world tour to generate interest in the games and more business for Spalding's sporting-goods firm. The tour included Australia and then Ceylon, described as a "queer sort of a place inhabited by a queer sort of people." Catcher Tommy Daly portrayed the Ceylonese as "howling, chattering, grotesquely-arrayed natives." Mascot Clarence Duval, who accompanied the White Stockings, amused the spectators with his tricks. In Egypt, the touring players played in front of the pyramids before a curious and fascinated crowd, some of whom were said to have been shocked when the players held an impromptu contest to see who could hit the Sphinx in the right eye with a baseball. Only left fielder Jack Fogarty succeeded.

Despite the excitement of the world tour, player-management relations continued to deteriorate in 1889, as owners cut costs and sought to exert even more control over their players. Spalding, for example, docked Ed Williamson all his pay (except for his $157 boat ticket) for breaking his ankle during the early part of the world tour. As a result of this increasing control, players rebelled, and formed the short-lived Players' League, which fielded its own teams for the 1890 season. Many of the White Stockings (now known as the Colts because of their youth) deserted Spalding and Anson and joined the new league, but the league survived only one year. However, Spalding, whose team had lost $65,000 that season, succeeded in co-opting many of the financial backers of PL teams by helping them buy into teams in the established leagues.

In late 1891, James A. Hart, a business associate of Spalding's and a minority stockholder in the White Stockings, became the team's new president, responsible for day-to-day operations. Spalding, ever more involved in managing his sporting-goods empire, continued to head the board, but devoted less and less time to White Stockings matters. Hart restructured the club in 1892, incorporating the team into a new organization and redirecting the existing corporation toward real-estate investments, such as spring-training property in Hot Springs and land in Chicago, including the site of the 16,000-seat West Side Grounds, which opened in 1893. In 1894, NL owners rejected Hart's suggestion that players wear numbers on the backs of their uniforms, arguing that it would encourage players to play for their own glory rather than for the success of the team.

Hart's accession marked the beginning of the end of the Anson era. Anson, who owned a few shares in the team, believed that he should have been given the opportunity to buy more stock, but that Hart had blocked him; consequently, he resented Hart, and the relationship between them deteriorated over the next five years. The White Stockings' fortunes on the field declined, and Anson accused Hart of undermining his authority with the players and of not spending the money to acquire better players. Some of Hart's frugality may have been at Spalding's behest. In the past, he had not hesitated to unload higher-salaried players to save money. Wags noted that "Al pulls the strings and Jim spiels."

In 1897, the team performed poorly, finishing in ninth place with a 59–73 record, 34 games out of first place. Anson later wrote in his autobiography, "That [the team failed to win] can only be explained by the underhanded work by some of the players looking toward my downfall. They were aided and abetted by President Hart who refused to enforce the fines levied by myself as manager and in that way belittling my authority . . . The ring-leader in this business was Jimmy Ryan, between whom and the Club's President the most perfect understanding seemed to exist." Whatever level of anti-Anson conspiracy may have existed, Hart fired Anson on February 1, 1898. "I'm glad it's over," Hart told the *Tribune*, which noted that Anson's 1894 illness had left him "stiffened," and that "his usefulness of body was impaired." Anson closed out a 22-year career with the White Stockings with a .329 batting average and 1,715 RBIs. Spalding wanted to have a fund-raising appreciation event for Anson, but he refused, stating, "I am not a pauper. The public owes me nothing." After a brief stint managing the New York Giants in 1898, Anson drifted around the vaudeville circuit, served a term as city clerk of Chicago, and died in 1922.

In 1898, Anson was replaced as manager by Tommy Burns. The team, now without their beloved manager, was popularly known as the Orphans. Burns led them to fourth- and eighth-place finishes. In 1900, Tom Loftus became manager, but his two seasons were very unsuccessful, including a 53–86 record in 1901. In 1901, the new American League began play with a Chicago franchise that Hart had sanctioned after it had agreed to build a ballpark on the South Side, where Hart was certain attendance would be low.

The AL Chicago team took over the old White Stockings name, now generally shortened to White Sox, and signed many NL players. The White Sox outplayed and outdrew the Orphans (who briefly became known as "the Remnants," since the White Sox had signed so many of their players). The Orphans lost their two best pitchers (Clark Griffith and Nixey Callahan) and a good outfielder (Sam Meeks) to the White Sox and four more players to other AL teams. The White Sox drew about 354,000 fans for the season, about 50,000 more than the Orphans, who lost even more players to the new league before the 1902 season.

THE ERA OF FRANK CHANCE AND CHARLES WEEGHMAN, 1901–19

In 1902, the team's fortunes took a turn for the better with the hiring of Frank Selee as manager. Selee had played very little professional baseball but was a good judge of talent and skilled at developing excellent players. He moved Frank Chance, a promising young player, to first base from split duty as a catcher and outfielder and Joe Tinker to shortstop from third base, and brought Johnny Evers in to play second base, creating the legendary Tinker-to-Evers-to-Chance double-play combination that was immortalized in a poem by Franklin P. Adams. During the 1902 season, the name "Cubs" became commonly used because of Selee's emphasis on youth, and the overall improvement in the team's play signaled better times to come.

Selee managed the Cubs for three and a half seasons, during which they steadily improved from sixth place to second. However, he resigned midseason in 1905, very ill with the tuberculosis that would kill him five years later. Frank Chance became manager, and the Cubs name was made official in that year.

Meanwhile, matters were not so positive in the front office. During the 1902 season, James Hart and AL president Ban Johnson engaged in a public feud. Johnson declared that his league would not contract with Spalding's sporting-goods company for uniforms as long as Hart remained a part of baseball, since Hart is Spalding's "representative and mouthpiece." For his part, Hart said, "[Johnson] does not keep his promises and he is utterly discredited in National league councils." Indeed, Hart and Spalding had been longtime business associates in baseball and real estate, a relationship that was "said to be" over. Spalding had an exclusive contract with the eight AL clubs for uniforms, worth more than $2,000. This dispute, as well as a failed attempt to win election as NL president, ended Spalding's active involvement with the Cubs and with baseball management in general. He retired to California, and while he continued to produce his annual baseball guide (and, indeed, was instrumental in creating the Abner Doubleday legend of baseball's origins in

1907), spent more of his time involved in theosophy and state politics until his death in 1915.

By 1905, Hart was having financial problems and sold the team to a former Cincinnati sportswriter named Charles W. Murphy. A large portion of the $125,000 sale price came from Charles P. Taft, a newspaper publisher in Cincinnati and half brother of then secretary of war (and later president) William Howard Taft. Murphy had worked for the New York Giants as a press agent and advance man prior to his purchase of the Cubs in 1905. Nicknamed "Chubby Charlie," he happened to be in Chicago when he heard that Hart was interested in selling the Cubs for about $100,000. He convinced Taft to invest in the Cubs, and a deal was worked out to buy the Chicago club for $120,000, plus $5,000 to Hart himself for facilitating the arrangements. Murphy became club president just as the club was entering its period of greatest success on and off the field. From 1906 through 1915, the team made $1.26 million.

Murphy's style was antagonistic to field manager Frank Chance and nearly everyone else. Several of Murphy's rivals called him a "rat," a "sneak," and a "windbag." He was involved in a controversy over the sale of World Series tickets in 1908, accused St. Louis manager Roger Bresnahan of throwing games in 1911, and was connected to the scandal that led Philadelphia Phillies owner Horace S. Fogel to be expelled from the game. Meanwhile, he made a great deal of money from the Cubs, but Chance accused him of unwillingness to acquire good players, which contributed to his firing on September 28, 1912.

Despite Murphy's questionable executive management, the Cubs dominated the NL from 1906 to 1910, with pennants in 1906, 1907, 1908, and 1910, and finished second (even with 104 wins) in 1909. The team won its only two World Series championships in 1907 and 1908.

In 1906, the Cubs went 116–36 for a .763 winning percentage, a record that still stands, and they won 50 of their final 58 games. The team had the best defense and offense in the NL. Led by 20-game winners Mordecai "Three-Finger" Brown and Jack Pfiester, the pitching staff posted a 1.75 ERA. Led by third baseman Harry Steinfeldt (.327), the team batted a league best .262 in the heart of the dead-ball era. However, the season ended in bitter disappointment when the Cubs lost the World Series to the crosstown White Sox, the "Hitless Wonders," four games to two.

The 1907–10 teams did not match the 1906 team's record, but they played superbly, winning an average of 103.5 games per season. Brown won 101 games in those four years while losing just 37, and team ERA was less than 2.00 every year but 1910. In the 1907 Series, the first game against the Detroit Tigers ended in a 12th-inning 3–3 tie, but then the Cubs swept the next four games and captured the world championship.

The 1908 season was highlighted by a close and exciting pennant race between the Cubs and the New York Giants. The climactic point of the season came on September 23, when, in a game between the two contenders, New

National League Park, 1908. Courtesy of the Library of Congress

York infielder Fred Merkle failed to touch second base while advancing on a hit late in the game. Evers noticed and called for the ball, and Merkle was declared out. As a result, the game ended in a tie, and the teams met in a playoff game two weeks later. The Cubs won and advanced to meet Detroit in the World Series, whom they handily defeated, four games to one. However, in 1910 they were overwhelmed in the Series by the Philadelphia Athletics, winning only the fourth game.

In 1909, Joe Tinker and Johnny Evers stopped talking with one another following a fight at an exhibition game in Bedford, Indiana. Evers took a taxi, or hack, to the ballpark by himself, leaving several other players to wait. When Tinker called him on it, a fight started that was concluded with an agreement between the two not to speak. Nevertheless, they played together on the Cubs through the 1912 season, and when Evers was made manager before the 1913 season, Tinker, at his request, was dealt to Cincinnati.

In 1911 Cub fortunes began to decline. Chance was injured most of the season—too many blows to the head by pitched balls resulted in the loss of some vision and may have altered his personality as well. He played only 31 games but had a stormy year as manager. In mid-August, he fined Tinker $150 and suspended him for the balance of the season for careless play but then reinstated him after three days. Chance also fined second baseman Heinie Zimmerman, substituting for an injured Evers, for "lackadaisical" play and then inexplicably excused the fine. Murphy fired Chance on September 28, 1912, after a year in which Chance played only five games before retiring as an active player. The team finished third with a 91–56 record, but the differences between Murphy and Chance had grown too great, with conflict over Chance's salary (less than one-third of John McGraw's) and Chance's constant complaint that Murphy refused to invest in good players despite having the resources to do so. Murphy offered Chance $20,000 for the 10 percent of the club he had received in 1906 when he became manager, but

Chance refused the offer and instead sold his shares to Harry Ackerland of Pittsburgh for $35,000.

The conflict between Murphy and Chance was suggestive of the deteriorating relationship between owners and players in professional baseball. Beginning about 1905, the owners tried to professionalize the game by having players project a better public image. They were ordered to wear suits in town, and carnival-like parades to the ballpark were banned. From the comfort of his California estate, Spalding praised the parade ban, and said, "Coons can do these things and feel proud of it, but it is the most servile thing to compel gentlemanly players to do so." Nevertheless, detectives were still hired to shadow the league's gentlemanly players.

In 1912, another salary battle between players and owners drew much attention and eventually led to the formation of a new players' union. The Cubs' Mordecai Brown, an acknowledged star, earned only $7,000 after nine years in the league. Players' demands induced Murphy to fire Chance and dismantle the team after the 1912 season, with Brown demoted to the minor leagues before being sold to Cincinnati. Arthur "Solly" Hofman, a part-time player who had signed a $5,000 contract, was sent down to the minors at lower pay only after being "laundered" through Pittsburgh. He sued and eventually won more than $2,900 in a judgment handed down by the Illinois Supreme Court.

In late 1913, a controversy boiled over between Murphy and player-manager Johnny Evers, who had a four-year contract worth $40,000. Evers talked about joining the new Federal League. Murphy claimed that Evers had quit the team, and terminated his contract without the required 10-day notice. In February 1914, NL president John K. Tener criticized Murphy and directed him to fulfill the terms of Evers's contract with the Cubs, and other club owners backed Tener's decision. Soon afterward, Murphy traded Evers to Boston, whose owner, James E. Gaffney, promised to give Evers what his contract with Murphy had stipulated. Evers, however, rejected the deal and said he wanted no part of any arrangement that would benefit Murphy in any way. He said he would rather become a free agent and make his own deal.

The *New York Times* reported that Evers had talked with millionaire chain restaurateur Charles A. Weeghman, the owner of the Chicago club in the Federal League, who had reportedly offered the ballplayer a four-year, $50,000 contract. In the end, Evers played for the Boston Braves in 1914 and helped that team win a pennant.

All of these controversies undermined Murphy's standing among the other owners, and they persuaded Charles P. Taft to buy Murphy's 53 percent interest in the team for $397,500. Taft appointed Charles H. Thomas as the new club president, although other owners protested that Thomas's reputation was not in baseball's best interests and that he would be just a stooge for the discredited Murphy. However, Taft replied that Thomas's appointment was a temporary move until he could sell the team.

In late 1915, Taft sold the team to Charles Weeghman as part of the settlement in which the Federal League was dissolved. Weeghman formed a syndicate that paid $500,000 for about 90 percent of the club's shares. One member of the syndicate was chewing-gum magnate William Wrigley Jr., who invested $100,000 for a 20 percent share. Weeghman's Chicago Whales (fans chose the name in a contest) had been one of the successes of the Federal League. His player-manager was former Cubs shortstop Joe Tinker, and the club played in his new $250,000 North Side stadium. Fans enjoyed the amenities, which included permanent refreshment stands, and they did not have to return foul balls hit into the stands. The Whales outdrew the Cubs in both Federal League seasons of 1914 and 1915, which undoubtedly encouraged the NL to sanction Weeghman's purchase of the Cubs from Taft.

Weeghman hired Joe Tinker as manager to replace Roger Bresnahan, whose 1915 fourth-place squad had the team's first losing record since 1902. Bresnahan was paid for the two years remaining on his contract and Weeghman helped him purchase the Toledo club of the American Association. The highlight of the 1917 season occurred at Weeghman Park on May 2, when Hippo Vaughn and Cincinnati's Fred Toney both threw nine-inning no-hitters. However, in the 10th, the Reds singled and scored on an error to win the game. Weeghman decided that after fifth-place finishes in his first two seasons as owner, he had to become more aggressive in building a contending team. On December 11, 1917, he obtained star pitcher Grover Cleveland Alexander and talented catcher Bill Killefer from the Phillies for pitcher Mike Prendergast, backup catcher Pickles Dillhoefer, and $50,000. The deal surprised the baseball world, as Alexander was thought to be untouchable, but he was mired in a contract dispute with the Phillies, demanding a three-year contract at $12,000 per year, a sum the club thought too much given the uncertainty of the war in Europe.

Weeghman took the risk to acquire Alexander, arguably the best pitcher in the game, having won 30 or more games for the past three seasons, a feat only matched by the immortal Christy Mathewson. Both Alexander and Killefer had been born in 1887 and with the Phillies since 1911. After the Alexander deal, Weeghman told the *New York Times* that he was considering offers to other star players, including outfielder Zach Wheat of Brooklyn. The club's board of directors authorized Weeghman to spend up to $200,000 to obtain the players necessary to win a pennant in 1918. Weeghman offered the St. Louis Cardinals $50,000 for second baseman Rogers Hornsby, but Cardinals president Branch Rickey turned down the bid. Nevertheless, he acquired pitcher Lefty Tyler and center fielder Dode Paskert.

Weeghman's activities, along with those of Boston Red Sox president Harry H. Frazee, aroused the ire of the *New York Times*, whose sports department lamented that Weeghman seemed willing to pay any price to win a pennant without having to wait for his manager to develop a winning team. Part of Weeghman's motivation, noted the *Times*, may have been based on cross-city rivalry with the 1917 World Series champion White Sox. "Every star ballplayer in the National league has become restless and is anxiously awaiting a call from the Cubs," claimed the newspaper, and other players were said to be ready to hold out or make themselves disagreeable in other ways so that their clubs might sell or trade them. Weeghman's and Frazee's dealings, concluded the *Times*, "give the game too much of a commercial aspect and overshadow the sporting end."

Even though Alexander joined the army and appeared in only three games, Weeghman's other acquisitions paid off, and the Cubs, managed by Fred Mitchell, won the NL pennant in 1918 by 10 1/2 games with an 84–45 record. The team had the best offense and defense in the NL, led by pitcher Hippo Vaughn, who led the league in strikeouts (148), wins (22), and ERA (1.64). However, the Cubs were bested in the World Series by a terrific Boston Red Sox club, four games to two. The Sox winning hurlers were Carl Mays and Babe Ruth. Chicago's home games were played in massive Comiskey Park instead of the smaller North Side field.

The 1918 season was not Weeghman's finest hour, because financial problems resulting from the war forced him to borrow money from Wrigley, with Weeghman's stock in the club as collateral. When Weeghman could not repay the loan, Wrigley took over the stock and purchased all of Weeghman's remaining shares. Weeghman's departure made Wrigley the largest shareholder in the organization, although he did not acquire majority control until 1919. In an interview with the *New York Times*' John Kieran years later, Weeghman traced his financial difficulties back to his original purchase of the Cubs. One of the members of the original syndicate failed to meet his pledge of $75,000, forcing Weeghman to borrow that sum from a bank. Wrigley cosigned for the note, Weeghman never could pay the bank loan in full, "and that's how Wrigley came to get the ball club from me."

Weeghman resigned from the club presidency after the 1918 season and was replaced briefly by Mitchell, an unusual situation. Only the Philadelphia Athletics' Connie Mack served as both field manager and chief executive of the club, but he never carried the title of club president. Mitchell, however, was known to have good business skills to go with his baseball knowledge. However, a few months later, Vice President William L. Veeck, a veteran baseball writer, was elevated to the presidency after Mitchell stepped down when the league decided that one person could not be both president and manager of a club. Veeck knew the game intimately, having covered it for 11 years, and had coordinated press relations for the Cubs during the 1918 World Series.

THE ERA OF WILLIAM WRIGLEY AND ROGERS HORNSBY, 1919–32

William Wrigley, whose family would own the Cubs for more than 60 years, was born in Germantown, Pennsylvania, in 1861, the son of a soap manufacturer. He ran away from home at the age of 11, operated a newsstand in New

York City, and returned to Germantown after four months. He worked for his father and became a partner in the business at age 21. In 1891, he established his own business in Chicago with the idea of manufacturing and marketing baking powder. Soon he turned to the manufacturing of chewing gum, which had first been offered as a premium for buying baking powder. However, the advantages of gum soon became obvious. Gum could be shipped anywhere and was worth 20 times more per pound than baking powder. Widely advertised and even given away to potential customers, the Wrigley product soon became extremely popular, reaching sales of $70 million per year by the time of Wrigley's death in 1932. Wrigley was also involved in the development of Catalina Island off the coast of California near Los Angeles, as well as banking, railroads, and coal. He was a generous partisan of the Republican Party and a philanthropist who supported hospitals and the Salvation Army. What he was not, in 1919, was a baseball man.

Wrigley had a deep appreciation for baseball, but he understood that one should not invest in a baseball club unless he loved the game, because it was not easy to make large profits from baseball. He continued to buy up shares from minority stockholders so that by 1921, he owned a vast majority of the club, and as his love for the game grew, he worked hard to earn those large profits. He instituted Ladies' Days. He spent $2 million on the Cubs' North Side ballpark, which by 1926 was known as Wrigley Field. He pioneered radio broadcasts of Cubs games, and attendance improved even though the team floundered.

William Veeck first met Wrigley in California, and the businessman was impressed with the sportswriter's style and thoughtfulness, and brought him into the Cubs' organization. After he replaced Mitchell as club president in 1919, Veeck ran the club for 14 years, until his death in 1933. Even as club president, he played the role of a contemporary general manager, and Cubs historians Jerome Holtzman and George Vass consider Veeck to have been the first general manager in the modern sense of the term. Under Veeck's direction, spring-training facilities were built at Catalina Island, and the Cubs began training there in 1921, with the Los Angeles minor league team, purchased in 1921, becoming the Cubs' principal feeder of talent. Wrigley even built a replica of Wrigley Field in Los Angeles for $1 million.

Veeck's investigation and suspension of pitcher Claude Hendrix for consorting with gamblers in 1919 is said to have led to the investigation that uncovered the Black Sox scandal, and he was instrumental in the hiring of Judge Kenesaw Mountain Landis as baseball's first commissioner. In 1921, Veeck reached an agreement with Chicago Bears owners George Halas and Edward Steinaman to rent Wrigley Field to the Bears for their home football games, and the Bears played there for 50 years.

Veeck agreed with Wrigley regarding the positive impact of radio broadcasts of Cubs home games as well as a comfortable stadium. Radio broadcasts began on station WMAQ in April 1924. Hal Totten, a 23-year-old *Chicago Daily News* reporter, handled the play-by-play on every Cubs (and White Sox) home game that season, and Wrigley was pleased to see attendance at the ballpark increase as a result. Totten went on to a long career as a sportscaster and worked World Series games for national networks on occasion. By 1929, Cubs games were broadcast on as many as five local stations, including WMAQ and WGN. In the 1930s, Bob Elson emerged as the voice of Chicago baseball, doing both Cubs and White Sox games. In addition, after the 1926 season, Wrigley Field was enlarged with an upper deck, increasing its capacity to 38,396 and bringing it close to the look it retains today.

After several years of mediocrity under managers Fred Mitchell (1920), Johnny Evers (1921), and Bill Killefer (1921–25), including last place in 1925, Wrigley's frustrations boiled over. Saying he would "shoot $1 million to put the Cubs over the top in 1926," he began by hiring Joe McCarthy as manager at a $20,000 annual salary. McCarthy had never managed in the major leagues before, but had completed six successful seasons with Louisville of the American Association. He believed in discipline and inherited a team of castoffs and inexperienced players. In June, Pete Alexander, whose alcoholism was becoming more and more of a distraction, was placed on waivers, and was claimed by St. Louis. McCarthy was pleased: "I absolutely refuse to allow him to disrupt our team and will not have him around in that condition." Newly acquired players like pitcher Charlie Root and outfielder Riggs Stephenson helped the team to a first-division finish for the first time since 1919. Steady improvement followed in 1927 and 1928, and in 1929, the Cubs captured the NL pennant by 10 1/2 games with a 98–54 record. Rogers Hornsby, purchased from Boston early that year for $200,000, led the team (which hit .303) with a .380 batting average and 39 homers. He led the NL in total bases (405), slugging (.679), and runs (156) and won the MVP Award. Hack Wilson drove in 159 runs, and three of the starting pitchers won 18 or more games. Wrigley had acquired Hornsby without consulting Veeck, and the club president, who disliked Hornsby, resigned in protest. However, Veeck rescinded his resignation when Wrigley promised not to interfere with player personnel matters again. Overall, the Cubs made $1,461,544 during the 1920s, half of it in 1928 and 1929. The team drew over a million fans each year from 1927 to 1931, including 1,485,166, a major-league record until 1947, and a mark the Cubs would not surpass until 1969.

In the 1929 World Series, the Cubs lost game four to the Philadelphia Athletics 10–8 after leading 8–0 in the eighth inning. However, center fielder Hack Wilson lost a fly ball in the sun that contributed to a 10-run Philadelphia uprising. The loss put the Cubs behind in the series, three games to one, and they lost game five 3–2 when the Athletics scored three times in the ninth inning. Wrigley was crushed, and it soured his opinion of McCarthy. Rumors of spring-training frivolity only served to confirm the notion that McCarthy was not tough enough to manage the Cubs.

Rogers Hornsby became manager of the Cubs on September 25, 1930, after McCarthy refused to finish the last four games of the season. He had been told on September 23 that his contract would not be renewed for the 1931 season and decided it would be "best for all concerned" if he departed immediately, even though Wrigley and Veeck tried to persuade him to finish the season. Mc-Carthy went on to manage the New York Yankees and Boston Red Sox for the next 20 years, winning several AL pennants and World Series titles.

Hornsby proved to be a failure as manager because he lacked the temperament to deal with players. He was very demanding, did not tolerate mistakes, and never developed rapport with his players. Nor did he get along with Veeck, who felt Hornsby was too pessimistic In 1931, Hack Wilson, who set an NL record with 56 home runs in 1930, hit only 13 (a deadened ball was partly to blame) and spent the entire season feuding with Hornsby. He was dealt to Boston after the season. Hornsby started the 1932 season as Cubs manager, but after allegations that he was involved with gamblers, Veeck fired him on August 2 and named easygoing first baseman Charlie Grimm as the new manager. After his firing, Hornsby requested that the club pay him the balance of his contracted salary in one payment so that he could pay off players who had lent him money to bet on horse races. At his dismissal, Hornsby told the *Tribune* that there were "big differences of opinion about the ball club and the way it should be run." Under Grimm, a ray of sunshine compared to Hornsby, the players responded and won the pennant by four games. The team's strength was the starting pitching, especially Lon Warneke, who led the league with a record of 22–6 and an ERA of 2.37. Alas, the Yankees swept the Cubs in the World Series. In the fifth inning of game three, Babe Ruth made a gesture that some interpreted as pointing to center field, where he promptly deposited the next pitch off Charlie Root for a home run. After the series, the players showed their disdain for Hornsby by refusing to vote him a share of the World Series proceeds, even though he had managed the team for two-thirds of the season.

THE ERA OF PHILIP K. WRIGLEY

William Wrigley Jr. died at his Arizona winter home from the effects of a stroke on January 26, 1932, leaving an estate worth more than $50 million, including the Cubs, said to be worth $5 million. His 38-year-old son Philip K. Wrigley inherited the team but initially left baseball decisions to the club's president. The younger Wrigley had flunked out of prestigious Phillips Academy and briefly studied chemistry at the University of Chicago. He assumed control of the chewing-gum operations in 1923 and built it into an enterprise in which the family name became synonymous with the product. Shortly after World War II, the Wrigley fortune was estimated at more than $100 million.

The Cubs organization suffered a significant loss on October 5, 1933, when William Veeck died unexpectedly after a three-week illness described as a "mysterious blood disease" that may have been leukemia. *Tribune* columnist Arch Ward praised him as the ideal baseball magnate and a person who had an excellent sense of players' values to the club. Veeck's "striking" personality drew players to perform according to his standards or be sent on their way. He insisted on good sportsmanship and sought players of good character. Veeck was also a strong supporter of the All-Star Game, an idea of Ward's that began in 1933 as a collateral event to the Century of Progress Exposition in Chicago, and was influential in obtaining the league's sanction for such a game. At the time of his death, Veeck was also looking into the idea of interleague play, advocating a month of games beginning July 4, with results to count in the standings.

Philip Wrigley selected William H. Walker to succeed Veeck as club president. Walker was the second-largest shareholder in the club and a successful businessman in the wholesale fish trade, but he was not a knowledgeable baseball person. He began his tenure with gusto, spending $65,000 to acquire aging outfielder and 1933 NL batting champion Chuck Klein from Philadelphia. Klein had hit .368 for the Phillies but only .301 and .298 in his two seasons with the Cubs. Walker also traded promising young first baseman Dolph Camilli to Philadelphia for Don Hurst, another veteran, who hit .199 in what would prove to be his final season. Walker did not get along with field manager Charlie Grimm and rejected Wrigley's suggestion of lower ticket prices for children. Late in 1934, an exasperated Wrigley bought Walker's 1,274 shares in the club and assumed the presidency. Wrigley later claimed that there had been no conflict with Walker; he had some ideas, "which may seem a little crazy in baseball circles," that he wanted to try out.

Wrigley's purchase brought his total to 7,455 2/3 shares, further consolidating the family's ownership of the club. The Cubs had been more or less a closed corporation since 1925, with very little open buying or selling of stock. Although the estimated value of Cubs stock was $125 per share, it was widely believed that it would cost four or five times that amount to wrest majority control from Wrigley. During the first two years of the depression, the Cubs made out brilliantly, earning about $700,000, but lost $665,000 from 1932 through 1934. Thereafter the team resumed making money.

Philip K. Wrigley owned the Cubs for 45 years, until his death in 1977. During that time, he was often criticized as an absentee owner who never attended games and who seemed not to care about the fortunes of the teams or the desire of fans to see a winner. Wrigley, it was said, cared only about the club as a business, and the object of any business is to make a profit. Given the Cubs' lack of success—only four NL championships and no World Series championships in those 45 years—it is hard to argue that he wanted the Cubs to win. Yet by most accounts he cared deeply about the Cubs, a "sacred trust" from his father, and for that reason held on to it despite many years in which the club lost a great deal of money. He told his biographer, Paul Angle, that his "father was very much interested in the team and so was I. The club appealed to me because the customers of the Cubs were exactly the same people that we sold chewing gum to." He assumed the club presidency because "no matter who's in there, if something, goes wrong, I'm going to get blamed for it, so I might as well take the job myself."

As president, Wrigley adopted a policy of admitting children for half price, a move other owners opposed. He thought that Cubs fans would respond to advertising of the same kind that he used to sell chewing gum, and in 1934, Chicago newspapers ran display ads touting the fun and enjoyment of going to Cubs games. Although some suggested that a winning team was the key to success at the turnstiles, Wrigley opted to rely on promoting the fun and healthfulness of spending a sunny afternoon watching the Cubs play baseball, regardless of whether they won or lost. He was, like his father, a strong believer in the advertising value of broadcasting games over the radio and, later, television. To make the experience of going to a ball game more enjoyable, he installed larger seats, loudspeakers in the stands, and moving ramps at Wrigley Field and was the first to indicate balls and strikes on the scoreboard. In 1937, outfield bleachers and a large mechanical scoreboard, largely operated by hand, were added to the park. Vines were planted at the base of the brick outfield wall to grow up the wall and present a very distinctive appearance. One of Wrigley's early major player transactions, the acquisition of star pitcher Dizzy Dean from the St. Louis Cardinals for $185,000 and three players just before the opening of the 1938 season, was as much a marketing ploy as an effort to improve the team. Dean had a bad arm, but Wrigley said, "Even if he can't pitch very well, we'll get a lot of publicity out of him."

Night baseball was another matter. In 1930, the Western League began playing night games under permanent lights, and in 1934, the NL voted to allow each team seven night games. However, Wrigley believed that baseball should be played in the daytime because "it brings people out into the air and sunlight." In 1941, however, he gave in and ordered lights for Wrigley Field at a cost of $185,000, partly because of President Franklin D. Roosevelt's suggestion that there be more night baseball so that workers on day shifts could see games. The lights were ready for installation on December 7, but Pearl Harbor intervened, the country went to war, and Cubs management, perhaps to Wrigley's great relief, quickly decided to donate the steel, copper wire, aluminum reflectors, and other material to the government for the war effort. Wrigley emerged as a good patriot for his generous contribution.

Nevertheless, the move to night baseball continued, and rumors floated around that the Cubs would play some night games at Comiskey Park, home of their crosstown rivals, the White Sox. Cubs management denied these rumors, noting the inconvenience for North Side fans to get to Comiskey Park. Although the Cubs said in the mid-1940s that they still might do it, the White Sox organization felt differently and effectively vetoed the notion of Cubs night games in its park. When Detroit added light to Briggs Stadium in 1948, Wrigley Field was left as the only major-league ballpark without lights. It was not as if there had never been night activity at Wrigley Field. Night wrestling and boxing matches, using portable lighting systems, had taken place there since 1934, when 35,000 fans saw Jim Londos pin Ed "Strangler" Lewis. In August 1943, heavyweight boxer Lee Savold knocked out Lou Nova, and a year later, he lost to Joe Baksi. Other night events at Wrigley Field included political rallies, a rodeo, and, in 1954, a basketball game featuring the Harlem Globetrotters. In addition, the All American Girls Professional Baseball League, which Wrigley had founded, played a doubleheader at Wrigley Field in 1943 under a temporary lighting system that did not throw light high enough for players to track fly balls.

As time went on, Wrigley became more adamantly against lights, fearing the impact of night games on the neighborhood. "How can anybody sleep with a loudspeaker going, thousands of people hollering, and cars being parked all over their yards?" he asked. He believed that the advent of television was good for daytime baseball because there was "more competition at night." From time to time, however, he did point out that lights would be useful to finish long afternoon games or to help the Bears on short winter days. Nevertheless, lights would not brighten Wrigley Field until 1988, 11 years after Wrigley's death and 7 years after the family sold the team.

Even though Wrigley took a more active role in operating the club after Walker's ouster, he was hardly an experienced baseball executive. He hired Charles "Boots" Weber as general manager in 1934. Weber had been operating the Los Angeles minor-league club since William Wrigley had acquired it in 1921. He became part of an advisory group that included manager Charlie Grimm until mid-1938, vice president and secretary John O. Seys, and scouts Jack Doyle and Clarence "Pants" Rowland. Grimm and Rowland had the greatest influence on Weber.

Weber played an important role in the trades and acquisitions that produced pennants in 1935 and 1938, although Wrigley's trade for Dizzy Dean was made over Weber's protest that it was too costly. The 1935 team had outstanding offense and pitching. Catcher Gabby Hartnett was MVP, with a .344 batting average, while Warneke and Bill Lee both won 20 games. In the World Series, Warneke shut out the Tigers in game one (3–0), but the Tigers won four of the next five to take the championship. The highlight of the 1938 championship season was player-manager Gabby Hartnett's "homer in the gloaming" on September 28 against the Pirates. With the score tied 5–5 in the bottom of the ninth, it was so dark that the game was sure to be called if the Cubs failed to score. However, with two out, Hartnett hit an 0–2 pitch into the right-field bleachers to win the game and move the Cubs into first place over the Pirates. They clinched the pennant two days later with a win over the Cardinals. Hall of Famer Hartnett was one of the greatest Cubs of all time, playing 19 years in Chicago before ending his career with the Giants, with a lifetime batting average of .297. The Series of 1938 was a disaster, as the Yankees again swept the Cubs, outscoring them 22–9.

After 1938, the Cubs had six straight losing seasons, ending with the pennant in 1945, when many key players were in military service. The Cubs struggled financially in the war era, losing $167,192 from 1939 through 1941, and even in the pennant year of 1945 only made $45,554. In 1940, Wrigley sent Weber into retirement and hired Jim Gallagher, a former journalist, as general manager. Gallagher launched a five-year plan and traded off veterans such as Billy Herman and Billy Jurges for younger players, most of who had scant success. A farm system was set up in the 1940s, long after others teams had done so. Grimm had returned as manager in 1944, and led the team to the pennant a year later. The hero was Phil Cavaretta, a Chicago boy, who led the NL in batting (.355) and was voted MVP. Stan Hack hit .323 and Andy Pafko drove in 110 runs. Seven Cubs made the All-Star team, including Phil Wyse, who won 22 games. The hurlers had a sparkling 2.98 ERA to lead the league. The exciting season brought out the fans, as the Cubs led the NL in attendance and reached the million mark for the first time since 1931.

In the World Series, the Cubs again came out second best. The match with the Tigers went to the seventh game, but in the first inning, the Tigers scored five and knocked out Hank Borowy on their way to a 9–3 victory. A fabled piece of Cubs legend was born during the series. This was the "Curse of the Billy Goat," which emanated from an incident in game four, with the Cubs holding a two-games-to-one lead. William Sianis, a local fan of Greek heritage and owner of the Billy Goat Tavern, brought Murphy, his pet goat, to Wrigley Field. Ushers denied entrance to Murphy, and Sianis appealed to Philip Wrigley. Wrigley supported the decision of the ushers, declaring that the goat "stinks" and therefore could not enter the stadium. Sianis reportedly said, "The Cubs ain't gonna win no more. The Cubs will never win a World Series so long as the goat is not allowed in Wrigley Field." This was seen as a curse, supported by the fact that the Cubs have not even been in a World Series since 1945. Sianis died in 1970, but in 1969, when the Cubs led the NL East most of the season, he announced that the curse was removed. It was not to be; the Cubs faded in September and lost to the Mets.

In 1973, Sianis's nephew Sam, now the tavern owner, brought Socrates, a descendant of Murphy, to Wrigley Field, where it too was denied admission, and the Cubs dropped out of pennant contention. When the Cubs made the playoffs in 1984 and 1989, the Tribune Company invited Sam Sianis and Socrates to the ballpark, and Sianis declared that the curse was lifted, to no avail. Similar efforts to lift the curse in the playoff years of 1998 and 2003 also failed.

Nothing much seemed to work after the 1945 pennant and a respectable third-place finish in 1946. The Cubs played no better than .500 ball for the next 16 seasons and went through a lengthy parade of managers. Wid Matthews, the farm director of the Brooklyn Dodgers, took over as general manager in late 1949 as Gallagher became vice president. Matthews attended the entire 1950 spring-training camp at Catalina, arranging activities for the players in an effort to promote camaraderie and spirit. Another result of this visit may have been the move of the team's spring-training facilities to Mesa, Arizona, in the early 1950s, where the environment was decidedly less resort-like. However, he failed to develop the team into a winner, and was followed in 1956 by John Holland, who had run the Cubs' farm team in Los Angeles.

Wrigley turned down many offers to buy the club. His standard line was "I'm not that hard up."

Despite seemingly unending losing seasons, the Cubs remained a popular attraction in Chicago in the postwar years, earning an average of $201,700 from 1946 through 1950. Part of the reason for this was Wrigley's decision to televise Cubs games over WGN, a local station that first went on the air in 1948. Jack Brickhouse, who began his baseball-broadcasting career as Bob Elson's partner in 1940, became the sole Cubs radio broadcaster in 1945. When television broadcasts began, he moved over to the television booth, and his clear and competent style was popular with fans. Brickhouse, whose voice was the first heard when WGN went on the air, also covered Bears football games for many years, as well as college football and other sports, and political conventions. He retired in 1981 and was elected to the broadcasters' wing of the Hall of Fame in 1983.

Individual players also made their mark with Cubs fans during these years, none more so than Hank Sauer, "the Mayor of Wrigley Field." Sauer, who played with the Cubs from 1949 through 1955, was a slugging outfielder that won the NL MVP Award in 1952 by hitting 37 home runs and driving in 121 runs. An avid tobacco chewer, Sauer was the recipient of countless bags of chewing tobacco thrown at him by adoring fans.

ERNIE BANKS AND THE HAPLESS CUBS

After Jackie Robinson's integration of baseball in 1947, Wrigley was reticent about bringing in African American players. He felt his first black player, like Robinson, had to have outstanding talent lest "it . . . reflect on his race." In 1950, the Cubs bought the contract of black infielder Gene Baker from the Kansas City Monarchs and sent him to their farm team in Springfield, Massachusetts. Later in 1950, Baker went to the Triple-A team in Los Angeles and played there for more than three years. At the end of the 1953 season, Baker was deemed ready to debut with the Cubs, and Matthews purchased Ernie Banks, a shortstop from the Monarchs, for $15,000 to provide Baker a roommate. Both players reported to the Cubs after the Pacific Coast League season ended on September 15, to bolster the middle of the infield, which had collapsed defensively that year. Baker had set a Los Angeles record by playing in 420 consecutive games, and in 1953, he hit .287 with 18 home runs and 68 RBIs. Banks, meanwhile, had hit .344 for the Monarchs, and both were considered excellent defensive players.

While Baker was a creditable player for the Cubs, hitting .265 in 630 games before departing for the Pittsburgh Pirates in 1957, Banks became the team's greatest star in the post–World War II Wrigley years. He played 19 seasons for the Cubs, first at shortstop and later at first base. He had a career batting average of .274, and his 512 home runs stood as a team record until 2003. His optimistic outlook on baseball and life in general made him very popular with the fans, to whom he became known as "Mr. Cub," and his baseball skills earned him the NL's MVP Award in 1958 and 1959, even though the Cubs were not contenders. He was elected to the Hall of Fame in 1977.

Despite the addition of Banks, Baker, and other talented African American players during the 1950s, the Cubs were a perennial second-division team, finishing fifth three times between 1950 and 1959, sixth once, seventh four times, and last twice. As the team floundered to another seventh-place finish in 1960, Wrigley and his management team decided to expand the coaching staff from three to eight. Other teams had as many coaches, whom they used in their farm systems, but Wrigley declared that "[coaches] are the heart of a ball club." As such, the coaches, not the front office, would select the manager (who might not even bear that title). The club felt that all the necessary qualities for an excellent manager could not be found in one individual, but would exist in a collective of coaches, or, as it came to be known, a college of coaches. From the beginning, sportswriters mocked the plan, but Wrigley resolutely stood by it.

A March 1961 document, "The Basic Thinking That Led to the New Baseball Set-Up of the Chicago National League Ball Club," emphasized the failings of the traditional patronage system of hiring coaches and stressed the importance of instructing players. Sportswriter Jerome Holtzman's article "The Cubs' Curious Experiment," in the August 1961 issue of *Sport*, pointed out that the entire management team (Wrigley, the front-office personnel, the coaches, and a player representative) met during spring training to deal with the most important question: the tenure of the head coach. Would he stay all season or would he rotate, along with the other coaches, to one of the minor-league teams?

As it turned out, he rotated, and the Cubs employed several head coaches during this period. The college-of-coaches system was implemented during the 1961 and 1962 seasons, but with no better results than before; the team finished seventh in 1961 and an embarrassing ninth in 1962, when the expansion franchise in Houston finished ahead of them. According to Paul Angle, the system benefited the farm-system players by putting them in closer contact with coaches who had major-league experience, and administratively helped bring about a closer relationship between the Cubs and their farm system. After two years, however, it was clear that the scheme was not bringing about an improved team, and Bob Kennedy was hired as manager for the 1963 season (although Wrigley refused to use that title for some time to come), and led the team to its first winning season since 1946 (albeit in seventh place). Wrigley also hired retired air-force colonel Robert Whitlow as "athletic director." He would be sort of a personnel director for coaches and minor-league managers and a person who could fill the gap between the front office and the playing field. Once again, Wrigley came under considerable criticism from the press. Whitlow had no baseball background, and his vague duties impressed some critics as a non-job. After two years, Whitlow resigned in the belief that he was not earning his salary. His lack of baseball experience made it hard for him to supervise coaches and managers and enforce player discipline, as was his responsibility.

LEO THE LIP AND THE CUBS RETURN TO RESPECTABILITY

Soon after Whitlow's resignation, the Cubs hired Leo Durocher as field manager. Durocher, one of the game's most colorful individuals, had played for the New York Yankees, Cincinnati Reds, St. Louis Cardinals, and Brooklyn Dodgers, and had managed the Dodgers and New York Giants before arriving in Chicago for the 1966 season. Wrigley announced to the press that he wanted a "take-charge guy," and Durocher said he was that guy, although his team came in last (59–103). Under Durocher, the team reached third place in 1967 and 1968, and after leading the NL East for much of the 1969 season, slipped back to second place in the final month and lost by eight games. The team had a strong daily lineup, led by Ron Santo, with 123 RBIs, and Banks, with 106, but the team only batted .253. Five pitchers won 10 or more games, including Bill Hands (20) and Hall of Fame Ferguson "Fergie" Jenkins (21). Jenkins won 20 or more six straight years and averaged around 300 innings a season. Wrigley thought the unaccustomed spotlight of celebrity early in the season, when the team was in first place, had distracted the players and contributed to the team's late fade, but a more likely reason was Durocher's failure to rest his top-line players. Whatever the causes, the 1969 season was the high point of Cubs success in the later Wrigley years. In 1970, the Cubs were again second in their division, and the following year dissension between Durocher and his players surfaced and reached a high point with a stormy clubhouse meeting in late August. Wrigley placed an advertisement defending Durocher in all four Chicago daily newspapers, but the fiery manager was let go in the middle of the 1972 season.

After several dreary seasons in the mid-1970s, in November 1976 Wrigley named former White Sox infielder and Cubs manager Bob Kennedy as director of the club's baseball operations. Kennedy replaced general manager E. R. "Salty" Saltwell, who had been promoted from director of concessions in 1969 in an act of admirable Wrigley loyalty but who had been able to accomplish little with team development. Kennedy's first move was to name Herman Franks the new field manager, replacing Jim Marshall. Franks had formerly managed the San Francisco Giants to four second-place finishes in the NL West.

THE WRIGLEY FAMILY STEPS OUT

Philip K. Wrigley died April 12, 1977, at his country home in Elkhorn, Wisconsin, of gastrointestinal hemorrhaging. Sports columnists praised his fan friendliness but pointed out that he had rarely attended Cubs games and seldom involved himself in club operations, although he used his veto power in major transactions. His son, William Wrigley, inherited the club and pledged to maintain the family dynasty. Under his father's tenure as club president, William Wrigley had played virtually no role in the club's management, and instead had prepared himself to run the other family enterprises. He appointed William Hagenah, Jr. as club president and contented himself with the largely ceremonial position of chairman of the board of directors. Much of his time was occupied by huge legal and financial problems stemming from the death of both his parents within a few months of one another. Hagenah, who had been the treasurer of the Wrigley Company, was not a baseball man, and thus Bob Kennedy handled the Cubs' operations almost exclusively, obtaining Hagenah's approval only for key personnel decisions. Sportswriters began to speculate within days of Philip Wrigley's death about the future of the Cubs. Most agreed that the club deserved leadership that was more dynamic. Would it come from the Wrigley family or from a new owner?

Under William Wrigley's distant guidance, the Cubs struggled on, playing nearly .500 ball and finishing in the middle of the pack between 1977 and 1979, and then collapsing in 1980 with a 64–98 record and a last-place finish in their division. During that season, Murray Chass, a sportswriter for the *New York Times*, pointed out that except for the Cubs, every team that had been in the NL since 1945 had been to the World Series or playoffs at least four times. The Cubs had finished in the second division 26 times out of 35 seasons and had ended each season an average of 22 1/2 games behind the league or division winner. Chass laid the blame on an overly conservative management style that had evolved under Philip Wrigley. The club hired only traditional baseball executives and managers, not the kinds of mavericks that win pennants. Player personnel directors had never risked signing talented high-school players and giving them generous bonuses. Wrigley's insistence on day baseball sapped the players' energy during the hot, humid summers of Chicago and freed players to carouse at night. In addition, as long as fans kept filling Wrigley Field, the club did not have to care about winning. Of course, William Wrigley denied the allegation that the family was not concerned about winning and claimed vaguely that "you have to go to the grass roots, and that's what we're doing."

Rumors about a sale of the Cubs became more frequent after the dismal 1980 season that saw the club post a $1.7 million loss. This time there was truth to them. Negotiations with the Tribune Company, parent corporation of the *Chicago Tribune*, began in the spring of 1981, well before the 50-day strike that interrupted the baseball season between June 12 and August 1. The terms were announced June 16 and stipulated that the Tribune Company would buy the assets of the Cubs and assume the club's liabilities for $20.5 million. The arrangement included Wrigley Field, but not the land on which it stands, which the club leases for $30,000 per year through a contract that continues until 2012. William Wrigley transferred his 81 percent share of the ownership, and minority stockholders likewise disposed of their 1,900 shares to the new owner. Each received about $2,000 per share. The sale of the Cubs was the 10th MLB ownership change since 1976 and followed closely the $20 million sale of the White Sox. The $20.5 million purchase price was just short of the record $21.1 million Nelson Doubleday paid for the New York Mets in early 1980.

However, what prompted the sale was the $40 million in inheritance taxes that the Wrigley family owed to the federal government and to California, Illinois, and Wisconsin following the deaths of Philip and Helen Wrigley in 1977 and the lack of liquid assets to pay the large estate tax. It took nearly four years for an agreement on the value of the estate to be completed between the family and the involved government agencies. By 1981, most of the taxes had already been paid, and the balance was paid out of the sale price of the Cubs.

THE ERA OF DALLAS GREEN AND SAMMY SOSA, 1981–2005

Under the new management of the Tribune Company, Andrew McKenna became president of the Cubs. A former part owner and board member of the White Sox, he was a practical finance expert and used his two years as president to stabilize the club's finances. In October 1981, he hired Dallas Green as executive vice president and general manager; here, perhaps was the maverick the Wrigleys could never bring themselves to hire.

Dallas Green came to the Cubs from Philadelphia, where he had managed the Phillies to a World Series championship in 1980. Known for his fiery aggressiveness and lack of diplomatic skills, he minced no words when he announced, "I'm going to look everybody in the eye and tell them if they don't want to work as hard as I do, they might as well go home now." He was given a five-year contract worth more than $1 million, including benefits. A driven, intense man, Green ran into conflict with nearly everyone in the organization. "My trouble was I have a big mouth, and I pop off about a lot of things," he said later. The new team slogan was "Build a New Tradition," and under Green's forceful leadership, trades, and free-agent signings, and the work of field managers Lee Elia and Jim Frey, the Cubs improved to a point where they made the playoffs in 1984, winning the NL East with a record of 94–65. The key acquisition was Rick Sutcliffe, who went 16–1 and won the Cy Young Award. Second baseman Ryne Sandberg hit .314 and had 200 hits. He and five other players had 80 or more RBIs. However, the season ended in bitter disappointment, when after winning the first two games against the San Diego Padres, the Cubs lost the next three and were eliminated. The exciting campaign brought out the team's first 2 million attendance, and except for the shortened 1994 and a short dip the following year, the Cubs have drawn over 2 million ever since. Attending games at lovable Wrigley had become the popular thing to do. In addition, there was a major improvement in the surrounding gentrified neighborhood, which became a popular entertainment area for young professionals.

By that time, Andrew McKenna had given way to Jim Finks as club president. Finks was formerly general manager of both the Minnesota Vikings and Chicago Bears of the NFL, and his appointment was seen as a way to contain the ambitious Dallas Green, since Finks was known to be a strong though low-key leader. However, Finks was really not much of a baseball man, and despite the successful 1984 season, he returned late that year to professional football as general manager of the New Orleans Saints. Dallas Green was promoted to president of the Cubs, at the same time retaining his post as general manager.

After the 1984 season, the Cubs went into a downward spiral, finishing fourth in their division in 1985, fifth in 1986, and last in 1987. Star players like Sutcliffe suffered injuries or the ravages of age and performed badly after 1984. Finally, on October 29, 1987, Dallas Green resigned as president and general manager because of what were politely called "basic philosophical differences with management." Money matters had been involved; the Tribune Company was concerned about the $15 million payroll, third highest in 1986, and Green had had to get rid of a number of high-salaried players such as third baseman Ron Cey, outfielder Gary Matthews, and pitchers Dennis Eckersley and Steve Trout. Their departure partially accounted for the last-place finish in 1987. The Tribune Company wanted to reduce Green's control over player personnel matters to prevent future payroll inflation, stipulating that contracts would have to be reviewed by another, as yet unhired, club official. Green, for his part, wanted to take on the field manager's job while remaining club president. Green could not agree with what the Tribune Company wanted. Since ownership would not allow his request (which was against MLB rules), he resigned.

The feud between Green and his superiors boiled over in the last month of the disastrous 1987 season. Manager Gene Michael quit in early September, and Green accused the players of "quitting with a capital Q." John Madigan, the Tribune Company's executive vice president, who oversaw the Cubs, was appointed to run the club in the interim and search for a new director of baseball operations.

The stormy 1987 season was complicated further by the problem of owner collusion over the signing of free agents. None of the several top-flight players who had declared free agency were offered a contract by any team. Among the most prized was outfielder Andre Dawson of the Montreal Expos, who had rejected a $1 million, one-year offer from them. He approached the Cubs during spring training, but Green expressed concern over finances. Sutcliffe offered to donate $100,000 of his salary to subsidize Dawson's contract. Dawson's agent Dick Moss announced that Dawson wanted to play for the Cubs so much that he would sign a blank contract. That ploy worked, and the Cubs signed Dawson for $500,000, plus some incentives, a figure that made him the 15th-highest-paid Cubs player. Dawson responded with a career year that included 49 home runs and 137 runs batted in, earning him the MVP Award and future lucrative contracts.

Then, in 1988, lights finally came to Wrigley Field. The Tribune Company was very much in favor of installing lights, especially since it owned WGN-TV, now a cable superstation with a national market, and Cubs management wanted more prime-time broadcasts. The Cubs' television broadcaster was

Harry Caray, who had succeeded Jack Brickhouse in 1982, a nationally popular personality known for his down-to-earth style, genuine enthusiasm for the game, and good-natured mispronunciations and attention lapses. Night baseball would serve to increase Caray's popularity and with it the popularity of the team.

Green had advocated lights early in his tenure as general manager, but without initiating discussions with either the city government or neighborhood leaders. His arrogance stimulated the formation of CUBS (Chicagoans United for Baseball in Sunshine), an antilights organization, which gradually emerged as a potent political force. CUBS influenced the state legislature to pass a law in August 1982 forbidding excessive noise after 10 P.M. for "any professional sport played in a city with more than one million inhabitants, in a facility in which night sports were not played before July 1, 1982," a description specifically aimed at Wrigley Field. Two days later, the city passed an ordinance forbidding sports events between 8 P.M. and 8 A.M. on any field that was not totally enclosed, featured more than 15,000 seats, and was closer than 500 feet to 100 residences. Clearly, this ordinance was also specifically aimed at Wrigley Field. The Tribune Company fought back, calling the laws "bills of attainder" and unconstitutional because they applied only to one specific property.

In 1984, when the Cubs made the playoffs, MLB worried about low television ratings from weekday afternoon ball games. As it turned out, the playoff schedule was so arranged that there was only a Friday afternoon game at Wrigley Field. However, there was a feeling that the problem of televising postseason day teams would recur if the Cubs continued to play well. In December, Commissioner Bowie Kuhn told the Cubs that in the future, the team would have three choices with respect to playoff games: (1) the Cubs could install lights at Wrigley Field, (2) they could agree to play postseason home games at another park with lights, or (3) they could agree to reimburse MLB and its teams for revenue lost because of poor television ratings. This virtual ultimatum stirred the Tribune Company to overturn the restrictive state and city laws.

In addition to challenging the constitutionality of the laws in court, the Tribune Company floated rumors that it might move the team to the western suburbs, where it owned property suitable for constructing a new stadium, and announced the cancellation of plans for new luxury boxes at Wrigley Field. In March 1985, a Cook County judge upheld the constitutionality of the city ordinance in a 64-page decision that included poetry and quotes from the song "Take Me Out to the Ball Game." A month later, after the appeals process had been hastened with the help of Governor James R. Thompson, the case went to the Illinois Supreme Court, which, in October, upheld the city ordinance and the state law. The disappointed Cubs management once again raised the specter of the club becoming a suburban team.

In March 1987, Tribune executive Don Grenesko was appointed to pursue the lighting issue. He offered a compromise to the city whereby the Cubs would play a maximum of 18 night games a season. Meanwhile, the state legislature passed a bill exempting playoff and World Series games from its 1982 noise-pollution law, and Governor Thompson signed it. Then, in Chicago, after a neighborhood survey revealed that a majority of local residents did not oppose 18 night games a season, Mayor Harold Washington introduced a revised ordinance in the city council. The mayor unexpectedly died, however, and the bill stalled in the deeply divided council. However, the issue did not go away, as local critics blamed the newspaper for controlling the Cubs and dominating the Wrigley Field lighting argument. In February 1988, the *Tribune,* in a lead editorial, ripped into local and state politicians for using the night-baseball issue to "leverage the newspaper's editorial policy." Calling the politicians "bums," the editorial said that if the paper really did control the Cubs, the team would have fled to the suburbs years earlier.

Amid all the controversy, the Cubs modified their compromise offer, opting for an early 7:05 P.M. starting time for night games and agreeing to cut off beer sales after the seventh inning. In addition, the club promised to add 300 parking spaces so fewer patrons would have to park on residential streets around the stadium. As the city council neared a vote on the compromise plan, A. Bartlett Giamatti, the new commissioner of baseball, promised the 1990 All-Star Game to Wrigley Field if the vote went for night baseball. By a vote of 29–19, the city ordinance banning night games was repealed and the compromise was approved.

The lighting system that was installed in the spring and early summer of 1988 provided for six banks of floodlights mounted above the existing grandstand, with a total of 540 halide lamps backed by black metal plates to block the light from the surrounding neighborhood. The design was chosen for its architectural compatibility with the 70-year-old stadium and cost about $5 million.

The first night game was to be played August 8, 1988, against the Phillies before a capacity crowd, some of whom had paid as much as $1,000 to scalpers for a ticket. The Cubs authorized a record 560 press passes, more than twice the number issued when Pete Rose broke Ty Cobb's career hits record. Unfortunately, the game was called because of rain after a two-and-a-half-hour delay, and the first completed night game was played on August 9, with the Cubs beating the Mets 6–4.

Following Green's departure, the Cubs operated without a president for a year and a half, until Grenesko, fresh from his successful arrangement for night baseball, was named to the post in 1989, mainly to oversee the club's finances. General manager Jim Frey, who had replaced Green in that position in 1987, hired his boyhood friend Don Zimmer as field manager for the 1988 season. This appointment was virtually inevitable. Frey and Zimmer had grown up in Cincinnati, where they played on the same Knothole Baseball team as youths. Zimmer had been Frey's third-base coach in the mid-1980s, when Frey was field manager, and Dallas Green had fired both of them in June 1986.

Before the 1989 season, Frey traded promising young outfielder Rafael Palmeiro, who had hit .307, to the Texas Rangers for hard-throwing but erratic closer Mitch Williams. The trade was widely criticized, even by some players, but when Williams had a career year, young outfielders Jerome Walton (.293) and Dwight Smith (.324) blossomed, first baseman Mark Grace and second baseman Ryne Sandberg had excellent seasons, and Greg Maddux won 19 with a 2.95 ERA, the Cubs returned to the playoffs for the first time in five years. The club led the NL in batting average (.261) and run production, even though no one drove in more than 79 runs. However, the club failed again in the postseason, losing to the San Francisco Giants in the first round four games to one.

The success could not be sustained under field manager Don Zimmer. After the team floundered badly in 1990, finishing fifth, Frey was authorized to spend more money than ever before in the free-agent market, and during the 1990–91 off-season, he put out $25.2 million to sign outfielder George Bell, the 1987 AL MVP, and pitchers Danny Jackson and Dave Smith. Nevertheless, the investment did not pan out, and the Cubs finished fourth with a 77–83 record. Zimmer clashed publicly with Grenesko, which cost him his job in May, and Jim Essian finished the season. Frey became senior vice president after the season, and former White Sox general manager Larry Himes was named executive vice president of baseball operations, assuming Frey's responsibilities. Despite the poor finish, the team was worth $125 million, ninth among MLB clubs.

Grenesko himself stepped down as club president at the end of the season. For nearly three years, the Cubs were run by committee, with Tribune Company board president Stanton Cook nominally in charge. Under that regime, Himes traded George Bell to the White Sox for outfielder Sammy Sosa and left-handed pitcher Ken Patterson. In his one season with the Cubs, Bell hit .285 with 25 home runs, but he committed more errors than any other outfielder. Sosa was acquired for his speed and defensive skills. It was only later in the 1990s that his ability to hit home runs would make him the most popular Cub of the Tribune era. While the Sosa trade paid substantial dividends for the Cubs, Himes was castigated for allowing All-Star pitcher Greg Maddux to sign as a free agent with the Braves and for failing to re-sign Andre Dawson after he had 22 home runs and 90 RBIs in 1992. The Cubs continued their losing ways in 1992, 1993, and 1994, which ultimately led to an administrative shake-up in the Cubs' organization, following the naming of Andy MacPhail as the president of the club.

Andy MacPhail, son of Lee MacPhail, the former president of the AL, had begun his baseball management career with the Cubs in 1976 as a minor-league business manager. He then become assistant general manager of the Houston Astros in 1982 and general manager of the Minnesota Twins in 1985, leading that club to two World Series titles in 1985 and 1987. The Tribune Company brought MacPhail in after the strike-ruined 1994 season. He quickly hired former Cubs pitcher Ed Lynch as general manager and Jim Riggleman as field manager. Lynch, who had earned a law degree from the University of Miami after his playing career ended in 1987, came to the Cubs from the Mets, where he had been special assistant to general manager Joe McIlvane since 1993. Riggleman had managed the San Diego Padres for two years before coming to the Cubs. The new management team also had to deal with the financial and psychological impact of the long strike, which shortened the 1994 season, canceled the World Series, and delayed the opening of the 1995 season.

Partly because of the strike, the MacPhail era started slowly, although he and Lynch worked hard behind the scenes to build up the minor-league system. The team had a winning season in 1995, but reverted to form the next year. In 1997, the Cubs began the season with a team record 14-game losing streak and never recovered, finishing with just 68 wins. However, in 1998, the Cubs engineered a remarkable turnaround, coming in second with 90 wins, and made the playoffs. MacPhail signed five former All-Stars, increasing the payroll by 15 percent, and all of them contributed. Sammy Sosa hit 66 home runs and led the majors in RBIs with 158, and enchanted fans followed his epic home-run battle with the Cardinals' Mark McGwire. Although the team was swept by the Atlanta Braves in the first round of the playoffs, fans, for the first time in the memory of most, believed that the Cubs were poised to be perpetual contenders, especially with rookie hurler Kerry Wood, who struck out 20 Astros in one game. Once again, however, disappointment stalked Wrigley Field, as the Cubs lost 23 more games in 1999 than in 1998, despite 63 home runs from Sosa, and finished with their worst record since 1980. Don Baylor came in to manage in 2000, and while Sosa hit 50 homers, the team dropped to 65 wins. The following year, Sosa had a sensational season, with 64 homers, 160 RBIs, and a .328 batting average, which along with Josh Lieber's 20 wins helped raise the team to an 88–74 mark. But in 2002, the club nose-dived to a 67–95 season and fifth place.

Through all the ups and downs, all the brief successes and lengthy frustrations, Wrigley Field remained the seemingly unchanged landmark of Chicago baseball. While stadium lights lit up the surrounding neighborhood, known as Wrigleyville, on 18 summer nights, other subtle changes were

Sammy Sosa slugs his 499 home run during the 2002 season. © AP / Wide World Photos

creeping into and around the ballpark. In 1989, a year after the addition of lights, private boxes were built on the mezzanine level where the broadcast booths had been. More were added in the mid-1990s, bringing the total to 63. And before the 2004 season, 213 new box seats were added in three rows built between the two dugouts. None of these changes significantly altered the appearance of the park.

Outside Wrigley Field, rooftop game watching began in 1974 with building owner George Loukas inviting friends to his rooftop to watch Cubs games from behind the lower parts of the outfield bleachers. What seemed like a quaint practice took off in the playoff year of 1989, when one entrepreneur turned his rooftop into a private club, denying access even to building residents who were not club members. By 1995, all buildings with a view—perhaps a dozen—were owned by businesspeople with an eye toward profiting from the vantage point offered by the roof. By the late 1990s, owners had installed aluminum bleachers and "luxury" seating for wealthy patrons, and the city had recognized the commerciality of the rooftops and was licensing, regulating, and taxing them.

Within Wrigley Field, the Cubs were enjoying excellent attendance during these years, so rooftop attendance could not be considered a drain on gate receipts. But increasing player salaries and other expenses forced the Tribune Company to look for ways to increase further revenue from the stadium. In August 2001, the company floated a plan to spend $11 million to enlarge the bleacher area by 2,000 seats, add luxury boxes, and create advertising space. Traditionalists opposed these plans, as did some rooftop owners, who feared the expanded bleacher area would block their view. Mayor Richard M. Daley suggested that Wrigley Field be granted historic-landmark status, which would give the city more input into proposed structural and aesthetic changes. The Cubs wanted an agreement that would give Wrigley Field landmark status but still allow the Tribune Company to make modifications without a great deal of bureaucracy. The Cubs also wanted to increase the number of night games to 30; this, they reasoned, would boost both attendance and the size of the television audience. Given that the announced profit of the Tribune Company for the year 2000 was $200 million, some residents were skeptical about the company's desire for more revenue from the Cubs and its promise not to disrupt neighborhood harmony. According to *Forbes*, the Cubs made $7.9 million in 2001 and the team was worth $247 million, escalating to $358 million at the start of 2004, eighth highest in the majors.

Landmark status was granted, but the proposed bleacher expansion did not take place. Early in 2004, a new variation on the bleacher-expansion issue was proposed. With this plan, the exterior walls behind the bleachers would be moved out 10 feet toward the street to provide support for the additional seats. Sidewalk space would be reduced somewhat, but this was not seen as a major problem. During the summer of 2004, discussion about stadium expansion was set aside after falling chunks of concrete revealed some potentially serious structural problems with the 90-year-old ballpark. The problems were quickly remedied, but they were reminders of the frailty of the old stadium, and led some to speculate that perhaps the time had come to think seriously about replacing Wrigley Field with a new stadium. Would a new Wrigley Field be a replica of the old one, or would the design be fundamentally altered to provide for some of the amenities found in newer stadia? Would a new Wrigley Field be subsidized with public funds, as had been the case with the new White Sox park and the major renovation to Soldier Field, the home of the Chicago Bears, or would a new park be privately funded? If a new park were built on the same site as Wrigley Field, where would the Cubs play during construction and what impact would that construction have on neighborhood residents and businesses? For the first time in 90 years, Cubs management and fans had to begin thinking about these very basic questions. For the short term, however, life went on as usual. In November 2004, the Tribune Company went to the city's landmarks commission to obtain approval to install permanent 10-foot-by-3-foot revolving advertising boards behind home plate. Temporary boards of this type had been used for the 2003 regular season and playoffs, and these boards are common in other ballparks. The Cubs hoped to generate between $3 million and $5 million from the device, and that, combined with a 17 percent increase in ticket prices, could allow for a significant payroll increases.

The on-field fortunes of the Cubs began to improve after the year 2000, coincidental with the rise of Jim Hendry in the organization. Hendry and MacPhail had worked together in the Florida Marlins system in 1994, when Hendry was special assistant to general manager Dave Dombroski, and MacPhail had brought Hendry into the Cubs organization, where by 1998 he was director of the farm system and scouting. In June 2000, Hendry became MacPhail's top assistant, and the following year, after the departure of Ed Lynch, Hendry was promoted to assistant general manager and then to vice president and director of player personnel under MacPhail, who acted as both president and general manager. A year later, in November 2002, MacPhail ceded the title of general manager to Hendry.

Hendry's first accomplishment as general manager was to hire Dusty Baker, the manager of the 2002 world champion San Francisco Giants. Baker brought a record of consistent success in 11 years of managerial experience, and in his first year with the Cubs, he steered the team to an 88–74 record and a spot in the playoffs. The team had excellent starting pitching, especially Mark Prior, who went 18–6, while Wood led the NL in strikeouts (266). The team beat the Atlanta Braves in the best-of-five first round of the playoffs and seemed well on its way to winning the second round against the Florida Marlins when yet another bizarre incident took place. In the eighth inning of the fifth game of the series with the Marlins, with the Cubs leading three games to one and 3–0 in that game with Prior on the mound, a fan named Steve Bartman appeared to interfere with a foul ball that left fielder Moises Alou might have caught. The Marlins went on to score eight runs that inning to win the game, and then won games six and seven to take the series from the Cubs and advance to the World Series. Cubs fans were devastated, and Bartman briefly became the billy goat of 2003.

Hendry had made some excellent trades to help the Cubs do well in 2003, and in the 2003–4 off-season, he acquired former Cubs pitcher Greg Maddux, first baseman Derrek Lee, second baseman Todd Walker, and pitcher LaTroy Hawkins, among others, to strengthen the team still further. Most analysts predicted that 2004 would finally be the year that the Cubs would make the World Series, but a number of serious injuries to key players, such as starting pitchers Kerry Wood and Mark Prior and closer Joe Borowski, ruined the season, and the Cubs finished 16 games off the pace. Still, Cubs fans could find hope in the fact that for the first time in more than 30 years the team had had two winning seasons in a row. Cubs management could rejoice in the fact that for the first time ever, attendance surpassed the 3 million mark.

During the winter of 2004–5, Hendry traded the increasingly difficult and disruptive Sammy Sosa and his $16 million salary to Baltimore for utility player Jerry Hairston Jr. and acquired slugger Jeromy Burnitz from Colorado. He also let argumentative pitchers Kyle Farnsworth and Kent Mercker find employment elsewhere. These moves, it was hoped, would foster a more harmonious team in 2005 without sacrificing talent. Injuries to key players Mark Prior, Kerry Wood, and Nomar Garciaparra, however, combined with inexperienced middle relievers to send the $100 million Cubs home before the playoffs with a fourth-place finish in the NL Central.

Perhaps another new season will be the one that will end the long championship drought and the curse of the billy goat.

NOTABLE ACHIEVEMENTS

Most Valuable Players

Year	Name	Position
1935	Gabby Hartnett	C
1945	Phil Cavarretta	1B
1952	Hank Sauer	OF
1958	Ernie Banks	SS
1959	Ernie Banks	SS
1984	Ryne Sandberg	2B
1987	Andre Dawson	OF
1998	Sammy Sosa	OF

Cy Young Winners

Year	Name	Position
1971	Fergie Jenkins	RHP
1979	Bruce Sutter	RHP

1984	Rick Sutcliffe	RHP
1992	Greg Maddux	RHP

Rookies of the Year

Year	Name	Position
1961	Billy Williams	OF
1962	Ken Hubbs	2B
1989	Jerome Walton	OF
1998	Kerry Wood	P

Batting Champions

Year	Name	#
1876	Ross Barnes	.429
1880	George Gore	.360
1881	Cap Anson	.399
1884	King Kelly	.354
1886	King Kelly	.388
1912	Heinie Zimmerman	.372
1945	Phil Cavarretta	.355
1972	Billy Williams	.333
1975	Bill Madlock	.354
1976	Bill Madlock	.339
1980	Bill Buckner	.324
2005	Derrek Lee	.335

Home-Run Champions

Year	Name	#
1884	Ned Williamson	27
1885	Abner Dalrymple	11
1888	Jimmy Ryan	16
1890	Walt Wilmot	13
1910	Frank Schulte	10
1911	Frank Schulte	21
1912	Heinie Zimmerman	14
1916	Cy Williams	12
1926	Hack Wilson	21
1927	Hack Wilson	30
1928	Hack Wilson	31
1930	Hack Wilson	56
1943	Bill Nicholson	29
1944	Bill Nicholson	33
1952	Hank Sauer	37

1958	Ernie Banks	47
1960	Ernie Banks	41
1979	Dave Kingman	48
1987	Andre Dawson	49
1990	Ryne Sandberg	40
2000	Sammy Sosa	50
2002	Sammy Sosa	49

ERA Champions

Year	Name	#
1902	Jack Taylor	1.33
1906	Mordecai Brown	1.04
1907	Jack Pfiester	1.15
1918	Hippo Vaughn	1.74
1919	Grover Alexander	1.72
1920	Grover Alexander	1.91
1932	Lon Warneke	2.37
1938	Bill Lee	2.66
1945	Hank Borowy	2.13

Strikeout Champions

Year	Name	#
1880	Larry Corcoran	268
1885	John Clarkson	308
1887	John Clarkson	237
1892	Bill Hutchison	316
1909	Orval Overall	205
1918	Hippo Vaughn	148
1919	Hippo Vaughn	141
1920	Grover Alexander	173
1929	Pat Malone	166
1938	Clay Bryant	135
1946	Johnny Schmitz	135
1955	Sam Jones	198
1956	Sam Jones	176
1969	Fergie Jenkins	273
2003	Kerry Wood	266

No-Hitters

Name	Date
Larry Corcoran	08/19/1880
Larry Corcoran	09/20/1882

Larry Corcoran	06/27/1884
John Clarkson	07/27/1885
Walter Thornton	08/21/1898
Jimmy Lavender	08/31/1915
Sam Jones	05/12/1955
Don Cardwell	05/15/1960
Ken Holtzman	08/19/1969
Ken Holtzman	06/03/1971
Burt Hooton	04/16/1972
Milt Pappas	09/02/1972

POSTS\EASON APPEARANCES

NL East Division Titles

Year	Record	Manager
1984	96–65	Jim Frey
1989	93–69	Don Zimmer

NL Central Division Titles

Year	Record	Manager
2003	88–74	Dusty Baker

NL Wild Cards

Year	Record	Manager
1998	90–73	Jim Riggleman

NL Pennants

Year	Record	Manager
1876	52–14	Al Spalding
1880	67–17	Cap Anson
1881	56–28	Cap Anson
1882	55 29	Cap Anson
1885	87–25	Cap Anson
1886	90–34	Cap Anson
1906	116–36	Frank Chance
1907	107–45	Frank Chance
1908	99–55	Frank Chance
1910	104–50	Frank Chance
1918	84–45	Fred Mitchell
1929	98–54	Joe McCarthy

1932	90–64	Rogers Hornsby
		Charlie Grimm
1935	100–54	Charlie Grimm
1938	89–63	Charlie Grimm
		Gabby Hartnett
1945	98–56	Charlie Grimm

World Championships

Year	Opponent
1885	St. Louis
1907	Detroit
1908	Detroit

MANAGERS

2003–	Dusty Baker
2002	Bruce Kimm
2002	Rene Lachemann
2000–2002	Don Baylor
1995–1999	Jim Riggleman
1994	Tom Trebelhorn
1992–1993	Jim Lefebvre
1991	Jim Essian
1991	Joe Altobelli
1988–1991	Don Zimmer
1987	Frank Lucchesi
1986–1987	Gene Michael
1986	John Vukovich
1984–1986	Jim Frey
1983	Charlie Fox
1982–1983	Lee Elia
1980–1981	Joey Amalfitano
1980	Preston Gomez
1979	Joey Amalfitano
1977–1979	Herman Franks
1974–1976	Jim Marshall
1972–1974	Whitey Lockman
1966–1972	Leo Durocher

1965	Lou Klein
1963–1965	Bob Kennedy
1962	Charlie Metro
1962	Lou Klein
1962	El Tappe
1961	Lou Klein
1961	El Tappe
1961	Harry Craft
1961	Vedie Himsl
1960	Lou Boudrean
1960	Charlie Grimm
1957–1959	Bob Scheffing
1954–1956	Stan Hack
1951–1953	Phil Cavarretta
1949–1951	Frankie Frisch
1944–1949	Charlie Grimm
1944	Roy Johnson
1941–1944	Jimmie Wilson
1938–1940	Gabby Hartnett
1932–1938	Charlie Grimm
1930–1932	Rogers Hornsby
1926–1930	Joe McCarthy
1925	George Gibson
1925	Rabbit Maranville
1921–1925	Bill Killefer
1921	Johnny Evers
1917–1920	Fred Mitchell
1916	Joe Tinker
1915	Roger Bresnahan
1914	Hank O'Day
1913	Johnny Evers
1905–1912	Frank Chance
1902–1905	Frank Selee
1900–1901	Tom Loftus
1898–1899	Tom Burns
1879–1897	Cap Anson
1879	Silver Flint
1878	Bob Ferguson
1876–1877	Al Spalding

Team Records by Individual Players

Batting Leaders

	Single Season			Career	
	Name		Year	Name	Plate Appearances
Batting average	Bill Lange	.389	1895	Riggs Stephenson .336	3,964
On-base %	Mike Kelly	.483	1886	Hack Wilson .412	3,719
Slugging %	Sammy Sosa	.737	2001	Hack Wilson .590	3,719
OPS	Hack Wilson	1.177	1930	Hack Wilson 1.002	3,719
Games	Billy Williams	164	1965	Ernie Banks 2,528	10,395
At bats	Billy Herman	666	1935	Ernie Banks 9,421	10,395
Runs	Roger Hornsby	156	1929	Cap Anson 1,719	10,112
Hits	Roger Hornsby	229	1929	Cap Anson 2,995	10,112
Total bases	Sammy Sosa	425	2001	Ernie Banks 4,706	10,395
Doubles	Billy Herman	57	1935	Cap Anson 528	10,112
Triples	Frank Schulte	21	1911	Jimmy Ryan 142	7,542
Home runs	Sammy Sosa	66	1998	Sammy Sosa 545	7,898
RBIs	Hack Wilson	191	1930	Cap Anson 1,879	10,112
Walks	Jimmy Sheckard	147	1911	Stan Hack 1,092	8,506
Strikeouts	Sammy Sosa	174	1997	Sammy Sosa 1,815	7,898
Stolen bases	Bill Lange	84	1896	Frank Chance 400	5,066
Extra-base hits	Sammy Sosa	103	2001	Ernie Banks 1,009	10,395
Times on base	Woody English 320		1930	Cap Anson 3,979	10,112

Pitching Leaders

	Single Season			Career	
	Name		Year	Name	Innings Pitched
ERA	Mordecai Brown	1.04	1906	Albert G. Spalding 1.78	539.7
Wins	John Clarkson	53	1887	Charley Root 201	3,137.3
Won-loss %	Rich Sutcliffe	.941	1984	John Clarkson .706	1,730.7
Hits/9 IP	Eddie Reulbach	5.33	1906	Orval Overall 6.86	1,135
Walks/9 IP	Albert G. Spalding	.44	1876	Albert G. Spalding .43	539.7
Strikeouts	Bill Hutchinson	314	1892	Fergie Jenkins 2,038	2,673.7
Strikeouts/9 IP	Kerry Wood	12.58	1998	Mark Prior 10.55	613.3
Games	Ted Abernathy	84	1965	Charley Root 605	3,137.3

(Continued)

Pitching Leaders (Continued)

	Single Season			Career	
	Name	Year	Name		Innings Pitched
Saves	Randy Myers 53	1993	Lee Smith	180	381.3
Innings	John Clarkson 623	1885	Charley Root	3,137.3	3,137.3
Starts	John Clarkson 70	1885	Fergie Jenkins	347	2,673.7
Complete games	John Clarkson 68	1885	Bill Hutchison	317	3,021
Shutouts	John Clarkson 10	1885	Mordecai Brown 48		2,329

Source: Drawn from data in "Chicago Cubs Batting Leaders (seasonal and career)," http://baseball-reference.com/teams/CHC/leaders_bat.shtml; "Chicago Cubs Pitching Leaders (seasonal and career). http://baseball-reference.com/teams/CHC/leaders_pitch.shtml.

BIBLIOGRAPHY

Ahrens, Art, and Eddie Gold. *The Cubs: The Complete Record of Chicago Cubs Baseball.* New York: Macmillan, 1986.

Angle, Paul. *Philip K. Wrigley: A Memoir of a Modest Man.* Chicago: Rand McNally, 1975.

Anson, Adrian C. *A Ball Player's Career.* Chicago: Era Publishing, 1900.

Bogen, Gil. *Tinkers, Evers and Chance: A Triple Biography.* Jefferson, NC: McFarland, 2004.

Brown, Warren. *The Chicago Cubs.* New York: G. P. Putnam's Sons, 1946.

Burk, Robert F. *Never Just a Game: Players, Owners, and American Baseball to 1920.* Chapel Hill: University of North Carolina Press, 1994.

Di Salvatore, Bryan. *A Clever Base-Ballist: The Life and Times of John Montgomery Ward.* Baltimore: Johns Hopkins University Press, 1999.

Federal Writers Project. *Baseball in Old Chicago.* Chicago: A. C. McClurg, 1939.

Feldman, Doug. *September Streak: The Chicago Cubs Chase the Pennant.* Jefferson, NC: McFarland, 2003.

Gentile, Derek. *The Complete Chicago Cubs.* New York: Black Dog and Leventhal, 2002.

Gold, Eddie, and Art Ahrens. *The Golden Era Cubs, 1876–1940.* Chicago: Bonus Books, 1985.

———. *The Renewal Era Cubs, 1985–1990.* Chicago: Bonus Books, 1990.

Golenbock, Peter. *Wrigleyville.* New York: St. Martin's Press, 1999.

Holtzman, Jerome. "The Cubs' Curious Experiment." *Sport* 32 (August 1961): 78.

Holtzman, Jerome, and George Vass. *Baseball, Chicago Style.* Chicago: Bonus Books, 2001.

———. *The Chicago Cubs Encyclopedia.* Philadelphia: Temple University Press, 1997.

Langford, Jim. *The Game Is Never Over.* South Bend, IN: Icarus, 1982.

Levine, Peter. *A. G. Spalding and the Rise of Baseball.* New York: Oxford University Press, 1985.

Miller, Donald C. *City of the Century: The Epic of Chicago and the Making of America.* New York: Simon and Schuster, 1996.

Muskat, Carrie, comp. *Banks to Sandberg to Grace.* Chicago: Contemporary Books, 2001.

Names, Larry D. *Bury My Heart at Wrigley Field: The History of the Chicago Cubs.* Neshkoro, WI: Sportsbook, 1990.

Pietrusza, David. *Lights On! The Wild Century-Long Saga of Night Baseball.* Lanham, MD: Scarecrow Press, 1997.

Skipper, John C. *Take Me Out to the Cubs Game.* Jefferson, NC: McFarland, 2000.

Spirou, Costas, and Larry Bennett. *It's Hardly Sportin': Stadiums, Neighborhoods, and the New Chicago.* DeKalb: Northern Illinois University Press, 2003.

4

Cincinnati Reds

Edward J. Rielly

The history of the Cincinnati Reds is a history of professional baseball itself, from the first professional team, the unbeaten Red Stockings of 1869, through the birth of the National League, the arrival of night baseball, and such modern business practices as public funding of stadiums and the selling of stadium naming rights.

Throughout the many years of Cincinnati's baseball history, its teams have enjoyed some of the sport's greatest moments on the field and have labored under some of baseball's most infamous scandals. For almost a century and a half, Cincinnati and baseball have traveled together—the Queen City and America's national pastime.

CINCINNATI AND ITS FIRST PROFESSIONAL TEAM (1866–70)

A forerunner of the current Cincinnati Reds came into existence in 1866, the offspring of attorneys from the firm of Tilden, Sherman, and Moulton, who by their own admission had more time than clients and set out to find an enjoyable way to use some of that spare time.

Cincinnati in the 1860s was known as "the Queen City of the West," residing in the grassy Ohio River Valley surrounded by tree-covered hills, with the Ohio River serving the city as a major conduit for commerce. The city was also the center for pork packing in the region (it was known as "Porkopolis"), and for industries tied to by-products, like fat, employed in the manufacturing of soap. Proctor and Gamble produced its floating Ivory soap in 1879 and soon established the largest soap factory in the world.

Cincinnati was also an intellectual center, "the Athens of the West," with a large book-publishing industry and many fine-arts facilities. Its citizens could enjoy Shakespeare at John Bates's National Theatre, examine Egyptian antiquities at the Western Museum, and view fine paintings at the National Art Union and other city galleries. Harriet Beecher Stowe gave readings in her native city, and the poet Henry Wadsworth Longfellow was quoted hailing the city by its queenly epithet.

Henry "Harry" Wright, 1876. Courtesy of the Baseball Hall of Fame

The attorneys' early baseball team, known initially as the Resolutes and then as the Cincinnati Base Ball Club, played four games in 1866, winning two. It was an inauspicious beginning, but by its second year, the team was on its way to helping establish baseball as an American institution. The club moved from its original playing field west of downtown Cincinnati to Union Grounds, where the Museum Center in the Union Terminal train station now stands. Competitive juices already were flowing, and the organization hired its first professional, Harry Wright, a local cricket star, to plan and manage the baseball club. The team did well, winning 17 of 18 games.

Cincinnati added three more paid players in 1868—Fred Waterman, Johnny Hatfield, and Asa Brainard—violating a prohibition on paying players set by the National Association of Base Ball Players. The NA was established by some of the oldest baseball clubs, including the New York Knickerbockers, to regulate rules of play and protect the amateur character of the game. The squad by this time was widely known as the Red Stockings and had introduced a uniform that, with a variety of modifications, would remain the Cincinnati uniform throughout the decades: white flannel shirt with a red C, white knickers, red stockings, and a white cap. Viewers, especially women, were shocked and not a little titillated by the knickers and red socks, unaccustomed to seeing clothing generally considered underwear on public display.

The continued success of the Red Stockings, by now the best team outside the East, further fueled the club's competitive juices. John Joyce, the club's secretary, persuaded team president Aaron Champion, a local businessman and politician, to sign all of the players to contracts to facilitate discipline and hard work. The civic boosters who ran the team knew they needed to expand revenue from gate receipts. They encouraged local interest by promoting the team as a representative of the city, allying the club with the broad local drive to make Cincinnati a thriving and respected commercial and cultural center. The owners pushed the concept that local folk who supported the ball club were also behind the hometown.

The 1869 club thus became the first baseball team with a totally professional roster. Hatfield was gone by this time, but shortstop George Wright, brother of the manager and perhaps the best player in the country, had arrived. The entire team consisted of only 10 players, including one substitute and one pitcher, the hurler expected to start and complete most of the games. So when pitcher Asa Brainard needed a breather, Harry Wright would usually switch positions with him. The total salary for the Red Stockings was $10,500, with manager, starting center fielder, and sometime pitcher Wright earning a top figure of $2,000, $200 more than George.

The Red Stockings did much to popularize the sport on their way to compiling a perfect record of 57 wins and no losses, plus unofficial wins because the opponents were not NA teams. Some victories were close, although the Red Stockings often scored 30 or more runs in a game. They demolished the hapless Cincinnati Buckeyes, for example, 103–8. The team broke even financially despite its outstanding record.

The large scores were the result of baseball being a hitter's game in the 1860s. There were rough fields, which caused balls to bounce away from fielders; no gloves to encase sharp grounders and long fly balls; underhanded pitching, which meant, by later standards, slow pitching; and no pitcher's mound to give the pitch a difficult downward slant. In addition, fouls were not strikes, and strikes were not called unless a batter obstinately refused to swing at anything, permitting batters to wait for a fat pitch. Spectators got a lot of action for their 25 cents' admission.

The Red Stockings journeyed across the country during that summer of 1869. A road trip to the East garnered 20 wins, a championship reception by President Ulysses S. Grant at the White House (the first championship club to be so honored by a president), and a welcoming home parade. In the middle of September, the West beckoned, and the Red Stockings embarked on a 32-day trip. Just a few months before, on May 10, 1869, the golden spike marking completion of the first transcontinental railroad had been driven into the ground at Promontory Point near Ogden, Utah. The Red Stockings took that route west to San Francisco, along with some rugged miles by stagecoach and steamer. Western teams proved vastly inferior, and the Red Stockings played their way home against midwestern teams that were little better.

This first important phase in the history of the Cincinnati Reds ended after the following season. The 1870 Red Stockings, increasingly known as the Reds, retained the same players from the previous year but had their winning \streak end at 81 games when they lost to the Brooklyn Atlantics 8–7 in 11 innings. Cincinnati lost six times that season, and despite doubling ticket prices to 50 cents, the club could not turn a profit. Faced with increased competition for players, and with the National Association of Professional Base Ball Players, a new, professional league, forming for 1871, new club president A. P. Bonte announced that Cincinnati would revert to amateur status. The first all-professional team would not join the new professional league. The issue of salaries and other expenses versus revenue had claimed a prominent early victim.

THE NATIONAL LEAGUE (1876–80)

The Reds, under the leadership of John P. Joyce, secretary of the original Red Stockings, returned to professionalism in 1875 with an independent professional team. During the intervening years, the Reds had sold off their 1869–70 trophies and even the lumber from their Union Grounds fence and grandstand. Until they opened a new ballpark near Spring Grove Avenue in the vicinity of the stockyards, the Reds played in Ludlow, Kentucky. Their contests included a 15–5 defeat at the hands of the Boston Red Stockings, led by former Cincinnati captain Harry Wright in the so-called War of the Hoses.

The Cincinnati club became a charter member of a new professional league, the National League, which began play in 1876. The first five years of Cincinnati's life in the NL were marked by inconsistency on the field and instability in the front office. After a last-place finish in 1876, Cincinnati climbed to second place in 1878, only to fall back to last place by 1880. However, despite their modest achievements, the early Reds did boast some memorable players, particularly pitcher Will White, who in 1879 started and completed 75 games, pitched 680 innings, and won 43 starts. His battery mate was his brother, Jim "Deacon" White, so named because of his abstinence from tobacco and liquor and his regular churchgoing. They formed the first brother battery in the major leagues, with Deacon Jim the first Reds backstop to sport a face mask. Other notables were Hall of Famer Michael "King" Kelly, who batted .348 for the Reds in 1879, his second season with the team, but jumped to the Chicago White Stockings the following year, and the reputed inventor of the curveball, William "Candy" Cummings, considered by journalist Henry Chadwick the best pitcher in the early 1870s, who completed his playing career with an undistinguished season for the Reds in 1877.

The club's highlights during these early years included playing the first major-league doubleheader against Hartford in 1876 with separate admissions charged for each contest. The 1877 Reds were among the most colorful NL teams ever since each player sported a different colored cap. Bobby Mitchell of the Reds was the first left-hander ever to start a major-league game, tossing a shutout on September 6, 1877, against Louisville batters befuddled by pitches coming at a different angle. In the same game, Lipman Pike became the first

Reds player to hit a home run over an outfield fence. Pike had opened the season as the majors' first Jewish manager, but resigned later in the season.

Off the field, the Reds underwent constant changes in ownership due to the ebb and flow of the owners' finances. Josiah Keck, the first owner of the NL club, operated a meatpacking plant near the club's Avenue Grounds. By the 1870s, though, Porkopolis was headed into financial trouble, partly because of declining population growth. A general economic malaise had beset the city since the 1850s, when railroads began replacing waterways as prime movers of commerce. Cities not on river routes learned to compete with Cincinnati in manufacturing, and after a temporary upturn in response to Civil War needs for pork, clothing, and wagons, the city's economy again dipped in the late 1860s.

These factors contributed to Keck's financial troubles, along with the club's payroll, which reached $20,000 by 1878. Attending games was expensive (admission was 50 cents) and inconvenient. The Avenue Grounds was approximately four miles from the residential center, requiring most attendees to rely on horse-drawn streetcars or commuter trains to reach the ballpark. Once there, spectators could enjoy refreshment stands and a covered grandstand that seated 3,000 fans. Attendance, except for special events such as Fourth of July games, usually filled only a fraction of the seats. Customers typically numbered somewhere between 800 and 900.

By the middle of June 1877, Keck gave up, and the club disbanded. In early July, a group headed by businessman J. W. Neff assumed ownership. Neff refused to pay the $100 league fee, arguing that the Reds were not a new club. The NL retaliated by declaring the club's games invalid, although today those games are counted as official.

After the 1877 season ended, Neff put his business acumen to work. He purchased Avenue Grounds and the surrounding land, improved the grandstand by adding backs and arms to the seats, and instituted a multigame admission plan by which fans were encouraged to purchase a coupon book with 20 game tickets for $10. Neff hired Cal McVey, a member of the famed 1869 Red Stockings, as his manager, implicitly promising a return to a golden age of Cincinnati baseball. Toward that end, Neff rebuilt his roster, retaining only Pike and two other players from the previous year, and brought in several newcomers, including the White brothers and King Kelly. The improved Reds routinely drew more than a thousand fans. However, Neff could not overcome the high annual payroll of about $20,000 and other expenses, as well as a drop in attendance in 1879. With his club $10,000 in debt, Neff disbanded the Reds in October 1879, but in December the league authorized a group headed by Justus Thorner of the J. G. Sohn and Company brewery, and the previous head of a semipro club, to take over the franchise.

The 1880 season was a disaster on and off the field despite a move to the new Bank Street Grounds, which was closer to the city center and featured a scoreboard that showed the name of each batter and scores of other games received by telegraph. The team plummeted to last place, attendance dwindled to little more than 500 per contest, and ownership shifted, seemingly with the wind. Thorner yielded control during the season to clothing manufacturer Nathan Menderson, and finally to John Kennett, an insurance salesman.

The 1880 season marked a change in baseball that would reverberate down through the years as a source of discord between owners and players. The NL implemented its first reserve clause, initially binding five players of the owner's choice to the club. Another development affected the Reds more than any other and led to the team's temporary demise as a league member. The NL, concerned with rowdyism and determined to foster a family atmosphere, forbade clubs from selling alcohol at games and from renting out their ballparks for Sunday activities, Sabbath games having been prohibited since the league's inception. The clamping down on alcohol especially affected the Reds, since breweries constituted one of the city's leading industries.

Furthermore, the prohibition constituted a cultural attack on Germans, the largest immigrant group in Cincinnati. Germans made up approximately 30 percent of the population by 1840, and by midcentury affected every aspect of city life. The largely German-owned breweries employed mainly fellow Germans, who expected to drink beer and profit from its sale at games. In addition, the club needed the revenue from beer sales as well as from Sunday park rentals to survive. Faced with overriding financial and cultural objections to the league ultimatum, the club refused to accept the new rules. As a result Cincinnati was expelled from the NL, and no doubt many locals drowned their sorrow in a glass of fine German beer.

THE BEER AND WHISKEY LEAGUE: CHANGE AND TRADITION (1882–89)

The Cincinnati Reds did not long remain out of the major leagues. Oliver Perry "O. P." Caylor, a *Cincinnati Commercial* journalist, helped lead the way in creating a new league for the 1882 season. The league focused on cities excluded from the NL and aimed especially at the working class. Known unofficially as "the Beer and Whiskey League," the American Association (AA) staked out a direction radically at odds with the NL. Games were permitted on Sundays, the only day many workers had off from their jobs. The sale of German beer and other spirits was permitted. Tickets were offered at half the going rate, just 25 cents. These policies fit well the new slate of owners, headed by the returning Justus Thorner, which included several brewers.

Membership in the new league also coincided with the spirit of Cincinnati, which featured a wide-open approach to recreation. During the AA days, saloons and brothels were widespread, and gamblers and "fancy women" enjoyed a brisk business. Crime and violence were epidemic, highlighted by nine murders in nine days during the summer of 1883 and by the Courthouse Riots of 1884 that followed when William Berner only got a 20-year sentence for killing his boss. Vigilantes tried to lynch Berner, resulting in the burning of the courthouse and the deaths of approximately 56 people.

In this somewhat schizophrenic culture, torn between artistry and violence, the Reds thrived during the 1880s. Beer sales, low ticket prices, Sunday games, and clever marketing devices that included Ladies' Days and, in the late 1880s, discounted admission for young boys helped Reds management turn a profit.

A new park also helped maintain excitement. The Reds initially played in the Bank Street Grounds but moved in 1884 into American Park (also known as Cincinnati Ball Park) at the corner of Findlay Street and Western Avenue, a move necessitated when the Cincinnati entry in the short-lived Union League took over the Bank Street Grounds lease. American Park had a covered grandstand behind home plate with comfortable leather cushions on the seats and a bar underneath the stands for gentlemen. Covered seats along the third-base line faced open seats behind first base, although the first-base seats were also roofed over by 1888. An attempt to help fans (often referred to as "cranks") identify players by assigning a different uniform color to each position proved enormously confusing to fans and players, and was soon discarded.

Cincinnati drew an average of almost 2,000 fans per game during the team's years in the AA and surpassed that mark in 1885 and 1887. The AA as a whole generally drew well, and the Reds, despite their turnstile success, ranked only fourth in attendance. The league's popularity led to an expanded season of 140 games in 1886, 60 more than in 1882.

The expanded schedule required additional pitchers. Cincinnati, like other AA teams, was forced away from the earlier practice of relying on one pitcher to start most games. By 1884, overhand pitching, which put more stress on the pitching arm than underhand throwing, had become legal in the NL, and the AA followed one year later. It created a need for more starters. Some pitchers, including the Reds' longtime ace Will White, could not make the transition. White hurt his arm in 1885 and quickly faded from the scene. It took a while for the Reds to establish a regular rotation with starters equally sharing the work, but by 1888, Tony Mullane, Lee Viau, and Elmer Smith were starting 42, 42, and 40 games respectively. All three were effective pitchers and gave the Reds their first three 20-game winners (27 for Viau, 26 for Mullane, and 22 for Smith), unmatched until 1923.

The Reds won the first AA championship. Will White led the pitching staff in 1882, and rookie John "Bid" McPhee sparkled at second base, as he would for 18 seasons. A great defensive player, McPhee followed the tradition of using only bare hands to field until 1896, when he yielded to sore hands and started using gloves. McPhee, a future Hall of Famer, had his disagreements with management and was the first major-league holdout. The Reds dominated their rivals that first year, winning the championship by 11 1/2 games. They would not enjoy another championship until 1919.

Following the league's inaugural season, the Reds engaged the champion Chicago White Stockings of the NL in the first postseason championship series ever between two professional leagues. The two clubs played two games in Cincinnati on October 6 and 7, the Reds winning the first and the White Stockings, led by manager and first baseman Cap Anson, taking the second. AA rules forbade postseason games against NL teams, and pressure from the league forced cancellation of a third and deciding contest. Nonetheless, the two leagues did establish a postseason championship series in 1884 that continued through 1890.

The Reds remained among the better AA clubs throughout the decade, finishing second twice, although club ownership changed hands several times. O. P. Caylor was co-president with Justus Thorner from 1882 through 1883 and remained with the organization until 1886, the last two years as team manager.

Ownership reached its unstable nadir in 1884, as the club passed among three owners within the year. Thorner left the club in April to help establish the new Cincinnati club in the rival Union Association, an idealistic organization that rejected the reserve clause. Aaron Stern followed Thorner as principal owner of the Reds. A penny-pincher who had made his money as a clothing merchant, Stern cut the number of special police at weekday games from six to three and ordered the new-style self-registering turnstile turned off to hide the actual attendance figures so he could deprive other teams of their proper share of the take. However, Stern's tenure was brief, as he sold out in October to George Herancourt, who was the first local brewer in the 1870s to purchase the newly designed Arctic Ice Machine, a remarkable ice-making device that produced 10–50 tons of ice per day and eliminated the inconvenience and excessive cost of buying lake and river ice.

Herancourt in turn sold the franchise in the spring of 1886 to John Hauck, owner of the John Hauck Brewing Company, and after the season, Stern reacquired the club. He fired Caylor and replaced him with a skipper who appealed to the city's German heritage, the red-bearded Gus Schmelz.

The front-office turbulence was matched by the battle of the Cincinnati newspapers. The impetus for the journalistic battle was O. P. Caylor's close association with the Reds and the animosity that his former employer, the *Cincinnati Enquirer,* had for him because of his departure for the rival *Cincinnati Commercial.* The *Commercial* supported the Reds while the *Enquirer* took every opportunity to attack the hometown team. The conflict became even more pronounced in 1885 when Caylor assumed the managerial position. The *Enquirer* viciously attacked Caylor, questioning his character and even his manhood by depicting him in a cartoon wearing a dress and asserting that he had worn dresses until he was 12. The papers also lined up on opposite sides regarding the *Enquirer's* charges that pitcher Tony Mullane had deliberately lost two games in May 1886 to Philadelphia and Brooklyn. An AA investigation found Mullane innocent. That year Mullane won 34 games for the fifth-place Reds. The following year, when the Reds came in second (81–54), he went 31–17, Elmer Smith was 34–17, and the staff ERA was 3.58, best in the AA. The Reds would not finish so high again until 1919.

Opening Day of 1889 occurred amid park decorations and musical entertainment courtesy of the Cincinnati Orchestra. Celebrating the season's first game soon became a permanent Cincinnati tradition, complete with a parade and an address by the mayor. Another developing tradition was the custom of Cincinnati opening the season at home. This initially had more to do with climate than anything, since Cincinnati was farther south, and presumably warmer, than some of its competitors. The cranks at Opening Day—and all of the following contests—could while away slow time by examining their baseball cards. Old Judge Cigarettes and other tobacco companies began inserting baseball cards into packages of their products in the late 1880s.

The 1880s comprised one of the most successful decades in Cincinnati baseball history, but when it ended, so did the Reds' membership in the AA. The departure of the Reds was principally caused by weak league administration and the growing dissatisfaction of individual teams with league leadership. Cincinnati's final motivation to exit grew out of two disputed games between the Brooklyn Bridegrooms and the St. Louis Browns that were awarded to Brooklyn on forfeit. The AA board of directors split the difference, giving one of the games to St. Louis. The eight AA teams met to elect a new president to replace the much-disliked Wheeler Wikoff, but were deadlocked between two candidates. At this point Cincinnati and Brooklyn chose to leave the AA and join the NL. It was a homecoming for the Reds to the league that had expelled them a decade earlier.

BACK TO THE NATIONAL LEAGUE: OUT OF CHAOS, ORDER (1890–1901)

The Reds returned to the NL in 1890, the same year the Players' League was organized to enable players to share more equitably in the financial rewards of baseball. Stars such as Connie Mack and Charles Comiskey jumped to the new league, which promised a player-run organization that would undermine the reserve clause and boost player salaries.

The Reds finished in second place in the turbulent season, 10 1/2 games back, the closest they would get to a championship during the 1890s. After the season ended, Cincinnati owner Aaron Stern switched the club to the Players' League, and then sold the team as well as the lease to League Park (the new name of the ballpark, renamed in deference to their NL affiliation) to streetcar magnate Albert Johnson. Johnson signed the Cincinnati players and brought in King Kelly as player-manager.

Johnson's motivation in getting into baseball included a heavy dose of idealism. A partner in running Cleveland's streetcar lines with his brother, Tom L. Johnson, he was a strong opponent of the reserve clause and sincerely concerned with the employment rights of the players. Idealism ran in the family. His brother, a wealthy businessman, was transformed into a strong proponent of the commonweal by reading a book entitled *Social Problems*, by Henry George.

Tom consequently entered public service, four times being elected mayor of Cleveland, and worked hard to improve life for his constituents with new parks, bridges, hospitals, and swimming pools.

The Players' League folded, however, leaving Johnson without a league, a problem he quickly solved by returning the Reds to the AA. The NL retaliated by granting a Cincinnati franchise to John Brush, a clothing merchant from Indianapolis. Events continued along a bizarre path. Johnson sold the team and its assets to Brush. The Reds had careened through three leagues in one short off-season. The AA fielded a Cincinnati team in 1891 under King Kelly, but the team died in August. At the end of the season, the entire AA followed suit.

The 1890–91 ownership machinations provided the most exciting aspect of Reds baseball during the decade. The new owner provided stability, an entertaining product, and a new park facility for Cincinnati fans. The team generally played winning ball during the next 10 years. Among the most prominent Reds players of the decade were longtime second baseman Bid McPhee, pitchers Frank Dwyer and Billy Rhines, first baseman Jake Beckley, slugging outfielder James "Bug" Holiday, and base-stealing star William "Dummy" Hoy, the latter the first deaf-mute to play in the majors.

Charles Comiskey, recently returned from the Players' League, managed and played first base for the Reds from 1892 to 1894. His first two teams had winning records, finishing in the middle of the pack, but in 1894 came in 10th (55–75). More successful was Buck Ewing, a Cincinnati native and star catcher, who guided the Reds to five straight victorious seasons. The 1896 team came in third and drew 373,000, most in the NL, and a nineteenth-century record for the Queen City.

John Brush proved an effective owner, whose accomplishments including hiring an able business manager, Frank Bancroft. In 1891, the club enjoyed its first Opening Day festival complete with an impressive parade. Players portrayed a crisp, professional sartorial image with white uniforms that sported *Cincinnati* on the front of a shirt, the previous drawstring replaced by buttons. The cap took on a more rounded shape. The excitement reflected in the festivities resulted in expanded press coverage. The addition of Sunday games in 1892 further contributed to the game's excitement and to increased attendance.

The 1892 season demonstrated that baseball could call forth both the pathetic and the sublime. Saloon fights in May led to several Reds players being suspended. During the final game of the season, Charles Leander "Bumpus" Jones, a sometime minor leaguer born in Cedarville, Ohio, stopped by the Cincinnati clubhouse to ask Comiskey to let him pitch. The manager, perhaps on a whim, agreed, and Bumpus Jones tossed a no-hitter against Pittsburgh. Comiskey brought him back the following year, when the distance from pitcher to home plate was increased to 60 feet, 6 inches. Jones made only six appearances, winning just once.

The highlight of the 1894 season was the opening of the new League Park, built on the same site as the old field of the same name. It was an opulent park for its time. Three turrets with flags flying above them adorned the roof of the new iron and wood grandstand. The lower level of the grandstand, known as "rooter's row," proved popular with often inebriated male fans, which led the following year to installing rows of barbed wire to keep them off the field. The better and more expensive seats were a level above. A row of "fashion," or what would later be called "luxury," boxes lined the top tier at the front railing. Tickets, depending on location, went for 25, 50, or 75 cents, with accommodations in the fashion boxes costing a dollar. Season tickets were available for 35 dollars.

Sheep, penned nearby, kept the grass down, and strategically placed barrels of water and buckets stood nearby to address the inevitable fires caused by carelessly dropped cigars and cigarettes. A number of fires did occur, the most serious one destroying the grandstand in the early morning of May 28, 1900. Brush wanted games resumed as soon as possible. He ordered the diamond shifted, which left the remnants of the grandstand in left field. Balls hit into the debris from the fire were declared in play, although retrieving them was often impossible.

With no time to grow grass, the infield remained all dirt, contributing to a neighborhood problem with dust from the nearby unpaved roads and soot and smoke from industrial pollution. With a temporary grandstand constructed, games at League Park resumed exactly one month from the date of the fire.

Other highlights during the 1890s included two exhibition games against the Page Fence Giants, an African American team, in 1895; the first major trade in Reds history (bringing in pitcher Philip "Red" Ehret and catcher Henry "Heinie" Peitz) in November 1895; a League Park tribute to the recently deceased Harry Wright in 1896; Elmer Smith's 30-game hitting streak in 1898 (a team record broken by Pete Rose in 1978); and a celebration of Theodore Roosevelt's successful dash up San Juan Hill with his Rough Riders by setting off firecrackers and firing pistols in the air at a July 4, 1898 doubleheader.

In 1901 the NL was challenged by the arrival of a rival, the American League. Once again players had an option to sign with a new team because the AL at first did not recognize the older league's reserve clause. Cincinnati lost only outfielder Jimmy Barrett, who switched to the Detroit Tigers.

With old friend Bid McPhee now managing the Reds, the team stumbled home in last place in 1901, 38 games behind Pittsburgh. The star of the team was outfielder Jake Beckley, a future Hall of Famer, who played for the Reds from 1897 through 1903 and batted over .300 every year but one. Punctuating the terrible season was the assassination of President William McKinley, who was shot on September 6 and died eight days later. On September 19, the Reds postponed their game against the Pirates in deference to his funeral that day.

THE ERA OF GARRY HERRMANN (1902–27)

The long ownership tenure of August "Garry" Herrmann saw the Cincinnati Reds finally win a World Series, albeit one tainted by the Black Sox scandal.

The Herrmann years also witnessed massive changes to the Cincinnati ball-park, attendance records, radio broadcasting, and some of the greatest pitching staffs in NL history. In addition, the nature of the game itself changed dramatically as the home run, propelled by the arrival of Babe Ruth, replaced small ball. Batting averages and ERAs went up, complete games and stolen bases declined, and a new baseball figure, the commissioner, became the absolute ruler of baseball.

The 1902 season opened with John Brush still the owner. A new iron and concrete grandstand was built, known as the Palace of the Fans, while the rest of the park consisted of the old seats and bleachers. The Palace featured classical Greek and Roman architecture with hand-carved columns and a peaked cornice behind the grandstand with *Cincinnati* in large capital letters. The grandstand could accommodate three thousands "bugs," as fans increasingly were called. Nineteen "fashion boxes" housed 15 or more fans each. Cheap lower seats constituted another "rooter's row." Home plate was shifted back to its earlier location, and the old temporary grandstand hurriedly constructed after the 1900 fire became the right-field stands. The new grandstand, abetted by beer selling for about eight cents per glass, attracted larger crowds in its second season, increasing from 3,104 per game to 4,627.

In 1906, additional seating was added by building an upper deck on the grandstand. The field's spacious dimensions, reaching 450 feet to the right-field corner and 412 feet to the left-field corner, prevented home runs being hit over the fence. So many fans arrived by carriages and automobiles that by 1910 the parking area under the grandstand had become insufficient.

Brush did not stay long enough to enjoy his changes to League Park, selling out in August 1902 to a politically connected group that included Garry Herrmann, head of the Cincinnati Waterworks; Cincinnati mayor Julius Fleischmann, whose family owned the Fleischmann Yeast Company; and George Barnsdale Cox, the powerful Republican boss of Cincinnati politics from 1886 to 1915. Brush, who may well have been pressured by the Cincinnati political machine to sell, subsequently purchased the New York Giants.

Herrmann, one of Cox's most able and trusted assistants, had proved adept with large budgets and at getting projects completed while serving on the board of administration and as head of the waterworks. While just a minority shareholder in the Reds, he was appointed president because of his administrative and financial skills as well as his reputation for integrity. One of his wisest moves was retaining Frank Bancroft as business manager, a position that included most of the duties of a modern general manager.

Herrmann quickly earned the respect of his fellow owners, aided by his long-time friendship with AL president Ban Johnson, formed when Johnson had worked as a Cincinnati sportswriter. Herrmann served from 1903 until 1920 as chairman of the National Commission, baseball's ruling body, which consisted of the two league presidents and a third owner chosen by the presidents. The commission was established as part of the 1903 National Agreement between the NL and the new AL. Herrmann's effectiveness in helping to bring about the National Agreement and establish peace between the leagues at a meeting in Cincinnati dubbed "the Cincinnati Peace Treaty" earned him the respect of most owners and made him an acceptable choice to chair the National Commission. The agreement prevented one league from raiding the other and kept player salaries down. The agreement also made possible the institution of a World Series between the two league champions.

On the field, the Reds were competitive during Herrmann's first few years, posting winning records from 1903, when the team finished third, to 1905. A social highlight of those years was the presence of Alice Roosevelt, daughter of Theodore Roosevelt, at a game in June 1905 accompanied by her future husband, Ohio congressman Nicholas Longworth.

The Reds then struggled mightily for a decade, posting only one winning season (77–76 in 1909) for the years 1906–16. Too little offense and, during the second decade, financial problems played significant roles in the team's lack of success. Even in hard times, though, Cincinnati featured some excellent players. Among the team's most prominent performers during the Herrmann era were outfielder James "Cy" Seymour, who batted .332 for the Reds (1902–6) with a league-leading .377 in 1905; outfielder Sam Crawford, who led the league with 22 triples in 1902 before going on to a Hall of Fame career with Detroit; outfielder like Donlon, signed away from Baltimore of the AL in 1902, who supplemented his baseball income by performing in vaudeville; and third baseman Henry "Heinie" Groh, a steady hitter and fine fielder with Cincinnati from 1913 to 1921.

During the long run of losing seasons, there were many memorable attempts at innovation. In 1908 Cincinnati businessmen supported the feasibility of playing under the lights. The Cahill brothers, who owned a floodlight-manufacturing plant, constructed three light towers at the park, but they failed to illuminate the field sufficiently, and the plans were put on hold. The following summer, the experiment went ahead, with two June games featuring amateur teams. But batters and fielders had trouble seeing the ball, and there were problems keeping all the lights operating simultaneously. Consequently the experiment was abandoned.

After the 1908 season, the Reds barnstormed in Cuba, the first major-league team to play there. The contests opened an important channel for baseball talent to flow into the United States. Two Almendares players, Armando Marsans and Rafael Almeida, joined the Reds in 1911 as the first Cuban major leaguers since 1882. Marsans was the more successful of the two, batting .317 and .297 in 1912 and 1913 before jumping to the Federal League during the 1914 season. Their success paved the way for others, including Dolf Luque. The Reds circumvented the ban on African Americans in organized baseball by claiming that both were entirely of European ancestry. Marsans was part black, but light-skinned enough to support Cincinnati's contention.

Clark Griffith was brought in to manage the Reds in 1909, but his three-year run as manager proved unsuccessful. After being let go, he purchased the

Washington Senators. In his final year as manager, the uniform was changed, as the word *Reds* inside the letter *C* appeared in 1911. The shirt collar disappeared in 1913, and pinstripes appeared in 1916.

As the 1911 season came to an end, Herrmann, dissatisfied with the capacity of his ballpark, commissioned Harry Hake to design a new grandstand. Like Herrmann, Hake was part of the Cox political machine and had designed many Cincinnati buildings, including the new county courthouse as well as the old grandstand.

The new $225,000 Redlands Field was ready for Opening Day 1912. The grandstand consisted of two decks, with single-deck pavilions reaching to the outfield walls. The ballpark was decorated with a shamrock-shaped pitcher's box, crushed white rock for 10 feet in front of the outfield walls, and a scoreboard that registered balls, strikes, and outs, the first major-league scoreboard to do so. The park dimensions remained large: 393 feet to right field, 415 to center, and 348 to left. It would be almost a decade before anyone hit a ball over any of the fences.

The new facilities welcomed Cincinnati native son President William Howard Taft on May 4, 1912. President Taft, who in 1910 had begun the tradition of throwing out the first pitch of the baseball season, also became the first president to attend a game in Cincinnati, and the last until Richard Nixon was present at the 1970 All-Star Game. That year manager Hank O'Day was assisted by Henry "Heinie" Peitz, the first coach in Reds history.

The 1913 season started with a flood that covered Redland Field with 12 feet of water, delaying the home opener until April 12, two days after its scheduled date. Joe Tinker, the great Cubs shortstop, was player-manager and batted .317, a career high. But he jumped to the new Federal League the following year. Reds attendance went into free fall in 1914, sinking to about 100,000, caused by the poor quality of play that included a 19-game losing streak, equaling the current record for futility. The team came in eighth, winning only 60 games, 4 less than the year before, when the Reds were seventh.

The Reds in 1914 had an agreement with Baltimore of the International League to claim two players, but did not pick their young pitching phenom, Babe Ruth. This ranked with the club's earlier decision in December 1900 to trade a youthful Christy Mathewson, whom they had drafted from the New York Giants but who had not pitched for Cincinnati, back to New York for old-time star pitcher Amos Rusie. The sore-armed Rusie would make all of three appearances with the Reds.

In 1916 the Reds took advantage of the collapse of the Federal League to start rebuilding, landing three starters from that league. The biggest addition was Hal Chase, a magnificent first baseman who led the NL in batting (.339) and hits (182) and was second in slugging (.459) and RBIs (84). The Reds also made a major trade with the Giants on July 20, trading catcher-manager Buck Herzog and outfielder Wade Killefer for outfielder Edd Roush, who would spend much of his Hall of Fame career with the Reds (1916–26);

Bill McKechnie, a future Reds manager; and star hurler Christy Mathewson, who became the new manager. Mathewson was at the end of his playing career and made only one appearance for the Reds, his final game as a player, for the 373rd victory of his storied career. Despite these changes, the Reds ended up in the cellar again (60–93).

In 1917, the Reds edged slightly above .500, finishing with a 78–76 record. One of Mathewson's outfielders for part of the season was Jim Thorpe, a Native American of Sauk and Fox ancestry and the Olympic gold medalist in the pentathlon and decathlon at the 1912 Olympics. Thorpe was a star at virtually every sport that he tried—except, unfortunately, baseball. He batted just .247 in 77 games for Cincinnati, five points below his career average.

Mathewson's attempt to resurrect the Reds was hindered by Hal Chase and World War I. Chase was reputedly as adept at throwing games as playing brilliantly. He and second baseman Lee Magee planned to fix the July 25, 1918, game against Boston. Conflicts with owner Herrmann over salary may have been a factor. Magee tried hard to lose, making two errors, but Chase seemingly failed to carry out his part of the bargain, and the Reds triumphed. Chase was suspended by the Reds on August 9, but returned to the majors for one more year with the Giants. Magee's role did not surface until after the 1919 season, when he was playing for the Cubs. Mathewson's testimony in conjunction with a lawsuit that Magee filed against baseball helped ensure that Magee never again played major-league baseball.

That dishonest play had occurred on the watch of the man known as "the Christian gentleman" for his consistently upright behavior was a bitter pill for Mathewson to swallow. It must have been with some relief that he accepted a commission as a captain in the chemical-welfare branch of the army and departed for war shortly after Chase's suspension, leaving Heinie Groh to fill in as manager in the war-shortened season that concluded on September 2.

Expecting the war to continue through the 1919 season and recognizing the difficulty of staffing teams and drawing fans, MLB planned an abbreviated 140-game season for 1919. When the war ended on November 11, 1918, it was deemed too late to change the schedule back to 154 games. The Reds, under new manager Pat Moran, reaped the fruit of Mathewson's rebuilding efforts and won the NL pennant, their first championship since the AA title of 1882.

The 1919 squad won 96 games and lost just 44. Roush hit .321 to lead the NL and drove in a team-leading 71 runs. The defense was outstanding. The team had the best defense and gave up the least number of runs in the NL with a 2.23 ERA. Six pitchers won in double figures, led by Slim Sallee at 21–7.

The end of the war and the improved play on the field led to attendance at home games more than triple the daily average of the previous year, 7,607, for a total of 532,501. The increase was a huge boost for the Reds, especially since in January Herrmann was unable to meet payments and faced possible foreclosure. He dissolved the organization, established a new entity, and asked shareholders, who had lost their investment during the dissolution, to purchase shares in the new organization. Louis Widrig, one of the stockholders, came to the rescue, buying hundreds of shares. He later became team treasurer.

The main events of the 1919 World Series are well known. The heavily favored Chicago White Sox lost to the Reds five games to three in a series that had been extended from best of seven to best of nine to help compensate for the attendance lost due to the abbreviated season. The series opened in Cincinnati, where the Reds had added about 9,000 temporary seats. Tickets sold for between two and six dollars.

The Reds surprised most observers by winning the first game handily, 9–1. Dutch Ruether pitched a six-hitter while also collecting three hits, including two triples. Sox ace Eddie Cicotte hit the first batter, Morrie Rath, which signaled that the fix was on. Game two also went to the Reds as Slim Sallee bested Lefty Williams, a control artist turned wild.

Chicago won the third game at Comiskey Park, behind a young hurler named Dickie Kerr, who was not in on the fix. The Reds, however, captured the fourth game as Cicotte again lost, this time to the Reds' Jimmy Ring. They added a fourth victory in game five, with Hod Eller pitching a three-hit shutout and Lefty Williams again losing.

Down four games to one, and just one loss away from dropping the series, the White Sox, with Kerr starting, beat the Reds 5–4 at Redland Field before over 32,000 spectators. Failure to deliver all of the promised money convinced some of the White Sox, including Cicotte and Williams, to try to salvage the series, and Cicotte pitched his team to a 4–1 triumph the following day. However, back in Chicago, when Lefty Williams was threatened prior to his next start, he changed his mind again and deliberately pitched badly, the Reds winning 10–5.

Members of the winning Reds received $5,207 apiece, with the losers each taking home $3,254. These figures were huge considering the level of salaries at the time; the great Shoeless Joe Jackson, for example, earned just $6,000. The series share for some players was more than their entire salary.

Christy Mathewson, home from the war with his lungs ruined by mustard gas, covered the series for the *New York World*. He sat in the press box with Chicago sportswriter Hugh Fullerton, and circled on his scorecard every play that he thought was deliberately bungled.

As the Roaring Twenties opened, the Reds set out to defend their championship. For a time, it appeared that they might well do that, spending about half of the season in first place. However, they had dropped back to third by the end. The case of former teammate Lee Magee went against him in June, ending his hopes of reinstatement. Testimony at the trial made it clear that betting on games had been commonplace among Reds players, hardly news to Cincinnati officials.

Before the season was over, a grand jury in Chicago indicted eight White Sox players for fixing the 1919 World Series. The players were found not guilty, but that did not hide the fact that Cincinnati's victory was, and would always be, tainted. No one would ever know whether the Reds would have won if the White Sox had really tried.

In an attempt to swing the pitcher-hitter pendulum toward hitters, MLB prior to the 1920 season had outlawed adding foreign substances to the ball and mandated having a clean ball in play at all times. While spitball pitchers were grandfathered in, the new rules badly hurt Slim Sallee and Hod Eller, who doctored their pitches with paraffin or whatever was available, or defaced the ball with a fingernail file or small emery board. Sallee went from 21 wins to 6 and Eller from 19 to 13, and the following year to 2.

As baseball entered the home-run era, the Reds, with their vast outfield spaces, were unable to capitalize on the change. The first home run over Cincinnati's left-field wall (the shortest distance in the park) was hit in an exhibition game by Negro Leaguer John Beckwith in May 1921. Then, in a July 25 exhibition game between the Reds and Yankees, Babe Ruth himself cleared the center- and right-field fences. Not until 1929 would a home run in a regular-season game clear center field. Nonetheless, the Reds continued to play winning, although not championship, ball. While attendance shot up throughout the major leagues, as fans fell in love with the home run, Cincinnati benefited less than did most teams. The Reds averaged over 6,000 per game in the 1920s, but ranked only sixth in NL attendance.

The Reds, especially during the final decade of Herrmann's rule, boasted a long run of outstanding pitchers. Cincinnati consistently had one of the best NL staffs during the 1920s, leading the league in ERA from 1923 through 1925 and featuring such stars as Eppa Rixey and Dolf Luque. Rixey won more games, 179 from 1921 to 1933, than any pitcher in modern Reds history. For his career, Rixey won 266 games, and made the Hall of Fame in 1963. Luque, Cuban born, pitched for the Reds from 1918 until 1929, winning 27 games in 1923.

On January 21, 1921, Kenesaw Mountain Landis became baseball's first commissioner. The new office replaced the National Commission, eliminating Herrmann's position as commission chairman, which he had held since 1903. About two months later, the Reds lost one of their organization's most important members when business manager Frank Bancroft died on March 30, 1921, 28 years after assuming that position.

In the early 1920s, salaries were a big problem for club officials. Three players—outfielder Edd Roush, third baseman Heinie Groh, and pitcher Ray Fisher—held out in 1921. The first two eventually returned, but Fisher left to become a long-running and highly successful baseball coach at the University of Michigan. In 1924, Roush, who was always difficult to sign, received Cincinnati's first-ever multiyear contract at three years for $19,000 annually. A Hall of Famer, he played most of his 18 years with the Reds and had a lifetime .323 batting average.

Shortly before the start of the 1924 season, on March 7, manager Pat Moran suddenly died of Bright's disease. Moran's five-year record was an impressive 425–329, including the 1919 World Series championship. Herrmann turned to veteran minor-league manager Jack Hendricks, who led the Reds for the rest of the decade.

Opening Day of 1924, which drew an all-time Reds record attendance of close to 36,000, was the first Reds contest broadcast over radio. The game with the Pirates was carried by WLW and WSAI in Cincinnati and KDKA in Pittsburgh. Thereafter the Reds regularly broadcast Opening Day. However, baseball was slow to embrace the radio for fear that broadcasts would hurt attendance. Organized baseball also felt that the proper way to appreciate a baseball game was in person.

Another tragedy hit the Reds in a game against St. Louis on May 28, 1924, when first baseman Jake Daubert, the popular captain, was beaned by pitcher Allen Sothoron. Daubert was hospitalized, but no serious injury was discovered. However, Daubert suffered from insomnia and weakness for the rest of the season and went home to rest late in the campaign. He returned, hoping to play in the final games of the season, but felt worse and was hospitalized on October 2 for surgery. The doctors misdiagnosed his ailment as appendicitis or gallstones. Daubert died on October 9, presumably because of the beaning. Years later, his son developed similar symptoms, leading to the conclusion that the illness involved the spleen and was hereditary.

In April 1925, Herrmann helped arrange for 25 barrels of beer to be delivered to a St. Louis hotel for a group of Cincinnati boosters and was arrested by Prohibition agents. A large fine ensued. Later that year, Herrmann presented a plan to construct a new Reds stadium north of Redland Field to accommodate more fans and more automobiles. Herrmann envisaged the new park as the site of not only Reds games, but also other sporting contests. In a harbinger of future conflicts between owners and city officials over ballpark construction, the city rejected Herrmann's plans. Cincinnati's Park Board wanted to construct a municipal athletic field on the site Herrmann had picked. When negotiations went nowhere, and having set a new season attendance record of almost 673,000 in 1926, Herrmann added 5,000 additional seats to Redland Field for the 1927 season. However, the team sank to fifth place, and attendance dropped as well.

On October 25, 1927, Herrmann resigned as president, citing increasing deafness and other health problems. By then, his major original partners had died, Cox in 1916 and Fleischmann in 1925. Attorney Campbell Johnson McDiarmid, club secretary and a team shareholder, purchased a majority holding in the Reds and became club president. The Reds lost close to $8,000 in Herrmann's final year as president, but had enjoyed a profit of $136,500 the year before. The Reds, from 1920 through 1927, earned an average annual profit of nearly $74,000. That happy financial picture would quickly change for the new owner.

THE CROSLEY ERA: NIGHT BASEBALL AND BROADCASTING COME TO CINCINNATI (1928–60)

The late 1920s and early 1930s were an interregnum between two lengthy periods of ownership. As the Reds struggled through seventh-place finishes in 1929 and 1930 and dropped into the basement every year from 1931 through

1934, ownership passed quickly through several hands. Shareholders were unhappy with the Reds losing money, as the team consistently brought up the rear in the NL and was saddled with substantial debt after purchasing Redland Field. A major disagreement developed late in the 1929 season over whether to retain manager Jack Hendricks. The turmoil offered Sidney Weil an opportunity to purchase the club. Weil, a successful stock investor who had inherited wealth from his father, who was in the car business, was an ardent Reds fan. But the Reds were a questionable investment, having lost money three straight years, including $203,091 in 1929, the only team in the NL to finish in the red that season.

On October 30, 1929, Sidney Weil became president of the Reds, and within a week installed the ballpark's first public-address system. But when the stock market crashed, Weil had lost most of his fortune. By 1933, the principal owner and his ball club were both bankrupt.

Despite the Reds' financial problems, Weil sought to improve the fans' baseball experience. Parking was an ongoing problem, so the Reds offered free parking for 400 automobiles. Management continued to tinker with uniforms, dropping the pinstripes in 1930. Later in the decade, the Reds briefly tried red trousers, and in 1939 went to blue caps, blue sleeves, and blue and red socks with the white home uniforms and gray road attire. Weil also demonstrated at least an occasional eye for talent, trading for catcher Ernie Lombardi and pitcher Paul Derringer, both of whom would be instrumental in the Reds' resurgence.

Weil's greatest innovation involved radio broadcasting. While home openers had been broadcast since 1924, other home games were unavailable to radio listeners until 1929, when WLW, with Bob Burdette at the microphone, broadcast 40 contests. In 1931, Harry Hartman of WFBE persuaded Weil to allow broadcasts of all home games except weekend contests. In the early years of radio broadcasting, Cincinnati, like other teams, charged stations no broadcasting fees. Hartman, the PA announcer, popularized several memorable expressions, most notably "Going, going, gone" for home runs.

For many years, multiple stations carried Reds games, with exclusive broadcasting rights not granted until 1945. Finally, in 1949, all home games were available on radio, and road games were carried live beginning in 1956. Hartman was enormously popular with local listeners, but he was only one of many broadcasters who gave Cincinnati one of the most illustrious radio-broadcasting histories of major-league teams. Red Barber (1934–38), Waite Hoyt (1942–65), Marty Brennaman (1974—1994), and Joe Nuxhall (1967–present) are among those who have occupied the broadcasting booth over the years. Barber and Brennaman both were selected for the broadcasters' wing of the Baseball Hall of Fame, while Hoyt made it into the Hall as a pitcher, his experience as a teammate of Babe Ruth's providing many entertaining stories.

Sidney Weil resigned as president in November 1933, his stock going to the Central Trust Company as collateral for loans he was unable to repay. The bank assumed control of the Cincinnati Reds and hired Larry MacPhail, son of a wealthy banker and a former World War I artillery captain and attorney, to run the club. His baseball experience included running Columbus in the AA, which he saved by introducing night games. Central Trust, which had no desire to retain the team, directed MacPhail to find a local owner.

MacPhail hired Frank Lane to develop a minor-league system and recruited Powel Crosley in February 1934 to buy the team. The Reds had lost $482,498 since 1930 and led MLB in the size of deficits for the last three years. Crosley was a wise choice, a creative businessman with experience in the young communications-technology industry and a range of other business enterprises. He helped create the radio industry by manufacturing radios and opening radio station WLW in Cincinnati, which beamed out the most powerful radio signal in the world. Crosley was also involved in other home-appliance products. Crosley sold the first refrigerators that included shelves on the inside of their doors. In addition, he manufactured a small fuel-efficient automobile, the Crosley.

Crosley wasted no time in making changes with the Reds. He made MacPhail vice president and the Reds' first general manager. The owner renamed Redland Field as Crosley Field and hired Red Barber to broadcast Reds games on WSAI (along with WLW, a Crosley-owned radio station). Several ballpark renovations were initiated, starting with the removal of a tier of advertisements atop the left-field wall and the addition of two large Crosley radios on each side of the scoreboard, with the dials set at Crosley's own WLW. Other changes included shortening the outfield dimensions in 1938 (from 339 feet to 328 in left field, 377 to 366 in right, and 395 to 387 at the deepest point in center) and adding 3,100 seats by constructing a second level to the pavilions down the right- and left-field lines in 1939. The new level had a steel floor, which added a pronounced auditory effect to stamping feet when Reds fans cheered their hometown favorites. Right field was further shortened in 1946 by another 20 feet when seating was added in front of the bleachers, creating an area known as "Goat Run."

The shortened distances greatly increased home-run production, much to the fans' enjoyment. In 1938, the Reds hit 50 homers in Crosley Field, compared to 13 the year before, and overall hit over 100 homers for the first time in the team's history. The new emphasis on the long ball culminated in 1956 in a record-tying 221 home runs.

Another Crosley innovation was transporting his team by airplane. On June 8, 1934, the Reds flew from Cincinnati to Chicago on two American Airlines planes, the first time a major-league team flew. This was a one-time stunt during a heat wave by an owner who had great interest in aviation and flew his own plane.

The most important innovation during the Crosley years was the introduction of night baseball in 1935. Attendance had barely exceeded 200,000 each of the previous two years as fans tired of watching the Reds repeatedly come in last. Something was needed to entice viewers. MacPhail knew how successful night games had been in saving his earlier Columbus club. At the urgent request of the Reds, the NL, trying to save the clearly faltering club, agreed to permit seven night games at Crosley Field for 1935. On May 24, with an impressive array of special guests (including NL president Ford Frick, AL president Will Harridge, and George Cahill), and after much pregame entertainment (including a band concert and fireworks), President Franklin D. Roosevelt pressed a button at the White House and Crosley Field glowed. The fans roared with the thrill of it, and the team gave them a victory, 2–1, behind Paul Derringer.

The lighting system cost $50,000 to construct and $250 per night to operate. However, the lights paid for themselves after the seven night games. The Reds drew approximately 130,000 to those seven games, while attendance for the 69 home day games was about 324,000. The Reds more than doubled home attendance from the previous season, but there were still many skeptics. Players worried about hurting their arms in the cool night air and being unable to see the ball. Many owners and the *Sporting News* raised high the banner of traditionalism. Yet the NL agreed to continue the Cincinnati experiment the following year, and the genie was out of the bottle. By 1940, eight major-league teams had installed lights.

Larry MacPhail resigned in September 1936, surfacing the next year as general manager of the Brooklyn Dodgers, where in 1938 he made the Dodgers the second major-league team to begin night baseball. Warren Giles, formerly president of the International League, replaced him with the Reds. The city's worst flood ever deposited 21 feet of water on home plate in January 1937, and the team continued to flood the loss column with a dismal 56–98 record under Chuck Dressen, fired after managing for three years.

A turning point for the on-field fortunes of the Reds came in 1938 with the appointment as manager of former Reds player Bill McKechnie. The Reds, now a power-hitting team in their own park as well as on the road, rose to fourth place (82–68) for the new skipper, who previously had won pennants with the Pirates and Cardinals. The team won 26 more games than the year before, with the most productive offense in the league.

The 1938 season featured a number of highlights. Cincinnati left-hander Johnny Vander Meer became the first and only major-league pitcher to throw two consecutive no-hitters, one on June 11 and the second four days later during the first night game ever played at Ebbets Field. Crosley Field played host to the All-Star Game, which included three shutout innings by Vander Meer, a sparkling catch of a Lou Gehrig drive by Cincinnati outfielder Ival Goodman, and an RBI by Reds catcher Ernie Lombardi. Lombardi became the first Reds player ever to win the NL MVP Award, as he compiled a league-leading .342 batting average. Paul Derringer went 21–7 with a 2.93 ERA.

On August 26, 1939, the Reds-Dodgers doubleheader in Brooklyn was telecast on W2XBS, an NBC experimental station. But it was not until September 21, 1947, that the first Reds games were telecast in Cincinnati, a doubleheader with Pittsburgh viewed on the city's 250 television sets. The approach in 1947 was primitive, with only two cameras, one behind home plate and the other behind first base. Opening Day and a selection of home games were televised in 1948, and all home games the following year, with the number of televised contests reduced over the next few decades to boost ballpark attendance. Waite Hoyt did double duty on radio and television from 1948 to 1955.

Reds executives worried that televised games might hurt attendance but also saw more quickly than with radio the medium's financial opportunities. Local television contracts generated revenue for the club, and the television station profited by selling advertisements. By 1953, 15 clubs, including Cincinnati, had television contracts, which brought in an average of $200,000 per team.

The Reds surprised the baseball world in 1939 by capturing their first pennant since 1919 with a record of 97–57. The team paced the NL in pitching, led by MVP Bucky Walters, who led the league in wins (27), ERA (2.19), strikeouts (137), and innings pitched (319). First baseman Frank McCormick paced the team in batting at .332 and RBIs with 128. Catcher Ernie Lombardi led in home runs with 20. Attendance increased by about 300,000 to approximately 980,000. The Reds earned $335,210 that year, nearly equaling Crosley's profits over the four previous years.

The New York Yankees, winners of 106 games during the season, proved too strong for Reds, and swept the World Series in four games. The major difference was in power, with New York clubbing seven home runs against none for Cincinnati.

The World Series demonstrated the continuing advancement of communications technology, as the games were broadcast nationally with Red Barber and Bob Elson describing the contests to the whole country. The Gillette Safety Razor company sponsored the series, beginning its long-running association with the Fall Classic.

Cincinnati fans liked their pennant winners, but not the idea of a new publicly funded 60,000-seat stadium covered with a glass roof and built atop a garage that would hold 15,000 cars. The proposed stadium was intended to accommodate other sports events and conventions. The $6 million bond issue was defeated by a margin of almost two to one, but the project proved prescient for two reasons: the forward-looking design concept and the battle over public financing of ballparks.

The 1940 season ended in joy for the Queen City. Cincinnati rolled to the pennant, winning 100 games and outdistancing Brooklyn by 12 games. For the third straight season, a Cincinnati player captured the MVP Award: first baseman Frank McCormick, who batted .309, drove in 127 runs, and led the league in both hits (191) and doubles (44). The team again had outstanding pitching, led by Derringer and Walters, who combined for 42 wins, and a league-leading team ERA of 3.05. The Reds went on to defeat the Tigers in the World Series in seven games, winning the finale at home by a score of 2–1. Bucky Walters and Paul Derringer led the Reds in the series with two wins each. Lombardi was injured, so the Reds relied on 40-year-old coach Jimmie Wilson, activated in August, to handle the catching, which he did while hitting .353.

The championship season, though, was not without tragedy. Catcher Willard Hershberger, suffering from depression and the increased pressure of filling in for Lombardi, committed suicide by cutting his throat with a razor in a Boston hotel room.

The Reds dropped to third place in 1941. Once the United States entered World War II, its effect on Cincinnati baseball was immense. Nineteen-year-old Ewell Blackwell pitched his first two games for the Reds, and soon was off to war, earning two battle stars with General George Patton's Third Army. A long line of other Cincinnati players followed Ewell into service over the next few years, including outfielder Mike McCormick, catcher Ray Lamanno, catcher Ray Mueller, pitcher Joe Beggs, pitcher Harry Gumbert, second baseman Lonny Frey, outfielder Eddie Lukon, and no-hit specialist Johnny Vander Meer. Fifty-year-old coach Hank Gowdy, a veteran of World War I combat in France, enlisted for a second tour of duty and was stationed at Fort Benning, Georgia.

Cincinnati's attendance, which was at the lower end of the NL, fell during the war years to approximately half of its 1940 level of about 850,000, finally bottoming out in 1945 at just over 290,000. Nonetheless, the team operated in the black during the war, earning about $141,831, half of what the Reds earned in the championship 1940 season alone. Transportation was part of the problem, with tire and gasoline rationing and restrictions on train travel. Travel restrictions prevented teams from going south for spring training, and the Reds trained at Indiana University in Bloomington.

Large numbers of workers put in longer hours at defense-related plants, making their attendance at games difficult if not impossible. The team responded by scheduling games at different times, such as in the morning to benefit second-shift factory workers.

Attendance was also hindered by the use of less talented and less renowned replacement players. One wartime player who later made good was Joe Nuxhall, who became the youngest player in the modern history of MLB when he pitched in a game on June 10 at the age of 15, about two months shy of his 16th birthday. Nuxhall later served his apprenticeship in the minors and returned to be an important member of the club's starting rotation during the 1950s and, in a second go-around with the team, in the 1960s.

The Reds did not fare well after the war, typically ending in sixth or seventh, and failed to make it out of the second division until 1956, their first winning season in 12 years. McKechnie resigned as manager in September 1946 and was replaced by coach Hank Gowdy for the rest of the season and Johnny Neun for the following season. In 1947, Ewell Blackwell won 16 games in a row, including a no-hitter, for the fifth-place Reds. He was an All-Star six straight years (1946–51). Attendance picked up after the war, but the team was last or next to last in attendance from 1945 through 1955.

Jackie Robinson made his Cincinnati debut on May 13, 1947, with Robinson supporters present. Unlike in some other cities, he stayed with the team in Cincinnati at the Netherlands Plaza Hotel, although he was not allowed into the dining room or swimming pool. Robinson drew a lot of fans into Crosley Field, but he also faced racial insults and even death threats in the Queen City. On May 20, 1951, the FBI informed Robinson that the Reds, the police, and the *Enquirer* had each received a letter threatening that Robinson would be shot while he played. Robinson played anyway and hit a home run in the seventh inning of the first game in a doubleheader sweep by the Dodgers. The spectators were aware of the letter and greeted Robinson's home run with thunderous applause.

The Korean War (1950–53) and the Red Scare had a direct impact on the team's moniker. Gabe Paul, who had become general manager when Warren Giles was named president of the NL in 1951, changed the team's nickname from Reds to Redlegs in 1953. The new name may have pleased Senator Joseph McCarthy, who was zealously tracking down alleged communists and their sympathizers, but it did not please the fans, who generally stayed with the old name. By the end of the decade, the term "Redlegs" had largely disappeared.

The club tried to improve itself by hiring Rogers Hornsby, one of the greatest hitters of all time, as manager during the 1952 season. However, the team continued to lose, and the players were in near revolt against their manager's authoritarian manner. Hornsby was let go late in the 1953 season. The new manager was Birdie Tebbetts, the recently retired long-term catcher of the Tigers and Red Sox.

That year the Reds brought in their first African American player, 30-year-old third baseman and outfielder Chuck Harmon. The team made it up to fifth place, led by slugging first baseman Ted Kluszewski, whose 49 homers and 141 RBIs led the NL. He hit 47 the following year, another fifth-place finish. In 1956, the Reds led the league at the All-Star break and finished third, only two games back of the champion Dodgers. Kluszewski dipped a bit, to 35 home runs, but others more than made up the difference. Outfielder Wally Post hit 36, outfielder Gus Bell 29, catcher Ed Bailey 28, and rookie outfielder Frank Robinson, Cincinnati's first African American regular, a team-leading 38, tying the league record for most home runs by a rookie. As important to the team's success, though, was the strong defense by the middle infielders, second baseman Johnny Temple and shortstop Roy McMillan.

The fans loved the power onslaught and came in droves as Cincinnati for the first time ever surpassed 1 million in attendance, repeating the accomplishment the next year. Fans also liked the new sleeveless uniforms, which allowed spectators to get a good look at Ted Kluszewski's considerable muscles. Adding players' names to the front of their uniforms at the same time made it easier to identify players not as distinctive in appearance as Big Klu.

The fans were so taken with their bombers that they flocked to cast All-Star ballots, abetted by radio station WSAI and the local press, which heavily promoted voting for the hometown favorites. The result was election of five Reds starters: Bailey, Temple, McMillan, Robinson and Bell. Nuxhall and Kluszewski were also added to the team. The heavy voting for Reds players upset fans from other cities but produced on-field results, as Kluszewski, Temple, and McMillan each had two hits in a 7–3 NL victory.

Having found that ballot-box stuffing worked, Reds fans repeated the process the following year, only more so. By late June, eight Reds were leading the All-Star voting at their positions: Bailey, first baseman George Crowe (substituting for the injured Kluszewski), Temple, McMillan, third baseman Don Hoak, Bell, Robinson, and Post. Commissioner Ford Frick took action, replacing Bell, Post, and Crowe with Hank Aaron, Willie Mays, and Stan Musial (although Musial ended up passing Crowe in voting anyway). Still, as in 1956, five Reds started, and manager Walter Alston added Bell to the team as a backup. The major effect of Cincinnatians' overly zealous voting was a complete overhaul of the voting process. Commissioner Frick turned selection of All-Star starters entirely over to players, managers, and coaches. Only in 1970 was the All-Star franchise finally returned to the fans.

A number of improvements were made to Crosley Field in the mid-1950s, including air conditioning in the dugouts and the press box in 1956 and a new scoreboard in 1957, the first to display hitters' batting averages. However, the long-term future of the field was increasingly in doubt. Crosley Field was in a bind, caught between inadequate parking, worsened by the larger cars of the 1950s, and nearby residences, factories, and railroad yards that prevented stadium expansion. Getting a new stadium, though, would not be easy. In August 1956, the Hamilton Country Board of Commissioners turned down a proposed purchase of 90 acres from Girls' Town for a new stadium. The following year was rife with rumors of the Reds' departure from Cincinnati for New York once the Dodgers and Giants had been given permission by MLB owners to move to California. Crosley repeatedly denied that the team was thinking of relocating. In January 1958, city officials, perhaps pressured by the rumors, approved 2,600 additional parking spaces at the stadium, although many of the spaces were eliminated when I-75 opened in 1963.

The Reds dipped to fourth in the league in 1957 and 1958, and Tebbetts resigned on August 14, 1958. Coach Jimmie Dykes completed the season, and Mayo Smith was brought in for 1959, but lasted only half the season. Fred Hutchinson replaced Smith, his 39–35 record for the second half more indicative of his future success with the Reds than his sixth-place finish the next year.

In 1959 Cincinnati played the Dodgers in a spring exhibition game in Havana, Cuba, a few months after Fidel Castro's successful revolution brought him to power. This was the last major-league appearance in Cuba until the spring of 1999, when Baltimore played the Cuban national team. The Havana Sugar Kings of the International League ended a five-year run as Cincinnati's Triple-A team in 1960, the victim of the U.S. boycott of communist Cuba.

Also in 1959, the Reds added 738 box seats down the foul lines and, to the delight of fans, a process for cooling spectators by placing jet air fans in the grandstand. Color telecasts were also introduced, just one year after color TV went on the market. Twelve home games appeared in living color on the Crosley Broadcasting Company network.

The early 1960s brought major front-office change to the club. General manager Gabe Paul resigned in October 1960 to join the new Houston franchise. Bill DeWitt became Cincinnati's new vice president and general manager, having resigned two weeks earlier as president of the Detroit Tigers.

A PENNANT, THE DEATH OF A MANAGER, AND THE ORIGINS OF THE BIG RED MACHINE (1961–69)

In a sad twist, the Cincinnati Reds returned to the World Series for the first time in 21 years a few months after the death of longtime owner Powel Crosley on March 28, 1961. Ownership shifted to a family nonprofit foundation. In March of the following year general manager Bill DeWitt, flush with optimism after winning the pennant, headed a corporation that bought the Reds for $4,625,000. DeWitt had started from the bottom years before selling soda at Sportsman's Park in St. Louis and worked his way up the baseball ladder. DeWitt did not capture another championship during his short reign as owner, but helped lay the foundation for the great Reds teams of the 1970s.

The 1961 pennant was a stunning surprise known widely as "the Miracle on Western Avenue." A 20–6 May record propelled the team into a first-place tie with the Giants. The team overcame a July slump to establish a lead in the middle of August that it never lost, finishing four games ahead of second-place Los Angeles. Frank Robinson captured the NL MVP Award after hitting 37 home runs and driving in 124 runs, outfielder Vada Pinson batted .343 with 208 hits, and Jerry Lynch, in an era of growing specialization, served as pinch hitter par excellence, with five pinch home runs during the season. Joey Jay, Jim O'Toole, and Bob Purkey gave the team a strong starting staff. DeWitt was named Executive of the Year by the *Sporting News,* and manager Fred Hutchinson provided hard-nosed leadership. Whether the Reds were in better shape than their opponents is impossible to prove, but conditioning coach Otis Douglas was the first in major-league history.

Over a million fans came out to see the Reds, and they had high hopes for the World Series, paying $10 for box seats, $7 for the grandstand, and $2–$4 for the privilege to standing or sitting in the bleachers. However, the Reds ran into one of baseball's all-time great teams, the 1961 New York Yankees of Mantle and Maris, winners of 109 games.

The Yankees made short work of Cincinnati, splitting the first two games in Yankee Stadium and sweeping the next three at Crosley Field. Cincinnati futility reached bottom when Whitey Ford was on the mound. The Yankees ace won twice, pitching 14 scoreless innings.

Although the Reds would not win another championship during the 1960s, DeWitt built the base for future championships by establishing strong scouting and farm systems. The Reds came close to repeating in 1962, finishing third, only three and a half games behind the Giants. A fifth-place finish the next year was followed by a down-to-the-wire race in 1964, the Reds coming in just one game behind the Cardinals. The club's on-field successes might have been even greater had cancer not cut short Fred Hutchinson's career at the age of 45. In October 1964 he resigned as manager, yielding the position to coach Dick Sisler, and on November 12 he passed away.

During the post-pennant years, the Reds featured a variety of on-field accomplishments. In 1962, Bob Purkey and Joey Jay became the first pair of Reds hurlers to win 20 or more games since 1940. Fireballer Jim Maloney won 23 games in 1963 and threw two extra-inning no-hitters in 1965, losing the first in 11 innings but winning the second in 10. Pete Rose became the team's second baseman in 1963, capturing the Rookie of the Year Award. However, Frank Robinson was traded to the Baltimore Orioles after the 1965 season, undoubtedly DeWitt's worst blunder, and one of the worst trades in the team's history. Robinson immediately won the Triple Crown and led the Orioles to a World Series triumph over the Los Angeles Dodgers.

Reflecting the city's long love affair with music, the Reds celebrated rock 'n' roll at Teen Night on June 8, 1962. Almost 3,700 teenagers availed themselves of the one-dollar-per-ticket promotion, listening to six rock 'n' roll bands before the game. A different musical clientele showed up on August 16 for Trumpet Night, needing only to bring a trumpet to get in free.

Probably DeWitt's most frustrating challenge was to settle on an acceptable plan for a new baseball stadium. DeWitt continued improvements to Crosley Field, adding additional parking lots for the 1961 season and constructing a 40-foot screen on top of the left-field wall to prevent balls from damaging cars in the newly finished lot. In 1965, DeWitt added the first glass backstop in baseball as well as 1,600 additional box seats.

Debate over the location of a new stadium continued. A growing consensus favored the riverfront area for both historic and financial reasons. The riverfront was the historic center of the city, and supporters of that location believed that a new stadium would help regenerate the downtown area by attracting other businesses. Economic revitalization in turn would at least partly re-create a walking city, with pedestrians able to move easily among the stadium and a wide range of shops. DeWitt opposed a downtown site, warning of parking and flooding problems. He preferred to locate the ballpark near Blue Ash Airport at Plainfield because he believed that location provided more space for parking, easier access for motorists, and security against the periodic flooding of the Ohio River.

Against DeWitt's wishes, the Cincinnati City Council in June 1966 overwhelmingly approved a riverfront site and an enclosed circular design. Among the most influential political supporters of the riverfront site was Eugene Peter

Ruehlmann, a longtime city-council member and vice mayor who would serve two terms as mayor (1967–71). DeWitt sold the club in December 1966 to a group of local investors, including his son, William DeWitt Jr., and Frank Dale, publisher of the *Cincinnati Enquirer.*

The new ownership group elected Dale president and agreed to a 40-year lease on the new downtown stadium. In January 1967 the new owner hired Bob Howsam as general manager, and Howsam set about further strengthening the Cincinnati farm system.

Johnny Bench, the future Hall of Fame catcher, made his Cincinnati debut in late August 1967, while Tony Perez in the same year established himself as the regular third baseman, driving in over 100 runs. Both would be pivotal figures in the championship seasons of the next decade, by which time Perez had moved to first base. Lee May, the Cincinnati first baseman in 1967, was named Rookie of the Year by the *Sporting News.*

Opening Day 1968 was scheduled for April 8, but when President Lyndon Johnson declared April 9 a national day of mourning for the martyred Martin Luther King Jr., the Reds postponed their opener until the 10th. Two months later, when Democratic presidential candidate Senator Robert F. Kennedy was assassinated on June 5, Johnson declared a day of mourning for June 8. When Cincinnati did not postpone its game, several Reds players, led by pitcher Milt Pappas and outfielder Vada Pinson, led a protest. A majority of the players voted not to play, and the game was delayed while management tried to persuade them to take the field. Finally, Pete Rose and a few others acceded to the urgings of manager Dave Bristol, who in July 1966 had succeeded Don Heffner, and general manager Bob Howsam and took their places on the diamond. Others followed, and the game began about 45 minutes late.

Three days after the short-lived rebellion, Milt Pappas was traded to the Braves. On October 11, the other leader of the attempted boycott, Vada Pinson, was sent to the Cardinals. For one brief moment, the Reds players had joined the countercultural world of demonstration and revolution. The team responded by removing the leaders of that movement. Earlier that year, Cincinnati management had made its political position known by changing the team's logo. Gone was the mustachioed baseball player, replaced by a clean-shaven image. Facial hair represented the counterculture, which was anathema to the organization, determined to position itself in a more traditional mode, even if doing so required abandoning the team's well-known logo. As with the team's earlier attempt to drop the communist-sounding "Reds" name in 1953 at the height of Senator Joseph McCarthy's public hunt for communists, management sought to give the club a strong conservative bent.

The Reds finished fourth in 1968, with Bench named Rookie of the Year. Pete Rose won the batting championship with a .335 mark. In 1969, a new divisional structure was introduced, and the Reds were placed in the six-team Western Division. The club went 89–63, good for third place, and was in the pennant hunt most of the season. Bob Hertzel in the *Cincinnati Enquirer* introduced the nickname "Big Red Machine" in an article on July 4 that season. Despite the successful season, Bristol was fired on October 8, and the next day, Sparky Anderson, a 35-year-old former minor-league manager who had played only one season in the majors, became the new field boss. He would help to fashion some of the greatest teams in the organization's long history.

RIVERFRONT STADIUM AND THE HEYDAY OF THE BIG RED MACHINE (1970–78)

The $45 million publicly funded Riverfront Stadium opened on June 30, 1970. Its original capacity was 51,050, with dimensions of 330 feet down the foul lines and 404 feet to center field. Although construction was not yet completed, with work remaining on the parking garage, elevators, and escalators, and fans having to forgo hot dogs in the absence of electricity in the concessions area, the stadium proved a big hit. Attendance soared over the decade despite rising ticket prices. In 1970, reserved seats cost three dollars and box seats four, but by the end of the decade, tickets ranged from three to seven dollars, and were among the highest in MLB. The Reds, with a new stadium and successful teams, set an attendance record of over 1.8 million in 1970, broke the 2 million barrier in 1973, and remained above it for the rest of the decade.

Riverfront Stadium was built to remain usable during floods of up to 80 feet, eliminating a problem of previous ballparks. Pedestrian bridges led from parking lots across the expressway, lessening the impact of insufficient adjacent parking. Nearby merchants generally reported an upswing in their business, and the downtown, as planned, became more of a walking city. However, shutting off a view of the city from inside the stadium was counterproductive, somewhat psychologically isolating the ballpark from its surroundings.

The stadium had artificial turf, one of four ballparks built in the 1970s to eschew natural grass, raising the number of NL parks with artificial playing fields to six. The new turf offered a smooth running surface and a speedy surface for ground balls. Consequently, stolen bases increased, and teams also had to give greater attention to defense. The emphasis on speed was accompanied by a decline in home runs. During the decade, stolen bases increased from an average of 87 per NL team to 124, and home runs dropped from 140 to 119.

General manager Bob Howsam and manager Sparky Anderson, without abandoning power, built a team that featured outstanding defense and speed. In 1970, the Reds won their division with 102 victories, leading the league a record 178 days. Catcher Johnny Bench combined power with some of the finest defense ever exhibited behind the plate. He led the NL with 45 homers and 148 RBIs, and was NL MVP. Defensive star Dave Concepcion manned shortstop, reliable first baseman Tony Perez clouted 40 homers, and versatile hometown hero Pete Rose played right field and led the NL with 205 hits. The pitching staff was strong, particularly Wayne Granger with 35 saves. The Reds went on to sweep Pittsburgh in the three-game NL Championship Series, but lost the World Series to Baltimore in five games. It was the first of a string of championships under Sparky Anderson that included five divisional titles, four pennants, and two World Series championships.

After slipping to fourth in 1971, Cincinnati rebounded to take the division in 1972 with 95 wins. Bench won his second NL MVP. An important trade added second baseman Joe Morgan, the total defensive and offensive package, from Houston. In 1972 he paced the NL with 122 runs and a .417 on-base percentage. He was second in steals with 58. The Reds captured the pennant against Pittsburgh in five games. The World Series against Oakland went seven games, with the A's taking the deciding game 3–2. Reds pitching was very strong, giving up only 16 runs in seven games. The 1973 club, paced by Rose, who had 230 hits, hit a league-leading .338, and was MVP, won 99 games, but lost to the New York Mets in the NLCS. The next season the Reds only came in second, leaving Cincinnati fans still waiting for the ultimate triumph.

By 1975, Anderson had his championship lineup fine-tuned. Rose had moved to third base, freeing up left field for slugger George Foster. Ken Griffey became the right fielder. Don Gullett, a talented left-hander, headed a competent starting staff, while Anderson, who cared little about complete games, relied on a revolutionary bullpen-by-committee approach. His Reds staffs usually ranked near the bottom in complete games, and his approach soon caught on and permanently altered how managers used pitching staffs.

Among the many Reds stars, the most popular at home, and most disliked away, was Pete Rose. The pugnacious, all-out style of play that endeared him to Cincinnati fans at times angered fans elsewhere. During the 1970 All-Star Game at Riverfront Stadium, Rose scored from second base on a 12th-inning single by Jim Hickman, bowling over catcher Ray Fosse. He scored the winning run but seriously injured Fosse, impairing his professional career. During the 1973 NLCS, Rose got into a fight at Shea Stadium with Mets shortstop Bud Harrelson. Mets fans responded by throwing bottles and other objects at Rose when he returned to left field, almost leading to a forfeit. The negative reaction continued the following year at several stadiums. Rose sometimes had to wear a batting helmet in the field for protection.

Sparky Anderson's team cruised in 1975, winning 108 games, finishing 20 games ahead of Los Angeles in the West. The Reds set an NL record by clinching the title on September 7, and then swept Pittsburgh in the championship series. Joe Morgan won the first of his two consecutive MVP Awards. Six pitchers won 10 or more games, and the team led the league in runs scored, stolen bases, fielding percentage, fewest errors, and most saves.

The World Series against Boston proved much more difficult. Five of the seven contests were decided by one run, and in five the winner had to come from behind. In addition, two of the games went into extra innings. The most memorable image of the series remains Boston catcher Carlton Fisk gesturing for his home run to remain fair in the bottom of the 12th inning of game six. It did, and Boston won. Nonetheless, Cincinnati won the deciding seventh game 4–3 and its third World Series, its first since 1940.

In 1976 Cincinnati won 102 games, taking the West by 10 games. Five of the starting players hit over .300, and the Reds led the NL in virtually every single offensive category, including batting (.280) and homers (141). Morgan repeated as MVP with 27 homers, 111 RBIs, and 60 stolen bases, and led the NL with a .576 slugging percentage and .444 on-base percentage. It was the third straight year he led the NL in the latter category. Six pitchers won 10 or more games, the relievers led the NL in saves, and the defense had the fewest errors.

The Reds then swept Philadelphia in the NLCS and the New York Yankees in the World Series, the first to use a designated hitter, becoming the first team to sweep both a championship series and the World Series. The triumph made the Reds the first NL team since the New York Giants of 1921–22 to win back-to-back world championships.

After the series was over, the team began to be broken up, hastened by the rise of free agency. One of the first players to take advantage was ace left-hand-er Don Gullett, winner of game one of the past World Series, who departed in November for the Yankees. The Reds management was the last to employ free agency, which handicapped the team. Also departing after the 1976 season was longtime first baseman Tony Perez, who was traded to the Montreal Expos.

Cincinnati dropped to second place (92–69) the following year despite the acquisition of pitcher Tom Seaver and an MVP season by George Foster, who hit 52 home runs. In 1978, when the Reds again finished second, Pete Rose surpassed 3,000 career hits and tied Willie Keeler's NL record by hitting safely in 44 consecutive games. The winds of change, though, were howling.

Bob Howsam stepped down and was succeeded in April 1978 by Dick Wagner as president and CEO. After the season, in a move that shocked most Reds fans, Wagner fired Sparky Anderson after the most successful managerial run in Cincinnati history. Wagner claimed that Anderson had lost control of the players by failing to maintain discipline. Then came the unthinkable. Pete Rose, whose request for a long-term $400,000-per-year contract was rejected, signed as a free agent with the Philadelphia Phillies, who gave him a four-year contract at more than $800,000 annually. The hometown hero was gone, and the heyday of the Big Red Machine was over.

PETE ROSE AND MARGE SCHOTT: AN ERA OF CONTROVERSY (1979–2005)

The first season after the departures of Howsam, Anderson, and Rose promised more than the future would provide for the Cincinnati franchise. The Reds, under new manager John McNamara, won their division in 1979 (90–71). Ray Knight took over third base and hit .318, and Foster drove in 102 runs. Cincinnati was swept in the championship series by Pittsburgh, but Reds fans were optimistic about the future. However, Cincinnati lurched into decline. The team dropped to third in 1980, rebounded to post the majors' best overall record (66–42) in 1981, but since they finished second in each half of the strike-shortened season, missed the playoffs. The squad then collapsed to two consecutive sixth-place finishes (including a franchise record 101 losses in 1982) followed by a fifth-place finish in 1984.

The second half of the decade was better, but still frustrating. Pete Rose returned in mid-August 1984 as a player-manager, and beginning in 1985, guided the club to four straight second-best finishes. Then, in 1989, Rose's baseball career ended in a maelstrom of gambling-related scandal.

Attendance followed the on-field fortunes of the Reds, failing to reach 2 million from 1981 until 1987. During the 1980s and 1990s, Cincinnati was one of five major-league teams that never reached 2.5 million in attendance.

Turmoil and change characterized the Reds ownership in this era. Cincinnati businessmen William J. and James R. Williams, who had been minority shareholders since 1966, became the principal owners in 1981. The following year Russ Nixon replaced manager John McNamara in July. In 1983, Howsam

Pete Rose, 1988. © AP / Wide World Photos

returned as general manager as the Williams brothers fired Dick Wagner, by then immensely unpopular because of his confrontational management style and failure to maintain the Big Red Machine. Vern Rapp was hired as field manager for the 1984 season, only to be replaced by Rose in August. In October, Howsam stepped down again as general manager, replaced by Bill Bergesch, although Howsam remained as a vice president. Marge Schott, famous for her car dealerships in Cincinnati, purchased controlling interest in the club.

Schott's years were marked by feuds with ownership partners; an authoritarian approach that led large numbers of team employees to leave; flamboyant, unpredictable behavior; bigoted comments; and a variety of fines and suspensions. Her dedication to keeping ticket prices down, accessibility to fans, and substantial contributions to charities could not counter her steadily developing negative image. Meanwhile, Bob Howsam resigned as vice president in 1985, remaining as a consultant through 1986 before severing his association with the Reds. Schott fired Bergesch as general manager in 1987 and replaced him with Murray Cook, formerly a general manager with the Yankees and Expos.

The spirit of the Big Red Machine receded into history. Joe Morgan departed after the 1979 season, Tom Seaver was traded in December 1982, Johnny Bench retired in 1983, and the last of the era's stars, Dave Concepcion, retired in 1988. Glimmerings of the past resurfaced as Tony Perez was brought back in 1984 as a part-time player, and player-manager Rose continued his assault on Ty Cobb's record for most career hits. On September 11, 1985, at Riverfront Stadium, Rose stroked a single off Eric Show for hit number 4,192 to establish a new record. The next year, both Rose and Perez brought down the curtain on their playing careers, Rose finishing with 4,256 hits and, everyone assumed, a certain first-ballot ticket into the Hall of Fame.

Then, in 1988, another curtain began falling on Rose. On April 30, Rose became embroiled in a heated argument with umpire Dave Pallone over a close play at first base. Rose, apparently provoked by a Pallone finger to his face, shoved the umpire, leading to ejection and a 30-day suspension and $10,000 fine levied by NL president A. Bartlett Giamatti. Never before had a manager received such a heavy penalty for on-field behavior.

By 1989, Rose's gambling habits were closing in on him. An investigation into his gambling had begun under Commissioner Peter Ueberroth and continued under his successor, Bart Giamatti. The investigation was announced publicly in March, and the Reds staggered through the season under the uncertainty clouding Rose's future, dropping from first place in June to fifth place at the end of the year under interim manager Tommy Helms. In June, Rose sued Giamatti, charging that he could not render an impartial decision because of his previous year's judgment. Hamilton Country judge Norbert Nadel ruled that Giamatti had prejudged Rose and blocked a scheduled hearing. The victory, though, was short-lived. Attorney John Dowd, hired by Giamatti to investigate Rose, issued his findings in a 225-page report, concluding that Rose had bet on baseball and on the Reds. According to the Dowd report, Rose had violated MLB's rule 21(d), which forbids betting on a team for which the bettor "has a duty to perform." The prescribed punishment was permanent ineligibility from organized baseball.

Rose strongly denied the charges, but agreed to a conclusion of the case that banished him from baseball for life, but with the opportunity to request reinstatement. Rose also acknowledged that the commissioner had a factual basis for imposing the penalty. Giamatti, while banning Rose on August 24, agreed not to issue a formal finding that Rose had bet on baseball, although the commissioner shortly afterward stated that he had concluded that Rose had done so. In early 1991, shortly before Rose became eligible for election to the Hall of Fame, the Hall directors amended selection rules to disqualify anyone on baseball's ineligible list. Rose never publicly admitted gambling on the Reds until the publication in 2004 of his book *My Prison without Bars*. He remains absent from the panoply of baseball greats enshrined at Cooperstown.

The story of Rose's banishment carried with it more sad chapters. Eight days after banning Rose from baseball, Commissioner Giamatti died of a heart attack. Within a year, Rose had pleaded guilty to tax evasion and was sentenced to prison, serving five months.

Before the 1990 season, more changes occurred in the front office and on the field, almost as if the Reds were attempting to exorcise their past. General manager Murray Cook was fired and replaced by Bob Quinn. Helms was replaced by former Yankees player, manager, and general manager Lou Piniella.

The transformation worked as Piniella cleverly used a deep bullpen and the team's ability to play without the Rose distractions, guiding the Reds to 91 wins; a divisional title; a victory over the Pirates in the championship series, four games to two; and, in a huge upset, a sweep of the Oakland A's in the World Series. Jose Rios, who won two games with a 0.59 ERA, was the Series MVP. The team featured 1988 Rookie of the Year third baseman Chris Sabo, the multitalented but often injured center fielder Eric Davis, and the bullpen trio known as "the Nasty Boys"—Rob Dibble, Norm Charlton, and Randy Myers. Shortstop Barry Larkin, possibly the team's best player, batted .301, stole 30 bases, and played outstanding defense. A strong bench and capable role players helped compensate for the lack of superstars who populated the Big Red Machine teams.

The championship season brought a jump in attendance to over 2.4 million. The Reds were carried on cable television for the first time. Sports Channel Cincinnati signed to air 25 games per year for three years.

Unfortunately, 1990 marked a high point for the Reds. Their play ever since has been marked by irregular on-field success and considerable front-office turmoil. The Reds dropped to fifth place in 1991. Although the team rebounded to finish second in 1992, Piniella resigned as manager after the season, and general manager Bob Quinn was let go two days later. His replacement, Jim Bowden, at 31, was until recently the youngest major-league general manager ever. The new field leader was the enormously popular Tony Perez, but after winning just 20 of his first 44 games, he was fired and replaced by Davey Johnson.

In 1994, the league split into three divisions. The Reds were in first place in the Central when a players' strike ended the season, depriving Cincinnati of a post-season trip. The next year, the Reds won their division in a strike-shortened season that did not begin until April 26. Shortstop Barry Larkin captured the MVP Award, and the club rolled past the Dodgers 3–0 in the new NL Divisional Series. However, the Reds were in turn swept by the Atlanta Braves in the NLCS.

During the remainder of the 1990s, the Reds sometimes challenged but consistently came up short, finishing third under manager Ray Knight in 1996 and compiling third- and second-place finishes under Jack McKeon from 1997 through 2000. In 1999, the Reds tied for the wild-card spot with the New York Mets but lost a one-game playoff. Four men hit 20 or more homers, led by Greg Vaughn with 45 and 118 RBIs.

As the new century dawned, Cincinnati's fortunes continued to sink. Under still another manager, Bob Boone, the Reds came in fifth in 2001, third (but again with a losing record) in 2002, and fifth in 2003 (although Boone had to share that losing season with midseason replacement Dave Miley). In an unusual conjunction of firings, Cincinnati dismissed both the field manager and general manager Jim Bowden on the same day, July 28. Given a full season in 2004, Miley led the Reds to an only slightly better finish, fourth place, while the new general manager, Dan O'Brien, hired in the fall of 2003, was attempting to rebuild the club's scouting and player-development programs. After a disappointing start to the 2005 campaign, Miley was fired on June 21. His replacement, Jerry Narron, led Cincinnati to its fifth consecutive losing season, but the team showed sufficient improvement for him to be rehired. Ken Griffey Jr., who had missed much of the previous four seasons with injuries, played 128 games, batting .301 with 35 home runs and 92 RBIs, and was NL Comeback Player of the Year, putting him back on track for the Hall of Fame. The team led the NL in offense, with outfielder Adam Dunn hitting 40 home runs, but poor pitching hampered the club throughout the season.

CAPITALISM AND THE CINCINNATI REDS

Attendance stagnated in the 1990s, with Cincinnati remaining under 2 million until 1999, while ticket prices increased. During the 1990s, the team's premier "blue seats" rose from $8.50 to $17, and "red" reserve seats from $5.50 to $7. Although the payroll rose from $15 million in 1990 to $35 million in 1999, the increase lagged behind most teams, placing the Reds near the bottom of NL payrolls, which factored into the team's on-field struggles. In an attempt to boost revenue, the organization in 1996 sold stadium naming rights to Cinergy Corporation for $6 million.

By the early 1990s Marge Schott was floundering on the shoals of suspensions and fines. Her flamboyance and lack of decorum had evolved into racial and ethnic slurs. In February 1993, MLB's Executive Council suspended her for one year and fined her $25,000. Schott retained ownership, but was removed from daily operations. Some positive statements about Adolf Hitler's early career as führer led to another suspension in June 1996, which lasted through the 1998 season. John Allen, controller of the Reds, ran the team's front-office operations.

Then in December 1996 General Motors filed a complaint alleging that Schott had falsified sales of cars in order to meet her quotas and had fallaciously used names of Reds employees in her scheme. Faced with a continuing suspension from the team, Schott agreed in October 1998 to sell her majority interest. On April 20, 1999, Carl Lindner, owner of the Great American Insurance Company, became head of the new ownership group. After 15 years as owner, the colorful but polarizing and often embarrassing Marge Schott was out.

The Reds are financially a small-city team. In 2001, when the team made $4.3 million according to *Forbes*, it was only 26th in salaries paid players. The team was 26th in media revenue and 28th in money made from ancillary activities (parking, concessions, and luxury seating). Its total local revenue was $46.5 million, half of what the average team brought in.

Schott's legal problems and her vacillations about a new ballpark slowed down the effort to replace the stadium. In May 1995, Schott, who periodically had threatened to move the Reds to another city, agreed to work with the Cincinnati Business Committee to build a new stadium west of Cinergy Field by 1998 or 1999.

Various arguments were brought forward for a new stadium, among them the desire to integrate the stadium more effectively with the environment, including the river. City and club officials also wanted to make the stadium a fuller experience that would incorporate club history, more comfortable seating, and enjoyable dining.

In June, city and Hamilton County officials developed a financing plan to construct two stadiums, one for the Reds and the other for the NFL's Bengals. They agreed to finance the stadiums with a one percent increase in the county sales tax. The plan raised the important issue of whether a privately owned business should receive public funding to create the building where it carries out its business.

Critics contended that the approach was inappropriate and that the funds could be better used for schools, public safety, and other city needs. The argument, repeated in other cities facing similar decisions, led to an extensive and successful petition drive to bring the issue to the voters in March 1996. Proponents of a new stadium reduced the proposed tax increase to one-half of one percent to improve chances to win the referendum. The strategy worked, as voters approving the dedicated tax increase by almost 55,000 votes.

A subsequent vote in November 1998 to determine the location of the stadium resulted in selection of a riverfront site by almost a two-to-one margin. The winning location was between the old stadium and Firstar Center, surrounded by Broadway, I-71, and Mehring Way, with a view of the Ohio River from inside the stadium.

The Reds signed the formal agreement to build the stadium on May 20, 1999. In July 2000, majority owner Carl Lindner bought the naming rights to the stadium for his Great American Insurance Company for $75 million. Groundbreaking for Great American Ballpark took place on October 4, 2000. Five years later, Lindner sold his controlling interest to a syndicate headed by Robert Castellini, a member of the Cardinals' ownership group and chairman of the Castellini Company, a locally based wholesale produce company. The new owners included Thomas L. Williams and Williams J. Williams, Jr., whose father and uncle were Reds stockholders from 1966 to 1984.

By 2003, the new 42,059-seat stadium was ready for play at a cost of $325 million, 86 percent of which was publicly funded. The stadium featured a natural grass surface and outfield dimensions of 325 feet down the right-field line, 328 feet down the left-field line, and 404 feet to center field. An accompanying Reds museum and hall of fame opened in September 2004. Among the exhibits planned is one called "The Business of Baseball." The irony inherent in this section may have gone unnoticed by management, with the exhibit designed to portray such aspects of Reds history as the city's first professional team and the introduction of night baseball. However, baseball as big business having built the stadium, the final object in the exhibit should properly be the entire stadium itself. The first professional team, those mighty Red Stockings of 1869, had given birth to so much more than they ever could have imagined.

NOTABLE ACHIEVEMENTS

Most Valuable Players

Year	Name	Position
1938	Ernie Lombardi	C
1939	Bucky Walters	P
1940	Frank McCormick	1B
1961	Frank Robinson	OF
1970	Johnny Bench	C
1972	Johnny Bench	C
1973	Pete Rose	OF
1975	Joe Morgan	2B
1976	Joe Morgan	2B
1977	George Foster	OF
1995	Barry Larkin	SS

Rookies of the Year

Year	Name	Position
1956	Frank Robinson	OF
1963	Pete Rose	2B
1966	Tommy Helms	3B
1968	Johnny Bench	C
1976	Pat Zachry	P
1988	Chris Sabo	3B
1999	Scott Williamson	P

Batting Champions

Year	Name	#
1905	Cy Seymour	.377
1916	Hal Chase	.339
1917	Edd Roush	.341
1919	Edd Roush	.321
1926	Bubbles Hargrave	.353

1938	Ernie Lombardi	.342
1968	Pete Rose	.335
1969	Pete Rose	.348
1973	Pete Rose	.338

Home-Run Champions

Year	Name	#
1892	Bug Holliday	13
1901	Sam Crawford	16
1905	Fred Odwell	9
1954	Ted Kluszewski	49
1970	Johnny Bench	45
1972	Johnny Bench	40
1977	George Foster	52
1978	George Foster	40

ERA Champions

Year	Name	#
1923	Dolf Luque	1.93
1925	Dolf Luque	2.63
1939	Bucky Walters	2.29
1940	Bucky Walters	2.48
1941	Elmer Riddle	2.24
1944	Ed Heusser	2.38

Strikeout Champions

Year	Name	#
1899	Noodles Hahn	145
1900	Noodles Hahn	132
1901	Noodles Hahn	239
1939	Bucky Walters	137
1941	Johnny Vander Meer	202
1942	Johnny Vander Meer	186
1943	Johnny Vander Meer	174
1947	Ewell Blackwell	193
1993	Jose Rijo	227

No-Hitters (Italics = Perfect Game)

Name	Date
Bumpus Jones	10/15/1892
Ted Breitenstein	04/22/1898

Noodles Hahn	07/12/1900
Fred Toney	05/02/1917
Hod Eller	05/11/1919
Johnny Vander Meer	06/11/1938
Johnny Vander Meer	06/15/1938
Clyde Shoun	05/15/1944
Ewell Blackwell	06/18/1947
Jim Maloney	08/19/1965
George Culver	07/29/1968
Jim Maloney	04/30/1969
Tom Seaver	06/16/1978
Tom Browning	*09/16/1988*

POSTSEASON APPEARANCES

AA Pennants

Year	Record	Manager
1882	55–25	Pop Snyder

NL West Division Titles

Year	Record	Manager
1970	102–60	Sparky Anderson
1972	95–59	Sparky Anderson
1973	99–63	Sparky Anderson
1975	108–54	Sparky Anderson
1976	102–60	Sparky Anderson
1979	90–71	John McNamara
1990	91–71	Lou Piniella

NL Central Division Titles

Year	Record	Manager
1994	66–48	Davey Johnson
1995	85–59	Davey Johnson

NL Pennants

Year	Record	Manager
1919	96–44	Pat Moran
1939	97–57	Bill McKechnie
1940	100–53	Bill McKechnie

1961	93–61	Fred Hutchinson
1970	102–60	Sparky Anderson
1972	95–59	Sparky Anderson
1975	108–54	Sparky Anderson
1976	102–60	Sparky Anderson
1990	91–71	Lou Piniella

World Championships

Year	Opponent	MVP
1919	Chicago	
1940	Detroit	
1975	Boston	Pete Rose
1976	New York	Johnny Bench
1990	Oakland	Jose Rijo

MANAGERS

2005–	Jerry Narron
2003–2005	Dave Miley
2003	Ray Knight
2001–2003	Bob Boone
1997–2000	Jack McKeon
1996–1997	Ray Knight
1993–1995	Davey Johnson
1993	Tony Perez
1990–1992	Lou Piniella
1989	Tommy Helms
1984–1989	Pete Rose
1984	Vern Rapp
1982–1983	Russ Nixon
1979–1982	Jack McNamara
1970–1978	Sparky Anderson
1966–1969	Dave Bristol
1966	Don Heffner
1964–1965	Dick Sisler
1959–1964	Fred Hutchinson
1959	Mayo Smith

1958	Jimmie Dykes
1954–1958	Birdie Tebbetts
1953	Buster Mills
1952–1953	Rogers Hornsby
1952	Earle Brucker
1949–1952	Luke Sewell
1948–1949	Bucky Walters
1947–1948	Johnny Neun
1946	Hank Gowdy
1938–1946	Bill McKechnie
1937	Bobby Wallace
1934–1937	Chuck Dressen
1934	Burt Shotton
1934	Bob O'Farrell
1933	Donie Bush
1930–1932	Dan Howley
1924–1929	Jack Hendricks
1919–1923	Pat Moran
1918	Heinie Groh
1916–1918	Christy Mathewson
1916	Ivey Wingo
1914–1916	Buck Herzog
1913	Joe Tinker
1912	Hank O'Day
1909–1911	Clark Griffith
1908	John Ganzel
1906–1907	Ned Hanlon
1902–1905	Joe Kelley
1902	Frank Bancroft
1901–1902	Bid McPhee
1900	Bob Allen
1895–1899	Buck Ewing
1892–1894	Charles Comiskey
1890–1891	Tom Loftus
1887–1889	Gus Schmelz (American Association)
1885–1886	O. P. Caylor (AA)
1884	Pop Snyder (AA)
1884	Will White (AA)
1882–1883	Pop Snyder (AA)

Team Records by Individual Players

Batting Leaders

	Single Season			Career		
	Name		Year	Name		Place Appearances
Batting average	Cy Seymour	.377	1905	Cy Seymour	.332	2,420
On-base %	Joe Morgan	.466	1975	Joe Morgan	.415	4,973
Slugging %	Ted Kluszewski	.642	1954	Frank Robinson	.554	6,409
OPS	Ted Kluszewski	1.049	1954	Frank Robinson	.943	6,409
Games	Leo Cardenas	163	1964	Pete Rose	2,722	12,325
At bats	Pete Rose	680	1973	Pete Rose	10,934	12,325
Runs	Bid McPhee	139	1886	Pete Rose	1,741	12,325
Hits	Pete Rose	230	1973	Pete Rose	3,358	12,325
Total Bases	George Foster	388	1977	Pete Rose	4,645	12,325
Doubles	Frank Robinson	51	1962	Pete Rose	601	12,325
Triples	John Reilly	26	1890	Bid McPhee	188	9,409
Home runs	George Foster	52	1977	Johnny Bench	389	8,669
RBIs	George Foster	149	1977	Johnny Bench	1,376	8,669
Walks	Joe Morgan	132	1975	Pete Rose	1,210	12,325
Strikeouts	Adam Dunn	195	2004	Pete Rose	1,306	12,325
Stolen bases	Hugh Nicol	138	1887	Bid McPhee	568	9,409
Extra-base hits	Frank Robinson	92	1962	Pete Rose	868	12,325
Times on base	Pete Rose	311	1969	Pete Rose	4,654	12,325

Pitching Leaders

	Single Season			Career		
	Name		Year	Name		Innings Pitched
ERA	Harry McCormick	1.52	1882	Andy Coakley	2.11	507.7
Wins	Will White	43	1883	Eppa Rixey	179	2,890.7
Won-loss %	Tom Seaver	.875	1981	Don Gullett	.674	1,187
Hits/9 IP	Mario Soto	5.96	1980	Mario Soto	7.26	1,730.3
Walks/9 IP	Red Lucas	0.74	1933	Red Lucas	1.55	1,768.7
Strikeouts	Mario Soto	274	1982	Jim Maloney	1,592	1,818.7
Strikeouts/9 IP	Mario Soto	9.57	1982	Jim Maloney	7.88	1,818.7
Games	Wayne Granger	90	1969	Pedro Bourbon	531	920.7
Saves	Jeff Brantley	44	1996	Danny Graves	172	714.7
Innings	Will White	577	1883	Eppa Rixey	2,890.7	2,890.7
Starts	Will White	64	1883	Eppa Rixey	356	2,890.7

(Continued)

Pitching Leaders (Continued)

	Single Season			Career		
	Name		Year	Name		Innings Pitched
Complete games	Will White	64	1883	Mullane	264	2,599
Shutouts	Will White	8	1882	B. Walters	32	2,355.7

Source: Drawn from data in "Cincinnati Reds Batting Leaders (seasonal and career)." http://baseball-reference.com/teams/CIN/leaders_bat.shtml; "Cincinnati Reds Pitching Leaders (seasonal and career)." http://baseball-reference.com/teams/CIN/leaders_pitch.shtml.

BIBLIOGRAPHY

Benson, Michael. *Ballparks of North America: A Comprehensive Historical Reference to Grounds, Yards, and Stadiums, 1845 to Present*. Jefferson, NC: McFarland, 1989.

Cagan, Joanna, and Neil deMause. *Field of Schemes: How the Great Stadium Swindle Turns Public Money into Private Profit*. Rev. ed. Monroe, ME: Common Cause Press, 1998.

Cincinnati Federal Writers' Project of the Works Progress Administration in Ohio. *They Built a City: 150 Years of Industrial Cincinnati*. Cincinnati, OH: Cincinnati Post, 1938.

Conner, Floyd, and John Snyder. *Day-by-Day in Cincinnati Reds History*. New York: Macmillan, 1983.

Cook, William A. *Pete Rose: Baseball's All-Time Hit King*. Jefferson, NC: McFarland, 2003.

Devine, Christopher. *Harry Wright: The Father of Professional Base Ball*. Jefferson, NC: McFarland, 2003.

Ellard, Harry. *Base Ball in Cincinnati: A History*. 1907. Reprint, Jefferson, NC: McFarland, 2004.

George, Henry. *Social Problems*. New York: Robert Schalkenbach Foundation, 1966.

Guschow, Stephen D. *The Red Stockings of Cincinnati*. Jefferson, NC: McFarland, 1998.

Hertzel, Bob. *The Big Red Machine*. Englewood Cliffs, NJ: Prentice Hall, 1976.

Johnson, Tom L. *My Story*. Ed. Elizabeth J. Hauser. New York: B. W. Huebsch, 1913.

Lowry, Philip J. *Green Cathedrals: The Ultimate Celebration of All 271 Major League and Negro League Ballparks Past and Present*. Reading, MA: Addison-Wesley, 1992.

Reston, James. *Collision at Home Plate: The Lives of Pete Rose and Bart Giamatti*. New York: HarperCollins, 1991.

Rhodes, Greg, and John Snyder. *Redleg Journal: Year by Year and Day by Day with the Cincinnati Reds since 1866.* Cincinnati, OH: Road West Publishing, 2000.

Riess, Steven A. *Touching Base: Professional Baseball and American Culture in the Progressive Era.* Rev. ed. Urbana: University of Illinois Press, 1999.

Rose, Pete, with Rick Hill. *My Prison without Bars.* Emmaus, PA: Rodale, 2004.

Ross, Steven J. *Workers on the Edge: Work, Leisure, and Politics in Industrializing Cincinnati, 1788–1890.* New York: Columbia University Press, 1985.

Tucker, Louis Leonard. *Cincinnati: A Student's Guide to Localized History.* New York: Teachers College Press, Columbia University, 1969.

Walker, Robert Harris. *Cincinnati and the Big Red Machine.* Bloomington: Indiana University Press, 1988.

Writers' Program of the Works Projects Administration in the State of Ohio. *Cincinnati: A Guide to the Queen City and Its Neighbors.* Cincinnati, OH: Wiesen-Hart Press, 1943.

5

Colorado Rockies

Thomas L. Altherr

The Colorado Rockies franchise was officially born the day after Independence Day in 1991 when the National League awarded Denver one of its two 1993 expansion entries. But in the hearts and minds of many Denverites, Coloradoans, and westerners, the arrival of major-league baseball was long overdue. In the 1980s Denver had tried unsuccessfully to lure the Chicago White Sox, Baltimore Orioles, Oakland Athletics, and San Francisco Giants. Despite the efforts of several well-heeled Denver businessmen, a major-league franchise eluded the area.

Except for interludes during the depression and World War II, Denver had boasted several successful minor-league clubs since the 1880s, when the renowned *Denver Post* tournament attracted good players every summer. Professional baseball returned in 1947 with a Western League entry, and then in 1955, under the auspices of Bob Howsam, the Denver Bears became a New York Yankees farm club in the Triple-A American Association. In the late 1950s there was some talk of including Denver in a new third-major-league proposal floated by Branch Rickey, but nothing materialized. Over the next four decades, the Denver Bears (later renamed the Denver Zephyrs in the late 1980s), under managers such as Ralph Houk and Charlie Metro, put fine Triple-A teams on the field at Bears Stadium, which was renamed Mile High Stadium.

In the late 1980s and early 1990s, the major leagues, which had not added any franchises since 1977, scouted the possibility of expansion. In addition to Denver, other candidates included Buffalo; Vancouver; Memphis; Orlando; Jacksonville; Tampa–St. Petersburg; Washington, DC; and Miami. According to one interpretation, Denver and Miami garnered the nods when Senators Tim Wirth of Colorado and Bob Graham of Florida hinted they might reopen a congressional examination of MLB's antitrust exemption status if the league did not place a franchise in their states. Denver's selling points included its successful minor-league teams, its climate, its growing population base, and the absence of any other major-league team in the region.

Anticipating a franchise, Colorado governor Roy Romer formed the Colorado Baseball Partnership to facilitate an ownership group in August 1990. A week earlier Denver-area voters had approved a 0.1 percent sales tax to fund construction of a baseball-only park to be built most likely in downtown Denver (although, ironically, the city and county of Denver did not support the levy). By March 1991 the Denver Metropolitan Stadium district chose to site the stadium at 20th and Blake Streets, two blocks from Union Station in lower downtown (LoDo). Construction costs were $215 million, of which 22 percent came from the owners. It was the first new NL stadium since Montreal's Stade Olympique opened in 1977, and the first NL park built exclusively for baseball since Dodger Stadium in 1962. A couple of days later, the ownership group announced that Coors Brewery had bought the naming rights to the new park for an indefinite period of time for $15 million.

The first ownership group included Youngstown-based businessmen John Antonucci and Mickey Monus, whose shady financial dealings with his Pharmor stores had landed him jail time. By September 1992, a local trucking magnate, Jerry McMorris, and other Coloradoan minority partners bought out the non-Coloradoan ownership. Eventually Charles and Richard Montfort, Greeley meatpacking tycoons, joined with McMorris in sort of a tripartite ownership arrangement. After some debate about a team name, which included the traditional Denver Bears and the Denver Grizzlies, the franchise settled on the Colorado Rockies to evoke a regional image. After all, the Rockies would be the only major-league club between Kansas City and California. The club's uniform colors were purple, black, and white, with occasional pinstripes. Former major-league pitcher Bob Gebhard was the club's first general manager, serving until midway through the 1999 season. Dan O'Dowd succeeded Gebhard. Don Baylor held the managerial reigns through the 1998 season.

In 1992 the Rockies held an expansion draft, made trades, and signed free agents that netted several young prospects, especially pitcher David Nied, and some veteran players, most notably first baseman Andres Galarraga and outfielder Dante Bichette. But as would be expected of an expansion team, rosters were very fluid the first few seasons. Players came and went until some stability emerged in the mid-1990s with a slugging lineup dubbed "the Blake Street Bombers" that featured Bichette, Galarraga, Vinny Castilla, Larry Walker, and Ellis Burks. The Rockies became known as an explosive offense-minded team (although not necessarily on the road). Finding long-term effective pitching, however, proved more frustrating.

THE FIRST THREE YEARS

In 1993 and 1994, the Rockies played at Mile High Stadium, a venue more geared to football. For the first home stand, the club constructed temporary bleachers in center field to seat 80,000 fans. Eric Young, leading off the first game at Mile High, hit a home run to left field, prompting much stomping and raucous cheers. The Rockies stayed at Mile High throughout 1993 and 1994. The Rockies finished in sixth in 1993 (67–95) with a payroll of just $8,829,000. Salaries were nearly tripled one year later to $23,654,508, when the team improved its record (53–64) in the strike-shortened season of 1994.

By 1995, however, Coors Field was completed, with 50,000 seats, including 63 luxury boxes and 4,500 club-level seats. It aimed at providing the atmosphere of the old-time ballparks with hand-positioned brick and an old-fashioned clock tower over the main entrance. The playing field is asymmetrical and has an underground heating system that instantly melts snow.

After the protracted 1994–95 strike, Dante Bichette sent Rockies fans home happy with an extra-innings home run to win the team's first game at Coors. Over the years Coors Field has been the subject of much praise for its beauty and design, but also much criticism. Hitters seemed to have an unfair advantage in the thinner air, and pitchers complained that their pitches broke less than at lower elevations. One recent interpretation, however, suggested that wind currents in the Platte River Valley are more to blame for the home runs than the thinner air. In some years, moreover, other parks, such as Houston's, produced more home runs than did Coors.

In 1995 the Rockies thrilled their fans by squeaking into the NL playoffs as the wild-card team. They became the first expansion team to reach the playoffs in their third year, with a 77–67 record, leading the NL in offense (5.45 runs per game) while giving up the most runs (5.44). Baseball purists who derided the wild card became enthusiasts overnight. Unfortunately, the club faced the strong Atlanta Braves in the first round. Colorado dropped the series in four games, winning only the third game. The first game remains controversial for Rockies fans because manager Don Baylor found himself with only pitcher Lance Painter available to pinch-hit in the bottom of the ninth. Despite losing in the first round, Baylor won the NL Manager of the Year Award. The Rockies won 83 games the next two years and led the NL in batting both years, but they also led the league in runs allowed. In 1997 the Rockies risked fan discontent by releasing popular first baseman Andres Galarraga, but his replacement, former star college quarterback Todd Helton, quickly made fans forget about Galarraga.

The highly popular Coors Field was the site of 1998's All-Star Game. For a week before the game baseball fans reveled in the FanFest activities. Ken Griffey Jr. beat out Jim Thome in the Home Run Derby contest. The actual game turned into a slugfest, the highest-scoring match in All-Star history. The American League won 13–8, and Roberto Alomar took home MVP honors.

Red, white, and blue Tyco "Glory" beanie babies, handed out as a promotional giveaway, touched off a frenzy of selling and speculation over the next few weeks as hot souvenirs.

During the 1998 season the club fell to fourth with a losing record of 77–85, despite again leading in hitting (.291), while the team's ERA (5.20) was second worst of 16 teams. Larry Walker's .363 and Dante Bichette's 219 hits led the NL. Veteran skipper Jim Leyland, whose Florida Marlins had won the 1997 World Series, took over as manager for 1999, but the club fell to fifth (72–90) despite Walker's league-leading .379 batting average. Leyland left after a year and was succeeded by Buddy Bell, who got the $71 million team into fourth place (82–80). First baseman Todd Helton had a sensational season in 2000, leading the league in batting (.372), RBIs (147), hits (216), doubles (59), slugging (.698), and total bases (405). But the squad fell to fifth in 2001. Leaders in offense, they were the worst in defense. Bell's tenure as manager lasted until late April 2002, when he was fired and replaced by Clint Hurdle. The Rockies placed fourth in Hurdle's first three seasons, including a dismal 68–94 in 2004 despite a payroll of $67,390,000. They did even worse in 2005, finishing last in the NL West with a dismal 67–95 record.

From time to time, critics have complained that the Rockies have fallen into a pattern of looking for one pitcher to save the club and catapult it to success. In the Rockies' inaugural season this mantle fell on Greg W. Harris, who repaid his enthusiastic greeting after his arrival from San Diego with a dismal 1–8 record. Later examples have included pitchers Bret Saberhagen, Bill Swift, Daryl Kile, Mike Hampton, and Denny Neagle. Each met with little success, although Hampton did make the All-Star team in 2001. More successful pitching came from Kevin Ritz, Pedro Astacio, and 2002 Rookie of the Year Jason Jennings. But overall, Coors Field chewed up many young hurlers.

Two Rockies, outfielder Larry Walker and first baseman Todd Helton, have performed well enough to warrant serious consideration from the Baseball Hall of Fame once their careers end. Walker, who was an established star in Montreal, came to the club for the 1995 season. Over nine seasons Walker thrilled hometown fans with his home-run power, astute baserunning, and superb defensive plays, especially his throwing arm. He won the NL MVP Award in 1997. Through 2003, in his nine years with the team, Walker batted .344, clubbed 252 home runs, and knocked in 828 runs, as well as amassing 459 walks and 124 stolen bases. Larry took home Gold Gloves in 1997–99 and 2001–2. But in early 2004 Walker and his $12.7 million salary were traded to the Cardinals. Through 2005, Helton has compiled a career batting average of .337, the highest lifetime average of any current major leaguer; slugged 271 home runs; and knocked in 915 runs, with a slugging percentage of .607 in nine seasons. In 2000, he flirted with .400 much of the season, and in 2003 he narrowly missed the league batting crown with a .358 average, all the while fielding his position excellently. He won Gold Gloves in 2001, 2002, and 2004.

Larry Walker slides safely into third in a game against the San Diego Padres, 1997. © AP / Wide World Photos

ATTENDANCE

In their first season, the Rockies set a major-league attendance record of 4,483,350, which still stands today. Colorado and Rocky Mountain–area fans starved for major-league baseball in Denver thronged to the ballpark. The team was headed for even larger attendance in 1994, averaging 57,570 per game when the players struck, shortening the season. Whenever popular out of town teams such as the Chicago Cubs or St. Louis Cardinals came to town, transplanted residents from the Midwest crowded the stadium. Seeing a Rockies game at Mile High Stadium or later at Coors Field and socializing at the nearby LoDo watering holes quickly became a trendy activity for Denverites. Attendance stayed strong for the club's first eight seasons, topping the majors for the first seven seasons. By seasons 10 and 11 the novelty had worn off. Combined with the Rockies fielding a noncompetitive team, attendance dropped. Still, the Rockies usually draw more fans than the overall league average.

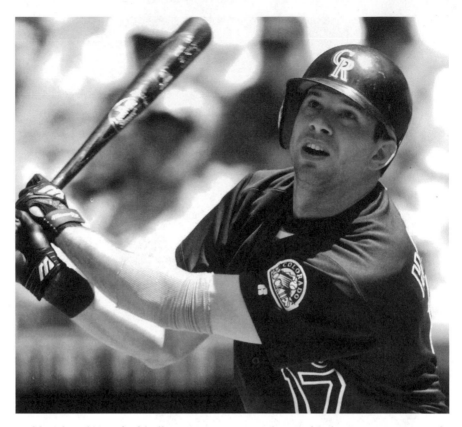

Todd Helton hits a foul ball in a game against the Cardinals, 2001. © AP / Wide World Photos

ECONOMIC IMPACT

It is difficult to assess accurately the exact economic impact the Rockies have had on Denver and Colorado. The most positive proof, however, is the economic rejuvenation of the LoDo area. During the first few seasons, new restaurants and stores proliferated in the district, new lofts became hot properties, and the area's old skid-row qualities vanished. The district attracted tourist and entertainment seekers even on non-game-days and during the off-season. But it is clear that the Rockies have failed to generate the same amount as the NFL Broncos and the NHL Avalanche. The Rockies have done some community-outreach programs, especially funding or building a number of baseball venues throughout the metro area for youths. As a business entity, the team has proved profitable. According to *Forbes* magazine, McMorris's consortium paid a $95 million franchise fee in 1993, and the franchise appreciated in value to $311 million in the early twenty-first century. It has hovered around the $300 million mark in recent years. In terms of payroll, the owners have kept the Rockies in the middle of the pack, splurging in some years and retrenching during others.

Now in its 12th season, the Colorado Rockies have provided fans with much excitement and much disappointment. The Broncos and the Avalanche have won Super Bowls and Stanley Cups respectively, and in the 2003–4 season the formerly dormant NBA Denver Nuggets made the play-offs. But the Rockies have bumbled along in mediocrity, typically in fourth or fifth place in the West. Whatever their on-field lapses, however, the Colorado Rockies have been an outstanding success as an entertaining franchise, with a beautiful ballpark, attendances that make most other major-league clubs salivate, and economically vibrant environs.

NOTABLE ACHIEVEMENTS

Most Valuable Players

Year	Name	Position
1997	Larry Walker	OF

Rookies of the Year

Year	Name	Position
2002	Jason Jennings	P

Batting Champions

Year	Name	#
1993	Andres Galarraga	.370
1998	Larry Walker	.363
1999	Larry Walker	.379
2000	Todd Helton	.372
2001	Larry Walker	.350

Home-Run Champions

Year	Name	#
1995	Dante Bichette	40
1996	Andres Galarraga	47
1997	Larry Walker	49

POSTSEASON APPEARANCES

NL Wild Cards

Year	Record	Manager
1995	77–67	Don Baylor

MANAGERS

2002–	Clint Hurdle
2000–2002	Buddy Bell
1999	Jim Leyland
1993–1998	Don Baylor

Team Records by Individual Players

Batting Leaders

	Single Season			Career		
	Name		Year	Name		Plate Appearances
Batting average	Larry Walker	.379	1999	Todd Helton	.337	5,424
On-base %	Todd Helton	.469	2004	Todd Helton	.433	5,424
Slugging %	Larry Walker	.720	1997	Larry Walker	.618	4,795
OPS	Larry Walker	1.172	1997	Larry Walker	1.044	4,795
Games	Vinny Castilla/ Neifi Perez	162	1998	Todd Helton	1,279	5,429
At bats	Neifi Perez	690	1999	Vinny Castilla	4,078	4,429
Runs	Larry Walker	143	1997	Larry Walker	892	4,795
Hits	Dante Bichette	219	1998	Todd Helton	1,372	5,424
Total bases	Larry Walker	409	1997	Larry Walker	2,520	4,795
Doubles	Todd Helton	59	2000	Todd Helton	373	5,424
Triples	Neifi Perez	11	1999	Neifi Perez	49	2,936
Home runs	Larry Walker	49	1997	Todd Helton	271	5,424
RBIs	Andres Galarraga	150	1996	Todd Helton	915	5,424
Walks	Todd Helton	127	2004	Todd Helton	773	5,424
Strikeouts	Andres Galarraga	157	1996	Larry Walker	659	4,795
Stolen bases	Eric Young	53	1996	Eric Young	180	2,450
Extra-base hits	Todd Helton	105	2001	Todd Helton	668	5,424
Times on base	Todd Helton	323	2000	Todd Helton	2,348	5,424

Pitching Leaders

	Single Season			Career		
	Name		Year	Name		Innings Pitched
ERA	Joe Kennedy	3.66	2004	Armando Reynoso	4.65	503
Wins	Kevin Ritz	17	1996	Pedro Astacio	53	827.3
Won-loss %	Julian Tavarez	.688	2000	Jason Jennings	.533	729
Hits/9 IP	Kevin Ritz	8.88	1995	Shawn Chacon	8.85	552.3
Walks/9 IP	Armando Reynoso	2.61	1996	John Thomson	2.77	611

(Continued)

Pitching Leaders

	Single Season			Career		
	Name		**Year**	**Name**		**Innings Pitched**
Strikeouts	Pedro Astacio	210	1999	Pedro Astacio	749	827.3
Strikeouts/9IP	Pedro Astacio	8.85	2000	Pedro Astacio	8.15	827.3
Games	Todd Jones	79	2002	Steve Reed	461	499
Saves	Jose Jimenez	41	2002	Jose Jimenez	102	300.7
Innings	Pedro Astacio	232	1999	Pedro Astacio	827.3	827.3
Starts	Kevin Ritz	36	1996	Pedro Astacio	129	827.3
Complete Games	Pedro Astacio	7	1999	Pedro Astacio	14	827.3
Shutouts	Bailey	2	1997	Bailey	2	356

Source: Drawn from data in "Colorado Rockies Batting Leaders (seasonal and career)." http://baseball-reference.com/ teams/COL/leaders_bat.shtml; "Colorado Rockies Pitching Leaders (seasonal and career)." http://baseball-reference. com/teams/COL/leaders_pitch.shtml.

BIBLIOGRAPHY

Gottlieb, Alan. *In the Shadow of the Rockies: An Outsider's Look inside a New Major League Baseball Team.* Niwot, CO: Roberts Rinehart Publishers, 1994.

Kravitz, Bob. *Mile High Madness: A Year with the Colorado Rockies.* New York: Random House, 1994.

Moss, Rivin, and Mark Foster. *Home Run in the Rockies: The History of Baseball in Colorado.* Denver: Publication Design, 1994.

Munsey and Suppes. "Ballparks." http://www.ballparks.com/baseball/index.htm.

Page, Brian, Frederick Chambers, and Clyde Zaidins. "Into Thin Air: What's All the Fuss about Coors Field?" In *Above the Fruited Plain: Baseball in the Rocky Mountain West,* ed. Thomas L. Altherr, 53–62. Cleveland, OH: Society for American Baseball Research, 2003.

Sumner, Jan. *Fat Pitch: My Six Seasons with the Rockies.* Denver: JaDan, 2000.

6

Florida Marlins

Kevin B. Witherspoon

The Florida Marlins' 2003 World Series victory capped a remarkable first decade for one of Major League Baseball's youngest franchises. Over that span, the Marlins twice won the World Series, endured the growing pains of an expansion franchise and rebuilding after their first championship, and changed ownership and philosophies several times. The South Florida market, with its endless urban sprawl and large immigrant and seasonal population, has produced unique conditions around the Marlins. It is a team in a large media market often forced to behave like a small-market franchise. The Marlins' history is closely linked with many other themes of a modern baseball club: expansion and contraction; free agency and salary issues; a fickle fan base; the influence of Hispanic players, fans, and coaches; corporate ties; and civic clashes over a new stadium.

Before gaining a major-league franchise, Florida was long the site of spring-training complexes and minor-league teams. Floridians who longed for a major-league team saw their hopes piqued in the mid-1980s as MLB executives began to discuss the expansion of the National League. In 1990, the NL announced a short list of candidates, including three groups from Florida: Tampa–St. Petersburg, Orlando, and South Florida. H. Wayne Huizenga, owner of Blockbuster Video and 15 percent of the Miami Dolphins, made the South Florida bid. Huizenga (worth $1.875 billion in 1998) appealed to baseball executives because he would be the sole owner of his team, rather than a group of owners. He also owned Joe Robbie Stadium (later renamed Pro Player Stadium and finally Dolphins Stadium), which with $10 million in improvements would be baseball-ready, so his bid did not hinge on the building of a new stadium. Finally, through his close friend and fellow Blockbuster executive Carl Barger of the Pittsburgh Pirates, Huizenga already had ties with MLB and the expansion committee. Skeptics argued that a major-league franchise in Florida would dampen enthusiasm for spring training and minor-league teams, that the weather in Florida was unsuitable for a full baseball schedule, and that Florida's "snow-bird" and transplant residents would not support a team. Such arguments could not overcome Huizenga's bid, however, and on June 10, 1991, Commissioner Fay Vincent announced that South Florida, along with Colorado, was awarded a franchise to begin major-league play in 1993. The team's salaries were $18 million, fourth lowest in the majors. At the end of the season the franchise was worth an estimated $81 million.

The Marlins, along with the Colorado Rockies, set about in late 1991 and 1992 to build a team. Modern expansion franchises in virtually every sport are expected to be more competitive than expansion teams of earlier eras, and fans tend to lose interest quickly in a losing team, even a relatively new one. While the pressure was great to produce a winning team, the Marlins struggled through the growing pains typical of an expansion franchise. Through signing free agents, open tryouts, and the amateur draft, the Marlins fielded several minor-league teams in 1992. In November, MLB held an expansion draft in which both the Marlins and Rockies selected players from the other major-league teams. Those expansion players made up the core of the Marlins' roster for its first several seasons. The players available were serviceable major leaguers or overpriced superstars that both expansion clubs avoided. The inaugural Marlins roster consisted of players such as Jeff Conine, Pat Rapp, Charlie Hough, Bryan Harvey, and one true superstar—Gary Sheffield, acquired midway through the season. The team's payroll was $42.1 million, the third lowest in MLB. The club, under manager Rene Lachemann, won a respectable 64 games and drew over 3 million in attendance.

The Marlins added gradually to their talent pool and win total, finishing the next three years with records of 51–64 (in the strike-shortened 1994 season), 67–75, and 80–82. With each season, though, attendance declined and financial losses mounted. It seemed that the skeptics might have been right in doubting the loyalty of South Florida fans, who were less and less inclined to pay steep prices to watch a losing team. Theories behind the flagging attendance abounded: the player strike of 1994 damaged attendance around the league; the team was losing; the weather made watching games miserable, as it was often hot and muggy, with many rain delays and rainouts; Miami was a football town, with fans supporting the Dolphins and the University of Miami Hurricanes and little else; the team had no real home, struggling to draw fans from a huge area of urban sprawl rather than a fiercely loyal community; Joe Robbie Stadium was located at the northern edge of Dade County, and poor public transportation hindered access for fans living in Miami; the Hispanic fan base was uncommonly impatient and fickle, and could not afford high ticket prices; and after the perfect 1972 Miami Dolphins season, no team was good enough to satisfy South Floridians. Comparisons to their companion expansion team left the Marlins deflated as well, as the Rockies shattered attendance records and made the playoffs in only their third season. For all these reasons, Marlins attendance fell to 1.7 million in 1996, 13th in the NL. Since then the team has always been 14th or 15th in attendance.

Huizenga, claiming losses of $20 million that season, made a desperate attempt to salvage fan interest, and money, by investing heavily in free agents prior to the 1997 season. He hoped that victories on the field would translate into more fans in the stands and encourage interest in a new baseball-only stadium, deemed necessary for the survival of the franchise. In 1996 he brought in top pitchers Kevin Brown (1.89 ERA) and Al Leiter (2.93). The following year he invested a record $89 million on free agents, including five-year contracts for Alex Fernandez ($35 million) and Moises Alou ($25 million) and $23.3 million over four years for Bobby Bonilla. The 1997 team had a $47.8 million payroll, seventh highest in the majors. Huizenga also hired Jim Leyland, who had had great success as manager of the Pittsburgh Pirates, for $1.2 million per year. The gambit paid off, and the Marlins finished the season at 92–70, second place in the NL East, good enough to secure the wild-card bid. They swept San Francisco in three games in the NL Division Series and defeated Atlanta four games to two in the NL Championship Series to reach the World Series. There, they outlasted the Cleveland Indians in a classic seven-game series, with shortstop Edgar Renteria hitting the game-winning single in the bottom of the 11th inning of game seven. Livan Hernandez was Series MVP.

Despite the championship, Huizenga reported losses of $34 million. Fielding a winning team loaded with stars, the team drew only about 2.3 million fans in the regular season, and struggled to fill the stadium during the playoffs. With no new stadium deal, Huizenga authorized a purge of his expensive roster, and within a year virtually every high-priced star in the lineup was gone. Long-time fan favorite Jeff Conine was traded to Kansas City, and others traded included Alou, Brown, Leiter, and Robb Nen. The biggest deal came after the beginning of the 1998 season, when Sheffield, Bonilla, Charles Johnson, and Jim Eisenrich were traded to the Los Angeles Dodgers for Todd Zeile and Mike Piazza, who was himself soon traded to the Mets. Victim of the inflated cost of operating a major-league franchise, the Marlins' roster was left with few quality players, and the team became the first defending World Series champion to lose more than 100 games the following season.

The fire sale drew the ire of Marlin fans and baseball purists, as well many observers who questioned the legitimacy of Huizenga's accounting. Huizenga publicly moaned about the losses incurred by the team, but made no mention of the considerable profit earned by Pro Player Stadium as well as many other assets. Economist Andrew Zimbalist estimated that Huizenga actually netted over $13 million for the 1997 season, crediting luxury suites, club seats, parking, concessions, and naming-rights money all to the ballpark, owned by a separate company, instead of the Marlins. Huizenga planned to sell the team for tax purposes and further gains rather than eliminate a losing part of his business empire.

As the wins left, so did the fans. Huizenga, once lauded in South Florida, was vilified by the fans, and his frustrations mounted after the World Series win. He finally jettisoned the team in January 1999, selling it to John W. Henry, a hedge-fund manager, Boca Raton resident, and minority owner of the New York Yankees. By then Huizenga had cut the payroll to $15 million, lowest in MLB.

In 2001 the Marlins lost $27.7 million from baseball operations according to MLB, offset by $18.6 million in revenue sharing, resulting in a deficit of $9,180,000 (*Forbes*, however, reported the Marlins made $14 million). The unfavorable lease on Huizenga's ballpark resulted in local revenues of just $4 million, second lowest in the majors, and overall the total local revenue was just $36.1 million, third lowest in the majors.

With no new park and increasing fan apathy, the Marlins were mentioned among several candidates for contraction in October 2001. In December, Henry sold the team to Jeffrey Loria, formerly the owner of the Expos, who quickly felt the brunt of fan disinterest. Only the anonymous purchase of 18,000 tickets on the final day of the 2002 season kept the Marlins from the lowest attendance of any team, finishing with 813,118, just ahead of Montreal.

From such dubious circumstances sprung the 2003 World Series champion team, a much more surprising champion than the 1997 version. That team, filled with free agents and superstars, the seventh-highest-paid squad in MLB at $47.8 million, emerged from spring training with great optimism and spent the entire season near the top of the rankings. At the start of the 2003 season, the team was worth $172 million. The team's mediocre early performance led to the firing of manager Jeff Torborg in May, replaced by 72-year-old Jack McKeon. The 2003 Marlins squad assumed something of a magical quality, though, and finished the season with the best record in the league after June 1. This team was made up of bargain players. Juan Pierre, acquired via a trade with the Rockies, was an excellent base stealer and leadoff hitter, and free agent Ivan "Pudge" Rodriguez, signed for one season at $10 million, anchored the team. Virtually every other impact player came from within the Marlins system. Two rookies, pitcher Dontrelle Willis (who won Rookie of the Year) and outfielder Miguel Cabrera, made key contributions. Young stars A. J. Burnett, Brad Penny, and Josh Beckett, who blossomed in the postseason, anchored a solid pitching staff. The Marlins won with defense, pitching, speed, intelligent play, and an intangible chemistry and faith in each other. In the playoffs, they overcame the San Francisco Giants 3–1 in the NLDS and the Chicago Cubs in seven games in the NLCS. In the World Series, the Marlins beat the New York Yankees, winning the deciding game six on the road at Yankee Stadium. Josh Beckett was Series MVP. The Yankees represented one of baseball's oldest and most storied teams, filled with high-priced and experienced players, and had one of the highest payrolls in the league. The Marlins were one of baseball's newest teams and a possible target for contraction, with a roster dominated by young players with little playoff experience and one of the lowest payrolls. In a league lately dominated by big-spending teams, the Marlins, along with the successful recent teams of the Oakland A's, Arizona Diamondbacks, and Anaheim Angels, proved that the team with the largest payroll does not always win the championship.

The Marlins missed the wild card in 2004 and 2005, finishing third both seasons. The failure in 2005 was a big disappointment, as the team faded in the last week. There were terrific performances by Dontrelle Willis, who went 22–10 with a 2.63 ERA, and free agent Carlos Delgado, who hit 33 homers with 115 RBIs. Jack McKeon resigned as manager after the season.

The Marlins represent some of the main current themes in MLB. From the beginning the franchise was particularly attentive to Hispanic fans in South Florida and throughout Latin America. For its inaugural season, the team launched a media campaign declaring the Marlins "the Team of the Americas," with sales agents throughout Latin America. The team arranged promotional travel packages with American Airlines for fans travel-

Alex Golzalez leaps on Derek Lee and Ivan Rodriguez after the Marlins defeated the New York Yankees to win the 2003 World Series. © AP / Wide World Photos

ing to Miami, and the airline was a core advertiser in the team's early years. No detail escaped the Latin influence, as the concession stands offered many traditional Cuban dishes, and the radio play-by-play man called home runs in both English and Spanish: "Wave it bye-bye" and *Hasta la vista.*" It is no coincidence that Hispanic players have not only been favorites with the fans, but have also played key roles in the team's success. The team has always been peppered with Hispanic players, and it has had an advantage in attracting free agents, many of whom feel at home in heavily Hispanic Miami. Its first signee in 1991 was Clemente Nunez, a 16-year-old pitcher from the Dominican Republic. Puerto Rican Benito Santiago hit the club's first home run in its inaugural game in 1993, and his teammate Cuban-born first baseman Orestes Destrade was another favorite of the fans. The most sensational player signing in the team's history was that of Livan Hernandez, who defected from Cuba in 1995, quickly signed a four-year, $4.5 million contract with the Marlins, and went on to star on the 1997 championship team. A close second was Miami native and Cuban American Alex Fernandez, whose signing prior to the 1997 season sparked ticket sales and interest from his hometown fans. The 1997 World Series–winning hit came off the bat of Edgar Renteria, from Colombia. More recent stars have included Luis Castillo, who had a team record 35-game hitting streak in 2002 and was a key part of the 2003 championship run; Ivan Rodriguez, who had clutch hits throughout the playoffs and the World Series; and Venezuelan Miguel Cabrera.

Another recurring theme for the Marlins, as well as many other professional franchises, has been the stadium dispute. The stadium was a key element in Wayne Huizenga's bid for an expansion franchise, as his was the only bid including a stadium already in place. Huizenga anticipated that Joe Robbie Stadium was only a temporary home, with a new baseball-only stadium to be built in the near future. The new stadium never came. The labor issues of the mid-1990s left most baseball fans unenthusiastic about supporting billionaire owners like Huizenga, and a bill proposing a $60 million tax break to pay for improvements to Pro Player Stadium failed in 1997, a key reason for Huizenga's sale of the team. Plans for a $325 million athletic park and new retractable-roof stadium in Miami, proposed in 2003, failed to pass the Miami–Dade County Commission. Most recently, the Marlins and the city of Miami have been unable to compromise the funding mechanisms for a $420 million stadium next to Dolphins Stadium. In the meantime, the Marlins play in Dolphins Stadium and suffer rain-filled South Florida summers.

The Florida Marlins face many challenges moving ahead. The stadium issue took a bitter turn when team officials met with Las Vegas mayor Oscar Goodman early in 2005 to discuss the possibility of moving the team. In response, Wayne Huizenga announced that the Marlins would no longer be allowed to use Dolphins Stadium after 2010. While the Marlins and the city of Miami seem reasonably close to a stadium deal, nearly 15 years of frustration may prove insurmountable. The Marlins also face the challenge of remaining competitive after their 2003 World Series title. While they avoided a purge like 1997, they did not re-sign catcher Ivan Rodriguez. The payroll fell to 25th in the majors ($42 million), and the team has not yet returned to championship form. Also in doubt is the loyalty of the South Florida fans, who have tended to abandon the team during losing seasons. Such obstacles are merely the price of operating a modern franchise, though, a task at which the young Florida Marlins have excelled thus far.

NOTABLE ACHIEVEMENTS

Rookie of the Year

Year	Name	Position
2003	Dontrelle Willis	P

ERA Champion

Year	Name	ERA
1996	Kevin Brown	1.89

No-Hitters

Name	Date
Al Leiter	05/11/1996
Kevin Brown	06/10/1997
A.J. Burnett	05/12/2001

POSTSEASON APPEARANCES

NL Wild Cards

Year	Record	Manager
1997	92–70	Jim Leyland
2003	91–71	Jeff Torborg
		Jack McKeon

NL Pennants

Year	Record	Manager
1997	92–70	Jim Leyland
2003	91–71	Jeff Torborg
		Jack McKeon

World Championships

Year	Opponent	MVP
1997	Cleveland	Livan Hernandez
2003	New York	Josh Beckett

MANAGERS

2006–	Joe Girardi
2003–2005	Jack McKeon
2002–2003	Jeff Torborg
2001	Tony Perez
1999–2001	John Boles
1997–1998	Jim Leyland
1996	John Boles
1996	Cookie Rojas
1993–1996	Rene Lachemann

Team Records by Individual Players

Batting Leaders

	Single	Season		Career		
	Name		Year	Name		Plate Appearances
Batting average	Luis Castillo	.334	2000	Juan Pierre	.303	2,212
On-base %	Gary Sheffield	.465	1996	Gary Sheffield	.426	2,358
Slugging %	Gary Sheffield	.624	1996	Gary Sheffield	.543	2,358
OPS	Gary Sheffield	1.090	1996	Gary Sheffield	.970	2,358
Games	Jeff Conine	162	1993	Luis Castillo	1128	4,966
At bats	Juan Pierre	678	2004	Luis Castillo	4,347	4,966
Runs	Cliff Floyd	123	2001	Luis Castillo	675	4966
Hits	Juan Pierre	221	2004	Luis Castillo	1,273	4,966
Total bases	Miguel Cabrera	324	2005	Mike Lowell	1641	4,003
Doubles	Cliff Floyd	45	1998	Mike Lowell	241	4,003
Triples	Juan Pierre	13	2005	Luis Castillo	42	4,966
Home runs	Gary Sheffield	42	1996	Mike Lowell	143	4,003
RBIs	Preston Wilson	121	2000	Mike Lowell	578	4,003
Walks	Gary Sheffield	142	1996	Luis Castillo	533	4,966
Strikeouts	Preston Wilson	187	2000	Derrick Lee	734	3,251
Stolen bases	Juan Pierre	65	2003	Luis Castillo	281	4,966
Extra-base hits	Cliff Floyd	79	2001	Mike Lowell	387	400
Times on base	Gary Sheffield	315	1996	Luis Castillo	1,814	4,966

Pitching Leaders

	Single Season			Career		
	Name			**Name**		**Innings Pitched**
ERA	Kevin Brown	1.89	1996	Dontrelle WIllis	3.27	594
Wins	Dontrelle Willis	22	2001	A. J.Burnett	49	853.7
Won-loss %	Dontrelle Willis	.700	2003	Josh Beckett	.547	609
Hits/9 IP	Al Leiter	6.39	1996	A. J. Burnett	7.58	853.7
Walks/9 IP	Kevin Brown	1.27	1996	Dontrelle Willis	2.64	594
Strikeouts	Ryan Dempster	209	2000	A. J. Burnett	753	853.7
Strikeouts/ 9 IP	A. J. Burnett	8.94	2002	Josh Beckett	8.97	609
Games	Braden Looper	78	2002	Braden Looper	368	388
Saves	Armando Benitez	47	2004	Robb Nen	108	3,140
Innings	Kevin Brown	237.3	1997	A. J. Burnett	853.7	853.7
Starts	Ryan Dempster	34	2001	A. J. Burnett	131	853.7
Complete games	Livan Hernandez	9	1998	A. J. Burnett	14	853.7
Shutouts	A. J. Burnett	5	2002	A. J. Burnett	8	853.7

Source: Drawn from data in "Florida Marlins Batting Leaders (seasonal and career)." http://baseball reference.com/ teams/FLA/leaders_bat.shtml; "Florida Marlins Pitching Leaders (seasonal and career)." http://baseball-reference.com/ teams/FLA/leaders_pitch.shtml.

BIBLIOGRAPHY

Angell, Roger. "Fish Story." *New Yorker*, November 27, 1997, 79–87.

Nichols, John. *The History of the Florida Marlins.* Mankato, MN: Creative Education, 1999.

Rosenbaum, Dave. *If They Don't Win It's a Shame: The Year the Marlins Bought the World Series.* Tampa, FL: Quality Books, 1998.

Unbelievable! The 2003 World Series Champion Florida Marlins. Chicago: Triumph Books, 2003.

Zimbalist, Andrew. "A Miami Fish Story." *New York Times Magazine*, October 26, 1998, 26–30.

7

Houston Astros

Benjamin D. Lisle

The first recorded game for a Houston baseball club was on April 21, 1867. Over 1,000 saw the Houston Stonewalls crush the Galveston Robert E. Lees 35–2, allegedly on the grounds of the Battle of San Jacinto, where Sam Houston's Texan army had routed Santa Ana's Mexican army in 1836. For the next two decades, various amateur club teams played in Houston, forming and dissolving without much record of their existence.

The Texas League played its inaugural season in 1888, starting the year with teams in Houston, Fort Worth, Dallas, Austin, San Antonio, and Galveston. By the end of the season, only Dallas and Austin clubs remained. The weaker teams, beset by poor attendance and incompetence, had gradually dropped out. The Houston club reappeared in 1889 under new management and, renamed "the Babies," won the Texas League title. The league and its teams remained highly unstable for the remainder of the century.

Houston's 1905 Texas League installment was renamed "the Buffaloes"—a name that stuck for the remainder of the club's existence through 1961. In 1925 the St. Louis Cardinals acquired the club for its farm system, an affiliation that lasted until 1958. Funded by Branch Rickey, the club broke ground on a new 18-acre, 12,000-seat stadium in early 1928 on the east side of Houston, adjacent to the interurban railroad tracks. Buff Stadium would be the home of Houston baseball until 1962.

Houston boomed in the postwar years and already had a larger population than most major-league cities. After moving to Houston in 1946, George Kirksey, a former sportswriter who had started a small public-relations firm, committed himself to landing the city a major-league club. Lacking the financial means himself, he tried to cobble together investor groups to purchase a club. However, the major leagues seemed uninterested in expanding so far south, and Kirksey was unable to sell the idea of relocation to discontented owners of existing clubs.

In 1956, Kirksey joined forces with Craig Cullinan, a Texaco heir, who two years later formed the Houston Sports Association (HSA), a syndicate of 28 investors. Cullinan and Kirksey's fundamental problem was that local civic leaders wouldn't support the building of a stadium until the city was promised a franchise, but no franchises would move without a ballpark in place. The Harris County Board of Park Commissioners was created to put together a proposal for a new stadium to encourage the arrival of MLB. On their recommendation, Houston voters on July 25, 1958, approved a $20 million bond issue to finance a domed stadium that would alleviate the problems of summer heat.

The HSA applied for admission to both the American and National Leagues in 1958, and later joined other minor-league cities to start a third major league, the Continental League. At that time, Senator Estes Kefauver of Tennessee chaired a subcommittee exploring the application of antitrust laws to professional sports leagues. Bill 3483 emerged from this subcommittee, and it clearly stated that preventing the creation and operation of a new major-league baseball club was an antitrust violation. Kefauver was a close friend of Senator Lyndon B. Johnson of Texas. Roy Hofheinz, who had aided Johnson's political campaigning in Harris County in the 1940s, lobbied Johnson heavily. Johnson pushed for an early vote on the bill, which nearly resulted in its passage. Major-league owners, once confident in an easy victory, were spooked by this near defeat, and were ready to negotiate with potential Continental League cities to head off the creation of a new major league. The expansion committee added two new teams to the AL in 1961 and the NL in 1962.

Houston's baseball group was strengthened when Kirksey convinced local oilman R. E. "Bob" Smith, whose net worth approached $1 billion, to increase his financial commitment to the HSA. Smith wanted his business partner, Roy Hofheinz, to be involved as well. The colorful Hofheinz had been the youngest man ever to become a U.S. county judge, at age 24, and as mayor of Houston he had encouraged the city's business boom. The duo provided the HSA with a unique combination of wealth and political savvy. Hofheinz also brought with him the vision of an air-conditioned stadium.

The NL awarded New York and Houston expansion franchises on October 17, 1960. The league required a $5 million deposit for the costs of getting the franchise running and an additional $1.75 million to be spent on players in an expansion draft following the 1961 season. When 12 of the original 27 HSA stockholders were unwilling to back their earlier pledges, Cullinan had to offer larger ownership roles to Smith and Hofheinz, who each ended up with 33 percent of HSA stock (Smith financed Hofheinz's share), while Cullinan held 15 percent and Kirksey just 2 percent.

Hofheinz began vigorously promoting his vision of a domed stadium to anyone who would listen, lugging a $35,000 model of the promised structure around the city. Houston voters, with an NL franchise in hand, approved Propositions 1 and 2 on January 31, 1961. Proposition 1 provided $18 million in bonds for the construction of a stadium and acquisition of a site. It passed by a vote of 62,023 to 54,204. Proposition 2 allowed for $4 million in bonds to build access roads and bridges to the site, and it was approved by a vote of 64,041 to 48,292. It was the largest turnout in the city for a bond election ever. Precincts in southern and western Houston (where the stadium would be located) tended to vote for the issue, while those in northern and eastern Houston either voted against it or passed it by a slim margin. It was particularly supported by black precincts.

African American reformers linked the desegregation of public facilities in Houston to the city's drive for a major-league baseball team. Quentin Mease, a Houston activist, threatened to mobilize the black vote against the stadium if it were not fully desegregated. Local television producer Jack Harris told Hofheinz, "Have you thought what will happen when the Giants come to Houston? . . . You can't have Willie Mays and the other ballplayers staying at a segregated hotel." Hofheinz and other business leaders agreed. More interested in financial spoils and prestige than Jim Crow, they collaborated with local media outlets to desegregate downtown stores and restaurants without news coverage, effectively preventing organized resistance. *Houston Chronicle* publisher John T. Jones, whose Houston Endowment owned the Rice, Lamar, and McKinney hotels, helped end the whites-only policies of the city's major hotels on April 1, 1962, mere days before the start of the club's first season.

The HSA held a contest in early 1961 to name the new team. "The Colt .45s" was chosen, from among 12,000 suggestions, to represent the city's bold and brazen character. Gabe Paul, general manager of the Cincinnati Reds, agreed to take the same position with Houston a week after the city was awarded the franchise. Paul brought with him William Giles, son of the NL president, and Tal Smith, his administrative assistant. Paul's fiscal conservatism and commitment to the baseball product clashed considerably with Hofheinz's promotional frivolity and baseball ignorance, and he quickly resigned in April 1961.

The HSA then turned to Paul Richards, the field manager of the Baltimore Orioles. Richards faced the difficult task of starting a team from scratch. Following the 1961 season, the club chose players in an expansion draft. The Houston and New York franchises alternately picked players in the expansion draft from a pool of players designated by other NL clubs. Houston ultimately paid NL owners $1.85 million for 23 marginal players. The Mets tended to choose older, experienced players who would be known by fans, hoping to boost attendance. Houston, conversely, focused on young talent and a handful of veterans, emphasizing pitching and defense.

The HSA and the county had planned to begin construction of the new domed stadium, the first covered baseball field, shortly after voters approved the general obligation bonds in January 1961. The team played in Colt Stadium, quickly erected in the Astrodome's future parking lot. The 33,000-seat temporary stadium was estimated to cost $800,000 to build, but the bill ran to $2 million. Hofheinz's appetite for extravagance drove its extra costs and explained its peculiar amenities. A *New York Daily News* reporter called the park "the damnedest you ever saw, its atmosphere is a blend of Disneyland and the old Wild West."

Seats were painted flamingo red, burnt orange, chartreuse, and turquoise—in Hofheinz's mind, to attract women. Employees wore western-themed costumes and fans parked in lots with names like "Wyatt Earp Territory." At a cost of $150 per year, season ticket holders became members of the Fast Draw Club, a bar and restaurant located in a temporary clapboard building behind home plate. Bartenders with handlebar mustaches and waitresses in fishnet stockings served the food as a player piano and saloon girl on a swing above the bar provided the entertainment. Hofheinz even had powder-blue cowboy outfits tailored—from boots to Stetsons—for all the players to wear on road trips. The owners tried anything to combat the unavoidable discomfort of watching baseball outdoors in Houston. Heat, humidity, and ravenous mosquito hordes preyed on fans and players alike, and few today recall the ballpark fondly.

The club drew 924,456 to Colt Stadium in the inaugural year. The Colt .45s, managed by Harry Craft, won their first game, played against the Cubs, by a score of 11–2 on April 10, 1962, in front of 25,271 fans. Houston finished eighth in the NL (64–96), ahead of the Cubs and the expansion New York Mets.

As construction on the domed stadium limped forward, it became clear that $22 million would not be enough to complete the massive project. A $9.6 million supplemental bond issue was approved on December 22, 1962, by a vote of 42,911 to 36,110. At this time, Cullinan left the HSA, convinced that Hofheinz's influence and interests were undermining baseball in Houston. Bob Smith bought Cullinan's shares at his request. Smith and Hofheinz then owned 96 percent of the HSA, and just three of the original shareholders still owned stakes in the club.

The Colt .45s slipped to ninth in 1963 and 1964 with identical 66–96 seasons, with attendance down to about 720,000 each year. The franchise announced a name change on December 1, 1964. Hofheinz originally favored the name "Stars," hoping to project an image of progressive savvy, while Kirksey and others wanted the team to embrace the Texas past. The Colt Firearms Company had originally approved the use of its gun's name in merchandising. However, as the opening of the domed stadium loomed, the company informed the HSA that it expected a share in receipts of all merchandise using the Colt .45 logo. This challenge gave Hofheinz the opportunity to bury the Wild West imagery for his preferred franchise persona—the technological future. Taking its lead from NASA's new $200 million Manned Spacecraft Complex just south of the city, the team became the Astros.

Ground for the Harris County Domed Stadium, popularly known as the Astrodome, was broken on January 3, 1962, when city officials fired faux Colt .45 pistols into the ground, and construction began a year later. The final cost of the project was $45,350,000: $31.6 million was financed through bonds approved by a referendum and spent on general construction, architectural and engineering fees, land acquisition, and parking-lot and access-road pavement; $6 million was spent by Hofheinz and the HSA to outfit the stadium with scoreboards, restaurants, skyboxes, and other concessions; and the remainder was spent by city and state agencies and property owners on road development.

The structure was located seven miles southeast of downtown Houston, on a site owned by Smith that had limited real estate value because it tended to flood. At its highest point, the roof was 218 feet tall and spanned 642 feet in diameter. It included a 260-acre parking lot with enough spaces for 30,000 cars. The stadium had 45,000 seats for baseball, 52,000 for football, and 65,000 for conventions. In addition to baseball, the dome would also host college and professional football, conventions, circuses, trade shows, rodeos, Billy Graham revivals, a Muhammad Ali fight, and the famed tennis match between Billie Jean King and Bobby Riggs. An exhibit center, Astrohall, was built adjacent to the stadium and opened in 1966. Two years later, the Astroworld amusement park and Astrodomain hotel and motel complex made their debuts. Finally, in 1975, the 6,600-seat Astroarena was introduced.

The president of ABC Television called the Astrodome "a practical monument to the imagination of the Space Age man, who dreams of better things and then goes out and makes them happen," precisely the reaction Hofheinz and other civic leaders hoped to provoke from visitors. Hofheinz boasted of the "Eighth Wonder of the World" and that "nobody can ever see this and go back to Kalamazoo, Chicago, New York, you name it, and still think this town is bush league, that this town is Indian territory."

The Astrodome employed and displayed technology at every opportunity. The ability to watch a baseball game indoors was itself a great feat, requiring a $4.5 million air-conditioning system maintained by "the Brain"—a massive computer reckoned to do the work of 280 men. The center-field scoreboard was four stories high and 474 feet long, covered 1,800 square feet, and cost $2 million. Its animated shorts enthralled visitors and prompted promotional writers to claim that "the scoreboard pyrotechnics are so spectacular that some fans will now say: 'Let's go to the Scoreboard tonight,' instead of the tried and true 'Let's go to the ball game.'"

The technological contributions to comfort and entertainment benefited fans from the cheapest seats to the most expensive. One of Hofheinz's favorite features of the Astrodome was that all the seats were padded, and he claimed, "If we've established grandeur we've done it for the bleacher fan and the country club member." A pavilion seat in center field cost $1.50, and most of the stadium's seats were priced between $2.50 (for reserved) and $3.50 (for box seats). High-end patrons could take out a five-year lease on one of the 53 luxury boxes ringing the top of the stadium. Five-year leases for 24-seat boxes were $15,000 per year, while 30-seat boxes cost $18,600 per year. There were also two larger 54-seat boxes that could be leased for $33,000 per year. Each box of seats was backed by a club room clad in pile carpeting and stocked with a telephone, radio, Dow Jones stock ticker, television, toilet, ice maker, and bar. The club rooms were each designed with a different motif, from the "Las Vegas" room, which had large dice as tables, to more exotic themes like "Bangkok" or "Old Mexico." Hofheinz extended his penchant for the gaudy and exotic to his own two-level, 2,000-square-foot apartment built into the stadium, outfitted with gold-plated fixtures, bronze Siamese lions, a cedar-lined Finnish sauna, and even an inlaid-pearl-covered bedside Bible. A five-level, 10,000-square-foot presidential suite was added for Lyndon Johnson, who, alas, never graced it with a stay.

Sports Illustrated wondered, "Just what, you may ask, has all this live-in luxury and astral salesmanship got to do with sport?" Hofheinz, unapologetically, was trying to alter the experience at the ballpark. Eighty-three percent of the country's population growth occurred in suburbs between 1950 and 1970, and the Astrodome was symbolic of this movement, motivated by conspicuous consumption, the ever-increasing use of the private automobile, the privileging of the nuclear family, the separation of work and leisure, and economic segregation. Like the air-conditioned mall, the Astrodome was a quasi-public space that welcomed women and children to enjoy a clean and safe environment that satisfied the needs of both consumption and community. Hofheinz related his philosophy to writer Roger Angell: "We have removed baseball from the rough-and-tumble era. I don't believe in the old red-necked sports concept, and we are disproving it there. We're in the business of sports entertainment." Baseball traditionalists feared this sanitization of the ballpark. Yet the Astrodome's luxury boxes and exploding scoreboards would become the norm in future stadiums, as would its artificial grass. Astroturf, in true domestic form, was tidied up not by lawnmower but by vacuum cleaner.

Aside from its alteration of traditional sports space, many opposed the stadium simply on the grounds of civic responsibility. Writer Larry McMurtry articulated the position of many who opposed, then and now, the publicly funded stadium: "It seemed a bit conscienceless for a city with leprous slums, an inadequate charity hospital, a mediocre public library, a needy symphony, and other cultural and humanitarian deficiencies to sink more than $31 million in public funds into a ballpark." Thoughtful visitors seemed both captivated by and anxious about its tidiness and technological prowess.

The first game at the Astrodome was an exhibition on April 9, 1965, in which the Astros defeated the Yankees 2–1. The player had a hard time seeing fly balls with the semitransparent cream-colored panels in the roof, so the ceiling tiles were painted. But then the grass died, which led to the installation of the Astroturf in 1966. It was replaced three years later by Monsanto's "Magic Carpet" system.

Attendance at the Yankees game was 47,876, including President Lyndon Johnson and Lady Bird Johnson. Hofheinz entertained the honored guests in the owner's suite, but did not invite Bob Smith until late in the game. This insult, in a suite Smith had largely paid for himself, exacerbated Smith's growing discontent with Hofheinz's ways. Soon thereafter, Smith demanded that Hofheinz either buy him out or be bought out.

Remarkably, Hofheinz was able to call Smith's bluff and raise the necessary $7.5 million through loans, silent partners, and his own wealth. Smith was amazed, but unwilling to rescind his ultimatum, and he was out of the picture by mid-1965. The HSA was then at the whim of Hofheinz's vision, which subordinated baseball to the larger Astrodomain entertainment concept. Broadcaster Gene Elston said of Hofheinz, "He was the dumbest genius I've ever known."

The move to the new park did not help on the playing field, as the club, under Lum Harris, remained mired in ninth place (65–97), although attendance skyrocketed to 2,151,470. Grady Hattan managed the next three years, and the team fell from 8th to 9th to 10th. The one bright spot was Rusty Staub, who hit .333 in 1967. The NL added two teams and split into two divisions in 1969, which helped the Astros, managed by Harry Walker, to an 81–81 record, the franchise's first nonlosing record. Larry Dierker won 20 games with a 2.33 ERA. Three years later, the club finished second with its first winning season at 84–69. However, by 1975, the club had slipped to its worst record ever, at 64–97, finishing a staggering 43 1/2 games back in the division. The team's top players then were Cesar Cedeno and Bob Watson, who both played over a dozen years for the Astros.

Ineptitude on the field mirrored failure in the club offices. Hofheinz's profligate spending finally caught up with him. On September 23, 1976, Hofheinz was forced to sell his stock interest in the Astrodomain complex—which included the Astros, the lease on the Astrodome, the Astroworld amusement park (then being leased and run by Six Flags), and 300 acres of undeveloped land in south Houston—to the two principal creditors, General Electric Credit Corporation and the Ford Motor Credit Corporation. The claims of GE, Ford, and other lesser creditors on Hofheinz and the HSA had been in excess of $38 million.

GE and Ford ran the Astrodomain Corporation jointly until November 21, 1978, when Ford bought out GE. The company hoped to raise the value of the Astros by improving the team's performance. The Astros clawed back to respectability under Bill Virdon, who managed from 1975 through 1982, with records of 80–82, 81–81, and 74–88, before the strong second-place, 89-win campaign of 1979. Before 1979, the club had finished with a winning record twice; after that season, it would enjoy winning records in 18 of the next 26 years.

John McMullen and Dave LeFevre bought Astrodomain from Ford on May 16, 1979, for just under $19 million. McMullen, who held 25 percent of the shares, was a 61-year-old marine architect and one of George Steinbrenner's 16 limited partners with the Yankees. LeFevre, a New York City lawyer, took possession of 10 percent of the total shares. The remaining 65 percent was spread among 25 limited partners.

McMullen's group inherited arguments between the HSA and Harris County regarding the lease of the Astrodome. County officials claimed that the HSA owed the county approximately $1.4 million from gross receipts and between $3 million and $4 million worth of repairs to the Astrodome parking lot and roof. County officials also hoped to renegotiate the Astrodome lease. The original yearly rent of $750,000 was intended to retire the $15 million in bonds approved in the 1961 vote. However, the lease was not renegotiated after the additional $9.6 million in bonds were issued in 1963. In 1979, the county claimed this discrepancy cost the taxpayers $8.9 million.

McMullen gained the good favor of Astros fans almost instantly, signing Nolan Ryan to a record-setting contract in November 1979. Ryan, from nearby Alvin, Texas, became baseball's first million-dollar man, signing a four-year deal worth over $4 million per year. He would arguably become the franchise's iconic figure, winning 106 games for the Astros. McMullen's failure to re-sign him in 1988 would outrage Houstonians.

McMullen's investment in Ryan and free agent Joe Morgan, who had played his first nine seasons for Houston before becoming a star for the Cincinnati Reds, paid off instantly, although neither had a banner season in 1980. The Astros won their first division title, despite losing a three-game lead over the Los Angeles Dodgers with three games to play in the season, as they bounced back to defeat them in a one-game playoff. The squad had terrific pitching, leading the NL with a sparkling 3.10 ERA. Joe Niekro's 20 wins was second in the league. The club then lost to the Philadelphia Phillies in a five-game NL Championship Series in which each of the final four games went into extra innings. The Astros took a two-run lead into the 8th inning of game five, with Ryan on the mound, but lost in the 10th. They had come within six outs of the World Series.

To the chagrin of most Houston fans, McMullen dismissed popular general manager Tal Smith. In the wake of this turmoil, the 1981 season was shortened by a player strike, and the Astros struggled through the first half before bouncing back to win the season's second half with a mark of 33–20. The winners of each half met in a best-of-five playoff series for the Western Division title. After defeating the Dodgers in the first two games in the Astrodome, Dodgers pitching shut them down in Los Angeles, as Houston lost the division with three straight losses.

Though the team remained competitive through the first half of the 1980s, attendance dropped significantly from a franchise record of almost 2.3 million in 1980. By 1985, when less than 1.2 million attended games in the Astrodome, John McMullen was threatening to move the team to the Washington,

DC, area. Things did not look good for the franchise, with the seventh-highest payroll in the majors in 1986, but the season proved a pleasant surprise—and attendance jumped over half a million.

Pitcher Mike Scott (18–10, and an NL best 2.22 ERA) received the NL's Cy Young Award, Glenn Davis finished second in MVP voting, and Hal Lanier was named Manager of the Year. The Astros finished 96–66 and won the NL West by 10 games; it was the franchise's most successful season on the field. The Astros battled the New York Mets in the best-of-seven NLCS. Mike Scott remained brilliant, winning game one 1–0 and giving up only three hits in game four. However, the Astros were unable to get the NLCS MVP the ball for game seven, losing a dramatic game six in 16 innings. Three of the Mets' four wins came in their last at bat.

The club struggled through the early 1990s. Then, in July 1992, Drayton McLane Jr. bought the club for $90 million and the Astrodome lease for $25 million. He refused to buy some of the HSA interests, however, including the three Astrodomain hotels. The 56-year-old McLane was the vice chairman of Wal-Mart Stores and was worth more than $370 million. McLane's Baptist religiosity and Texas address were emphasized in newspaper articles, painting him as a blue-collar millionaire (and implicitly contrasting him with the much-maligned outgoing New Yorker, John McMullen).

McMullen's reign was a bittersweet one for Houston fans. He was widely praised for signing Nolan Ryan in 1979, but equally vilified for letting him leave in 1988. He spent money on players early in his tenure, giving lucrative contracts to Hall of Famers like Joe Morgan and Don Sutton, but fired the popular and talented Tal Smith, and in later years pruned the roster severely while turning a healthy profit. McMullen's purchase of the team had excited fans in 1979; McLane's acquisition invoked the same hope in 1992.

The cornerstone of the club since the mid-1990s were their Killer Bs, Craig Biggio and Jeff Bagwell. Biggio started in 1988 as a 22-year-old catcher, but spent most of his career at second base or in the outfield, and made seven All-Star teams. Bagwell joined the club three years later at first base, and was a four-time All-Star. He became Houston's first NL MVP in 1994—only the third unanimous selection in league history—when he batted .368 with 39 homers and 124 RBIs in just 110 games. The Astros finished second in that strike-shortened season, and again in 1995, just a game back of the Colorado Rockies for the league's first-ever playoff wild-card berth. McLane estimated that he had lost $65 million on the club by the end of 1995 and had entered serious negotiations to sell the team to Virginia businessman Bill Collins, reportedly asking for $150 million.

After another second place in 1996, the club broke through in 1997 to win the division (84–79), led by Bagwell with 135 RBIs; good young pitching, especially Darryl Kile (19–7, 2.53 ERA); and manager Larry Dierker, a former Astros pitcher and a team broadcaster since 1979. However, the Atlanta Braves swept them out of the NL Division Series, 3–0. The Astros repeated the performance, winning the division again in 1998 (102–60), with the NL's most productive offense and second-best pitching. Bagwell, Moises Alou, and Derrick Bell combined for 343 RBIs. Dierker was named NL Manager of the Year, and general manager Gerry Hunsicker was given the *Sporting News* Executive of the Year Award. However, the San Diego Padres defeated them in the NLDS 3–1.

In 1999, the Astrodome's final season, the Astros won their third straight division title (97–65). Jose Lima and Mike Hampton combined for 43 victories. Bagwell hit .304 with 42 homers and 126 RBIs. But, as before, the Astros were routed in the NLDS, victims of the Atlanta Braves, 3–1. Since 1995, when McLane had offered the club for sale, attendance had boomed, nearly doubling from 1.4 million to 2.7 million in 1999. However, the Astros' stay in the Astrodome, described by one Houston writer as "anachronistic . . . the sporting world's equivalent of leisure suits and bell-bottoms," was over. Although the team lost 25 more games in 2000 than in 1999, attendance jumped by 350,000 as fans flocked to the club's new home.

Houston had voters passed Proposition 1 on November 5, 1996, by a vote of 51 percent to 49 percent. The vote gave county commissioners approval to proceed with plans to build a $265 million, 42,000-seat retractable-roof stadium downtown and work out financing for a proposed $200 million refurbishing of the Astrodome.

Drayton McLane and Astros officials had worked hard to secure the support of Houston's various minority communities. Black leaders from the Urban League and NAACP backed the plan after the club promised that 30 percent of project contracts would go to minority businesses—a higher percentage than the 20 percent typically required of city projects. Houston's Asian American business leaders, many of whose interests were on Houston's east side, vocally supported the proposition as well. Such deals seemed vital to the proposition's passage, as a *Houston Chronicle* reporter chalked up the surprising stadium victory to an "uncommon inner city coalition of affluent white voters joined with lower- and middle-class minority voters to counter suburban middle-class voters."

The proposition, of course, had other powerful and high-profile proponents as well. An enthusiastic and well-funded campaign for the stadium enlisted the aid of Nolan Ryan, former president George H. W. Bush, Enron chairman Ken Lay, Mayor Bob Lanier, and County Judge Robert Eckels, and barraged the airwaves with $100,000 worth of ads per week as the vote approached.

Ground was broken on the project in October 1997, and construction began the following January. The site, formerly occupied by a homeless encampment, was immediately east of downtown Houston. The Ballpark at Union Station, as the stadium was originally called, ultimately cost $248.2 million. The team paid 36 percent of the ballpark's total construction costs. In the end, the ballpark came in $1.8 million under budget, and cost significantly less than the other retractable-roof stadiums built at about the same time: Phoenix's Bank One Ballpark ($465 million) and Seattle's Safeco Field ($500 million).

Under the terms of its contract, the team agreed to pay the Harris County–Houston Sports Authority $4.6 million per year for rent and $2.5 million for repairs, and in return kept all revenues. McLane, who had claimed to have lost $130 million on the team from 1992 to 2000 because of the Astrodome's inadequacies, estimated that the new park would mean at least $20 million per year in additional revenues for the team.

Enron paid the Astros $100 million over 30 years for the naming rights of the stadium. The company hoped to get as much as $200 million over those 30 years through energy and management service contracts with the franchise. Enron chairman Ken Lay had been central to the stadium project, putting together a consortium in 1996 that contributed a $34.7 million zero-interest loan to purchase downtown land and subsidize construction costs. Lay hoped to stimulate development in downtown Houston, and officials supporting the stadium construction were quick to point out the $1.6 billion that had been spent in downtown construction when the ballpark opened, with an additional $1 billion in construction planned. Property values in the area were surging—some plots adjacent to the ballpark site had tripled from $30 per square foot since before construction began to $100 by September 1999. Developers pushed projects integrating office, residential, and entertainment space.

The stadium's main entrance was Houston's old Union Station, a brick and limestone structure completed in 1911. It established the central design theme of the stadium—the ironwork and humpbacked roof were purportedly inspired by train sheds, and a replica 1860s locomotive, 57 feet long and weighing 48,000 pounds, chugged along 800 feet of track above the left-field seats. A minority was less enthusiastic about its retro design, criticizing it both for contrasting with downtown Houston's contemporary architecture and for recalling a history that the city never really had.

Bursting out of this stylized shell, however, was the park's highly technologized character. In addition to the retractable roof (which required only 12 minutes to open and close), the stadium boasted a massive 35-foot-high, 131-foot-long scoreboard above the right-center-field seats, a 45-foot-long video board above the center-field seats, a closed-caption scoreboard, three auxiliary scoreboards, and a sound system calibrated to each individual section of seating. Ironically, perhaps the most prized technological advancement in Houston was the presence of actual grass. After years on the artificial turf in the Astrodome, players were excited about the more forgiving surface, while fans could enjoy a more natural setting without sacrificing climate control on Houston's tropical days.

Enron Field opened on March 30, 2000, with an exhibition game against the New York Yankees. Roger Clemens, the hypermasculine Texas cult figure in the vein of Nolan Ryan, started for the visitors. Despite traffic problems, the stadium was hailed as a success and, according to the *Chronicle*, "a testament to the city's can-do spirit." Before the season, 20,500 season tickets had been sold, breaking the club record of 15,500 from the previous season. Perhaps most importantly for the Astros' finances, the stadium had 63 luxury suites, which in 2001 put the Astros in ninth place ($36.8 million) among major-league teams in ballpark-generated local revenue.

The Astros struggled in Enron Field's opening season, finishing with a losing record for the first time since 1991. However, the club bounced back in 2001, winning its fourth division title in five years, despite modest pitching other than rookie Roy Oswalt, who was 14–3 with a 2.73 ERA. Bagwell, Lance Berkman, and Alou combined for 364 RBIs. Once again, the Atlanta Braves waited for them in the NLDS, and once again, the Braves sent the Astros packing, 3–1. According to MLB, the team's overall total revenue was $100 million, slightly above the average. The team lost $1.2 million from baseball operations, plus $5.2 million in revenue sharing.

Following the collapse of Ken Lay's Enron, Houston's ballpark was renamed Minute Maid Park on June 5, 2002, at a cost of $170 million for 28 years. The Astros finished second in 2002 and 2003, and expectations were high in 2004 with a team valued at $320 million. The team spent freely that season, with the payroll up to $75 million (12th in MLB), led by Bagwell at $16 million. However, the talented and balanced squad limped to the All-Star break with a .500 record, before catching fire in the season's second half, winning the NL wild card. The

Craig Biggio makes a diving catch during the National League Division Series, 2004. © AP / Wide World Photos

club was led by pitchers Oswalt (20–10) and 41-year-old free agent Roger Clemens, who went 18–4 with a 2.98 ERA and won his seventh Cy Young Award. The team then won its first playoff series in franchise history, finally defeating its historical postseason nemesis, the Atlanta Braves, 3–2. Houston lost game seven of the NLCS in St. Louis. Roger Clemens, who abandoned retirement to join the team, won his seventh Cy Young Award.

The 2005 Astros limped out of the gates, beginning the season with a 15–30 record as the club battled the losses of Jeff Kent and Carlos Beltran to free agency. The offense struggled throughout the season and was shut out 17 times. However, the club's pitching was superb. Roy Oswalt won 20 games, Roger Clemens had a major league-leading ERA of 1.87, Andy Pettite tallied 17 wins with a 2.39 ERA, Brad Wheeler was among the game's best setup men, and Brad Lidge saved 42 games. After

Roger Clemens of the Houston Astros pitches during the 2005 MLB All-Star Game.
© AP / Wide World Photos

the dismal start, the Astros went 74–43 for the remainder of the regular season, winning the NL Wild Card on the final day of the season. It was the club's sixth playoff appearance in nine years, and their postseason opponents were familiar foes. The Astros again defeated the Braves in the Divisional Series, after a dramatic game-four, 18th-inning homer by Chris Burke in the longest game in playoff history. The club then exacted revenge on the heavily favored Cardinals in six games for the club's first pennant. Craig Biggio and Jeff Bagwell had finally reached the World Series. However, the franchise would have to wait for its first world title. Houston's remarkable comeback season came to an end when it lost to a superior Chicago White Sox club in four close games.

NOTABLE ACHIEVEMENTS

Most Valuable Players

Year	Name	Position
1994	Jeff Bagwell	1B

Cy Young Winners

Year	Name	Position
1986	Mike Scott	RHP
2004	Roger Clemens	RHP

Rookies of the Year

Year	Name	Position
1991	Jeff Bagwell	1B

ERA Champions

Year	Name	#
1979	J. R. Richard	2.71
1981	Nolan Ryan	1.69
1986	Mike Scott	2.22
1987	Nolan Ryan	2.76
1990	Danny Darwin	2.21
2005	Roger Clemens	1.87

Strikeout Champions

Year	Name	#
1978	J. R. Richard	303
1979	J. R. Richard	313
1986	Mike Scott	306
1987	Nolan Ryan	270
1988	Nolan Ryan	228

No-Hitters

Name	Date
Don Nottebart	05/17/1963
Ken Johnson	04/23/1964
Don Wilson	06/18/1967
Don Wilson	05/01/1969
Larry Dierker	07/09/1976
Ken Forsch	04/07/1979
Nolan Ryan	09/26/1981
Mike Scott	09/25/1986
Darryl Kile	09/08/1993

POSTSEASON APPEARANCES

NL West Division Titles

Year	Record	Manager
1980	93–70	Bill Virdon
1981	61–49	Bill Virdon
1986	96–66	Hal Lanier

NL Central Division Titles

Year	Record	Manager
1997	84–78	Larry Dierker
1998	102–60	Larry Dierker
1999	97–65	Larry Dierker
2001	93–69	Larry Dierker

NL Wild Cards

Year	Record	Manager
2004	92–70	Phil Garner
2005	89–73	Phil Garner

NL Pennants

Year	Record	Manager
2005	89–73	Phil Garner

MANAGERS

2004	Phil Garner
2002–2004	Jimy Williams
1997–2001	Larry Dierker
1994–1996	Terry Collins
1989–1993	Art Howe
1986–1988	Hal Lanier
1982–1985	Bob Lillis
1975–1982	Bill Virdon
1974–1975	Preston Gomez
1972–1973	Leo Durocher
1972	Salty Parker
1968–1972	Harry Walker
1966–1968	Grady Hatton
1964–1965	Lum Harris
1962–1964	Harry Craft

Team Records by Individual Players

Batting Leaders

	Single Season			Career		
	Name		**Year**	**Name**		**Plate Appearances**
Batting average	Jeff Bagwell	.367	1994	Lance Berkman	.302	3,813
On-base %	Jeff Bagwell	.454	1999	Lance Berkman	.416	3,813
Slugging %	Jeff Bagwell	.750	1994	Lance Berkman	.557	3,813
OPS	Jeff Bagwell	1.201	1994	Lance Berkman	.973	3,813
Games	Jeff Bagwell	162	1992	Craig Biggio	2,564	11,341
At bats	Enos Cabell	660	1978	Craig Biggio	9,811	11,341
Runs	Jeff Bagwell	152	2000	Craig Biggio	1,697	11,341
Hits	Craig Biggio	210	1998	Craig Biggio	2,795	11,341
Total bases	Jeff Bagwell	363	2000	Craig Biggo	4,283	11,341
Doubles	Craig Biggio	56	1999	Craig Biggio	564	11,341
Triples	Roger Metzger	14	1973	Jose Cruz	80	7,448
Home runs	Jeff Bagwell	47	2000	Jeff Bagwell	449	9,431
RBIs	Jeff Bagwell	135	1997	Jeff Bagwell	1,529	9, 431
Walks	Jeff Bagwell	149	1994	Jeff Bagwell	1,401	9, 431
Strikeouts	Lee May	145	1972	Jeff Bagwell	1,558	9, 431
Stolen Bases	Gerald Young	65	1988	Cesar Cedano	487	6,389
Extra-base hits	Lance Berkman	94	2001	Jeff Bagwell	969	9, 431
Times on base	Jeff Bagwell	331	1999	Craig Biggio	4,165	11,341

Pitching Leaders

	Single Season			Career		
	Name		**Year**	**Name**		**Innings Pitched**
ERA	Roger Clemens	1.87	2005	Joe Sambito	2.42	536
Wins	Mike Hampton	22	1999	Phil Niekro	144	2,270
Won-loss %	Mike Hampton	.846	1999	Roy Oswalt	.680	980.7
Hits/9 IP	Mike Scott	5.95	1986	Billy Wagner	5.94	504.3

(Continued)

Pitching Leaders   (Continued)

| | Single Season | | | Career | | |
	Name		Year	Name		Innings Pitched
Walks/9 IP	Jose Lima	1.23	1998	Turk Farrell	1.88	1,015
Strikeouts	J. R. Richard	313	1979	Nolan Ryan	1,866	1,854.7
Strikeouts/9 IP	Nolan Ryan	11.48	1987	Billy Wagner	12.38	504.3
Games	Octavio Dotel	83	2002	Dave Smith	563	762
Saves	Billy Wagner	44	2003	Billy Wagner	225	504.3
Innings	Larry Dierker	305.3	1969	Larry Dierker	2,294.3	2,294.3
Starts	Jerry Reuss	40	1973	Larry Dierker	320	2,294.3
Complete games	Larry Dierker	20	1969	Larry Dierker	106	2,294.3
Shutouts	Dave Roberts	6	1973	Larry Dierker	25	2,294.3

Source: Drawn from data in "Houston Astros Batting Leaders (seasonal and career)." http://baseball-reference.com/ teams/HOU/leaders_bat.shtml; "Houston Astros Pitching Leaders (seasonal and career)," http://baseball-reference. com/teams/HOU/leaders_pitch.shtml.

BIBLIOGRAPHY

Angell, Roger. "The Sporting Scene: The Cool Bubble." *New Yorker*, May 14, 1966, 125–42.

Carroll, John M. "Houston Colt .45s—Houston Astros: From Showbiz to Serious Business." In *Encyclopedia of Major League Baseball Team Histories: National League*, ed. Peter C. Bjarkman, 239–62. Westport, CT: Meckler, 1991.

Houston Astros. *Houston Astros 2000: Commemorative Program*. Playa del Rey, CA: CWC Sports, 2000.

Houston Sports Association. *Inside the Astrodome*. Houston: Houston Sports Association, 1965.

Lipsyte, Robert. "Astrodome Opulent Even for Texas." *New York Times*, April 8, 1965.

McMurtry, Larry. "Love, Death, and the Astrodome." *Texas Observer*, October 1, 1965.

Ray, Edgar W. *The Grand Huckster: Houston's Judge Roy Hofheinz, Genius of the Astrodome*. Memphis: Memphis State University Press, 1980.

Reed, Robert. *Colt .45s: A Six-Gun Salute*. Houston: Lone Star Books, 1999.

Smith, Liz. "Giltfinger's Gold Dome." *Sports Illustrated*, April 12, 1965, 45–63.

Titchener, Campbell B. *The George Kirksey Story: Bringing Major League Baseball to Houston*. Austin: Eakin Press, 1989.

8

Los Angeles Dodgers

Steven P. Gietschier

The Dodgers, one of the oldest and most celebrated major-league franchises, occupy a place in American baseball history that transcends their record of success and failure on the playing field. For decades they were the quintessential neighborhood team and an integral part of Brooklyn's cultural identity, and their tortuous departure following the 1957 season epitomized that community's social and economic decline. In Los Angeles, they became the prototype in baseball's transformation from an enterprise seen as a sport to one defined as a business. Moreover, the Dodgers broke baseball's color line by offering a contract to Jackie Robinson, an African American, and bringing him to the major leagues in 1947, an episode generally regarded as a catalyst in the wider struggle for civil rights and equality.

THE RISE OF BASEBALL IN BROOKLYN

Brooklyn received its charter in 1835, and two decades later it was the nation's third-largest city, with a population exceeding 200,000. Many amateur baseball clubs called Brooklyn home, and their memberships reflected the city's ethnic and socioeconomic diversity. The Excelsiors, for example, included players from the city's old and wealthy families. The Eckfords were shipwrights and mechanics who named their club after Henry Eckford, a deceased shipbuilder. The Atlantics came from the section of the city called Bedford and reflected its Irish working-class heritage. Within a few years, competitive clubs began to engage players based on their ability and not their background. The best Brooklyn clubs were seriously competitive, and their rivals were the best clubs from across the East River in the city of New York. By the end of the 1850s, the metropolitan area boasted more than 50 baseball clubs, some of whom had organized the National Association of Base Ball Players in 1857 to promote common playing rules and standards for membership.

The following summer, baseball promoters on both sides of the river staged a three-game series matching the best players from Brooklyn against the best from New York. The games were played at the Fashion Race Course in the Corona section of Queens County, not far from the future location of Shea Stadium, and the New York "picked nine" won the first and third games. The promoters took advantage of the enclosed grounds and charged 50 cents admission to each game, marking these contests as the first that spectators paid to watch. As rivalries between competing clubs grew more intense, some began to offer players financial inducements. Political patronage jobs were one way to compensate players. Benefit games with an admission charge were another. The best players were paid outright, albeit surreptitiously, and the first of these was probably Jim Creighton, whom the Excelsiors paid starting in 1860. The next year, a Brooklyn political leader named Henry Cammeyer leased six acres of land in the city's Williamsburg section, just across the East River from lower Manhattan. He built an ice-skating rink that he drained in the spring and converted into an enclosed baseball park. Cammeyer invited the Eckfords, the Putnams, and the Constellations to use his Union Grounds for their home games, and he charged all fans 10 cents admission to every game. Baseball, once an amateur recreation, had thus evolved into a professional sport at which both players and entrepreneurs could make money.

Brooklyn's newspapers reported enthusiastically on the exploits of the city's teams and promoted baseball as healthy and moral exercise. In 1846, Walt Whitman, editor of the *Brooklyn Daily Eagle,* called the game "glorious" in an oft-quoted commentary. The most prominent journalist to devote his entire career to baseball was Henry Chadwick, a native of England who lived in Brooklyn. He began covering cricket matches for the *Eagle* and the *New York Times* in 1856 before switching his allegiance to the newer sport. Over the course of a half century, he reported on the game for nearly every newspaper in Brooklyn and New York, and he edited a series of annual guides that summarized each season and appealed to a national audience. Chadwick positioned himself as the conscience of the game and was, as he advanced in years, affectionately called "Father Baseball." More practically, he developed the notation system by which each play in a game can be recorded in a scorebook, and he augmented his news stories with the first box scores. He also compiled elaborate statistics as a way to summarize games and seasons and evaluate player performance.

Brooklyn's clubs did not rush to join the professional game. When the first all-professional league, the National Association of Professional Base Ball Players, began play in 1871, Brooklyn was not represented except that the New York Mutuals, a club founded by Manhattan firefighters in 1857, played their home games at Union Grounds. The Excelsiors, the Eckfords, and other top amateur clubs now called themselves "cooperative nines," meaning they used gate receipts to pay their expenses and recruit players, and they often played professional opponents. When one NA club, the Kekiongas of Fort Wayne, Indiana, folded in August, the Eckfords agreed to play out the remainder of their schedule. In the NA's second season, the Eckfords stayed in the league, but the professional teams outplayed them. They won only three games against 26 losses and thereafter abandoned competitive baseball entirely to become a men's social club that survived many more years. Two of the Eckfords' victories came against the Atlantics, who had also joined the NA while remaining an amateur club. They did not fare much better, finishing the season with a dismal record of 9–28. The NA lasted three more seasons, and both the Mutuals and the Atlantics stayed the course. The New York team challenged for the championship in 1874, but finished second to the Boston Red Stockings. The Atlantics' best season was also 1874, when they compiled a record of 22–33, but over the winter two of their best players signed with the Hartford club. In 1875, their roster was in disarray. Most clubs used just one pitcher, but the Atlantics used eight. Desperate to find players with sufficient ability, their business manager, Benjamin Van Delft, tried 35 different ones, some of whom played only a single game, but to no avail. The Atlantics won 2 games against 42 losses, including 31 in a row, after which they went out of business.

BROOKLYN JOINS THE AMERICAN ASSOCIATION

Following the 1875 season, baseball entrepreneurs led by William Hulbert, president of the Chicago White Stockings, met in New York to create a new league that would be stronger than the NA, more stable and refined, and controlled by owners and not players. The National League eventually met their goals, but did not include a club from Brooklyn. The Mutuals, a charter member, continued to use Union Grounds as their home field, but they were neither an artistic nor a financial success, finishing sixth and alienating their fans by adhering to the league policy mandating a 50-cent admission price. With funds running short, the club declined to make its last scheduled road trip to the league's western cities and was expelled. During the following season, the Hartford Dark Blues abandoned their Connecticut home and relocated at Union Grounds. Fans again stayed away, and this club disbanded at the end of the year. The NL enjoyed a monopoly for six seasons, but with no more than eight teams, it could not satisfy other businessmen who wanted their clubs to play major-league baseball. In the fall of 1881, six such owners formed the American Association and declared it to be a second major league. Since all of its teams were backed by beer or liquor interests, the AA was dubbed "the Beer and Whiskey League." It played its first season to a successful conclusion without any team moving or going out of business. Appealing more to the working class than did the NL, the AA set a 25-cent ticket price, sold beer to its fans, and played games, where legal, on Sundays.

The AA added two teams in 1883 and then, in response to a challenge from the Union Association, yet a third major league, four more teams in 1884. These clubs were located in Brooklyn, Indianapolis, Toledo, and Washington. The Brooklyn Grays, so called because of their uniforms, had already played a season in the Interstate Association, a minor league. Founding the team had been the idea of George Taylor, an editor at the *New York Herald*, and Charles Byrne, a real-estate agent who shared an office with Taylor's attorney. Byrne turned for funding to Joseph Doyle, his brother-in-law, who owned a casino in New York. Additional money came from another gambler, Ferdinand Abell, whose lavish casino was in Narragansett, Rhode Island. These owners secured a piece of land bordered by Third and Fifth Streets and Fourth and Fifth Avenues for their home games. This site had been the scene of the Battle of Brooklyn in 1776 and had also been the Excelsiors' first ball grounds. The Grays spent $30,000 to construct a grandstand, calling it Washington Park, and made the Gowanus House, a Revolutionary War–era stone building on the grounds, part of the facility. The Grays were popular and a good team besides. They won the 1883 IA championship on the season's last day, defeating Harrisburg 11–6. The winning pitcher for Brooklyn was William "Adonis" Terry, a handsome man whose popularity with the ladies tended to outshine his skills as a player.

When the Grays or the Brooklyns, as they were also called, entered the AA, the city was still basking in the glory surrounding the opening of the Brooklyn Bridge in May 1883. At that time the longest suspension bridge in the world, it cost $15 million and connected Brooklyn with lower Manhattan. Brooklyn's population was booming, and its economic base included more than 5,000 factories. The city's trolley companies were investing large sums to convert from horse-drawn carriages to electric trolleys as the primary method of public transportation. Many city streets added trolley tracks, and crowded intersections made crossing the street somewhat treacherous. Brooklyn's citizens, as a result, were sometimes called "trolley dodgers," and this amusing nickname soon was applied, albeit unofficially, to the city's major-league baseball team.

The AA played much better baseball than the IA, and the Grays struggled to repeat their success. Taylor managed the team to a ninth-place finish in 1884 with a record of 40–64. The highlight of the season came on October 4 against Toledo. Pitcher Sam Kimber allowed no hits and no runs, but his teammates also failed to score. After 10 innings, the umpire declared the game a 0–0 tie, but it was Brooklyn's first major-league no-hitter. In the off-season, Cleveland's NL team disbanded, and the Grays picked up several players along with Cleveland's manager, Charlie Hackett. Discord was the result, as the newcomers and the holdovers refused to get along. Byrne got so disgusted after one lopsided loss that he fined a number of players, fired Hackett, and became manager himself. Three seasons later, he realized that he was more suited to be an owner than a manager and hired Bill McGunnigle to take his place. Byrne also purchased the entire roster of the New York Metropolitans, an AA team going out of business, in order to obtain several key players, including first baseman Dave Orr. Finally, he bought three players from St. Louis, pitchers Bob Caruthers and Dave Foutz and catcher Doc Bushong. Fans of the Grays had great hopes for the coming season. Moreover, since several players had gotten married during the winter, the press rechristened the team "the Bridegrooms," a nickname that further endeared the club to its supporters.

McGunnigle had been an innovative player and a successful manager in several leagues. Some sources credit him with being the first player to wear a glove and don removable spikes. As a manager, he wore a suit, not a uniform, and directed his players on the field by gesticulating with a baseball bat. Under his leadership, the team improved to second place in 1888, behind the St. Louis Browns. Brooklyn and St. Louis were becoming rivals on and off the field. Byrne and Chris Von der Ahe, the Browns' owner, disagreed on several matters to the point of feuding, and their teams engaged in spirited pennant races in 1888 and again in 1889. Washington Park burned down in May 1889, and the Bridegrooms were forced to play most of the season's first half on the road until their home could be rebuilt. Still, they held a slim lead over St. Louis when the Browns came to Brooklyn in early September for three games. St. Louis built a 4–2 lead in the first game, but several arguments and other shenanigans left the game unfinished as darkness fell. Umpire Fred Goldsmith refused to call the game, and when a Brooklyn batter reached first base in the ninth inning, the Browns' manager, Charles Comiskey, pulled his team from the field in protest. Goldsmith then ruled the game a forfeit in Brooklyn's favor. Comiskey reacted by refusing to play the following day, and this game, too, was forfeited to the Bridegrooms. The third game was rained out. AA officials dickered for weeks before agreeing to award the first game to St. Louis and the second to Brooklyn, a decision that pleased neither club. The Bridegrooms held on to win Brooklyn's first major-league pennant by two games with a record of 93–44. The star of the team was Bob Caruthers, who won 40 of 51 decisions.

Starting in 1884, the champion of the NL had engaged the AA champion in a postseason match called the World's Series. In 1889, Byrne looked forward to a lucrative series because Brooklyn's opponent would be the New York Giants, who had beaten the Browns the year before. In a continuation, of sorts, of the intercity rivalry started during the amateur era, the teams agreed to play a best-of-11 series. The Bridegrooms, who won three of the first four games, marred the opening contests by stalling for time in the late afternoon whenever they took a lead. The Giants complained, and Byrne agreed to advance the games' starting time so they could be finished before darkness. The Giants rebounded by winning the next five games, thereby taking the series, six games to three. New York became the first major-league team to win two consecutive World's Series, and Brooklyn, in defeat, started its own tradition, that of the lovable loser, the underdog destined for decades of postseason futility.

When AA owners disagreed over whom to select as their new president, Byrne and Aaron Stern of the Cincinnati Reds withdrew their clubs and joined the eight-team NL, replacing Indianapolis and Washington. Both teams had also anticipated the announcement by the Brotherhood of Professional Base Ball Players, the sport's first union, that it would field teams in the new Players' League in 1890. The Bridegrooms and the Reds had signed their regulars to hefty contracts before the Players' League could approach them. As a result, they entered the NL with strong rosters while other teams found themselves depleted. The AA replaced Byrne's club with the Gladiators, a makeshift franchise that did not survive the season, and the Players' League also put a team in Brooklyn, the Wonders, owned by George Chauncey. McGunnigle used his veterans wisely. He employed a three-man pitching rotation, a novel concept, and the Bridegrooms won their second consecutive pennant easily, albeit in a different league. The public ignored them, however, believing that most of the best players had jumped to the Players' League. The Bridegrooms' attendance fell from 354,000 in 1889, best in the association, to only 37,000 in 1890. The Bridegrooms advanced to the World's Series against the AA's Louisville, but it was called off after each team had won three games because of bad weather and insignificant crowds.

The Players' League lasted only one season, after which Chauncey, a real-estate mogul, offered to invest in the Bridegrooms. Byrne, Doyle, and Abell, who had lost a significant amount of money in 1890, agreed to Chauncey's two conditions: that the team abandon Washington Park and begin playing its home games at Chauncey's Eastern Park, and that John Montgomery Ward, the leader of the Brotherhood and the manager of the Wonders, replace McGunnigle. Ward lasted but two seasons and, as other clubs improved markedly, could not duplicate McGunnigle's success. Foutz, the star of the 1889 team, succeeded him, but his tenure yielded nothing higher than a fifth-place finish in four seasons. During these desultory years, the team also struggled to find a catchy nickname after "Bridegrooms" no longer seemed appropriate. The Brooklyn press tried out "Ward's Wonders" and then "Foutz's Follies," but neither caught on, and "the Trolley Dodgers," left over from the team's days in the AA, was not generally embraced either. The Brooklyn club's ineptitude during the 1890s formed the foundation for the team's reputation as incompetent losers to whom unusual things often happened, both on and off the field. Historians have remembered pitcher William "Brickyard" Kennedy as an early example. Good enough to win 20 games four times, he once got lost traveling from his Brooklyn home to the Polo Grounds in upper Manhattan for a game against the Giants. A policeman who intervened learned that Kennedy had been born in Ohio and inexplicably put him on a westbound train before team officials rescued him.

THE NATIONAL LEAGUE COMES TO BROOKLYN: EBBETS AND THE MAKING OF THE BROOKLYN DODGERS

Moving to the forefront of the team's management was a former ticket taker named Charles Hercules Ebbets. Born in New York City on October 29, 1859,

Ebbets studied drafting and architecture, published novels, and held political office at a very young age. He served four years as an alderman and one as a New York State assemblyman before running unsuccessfully for the state senate. But his true love was baseball. He started selling tickets for the Brooklyn club in 1883 and soon was serving as Byrne's jack-of-all-trades assistant. No task was beneath his dignity as he learned the baseball business from top to bottom. He printed scorecards, swept floors, manicured the playing field, and kept the club's books. Late in 1897, after the team had suffered through its fourth straight sub-.500 season, he announced that he had purchased Chauncey's shares for $25,000 and taken an option on Abell's shares as well. Full of ambition, Ebbets told the Brooklyn press on January 1, 1898, that he controlled 85 percent of the club, a claim that proved to be greatly exaggerated. Nevertheless, Ebbets assumed the club presidency when Byrne died three days later, and he set to work right away to revive the stumbling franchise. Although in truth he held only 18 percent of the stock, he acted as if he were the team's sole owner. Seeking to avoid the steep rent the team paid at Eastern Park and to reconnect his business with its traditional fan base in south Brooklyn, he laid plans for a new Washington Park built on leased land across the street from the original. When the team got off to a lousy start, he replaced manager Billy Barnie with outfielder Mike Griffin and then with himself. Still, Brooklyn finished 10th in the 12-team league.

With no other league to challenge their monopoly status, NL owners fashioned themselves as Gilded Age barons running a business in ways similar to the trusts that controlled other industries. They lived extravagantly and expected to reap huge profits from baseball. Moreover, owners saw no reason not to assist each other when necessary. They switched scheduled games from one city to another in search of greater attendance, lent each other players, and invested in each other's clubs. These practices, known as syndicate baseball, had a precedent in 1890 when several clubs combined to bail out Giants owner John Day during the Players' League war. They came to a climax in 1899 when Ebbets forged an alliance with Harry Von der Horst, owner of the Baltimore Orioles, agreeing to an exchange of stock. The result of this deal was that each ownership group—Ebbets and Abell from Brooklyn and Von der Horst and his manager, Ned Hanlon, from Baltimore—held half of each club, with Ebbets being granted operating control of the Brooklyn club.

The agreement with Ebbets gave Von der Horst entry into the lucrative Brooklyn market, but more importantly, it brought Hanlon and several star players to the Brooklyn roster. Among them were first baseman Dan McGann, shortstop Hughie Jennings, and outfielders Willie Keeler and Joe Kelley. Hanlon, born in Connecticut in 1857, had been an average player with leadership skills that made him a natural candidate to become a manager. While he was still playing, he took the reins of Pittsburgh's NL club in August 1889, but he jumped to that city's Players' League club the following year. In 1891 he returned to the NL, only to be fired in July in a dispute with some players he was trying to discipline.

His playing career ended the following spring, but he was hired to manage the Orioles, one of the four AA teams absorbed into the NL. Baltimore was awful in 1892, finishing in last place, 54 1/2 games behind first-place Boston. During the next two seasons, Hanlon remade the Baltimore roster, discarding veterans and gambling on young players, including first baseman Dan Brouthers, third baseman John McGraw, catcher Wilbert Robinson, Jennings, Keeler, and Kelley. All six eventually were inducted into the Baseball Hall of Fame. The Orioles won the pennant in 1894 and again in 1895 and 1896. They finished second each of the following two years.

When Hanlon moved from Baltimore to Brooklyn in 1899, he was simultaneously president of the Orioles and manager of his new team, and he held 10 percent of the stock of each club. In an era renowned for tough, no-holds-barred play, Hanlon was regarded as the most innovative manager the game had yet seen. Admiring fans in Baltimore wore buttons that said "Ask Hanlon," a tribute to his wily skills and baseball acumen. By bringing his star players with him, he quickly transformed Brooklyn from a listless also-ran that came in 10th in 1898 into a powerhouse club that earned a new nickname, the Superbas. The name was borrowed from the Hanlon Brothers, a vaudeville troupe that specialized in spectacular acrobatics, gymnastics, and trapeze artistry, a mixture of comedy, suspense, and flamboyance. One of the Hanlons' productions that played to packed houses was called "Superba." By the time Hanlon's team took over first place on May 22, Brooklyn fans, hungry for a winner, had embraced the Superbas with glee. Both Boston and Philadelphia challenged for the lead, but Brooklyn held them both off, winning 101 games and the pennant by eight games. Keeler batted .379 and Kelley .325 to lead the offense, and pitcher Jay Hughes, another transfer from Baltimore, won 28 games, tying for the league lead.

On the same day that Ebbets had proclaimed his control of the club, the city of Brooklyn had ceased to exist as an independent municipality. The complex unification of the nation's first- and fourth-largest cities plus three other counties—Queens, Richmond (or Staten Island), and the Bronx—was the culmination of a movement begun decades before and accomplished against sustained opposition from various quarters. Brooklynites had barely approved of the merger that made their city part of Greater New York, and the triumph of their baseball team shortly thereafter provided some reassurance that Brooklyn still possessed its own identity. By latching onto the Superbas as their favorite team, they were beginning to redefine the place where they lived as a cultural entity in which major-league baseball and later the lack thereof would play an important role.

Hanlon's Superbas won the pennant again in 1900 (82–54), by four and a half games over Pittsburgh and star shortstop Honus Wagner. Keeler was fourth in batting (.362) and led in hits (204), pacing the NL's leading offensive team. The pitching was generally mediocre, but Ironman Joe McGinnity went 28–8, and Brickyard Kennedy was 20–13. Nonetheless, Brooklyn's home attendance declined by about one-third to 183,000, second worst in the NL, and the owners lost money. Ebbets agreed to play a postseason series against the Pirates to raise additional revenue, but when he could not find a sponsor for his half of the expenses, the *Pittsburgh Chronicle Telegraph*, the Pirates' sponsor, insisted that the entire best-of-five series be contested in Pittsburgh. Brooklyn won, three games to one, but each member of the Superbas earned only about $30 a game. The team was awarded a silver cup symbolizing the "world's championship." This was the club's last pennant until 1916 and its last championship until 1955.

Ebbets had debunked rumors that he would consider moving the club, but he refused to discount the possibility of selling the team or some players. Moreover, he chafed at the threefold difference between Hanlon's salary, the highest in baseball, and his own as club president. Hanlon didn't much like Ebbets either and suggested to Von der Horst that he move back to Baltimore. The NL had eliminated the Orioles after the 1899 season—and paid its owners a $30,000 buyout fee—and Hanlon wanted to seek a franchise in the new American League, which played its first major-league season in 1901. Von der Horst declined Hanlon's proposition and decided instead to get out of baseball by offering to sell his stock to Ebbets. This transaction was not consummated until after Ebbets had bought out Abell in 1902. With total command of the Superbas, Ebbets exercised his authority by cutting Hanlon's salary and raising his own above it.

When Ban Johnson, founder and president of the AL, put a team in Baltimore, its manager was not Hanlon, but his former player McGraw. Hanlon stayed in Brooklyn and watched helplessly as several of his key players signed contracts with teams in the new league. Before the 1901 season, the Superbas lost outfielder Fielder Jones, third baseman Lave Cross, and McGinnity, who rejoined McGraw in Baltimore. The following year, Kelley and second baseman Tom Daly left, and when the two leagues made an uneasy peace early in 1903, Keeler's contract, in a complicated transaction, was awarded to the AL's New York Highlanders. Hanlon brought his team home in third place in 1901 and second in 1902, but thereafter the club fell into the second division. After a 48–104 finish in 1905, Ebbets fired him and hired Patsy Donovan, a former player who had previously managed in Pittsburgh, St. Louis, and Washington.

Although the Superbas' attendance held fairly steady during these dismal seasons, they were but a shadow of their former selves and were, quite clearly, the third team in major-league baseball's only three-team city. The Brooklyn club not only had to compete with the Giants within the NL, but also the AL Highlanders. The rivalry with the Giants, an extension of the intercity competition that predated professional baseball, pitted blue-collar Brooklyn against white-collar New York. It heated up during the cities' protracted struggle over their consolidation and took a particular turn when the Giants' owner, Andrew Freedman, lobbied hard to oppose a subway station near Washington Park that would have greatly aided Ebbets's quest for more fans. Into this mix came the vitriolic McGraw. He had become player-manager in Baltimore after

Hanlon left for Brooklyn, spent one year in St. Louis, and was recruited by Johnson to return to Baltimore in 1901. By the middle of the following season, McGraw and Johnson had sparred so frequently that a break was inevitable. The maneuvers were clandestine and complex, but the result was that McGraw and some of his best players jumped to the Giants. McGraw soon found the Superbas to be a convenient target, and when the AL moved the Baltimore club to New York, the Superbas lost any claim to representing the entire city. They were Brooklyn's team solely.

The team's eighth-place finish in 1905 was the first of 10 straight years under .500. Donovan lasted three seasons, and Harry Lumley but one. Bill Dahlen, who had played shortstop for Brooklyn before being traded to the Giants in 1903, followed him. Nearly as abrasive as McGraw, Dahlen had dismissed Brooklyn when he left for New York, but in 1910 he accepted an offer to return to the Superbas as manager. The team did not improve, and Dahlen's temper often got him into trouble. In 1912, for example, he got into a fistfight on the field with an umpire. The AL's raids had left Brooklyn with few players of note. One exception was left-handed pitcher George Rucker, nicknamed "Napoleon" by sportswriter Grantland Rice. Rucker pitched a no-hitter in 1908 and struck out 16 Pittsburgh batters in a July 1909 game. He was a hard-luck pitcher, though, losing 10 games in his career by the score of 1–0 and pitching the losing end of a no-hitter in 1915. Despite his abilities, his career record was only 134–134 over 10 seasons. Another fine player was outfielder Zack Wheat, who began his Hall of Fame career in 1909 and was probably Brooklyn's best position player before World War II. Over 19 seasons, Wheat collected 2,884 hits. He batted .317 and led the league in hitting in 1918.

This decade of futility kept Ebbets on the financial brink. He had overextended himself with a hefty loan from furniture dealer Henry Medicus to purchase Von der Horst's share of the club, and he lacked enough capital to improve the team significantly. Ebbets added seats to Washington Park in search of more revenue, and he often criticized the ordinance that prohibited charging admission for sporting events on Sundays. In 1904, he played a Sunday game without selling tickets, instead requiring fans to buy color-coded scorecards keyed to the various prices tickets normally cost. When he tried the same stunt a second time, local officials arrested the team's pitcher and catcher and the opponent's leadoff batter. Despite these financial difficulties, Ebbets remained optimistic about baseball's future and his own. He expressed the view that "baseball is in its infancy" and once wrote in *Frank Leslie's Weekly*, "I am a firm believer in the future of baseball, both in Brooklyn and in the country at large." His ambitious plan to realize this potential was to construct a new ballpark that would be named Ebbets Field, a facility that defined the club's fortunes for the rest of its time in Brooklyn.

Baseball's first concrete and steel ballpark, Philadelphia's Shibe Park, opened in 1909. Ebbets announced his intention to replace Washington Park with his own concrete and steel facility on January 2, 1911. The team's old home was truly outdated, handicapped by a seating capacity of less than 19,000, the stench from the nearby Gowanus Canal, and the increasing costs of insuring against fire. Ebbets had already found a suitable site in 1908, an undeveloped spot east of Prospect Park in an area sometimes called "Pigtown" and other similarly descriptive nicknames. Ebbets liked the location because of its proximity to a nexus of railroad and subway lines that he hoped would bring fans from Manhattan. Working with his attorney, Bernard York, he bought 1,200 small parcels of land, even setting up a corporation called Pylon Construction in a futile attempt to keep his real purpose secret. The last piece of property, worth no more than $100, cost him somewhere between $500 and $2,000.

These purchases, totaling about $200,000, secured for Ebbets an irregular rectangle bounded by Sullivan Street, Cedar Street, Montgomery Street, and Bedford Avenue, where right field would be located. This odd shape would help create what historians and fans have called charm or personality, but hemming the new park into approximately four and a half acres forced Ebbets to build an extremely compact structure that would not allow for much renovation or expansion. Selecting another location or buying more land, even if a street had to be rerouted, might have given Ebbets some flexibility. Instead, he built a ballpark considerably smaller than its contemporaries, one that outlived its usefulness much sooner than the others. Still, Ebbets and architect Charles Randall Van Burick planned an elaborate edifice. Incorporating columns and arches with a Roman look, the centerpiece of its exterior was a massive rotunda with a dozen doors and ticket booths decorated in a baseball motif. Inside, the double-decked grandstand brought fans very close to the action, and the irregular dimensions of the playing field created quirkiness that ballparks built nearly 80 years later sought to imitate.

Realizing Ebbets's dream proved difficult, as his limited financial resources did not allow him to proceed without cutting corners. The ballpark lacked fan amenities, there was no press box until 1929, and parking for automobiles, once people began to drive to games in large numbers, proved wholly inadequate. Before construction began, Ebbets had hoped to lure, at least temporarily, the Yankees as tenants. They played their games in wooden Hilltop Park, which suffered by comparison after the Giants rebuilt the Polo Grounds in 1911 with concrete and steel. The Yankees' owners had expended substantial funds toying with a couple of ill-considered schemes for a new home, but when these plans fell through, they chose to rent from the Giants. Ebbets also had trouble working with Tammany Hall, New York's Democratic political machine, which hindered construction. Contractors seemed unable to do anything but delay until Ebbets forged a partnership with Stephen and Edward McKeever. Each of these brothers had developed a lucrative construction business once Stephen decided to join Tammany and reap the benefits of political connections. The brothers then sold their separate businesses and joined forces investing in Brooklyn real estate. Rich and reasonably respectable, they came to Ebbets with a simple offer: sell half the club and see the ballpark completed expeditiously. Ebbets accepted and entered into an agreement to form two corporations. The Brooklyn Baseball Club listed Ebbets as president and Edward McKeever as vice president, and the Ebbets-McKeever Exhibition Company, holding the ballpark and the land on which it sat, listed Edward McKeever as president and Ebbets as vice president. Stephen McKeever was treasurer of both companies.

Ebbets Field opened on April 5, 1913, with an exhibition game between the visiting Yankees and the home team, by this time generally known once again as the Dodgers. More than 25,000 fans—7,000 more than capacity—crammed their way in, and another 10,000 were turned away. After a few problems appropriate to this "Grand Opening," Edward McKeever's wife raised the American flag, and Ebbets's daughter Genevieve threw out the ceremonial first pitch. The Dodgers won, 3–2. Four days later, the park observed its "Special Opening," the first regular-season game, won by the Philadelphia Phillies, 1–0. Other celebrations followed throughout the year, which collectively outshone the Dodgers' performance on the field. After a fine start that found them near first place at the end of May, they fell steadily in the standings and wound up sixth, 34 1/2 games behind the pennant-winning Giants. First baseman Jake Daubert led the league in batting, and attendance climbed to almost 350,000. Nevertheless, the McKeever brothers pressured Ebbets to dismiss Dahlen after the end of the season.

Ebbets's choice for a replacement was former catcher Wilbert Robinson, recently fired as a coach by McGraw. Robinson had earned much praise in the press for the way he handled young Giants pitchers, which McGraw took as implicit criticism of his own work as manager. The two came to verbal blows after New York lost the 1913 World Series, and McGraw discharged his old teammate on the spot. Robinson decided not to return to his business interests in Baltimore and instead took his easygoing manner to Brooklyn, where his charm put a new face on Ebbets's operation. Sportswriters called him "Uncle Robbie," and his team soon became the Robins or, more colloquially, the Flock. As Robinson settled in, Ebbets had to deal with a potentially larger problem, a new league with a new team in Brooklyn. The Federal League had begun play in 1913 and commenced an effort to become a third major league the following year. As part of this campaign, the Federals granted a Brooklyn franchise to Robert Ward of the Ward Baking Company. He called his team the Tip Tops, after his company's best-selling brand of bread, and took a lease to play in Washington Park. Just as Ban Johnson had done a decade before, the Federal League began signing players from established teams to lucrative contracts. Many AL and NL teams lost key players to the upstarts, but Ebbets, backed by the McKeevers' money, fought back. He signed Daubert to a five-year contract worth $9,000 a year and finalized similar deals with Wheat and a young outfielder named Charles Stengel, soon to be dubbed Casey after Kansas City, his hometown.

Beyond Robinson's skills as a manager, it was his personality and willingness to poke fun at himself that gave his team a distinct identity. When the

Robins were good, they earned respect from opponents and fans alike. More often, they would play amateurish baseball, sometimes comically so, and would be stamped as laughingstocks—not just bad, but ridiculous. An episode from spring training in 1914, Robinson's first season, typified the funny business in which the team got involved. The idea behind this publicity stunt may have originated with Ebbets, but its exact details are no longer clear. The principals were a barnstorming pilot named Ruth Law, eager to attract customers for short joyrides, and Robinson, who agreed to attempt to catch a baseball Law would drop from an altitude of roughly 500 feet. Somehow, what Law tossed was not a baseball, but a grapefruit. Robinson circled under the object, and it hit his glove before bursting upon his chest. The manager fell to the ground and thought he had been seriously wounded, mistaking grapefruit juice and seeds for his own blood.

Various players took credit for the switch, but blame has most often been assigned to Stengel. More than any other single player, it was he who combined talent with high jinks to define the Robins' persona. He got four hits in his major-league debut midway through the 1912 season and hit the first home run in Ebbets Field, albeit in an exhibition game against the Yankees. Stengel, according to Brooklyn's catcher, John "Chief" Meyers, was a prankster who kept his teammates alert and entertained. In dental school, he had put a cigar into the mouth of a cadaver. In the minors, he once hid beneath a manhole cover on the field and popped out to catch a fly ball. Stengel conversed with the fans and was a visible presence throughout Brooklyn. He made the team an integral part of the neighborhood, beloved even when it was losing, and played right into Brooklyn's image as poorer, more down-to-earth, and more endearing than upscale Manhattan. After being traded to the Pirates, he returned to Brooklyn for the first time to a chorus of boos. He grabbed a sparrow, placed it under his cap, and at the appropriate moment let the bird loose, to great laughter.

Robinson guided the Robins to fifth place in 1914, third place in 1915, and first place in 1916, the team's first pennant since 1900. The fans turned out in droves, setting a team record of 447,747. Moreover, as Brooklyn rose in the standings, McGraw's Giants fell, to second in 1914 and last in 1915. The affable, rotund Robinson provided a sharp contrast to his acerbic mentor, and the Dodgers-Giants rivalry grew even more intense. Robinson developed a pair of young pitchers, Jeff Pfeffer and Sherry Smith, and picked up three veterans whose careers other clubs thought were finished, Jack Coombs from the Philadelphia Athletics, Larry Cheney from the Chicago Cubs, and Rube Marquard from the Giants. In 1916, this quintet won 82 games. The pitching staff had a sizzling 2.12 ERA, best in the NL. The team also had the league's highest batting average, .261. Daubert hit .316, and Wheat hit safely in 29 consecutive games, still the franchise record. The pennant race was a three-way battle between the Robins, the Boston Braves, and the defending champions, the Phillies. In the season's last days, Boston and Philadelphia defeated each other while the Dodgers beat the Giants twice to clinch first place. McGraw

Casey Stengel, 1915. Courtesy of the Library of Congress

left the Giants' dugout midway through the second of these two victories, incensed that his team had not played smart baseball or given maximum effort. McGraw suggested to reporters that certain of his players had let their affection for Robinson get the best of them, but another rumor circulated that McGraw's anger stemmed from his losing a late-season bet that New York would finish third. Thus, as Brooklyn won the pennant, the Giants grabbed the headlines, which irritated Robinson.

The Robins met the Boston Red Sox in the World Series. A powerful team that had captured the Series in 1912 and 1915, Boston had a superlative pitching staff, including a youngster named Babe Ruth who had won 23 games. The Red Sox made quick work of Brooklyn, winning the best-of-seven series in five games. Both managers manipulated their pitching staffs to create what they thought would be favorable matchups. These strategies resulted in Ruth and Smith pitching in game two, a memorable contest that went into the 14th inning tied 1–1. Ruth retired the Robins in order in the top of the inning, and then Red Sox pinch hitter Del Gainer doubled off Smith, scoring Dick Hoblitzell with the winning run. Boston's pitchers held Brooklyn to 13 runs and a .200 batting average.

Attendance at Ebbets Field had risen to nearly half a million in 1916, and advancing to the World Series gave Ebbets and the McKeevers an extra opportunity to recoup some of their investment. Boston played its home Series games at Braves Field, where seating capacity was much larger than at Fenway Park, but cold weather and Boston's dominance significantly cut crowds in Brooklyn. During the series, newspapers speculated that the team and the ballpark might be sold, with Stephen McKeever suggesting an asking price of $2 million. After the series was lost, Ebbets continued to cut the salaries of players without multiyear contracts, which he had started when the Federal League had gone out of business in December 1915. As a result, all three of his starting outfielders threatened to strike rather than report for spring training in 1917.

The loss in the World Series besmirched Robinson's reputation and indicated to some that his best days were behind him. His team's performance over the next three seasons did not dispel these doubts. After Ebbets cut player costs mercilessly, the Robins dropped to seventh place in 1917. The United States' entry into World War I cast a pall of uncertainty over the following two seasons, during which teams played a reduced schedule of 140 games. Brooklyn finished fifth both years, but in spring training of 1920, Robinson was optimistic that his pitching staff would once again be good enough to win. Tests came early as the Robins played several extra-inning games in April, but no game, before or since, surpassed what unfolded on May 1 in Boston. On that date, the Robins and the Braves played a 1–1 tie that lasted a record 26 innings. Both pitchers, Leon Cadore for Brooklyn and Joe Oeschger of the Braves, went the distance, each throwing more than 300 pitches. Cadore gave up 15 hits, but only 2 over the final 13 innings, while Oeschger surrendered no hits and only one walk over the last nine innings. The umpires called the game because of darkness after four hours of play. Returning to Brooklyn, the Robins played 13 innings the next day against the Phillies, and then, back in Boston, 19 more innings on May 3. Even though Brooklyn lost two and tied one, these games seemed to bear out Robinson's hope of an outstanding pitching staff. After a wartime lull, attendance skyrocketed. Brooklyn enjoyed a postwar economic boom based on industrial production surrounding the Brooklyn Navy Yard, and a new law finally allowed major-league baseball games on Sundays. By the end of the season, Ebbets had sold more than 800,000 tickets and made $189,785, and the Robins were champions. Wheat batted .328, and Burleigh Grimes led the league's best pitching staff with 23 wins. Brooklyn battled Cincinnati through most of the season and used a 16–2 spurt in September to hold off a second-half surge by the Giants.

On the day Brooklyn clinched first place, newspapers across the country were revealing that eight members of the Chicago White Sox, winners of the AL pennant the year before, had allegedly taken $100,000 in bribes to throw the World Series to the Reds. With a shadow automatically cast over the upcoming Series against the Cleveland Indians, Brooklyn district attorney Harry Lewis questioned Ebbets and his team about the integrity of this Series. He uncovered no such evidence, and the games proceeded as a best-of-nine affair with the first three games and the last two, if necessary, to be played in Brooklyn. Both Robinson and Tris Speaker, the Indians' manager, juggled their pitching rotations. The Robins won two of the first three games, all of them low-scoring pitching duels. As the series shifted to Cleveland, Marquard, the pitcher Robinson wanted to start game four, was arrested for scalping tickets, and Cadore got the assignment instead. Cleveland won 5–1, and took the next three games to win the championship. Game five remains one of the most famous because of three firsts: the Indians' right fielder Elmer Smith hit the first grand slam in World Series play, their Jim Bagby became the first pitcher to hit a Series home run, and their second baseman, Bill Wambsganss, recorded the only unassisted triple play in Series history. Once again, Brooklyn's hitters failed to rise to the occasion. The Robins scored only eight runs in all, and none in the last two games. Critics also noted that Robinson mismanaged his pitchers. Two pennants in five years were a triumph of sorts, but they also came to stand as a prelude for the two grim decades to come.

WHEN THEY WERE BUMS

Over the next 20 seasons, Brooklyn finished second twice, third twice, and sixth an astonishing 10 times. The Yankees and the Giants, in the same period, won 18 pennants and 11 World Series between them. The Yankees, with Babe Ruth, Lou Gehrig, and Joe DiMaggio as their most prominent stars, became baseball's most successful and most popular team. The Giants enjoyed one resurgence under McGraw in the early 1920s and then another in the 1930s after his retirement and death. Together these two teams dominated press coverage and fan interest throughout New York City, leaving only the borough of Brooklyn, and to some extent the suburban counties of Long Island, to the Robins. Among New York's many daily newspapers, only the *Eagle* covered the Robins with any degree of thoroughness, and its beat writer, Thomas Rice, treated the team's failures with kid gloves. Fans came to expect failure, so much so that wins and losses took a backseat to what would later be called entertainment value: the ambience of Ebbets Field, the colorful nicknames many players proudly bore, and the antics of players and some fans alike. Robinson, older, heavier, and devoted to playing the game as he had played it in the 1890s, was unable to stem this tide, especially when he was forced to accept more responsibilities as Ebbets aged. Mistakes he and his players made were magnified into a culture of incompetence. "Uncle Robbie" became a derisive appellation, and at some point, newspapers began to refer to the team and its leadership as the Daffiness Boys.

The Robins' best season during this period was 1924, when they finished second to the Giants by just a game and a half. Loitering near the .500 mark for most of the season, the team put together a couple of modest winning streaks in mid-August just as New York went into a swoon. Beginning on September 1, Brooklyn played doubleheaders on four consecutive days and won all 8 games, part of a 15-game winning streak. The Giants broke this skein on September 7 in Brooklyn when an overflow crowd spilled out onto the field and was barely restrained by ropes and an insufficient contingent of police. The Robins stayed in contention until the next-to-last day of what would be Charles Ebbets's final season at the helm. Long troubled by heart disease, the 64-year-old had resisted several overtures by the McKeevers to retire. After a busy off-season, he went to Florida for spring training but returned to New York after falling ill. He moved into his suite at the Waldorf-Astoria Hotel and died on April 18, 1925, the eve of the Robins' home opener. The hearse carrying his body home passed by Ebbets Field during the game, and again two days later for the funeral. Ebbets was buried in Brooklyn's Greenwood Cemetery in the cold and rain. At the graveside service, Edward McKeever caught a chill and developed influenza. Eleven days later, he too was dead.

The aftermath of these twin tragedies was the dispersal of team stock to a host of Ebbets and McKeever heirs. At a stockholders' meeting held in May, Stephen McKeever was sure that he would be elected president, but the Ebbets heirs held firm and offered the job to Robinson. No one had yet been both president and manager of any major-league team, and Robinson was particularly unsuited to set this precedent. He decided to remove himself from the dugout and appointed Wheat to be "assistant manager," but this arrangement proved unworkable. Moreover, Robinson demonstrated no skill for acquiring players, and he lost his ability to charm the press. McKeever, increasingly dissatisfied with Robinson, could do nothing to oust him. Board-of-directors votes always ended in a 2–2 tie, with Robinson and Ebbets's son-in-law, Joseph Gilleaudeau, standing on one side, and McKeever and attorney Edward York, representing Edward McKeever's heirs, on the other. Finally, in February 1930, NL president John Heydler intervened. Concerned that the team's inertia could compromise its competitive integrity, he persuaded Robinson to give up the club presidency in return for a two-year contract as manager. York became the new president, McKeever remained as treasurer, and Commissioner Kenesaw Mountain Landis added Walter Carter, brother-in-law of Chief Justice Charles Evans Hughes, as a neutral fifth member of the board to end the string of tied votes.

Following Wheat, whose Brooklyn career ended in 1926, the only two players who brought distinction to the Dodgers uniform in this period were Arthur (Dazzy) Vance and Floyd (Babe) Herman. Vance was a flamboyant right-handed pitcher whose major-league career did not truly begin until 1922, when he was 31. He did not hit his stride until he overcame a serious arm injury and until he began to pitch every fifth day, instead of the customary every fourth day. Vance came to the Robins in a trade and began to pay dividends right away. He won 18 games as a rookie and led the league in strikeouts. In 1923, he won 18 again, including 10 in a row, but his best year was 1924, when he led the league in complete games, strikeouts, and ERA; compiled a 28–6 record; and was named MVP. Vance won 20 games twice more and led the league in strikeouts seven consecutive years. He threw a no-hitter in 1925 and was later the league's highest-paid pitcher.

Herman, a native of Buffalo, New York, spent five seasons in the minor leagues before the Robins bought his contract after the 1925 season. His best offensive season was 1930, when he batted .393 and hit 35 home runs. He got 241 hits that year, ninth most in NL history. He was an outstanding hitter but an indifferent fielder who fit in well with Brooklyn's daffiness image. When he was accused of letting a fly ball hit him on the head, he took exception, responding that the ball had hit him on the shoulder. On August 15, 1926, Herman was the key actor in the Robins' zaniest play. He came to bat in the seventh inning with one out and the bases loaded. Hank DeBerry was on third, Vance on second, and Chick Fewster on first. Herman lined the ball to right field and slid into second with a double. When he heard the second baseman telling the shortstop to throw the ball home, Herman assumed that DeBerry and Vance had already scored and that a play would be made on Fewster. Herman got up and raced to third. In fact, DeBerry had scored, but Vance had inexplicably hesitated between third and home. When the throw home came from the shortstop, Vance retreated to third, there to meet both Fewster and the sliding Herman. The umpire called Herman out for passing Fewster, and when Fewster, thinking he was also out, wandered off third, the shortstop tagged him out, too. Observers cracked that Herman had tripled into a triple play, but in fact he had doubled into a double play. That DeBerry had scored the winning run on the play got lost in the confusion.

Brooklyn finished fourth in 1930, and actually took applications for World Series tickets before fading in the season's last weeks, and then fourth again in 1931. When attendance topped a million for the first time in 1930 and the team made $426,976, McKeever announced a two-year project to demolish the left-field bleachers and extend the double-decked grandstand all the way to center field. In 1931, though, baseball felt the effects of the Great Depression. Attendance at Ebbets Field plummeted, and the club's string of annual operating profits disappeared. The team lost $5,308 that year, and by the end of 1938, would lose a total of $576,650. When the season ended, Robinson's contract was not renewed. York's choice to replace him was Max Carey, a former outfielder and a strict disciplinarian. He lasted only two seasons as the team's front office went through a series of disruptive changes. York resigned the presidency, and 78-year-old McKeever assumed the job, while Gilleaudeau and McKeever's son-in-law, James Mulvey, privately agreed to share power peacefully. They left day-to-day baseball operations in the hands of two office aides, and when the team did not improve, McKeever still had enough authority to oust them in favor of Robert Quinn, the team's first general manager, who fired Carey and hired Casey Stengel. The franchise, once again known as the Dodgers, was in disarray, and other teams complained that they sold few tickets when hapless Brooklyn came to town. Before the start of the 1934 season, a reporter asked Giants manager Bill Terry about the Dodgers' prospects. "Is Brooklyn still in the league?" was his retort. Stengel had the satisfaction of making Terry eat his words when the Dodgers took two games from New York in late September to give the pennant to the St. Louis Cardinals. In other respects, Stengel's tenure was no better than his predecessors. Willard Mullin, sports cartoonist for the *New York World-Telegram*, immortalized these years of futility by drawing the bereft Brooklyn fan as an ill-clad, unshaven, cigar-smoking bum. Eventually, this unofficial nickname, the Bums, would be transferred to the team itself, but only after things on the field got remarkably better.

Quinn and Stengel did not last, either. The former resigned after the 1935 season and was replaced by the team's road secretary, whose job had been to arrange the team's railroad transportation. Stengel was dismissed a year later and replaced by Grimes. The team did not improve, and attendance fell so low that the future of the club was jeopardized. Holding a substantial amount of the team's debt, the Brooklyn Trust Company approached NL president Ford Frick with a plea to help hire a competent baseball man to head the franchise. Frick thought first of Wesley Branch Rickey, general manager of the Cardinals, but Rickey suggested his protégé, Leland Stanford "Larry" MacPhail. A native of Michigan and an army captain in World War I, MacPhail had proved to be an innovator running the minor-league club in Columbus, Ohio, and then the Reds. He signed a three-year contract as executive vice president early in 1938 and took charge of the entire Brooklyn operation.

Ignoring the club's heavy indebtedness, MacPhail began immediately to spend more of the bank's money. He hired new ushers and refurbished the poorly maintained ballpark. He installed new plumbing and, later in the year, lights for night games. Just as significantly, he redesigned the team's uniforms by putting a script *Dodgers* across the chest and abandoning a green-and-gold color scheme for a shade of blue that has ever since been known as Dodger blue. Then, the day before McKeever died at the age of 83, he began overhauling the roster by purchasing Phillies first baseman Dolph Camilli for $50,000. It was the first of many personnel changes, including the hiring of Babe Ruth as a coach and fan attraction. Ebbets Field hosted its first night game on June 15. Fireworks and a track-and-field demonstration by Olympic champion Jesse Owens entertained the capacity crowd, and then Cincinnati's Johnny Vander Meer pitched his second consecutive no-hitter, a feat never again equaled. The Dodgers finished seventh, but attendance jumped by nearly 200,000. After the season, MacPhail fired Grimes and named Leo Durocher, Brooklyn's scrappy shortstop, the next manager. Then he voided an agreement with the Yankees and the Giants to keep all their home games off the radio and hired Walter "Red" Barber to announce the team's games. No other single move added more to the team's popularity. Barber broadcast baseball objectively and crisply explained its nuances. He was a particular hit with housewives, many of them new to the game.

The Dodgers finished third in 1939 (with a profit of $143,637), second in 1940 ($125,221), and first in 1941 ($146,794), their first pennant in 21 years. MacPhail acquired a host of new players, a potent mix of talented veterans, like pitcher Whit Wyatt, outfielder Joe Medwick, and second baseman Billy Herman, and youngsters with enormous potential, like shortstop Harold "Pee Wee" Reese and outfielder Pete Reiser, who hit .343 in 1941, the best year in a career brutally abbreviated by injuries. He led the NL in batting, total bases, and runs, while Dolf Camelli led in homers (34) and RBIs (120). The Dodgers led the NL in batting (.272) and pitching (3.14 ERA). Wyatt and Kirby Higbe both won 22 games, the most in the league. Durocher and MacPhail quarreled often and vociferously, frequently under the influence of alcohol. The manager inspired his players, cajoled them, and bullied them—whatever was necessary to elicit their best performances. The 1941 pennant race against the Cardinals was tight all the way. Brooklyn, with 100 wins, eked out a two-and-a-half game margin. The Dodgers captured new fans locally and nationally. Brooklyn's popular outfielder

Fred "Dixie" Walker was known as "the People's Cherce," and the Dodgers were the "cherce" of Brooklynites near and far. In addition, the resurgent Dodgers supplanted the Giants as the Yankees' intracity rival. Throughout the Daffiness years, Brooklyn had been not much more than an afterthought in New York baseball, but MacPhail and Durocher changed that irrevocably.

By winning the 1941 pennant, the Dodgers found themselves in the World Series against the Yankees, a team that had won 11 pennants and eight Series since Brooklyn was last in the Series, in 1920. This was the first of seven Subway Series, so called because fans of each team could reach the other's ballpark easily via New York's extensive public transportation. The Yankees were a powerful team in 1941, and the Dodgers were mere upstarts who made mistakes under pressure. The teams split the first two games, and the Yankees won the third game, 2–1. In the pivotal game four, the Dodgers carried a 4–2 lead into the ninth inning Relief pitcher Hugh Casey retired the first two batters. Then Tommy Henrich struck out, except catcher Mickey Owen let the third strike trickle away from him. As the ball rolled into a crowd of police who had rushed onto the field anticipating the end of the game, Henrich scampered safely to first. DiMaggio, with two strikes on him, singled to left, and Charlie Keller, also with two strikes, doubled to right, scoring both runners. When the dust settled, the Yankees had a 7–4 win. They wrapped up the series by winning game five, 3–1. Brooklyn partisans could be philosophical that their team, so bad for so long, had come so far, yet Owen's miscue would, as time went on, loom very large in Dodgers history.

BRANCH RICKEY, INTEGRATION, AND THE BOYS OF SUMMER

Japan's attack on Pearl Harbor in December 1941 threw baseball into uncertainty, but President Franklin Roosevelt declared that the game should continue despite the war and its restrictions. Major-league seasons were played in their entirety, but teams began to lose players to military service, and the level of competitive play fell substantially over the next four seasons. The Dodgers lost only one regular in 1942, infielder Harry "Cookie" Lavagetto, and they won 104 games, only to be outdone by the Cardinals' winning 106. Then Durocher's team was stunned in September when MacPhail announced that he was resigning to accept an army commission. In truth, the club's board of directors was not sorry to see him go. Although MacPhail had made enough money to retire much of the team's debt, he had not paid much of a dividend to its stockholders. He plowed revenues back into the operation, took a huge salary for himself, and swaggered around in a way offensive to some of his employers. They lost no time in replacing him, and this time Rickey, a teetotaler, was their man. He had just resigned from the Cardinals, and Mulvey especially was anxious to hire him. Rickey's strength was building a farm system, a network of minor-league clubs that could supply the parent major-league team cheaply.

This was how he had turned the Cardinals into a winning team, and it was one of the chief skills he brought to Brooklyn. He sold several of MacPhail's veterans and invested the cash in young players. The team fell to third place in 1943 and seventh the year after, but the dislocations of the war, rather than Rickey, took the blame. Despite the war, the Dodgers only lost money in 1943, and broke even in the dismal 1944 season. Then in 1945, the Dodgers came in third, with four .300 hitters, led by Goody Rosen at .325. The team made $252,721, second most in the majors after the Giants.

Rickey wanted to operate from a position of strength instead of being just an employee. Early in 1944, he came to an agreement with John Smith, of Brooklyn's Pfizer Chemical Company, and Walter O'Malley, the team's attorney, to buy the quarter of the shares owned by the heirs of Edward McKeever. About a year later, this trio also purchased the half interest held by Gilleaudeau and the Ebbets heirs. Each of the three thus held 25 percent of the club, and they were able to concentrate operating control of the team in Rickey's hands. Once the key Brooklyn players were called into the service, Rickey confided in Durocher that immediate help would not be forthcoming. Instead, he reasoned that the war had removed the game's excellent players and that the Dodgers would best be served by planning for the postwar future. With the exception of Reese, who played the 1942 season before joining the navy, and Gil Hodges and Ralph Branca, both of whom played briefly during the war, all of the players associated with the great Dodgers teams known as "the Boys of Summer" came to Brooklyn after the war.

Born in rural southern Ohio and raised as a devout Methodist, Rickey had played and coached baseball at Ohio Wesleyan College. As the story goes, one of his players, an African American named Charles Thomas, was refused admission to the team's hotel on a road trip. This incident stayed with Rickey as he became a professional baseball player, an attorney, a manager, and then an executive with the St. Louis Browns. Rickey was an innovator who loved to talk about baseball to the point of sermonizing. Named manager of the Browns in 1913, he began to develop all sorts of devices and drills to teach players how to play better. In addition, he spent time during spring training giving his players formal lectures on various aspects of the game. Moving to the Cardinals, Rickey, operating under a very tight budget, formulated the notion of the farm system. Most minor-league teams were at that time independent business operations whose owners sought to win games, develop players, and sell the best of them to teams in better leagues. Rickey sought a more economical way. His goal was to directly control many minor-league players on many teams (once, in fact, holding an entire league) and promote those players who met certain standards. Commissioner Kenesaw Mountain Landis opposed Rickey's strategy as bad for the minor leagues, but most other major-league teams saw the wisdom of it and followed suit.

Rickey's baseball philosophy, sometimes reduced to a series of aphorisms like "Luck is the residue of design," became known as "the Cardinals' Way," and after he moved to Brooklyn, as "the Dodgers' Way." For his campus, he secured an abandoned military base in Vero Beach, Florida, and converted it into Dodgertown, the team's spring-training home and instructional complex. There he saw to it that every player under contract to the Brooklyn organization learned the game according to his standards. Part of his plan was to integrate baseball. Rickey's motivation was complicated and has been subject to a number of explanations. Certainly his upbringing played a role in fashioning his beliefs, as did his experience with Charles Thomas. The fact that African Americans were beginning to struggle for equal rights throughout American society was also important. There were practical factors as well. The Dodgers needed good players, and Rickey was not inclined to dismiss any portion of the potential pool or to ignore the appeal his team, located in a diverse city, could make to African American fans. Thus, in 1943, Rickey began to gather data on players who might suit his purpose. He worked under the guise of establishing the Brooklyn Brown Dodgers as a Negro Leagues team, but this was never his intention. When Landis died in November 1944, a major obstacle to integration disappeared. Rickey's scouts located Jackie Robinson, a former star athlete at UCLA and a former army officer playing for the Kansas City Monarchs, and in October 1945, Robinson signed a contract to play with the Montreal Royals, the Dodgers' farm team in the International League.

The postwar years brought an economic and social renaissance to Brooklyn. Scores of Hollywood war movies had included a character with a Brooklyn accent and an infectious optimism that defined so many veterans anxious to build successful lives now that the war was over. Many Brooklyn natives returned home, went to college with benefits from the GI Bill, found good-paying jobs, bought houses, and began families. Others, utilizing new highways, moved to the suburbs to do the same things and took their Brooklyn pride with them. One headline in the *Eagle* said, "Brooklyn Is America," and a big part of that identity was the interest that so many people took in the fortunes of the Dodgers. Walking along residential streets on summer afternoons or evenings, neighbors could hear one radio after another tuned to the game. Brooklyn's players returned from military service in 1946, and the team finished second to the Cardinals in a pennant race even closer than it had been in 1942. The teams ended the regular season tied, forcing the first playoff in NL history. In this best-of-three contest, the Cardinals won the first game in St. Louis and the second one back in Brooklyn.

Over the winter, Rickey asked his fellow owners at a special meeting to give assent to the promotion of Robinson to the Dodgers. The vote was 15–1 against. He then approached the new commissioner, Albert "Happy" Chandler, privately, and got his assurance that Robinson's contract would be approved. The Dodgers trained in Cuba in 1947 in order to avoid Florida's Jim Crow laws, and in March, several players signed a petition indicating their unwillingness to play with Robinson. Durocher told his team that Robinson was good enough to get them to the World Series, and Rickey promised to trade anyone who did not want to stay. Robinson's name was added to the roster just before Opening Day, and on April 15, he made his major-league debut, going hitless against the Braves. Robinson played first base, a position he had never played before spring training. The Dodgers opened the season without Durocher at the helm. In a ghostwritten newspaper column, the manager had mentioned that MacPhail had sat with several known gamblers at exhibition games between the Yankees and the Dodgers in Havana. MacPhail, then co-owner of the Yankees, retaliated. He filed a charge with Chandler that the Dodgers manager had engaged in "conduct detrimental to baseball." Durocher was going through a messy divorce, and he had friends who were gamblers, notably actor George Raft. The commissioner suspended Durocher for a year. Coach Clyde Sukeforth managed the team on Opening Day, and Burt Shotton took the reins for the balance of the season.

Robinson batted .297 and won the Rookie of the Year Award, but not before absorbing hazing and abuse, both verbal and physical, unprecedented in baseball history. Phillies manager Ben Chapman was particularly vocal and vicious. In May, *New York Herald Tribune* sports editor Stanley Woodward wrote a column uncovering an alleged conspiracy by the Cardinals to strike rather than play against the integrated Dodgers. By the midpoint of the season, Robinson and his teammates had worked out an accommodation, and he began to make real contributions to the team's success. The 1947 Dodgers were not yet the Boys of Summer, but they won the pennant by five games over the Cardinals, beginning a run of six first-place finishes in 10 years. Reese was back at short; Carl Furillo, a surly Pennsylvanian with a great throwing arm, played center field; and Edwin "Duke" Snider and Hodges saw limited service off the bench. Branca led the pitching staff with 21 wins and a 2.67 ERA. The team made $519,143, following the $412,314 the previous season.

The Dodgers drew the Yankees as their World Series opponent again, and the result was a series generally considered to be one of the best ever. Game four stood out as the highlight. With the Yankees ahead, two games to one, New York pitcher Bill Bevans no-hit the Dodgers for eight and two-thirds innings, an unprecedented feat in World Series play. With two out in the ninth inning and two Dodgers on base as a result of walks, pinch hitter Lavagetto doubled off the right-field wall and both runners scored, giving Brooklyn a 3–2 win. The Yankees won game five, lost game six, and came through in game seven, thus depriving the Dodgers and their fans of baseball's ultimate triumph again.

Durocher returned to the dugout in 1948, but he lasted only half a season. Never really comfortable with his manager's personality or his conduct, Rickey became enraged when Durocher criticized the decision to sell second baseman Eddie Stanky to Boston rather than grant him a raise. Rickey tried to maneuver Durocher into resigning, but that didn't happen right away. Instead the two bickered throughout the first half of the season. At the All-Star break, when Giants owner Horace Stoneham asked Rickey's permission to speak with Shotton

Jackie Robinson, 1947. Courtesy of the Baseball Hall of Fame

about replacing Mel Ott as New York's manager, Rickey suggested talking with Durocher instead. Within days, the change was effected, and Durocher had left Ebbets Field for the Polo Grounds. It was a stunning move with implications that would haunt the Dodgers for a long time. Shotton returned to the bench, but the Dodgers could do no better than finish third. With Stanky gone, Robinson had moved to second base, Hodges had taken over at first, and Billy Cox, a superb fielder, had won the job at third base. Roy Campanella opened the season at catcher, but Rickey inexplicably sent him to the St. Paul farm club in May. After Shotton took over, Campanella was recalled, Snider became the center fielder, Furillo moved to right, and pitcher Carl Erskine was promoted from the minors. The club played terrific baseball for quite a while, but was unable to make up the gap separating it from the pennant-winning Braves.

Despite these two terrific seasons, Dodger fans had not exactly embraced Rickey's revolution. Postwar baseball boomed in many cities, but not Brooklyn. Attendance for the other seven NL clubs increased 21 percent in 1947, but the number of tickets sold at Ebbets Field rose hardly at all. The Dodgers, in fact, drew better on the road than at home. In 1948, Brooklyn's attendance fell by more than 400,000, and the fans who attended games seemed younger and perhaps more willing to accept the sight of black faces on the playing field. Nonetheless, the team still made $543,201. The Dodgers rebounded to win another pennant in 1949 by one game over the Cardinals, and set a team record for profits ($642,614). Five hurlers won 10 or more games, including Rookie of the Year Don Newcombe. Robinson was MVP, leading the league in batting (.342) and stolen bases (37). However, the club was bested by the Yankees in the World Series, four games to one.

The Dodgers lost the next two pennants by razor-thin margins, but once again fell behind the two other New York teams as a fan attraction. More ominous was the growing exodus of mainly white middle-class Brooklynites to suburban Long Island and the influx of less affluent African Americans and Latin Americans, people less able to spend dollars on baseball tickets.

Co-owner Smith died in July 1950, and shortly after a 10th-inning home run by Philadelphia's Dick Sisler on the last day of the season deprived the Dodgers of another pennant, O'Malley set in motion a plan to oust Rickey, whose style he had never appreciated. Before the season was over, O'Malley and Smith's widow had forged an alliance, and Rickey knew that his days as president were numbered. Although he owned part of the team, he depended upon a salary to pay for loans he had taken out. Rickey balked when O'Malley suggested buying Rickey's interest for the same $350,000 he had paid for it. Through a third party, Rickey found an alternative buyer, New York real-estate mogul William Zeckendorf, who offered him $1.05 million and indicated that he was willing to buy out Mrs. Smith as well. O'Malley had the right of first refusal, and he was forced to match Zeckendorf's bid or risk losing control to him. The transaction was completed in October, and O'Malley, almost out of spite, immediately started to transform the Dodgers from a Rickey organization to an O'Malley organization. He began installing his own men. E. J. "Buzzie" Bavasi became general manager, Lafayette Fresco Thompson took control of the farm system, and Charlie Dressen was named the new manager.

Rickey's players stayed, though, and the lineup Brooklyn featured over the next several seasons was the league's best. The infield included Hodges at first base, Robinson at second, Reese at shortstop, and Cox at third. Andy Pafko played left field, Snider center, and Furillo right, and Campanella was the catcher. In time, Jim Gilliam took over at second, and Robinson moved to left field and then third base. The starting pitchers included Branca, Erskine, Elwin "Preacher" Roe, Don Newcombe, and, in turn, Russ Meyer, Billy Loes, and Johnny Podres. Some of these Dodgers had come tantalizingly close to winning the World Series in 1947, and more of them had just missed the pennant in 1950. But no season scarred them and their fans as much as 1951, the ultimate confrontation between Brooklyn—and all the team represented—and the Giants. Games between these two clubs always took on their own significance, irrespective of the league standings, and Durocher's presence in the New York dugout brought the rivalry to the boiling point. The Dodgers built a very healthy lead in the pennant race, 13 1/2 games on August 11, and a good chunk of their advantage had been accumulated at the Giants' expense. After that point, the Dodgers finished 26–23, but the Giants won 39 of their final 47 games to force a best-of-three playoff. New York won the opening game, Brooklyn came back to take the second, and in the third the Dodgers took a 4–1 lead into the bottom of the ninth inning. The pennant looked as good as won, but two singles, a popup, and a double scored one run, and then Bobby Thomson hit a three-run home run to give the Giants a victory that Brooklyn fans never forgot. The Dodgers had several outstanding individual performances that year, including ones by Campanella, who was MVP; Robinson, who hit .338; Hodges and Snider, who along with Campanella drove in over 100 runs; and Newcombe and Roe, who won 20 or more games.

Giants radio broadcaster Russ Hodges helped immortalize this moment by screaming into his microphone, "The Giants win the pennant! The Giants win the pennant!" but no words can adequately explain the damage this home run, often called the most dramatic in baseball's entire history, did to the collective psyche of the Dodgers and their fans. A half century later, Brooklyn fans who were present and many others who were not recalled for a documentary the wrenching emotional pain of the moment and its power to disrupt friendships, cause rifts in families, and endure. The home run came to be known as "the Shot Heard 'Round the World," and the Giants' comeback was dubbed "the Miracle of Coogan's Bluff," but for the Dodgers, this was the blackest day in their history. Even the revelation in 2001 that the Giants had been stealing the signs of other teams, using a spotter in the center-field clubhouse and a buzzer in the bullpen, did little but reopen old wounds.

WHEN "NEXT YEAR" CAME

The cry of frustration associated with Brooklyn's inability to win the World Series was "Wait till next year," but "next year" seemed never to come. The Dodgers took the pennant in 1952 with excellent batting, pitching, and defense. Reliever Joe Black (15–4) was Rookie of the Year. But they lost the World Series to the Yankees in seven games. One year later, the Dodgers were back in the Series after winning 105 games. They totally dominated offensively. Roy Campanella was MVP, Gilliam was Rookie of the Year, Furillo was batting champion (.344), and Snider led in slugging (.627), total bases (370), and runs (132). Yet again they faced the Yankees, who took the Series in six games. Some analysts have suggested that, as good as the team was, the roster still had shortcomings that O'Malley and his lieutenants seemed unwilling to address. One change they did make, when Dressen boldly asked for a two-year contract, was to replace him with Montreal manager Walter Alston. He would pay dividends in time, but not in 1954, when the Dodgers finished second to the Giants. Meanwhile, Brooklyn itself and the area around Ebbets Field continued to change, and not for the better. The *Eagle* ceased publication in early 1955, emigration to the suburbs picked up pace, and crime became a persistent problem. Attendance at Dodgers' home games stayed flat, despite the team's success, and the big crowds usually appeared only on weekends. O'Malley took notice, too, when the Braves left Boston for Milwaukee after the 1952 season and saw their attendance skyrocket from 280,000 to 1.8 million.

The Dodgers finally won the World Series in 1955. The players had had a tough time adjusting to Alston, and in the spring some serious discontent remained, but the team won its first game, then 22 of 24, and never left first place, finishing up 13 1/2 games. The team, led by Campanella, who won his third MVP Award, had the best batting, pitching, and defense in the NL. In the World Series, they defeated the Yankees, a feat many observers simply thought impossible. The series started with the Dodgers down two games to none, and then Johnny Podres, Clem Labine, and Roger Craig all pitched complete-game victories. The Yankees came back in game six under Whitey Ford, but in the deciding game seven, 22-year-old lefty Johnny Podres shut out the Yankees on five hits to win 2–0. The key play came in the sixth, when, with runners on first and second, defensive replacement Sandy Amoros, running at full speed, caught Yogi Berra's slicing fly near the left-field stands and doubled up Gil McDougald on first base. The delirium that swept the borough was unprecedented. In the hours after the final game, Brooklynites made more telephone calls than they had following the announcement that World War II had ended. To mark the occasion, the *New York Daily News* ran two headlines: "Who's a Bum!" and "This IS Next Year." The Dodgers and the Yankees met in one final Subway Series the following year, when they drew 1.2 million, the most since 1951 and second highest in the NL. Newcombe led the Dodgers with a record of 27–7, and was the MVP and Cy Young Award winner. The Yankees emerged triumphant once again, with the highlight of the confrontation being game five, when Don Larsen pitched the first and only perfect game in World Series history. The Dodgers tied the series the next day when Clem Labine pitched a 1–0 10-inning shutout, but the seventh game went to the Yankees, 9–0. In the last three games, the Dodgers managed a total of only seven hits.

THE DODGERS MOVE WEST

Ever the businessman, O'Malley had begun to angle for a new ballpark. The Braves' success in Milwaukee was educational, as were the shifts of the Browns to Baltimore in 1954 and the Athletics to Kansas City in 1955. These teams had all moved to new ballparks built with public funds and surrounded by large parking lots. People driving cars to games would pay to park, and they would also buy more food and drink inside the ballpark than would fans arriving by public transportation. Since Ebbets Field lacked adequate parking, O'Malley was missing out on two substantial sources of revenue. He tipped his hand a bit by scheduling a few "home" games in 1956 and 1957 in Jersey City's Roosevelt Stadium, and by selling Ebbets Field in October 1956 to a Boston-based real-estate developer. O'Malley took a lease on the park for three years with an option for two more after that, but clearly what he wanted was a new home for his team financed not entirely with his own funds. The question, of course, was where that new ballpark would be.

Much has been written, both emotional and analytical, about the protracted negotiations between O'Malley and various New York State and New York City officials, including Governor Nelson Rockefeller, Mayor Robert Wagner, and Robert Moses, a powerful figure who held several state and municipal jobs simultaneously and who had the political clout to decide whether the Dodgers' owner would get his way. Painting O'Malley as the bad guy who never seriously entertained proposals to stay in New York and who plotted from early on to abandon Brooklyn for Los Angeles is too simple a picture. Neither is it accurate to indict only Moses and blame him for forcing O'Malley out. A more accurate, if complicated, view is that O'Malley played his cards too close to his vest, never reaching out to make alliances with New York's political and business leaders who could have been his friends and helped him achieve his goal without leaving Brooklyn. Nor did O'Malley enhance his credibility when he enlisted futuristic architect Buckminster Fuller to design a geodesic dome in which he said the Dodgers would play, an idea that struck most observers as ridiculous. When O'Malley announced that he wanted New York City to condemn land surrounding an old Long Island Railroad terminal in Brooklyn as a location for a new ballpark, Moses said no. He instead offered the Dodgers a site in the Flushing Meadows section of Queens, but O'Malley called a new park in any borough besides Brooklyn unacceptable.

Immediately after the 1956 World Series, the Dodgers made a goodwill trip to Japan with a stopover in Los Angeles. There O'Malley met with Kenneth Hahn, a city councilman whose was trying to attract a major-league team. O'Malley may have suggested that the city build his team a ballpark at public expense, but Mayor Norris Poulson nixed this idea. Instead, O'Malley got free land, on which he would build a ballpark, and a network of access roads. The sale of Ebbets Field had given him the funds to pay for the park himself. Discussions continued with New York, but they were no longer serious. O'Malley delayed a formal announcement because he wanted to protect his attendance in 1957, but at the end of the season, the Brooklyn Dodgers were no more. Moreover, the Giants announced nearly simultaneously that they were relocating to San Francisco. NL officials had told the Dodgers that their move to the West Coast would not be approved unless a second team accompanied them, and O'Malley had convinced Stoneham to join him.

To get the territorial rights he needed, O'Malley swapped minor-league franchises with the Chicago Cubs. He also acquired Los Angeles's Wrigley Field, a scaled-down version of the one in Chicago and too small to house a major-league team. Los Angeles officials offered the Dodgers a site in a section of the city called Chavez Ravine. The city would spend $2 million grading the land,

and the county an additional \$2.7 million constructing roads. In exchanged, O'Malley would give Wrigley Field to the city and pay an estimated \$350,000 in annual property taxes. Opponents of this deal included some who objected to evicting the residents of Chavez Ravine, mostly poor Mexican immigrants, and others who argued against the use of public funds for this private purpose. They forced a referendum called Proposition B in June 1958 that squeaked through by a margin of about four percent. After a court battle, O'Malley was sure he had the acreage on which he would build Dodger Stadium. In the interim the team needed a temporary home. The Rose Bowl was deemed unsuitable, so the team wound up in the Los Angeles Coliseum, built for the 1932 Summer Olympics and not at all conducive to accommodating the dimensions of a baseball field. The diamond was positioned at the Coliseum's west end, resulting in a very short distance to the left-field foul pole and a very long one to right center. The club erected a screen 40 feet high in left, and balls that hit it were in play.

The idea of major-league baseball was so popular in Los Angeles that the Dodgers sold nearly \$2 million in tickets before Opening Day. The veteran Dodgers had a tough time adjusting to their new home. They played four seasons in the Coliseum, and no one hit more than 14 home runs there in any season. Although the short left-field screen looked very inviting, batters found it challenging to loft fly balls over it. Homering to right field was even more difficult since the club had erected a chain-link fence that bowed out to 440 feet from home plate. Then, too, the Boys of Summer were getting older. Robinson had retired back in 1956 rather than accept a trade to the Giants. Reese turned 40 during the first season in Los Angeles and was no longer a regular. Furillo was 36, Hodges was 34, and Campanella never played in Los Angeles, having been permanently paralyzed in a January automobile accident. The Dodgers drew 78,672 to their Opening Day game against the San Francisco Giants, and enthusiasm for the team remained high throughout the season, despite its poor finish. Total attendance for the year exceeded 1.8 million, even though the team wound up in seventh place.

The club's management learned in 1958 that a pitching staff needed to be assembled to deal with the peculiarities of the Coliseum. By the middle of the season, Alston had pretty much benched his veteran pitchers in favor of youngsters Don Drysdale, Sandy Koufax, and Stan Williams. They all excelled at striking batters out, the best way to keep hitters from taking a shot at the left-field fence. This was the genesis of a new style of Dodgers baseball that would hold the club in good stead for decades: a reliance on pitching, speed, and defense at the expense, if necessary, of offense, and especially power. It worked at the Coliseum and later at Dodger Stadium, generally regarded as a pitcher's park. In fact, using a careful mixture of the old and the new, the team rebounded in 1959 to tie the Braves for first place, resulting in yet another best-of-three playoff. This time, the Dodgers were victorious, two games to none, and they went on to defeat the White Sox in the World Series in six games. Chuck Essegian hit a pair of pinch-hit home runs, and pitcher Larry Sherry relieved in four games, winning two and saving two. Attendance for the three series games played in Los Angeles totaled 287,750, with each game attracting slightly more fans than the one before. The club made lots of money and plowed a good portion of it into resurrecting its farm system, just the opposite of what O'Malley had ordered after ousting Rickey.

When Dodger Stadium opened on April 10, 1962, it was a ballpark unlike any of its predecessors and better by far than many stadia that came after it. Built at a cost of $18 million, it was attractive, spacious, comfortable, and fan friendly. Surrounding the ballpark were parking lots to accommodate 16,000 cars. The lots were color coded, and the color scheme directed fans to the section where their seats were located. Inside the stadium, fans found cantilevered decks that eliminated poles, wide seats, gently sloping ramps, many concessions stands, and a very large scoreboard displaying lots of information. Those who purchased more expensive tickets received more elaborate service. The Stadium Club and the Diamond Room were reserved for the most select patrons, and special dugout-level box seats attracted an array of Hollywood stars. Dodger Stadium had 56,000 seats, all with unobstructed views of the field. O'Malley predicted confidently that one day his team would draw 3 million fans.

The 1962 Dodgers rose to the occasion. They won 101 games in the regular season and tied the Giants for first place, necessitating a playoff. Drysdale won 25 games and the Cy Young Award, while outfielder Tommy Davis led the league with a batting average of .346 and 153 RBIs. The star of the team, though, was diminutive shortstop Maury Wills, who scored 130 runs and stole 104 bases, surpassing the major-league record of 96 set by Ty Cobb in 1915. The catcher was four-time All-Star John Roseboro, who is best remembered for his brawl with pitcher Juan Marichal on August 22, 1965, at Candlestick Park. Marichal had hit a Dodgers batter, and while at bat was nearly hit by Roseboro's tosses back to the mound. He told Roseboro to stop, and when the catcher stood up and took off his mask, Marichal felt threatened and hit him in the head with the bat. This led to a violent 14-minute bench-clearing brawl. Roseboro suffered a nasty gash to his head and a concussion; Marichal was suspended for a week and fined $1,750.

In the best-of-three playoff, the Dodgers lost the first game, won the second, and took a 4–2 lead into the ninth inning of the finale. The Giants then erupted for four runs, with the lead run scoring on a bases-loaded walk by Stan Williams, and advanced to the World Series. In the aftermath of this bitter defeat, reminiscent of 1951, heads rolled. O'Malley considered firing Alston and replacing him with Durocher, who had rejoined the team as a coach, but Bavasi persuaded him not to do so. Instead, Durocher, a thorn in Alston's side, was fired, as was the manager's longtime coach and confidante Joe Becker. Several of the players involved in the game three collapse were traded or sold, too, including Williams and aging star Snider.

THE KOUFAX ERA

In 1963, Koufax became the most dominant and overpowering pitcher in the major leagues. A native of Brooklyn who attended the University of Cincinnati on a basketball scholarship, he signed a contract with the Dodgers in December 1954. Because he received a bonus in excess of $4,000, baseball's rules required that the team keep him on the major-league roster for two full seasons. This restriction did Koufax no good. He lost the opportunity to hone his craft in the minor leagues, and he struggled for six seasons to control his explosive fastball and sweeping curve. He did not post a winning record until 1961, when he was named to the All-Star team for the first of six straight years and led the league in strikeouts. Over the next five seasons, Koufax won five ERA titles; pitched four no-hitters, one of them a perfect game; and led the league in strikeouts three times. He won 25 games in 1963 (306 strikeouts, 1.88 ERA, MVP), 26 in 1965 (385 strikeouts, 2.04 ERA), and 27 in 1966 (317 strikeouts, 1.73 ERA), and won the Cy Young Award each of those years. The Dodgers made the World Series all three years because of their outstanding pitching, winning twice. Their offense was weak, mainly the product of Maury Wills swiping bases and the hitting of Tommy Davis, who won his second batting crown in 1963 (.326). They swept the Yankees in 1963 and defeated the Minnesota Twins in seven games two years later. In this Series, Koufax declined to play in the first game, opting instead to observe Yom Kippur, but he pitched a three-hit shutout in the decisive game and was Series MVP. Following the 1966 Series, he announced his premature retirement, a victim of crippling arthritis in his pitching arm. Though his 12 seasons and 165 wins left him far short of the usual benchmarks by which pitching excellence is measured, he was easily elected to the Hall of Fame.

Drysdale, Koufax's partner in these pitching-rich years, was a California native whose talents combined speed with a willingness to intimidate batters by hitting them. He became successful sooner than did Koufax, leading the league in strikeouts in 1959, 1960, and 1962. An eight-time All-Star, he played 14 years, won 209 games, and was elected to the Hall of Fame in 1984. Before the 1966 season, he and Koufax audaciously pursued an unprecedented joint negotiation with the Dodgers. They wanted a three-year agreement paying $500,000 each. With very little bargaining power except the threat not to play at all, the pair remained in Los Angeles when the team reported for spring training. They signed a contract to appear in a movie, and Koufax got an advance from Viking Press on his autobiography. Finally, in late March, the impasse was resolved, and both players signed one-year contracts at the team's terms, Koufax for $125,000 and Drysdale for $110,000. The club's intransigence virtually guaranteed that Koufax would make 1966 his last season, and after it was over, the team also ridded itself of another longtime Dodger stalwart, shortstop Maury Wills, trading him to the Pirates.

Sandy Koufax holds four baseballs with zeroes on them to signify his 4th no-hitter, 1963. Courtesy of the Baseball Hall of Fame

TOMMY LASORDA AND THE "DODGER WAY"

Over the next few seasons the team floundered in the standings, and the club's executive leadership underwent substantial change. Bavasi, who was unable to rebuild the team after it was swept by the Baltimore Orioles in the 1966 World Series, left to become a part owner of the San Diego Padres, an NL expansion team. Thompson replaced him, but soon died of cancer, and Al Campanis, formerly the director of scouting, succeeded him with the title of vice president for player personnel and scouting. O'Malley named his son Peter president of the club and became chairman of the board. One result of these transitions was that the club lessened its commitment to cultivating its own talent and to the Dodger Way. On the field, the club deemphasized its reliance on pitching and defense and put more stress on power hitting. A series of trades brought several sluggers to Los Angeles, but mostly players past their prime. Their eroded skills left the Dodgers playing second fiddle in the NL's Western Division to the Reds. Alston struggled through these years and was never offered more than a one-year contract. This made him a cautious manager, trying to win as many games as possible with the talent on hand, but declining to take any risk that might cost him his job. In 1973, the club installed Tommy Lasorda, onetime pitcher and longtime minor-league manager, as third-base coach and heir apparent.

That season, the team finally assembled a roster capable of winning the pennant. The core was the infield of Steve Garvey (MVP in 1974) at first base, Davey Lopes at second, Bill Russell at shortstop, and Ron Cey at third. They were complemented by starting pitchers Don Sutton, Claude Osteen, Tommy John, and Andy Messersmith, along with closer Mike Marshall, who won the Cy Young Award in 1974, finishing 83 games, with 21 saves. The Dodgers finished second in the West in 1973 and first in 1974 with 102 victories, leading the NL in scoring, home runs, and pitching (2.97 ERA). They defeated Pittsburgh in the NL Championship Series, three games to one, but lost the World Series in five games to the defending champion Oakland A's. Alston remained at the helm for two more seasons, but the Reds were a superior team, and it became clear that the club would not offer him a contract for 1977. With four games left in the 1976 season, he retired, and Lasorda took over.

The new manager brought with him an incredible amount of enthusiasm for his job, his team, and his players, an attitude encapsulated by his frequent use of the phrase "bleeding Dodger blue" and his prayerful glances toward "the big Dodger in the sky." In the last years of Alston's tenure, Los Angeles fans had become famously complacent. They arrived late for games and left early to beat the traffic. While sitting in Dodger Stadium, many listened quietly to broadcaster Vin Scully on their transistor radios. Lasorda tried to change all that. He acted as a cheerleader and refurbished the club's Hollywood image. He opened the clubhouse to celebrities like Frank Sinatra and comedian Don Rickles and frequented restaurants and clubs where the stars gathered. Lasorda was also a fine manager, and his team included quality players, many of whom had played for him in the minors. An early winning streak put the Dodgers in first place, and their powerful lineup kept them there. Four players, Garvey, Cey, Reggie Smith, and Dusty Baker, hit 30 or more home runs; Lopes stole 47 bases; and the starting pitching was more than adequate. Los Angeles dethroned Cincinnati's vaunted Big Red Machine by 10 games and defeated the Phillies to win the pennant. In the World Series, the Dodgers faced the Yankees yet again and lost, four games to two, as New York's Reggie Jackson set a Series record by hitting five home runs, three of them in the last game on three consecutive pitches against three different pitchers.

The 1978 season was, in some ways, a carbon copy of 1977. The Dodgers won the West (95–67), having led in batting (.262). runs per game (4.49), and ERA (3.12). The Reds finished second, the Phillies won the East, and the Dodgers advanced to the World Series, only to lose once more to the Yankees. Beneath the surface, though, there was turmoil. Lasorda's act had begun to wear thin. He acted far differently in private than in public, and he was prone to treat certain players, especially the younger ones, with utter disdain. He alienated many and lost support in the media. In the clubhouse, a serious rift developed between Garvey and several of his teammates, who took exception to his fondness for the media spotlight. Still, the Dodgers fulfilled their owner's prophecy by becoming the first team to draw more than 3 million fans. O'Malley was suffering from cancer, and he died in August 1979. The astute businessman left a personal estate to his two children, a family trust, and a ball club worth at least $60 million that made money every year. Formal control of the team passed to Peter O'Malley, who had already begun to run it like the graduate of the Wharton School of Business that he was. The club was still a family-owned enterprise, but it looked and acted much like any other modern corporation.

The spark that continued to attract fans in the early 1980s came from a charismatic Mexican pitcher, Fernando Valenzuela. Los Angeles had become the most ethnically diverse city in the country, and "Fernandomania" gripped fans for several seasons. Valenzuela had an unusual pitching motion, lifting his eyes skyward as he raised his right leg, and his success in 1981 helped to salve the wounds resulting from a midseason strike by the MLB Players Association. With a record of 13–7, Valenzuela won the Rookie of the Year Award and the Cy Young Award, and he pitched a complete game in the World Series against the Yankees. This time the Dodgers came out ahead in six games.

Valenzuela's ascent was meteoric, but his team's fortunes during the rest of his career were erratic. Los Angeles won division titles in 1983 and 1985, but failed to advance to the Series either time. But in 1984, Valenzuela went 12–17, and the Dodgers finished fourth in the six-team division. Two seasons later he rebounded, winning 21 games, but the Dodgers were terrible, winning only 73 games and nearly finishing last. The team, victimized by poor trades, played bad defense and had a weak bullpen. It was beset by injuries, racked with more dissension, and confounded by the multiple suspensions imposed on pitcher Steve Howe for repeatedly using cocaine. On April 7, 1987, Campanis appeared on the ABC television show *Nightline* to mark the 40th anniversary of Jackie Robinson's major-league debut. After interviewing Jackie's widow, Rachel Robinson, and sportswriter Roger Kahn, host Ted Koppel asked Campanis, "Is there still that much prejudice in baseball?" Campanis responded, "No. I don't believe it's prejudice. I truly believe they [African Americans] may not have some of the necessities to be, let's say, a field manager or perhaps a general manager." Koppel gave Campanis several chances to retract or amend his remarks, but he held firm. O'Malley, reacting to a firestorm of media criticism and the threat of a boycott, fired him two days later. Baseball had dragged its feet on hiring minorities for management positions on and off the field, and the Dodgers had now publicly abdicated their position as racial pioneers. Replacing Campanis was Fred Claire, a former journalist who had long worked for the club in marketing and public relations.

Despite all of this, Los Angeles put together an extraordinary season in 1988, with baseball's fifth-highest-paid team ($15,462,515), and won the World Series for the sixth time. The team's offense was hardly special, but the pitching was outstanding, with a league-leading 2.93 ERA. Outfielder Kirk Gibson, acquired as a free agent mostly for his leadership, won the MVP, despite hitting only .290 and driving in but 76 runs. The real star was NL Cy Young winner Orel Hershiser, who won 23 games and set a major-league record by pitching 59 consecutive scoreless innings. In September, he won five games while giving up no earned runs. Hershiser carried the Dodgers to a victory over the New York Mets in the NLCS, pitching four times in nine days. Before the first game of the World Series against Oakland, Gibson remained in the clubhouse to care for a pulled hamstring muscle. He had received injections of both cortisone and xylocaine earlier than day, and Lasorda did not expect him to play. Nevertheless, Gibson volunteered to pinch-hit in the bottom of the ninth inning with a man on first base and the Dodgers down a run. He hobbled to the plate, fouled off three pitches from ace reliever Dennis Eckersley, took two balls, and then hit an inside slider just over the fence in right field to win the game in melodramatic fashion. The Dodgers defeated Oakland in five games, with Hershiser winning two of them. The Series success resulted in the team moving up to the highest-paid club in 1989 ($21.6 million), and their payroll remained high until 1995, when they were only 17th at $30.5 million. By 2000 they were second only to the Yankees ($90.4 million), falling off to sixth in 2004 ($92.9 million).

Since the epic finish of 1988, Los Angeles has had its ups and downs, finishing 1992 with the worst record in the league, but finishing first in its division three times: 1994, when a strike by the Players Association led to an abbreviated season; 1995, when the club lost the NL Division Series, the new first round of postseason play, in three games to the Reds; and 2004, when the team lost the NLDS again, 3–1 to the Cardinals. The next year they collapsed to fourth place with a dismal record of 71–91. The star of the team in the 1990s was catcher Mike Piazza, Rookie of the Year in 1993. In five full seasons with the Dodgers and parts of two others, he batted an astounding .331. Lasorda remained as manager until midway through the 1996 season. He had been severely shaken by the death of his son from AIDS in 1991,and his shtick had grown quite stale. With the club searching for a way to ease him out gracefully, he suffered a heart attack in late June 1996, and a month later resigned. Bill Russell was named to replace him, and he was followed in turn by Glenn Hoffman, Davey Johnson, and Jim Tracy, who resigned after the 2005 season.

THE DODGERS SANS O'MALLEY

On January 6, 1997, O'Malley announced that the club was for sale. Overall, his tenure had been quite successful, but it was the Atlanta Braves, not the Dodgers, who were the best team in the league during the 1990s. Ever since moving to Los Angeles, the Dodgers always had enough money to do as they pleased, and Walter O'Malley had become one of the most influential owners in the game's inner circle. Throughout the 1990s, they were among the more valuable franchises. Peter O'Malley eschewed that role, and he was not keen to practice the fiscal restraint being preached by Commissioner Allan H. "Bud" Selig. Moreover, O'Malley said that his children were not interested in running the club, even though it had continued to be extremely profitable. By the fall, News Corporation Limited, the international media conglomerate owned by Australian Rupert Murdoch, had been identified as the probable buyer. News Corp. already owned the Fox Broadcasting Company and the rights to telecast baseball nationally and locally, but observers were not quite sure why Murdoch wanted to add a baseball team to his holdings. Perhaps he reacted to news that the Disney Company, one of his major competitors, had purchased an NHL franchise and the Anaheim Angels with the intention of building a cable-television empire in Southern California. Regardless, other clubs feared that Murdoch's great wealth would give the Dodgers an extreme competitive advantage.

The transaction took more than a year to complete, but on March 19, 1998, baseball's owners approved the sale of the franchise and all its assets for $311 million. Fox executives immediately took control and made changes. Chase Carey, chairman of Fox TV, negotiated a blockbuster trade that sent All-Star catcher Mike Piazza to the Florida Marlins. On June 21, with the team off to a poor start, the new owners fired both Russell and Claire, with Lasorda coming out of retirement to serve as Claire's interim replacement. Six months later, Lasorda stepped aside as the club hired Kevin Malone, Baltimore's assistant general manager. His tenure lasted until April 14, 2001, when he resigned after an altercation with fans in San Diego flared into an incident that demanded action. Dan Evans was hired from the White Sox.

As a News Corp. property, the Dodgers failed on the field, struggled at the box office, and lost money in 2001, estimated by *Forbes* at $29.6 million. The team took in about $41 million in revenue from activities associated with Dodger Stadium, such as parking and concessions, which amounted to the fifth highest in MLB. The average ticket price of $15.43 was only 19th among big-league teams, which was why the Dodgers only took in $50.7 million at the gate while drawing over 3 million fans. The company invested $100 million in refurbishing Dodger Stadium, but also suggested that the team might sell Dodgertown and do its spring training in Arizona or California. Rumors surfaced in 2001 that Murdoch wanted to sell. He had used the club to build up the Fox Sports West regional cable network, which he would retain, and continued ownership made little sense. Besides, Disney had also announced its intention to sell its teams. Finding a buyer for the Dodgers, though, took quite a while. The team's payroll was very high, and Murdoch's alleged asking price was steep. In October 2003, Frank McCourt, a Boston real-estate developer whose grandfather had once owned part of the Braves, offered $430 million for the club, and News Corp. accepted. MLB questioned the details of this proposed transaction at length since McCourt would not be using very much of his own money. Others wondered if his real interest was not the club, but the land on which Dodger Stadium sat. On January 29, 2004, baseball's owners gave their approval to a deal that had News Corp. loaning McCourt about one-third of the purchase price. The new owner seemed to be committed to restoring the Dodgers to financial stability and eventually to their former glory on the field. For his first move, he fired Evans and hired Paul DePodesta, a young, aggressive executive who had worked for Billy Beane, Oakland's general manager. Beane had gained notoriety for building a successful team within a very limited budget by using new ways to evaluate players. However, following some unpopular trades, DePodesta was replaced after the 2005 season by Nick Colletti. McCourt hoped that Colletti could restore a proud franchise to its days of glory.

NOTABLE ACHIEVEMENTS

Most Valuable Players

Year	Name	Position
1941	Dolph Camilli	1B
1949	Jackie Robinson	2B
1951	Roy Campanella	C
1953	Roy Campanella	C
1955	Roy Campanella	C
1956	Don Newcombe	P
1962	Maury Wills	SS
1963	Sandy Koufax	P
1974	Steve Garvey	1B
1988	Kirk Gibson	OF

Cy Young Winners

Year	Name	Position
1956	Don Newcombe	RHP
1962	Don Drysdale	RHP
1963	Sandy Koufax	LHP
1965	Sandy Koufax	LHP
1966	Sandy Koufax	LHP
1974	Mike Marshall	RHP
1981	Fernando Valenzuela	LHP
1988	Orel Hershiser	RHP
2003	Eric Gagne	RHP

Rookies of the Year

Year	Name	Position
1947	Jackie Robinson	1B
1949	Don Newcombe	P
1952	Joe Black	P
1953	Jim Gilliam	2B
1960	Frank Howard	OF
1965	Jim Lefebvre	2B
1969	Ted Sizemore	2B
1979	Rick Sutcliffe	P
1980	Steve Howe	P
1981	Fernando Valenzuela	P
1982	Steve Sax	2B
1992	Eric Karros	1B
1993	Mike Piazza	C
1994	Raul Mondesi	OF
1995	Hideo Nomo	P
1996	Todd Hollandsworth	OF

Batting Champions

Year	Name	#
1892	Dan Brouthers	.335
1913	Jake Daubert	.350
1914	Jake Daubert	.329
1918	Zack Wheat	.335
1932	Lefty O'Doul	.368
1941	Pete Reiser	.343
1944	Dixie Walker	.357
1949	Jackie Robinson	.342
1953	Carl Furillo	.344
1962	Tommy Davis	.346
1963	Tommy Davis	.326

Home-Run Champions

Year	Name	#
1890	Oyster Burns	13
1903	Jimmy Sheckard	9
1904	Harry Lumley	9
1906	Tim Jordan	12
1908	Tim Jordan	12

1924	Jack Fournier	27
1941	Dolph Camilli	34
1956	Duke Snider	43
2004	Adrian Beltre	48

ERA Champions

Year	Name	#
1924	Dazzy Vance	2.16
1928	Dazzy Vance	2.09
1930	Dazzy Vance	2.61
1957	Johnny Podres	2.66
1962	Sandy Koufax	2.54
1963	Sandy Koufax	1.88
1964	Sandy Koufax	1.74
1965	Sandy Koufax	2.04
1966	Sandy Koufax	1.73
1980	Don Sutton	2.20
1984	Alejandro Pena	2.48
2000	Kevin Brown	2.58

Strikeout Champions

Year	Name	#
1921	Burleigh Grimes	136
1922	Dazzy Vance	134
1923	Dazzy Vance	197
1924	Dazzy Vance	262
1925	Dazzy Vance	221
1926	Dazzy Vance	140
1927	Dazzy Vance	184
1928	Dazzy Vance	200
1936	Van Mungo	238
1951	Don Newcombe	164
1959	Don Drysdale	242
1960	Don Drysdale	246
1961	Sandy Koufax	269
1962	Don Drysdale	232
1963	Sandy Koufax	306
1965	Sandy Koufax	382
1966	Sandy Koufax	317
1981	Fernando Valenzuela	180
1995	Hideo Nomo	236

No-Hitters (Italics = Perfect Game)

Name	Date
Tom Lovett	06/22/1891
Mal Eason	07/20/1906
Nap Rucker	09/05/1908
Dazzy Vance	09/13/1925
Tex Carleton	04/30/1940
Ed Head	04/23/1946
Rex Barney	09/09/1948
Carl Erskine	06/19/1952
Carl Erskine	05/12/1956
Sal Maglie	09/25/1956
Sandy Koufax	06/30/1962
Sandy Koufax	05/11/1963
Sandy Koufax	06/04/1964
Sandy Koufax	*09/09/1965*
Bill Singer	07/20/1970
Jerry Reuss	06/27/1980
Fernando Valenzuela	06/29/1990
Kevin Gross	08/17/1992
Ramon Martinez	07/14/1995
Hideo Nomo	09/17/1996

POSTSEASON APPEARANCES

NL West Division Titles

Year	Record	Manager
1974	102–60	Walter Alston
1977	98–64	Tommy Lasorda
1978	95–67	Tommy Lasorda
1981	63–47	Tommy Lasorda
1983	91–71	Tommy Lasorda
1985	95–67	Tommy Lasorda
1988	94–67	Tommy Lasorda
1994	58–56	Tommy Lasorda
1995	78–66	Tommy Lasorda
2004	93–69	Jim Tracy

NL Wild Cards

Year	Record	Manager
1996	90–72	Tommy Lasorda
		Bill Russell

Pennants

Year	Record	Manager
1889	93–44	Bill McGunnigle (AA)
1890	86–43	Bill McGunnigle
1899	101–47	Ned Hanlon
1900	82–54	Ned Hanlon
1916	94–60	Wilbert Robinson
1920	93–61	Wilbert Robinson
1941	100–54	Leo Durocher
1947	94–60	Clyde Sukeforth
		Burt Shotton
1949	97–57	Burt Shotton
1952	96–57	Chuck Dressen
1953	105–49	Chuck Dressen
1955	98–55	Walt Alston
1956	93–61	Walt Alston
1959	88–68	Walt Alston
1963	99–63	Walt Alston
1965	97–65	Walt Alston
1966	95–67	Walt Alston
1974	102–60	Walt Alston
1977	98–64	Tommy Lasorda
1978	95–67	Tommy Lasorda
1981	63–47	Tommy Lasorda
1988	94–67	Tommy Lasorda

World Championships

Year	Opponent	MVP
1955	New York	Johnny Podres
1959	Chicago	Larry Sherry
1963	New York	Sandy Koufax
1965	Minnesota	Sandy Koufax
1981	New York	Ron Cey
		Pedro Guerrero
		Steve Yeager
1988	Oakland	Orel Hershiser

MANAGERS

2006	Grady Little
2001–2005	Jim Tracy
1999–2001	Davey Johnson
1998	Glenn Hoffman

1996–1998	Bill Russell
1976–1996	Tommy Lasorda
1954–1976	Walter Alston
1951–1953	Chuck Dressen
1948–1950	Burt Shotton
1948	Ray Blades
1948	Leo Durocher
1947	Burt Shotton
1947	Clyde Sukeforth
1939–1946	Leo Durocher
1937–1938	Burleigh Grimes
1934–1936	Casey Stengel
1932–1933	Max Carey
1914–1931	Wilbert Robinson
1910–1913	Bill Dahlen
1909	Harry Lumley
1906–1908	Patsy Donovan
1899–1905	Ned Hanlon
1898	Charles Ebbets
1898	Mike Griffin
1897–1898	Billy Barnie
1893–1896	Dave Foutz
1891–1892	John M. Ward
1888–1890	Bill McGunnigle (American Association 1888–1889)
1886–1887	Charlie Byrne (AA)

Team Records by Individual Players

Batting Leaders

	Single Season			Career		
	Name		Year	Name		Plate Appearances
Batting average	Babe Herman	.393	1930	Willie Keeler	.352	2,594
On-base %	Mike Griffin	.467	1894	Gary Sheffield	.424	2,276
Slugging %	Babe Herman	.678	1930	Gary Sheffield	.573	2,276
OPS	Babe Herman	1.132	1930	Gary Sheffield	.998	2,276
Games	Maury Wills	165	1962	Zach Wheat	2,322	9,720
At bats	Maury Wills	695	1962	Zach Wheat	8,859	9,720
Runs	Hub Collins	148	1890	PeeWee Reese	1,338	9,470
Hits	Babe Herman	241	1930	Zach Wheat	2,804	9,720
Total bases	Babe Herman	416	1930	Zach Wheat	4,003	9,720
Doubles	Johnny Frederick	52	1929	Zach Wheat	464	9,720

(Continued)

Batting Leaders (Continued)

	Single Season			Career	
	Name		Year	Name		Plate
Triples	George Treadway	26	1894	Zach Wheat	171	9,720
Home runs	Shawn Green	49	2001	Duke Snider	389	7,633
RBIs	Tommy Davis	153	1962	Duke Snider	1,271	7,633
Walks	Eddie Stanky	148	1945	Pee Wee Reese	1,210	9,470
Strikeouts	Billy Grabarkewitz	149	1970	Duke Snider	1,123	7,633
Stolen bases	Maury Wills	104	1962	Maury Wills	490	6,744
Extra-base hits	Babe Herman	94	1930	Duke Snider	814	7,633
Times on base	Babe Herman	311	1930	Zach Wheat	3,509	9,720

Pitching Leaders

	Single Season			Career		Innings Pitched
	Name		Year	Name		
ERA	Rube Marquard	1.58	1916	Jeff Pfeffer	2.31	1,748.3
Wins	Bob Caruthers	40	1889	Don Sutton	233	3,816.3
Won-loss %	Freddie Fitzsimmons	.889	1940	Preacher Roe	.715	1,277.3
Hits/9 IP	Sandy Koufax	5.79	1965	Sandy Koufax	6.79	2,324.3
Walks/9 IP	Watty Clark	1.22	1935	Curt Davis	1.77	1,007.3
Strikeouts	Sandy Koufax	382	1965	Don Sutton	2,696	3,816.3
Strikeouts/9 IP	Hideo Nomo	11.1	1995	Eric Gagne	10.37	5,43.3
Games	Mike Marshall	106	1974	Don Sutton	550	3,816.3
Saves	Eric Gagne	55	2003	Eric Gagne	160	543.3
Innings	Henry Porter	481.7	1885	Don Sutton	3,816.3	3,816.3
Starts	Adonis Terry	55	1884	Don Sutton	533	3,816.3
Complete games	Adonis Terry	54	1884	Brickyard Kennedy	279	2,857
Shutouts	Sandy Koufax	11	1963	Don Sutton	52	3,816.3

Source: Drawn from data in: "Los Angeles Dodgers Batting Leaders (seasonal and career)." http://base ball-reference.com/teams/LAD/leaders_bat.shtml; "Los Angeles Dodgers Pitching Leaders (seasonal and career)," http://baseball-reference.com/teams/LAD/leaders_pitch.shtml.

BIBLIOGRAPHY

Bavasi, Buzzie, with John Strege. *Off the Record*. Chicago: Contemporary Books, 1987.

Creamer, Robert. *Stengel: His Life and Times*. New York: Simon and Schuster, 1984.

Dewey, Donald, and Nicholas Acocella. *Encyclopedia of Major League Baseball Teams*. New York: HarperCollins, 1993.

Drysdale, Don, with Bob Verdi. *Once a Bum, Always a Dodger*. New York: St. Martin's Press, 1990.

Kahn, Roger. *The Boys of Summer*. New York: Harper and Row, 1972.

Koppett, Leonard. *Koppett's Concise History of Major League Baseball*. Philadelphia: Temple University Press, 1998.

Koufax, Sandy, with Ed Linn. *Koufax*. New York: Viking, 1966.

McGee, Bob. *The Greatest Ballpark Ever: Ebbets Field and the Story of the Brooklyn Dodgers*. New Brunswick, NJ: Rutgers University Press, 2005.

McKelvey, G. Richard. *The MacPhails: Baseball's First Family of the Front Office*. Jefferson, NC: McFarland, 2000.

McNeil, William F. *The Dodgers Encyclopedia*. Champaign, IL: Sports Publishing, 1997.

Oliphant, Thomas. *Praying for Gil Hodges: A Memoir of the 1955 World Series and One Family's Love of the Brooklyn Dodgers*. New York: St. Martin's Press, 2005.

Prince, Carl. *Brooklyn's Dodgers: The Bums, the Borough, and the Best of Baseball, 1947–1957*. New York: Oxford University Press, 1996.

Shapiro, Michael. *The Last Good Season: Brooklyn, the Dodgers, and their Final Pennant Race Together*. New York: Doubleday, 2003.

Stout, Glenn. *The Dodgers: 120 Years of Dodgers Baseball*. Boston: Houghton Mifflin, 2004.

Sullivan, Neil J. *The Dodgers Move West*. New York: Oxford University Press, 1987.

Terry, James L. *Long Before the Dodgers: Baseball in Brooklyn, 1855–1884*. Jefferson, NC: McFarland, 2002.

Walter O'Malley official Web site. http://www.walteromalley.com/.

9

Milwaukee Brewers

John McCarthy and Christopher Miller

The Milwaukee Brewers were the third major-league baseball team to play in Milwaukee, starting with the short-lived 1901 AL team. Several minor-league teams had used the nickname dating back to the nineteenth century, most recently a Triple-A club that had played in Milwaukee until 1952. The Braves moved in from Boston in 1953, and, under new management, moved to Atlanta in 1965. The proposed move provoked a strong response by local officials as Milwaukee County filed suit to enforce its lease agreement with the team, which required the Braves to play in Milwaukee through 1965. Attendance for the lame-duck team was abysmal, amounting to only 555,584 fans. The Braves used this statistic as evidence that Milwaukee could not support a baseball team, a contention only strengthened in the minds of baseball owners by Milwaukee County's decision to file a second lawsuit, which alleged that the proposed move violated federal antitrust laws. In response to the multiple lawsuits that challenged MLB's antitrust exemption, organized baseball in 1968 did not grant Milwaukee any of its four new expansion franchises. It appeared that Milwaukee would be without major-league baseball indefinitely.

However, local leaders did not give up in their quest to return their hometown to major-league status. Local boosters, led by Allan H. "Bud" Selig, a local car dealer, and such notables as Edmund B. Fitzgerald, a local insurance executive, and the Greater Milwaukee Committee, an elite group of civic promoters, enticed the White Sox to play 10 home games in 1968 and 1969 at Milwaukee County Stadium, 90 miles north of Chicago. The White Sox drew over 20,000 fans per game for the two seasons, demonstrating that Milwaukee's interest in major-league baseball had not waned despite the bitter departure of the Braves.

MAJOR-LEAGUE BASEBALL RETURNS TO MILWAUKEE

After the 1969 season, the year-old expansion Seattle Pilots declared bankruptcy, and Selig's syndicate was ready to pounce. Dewey Soriano, former president of the Pacific Coast League, and his brother Max, the league's legal counsel, led the Pilots. Seattle voters in 1968 had approved construction of a domed stadium, but meanwhile the team played in 22,500-seat Sick's Stadium. The American League demanded the Pilots make substantial renovations in the park and find more investors, since the team had lost millions on paper. When the owners could not meet these demands, the path was cleared for Selig's syndicate to buy the team and move it to Milwaukee for $10.8 million. The deal was closed on March 31, 1970, just five days before the start of the 1970 season.

The newly christened Brewers arrived in Milwaukee on April 5, 1970, and in a sign of the times, were met at General Mitchell Airport by 8,000 eager fans. By comparison, in 1953 a throng at the downtown railroad terminal had met the Braves. The successful attempt to acquire a franchise did not translate to success on the field, and the team compiled a dismal 65–97 record, just one more victory than the Pilots had the year before. A losing record proved no barrier to attendance, as about 935,000 Milwaukeeans passed through the turnstiles, a figure that AL president Joe Cronin called "remarkable, when you think the move was made only five days before the start of the season."

The early years were characterized by continued sub-.500 seasons. The team did not win more than 70 games under manager Dave Bristol, and he was fired in early 1972, replaced by old-time Milwaukee Brave Del Crandall. He fared little better, winning 74 games in 1973 and 76 in 1974, while attendance rose to just under 1.1 million by 1974. Selig maintained that even then the team was not profitable, and has denied reports that his investment group had ever received dividends. Perhaps the lone bright spot in the nascent years of the franchise was the return of home-run king Hank Aaron, who had starred for the Braves in the 1950s. However, at age 41 Aaron was a shadow of his former self, and his two-year stint with the Brewers was mainly symbolic.

BUILDING A CONTENDER

While the team's won-lost record remained poor in the mid 1970s, the Brewers quietly pieced together the elements that would make them a successful team. From 1973 to 1978, outfielder Gorman Thomas, infielder Jim Gantner, catcher Charlie Moore, and pitchers Moose Haas and Jim Slaton all emerged as talented young players, but the most important young Brewer was shortstop Robin Yount, who in 1974 was rushed to the majors at age 18. Despite his inexperience, Yount became an everyday player almost from his arrival, and throughout the mid-1970s showed flashes of the fielding and hitting skills that characterized his career. Although disgruntled fans did not realize it during the dark days of 1976 and 1977, Yount was slowly becoming an all-around star.

However, any improvements individual players made on the field were overshadowed by collective futility. After a second consecutive last-place finish in 1977, Selig decided that sweeping changes were needed at virtually all levels of the franchise. First, the team plunged into baseball's newly created free-agent market, landing slugging Minnesota outfielder Larry Hisle in a six-year, $3 million deal. A day after the Hisle signing was announced, the ax fell on management. Director of player development Al Widmar and manager Alex Grammas were fired, and general manager Jim Baumer resigned. No-nonsense Harry Dalton assumed the role of general manager, and immediately laid out his new standards for the team: "I'm no miracle worker, but first you've got to get rid of the dogs, the chronic losers." Dalton provided the Brewers with an experienced baseball mind and gave the franchise much-needed stability in the front office, remaining through 1991. For the immediate future, Dalton picked George Bamberger, longtime pitching coach of the Baltimore Orioles, to manage the struggling Brewers.

Nonetheless, with the vast majority of the previous year's last-place team back again, there was little reason to believe that 1978 would bring much success. Yet the Brewers stunned the baseball world by winning 93 games and finishing in third place in the tough AL East. Pitchers Mike Caldwell and Larry Sorensen and sluggers Thomas and Hisle all had career seasons. Rookie Paul Molitor stole 30 bases, hinting at future greatness and demonstrating all-around skills similar to Yount. However, the most popular Brewer in 1978 was not a player, but manager George "Bambi" Bamberger. He charmed fans all season long with his blunt assessment of player performances, no-nonsense approach to the game, and above all, lack of pretension. Bamberger drove a modest Ford Fairmont and enjoyed hanging out in neighborhood taverns. The *Milwaukee Journal,* the city's afternoon newspaper, delighted in recounting Bamberger's willingness to "have a beer and a ham sandwich with the boys who get their hands dirty making a living." Bamberger's blue-collar approach to the game proved a perfect fit for a city like Milwaukee. Dalton would later recall, "I haven't ever seen a baseball manager touch a community the way George has." Brewer fans' warm response to Bambi was no doubt helped by the team's 27-game improvement.

A year later, the Brewers proved that 1978 was not a fluke by winning a team record 95 games and finishing second in the AL East to the Baltimore Orioles. The team's core of young players had emerged as legitimate stars. Thomas led the league in home runs in 1979 and 1980. Molitor developed into a terrific leadoff hitter and joined Yount as a cornerstone of the franchise. But despite this progress, the postseason remained elusive. In 1980, the team, favored by many to win the AL East, won a disappointing 86 games and finished in third place, 17 games off the pace. Equally disappointing, heart problems forced Bamberger into retirement at the end of 1980. Injuries slowed the offense, but the Brewers primarily lacked dominant pitching. Cognizant of this problem, Dalton pulled off one of the most lopsided trades in recent baseball history. He sent pitchers Dave LaPoint and Larry Sorensen and outfielders Sixto Lezcano and Davey Green to the St. Louis Cardinals for catcher Ted Simmons, starting pitcher Pete Vuckovich, and reliever Rollie Fingers. Upon hearing of the Brewers' acquisitions, new manager Buck Rodgers observed that in the space of 15 minutes the Brewers had become contenders again. With the exception of Lezcano, none of the players the Cardinals acquired achieved more than journeyman status. Meanwhile, the veteran Simmons gave the Brewers added power and clubhouse leadership, and Fingers and Vuckovich won consecutive Cy Young Awards in 1981 and 1982. Dalton arguably surpassed his earlier masterpiece when as Orioles general manager he acquired Hall of Fame slugger Frank Robinson for Milt Pappas.

Dalton's trade increased anticipation for 1981, but labor problems loomed. In midseason, players struck after bitter conflicts with owners over the nature of free agency. With 53 games wiped out, prestrike standings were counted as first-half division winners, and division leaders of the remaining games advanced to an expanded playoff as second-half winners. Stuck in third place when the strike began, the Brewers suddenly found their slate wiped clean. The Brewers, in a tight three-team race with Baltimore and Detroit, managed a 31–22 record the rest of the way, enough to win the abbreviated title and advance to the postseason for the first time. Dalton's heist of the Cardinals had put the team over the top. Vuckovich posted a 14–4 record and Fingers dominated hitters all season, saving 28 games with a 1.04 ERA. First baseman Cecil Cooper hit .320, more than 50 points higher than any other starter. In the first round of the expanded playoffs, however, the Brewers' momentum wore out, as they fell to the New York Yankees three games to two. The two playoff games in County Stadium drew a total of only 61,000 fans, well below capacity.

HARVEY'S WALLBANGERS AND THE 1982 WORLD SERIES

The Brewers expected to remain contenders in 1982, but at the end of May they were limping along at 23–24, with several players grumbling about manager Buck Rodgers's handling of the team. Desperate to shake things up, Dalton fired Rodgers on June 1, replacing him with longtime assistant Harvey Kuenn, whose easygoing approach hit the right tone with the increasingly veteran Brewers. Upon Kuenn's hiring, an impatient Milwaukee sportswriter proclaimed, "Now, let's get on with the winning." The Brewers delivered, sweeping six and a half games ahead of the Orioles by the end of August. For the season, Vuckovich went 18–6 and led AL pitchers in winning percentage, and veteran left-hander Mike Caldwell also provided consistency. In September, Dalton acquired veteran star Don Sutton from the Astros. Fingers again delivered out the bullpen, posting 29 saves, but an elbow injury prematurely ended his season and left a gaping hole in the Brewers' bullpen. Consistent pitching kept the Brewers in games, but the strength of the team was offense. In 1982 Milwaukee hitters, dubbed "Harvey's Wallbangers," outdid themselves. The Brewers slugged 216 home runs, 30 more than any other team in the AL, and also led the league in total runs, hits, RBIs, and slugging percentage. Thomas, outfielder Ben Oglivie, and first baseman Cecil Cooper all surpassed 30 home runs, but it was Yount's maturation into a truly great player that was most impressive. Always a brilliant fielder, Yount finally found a consistent stroke behind the plate in 1982, hitting .331 with 29 home runs and leading the AL in hits, doubles, and slugging percentage.

If there were any doubters of Yount's greatness, they were silenced at the end of the season. In September, the Orioles slowly gained on the Brewers, weakened by Fingers's absence. The Brewers had a three-game lead entering a final four-game series in Baltimore. Inspired in part by legendary manager Earl Weaver's announcement that he would retire at the end of the year, the Orioles stunned the Brewers by winning three straight games, pushing the series to a dramatic denouement on the final day of the season. With veterans Sutton and Jim Palmer facing off, fans anticipated a pitcher's duel, but it was Yount who saved the season, hitting a triple and two home runs in a 10–2 victory. The Brewers had finally won an undisputed championship. Fans flooded downtown Milwaukee after the victory, honking horns, setting off fireworks, and soaking up the city's time in the national spotlight. The title was especially sweet for the die-hard Brewer fans who had watched the team bumble its way through much of the previous decade. One tearful fan hoped Milwaukee would earn respect from the East Coast media, and that they would "recognize Wisconsin as having something since the Vince Lombardi days of football. God, I love it!" For their part, players celebrated in the locker room, and Kuenn called Yount "the best all-around shortstop I've ever seen."

The Brewers were favored in the AL Championship Series to dispatch the veteran California Angels with relative ease, but the Angels surprised Milwaukee by winning the first two games at home, pushing Milwaukee to the brink of elimination. Back at home for game three, the Brewers found their stride, but it was close. Milwaukee took a 5–0 lead. Angels catcher Bob Boone hit a long fly ball to the left-field wall that Oglivie drifted back to catch, but a fan in the first row of the bleachers leaned over the railing and caught the ball, giving Boone a home run and putting the Angels back in the game. The spectator was a 27-year-old man from Racine named Eddie Becker, a devout Brewers backer who attended over 25 games a year and followed the team on road trips, drinking and joking with the players in hotel bars. But for a brief moment, Becker was in danger of becoming a dubious figure in Milwaukee sports history. With 50,000 fans now a potential lynch mob, stadium security escorted the forlorn Becker out of the stadium, where he sat in his car and prayed for a victory. Luckily, the Brewers hung on to win 5–3, and Becker discreetly sat in the upper deck for the rest of the series. After an easy 9–5 victory in game four, the Brewers, behind a key seventh-inning single by Cooper, won a tense deciding game 4–3, delivering Milwaukee its first pennant since 1958 and launching the city into delirium once again.

The Brewers faced the St. Louis Cardinals in the World Series, which provided the media with several interesting angles. The Brewers had won by out-slugging their opponents, while the Cardinals were known for their defense and speed. It was the Cardinals who had traded Fingers, Vuckovich, and Simmons to the Brewers. Moreover, St. Louis and Milwaukee headquartered America's two largest brewers, Anheuser-Busch and Miller Brewing. The national media dubbed the matchup "the Suds Series," which renewed Milwaukee's long-standing reputation as a blue-collar city brimming with breweries. The Cardinals and Brewers battled to a standstill in the first six games. Mike Caldwell won twice for Milwaukee, while Molitor hit .355 and Yount .414 for the series. However, in game seven Fingers's absence was painfully obvious, as Milwaukee's bullpen failed to hold a two-run lead, giving the Cardinals the World Series with a 6–3 victory.

STRUGGLING IN THE MID-1980S

Milwaukee's great run had ended, but the team had finally won over the city, and fans eagerly anticipated the 1983 season. Virtually all the team's key players were set to return, many rewarded with multiyear contracts. The long-term health of the franchise seemed assured. Instead, the 1982 pennant proved to be the end of an era rather than the beginning of sustained greatness. The Brewers' problems in the mid-1980s—both on and off the field—in many ways reflected the team's struggles throughout the history of the franchise. First, a disproportionate number of injuries plagued the Brewers. Molitor, Caldwell, Fingers, and Vuckovich were afflicted with serious injuries and missed significant amounts of time. Second, team management stubbornly refused to look outside the organization for help, failing to sign a single free agent from 1981 through 1991. Third, the Brewers' minor-league system failed to supply the team with the young players it desperately needed. Even more ominously, attendance, which peaked at 2.39 million in 1983, slipped dramatically as the losses piled up, demonstrating that the Brewers had never wholly won over Milwaukee sports fans, who remained preoccupied with the Green Bay Packers. Even during the winning years of the early 1980s, fans in County Stadium often preferred to discuss the numerous shortcomings of the Packers. After the pennant-winning season of 1982, the Brewers suffered through four consecutive losing seasons, and the long-term prospects of the franchise seemed dim.

The 1987 Brewers opened the season with just four players from the 1982 squad. The turnover reflected the team's age and the Brewers' refusal to play the free-agent market. The new wave included Rob Deer, B.J. Surhoff, Greg Brock, and Mark Clear as well as pitchers Teddy Higuera, Bill Wegman, Juan Nieves, and Chris Bosio, who would make up the core of the Tom Treblehorn–managed

Brewers for the next five years. The veteran holdovers (Yount, Molitor, and Gantner) were the highest-paid members of a team whose payroll ranked 22nd out of the 26 major-league teams. The season started off with a bang as the team won six straight, their best start ever. On Easter Sunday, April 28, the Brewers capped a 12-game win streak with a come-from-behind victory that cemented the team's identity as "Team Streak." The success forced local restaurateur George Webb to pay up on a longtime prediction that Milwaukee's team would win 12 games in a row—a promise that dated back to the old Triple-A Brewers. His chain had promised free hamburgers to anyone in the event of such a streak, and on May 1 gave away roughly 115,000 sandwiches to eager fans.

The new-look Brewers attempted to meld considerable young talent with the veteran core of the 1982 championship team. While competitive over the next few years, the pitching staff was especially ravaged by injuries, a curse that seemed to hover over the team like a black cloud. Ace Teddy Higuera was unable to reach his potential, and Bill Wegman, Chris Bosio, Juan Nieves, and Bill Spiers all saw their careers limited. Molitor and Yount remained franchise cornerstones and added to their Hall of Fame credentials. Between 1987 and 1991 Molitor hit over .310 four times, and Yount, moved to the outfield, continued his elite play, winning a second MVP Award in 1990. Both eventually finished their careers with over 3,000 hits and unquestionably remain the team's two greatest players. However, despite Yount and Molitor's sustained excellence, the Brewers failed to meet expectations in the late 1980s. In each of those five years, the team began with high expectations and failed to meet them, while its win totals dropped each year from 91 to 87 to 81 to 74 before rebounding to 83 in Treblehorn's final year. The effort to rebuild around players such as Gary Sheffield, Surhoff, Brock, and Glenn Braggs had failed, and Treblehorn was fired as the team sought a new direction on the field.

Off the field, the years following Milwaukee's World Series appearance in 1982 saw a steady erosion of the franchise's financial position, and by the late 1980s the escalation of player salaries and large-market media contracts had squeezed the Brewers' budget. Baseball owners had tried to restrict player salaries in the mid-1980s, but after the collusion decisions and the damages the courts imposed on the owners, salaries rose stratospherically into the early 1990s, setting the stage for economic disaster. In response to its allegedly deteriorating financial situation, the team began a public campaign for a new stadium in the late 1980s, when a series of reports identified both the economic peril the team faced and the economic impact the team had on the Milwaukee area. Arguments that the franchise was in trouble were, however, hard to maintain in the face of financial records that pointed to profits of nearly $5 million in the 1987 and 1988 seasons as the team had cut payroll and gone with younger, cheaper players. In this environment, the Brewers floated a plan in which they would privately finance a $110 million stadium if the county paid for needed infrastructure improvements to the stadium site.

While the team went to the public, hat in hand, the results on the field were discouraging. Milwaukee fans eagerly awaited the arrival of the young players, especially first-round draft pick Gary Sheffield. Reminiscent of Robin Yount, Sheffield arrived in 1988 as a super talented 19-year-old shortstop. However, Sheffield's slow start and vocal displeasure about his treatment by the team distracted fans from the action on the field and focused their attention on the image of the multimillionaire malcontent. Sheffield's relationship with both the team and the community was tumultuous almost from the minute he set foot in County Stadium. Scarcely two months into his major-league career, he publicly demanded a trade and blasted the organization for failing to treat him with enough respect. Two years later, prior to the 1992 season, after Sheffield complained that general manager Harry Dalton was ruining the team he was traded to the San Diego Padres. Sheffield's departure was ugly, especially since he later claimed that he had underperformed in an effort to get traded, though he later retracted those statements. Despite that retraction, even 10 years later fans still booed Sheffield when his teams visited Milwaukee.

COMMISSIONER BUD SELIG

While the Brewers were trying to build support for a new stadium, the sport as a whole was undergoing a series of wrenching changes, including the selection of a new commissioner. The series of events that led to Bud Selig's election as acting commissioner in 1992 were inextricably tied up in baseball's tangled labor history. Commissioner Fay Vincent's actions in "solving" the 1990 labor dispute led many owners to support Vincent's removal and replacement with Selig in 1992. During the late 1980s, Selig had united a group of small-market franchises whose financial woes ostensibly mirrored the Brewers' and who agreed that significant changes were needed in running baseball. Most significantly, they began pushing for a cap on player salaries to rein in rapidly escalating salaries and increased revenue sharing between the teams to even out the increasing discrepancies between the high- and low-revenue teams. Selig's elevation meant that the agenda of the self-proclaimed small-market teams, both in the relationships of teams to their cities and in player-owner negotiations, which had always been contentious, would be pushed to the forefront in the public eye. As a result, Selig's years as acting commissioner were rocky, exemplified by the players' strike in 1994 and the cancellation of the World Series.

Strangely enough, with economic whirlwinds swirling around the team, the 1992 Brewers gave Milwaukee its most recent shot at contention. Led by Molitor, who batted .320, and AL Rookie of the Year Pat Listach, and bolstered by the league's best pitching, particularly rookie Cal Eldred's outstanding debut (11–2, 1.73 ERA), new manager Phil Garner's team went 92–70. Any hopes for a renaissance were quickly dashed, however, as the next three years produced seasons of 69, 53, and 65 wins and baseball suffered the catastrophic players' strike of 1994 just as plans for the new stadium were moving into high gear. Incidentally, the Brewers' value fell to just $71 million at the start of 1995, the first poststrike season.

Public disgust at the team's performance manifested itself in taxpayer opposition to funding for a stadium. Finally, in August 1995, the state legislature passed by one vote legislation that allowed a five-county sales tax dedicated to funding a new stadium. George Petak of Racine, who cast the deciding vote, faced a recall election that he lost almost exclusively because of his support for the bill. Even after the plan was approved, other political holdups stalled the new stadium, provoking a public rally organized by Milwaukee attorney Gerald Boyle at County Stadium in favor of the project. Dubbed the "We Love Ya' Bud" rally, the event drew approximately 10,000 fans. Fans carrying signs that said "Build it NOW" were treated to an address from Petak. By late 1996, the last hurdles had been overcome, and the new Miller Park, scheduled to cost $313 million and open for the 2000 season, began to take shape outside County Stadium's center-field bleachers.

Selig was elected commissioner in 1998, after serving as acting commissioner for six years. In accordance with his new legitimacy, he removed himself from governance of the Brewers, placed his shares of the team into a blind trust, and ceded day-to-day control to his daughter, Wendy Selig-Prieb. Major changes in baseball during his tenure included the addition of interleague play, the creation of the wild-card playoff spot, increased revenue sharing, a luxury tax, two different expansions, and tightening the rules against drug usage. In the last round of expansion in 1998, the Brewers became the first team to switch from the American to the National League.

THE NATIONAL LEAGUE BREWERS

Armed with the promise of the stadium to come and a new crop of young players, the team "took this thing National" in 1998 armed with some optimism. The team upped its payroll in anticipation of new revenues from Miller Park and proclaimed itself a contender. After a 74–88 finish that year and a nearly identical record the next year, it became clear that the rebuilding plan had not taken root. In addition, during the summer of 1999, a fatal crane collapse on the Miller Park site killed three construction workers and delayed the project for at least a year. The accident and the team's dreadful play created a public-relations nightmare, robbing the franchise of the positive momentum gathering toward the scheduled opening of the new stadium in 2000. The ideal stadium-building plan involved developing an improving team for the move into the new facility so that the increased revenue could be used to make the first year a memorable one. However, the Brewers were heading in the opposite direction, and hit rock bottom in 1999. Faced with the prospect of opening brand-new Miller Park without a competitive team in place, management fired both Garner and general manager Sal Bando. The firings, which resulted in the hiring of Davey Lopes and Dean Taylor, an assistant general manager for the Atlanta Braves, were an admission of the depths to which the team had sunk. In an attempt to salvage the situation, the team announced that the popular seventh-inning sausage races, run by humans wearing sausage costumes, would take place at every game instead of just on Sundays for the rest of the season.

Taylor's reign began with a splash as he set out to remake the club. Trades were quickly made that sent Jeff Cirillo, Jose Valentin, Fernando Vina, Cal Eldred, and others away for pitching prospects Jimmy Haynes and Jamey Wright. Before the 2001 season, Taylor also signed free agent Jeffrey Hammonds to a three-year, $21.75 million contract, then the largest in Brewer history. The team's salaries amounted to $51 million, 22nd in the majors. These moves gave at least the illusion of progress, if not the real thing, and were accompanied by fervent public promises that revenue generated by the new stadium would allow the team to become competitive.

The 2001 season was when the long-promised era of competitive baseball was supposed to begin, but instead the team continued to decline. Miller Park, completed a year late and costing roughly $400 million, opened to rave public reviews that season. More than 2.8 million patrons took in a game there, a franchise record. After years in the red, the team made $16,129,000 according to MLB ($18.8 million by *Forbes*), the most in the majors. This extraordinary profit was based on revenue from baseball operations of $14,385,000 and $1,744,000 from revenue sharing. In an ironic twist, the 2002 team had a franchise-worst season (56–106), though its payroll rose to a franchise record $50 million. This failure caused the firing of Lopes, his interim replacement Jerry Royster, and Taylor as yet another rebuilding plan collapsed into rubble. As if this dismal performance on the field were not enough, the retractable roof on the new stadium suffered from problems almost from the start, as rain leaked into the stadium and several major components had to be replaced.

Growing public pressure throughout 2003 led to the dawn of a new era, as a total housecleaning swept out Wendy Selig-Prieb, Dean Taylor, and Jerry Royster and saw them replaced by Milwaukeean Ulice Payne (the first non-Selig chairman of the team), former Texas Rangers general manager Doug Melvin, and former Brewers catcher Ned Yost. The George Webb prediction was nearly achieved once again late in the 2003 season as the team managed a 10-game winning streak, but finished with a dismal 68–94 record.

The new regime resolved to focus on player development and build on high draft picks to repair the public damage caused by years of losing and the controversial new stadium project. After the 2003 season, ongoing problems with the roof combined with the memory of the crane collapse and Payne's public airing of plans to reduce payroll to create a public outcry. The situation ended with Payne's acrimonious departure from the franchise after only one year.

Most prognosticators believed that success was several years away for the Brewers and their prospects, who comprised one of the best farm systems in the game. However, the Brewers made a blockbuster trade in the off-season that paid much larger dividends than expected. Melvin traded slugging first baseman Richie Sexson to the Arizona Diamondbacks following a directive to reduce payroll and get what he could before Sexson departed as a free agent. But in acquiring Lyle Overbay, Junior Spivey, Craig Counsell, Chad Moeller, Chris Capuano, and Jorge De La Rosa, Melvin significantly improved the team's depth. The new players and a suddenly dominant right-hander, Ben Sheets (2.70 ERA), led the team to a surprisingly good first-half start in 2004. But the second-half collapse of the offense left the team with virtually the same record as 2003 (67–94). Late in the season, California financier Mark Attanasio announced that he had purchased the team from the Seligs for approximately $220 million, and he took control of the team's operations in the off-season.

Ben Sheets throws a pitch before the first inning of a spring training game against the Kansas City Royals in Maryvale, Arizona, 2005. © AP / Wide World Photos

He immediately made his mark by allowing the trade of center fielder Scott Podsednik for powerful left fielder Carlos Lee of the Chicago White Sox, taking on significant salary in the process. Lee produced, with 32 homers and 114 RBIs. The 2005 season was the franchise's first without a Selig in the front office. The team showed marked improvement, despite a $42 million payroll, by climbing to third and a .500 season, the best record since 1992. The youthful team provided a lot more optimism than Brewer fans have felt for years.

NOTABLE ACHIEVEMENTS

Most Valuable Players

Year	Name	Position
1981	Rollie Fingers	P
1982	Robin Yount	SS
1989	Robin Yount	OF

Cy Young Winners

Year	Name	Position
1981	Rollie Fingers	RHP
1982	Pete Vuckovich	RIIP

Rookies of the Year

Year	Name	Position
1992	Pat Listach	SS

Home-Run Champions

Year	Name	#
1975	George Scott	36
1979	Gorman Thomas	45
1980	Ben Oglivie	41
1982	Gorman Thomas	39

No-Hitters

Name	Date
Juan Nieves	04/15/1987

POSTSEASON APPEARANCES

AL East Division Titles

Year	Record	Manager
1981	62–47	Buck Rodgers
1982	95–67	Buck Rodgers
		Harvey Kuenn

AL Pennants

Year	Record	Manager
1982	95–67	Buck Rodgers
		Harvey Kuenn

MANAGERS

2003–	Ned Yost
2002	Jerry Royster
2000–2002	Davey Lopes
1999	Jim Lefebvre
1992–1998	Phil Garner
1986–1991	Tom Trebelhorn
1985–1986	George Bamberger
1984	Rene Lachemann

1982–1983	Harvey Kuenn
1980–1982	Buck Rodgers
1978–1980	George Bamberger
1976–1977	Alex Grammas
1975	Harvey Kuenn
1972–1975	Del Crandall
1970–1971	Dave Bristol
1969	Joe Schultz

Team Records by Individual Players

Batting Leaders

	Single Season			Career		
	Name		**Year**	**Name**		**Plate Appearances**
Batting average	Paul Molitor	.353	1987	Jeff Cirillo	.306	3,437
On-base %	Paul Molitor	.438	1987	Jeff Cirillo	.384	3,437
Slugging %	Geoff Jenkins	.588	2000	Richie Sexson	.536	2,288
OPS	Paul Molitor	1.003	1987	Richie Sexson	.902	2,288
Games	Gorman Thomas	162	1980	Robin Yount 2,856		12,249
At bats	Paul Molitor	666	1982	Robin Yount 11,008		12,249
Runs	Paul Molitor	136	1982	Robin Yount 1,632		12,249
Hits	Cecil Cooper	219	1980	Robin Yount 3,142		12,249
Total bases	Robin Yount	367	1982	Robin Yount 4,730		12,249
Doubles	LyneOverbay	53	2004	Robin Yount 583		12,249
Triples	Paul Molitor	16	1979	Robin Yount 126		12,249
Home runs	Gorman Thomas	45	1979	Robin Yount 251		12,249
RBIs	Cecil Cooper	126	1983	Robin Yount 1,406		12,249
Walks	Jeromy Burnitz	99	2000	Robin Yount 966		12,249
Strikeouts	Jose Hernandez	188	2002	Robin Yount 1350		12,249
stolen bases	Tommy Harper	73	1969	Paul Molitor 412		8,438
Extra-base hits	Robin Yount	87	1982	Robin Yount 960		12,249
Times on base	Paul Molitor	299	1991	Robin Yount 4,156		12,249

Pitching Leaders

	Single Season			Career		
	Name		**Year**	**Name**		**Innings Pitched**
ERA	Mike Caldwell	2.36	1978	Dan Plesac	3.21	524.3
Wins	Mike Caldwell	22	1978	Jim Slaton	117	2,025.3
Won-loss %	Moose Haas	.812	1983	Teddy Higuera	.595	1,380
Hits/9 IP	Teddy Higuera	6.65	1988	Dan Plesac	7.9	524.3

(Continued)

Pitching Leaders   (Continued)

	Single Season			Career		
	Name		Year	Name		Innings Pitched
Walks/9 IP	Ben Sheets	1.22	2004	Lary Sorenson	1.82	854
Strikeouts	Ben Sheets	264	2004	Teddy Higuera	1,081	1,380
Strikeouts/9 IP	Ben Sheets	10.03	2004	Dan Plesac	7.69	524.3
Games	Ken Sanders	83	1971	Dan Plesac	365	524.3
Saves	Danny Kolb	39	2004	Dan Plesac	133	524.3
Innings	Jim Colborn	314.3	1973	Jim Slaton	2,025.3	2,025.3
Starts	Jim Slaton	38	1973	Jim Slaton	268	2,025.3
Complete games	Mike Caldwell	23	1978	Mike Caldwell	81	1,604.7
Shutouts	Mike Caldwell	6	1978	Jim Slaton	19	2,025.3

Source: Drawn from data in "Milwaukee Brewers Batting Leaders (seasonal and career)." http://baseball-reference.com/teams/MIL/leaders_bat.shtml; "Milwaukee Brewers Pitching Leaders (seasonal and career)." http://baseball-reference.com/teams/MIL/leaders_pitch.shtml.

BIBLIOGRAPHY

Adomites, P. D. "Seattle Pilots—Milwaukee Brewers: The Bombers, the Bangers, and the Burners." In *Encyclopedia of Major League Baseball Team Histories: American League,* ed. Peter Bjarkman, 422–44. Westport, CT: Meckler, 1991.

Carlson, Chuck. *True Brew: A Quarter Century with the Milwaukee Brewers.* Dallas: Taylor Publishing, 1993.

Fetteroff, Robert J. "Baseball Public Relations: A Case Study of the Milwaukee Brewers (1970–1975)." Master's thesis, University of Wisconsin–Madison, 1975.

Helyar, John. *Lords of the Realm: The Real History of Baseball.* New York: Villard, 1994.

Hoffmann, Gregg. *Down in the Valley: The History of Milwaukee County Stadium; The People, the Promise, the Passion.* Milwaukee, WI: Milwaukee Brewers Baseball Club, Milwaukee Journal Sentinel, 2000.

Milwaukee Brewers Clippings Files of the *Milwaukee Journal* and *Milwaukee Sentinel.* Milwaukee Public Library, Milwaukee, WI.

Mishler, Todd. *Baseball in Beertown: America's Pastime in Milwaukee.* Black Earth, WI: Prairie Oak Press, 2005.

Okrent, Daniel. *Nine Innings.* Boston: Houghton Mifflin, 2000.

Ranker, Ryan Donald. "A Car Salesman and a White Elephant: Brewing Up Trouble in Milwaukee; The Mythical Promises of Publicly Subsidized Major League Baseball Stadium and the Reality." Master's thesis, University of Wisconsin–Milwaukee, 2001.

10

New York Mets

Maureen Smith

When the New York Giants and Brooklyn Dodgers moved west after the 1957 season, America's heralded sport capital and most populated city was left with only one team, the New York Yankees of the American League. New York had been home to three successful teams and tremendous rivalries played out each autumn. When the Giants and Dodgers departed for San Francisco and Los Angeles, respectively, they were seeking uncharted and singular territories; they would be sharing their California backyards with no other teams. Local fans felt betrayed. Some turned to the Yankees, but most kept their National League loyalties, listening to Les Keiter's re-creation of Giants games on WINS radio. Eventually a new team would take the place of the two departed clubs.

THE BIRTH OF THE METS

On July 27, 1959, the creation of the Continental League as a new major league, with Branch Rickey as president, was announced. Attorney A. William Shea, who headed the Mayor's Special Committee on Baseball and had tried to get an existing major-league team to move to New York, was instrumental in the development of the CL. The league was to be comprised of eight teams, including one in New York, and play was slated for 1961. In support of a second team, Mayor Robert Wagner unveiled in the spring of 1960 a proposal to build a $15 million stadium in Flushing Meadows Park, Queens. The park was planned as an open-ended, three-tier, circular stadium and would seat 55,000 fans. The primary owner of the proposed stadium was Joan Payson (wife of Charles Shipman Payson), a wealthy fan of the Giants, who wanted to find a replacement for her departed team. She was the sister of John Hay "Jock" Whitney, ambassador to Britain and publisher of the *New York Herald Tribune*, who owned a substantial amount of stock in the San Francisco Giants. They were avid supporters of the turf, and were partners in the well-known Greentree Stable. Charles A. Hurth, the president of the Southern Association, was named general manager of the New York syndicate, and Donald M. Grant, a New York investment broker, was named team president.

Organized baseball responded to this threat by opening discussions with the CL regarding a merger, but instead decided to expand with four additional teams, including one for New York. Two groups sought the new NL franchise in New York: the Payson syndicate and Madison Square Garden, a division of Graham-Paige. The decision for expansion resulted in the death of the CL in the summer of 1960. In addition to the New York franchise, which was awarded to the Payson consortium, the NL also expanded to Houston, which had also been an expected CL location, with the Colt .45s.

In March 1961, the New York Metropolitan Baseball Club Inc. was welcomed into the NL. A contest was held to come up with a suitable nickname for the new team, and ultimately "Mets" emerged as the moniker. This was a historical reference to the Metropolitan team of the nineteenth-century American Association. The new president was former Yankees general manager George Weiss, who had been recently forced out because of age. The expansion teams were formed by a draft of expendable players from the other NL teams. On October 10, 1961, the Mets paid $1.8 million to draft 22 players from NL teams, while the Houston Colt .45s paid $1.85 million to purchase 23 men. Each club made 7 players from their 25-man roster available, plus 8 additional players in their entire organization. The Mets selected 16 men at $75,000, two for $50,000, and four premium players who each cost $125,000. The Mets focused on drafting experienced, well-known players like Gil Hodges and Don Zimmer, who they hoped would help them compete in the New York market with the more established Yankees. Over the next few years, the Mets brought in other renowned ballplayers, including Duke Snider, Richie Ashburn, Yogi Berra, and Gus Bell, in a concerted effort to draw in nostalgic old NL fans. While the plan did attract fans to the ballpark, it did not work as a strategy to win games.

Eighteen days later, ground was broken for Flushing Meadows Park, the future home of the New York Mets. By November, the Mets logo, created by sports cartoonist Ray Gatto, was released. The emblem sought to represent all five New York boroughs by including the image of a bridge and skyline. The skyline image included a church spire, symbolic of Brooklyn; the Williamsburg Savings Bank, the tallest building in Brooklyn; the Empire State Building, symbolic of midtown; and the United Nations Building. The colors were Dodger blue and Giant orange, paying tribute to the old New York ball clubs.

Late in 1961, as the team seemed to take shape, the Mets hired former Yankees manager Casey Stengel. Between 1949 and 1960, Stengel had led the Yankees to 10 AL pennants and seven world championships. But in 1961 his contract was not renewed because, at 71, he was deemed too old. The Mets offered Casey a multiyear contract, but he opted for a one-year deal for about $85,000. Stengel was happy to be back in baseball and was his philosophic self when he mused, "An experienced man was needed. Nobody needs me, but maybe they need my experience. Baseball is very big. Baseball will live longer than Casey Stengel or anybody." When asked how he might handle working with a team that might struggle in its first few years, Stengel replied, "You're gonna have troubles in the baseball business every day. No matter who you're with. Myself, I'll expect to win

Manager Casey Stengel, 1962. Courtesy of the Baseball Hall of Fame

every day. I hope not to get sick worrying about it, if I don't. The main thing is to keep up the spirit of your men. Keep your head up and feel you're gonna win the next one."

1962: THE FIRST AND WORST SEASON

The Mets' first spring training was in St. Petersburg, former spring home of the Yankees, who had moved to Fort Lauderdale. The club played that season at the Polo Grounds, former home site of the Giants, where they expected to play one season. The squad's first official game, on April 11, 1962, was an 11–4 loss to the hosting St. Louis Cardinals. The Opening Day lineup had Richie Ashburn playing center field, Felix Mantilla at shortstop, Charlie Neal at second base, and left fielder Frank Thomas batting cleanup, followed by right fielder Gus Bell, first baseman Gil Hodges, third baseman Don Zimmer, catcher Hobie Landrith, and, hitting last, pitcher Roger Craig. The Mets played their first home game on April 13, 1962, a 4–3 loss to the Pittsburgh Pirates. The Mets lost their first nine games until Jay Hook pitched them to a 9–1 home victory over the Pirates on April 23, 1962.

The first season was full of challenges, because the team was abysmal. As one wag noted, "Can't anybody play this game?" Sport scribes such as Dick Young of the *New York Daily News* and Robert Lipsyte of the *New York Times* covered the hapless Mets, and more often than not reported on the comedy of the team's pitiful play. The club had the worst batting (.240), pitching

(5.04 ERA), and fielding (210 errors, .967 fielding percentage) in the league. Despite their uncanny knack for losing, fans loved the Mets, who drew 922,530, average for the NL. Fans hung homemade banners cheering on the team until George Weiss ordered them all removed, at which point in the season fans brought them in greater numbers. The banners signified that the fans were simply content to have a team to cheer for and call their own. One bedsheet read, "We don't want to set the world on fire—we just want to finish ninth"; another read "To err is human—to forgive is a Mets fan." By the next season, the Mets were the first team to host an official Banner Day.

Reporters considered the Mets to be "the people's team," and Young nicknamed the losers "the New Breed." The team had a lot of characters, like catcher Choo Choo Coleman and first baseman "Marvelous" Marv Throneberry, who one time hit a triple but was called out for missing first base. When Stengel went out to complain, Marv told him not to bother, since he also missed second. At the end of the inaugural season, the Mets had accumulated 40 wins and a record 120 losses, breaking the Boston Braves' 1935 record of 115 losses in a season. Roger Craig and Al Jackson both lost 20 or more games. The only bright spots were Frank Thomas, who hit 34 homers, and Richie Ashburn, who batted .306. Roger Angell, the well-known baseball writer, found himself cheering for the lovable losers. As he noted, "An amazing thing happened, which was that New York took this losing team to its bosom. Everybody thinks New York only cares about champions, but we cared about the Mets . . . People brought horns and blew those horns and after a while I realized was antimatter to the Yankees who were across the river and had won so long . . . Winning is not a whole lot of fun if it goes on too long. But the Mets were human and that horn, I began to realize, was blowing for me because there's more Met than Yankee in all of us." Things could only get better, but not by much. In 1963 the team went 51–111, with a dismal .219 batting average. The show on the field surpassed the play—for instance, when outfielder Jimmy Piersall hit his 100th homer, he ran the bases backward.

THE BUILDING YEARS

The 1964 season welcomed the Mets into their new home, the $28.5 million, 55,061-seat Shea Stadium, located adjacent to the World's Fair and named for William Shea, who had been instrumental in bringing the NL back to New York. Shea Stadium was the first ballpark to utilize motor-operated stands that converted it from a baseball field to a football field. It also was the noisiest, located right in the flight path of La Guardia Airport, and had the worst visibility for hitters of any major-league park. When the site had first been considered, it was inspected in the winter, when flight patterns were different, and there was no noise problem. The foul lines were 341 feet long, and center field was 410. At the Opening Day ceremonies on April 17, Shea christened the new stadium with two bottles of water, one from Gowanus Canal near Ebbets Field, former home of the Brooklyn Dodgers, and the other from the Harlem River, near the Polo

Grounds. In their first game at Shea Stadium, the hosts lost to the Pittsburgh Pirates, 4–3. Despite the new stadium, the Mets were still not competitive. They won just 53 games, and followed a year later with just 50. Stengel finally retired his spikes in mid-1965 and was replaced by coach Wes Westrum.

The Mets' first season at Shea drew 1,732,597 fans, an increase of 700,000 over the prior year at the Polo Grounds, and despite their losing ways, the Mets outdrew their crosstown rivals, the Yankees. Shea Stadium was the site of the All-Star Game in 1964, and became the home of the Jets of the NFL. On April 2, 1966, the Mets won a lottery for the rights to University of Southern California pitcher Tom Seaver. Originally signed by the Atlanta Braves in February 1966, Seaver's contract was voided by Commissioner William D. Eckert because his college baseball season had already begun when Seaver had signed with the Braves. Eckert ruled that any team willing to match the Braves' offer could bid for his services. The Philadelphia Phillies, the Cleveland Indians, and the Mets all made an offer. Their names were thrown in a hat, and the Mets were picked, and they won the talented youngster. The Mets had their best campaign ever (66–95), their first season with fewer than 100 losses. But they reverted to form a year later with 101 losses. By 1968, led by new manager Gil Hodges, the Mets were closing in on mediocrity, with a franchise-high 73 wins, led by a promising young pitching staff that included Seaver and rookies Jerry Koosman and Nolan Ryan.

1969: THE MIRACLE METS

As the Mets entered their eighth season, few would have predicted a stellar year for a team that had never finished higher than ninth, yet they went from the doormat of the NL to the darlings of New York. Following the 1969 expansion, each league created an Eastern and Western Division, with the winners of a playoff going on to the World Series. The Mets were assigned to the NL East and were not expected to challenge their divisional rivals, the St. Louis Cardinals, Pittsburgh Pirates, and Chicago Cubs.

Unexpectedly, in 1969 the pitching staff jelled, the hitters were hitting, and for the first time, the team was winning more than they were losing. Early in the season, the experienced Cubs led the pennant race, but the Mets stayed on their tail. Heading into the All-Star break, the Mets were within three and a half games of the Cubs and first place. The club then struggled, losing 12 of 21, falling into third place, nine and a half games out of first. But the Mets got hot during a 20-game stretch against the West Coast teams, winning 15. The club was back in the pennant race, only two and a half games behind the leading Cubs. The Mets reached first place on September 10, 1969, when they swept a doubleheader over the Montreal Expos, and clinched their first NL East championship two weeks later with a 6–0 victory over the St. Louis Cardinals. The team finished at a torrid 17–5 clip, on its way to a 100-victory campaign, eight games ahead of the Cubs. The offense remained weak, with just a .242 average, led by left fielder Cleon Jones, with a sparkling .340. But the key was the pitching, which was second in the NL with a team 3.34 ERA. Seaver was spectacular, winning his last 10 starts and going 25–7. He had an ERA of 2.21 and was voted the Cy Young Award. The exciting campaign resulted in a league-leading attendance of 2,175,373.

The Mets went into the postseason as heavy underdogs. In their first postseason game ever, on October 4, the Mets beat the host Atlanta Braves 9–5, and repeated, 11–6, the next day. The series moved to Flushing Meadows for the first postseason appearance by an NL New York team since 1956. On October 6, 1969, the Mets completed their three-game sweep by a score of 7–4 to earn their way into the World Series against the powerful AL champions, the Baltimore Orioles.

Before the World Series started, rumors started that if the Mets won, Seaver would sign on to a full-page ad in the *New York Times* that read, "If the Mets can win the World Series, the United States can get out of Vietnam." When asked about the controversy, Seaver answered that he did not wish to be used for political purposes. Many people in baseball were relieved to have the Series begin to move past the war issue. Baltimore was a prohibitive favorite, and captured the first game in Baltimore, 4–1, with Seaver suffering the loss. But in game two, Koosman helped bring the Mets back with six innings of no-hit baseball, which along with a home run by veteran Donn Clendenon led to a 2–1 victory to tie the series. The series headed to New York for game three, and Gary Gentry pitched a four-hit gem, which the Mets won 5–0. Seaver started game four, and held the

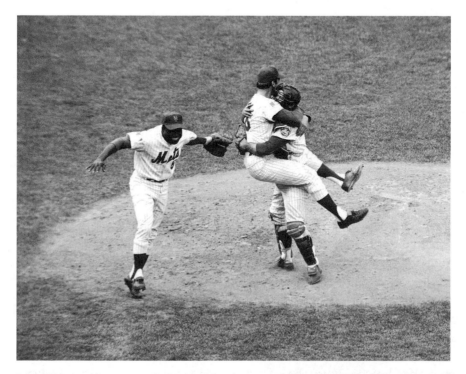

Jerry Grote embraces pitcher Jerry Koosman as the Mets defeated the Baltimore Orioles to win the 1969 World Series. © AP / Wide World Photos

Oriole scoreless for eight innings. The Orioles tied the pitching duel 1–1 in the ninth, but were thwarted by a brilliant catch by right fielder Ron Swoboda, one of the greatest in World Series history. In the bottom of the 10th, pinch hitter J. C. Martin bunted for a sacrifice, and while running inside the baseline, was hit by the throw, enabling Rod Gaspar to score from second, giving the Mets a 2–1 win. Then on October 16, 1969, in front of a hometown crowd of 57,397 fans, Donn Clendenon and Al Weis each hit home runs in support of Koosman's five-hitter, as the Mets won their first World Championship with a 5–3 victory over the Orioles. The Mets had won with outstanding pitching, brilliant fielding, and timely hitting. Each player received a series bonus of $18,332.

THE METS IN THE 1970S

The Mets remained competitive after their miracle season, tallying 83 victories in each of the next three years. These teams continued to hit poorly but pitch well, leading in ERA in 1970 (3.45) and 1971 (2.99). One of the mainstays on the team was local boy Ed Kranepool, who first appeared in a Mets uniform in 1962 at the tender age of 17. He played 18 seasons with a .261 batting average. In 1972 the team brought in popular Yogi Berra to manage, but made a disastrous trade before the season, sending Nolan Ryan to the California Angels for third baseman Jim Fregosi. Early in the season they traded pitcher Charlie Williams to the Giants for the great Willie Mays, who had been Joan Payson's favorite player. His acquisition allowed him to finish his playing days in the city where he started his career, but he was well past his prime.

In 1973 the Mets went 82–79, which was good enough for the divisional championship. The team batted .246, 11th in a 12-team league, but the pitching was again outstanding, led by Seaver (19–10), with a 2.08 ERA, and reliever Tug McGraw, who saved 25 games. The Mets took on the powerful Cincinnati Reds in the NL Championship Series, and used terrific pitching to set up a decisive game five at home. Seaver and McGraw thrilled 50,232 fans in combining for a seven-hitter and leading the Mets to a 7–2 win.

The team with the worst record of any club to play in the Fall Classic faced the heavily favored Oakland A's in the 1973 World Series. The Mets lost game one in Oakland, 2–1, but came back the next night with a 10–7 victory. Game three was played in New York and matched Tom Seaver against Catfish Hunter. In an exciting 11-inning game, the A's pulled out a 3–2 victory. The Mets came back the next day, winning by a convincing 6–1 score. Rusty Staub went four for four with a home run, three singles, and five RBIs. Then Koosman led the Mets to a 2–0 victory in game five. The Mets now needed one win to claim their second World Series title in four years. Hosting game six, the A's refused to be intimidated by Tom Seaver and won, 3–1, to tie the series, heading to a decisive game seven. Oakland, led by a towering Reggie Jackson homer, won the decisive game 5–2, capturing their second consecutive World Series title.

In 1974 and 1975, the Yankees played at Shea while their ballpark was being renovated. The Mets of 1974 hardly resembled the team that had just played in the World Series, and finished a poor 71–91. Berra was replaced after the 16th game of the 1975 campaign, and the team went on to record consecutive third-place finishes (82–80, 86–76) under managers Roy McMillan and Joe Frazier. From 1976 to 1978 the Mets struggled for mediocrity while the Yankees won two World Series titles in three trips. In September 1975, owner Joan Payson died, and the team collapsed without her financial backing. The decline was highlighted by the trade on June 15, 1977, of superstar hurler Tom Seaver to the Cincinnati Reds for infielder Doug Flynn, outfielders Steve Henderson and Dan Norman, and pitcher Pat Zachary. During Seaver's tenure with the Mets, he was Rookie of the Year (1967), won two Cy Young Awards (1973, 1975), and led the NL three times in ERA (1970, 1971, 1973) and five times in strike-outs (1970, 1971, 1973, 1975, 1976). In his 12 seasons with the Mets, Seaver compiled a record of 198–124 with a 2.57 ERA, and was selected to 10 All-Star teams. He still holds the Mets' career marks for wins, ERA, starts, complete games, strikeouts, and shutouts, among other categories. For his career, Seaver won 311 games, compiled a 2.86 ERA, and was a first-ballot inductee into the Baseball Hall of Fame in 1992.

Between 1977 and 1983, the Mets went through several managers and had seven consecutive losing seasons, tying the franchise record for futility set between 1962 and 1968. The team won between 63 and 68 games except for the strike-shortened 1981 campaign, when their record was 41–62. Joe Torre, the future Yankees manager, led the Mets from 1977 to 1981, and recorded a dismal .403 winning percentage.

THE METS IN THE 1980S

On January 24, 1980, the franchise was sold to a group led by Nelson Doubleday and Fred Wilpon for an estimated purchase price of $21.1 million, the highest amount ever paid then for an American professional-sports franchise. Doubleday's publishing company provided 80 percent of the purchase price, and he served as the new chairman of the board. Wilpon, a real-estate magnate who had been a teammate of Sandy Koufax at Lafayette High School in Brooklyn, became president and chief operating officer. They hired Frank Cashen, formerly with the Baltimore Orioles, as general manager, and he set out to rebuild the Mets through the draft and trades. One major step was the selection of pitcher Dwight Gooden as the fifth pick in the 1982 draft. One year later, pitchers Neil Allen and Rick Ownbey were traded to the St. Louis Cardinals for outstanding first baseman Keith Hernandez, whose involvement with drugs had made him available. Then, in 1984, the Mets traded infielder Hubie Brooks, catcher Mike Fitzgerald, outfielder Herm Winningham, and pitcher Floyd Youmans to the Montreal Expos for star catcher Gary Carter. These acquisitions help build the foundation for the Mets' push for a third World Series appearance.

In 1984 major renovations of Shea Stadium were initiated. The team added luxury suites and altered the stadium's outer facade with images of baseball players. The Mets that year brought in the inexperienced Davey Johnson, a former All-Star second baseman, as manager. He led the team to a 90–72 record, six and a half games out of first place, and improved the mark a year later to 98–64, and just three games out. His teams were a mixture of veterans, players developed in the farm system, and effective trades. The team had a rising star in slugger Darryl Strawberry, the Mets' top pick in the 1980 draft, who was Rookie of the Year in 1983. One year later, the phenomenal 19-year-old Doc Gooden was Rookie of the Year, setting a major-league rookie record with 276 strikeouts. He also pitched a one-hitter against the Cubs. He was even better the following season, when he won the Cy Young Award, leading the league in wins (24–4), ERA (1.53), strikeouts (276), and innings pitched (277). He seemed on his way to becoming one of the greatest pitchers of all time, and did end his 16-year career with a sparkling .634 winning percentage (194–112), but his brilliance had faded by the time he was in his mid-twenties. Gooden tested positive for cocaine during spring training in 1987 and entered a rehabilitation center to avoid suspension. He suffered two shoulder injuries in 1989 and 1991 that significantly decreased his pitching abilities. In 1994, Gooden tested positive for cocaine and was suspended for 60 days. During the suspension, he tested positive again and was suspended for the entire 1995 season.

In 1986, the Mets stayed at the top of the pack for most of the season, and clinched the NL East title with a 4–2 win over the visiting Chicago Cubs on September 18, 1986. The team finished with 108 wins and only 54 losses, an astonishing 21 1/2 games ahead of second-place Philadelphia. The Mets fielded a superb team that led the NL in virtually every batting statistic (runs, hits, batting average, on-base percentage, and slugging) and several pitching statistics. Led by Bob Ojeda, the team had three of the five lowest ERAs in the NL, along with the four highest winning percentages. The starters were bolstered by strong relief pitching from Roger McDowell and Jesse Orosco, who together earned 43 saves. The team had one of the biggest payrolls in baseball, including the two highest-paid players, outfielder George Foster ($2.8 million), who was injured most of the season, and Carter ($2.2 million), who drove in 105 runs. The squad had a mixture of personalities who had a reputation for big parties, chasing women, drinking and drug use, and vandalizing the team's chartered flights.

The Mets faced the Houston Astros in the NLCS and took the series four games to two. The deciding sixth game on October 15 was a memorable game that lasted 16 innings, with the Mets winning 7–6. The opponent in the World Series was the Boston Red Sox, who had lost the 1975 Series in seven games to the Cincinnati Reds. The Mets lost the first two games at home to the Sox, but came back and tied the series at two games apiece in Boston. Game five was won by the Red Sox, making them one game shy of their first World Series title since 1918. In the potential deciding match back at Shea, play went into extra innings tied 3–3, and the Sox scored twice in the top of the 10th to take the lead. The first two men up were retired, and the Sox were one out from the championship. Then Carter, Kevin Mitchell, and Ray Knight all singled. Pitcher Bob Stanley then threw a wild pitch with Mookie Wilson at bat, tying the score and advancing Knight, the potential tying run, to second. Wilson then hit a slow grounder to an injured Bill Buckner at first, and the ball went through his legs, bringing in the winning run for a true miracle comeback. The deciding game was played at Shea on October 27. The Red Sox took a 3–0 lead in the sixth behind Bruce Hurst, but the Mets tied it up with three runs in the bottom of the frame. In the seventh inning, Calvin Schiraldi, loser of the previous game, entered in relief, but Ray Knight homered, and the Mets scored two more runs. The Sox scored two in the eighth, but a Strawberry homer iced the game, and the Mets won 8–5, for their second world championship.

One result of the great 1986 season was that the Mets, seemingly poised for continued success, drew over 3 million for the first time in 1987. However, they dropped to 92 victories and second place in the East, despite leading the league in batting and finishing among the leaders in pitching. In 1988, the Mets regained the division championship with 100 victories, coming in second in batting in the NL, first in runs scored, and first in pitching and defense. Strawberry provided the power with 39 homers and 101 RBIs. The hurlers had a fabulous 2.91 ERA, and second-year man David Cone blossomed with a 2.22 ERA and 20 wins. The Mets played the Dodgers in the NLCS, but lost in seven games. In the next two seasons, despite leading the league in homers and maintaining a strong pitching staff, the club, hurt by injuries to key players, fell to second place both years, and as a result Johnson was fired as manager one-fourth of the way into 1990, the seventh straight consecutive winning season for the Mets. He was replaced by former star shortstop Bud Harrelson. Despite the bad finish, the franchise was worth $200 million, second only to the Yankees.

By the start of the 1990s, the Mets were in a rebuilding mode. The club fell to fifth in 1991, despite solid pitching, because of a weak lineup. Jeff Torborg took over as skipper the next year, another fifth-place finish, with five fewer wins (72). The team batted a league low .235, and the pitching was nearly as dismal. Torborg was replaced early in the 1993 season by Dallas Green, who seemed intent on challenging the 1962 Mets for the most losses in franchise history. The 1993 Mets lost 103 games and finished in seventh place, despite the presence of such high-priced talent as Gooden, Bobby Bonilla, John Franco, Eddie Murray, and Bret Saberhagen, who all earned over $3 million. Green improved the club to third place (55–58) in the strike-shortened 1994 season, and raised the team to second place in 1995 despite a losing record (69–75). That team hit better than most recent Mets clubs, led by Randy Hundley and Bernard Gilkey, who together had 71 homers and 229 RBIs. The years of struggle had reduced the value of the franchise to $144 million, 12th highest in MLB. Late in 1996, in the midst of his fourth straight losing season, Green was fired, replaced by former Mets player Bobby Valentine, who was charged with bringing the team back to respectability and the playoffs. He led the Mets in his first full season to a winning record

(88–74) and third place. Attendance between 1992 and 1997 was below 2 million in every season.

THE METS AND CONTEMPORARY MAJOR LEAGUE BASEBALL

In 1997 MLB, in its effort to attract more fans, capitalize on rivalries, and expose fans to the best players from both leagues, revised the schedule to include interleague play, which pitted teams from the NL versus the AL. On June 16, 1997, the Mets and Yankees met in their first regular-season game. This "Subway Series" hearkened back to the days of the storied rivalry of the Yankees and Brooklyn Dodgers in the 1950s. In the first game against the Yankees, the Mets scored three runs in the first inning and Dave Mlicki pitched a complete-game shutout in a 6–0 victory. The three-game series drew 160,740 fans, an all-time franchise high.

The Mets had the same record in 1998 as the year before, but finished in second place. A key addition, in one of the franchise's greatest trades, was catcher Mike Piazza from the Florida Marlins, godson of Dodgers manager Tommy Lasorda and the best offensive catcher of his generation. Piazza, who made $8 million in his first year in New York, has hit more home runs while playing that position than anybody else in major-league history. The Mets won the wild-card spot in 1999, coming in second in the NL East (97 66). The team had an excellent lineup, with five starters batting over .300, three players driving in over 100 runs each, and Piazza stroking 40 homers. They won the NL Division Series against the Arizona Diamondbacks in four games, advancing to the NLCS against the Braves. Down three games to none, the Mets fought back, winning the next two games, including a thrilling 15-inning victory in game five. In the finale, the Mets rallied from a five-run deficit to send the match into extra innings, only to lose in the 11th, 10–9.

In 2000 the Mets came in second in the East to the Braves by one game, and again made the postseason as the wild-card team. The team was carried by Piazza, the $12 million man, who batted .324, with 38 homers and 113 RBIs. One of the highlights of the year occurred on July 8, when the two New York franchises engaged in a historic doubleheader that started at Shea Stadium for game one and ended in Yankee Stadium for game two. This marked the first time in major-league history that two teams played each other in one day in two different ballparks. Another highlight took place on October 8 when Bobby Jones threw a one-hitter against the Cardinals, advancing the Mets to the NLDS. The Mets lost the first game of that series to the Giants, but won the next three and advanced to the NLCS. They took on the Cardinals for the pennant, and led by their new lefty starter, Mike Hampton, beat them four games to one. The Mets headed to their fourth World Series appearance against a familiar face.

In a World Series reminiscent of the numerous battles between the Yankees and the Dodgers or the Giants, New York fans were treated to a modern version of the crosstown matchup in the 2000 Subway Series pitting the Mets against the Yankees. The two teams had played in recent years due to interleague play, allowing the fans to engage in the rivalry and battle for city bragging rights, but the meeting in the postseason was significant, marking the first time the two teams played each other in the postseason. Two New York teams had not played each other in the World Series since 1956. The two-time defending world champion Yankees won the series, four games to one, as their hurlers stymied the Mets' bats. The series was actually very competitive, and the Mets were only outscored 16–19.

After their stellar 2000 season, the Mets hoped to continue their winning ways into the twenty-first century. They had a slow start in 2001, and despite pulling within a game of first place, the team could not pull it out and failed to make the playoffs, coming in third (82–80). The offense was the least productive in the entire NL. Following the September 11 terrorist attack on the World Trade Center, baseball took a brief respite from games as the nation tried to comprehend the recent events. Shea Stadium became a relief center and gate areas were filled with supplies, food, and lodging for the rescue effort. On September 21, 2001, the Mets hosted the Braves in New York's first professional sporting event since the attack, attended by 41,275 supportive fans. The game had a lot of symbolic meaning, and the ballplayers sported hats with the emblems of New York's fire and police departments. Mike Piazza won the game with a two-run homer in the eighth inning for a 3–2 Mets victory. During the off-season, the Mets set out to acquire veterans in an effort to return to the playoffs and signed big-name free agents Roberto Alomar for $7.9 million and Mo Vaughn for $12.1 million, but both proved to be big disappointments, and the club languished in fifth place, with its first losing record since 1996. That season, to celebrate the franchise's 40th anniversary, the fans were invited to select their "All Amazin' Team." It was comprised of manager Gil Hodges; first baseman Keith Hernandez; second baseman Edgardo Alfonzo; shortstop Buddy Harrelson; third baseman Howard Johnson; catcher Mike Piazza; outfielders Mookie Wilson, Lenny Dykstra, and Darryl Strawberry; pinch hitters Rusty Staub and Ed Kranepool; right-handed starter Tom Seaver; left-handed starter Jerry Koosman; right-handed reliever Roger McDowell; and left-handed reliever John Franco.

Valentine was replaced in 2003 by Art Howe, former manager of the Oakland A's, who failed to halt the skid as the team finished in fifth place (66–95). The one bright spot was 20-year-old rookie shortstop Jose Reyes, who hit .307 in half a season. Despite having one of the highest payrolls in the majors, the Mets barely improved in 2004, moving up to fourth place with a dismal 71–91 season. That same season, front-office changes occurred. Co-owner Nelson Doubleday agreed to sell his half of the team's ownership to his partner Fred Wilpon. A month earlier, the team had been appraised at $391 million, and Wilpon then sued to force Doubleday to sell his half based on an agreement made at the time of the 1986 acquisition. Doubleday accused the commissioner's office of being "in cahoots" with Wilpon and purposefully underestimating the team's value. After settling the team's debt, Doubleday received $137.9 million for his share of the team. Doubleday's lawyers chastised the commissioner's office, claiming that "MLB orchestrated a sham process that not only mistreated Doubleday and betrayed his trust; it actively favored Wilpon and engineered a result that served MLB's other and conflicting interests."

The Mets hope to replace the dilapidated Shea Stadium with a new field, resembling Ebbets Field, in the adjacent parking lot. The proposal includes several features, such as a rotunda at the entrance, reminiscent of Ebbets Field, as well as new features including 78 luxury boxes, over 5,000 club seats, and 12,000 parking spaces. The most innovative feature planned was a portable 4,255-foot-wide grass platform that would enable other events to take place at the stadium without harming the natural turf. The Mets claim they will contribute substantially toward the construction costs. Former mayor Rudy Giuliani had promised to build both New York teams $800 million retractable-roof stadiums, financed by public bonds, but his successor, Michael Bloomberg, put those plans on hold.

In their 23 seasons, the Mets have won two wild-card playoff spots (1999 and 2000), four NL East championships (1969, 1973, 1986, and 1988), four NL championships (1969, 1973, 1986, and 2000), and two World Series titles (1969 and 1986). Recent free-agent acquisitions, such as pitcher Pedro Martinez, who went 15–8 with a 2.82 ERA in 2005, and center fielder Carlos Beltran indicate that the Mets are still striving to make their way into the playoffs, and are willing to pay top dollar to do so. Their 2005 payroll was $101,305,821, third highest in the majors, and under new manager Willie Randolph produced a third-place tie in the rugged NL East with a respectable 83–79 record.

Despite these expenditures, the club is far from being one of the elite franchises on the field. Yet the team's value in 2005 was $505 million, third highest in baseball, and more than 20 times the cost of the team in 1980. An important ingredient in the team's value is the lucrative media contracts, which amounted to $46 million in 2001, second only to the Yankees. Today the 2000 World Series appearance is a faint memory to fans and the front office, and attendance lags far behind their more popular crosstown rivals.

NOTABLE ACHIEVEMENTS

Cy Young Winners

Year	Name	Position
1969	Tom Seaver	RHP
1973	Tom Seaver	RHP
1975	Tom Seaver	RHP
1985	Dwight Gooden	RHP

Rookies of the Year

Year	Name	Position
1967	Tom Seaver	P
1972	Jon Matlack	P
1983	Darryl Strawberry	OF
1984	Dwight Gooden	P

Home-Run Champions

Year	Name	#
1982	Dave Kingman	37
1988	Darryl Strawberry	39
1991	Howard Johnson	38

ERA Champions

Year	Name	#
1970	Tom Seaver	2.81
1971	Tom Seaver	1.76
1973	Tom Seaver	2.08
1978	Craig Swan	2.43
1985	Dwight Gooden	1.53

Strikeout Champions

Year	Name	#
1970	Tom Seaver	283
1971	Tom Seaver	289
1973	Tom Seaver	251
1975	Tom Seaver	243
1976	Tom Seaver	235
1984	Dwight Gooden	276
1985	Dwight Gooden	268
1990	David Cone	233
1991	David Cone	241

POSTSEASON APPEARANCES

NL East Division Titles

Year	Record	Manager
1969	100–62	Gil Hodges
1973	82–79	Yogi Berra

| 1986 | 108–54 | Davey Johnson |
| 1988 | 100–60 | Davey Johnson |

NL Wild Cards

Year	Record	Manager
1999	97–66	Bobby Valentine
2000	94–68	Bobby Valentine

NL Pennants

Year	Record	Manager
1969	100–62	Gil Hodges
1973	82–79	Yogi Berra
1986	108–54	Davey Johnson
2000	94–68	Bobby Valentine

World Championships

Year	Opponent	MVP
1969	Baltimore	Donn Clendenon
1986	Boston	Ray Knight

MANAGERS

2005–	Willie Randolph
2003–2004	Art Howe
1996–2002	Bobby Valentine
1993–1996	Dallas Green
1992–1993	Jeff Torborg
1991	Mike Cubbage
1990–1991	Bud Harrelson
1984–1990	Davey Johnson
1983	Frank Howard
1982–1983	George Bamberger
1977–1981	Joe Torre
1976–1977	Joe Frazier
1975–1976	Roy McMillan
1972–1975	Yogi Berra
1968–1971	Gil Hodges
1967	Salty Parker
1965–1967	Wes Westrum
1962–1965	Casey Stengel

Team Records by Individual Players

Batting Leaders

	Single Season			Career		
	Name		Year	Name		Plate Appearances
Batting average	John Olerud	.354	1998	John Olerud	.315	2,018
On-base %	John Olerud	.447	1998	John Olerud	.425	2,018
Slugging %	Mike Piazza	.614	2000	Mike Piazza	.542	3,041
OPS	Mike Piazza	1.024	1998	John Olerud	.926	2,018
Games	Felix Millan	162	1975	Ed Kranepool	1,853	5,997
At bats	Lance Johnson	682	1996	Ed Kranepool	5,436	5,997
Runs	Edgar Alfonzo	123	1999	Darryl Strawberry	662	4,549
Hits	Lance Johnson	227	1996	Ed Kranepool	1,418	5,997
Total bases	Lance Johnson	327	1996	Ed Kranepool	2,047	5,997
Doubles	Bernard Gilkey	44	1996	Ed Kranepool	225	5,997
Triples	Lance Johnson	21	1996	Mookie Wilson	62	4,307
Home runs	Todd Hundley	41	1996	Darryl Strawberry	252	4,549
RBIs	Mike Piazza	124	1999	Darryl Strawberry	733	4,549
Walks	John Olerud	125	1999	Darryl Strawberry	580	4,549
Strikeouts	Tommy Agee	156	1970	Darryl Strawberry	960	4,549
Stolen bases	Roger Cedano	66	1999	Mookie Wilson	281	4,307
Extra-base hits	Howard Johnson	80	1989	Darryl Strawberry	469	4,549
Times on base	John Olerud	309	1999	Ed Kranepool	1,886	5,997

Pitching Leaders

	Single Season			Career		
	Name		Year	Name		Innings Pitched
ERA	Doc Gooden	1.53	1985	Tom Seaver	2.57	3,045.3
Wins	Tom Seaver	25	1969	Tom Seaver	198	3,045.3
Wont-loss %	David Cone	.870	1988	Doc Gooden	.649	2,169.7
Hits/9 IP	Sid Fernandez	5.71	1985	Nolan Ryan	6.51	510
Walks/9 IP	Brett Saberhagen	0.66	1994	Brett Saberhagen	1.32	524.3
Strikeouts	Tom Seaver	289	1971	Tom Seaver	2,541	3,045.3
Strikeouts/9 IP	Doc Gooden	11.39	1984	David Cone	8.72	1,209.3
Games	Mike Stanton	83	2004	John Franco	695	702.7
Saves	Armando Benitez	43	2001	John Franco	276	702.7

(Continued)

Pitching Leaders (Continued)

	Single Season			Career		
	Name		Year	Name		Innings Pitched
Innings	Tom Seaver	290.7	1970	Tom Seaver	3,045.3	3,045.3
Starts	Jack Fisher	36	1965	Tom Seaver	395	3,045.3
Complete games	Tom Seaver	21	1971	Tom Seaver	171	3,045.3
Shutouts	Doc Gooden	8	1985	Tom Seaver	44	3,045.3

Source: Drawn from data in "New York Mets Batting Leaders (seasonal and career)." http://baseball-reference.com/teams/NYM/leaders_bat.shtml; "New York Mets Pitching Leaders (seasonal and career)." http://baseball-reference.com/teams/NYM/leaders_pitch.shtml.

BIBLIOGRAPHY

Allen, Maury. *After the Miracle: The 1969 Mets Twenty Years Later.* New York: Franklin Watts, 1989.

———. *The Incredible Mets.* New York: Paperback Library, 1969.

Bjarkman, Peter C. *The New York Mets Encyclopedia.* Champaign, IL: Sports Publishing, 2002.

Cohen, Stanley. *A Magic Summer: The '69 Mets.* San Diego: Harcourt Brace Jovanovich, 1988.

Durso, Joseph. *Amazing: The Miracle of the Mets.* Boston: Houghton Mifflin, 1970.

Fox, Larry. *Last to First: The Story of the Mets.* New York: Harper and Row, 1970.

Golenbock, Peter. *Amazin': The Miraculous History of New York's Most Beloved Baseball Team.* New York: St. Martin's Press, 2002.

Klapisch, Bob, and John Harper. *The Worst Team Money Could Buy: The Collapse of the New York Mets.* New York: Random House, 1993.

Koppett, Leonard. *The New York Mets: The Whole Story.* New York: Macmillan, 1970.

Lang, Jack, and Peter Simon. *The New York Mets: Twenty-five Years of Baseball Magic.* New York: Henry Holt, 1987.

Lichtenstein, Michael. *Ya Gotta Believe! The 40th Anniversary New York Mets Fan Book.* New York: St. Martin's Press, 2002.

Shecter, Leonard. *Once upon the Polo Grounds: The Mets that Were.* New York: Dial Press, 1970.

Vecsey, George. *Joy in Mudville: Being a Complete Account of the Unparalleled History of the New York Mets from Their Most Perturbed Beginnings to Their Amazing Rise to Glory and Renown.* New York: McCall, 1970.

———. *Subway 2000: The Dramatic Story of the First Subway Series since 1956.* London: Carlton, 2002.

11

Philadelphia Phillies

John P. Rossi

THE EARLY YEARS, 1883–1916

Philadelphia was not only the cradle of liberty but also one of the cradles of baseball. Some variant of baseball was played in the city as early as the 1830s. The "Philadelphia Game," with a diamond-shaped field and round home plate, proved a popular version of baseball in parts of the northeastern United States. Alexander Cartwright's rules, with their three outs per inning, bases 90 feet apart, and nine players to a side gradually were adopted in Philadelphia by the 1850s and early 1860s and helped spread the popularity of the new sport, rapidly outdistancing cricket as the city's most popular bat-and-ball game.

By the 1860s Philadelphia had many successful baseball teams, including a celebrated Athletics squad regarded as one of the best in the nation. In 1866 an estimated 40,000 fans watched an Athletics contest against the highly regarded Brooklyn Atlantics. When the first successful professional league, the National Association of Professional Base Ball Players, was organized in 1871, Philadelphia had an entry. In 1876, when William Hulbert and A.J. Spalding organized the owner-dominated National League, they wanted a team in Philadelphia. The Athletics went 14–45 under manager Al Wright and played at the Jefferson Street Grounds. The club was expelled from the NL for failing to complete its first season.

Seven years later a new Philadelphia franchise was created by NL officials determined to be represented in America's second-largest city. The formal history of the Phillies dates from 1883 when the failed three-year-old Worcester, Massachusetts, Ruby Legs franchise was transferred to Philadelphia. A politically well-connected Philadelphia lawyer, John I. Rogers, and the owner of a thriving sporting-goods business, A.J. Reach, who had played professionally back in 1866, shared control of the new team, which was originally named the Quakers but renamed in 1890 as the Phillies (a takeoff on the city's name), or "Fillies."

Under Rogers and Reach the Phillies became one of the bulwarks of the NL, outlasting teams placed in Philadelphia by rival leagues such as the American Association (1882–91), the Union Association of 1884, and the Players' League of 1890.

In 1883 the Phillies literally started from scratch, as they had to recruit new players. As a result the team had a terrible record during its first years in the NL. Reach made a crucial decision when in 1884 he hired Harry Wright, the former player and manager of the famous Cincinnati Red Stockings team of 1869, baseball's first all-professional team. Wright was an excellent judge of baseball talent and gradually put together a respectable squad. In his 10 years as manager the Phillies won 1,225 and lost 885 games for a .581 average, the best record of any Phillies skipper. While the Phillies never won a pennant under Wright, they were a consistent first-division team, coming in second, third, or fourth every year from 1885 through 1895. In the mid-1880s the Phillies produced a handful of players who would rank among the best in nineteenth-century baseball.

The first great Phillies player was pitcher Charlie Ferguson, who won 20 games four times and 30 games once, but unfortunately died of typhoid fever in 1888 at 25. That season the Phillies signed Ed Delahanty, their first superstar. In 13 years with the Phillies Delahanty was the premier right-handed power hitter in baseball. He hit .300 or better for 10 consecutive seasons (1892–1901), including .400 in three of those years. He hit four home runs in a game, only the second player in baseball to do so. A Hall of Fame player with a lifetime average of .346, he still holds the Phillies record for most doubles and triples in a career.

Delahanty jumped to the Washington Senators in the new American League in 1902, and died tragically in July 1903 after falling from a bridge crossing the Niagara River. It is believed he was drunk and tried to walk across the bridge after being thrown off the train.

Delahanty was joined in the early 1890s by Sam Thompson and "Sliding" Billy Hamilton, all future Hall of Famers. Together the trio constituted one of the best outfields in baseball history. Thompson, a power hitter like Delahanty, hit .300 five times and reached the .400 level once, and averaged .331 in his career. He also drove in 100 runs seven times. Hamilton was the premier defensive center fielder of his era. Famous for his speed, he set numerous stolen-base records, including twice stealing 100 bases. In his six years in Philadelphia he averaged 85 stolen bases a year. Between 1891 and 1895 the outfield of Delahanty, Hamilton, and Thompson averaged .354, the highest batting average for any outfield in baseball history. The Phillies led the majors in batting from 1892 to 1895. In 1894 the team hit an incredible .349, led by its outfielders, all of whom batted above .400.

Beginning in 1883, the Phillies played at Recreation Park, in the heart of one of the fastest-growing sections of north Philadelphia. Regarded then as "the best athletic ground in the world," it seated 16,000 fans with standing room for another 5,000. The team originally charged 50 cents for admission, but soon cut the price in half to compete with their rivals, the Athletics of the American Association. In the mid-1890s, the Phillies were the biggest draw in baseball, surpassing 250,000 from 1893 to 1898.

In 1887 Rogers and Reach moved to a more fashionable neighborhood at the intersection of Broad Street and Lehigh Avenue, adjacent to a major railroad station. Their new 12,500-seat Philadelphia Base Ball Park, perhaps the finest in the United States, cost $100,000, an enormous amount at the time. A fire destroyed much of the park in 1894. The club replaced the old park with the modern 18,000-seat Huntingdon Avenue Grounds, using mostly steel and brick to construct a fire-resistant structure that featured a cantilevered pavilion. It sported an all-brick entrance tower that resembled a medieval castle, while the outside walls were covered in ornamental brickwork. It was renamed Baker Bowl in 1913, after William F. Baker, one of the team's owners. In 1903, a balcony at the park collapsed, killing 12 and injuring 232. The Phillies would play there until 1938 while the neighborhood deteriorated around them. In 1895, the new park was a big hit with fans. Attendance reached 474,971, one of the highest of any nineteenth-century team, and a Phillies record until 1916.

In 1893 Wright's health gave out and he resigned as manager. The team had five managers over the next decade. The most successful was Billy Shettsline, a former executive with the Phillies, who guided them to a 94–58 record in 1899. His .618 winning percentage established a Phillies record that lasted until 1976. Two years later he guided the club to second place, its highest finish until 1915.

The Phillies were confronted by a grave challenge in 1901 when the AL placed a team in the city. The Philadelphia Athletics were well financed by local businessmen Tom and Ben Shibe, and guided by a keen student of the game, Connie Mack. Reach's retirement in 1902 after a falling-out with Rogers began a long period where the Phillies changed hands repeatedly. Most of the owners after Reach, until Robert Carpenter bought the team in 1943, either had limited financial resources or would not spend to develop the team.

Trouble began almost immediately for the Phillies when the Athletics came to town. Rogers, notoriously short-tempered, refused to compete with the AL for players and lost key personnel, including Delahanty and future Hall of Famers Elmer Flick and Napoleon Lajoie, to the rival league. These players jumped to the AL when Rogers refused raises of $600 each. As a result the Phillies were a nondescript team in the opening years of the twentieth century, while Mack's Athletics became one of baseball's first dynasties. The Athletics quickly became more popular than the Phillies. In 1902, for example, they outdrew the Phillies by 300,000 fans. Some of the hard feelings that existed between the two teams abated after the 1903 season when the first City Series was played, a fixture for half a century.

While Mack's Athletics were winning the hearts of Philadelphia fans, the Phillies fielded a mediocre team. After Reach's retirement the Phillies went through six presidents in a decade. One of them, Horace Fogel, was barred from baseball for claiming that the 1912 pennant race was fixed and that league officials favored John McGraw's New York Giants.

During the first decade of the twentieth century the highest the Phillies finished was third, in 1907. They produced a few quality players, most notably outfielder Sherwood "Sherry" Magee, who arrived in 1904 and gave them 11 good years. During his tenure with the Phillies Magee led the NL in RBIs three times and runs scored once, and won the batting title in 1910. He hit .300 or better five times.

The Phillies slowly began their rise to the top of the NL in 1913 when they finished in second place behind McGraw's Giants, led by one of the greatest pitchers in baseball history, Grover Cleveland Alexander. Joining Alexander were three other outstanding pitchers, Erskine Mayer, Eppa Rixey, and Al Demaree. Sherry Magee, hard-hitting first baseman Fred Luderus, third baseman Hans Lobert, and the greatest power hitter in baseball before Babe Ruth, Gavvy Cravath, led the offense. Cravath, a left-handed hitter, was 31 when he joined the Phillies and immediately zeroed in on the short right-field fence at Baker Bowl. He led the NL in homers six times, finishing second in 1916.

The Phillies slipped to sixth place in 1914 partly due to raids by the rival Federal League, which cost the Phillies some of their key players, including their keystone combination of Otto Knabe and Mickey Doolan. In 1915, under new manager Pat Moran, the Phillies ran away with the NL pennant. They led the league on and off for most of the season and breezed to the pennant by seven games over the Boston Braves. Team salaries rose due to the rival league and the pennant-winning year, from an average of $3,400 in 1914 to $4,300 in 1916.

Alexander won 31 games, including 12 shutouts. Rixey won 11, Mayer 21, and Demaree 14. Cravath set a modern major-league record with 24 homers and led the NL in RBIs with 115. Luderus hit .315, and rookie Dave "Beauty" Bancroft anchored the infield at shortstop.

The World Series paired the Phillies against the Boston Red Sox, one of the best teams in the first two decades of AL history. The Red Sox, winners of 101 games in 1915, had the best pitching staff in the majors, with Ernie Shore, Rube Foster, Dutch Leonard, Smokey Joe Wood, and 20-year-old left-hander Babe Ruth. The offense was led by future Hall of Famers Tris Speaker and Harry Hooper, who with Duffy Lewis gave the Red Sox one of the best defensive outfields in history.

The series was a letdown for the Phillies. The first two games were played in Philadelphia before enthusiastic overflow crowds of 20,000. In game one Alexander beat Shore 2–1. After the game fans poured onto the field and celebrated by carrying Alexander on their shoulders.

The celebration proved premature. The Phillies would not win another World Series game for 65 years. President Woodrow Wilson, a baseball fan, came from Washington to watch game two, the first time a sitting president had attended a World Series. Mayer and Foster both pitched well. With the game tied 1–1, the Red Sox pushed across a run in the top of the ninth to win.

When the series moved to Boston, Moran started Alexander on two days' rest. He pitched well but couldn't match Leonard, who held the Phillies to just three hits and retired the last 20 batters in a row. The Red Sox won in the bottom of the ninth when Duffy Lewis singled in the winning run.

For some reason, in game four Moran started George "Dut" Chalmers, who had an 8–9 record, instead of Rixey. The Red Sox countered by coming back with Shore, who again won by a 2–1 score. The Phillies' bats were silent. Cravath was completely shut down by Red Sox pitching. He hit .125 for the series, with no homers and one RBI. As a team the Phillies hit a pathetic .182.

The Red Sox won the series in game five back in Philadelphia. Alexander came down with a sore arm, forcing Moran to start Mayer on three days' rest. The Red Sox countered with Foster, also pitching on three days' rest. Mayer wasn't sharp, giving up six hits and two runs in two and a third innings. Rixey replaced him and pitched well, but again the Phillies gave up the winning run in the top of the ninth.

After the series some Phillies fans blamed team president W. F. Baker for the loss. He had put temporary bleachers in left and center field to boost attendance, and the Red Sox hit three homers there, including the ones that won the fifth and deciding game.

Despite their World Series loss, the Phillies seemed poised to be a powerhouse. In 1916 the Phillies made a run at a second pennant. They fell short, although they won one more game than in 1915, finishing two and a half games behind Brooklyn. Again Alexander was overpowering, winning 33 games, while Rixey won 22. However, the offense was anemic. No one hit .300 and Cravath hit just 11 homers. Still, the Phillies set an attendance record for Baker Bowl, drawing over 515,000 fans, a figure unsurpassed by the club until 1946.

A decades-long downward slide began for this fine Phillies squad in 1917. They never contended for the lead in the pennant race and trailed McGraw's Giants throughout the season, finishing 11 games behind, in second place. Again Alexander was the heart of the team, winning 30 games while compiling an ERA of 1.64. The offense was lifeless for the second season in a row as the team hit just .248.

At the end of the season, Baker shocked the fans by trading Alexander to the Chicago Cubs for pitcher Mike Prendergast, catcher Bill "Pickles" Dillhoefer, and $60,000, then the most cash ever in a player deal. Prendergast pitched two seasons for the Phillies, going 13–15, while Dillhoefer hit under .100 and was traded away. In the meantime Alexander went on to win another 183 games. The Alexander deal was the beginning of a two-decade period when the Phillies would trade away their best players for money. Baker justified the trade by claiming that Alexander, who had been drafted, might not be effective after the war. He later admitted it was for the cash.

ONE HUNDRED YEARS IN THE CELLAR

A writer once titled a history of the Phillies in the twentieth century *One Hundred Years in the Cellar*. He was really dealing with the years after the breakup of the Phillies team of the midteens. Between 1909 and 1913, the Phillies had passed through the hands of four different owners. The instability came to end when William Baker, a former New York police commissioner, took control. From 1913 until his death in 1930 Baker ran the Phillies on a shoestring. In spite of his wealth, he refused to invest in player development and allowed the ballpark to deteriorate. Between 1909 and 1923 13 new ballparks were built or older ones modernized. Baker Bowl, once considered a gem, began to rot away. By the end of the 1920s it was nicknamed "the Dump." In 1927 the stands collapsed for the second time in Baker Bowl's history, with one person dying and over 50 injured.

Baker's failure to modernize and his penny-pinching cost the Phillies the services of manager Pat Moran, who left for Cincinnati, where he won the World Series in 1919. Throughout the 1920s the Phillies were one of the jokes of baseball. Beginning in 1918 they began a 27-year stretch during which they finished last 16 times and seventh 7 times. Not surprisingly, the team had had the worst attendance in the NL 18 times by 1945, including every year from 1932 through 1942. In contrast in the mid-1920s, the Athletics' Connie Mack began to put together his last dynasty, the team that would win three consecutive pennants (1929–31) and two World Series (1929–30). While the Athletics were playing exciting baseball against powerhouses like the Babe Ruth–led New York Yankees, the Phillies sputtered along. In the 1920s the Phillies sold space on the right field wall for advertising. One of the signs read, "The Phillies Use Lifebuoy Soap." "Yeah, and they still stink," was the response of the fans.

In the decade from 1919 to 1928 the Phillies finished last seven times and lost 100 games three times. Their best season was sixth-place finish in 1925. Yet the team continued to put up decent offensive numbers. Cy Williams, a worthy successor to Cravath, led the NL in homers three times, including hitting 41 in 1923, the second-highest total in NL history at that time.

The Phillies had some decent players during these years, including Casey Stengel, Irish Meusel, catchers Jimmy Wilson and Butch Henline, and second baseman Fresco Thompson. But Baker would sell or trade them as soon as they proved their value.

Baker was no fool. He made some shrewd trades. He got Lefty O'Doul, one of the greatest hitters in NL history, from the New York Giants in 1928; O'Doul then hit .398 and .383. Then Baker packaged him along with Thompson to the Brooklyn Dodgers for three players and $25,000. It is difficult to imagine any other team trading a hitter like O'Doul, a batting champ in 1929 and holder of the NL record for hits in a season, 254. Baker claimed he needed the cash.

The same year he got O'Doul, Baker signed a young outfielder, Chuck Klein. Until he too was unloaded for cash and players after the 1933 season, Klein's offensive stats were among the greatest in baseball history. From 1929 through 1933 Klein averaged .359, hit 180 homers, scored 658 runs, and drove in 693. He won the Triple Crown in 1933 and had 107 extra-base hits in 1930. He was also a great defensive outfielder who mastered the right-field wall in Baker Bowl and set an NL record with 44 assists in one season.

While the Phillies didn't draw well in the 1920s, their attendance, which averaged 266,000, was enough to pay the bills and even show a small profit of $110,792. Baker's problem was a lack of consistency. There was a constant turnover of players and managers (six in the 1920s) during the last years of his tenure.

The 1930 Phillies squad, 100-game losers, nonetheless managed a collective .315 average, the best of any Phillies team in the modern era. Six regulars hit .300, led by Klein, who hit .386 and paced the NL with 158 runs scored and 59 doubles. He also drove in 170 runs. O'Doul was at .383, first baseman Don Hurst .327, and third baseman Pinky Whitney .342. The Phillies scored 944 runs, the best total in team history. Unfortunately, the pitching was horrendous, with a staff ERA of 6.71.

Baker died in 1930 and was succeeded briefly by the team's vice president, Lewis Ruch, who sought to upgrade the Phillies. There was a temporary lull in selling off the team's best players. In 1932, under manager Burt Shotton, the Phillies finished fourth, topping .500 for their best record since 1917. Six players batted over .300, but the Phillies had the highest ERA in the NL.

At the end of the 1932 season Ruch retired due to ill health. He and Baker's widow sold the team to Gerald Nugent, who had served as the business manager for five years. Nugent would lead the Phillies for a disastrous decade. In many ways Nugent was the quintessential Phillies owner. He had started as an assistant to Baker, married Baker's secretary, and helped run the club for Ruch. He was a knowledgeable baseball man but chronically short of cash. As a result he ran the Phillies on a year-to-year basis, selling off players to pay his bills and neglecting Baker Bowl. When Nugent took over he sold Klein, Whitney, and shortstop Dick Bartell to keep the Phillies afloat in the midst of the depression. During the 1930s he secured talented players such as Dolph Camilli, Claude Passeau, Bucky Walters, Ethan Allen, and Kirby Higbe. After they showed signs of promise, they were peddled to the highest bidder for cash. He got $65,000 for Klein; $50,000 each for Allen, Camilli, and Walters; and $100,000 for Higbe.

The Phillies of the 1930s and early 1940s fielded some of the worst teams in baseball history. From 1936 to 1942 the Phillies lost 100 games every year but one and finished last six of the seven years. In July 1938 the Phillies moved to Shibe Park. Nugent could not maintain Baker Bowl any longer and hoped that playing in Shibe Park would attract greater attendance. While the Phillies drew better, Nugent still was living from year to year. His debts were mounting and he no longer had players to sell to pay his bills. The team actually made a little money ($15,911) in 1930–37, but ended the era with a deficit by losing $113,661 in 1938 and 1939.

By the early 1940s NL president Ford Frick was looking for a way to force Nugent to sell the team. The league had been bailing Nugent out for years, who owed back rent to Connie Mack for the use of Shibe Park. There were plenty of potential buyers, including construction magnate Jack Kelly, the father of the future Princess Grace of Monaco. Years later, Bill Veeck claimed in his autobiography, *Veeck—as in Wreck,* that he tried to buy the Phillies and stock it with players from the Negro Leagues. This tale was largely a figment of Veeck's ripe imagination.

With bills mounting, Nugent was forced to sell the club in 1942. The eventual buyer was William Cox, lumber merchant, sportsman, and Yale graduate, who would prove himself as inept an owner as Nugent. Cox loved to gamble and bet on his team, known as the Blue Jays, from 1943 to 1944. His wagering became public knowledge when Cox and the new manager, Bucky Harris, had a falling-out in the middle of the 1943 season. Commissioner Kenesaw Mountain Landis forced Cox to sell the team for $400,000 to Bob Carpenter Sr., president of the DuPont Chemical Company. Luckily for the Phillies, he installed his son, Robert Jr., as president. The Carpenter family owned the Phillies for 38 years and gave the team a much-needed modernization. For once the team would not be short of cash. This was important, since the club lost $490,889 between 1940 and 1945.

THE CARPENTER ERA

When Bob Carpenter took over the Phillies, his first act was to hire as general manager Herb Pennock, then running the Boston Red Sox's minor-league system. A Hall of Fame pitcher for the Athletics, Red Sox, and Yankees, Pennock's first task was to build up the farm system. The Phillies had no farm teams, just a working agreement with Trenton in the Class B Interstate League. By 1949 the Phillies had 11 well-stocked teams in their minor-league system. Pennock also shelled out Carpenter's money liberally on "bonus babies." Before his untimely death in January 1948, Pennock had showered $1,250,000 on untried young players, including future regulars Curt Simmons, Robin Roberts, Willie Jones, Stan Lopata, and Richie Ashburn.

The Phillies showed the first signs of improvement in 1946, making fifth, their best performance since 1932. Philadelphia fans responded enthusiastically, and the Phillies drew 1 million fans for the first time in their history. The 1946 team was a mix of older veterans, like Schoolboy Rowe, Frank McCormick, and Jim Tabor, and youngsters, like catcher Andy Seminick and outfielder Del Ennis. Ennis, a product of the Olney section of Philadelphia, hit .313 and was named Rookie of the Year.

In 1947 and 1948 the Phillies seemed to spin their wheels, finishing tied for seventh in 1947 and sixth in 1948. In reality they were gradually working new players into the team. In 1947 bonus-baby Curt Simmons made his first appearance, and one year later shortstop Granny Hamner became a regular, pitcher Robin Roberts arrived in midseason to win seven games, and Richie Ashburn took over center field and hit .333 to finish second to Stan Musial in the batting race. He was named the second Phillies Rookie of the Year in three years. First baseman Dick Sisler also joined the Phillies in 1948 after a trade with the Cardinals. He hit .274 with 11 homers. In September the Phillies brought up their third baseman of the future, Willie Jones. Although the Phillies only won 66 games, they had the look of a team with a future.

In midseason Carpenter fired his fiery, racist southern-born manager, Ben Chapman, and replaced him with the quieter, fatherly Eddie Sawyer. Pennock had brought Sawyer over from the Yankees organization with the idea of him eventually taking over as manager. Carpenter believed that Sawyer was perfect to guide the youthful Phillies team.

The Phillies also maintained fan loyalty against Connie Mack's revived Athletics. Mack had put together his last good team after the war, and in 1947–49 the Athletics were again a competitive team. In 1948 they were in the middle of the pennant race until late August. Still, the Phillies, despite their sixth-place finish in 1948, managed to draw 767,000 fans to the Athletics' 940,000. Over the next two years the Phillies would win over the loyalty of the Philadelphia baseball fans from the Athletics, something they had been unable to do in the past.

After Herb Pennock's untimely death, Carpenter became his own general manager. He took over a first-class organization with talented scouts and a string of good players in the pipeline. But Carpenter's limitations as a judge of baseball talent would eventually prove costly.

Everything seemed to come together for the Phillies in 1949. Before the season Carpenter made two good trades. He got Eddie Waitkus, a .300-hitting first baseman; Russ Meyer, a pitcher with potential; and slugging outfielder Bill Nicholson from the Chicago Cubs for cash and some excess players. The deal enabled Sisler to move to the outfield and provided the team with a powerful pinch hitter and a talented player at every position.

After a slow start, the 1949 Phillies were tied for third place on July 4, just five and a half games out of first place. The Phillies' starting pitchers were a combined 30–19 while Ennis was fourth in the league in homers and second in RBIs. The Phillies had slid back to fifth place by mid-August when an angry tirade by Sawyer jolted them from their lethargy. He told them that if play didn't improve some of the players would be back in the minors. His warning worked. The Phillies went 16–10 to finish in third place, 81–73, their best record since 1917.

The Phillies accomplished this despite some serious setbacks. In June Waitkus was shot by a deranged female fan while the team was in Chicago. Sisler took over at first and filled in nicely, hitting .287. Jones, in his rookie year, hit 19 homers while driving in 77 runs and playing a flawless third base. Ennis had his second solid year with a .302 batting average, 25 homers, and 110 RBIs. Seminick led all major-league catchers with 24 homers.

The starting pitching was excellent. Roberts won 15 games in his first full season while veterans Ken Heintzelman and Russ Meyer each won 17 games. Jim Konstanty, whom Sawyer had rescued from the minors, chipped in with nine wins and seven saves. The Phillies were a team to be reckoned with, and the players believed that they were legitimate pennant contenders.

In 1950 the Phillies were picked to finish third or fourth behind the champion Dodgers. The Phillies entered the 1950 season without making any major trades. Rookie pitchers Bob Miller and Emory "Bubba" Church made the team out of spring training. They were the last products of Pennock's farm system to make an impact on the Phillies. The roster averaged just 26 years of age and became known as "The Whiz Kids."

Opening Day in Philadelphia against the Dodgers set the tone for the season. Before 30,000 fans, the largest Opening Day in Phillies history, Roberts defeated Don Newcombe for his first victory over the Dodgers. He would beat them three more times that season.

The Phillies started slowly, but by June 1 were in third place, just half a game out of first. Roberts and Simmons were pitching brilliantly, and Konstanty was on his way to the greatest season any relief pitcher had had to date. Throwing a deceptive palm ball, he was virtually unhittable. Meyer and Heintzelman, the aces of the 1949 staff, struggled, but Church and Miller, who won his first eight decisions, picked up the slack.

By July, behind the hitting of Ennis, Sisler, and Willie Jones, the Phillies had begun challenging the Cardinals and Dodgers for first place. Ennis had an unbelievable July, driving in 39 runs. The Phillies took over first place to stay on July 25 as Roberts and Church swept a doubleheader from the Chicago Cubs.

When Miller hurt his back in July and then his shoulder in September, Church stepped in and won seven crucial games. Between them the two rookies went 19–12 for the season. More serious than Miller's injury was the loss of Simmons when his National Guard unit was called to active duty in August. He was able to pitch on weekends for a while. At the time, he was 15–6, and according to Sawyer was pitching better than Roberts.

The Phillies stretched their lead to seven games over the Dodgers on September 1. Philadelphians were talking pennant and crowds were coming out in record numbers. Eventually the Phillies led the NL in attendance, and shattered their single-season attendance record by drawing 1,217,000 fans. It marked the first time since 1917 that the team was higher than fifth best in attendance.

Things suddenly turned sour in September. The Dodgers got hot and the Phillies were hit by one setback after another. Simmons was lost for good by the middle of September. Miller was virtually useless, Seminick suffered a severe ankle injury in a play at the plate and was hobbled for the rest of the season, and Church was hit in the face by a line drive off the bat of Ted Kluszewski. The Phillies were suddenly vulnerable. They went 12–16 for the month while the Dodgers won 20 games. Going into the last two days of the season against the Dodgers in Brooklyn, the Phillies led by two games. They had to win once or there would be a three-game playoff that they almost surely would lose given the state of the team.

The Phillies lost the first game as Miller made a valiant effort but fell short. Roberts started the last game of the season, his fourth start in eight days. In the bottom of the ninth with the score tied 1–1, the Dodgers got their first two batters on. Duke Snider lined a single to center but Ashburn, playing shallow, fielded the ball on one hop and threw out Cal Abrams at the plate by 10 feet. Roberts loaded the bases by walking the dangerous Jackie Robinson and then got Carl Furillo to pop up and Gil Hodges to fly out to right field. In the top of the 10th the Phillies won the game when Dick Sisler hit a three-run homer. The Phillies had won the pennant, but the team was exhausted.

The Phillies had won because of solid pitching, leading the NL with 3.50 team ERA. Roberts became the first Phillies pitcher since Alexander in 1917 to win 20 games. Simmons was 17–8, and Konstanty won 16 while saving 22 others. In 151 innings Konstanty gave up just 109 hits, and he was named NL MVP. The team earned a franchise record $303,000, and had averaged nearly $100,000 a year in profit since 1946.

The World Series against the New York Yankees proved a letdown. The Yankees swept the Phillies in four close games by scores of 1–0, 2–1, 3–2, and 5–2. The Phillies were silenced by Yankees pitching, hitting just .203, but their hurlers held the vaunted Yankees to just 11 runs in four games.

Even with their loss in the World Series, the Phillies confidently expected to be pennant contenders for the next five to seven years since they were a young team, with an average age of 26. It wasn't to be. Roberts believed that the Phillies won too soon and were not mature enough to handle success. Ashburn believed that the Phillies' failure to tap into the great black players coming out of the Negro Leagues was the main reason the Phillies failed to contend in the 1950s.

THE DECLINE OF THE WHIZ KIDS

In 1951 the Phillies slipped badly, finishing fifth with a 73–81 record, a 17-game drop from the previous year. There were problems from the start, as players arrived in spring training out of shape and overconfident. The team got off to a slow start and never was a factor in the pennant race.

Key Phillies suffered through poor seasons. Ennis had his worst year since entering the majors, hitting just .267 with 15 homers and 73 RBIs. Mike Goliat, a key figure at second base in 1950, hit .212 and found himself back in the minors. Andy Seminick hit .237 with 11 homers and was traded to Cincinnati after the season. Jim Konstanty, the miracle reliever of 1950, could not get anyone out and slipped to 4–11 record. Among the regulars, only Roberts, who won 20 games for the second season in row; Richie Ashburn, who hit .344 and finished second in the batting race; and third baseman Willie Jones, who led the team in homers and RBIs, had solid years.

The consensus was that the Phillies had slipped but would quickly rebound in 1952. Over the winter of 1951–52 Carpenter tried patching together a winning team around the Whiz Kids nucleus, but the minor-league system was weak.

Carpenter's key moves were designed to fill gaps in the Whiz Kids' facade. He traded Seminick and Sisler to a weak Cincinnati team for second baseman Connie Ryan, pitcher Howie Fox, and throw-in catcher Smoky Burgess.

Carpenter showed his support for Sawyer by giving him a three-year contract extension. At spring training Sawyer cracked down on the team for its lethargy, banning the players' wives from the training complex and ordering no swimming or golf. Nothing worked. Sawyer, the father figure, had lost control of the team.

The Phillies started poorly in 1952. They were 30–46 when, at the end of June, Carpenter fired Sawyer. He brought in "Stout" Steve O'Neill, a longtime major-league manager, to see if the team would prosper under his loose hand. O'Neill had been successful in the past, having won a World Series with the 1945 Detroit Tigers. He was good at getting the most out of veterans. But at 61 he was probably past his prime. A big, heavyset man, he often fell asleep on the bench.

In the second half of the season, the Phillies were the hottest team in the NL, going 59–32. Roberts had his greatest season, winning 28 games against just 7 losses for the best year of any NL pitcher since Dizzy Dean won 30 games in 1934. Simmons came out of the army to win 14 games. Overall the Phillies' pitching staff led the NL with a 3.07 ERA.

Among the hitters, Ennis had a solid year, driving in 100 runs, and Burgess hit .296 while sharing catching duties with Stan Lopata. Granny Hamner hit .275 with 17 homers and played brilliantly at shortstop.

The Phillies' 87 victories put them in fourth place, nine and a half games back of the pennant-winning Dodgers. Carpenter believed the team was one or two players shy of competing with the Dodgers and Giants. However, he didn't grasp that other teams were starting to pass the Phillies in talent and organizational leadership.

Nowhere were the Phillies more out of touch with reality than in their failure to tap into the African American talent pool. Carpenter always claimed the Phillies were not reluctant to sign African American players. Nonetheless, the team signed none and was the last in the NL to integrate. The Phillies did not produce a great black player until Dick Allen in 1964, a full generation after Jackie Robinson joined the Dodgers. The Phillies paid the price for their racism.

Between 1953 and 1956 the Phillies' performance fluctuated between mediocre and poor. They tied for third once, fourth twice, and fifth once. They topped the .500 mark once, in 1953. They were never a serious pennant contender despite still having talented players like Ennis, Ashburn, Roberts, Simmons, and Hamner.

Carpenter continued his tinkering with the Whiz Kids. In 1953, Earl Torgeson replaced the fading Eddie Waitkus. Roberts won 20 games for the fourth straight season. Roberts was now the premier right-handed pitcher in baseball. However, Simmons never returned to his former dominance. The talent gap between the Phillies and the top teams in the NL continued to grow.

Early in 1954 Carpenter named his first general manager since Pennock's death, hiring Roy Hamey, assistant general manager to George Weiss of the Yankees, who had previously spent four years developing the Pittsburgh Pirates' minor-league system. Hamey got rid of O'Neill partway through the lackluster 1954 campaign, replacing him with former Cardinals outfielder Terry Moore. Moore had no more success in handling the Whiz Kids than O'Neill, and he was gone after the season. The Phillies finished in fourth place, with a poor record of 75–79. Roberts again won 20 games, but Simmons fell to 14–15. Hamner had a career year, hitting .299 with 13 homers and 98 RBIs, while Burgess hit an astounding .368, but without enough at bats to qualify for the batting title.

Even with the A's, in their last year in Philadelphia, playing awful baseball, the Phillies were unable to attract fans. Attendance declined by 115,000 from 1953. Even more disturbing was that attendance had declined by a half million since 1950.

In 1955, Hamey dipped into the Yankees organization for a new manager, Mayo Smith, the Phillies' fourth in four years. Smith was an adequate field general whose one great moment in nine years of managing was directing the underdog Detroit Tigers to a World Series victory in 1968. A low-key individual, Smith recognized that he had inherited the difficult situation of an aging team in transition. In a little over three and a half seasons Smith guided the Phillies to two .500 finishes while gradually infusing new blood into the franchise. Unfortunately for him, the new players were not of Whiz Kid caliber. Nor did Hamey help, with disastrous trades like dealing Burgess to Cincinnati in 1955 for unproductive outfielder Jim Greengrass.

In 1955 the Phillies improved, but were never in the pennant race because the Dodgers held first place the entire season. The Phillies doomed their season by losing 13 games in a row in late April and early May. Led by Richie Ashburn, who won his first batting title with a .338 average, and Roberts's sixth straight 20-victory season, the Phillies went 45–38 in the last three months of the season to finish in fourth place at 77–77.

It was difficult to be optimistic about the Phillies, who were a complete bust in 1956, finishing below .500 at 73–81 in fifth place as Roberts failed to win 20 games for the first time since 1950. Hamey planned dramatic changes for 1957. First he engineered another poor trade, sending Ennis, a Phillies favorite for 11 years, to the Cardinals for Eldon "Rip" Repulski, who flopped, while Ennis hit 24 homers with 105 RBIs. Hamey also launched a youth movement that brought excitement to Philadelphia for the first time since 1950. Seven rookies made the 1957 squad. Jack Sanford won 19 games, led the NL in strikeouts, and was named the *Sporting News*'s outstanding rookie. First baseman Ed Bouchee hit .297 with 17 homers and was named the Baseball Writers Association of America's Rookie of the Year. Outfielder Harry Anderson showed signs of power, hitting 17 homers in just 400 at bats. Another rookie, relief pitcher Dick Farrell, won 10 games and saved 10 others.

Philadelphia fell in love with the young team as fans came out in numbers unseen since 1950. The 1957 team drew 1,146,000, only the third time the Phillies had topped 1 million. Excitement peaked in early July as the Phillies made a run for the pennant. On July 14 Sanford beat the Cardinals to put the Phillies in first place for the first time that late in the season since 1950. Talk of another Whiz Kids miracle died as the Phillies went into a tailspin, losing 20 of 27 games to drop out of contention. They finished 77–77 in fifth place.

During the 1957 season, the team finally integrated its roster. Pressure had mounted from political circles in Philadelphia, with its large African American population. The African American papers, especially the *Philadelphia Tribune*, had been pressing the Phillies for years to integrate. In 1956 the Phillies purchased the contract of shortstop John Kennedy from the Kansas City Monarchs, and after a good year in the minors, brought him to spring training, intending to make him the everyday shortstop. However, Kennedy was not major-league material, and lasted just five games in the majors. This forced Hamey to make a major trade with the Dodgers to avoid charges of tokenism, and he secured shortstop Chico Fernandez. A black Cuban, Fernandez became the first African American Phillies regular. He had a solid rookie year, hitting .262, driving in 51 runs, and playing an exciting shortstop.

The local fans were shocked that year by the total collapse of Robin Roberts. After six consecutive 20-victory seasons and a 19-win season in 1956, Roberts plummeted to 10–22 in 1957. He was hit hard all season and led the majors in losses. Roberts originally claimed he suffered from back problems, but later admitted his arm hurt him the entire season. Roberts rebounded the next year to win 17 games, but was never again a dominant pitcher. Roberts's decline certified that the Whiz Kids era was long over.

The 1958–59 seasons saw the final collapse of the Phillies as they finished in the cellar both years, starting a run of four consecutive basement finishes. The Phillies began to resemble the cellar dwellers of the 1930s and early 1940s. The 1958 season started well enough, but by July the Phillies were stumbling badly. Trouble started even before the season when Bouchee was arrested on a morals charge. Sanford couldn't recapture his pitching dominance and ended the year 10–13. Dick Farrell went 8–9 and was ineffective the second half of the season. The team hit well, especially Ashburn, who won his second batting title with a .350 average, but the Phillies were next to last in the league in pitching. Hamey fired Smith, and at the urging of Carpenter, brought back Eddie Sawyer in a desperate effort to recapture the glory of the Whiz Kid days. However, the Phillies lost 41 of their last 69 games.

Things were worse the next season. In January 1959 Carpenter fired Hamey and brought in John Quinn, general manager of the Milwaukee Braves. Quinn had developed the Braves into a powerhouse that won NL pennants in 1957 and 1958 and the World Series in 1957. Unlike Hamey, who took over a team in transition, Quinn's task was simpler, yet more difficult—disband a team in free fall. In 1959 he got rid of former Whiz Kids Hamner, Lopata, and Jones, leaving only Roberts, Ashburn, and an ailing Simmons from the glory days. Quinn believed that trades could not revive the Phillies, but instead focused on the farm system.

The Phillies had begun the 1950s by winning the pennant, and ended the decade with the team's worst record since 1947, just 64 victories. Ashburn had his poorest season, hitting .266 and driving in 20 runs. Ruben Gomez, whom Hamey got from the Giants for Jack Sanford, won 3 games, as did Ray Semproch, a 13-game winner in 1958. The team collapse was total. The Phillies were sixth in ERA, last in team batting average, and last in fielding percentage. With the blessing of Carpenter, Quinn began a wholesale housecleaning. A decade of baseball in Philadelphia ended in chaos. Change was coming.

THE QUINN-MAUCH ERA

Reviving the Phillies proved to be a major problem. Bad trades had devastated the team while the farm system failed to produce quality players. The 1959 Phillies team that Quinn inherited was old, talentless at key positions, and guided by an unenthusiastic manager. Quinn immediately began getting rid of the deadwood.

After the 1959 season he sent one of the few bright lights of the Phillies' season, third baseman Gene Freese, who had hit 23 homers, to the Chicago White Sox for Johnny Callison, a young outfielder who had failed a brief trial with the White Sox in 1959 yet was compared by some experts to a young Mickey Mantle.

By the middle of 1960 Quinn had unloaded almost the entire 1959 team in trades. In place of older players, Quinn sought younger players with potential. His record was mixed. For Wally Post and Harry Anderson he got Tony Gonzalez, a talented black Cuban outfielder who gave the Phillies nine solid years. For Bouchee and pitcher Don Cardwell, Quinn got Tony Taylor, another black Cuban who proved to be a fine second baseman and one of the most popular players in Phillies history. These trades demonstrated that the hesitation to sign black talent was over.

Quinn also sent Ashburn to the Cubs in return for a young pitcher, John Buzhardt, whom the Phillies mistakenly hoped would deepen their pitching staff. The trade was unpopular because Ashburn was a Philadelphia icon.

Quinn fired Sawyer, and to manage the 1960 team, the youngest Phillies since the Whiz Kids, and lead the rebuilding process, he hired Gene Mauch, a 34-year-old minor-league manager, a young, imaginative baseball man enthusiastic enough to take on the arduous task of developing young players. It soon became clear that few knew baseball better than Mauch. Sparky Anderson said Mauch "was simply brilliant as a strategist and an innovator."

Mauch had an undistinguished playing career, but like many other mediocre players, became a keen student of the game. In 1953, at age 28, he became manager of the Atlanta Crackers of the Southern Association. However, he expected too much of his players, fought constantly with the umpires, and was a failure. After a couple more years as a part-time player he took over Minneapolis of the American Association in 1958, and was ready for that task.

The 1960 season wasn't a pretty sight. The Phillies finished with their worst record since 1945, losing 95 games. The 1961 team was even worse. After suffering through a 10-game losing streak in May, the Phillies lost 23 in a row in July and August to set an all-time record for baseball futility. The Phillies lost 107 games and finished a distant 46 games out of first place. The 1960 Phillies were out of the cellar for a few weeks; the 1961 club never escaped the basement.

Despite this awful record, Quinn and Mauch were rebuilding. In 1960 Callison and Gonzalez became regulars while Taylor was one of the league's best second basemen. Clay Dalrymple showed potential behind the plate. Chris Short, a pitcher from the Phillies system, showed occasional signs of brilliance. In midseason Quinn promoted the best pitcher in the Phillies farm system, 22-year-old Art Mahaffey, who won 7 of 10 decisions with an excellent ERA of 2.32.

Quinn continued the transformation of the Phillies in 1961. He signed Wes Covington, who had been a regular with the pennant-winning Braves in 1957–58 but had fallen out of favor. Covington hit .303 and began regaining the stroke that made him one of the most feared left-handed hitters in baseball. Mauch platooned him in left field against tough right-handers with great success over the next five years. Early in the 1961 season Quinn sent Farrell to the Dodgers for outfielder Don Demeter, who took over center field and led the Phillies in home runs in 1961. The next season he hit 29 homers and became the first Phillies player to drive in 100 runs since Del Ennis.

Despite these moves, the record losses doomed the Phillies in the eyes of the fans. Attendance in 1961 reached the lowest level in 16 years. The Phillies needed a boost, and finally got one the next season.

The 1962 Phillies team surprised the baseball world by finishing over .500, 81–80, for the first time since 1953, a 34-game improvement over its 1961 record. It was the first of six consecutive seasons finishing above .500 for the Phillies, the second-longest winning stretch in the team's history, bettered only by the 1975–84 teams.

Quinn made one major change before the 1962 season, trading Buzhardt to the White Sox for 35-year-old slugging first baseman Roy Sievers. Sievers was on the downside of his career, but had hit .295 in his last two seasons with

28 and 27 homers. Mauch wanted Sievers's presence in the lineup to take the pressure off his young players. Sievers provided stability at cleanup, hitting 21 homers and driving in 80 runs, and Callison, Gonzalez, and Demeter blossomed. All three outfielders hit .300 and topped the 20 mark in homers, giving the Phillies one of the best young outfields in the NL.

The pitching staff, led by Mahaffey, also showed improvement. Mauch carefully nurtured Mahaffey in 1962, spotting him mostly against second-division teams to boost his confidence. He went 12–2 against second-division teams and won 19 games in all, losing his chance for 20 wins on the last day of the season. Sophomore Jack Baldschun became one of the better relievers in the NL, winning 12 games and saving 13 others. In midseason the Phillies promoted one of their top pitching prospects, left-hander Dennis Bennett. Bennett won nine games, struck out 149 batters in 174 innings, and ranked third in the NL in fewest hits per nine innings. Baseball was once again becoming fun in Philadelphia. Attendance shot up by 170,000 over the 1961 figure, the Phillies' biggest one-year increase since 1950. Mauch was named NL Manager of the Year. However, some baseball writers perceptively noted that 31 of the Phillies' 81 victories came at the expense of the two expansion teams—the New York Mets and Houston Colt .45s.

Quinn and Mauch made only minor changes in 1963, expecting the Phillies to mature. The Phillies started slowly and remained near the cellar with a record of 35–41. In July they lost Mahaffey when he caught his spikes on the pitching rubber and broke his ankle. He dropped to 7–10 and was never again a consistent winner.

Beginning in late June the Phillies suddenly started playing better baseball, and finished fourth (87–75). The improvement coincided with the return from the disabled list of Bennett, who had suffered a broken ankle in a car accident in December 1962. He won nine games in the second half of the season and crafted a low 2.95 ERA. Bennett's return came as rookie right-handed pitcher Ray Culp won 14 games while striking out 176 batters. It was the best performance by a Phillies rookie pitcher since Jack Sanford. Baldschun had another fine year in the bullpen, winning 11 games and saving 16. The Phillies' staff ERA of 3.09 was third best in the NL. Callison hit 26 homers, the most for any Phillies left-handed batter since the team moved to Shibe Park. He also demonstrated one of the best throwing arms in baseball, leading the NL in assists for the second of four consecutive years.

Quinn and Mauch expected the Phillies to peak as pennant contenders in 1965 or 1966. The team's farm system was filled with solid prospects, including outfielders Adolpho Phillips and Alex Johnson, pitcher Ferguson Jenkins, and the team's best pure talent, Dick Allen.

In the off-season Quinn made one of his best trades, sending Demeter to the Detroit Tigers for pitcher Jim Bunning. At 32, Bunning was coming off his poorest season, winning just 12 of 25 games, and many considered him through, but Mauch believed he could help the young pitchers mature.

The Phillies were picked to finish fourth or fifth by most baseball experts. For Phillies fans, 1964 would prove one of the most exciting and traumatic in team history. The Phillies won 10 of their first 12 games. Led by the slugging of Allen, Callison, and Tony Gonzalez, the Phillies were in and out of first place for the first half of the season. Bunning was virtually unbeatable, capping his first half with a perfect game against the Mets on Father's Day. Bennett began the season 9–4 while Chris Short came into his own and gave the Phillies three top starters. Culp started well but came down with a sore arm and did not win a game after July 22.

At the All-Star break the Phillies were in first place with a 47–28 record. Fittingly, Callison won the All-Star Game with a three-run homer in the bottom of the ninth. From that point until the Phillies returned home from their last western road trip, the team steadily widened its lead. Yet problems were brewing. Mauch was reduced to two pitchers, Bunning and Short, who between them would win 36 games, because Culp was hurt, Mahaffey was inconsistent, and Bennett was virtually useless during the second half of the season. The bullpen, anchored by veterans Ed Roebuck and Baldschun, was one of the best. By September 21, with 12 games remaining, the Phillies opened a 7-game home stand with a six-and-a-half game lead. Then disaster struck, and the Phillies experienced one of the worst collapses in baseball history.

A 10-game losing streak began against Cincinnati when Chico Ruiz stole home with two outs and Frank Robinson at bat. Over the next two weeks the Phillies went into free fall. St. Louis went on to win 10 of 13 to win the pennant by one game over the Phillies.

Mauch was criticized for pitching Bunning and Short with just two days' rest, but his pitching staff was decimated. The team's veterans failed to hit. Covington went 1 for 17 during the losing streak, although the younger players like Callison, who homered three times in one game, and Allen came through.

All teams have losing streaks—the Phillies' came at the wrong time. Their collapse was the result of several factors, including the injuries to key pitchers and the lack of production at first base. Sievers developed a calf injury that effectively ended his career, and his replacement, Frank Thomas of the Mets, broke his finger.

Philadelphia was in shock. The 1964 team had won the hearts of the city's fans as no other since the Whiz Kids. To hold first place for 73 consecutive days and then lose everything in less than two weeks was more than the city could bear. A scapegoat was needed, and Mauch, who had been a popular manager, was the easy target.

The Phillies' near miss convinced Mauch and Quinn that with one more piece the team could go all the way. They overestimated the team's talent level and did not consider that 1964 might have been a freak year. A team built by surrounding its young players with a few key veterans began to sacrifice its farm system in a desperate search for experience.

First, Quinn sent Bennett to Boston for slugger Dick Stuart and got lefty Bo Belinsky from the Los Angeles Angels to replace Bennett. Quinn hoped he had filled two holes in the 1964 team, but the trades didn't work. Belinsky went 4–9, and while Stuart hit with power, with 28 homers, he batted just .234 and confirmed his reputation as a terrible defensive player.

The Phillies got off to slow start in 1965 in part because of their awful defense, making 51 errors in their first 40 games. Despite great years from Bunning and Short, who combined for 37 wins, and a comeback from Culp, with 14 victories, the Phillies could not match the talent of the Dodgers, Giants, and Reds. The Phillies finished in sixth place with an 85–76 record.

While still topping the 1 million mark in attendance, fan disillusionment set in as attendance declined by 280,000. A partial explanation for this drop-off was the changing nature of the neighborhood surrounding the ballpark. Connie Mack Stadium was located in the heart of north Philadelphia, an area shifting from white to black. Public transportation was adequate, but there were few parking spaces. Vandalism, especially slashed tires and broken windows, became a problem for car commuters. Racial tensions also were high. Philadelphia had experienced its first serious urban riot in August 1964 in an area south of the ballpark. Race relations remained strained for the rest of the decade.

Carpenter had purchased Connie Mack Stadium for $1,657,000 when the A's left town, but he believed the Phillies could no longer survive there. However, there was little public support for a new baseball stadium.

In 1966 Quinn and Mauch again searched for the one move that would return the Phillies to pennant contention. Quinn secured half of the Cardinals infield, shortstop Dick Groat and first baseman Bill White, for Mahaffey and outfielder Alex Johnson. In April, Quinn sent rookie outfielder Adolpho Phillips, first baseman John Herrnstein, and pitcher Ferguson Jenkins to the Cubs for veteran pitchers Larry Jackson and Bob Buhl. Mauch was thrilled that he had gotten "a diamond and a ruby for three bags of garbage." Jackson gave the Phillies three solid years while Buhl, at 38, was finished by the end of season. But Jenkins went on to win 284 games and wound up in the Hall of Fame.

White and Groat solidified the Phillies infield and Jackson joined Bunning and Short to give the Phillies three good starters. Early in the season the Phillies lost Allen for 24 games when he injured his arm sliding back to second base. He recovered to have one of the greatest offensive years of any Phillies player since Chuck Klein, hitting 40 homers and driving in 110 runs while batting .317. But Callison, after averaging 31 homers and 100 RBIs for the past two seasons, went into a bewildering offensive slump, hitting just 11 homers and driving in 55 runs. At 27, Callison was finished as a power hitter. The Phillies won 87 games and climbed to fourth place, but were never in the pennant race. In two seasons after almost stealing the pennant, the Phillies were just a mediocre team.

One year later the Phillies begin a decline that sank them to the bottom of the NL. Between 1967 and 1975, when the Phillies again became a serious pennant contender, they finished in the cellar three times and next to last twice.

The 1967 Phillies were an old team, and barely finished over .500 at 82–80. Bunning went 17–15 but lost five 1–0 games, with a superb 2.29 ERA and six shutouts. No other starter topped .500. Yet the real problem was the decline in offense. Before the season Bill White tore his Achilles tendon, and he was finished as an everyday player. Groat was also injured, and played just 10 games. Two regulars, catcher Dalrymple and shortstop Bobby Wine, hit less than .200. Allen was having a good year, with 23 homers and a .307 batting average, when he cut his hand in a freak accident pushing his car in August and was lost for the season. The final offensive figures for the Phillies, a .242 batting average and 103 homers, were the worst since 1961, when the team lost 104 games. Attendance sagged for the third straight season, dropping to 829,000, the lowest figure since 1962.

REBUILDING A CONTENDER

Although the 1967 Phillies finished at two games over .500, the team seemed to have no future. Quinn and Mauch had gambled that they could cobble together a pennant contender with a couple of clever moves, but they had lost. The Phillies were drifting back to 1960–61 levels.

A first step in the transformation of the team was trading Bunning to the Pittsburgh Pirates for pitcher Woodie Fryman and three young players, most notably 20-year-old shortstop Don Money. Mauch was ready to lead another rebuilding program, but had worn out his welcome with the fans. There also was growing friction between Mauch and Allen, who was disenchanted with Philadelphia and its racism. Philadelphia fans never embraced the moody Allen's style of play or his contempt for team rules. Allen didn't help matters by missing games. He and Mauch battled each other all through the opening weeks of the 1968 season, with Mauch fining and benching him. When it came to choosing between an unpopular manager and a controversial 26-year-old slugger, it was clear who would go. On June 14, after almost nine years as manager, Mauch was fired and replaced by Bob Skinner, manager of the Phillies' successful farm team in San Diego. An era in Phillies history was over. No other Phillies manager in the twentieth century served as long as Mauch.

The Phillies played out the string in 1968 as Skinner tried to evaluate the team's talent and develop rapport with Allen, its key player. The Phillies fell to seventh place and lost 86 games, their worst record since 1961. Aside from Allen, who hit 33 homers but dropped below .300 for the first time, and Short, who won 19 games, the team's performance was awful. No regular hit higher than .264, and their batting average of .233 was the lowest since 1942.

The decline continued in 1969. An attempt to replace veterans with players from the farm system began in earnest. Money was installed at shortstop but struggled all season, hitting just .229. Larry Hisle, the best hitting prospect in the organization, showed flashes of brilliance with 20 homers, the most of any Phillies rookie other than Allen. The pitching staff had to be revamped when Short developed a herniated-disc problem that ended his career as a dominant pitcher.

The unhealthy atmosphere around the club escalated when in August Skinner quit, criticizing the front office for not disciplining Allen. The team's decline reached new levels as they finished fifth of six teams in the new NL Eastern Division, losing 99 games. Attendance dipped to just over 500,000—the poorest since the last year of World War II.

Radical measures were necessary if the Phillies were to recover. To replace Skinner the Phillies promoted Frank Lucchesi, a 14-year veteran of their farm system. It proved a popular choice, as Lucchesi's genuine enthusiasm and empathy with fans proved infectious. Lucchesi was a warm individual with a gift for malapropisms. He once bragged that he wasn't going to be "a scrapegoat" for some Phillies failure.

Allen, who had been campaigning to be traded, was sent to the Cardinals for a package including center fielder Curt Flood, catcher Tim McCarver, and relief specialist Joe Hoerner. Flood refused to report despite being offered $110,000, saying he didn't want to play in a racist city, and eventually sued MLB seeking free agency. The Cardinals sent Willie Montanez as Flood's replacement. Montanez, "Willie the Phillie," would go on to become one of the more popular players with the team in the early 1970s.

From the farm system in 1970 the Phillies promoted their young double-play combination of shortstop Larry Bowa and second baseman Denny Doyle. With Money moved to third base and veteran slugger Deron Johnson at first, the Phillies had a decent infield for the first time in years. The outfield was questionable. Hisle suffered through a terrible case of the sophomore jinx, hitting just .205. The pitching staff struggled all season. Bunning, brought back for a second tour, went 10–15, Short went 9–16, and Grant Jackson slipped to 5–15. The relief core, led by Dick Selma, who came from the Cubs in exchange for Callison, won 17 games and saved 31 others.

The 1970 Phillies improved by 10 games over 1969 with a 73–88 record and brought back some excitement to the city. Part of the credit belongs to Lucchesi and part to a team that was showcasing its young players for the first time in years. Bowa, after a terrible start, hit .250 while playing great shortstop. Veteran Tony Taylor played all over the infield and had his last great season, hitting .301. Johnson clouted 27 homers and drove in 93 runs, while Money had his best year, batting .295.

The Phillies looked optimistically toward the 1971 season. Not only had the team shown improvement, but the Phillies were scheduled to move into their new 62,382-seat ballpark on the site of a former landfill, part of a complex that included the Spectrum, built in 1967. Veterans Memorial Stadium, known as "the Vet," had the largest capacity of any NL field.

The city decided in the mid-1960s to build a multipurpose stadium in south Philadelphia to serve both the Phillies and the Eagles and to promote economic development. The Vet, built for $52 million, a cost shared by the city and state, opened in April 1971. It was the newest and at the time most modern stadium, with an Astroturf playing surface and seating for 60,000 fans. Its shape was octorad, or eight-sided, with equal dimensions of 330 feet to left and right field. Sight lines were clear, with no pillars to block the fans' view.

The Phillies broke their attendance record in 1971 by drawing over 1.5 million fans, double what the team had drawn in its last year at Connie Mack Stadium. But on the field, the Phillies went backward, finishing in last place and losing 95 games, last in the NL. There were some remarkable individual performances: Johnson hit 34 homers, including 3 in one game, and Montanez set a Phillies rookie record with 30 homers and drove in 99 runs. Yet overall the team retrogressed, batting just .233, and Short and Bunning went 12–26.

The Phillies' poor performance foreshadowed an even grimmer year in 1972. Shortly before the season began Quinn made his last and best trade, sending Wise to the Cardinals for 20-game winner Steve Carlton. The Phillies also promoted their top prospect, Greg Luzinski, to the major-league roster. Carlton had a remarkable season, winning 27 games, including 15 in a row, and striking out 310 batters while compiling a 1.97 ERA. He accounted for 46 percent of the team's 59 victories, the best ratio in baseball history. He won the Cy Young Award for the first of four times. Luzinski had a fine rookie season, hitting .281 with 18 homers and leading the team in RBIs. Bowa had another steady year at short. Aside from these three, the team was a disaster zone.

The team's miserable performance led to major front-office changes. In early June Quinn retired and was replaced by farm director Paul Owens. On July 10 Owens fired Lucchesi and took over as manager to evaluate the squad. The Phillies finished a distant sixth with a 59–97 record. They probably would have lost 100 games, but a strike shortened the season by six games.

After the season, Owens returned to the general manager's job and the Phillies hired longtime Dodgers coach Danny Ozark as their manager to teach the fundamentals that the Dodgers had traditionally stressed.

The Phillies' resurrection slowly began in 1973. Owens had a reservoir of talent in the minor-league system and he proved a shrewd trader. With the nucleus of Carlton, Luzinski, and Bowa in place, Owens believed the team needed greater depth at pitching and in the outfield. He got Del Unser from Cleveland to play center field, and Bill Robinson, from the farm system, took over right field. He solved the pitching problem by trading Don Money to Milwaukee for pitchers Ken Brett and Jim Lonborg. In 1973 Brett and Lonborg each won 13 games, while a lightly regarded Wayne Twitchell also won 13 while compiling the league's second-lowest ERA, 2.50. Carlton came down with bronchitis in spring training and labored throughout the season. He won 13 games but led the league with 20 losses.

To replace Money, Owens and Ozark turned third base over to a 23-year-old rookie, Mike Schmidt. Schmidt had a bizarre season. He hit just .196 but had flashes of power with 18 homers and 52 RBIs. He led the team in strikeouts, walks, and game-winning hits. Luzinski had his first big year, with 29 homers and 97 RBIs, and Robinson contributed 26 homers. The Phillies played exciting baseball throughout the season. They finished last again at 71–91, but only 11 games out of first place.

The 1974 Phillies were an exciting team, and were in first place for 51 days. Dave Cash, whom they got from Pittsburgh for Ken Brett, proved to be a team leader, a good leadoff hitter, and durable. He started every game, hit .300, and finished second in the league in hits with 206. They finished 80–82 in third place. Carlton and Lonborg anchored a strong pitching staff with 33 victories between them. Rookie Dick Ruthven showed flashes of brilliance, winning seven of his nine victories in the second half of the season. The real surprise was the emergence of Mike Schmidt as a premier power hitter. He led the league in homers and slugging percentage and was second in RBIs and total bases. He also led all NL third basemen in total chances.

The one problem area that hurt the Phillies in 1974 was an erratic bullpen. Owens tried to solve that first by adding Gene Garber in July from Kansas City, and in 34 games he was 4–0 with a 2.06 ERA. After the season Owens traded one of the team's top prospects, catcher John Stearns, to the New York Mets for reliever Tug McGraw.

The Phillies entered the 1975 campaign with their strongest club in a decade. Early in the season Owens made two major trades. He sent Montanez to the Giants for center fielder Garry Maddox, who eventually won eight Gold Gloves, and brought back Dick Allen to play first base. But Allen was a shadow of the player he once had been.

The Phillies stayed close to the Pirates throughout the 1975 season, briefly tying them for first place on August 18. The Pirates steadily pulled away and the Phillies finished in second (86–76). The Phillies were now one of the best teams in the NL. Schmidt won the home-run title again and Luzinski led the league in RBIs and total bases. Cash and Bowa hit .305 and Cash led the league with 213 hits. Garber and McGraw stabilized the bullpen with 28 saves between them. Tommy Underwood came out of the minors to win 14 games and Carlton contributed 15. The Phillies were on the brink.

A PHILLIES DYNASTY

In the bicentennial year the Phillies hosted the All-Star Game and had the greatest performance in the team's history, initiating a decade of winning baseball that lasted from 1976 through 1984. They finished first six times, won more games than any NL team, and captured five NL East titles. They went to the World Series twice and won a world championship in 1980.

Owens created a great team built around future Hall of Famers Mike Schmidt and Steve Carlton and great defense. The infield of Bowa, Cash, and Schmidt gave the team interior strength; Bob Boone was a Gold Glove winner behind the plate; and Maddox was the best defensive center fielder in baseball. Owens filled the gaps with players from the team's rich minor-league system, directed by former Phillies pitcher Dallas Green. Owens also made a series of shrewd trades in the late 1970s, getting solid players such as Bake McBride and Manny Trillo to fill needed slots.

Danny Ozark, a poor communicator who massacred the English language, was not given much credit for managerial skills, but the Phillies played sound, fundamental baseball. The players may have policed themselves, but Ozark deserves some credit for sticking with Schmidt during his rookie year. During his five and half years as Phillies manager the team won 590 games, the third-highest total in team history. He was doing something right.

The 1976 Phillies surprised the baseball world. After losing three of their first four games, they fell behind the Chicago Cubs 12–1 and then roared back behind Schmidt's four home runs to win the game 18–16. The Phillies won 51 of their next 69 and took over first place permanently on May 9. In late August their lead over the second-place Pirates was 15 1/2 games. They then lost eight consecutive games while the Pirates suddenly got hot and narrowed the Phillies' lead to three games on September 17, bringing back memories of the 1964 collapse. At that point the Phillies rallied to win the NL East with a record of 101–61, the best in team history.

The offense was awesome. The Phillies scored 10 or more runs 15 times. They were second in the league in team batting average and tied for second in homers. Schmidt won the home-run title for the third consecutive year, the first NL player to do so since Ralph Kiner, and also led in total bases. Luzinski hit .304 and drove in 97 runs, Maddox hit .330, and Jay Johnstone hit .318. The pitching staff was also solid, third in team ERA. Carlton set the pace for the pitchers by winning 20 games, while Jim Lonborg contributed 18 wins. Ozark's five-man rotation of Carlton, Lonborg, Larry Christenson, Jim Kaat (whom the Phillies got from the Chicago White Sox), and Underwood started 156 of the team's 162 games. The Phillies also had one of the best bullpens in baseball, with 44 saves.

Philadelphia, by midsummer, was in love with the Phillies. Attendance zoomed to all-time levels and topped the previous record of 1.9 million by 571,000. Fans looked forward to the playoffs against Sparky Anderson's Big Red Machine. Few Phillies' players had playoff experience, and the Reds intimidated them, sweeping the Phillies in three games.

Owens basically stayed pat in 1977. The team played listless baseball for the first month of the season, landing in last place on May 6, but then jelled and moved into contention. The season's turning point came on June 15 when Owens swung one of his best deals, sending Underwood and two minor leaguers to the Cardinals for Arnold "Bake" McBride.

With McBride leading off and hitting a torrid .339 for the Phillies, Luzinski supplying the power in the second half of the season, and Carlton off to his best start since winning 27 games in 1972, the Phillies pulled away from the rest of the league. They were 61–29 for the last three months of the season, went into first place on August 5, and ended with record of 101–61.

Owens considered the 1977 Phillies his best team. They dominated the NL in team batting average (.279) while scoring 847 runs. Led by Luzinski's 39 homers and Schmidt's 38, they set a team record of 186 home runs. Carlton won 23 games and Christenson 19 to give the Phillies their best lefty-righty combination since Bunning and Short.

The Vet rocked with fan enthusiasm as the Phillies set an all-time attendance record of 2.7 million, an increase of 280,000 over 1976. In two years the Phillies had drawn 800,000 additional fans, a greater increase than any other team in the majors.

All the positives turned sour in the playoffs as the Phillies experienced one of the most painful breakdowns in their long history. The Phillies split the first two games against the Dodgers in Los Angeles and returned home, where they were 60–21. In game three, before a huge throng of 64,000 screaming fans, the Phillies scored two runs in the bottom of the eighth to take a 5–3 lead. With two out in the ninth and Garber pitching, Vic Davillio beat out a perfect drag bunt. Manny Mota followed with a long drive to left. During the season Ozark had usually replaced Luzinski with Jerry Martin for defensive purposes, but not this time. Luzinski got his glove on the ball against the fence and then dropped it, with Davillio scoring on the play. Luzinski then threw the ball past second, allowing Mota to reach third base. Davey Lopes then scorched a ground ball to Schmidt, who deflected it off his glove directly to Bowa, who hurled to first, but Lopes beat the throw and the game was tied. Garber then made an errant pickoff move and Lopes went to second. Shortstop Bill Russell grounded a single up the middle, and the Dodgers led 6–5. The Phillies went in order in the ninth. The next night the Dodgers took the pennant with an easy win.

The Phillies and their fans were stunned. Bill Conlin of the *Philadelphia Daily News* penned the best epitaph: "The 1964 collapse took ten games. This one took ten minutes. It was like watching the shambles of 1964 compressed into an elapsed-time film sequence."

The Phillies started slowly in 1978 and didn't take over first place until June 23. They held it throughout the season, but their biggest lead was just five games. The Phillies played solid defense and had good pitching but declined offensively. Owens pulled another June 15 deal to bolster the team, acquiring Dick Ruthven from Atlanta for Garber. Ruthven was a major reason for Phillies winning the divisional title, going 13–5.

Schmidt and Luzinski had mediocre seasons. Schmidt had just 21 homers and 78 RBIs; Luzinski had good power numbers, 35 homers and 101 RBIs, but batted just .265. The team batting average, .258, was the lowest since 1973, and they hit 53 fewer homers than they had in 1977. Nonetheless, they captured the East with a 90–72 record.

The playoffs against the Dodgers opened with two games in Philadelphia, which they lost. Carlton managed to win game three in Los Angeles and even hit a homer. Game four was another nightmare for the Phillies. In the bottom of the 10th Tug McGraw walked Ron Cey. Dusty Baker hit a routine soft liner to center field, which Maddox dropped. Once again Bill Russell got the hit that gave the Dodgers the game and the pennant. The Phillies were downcast, having for the third consecutive year failed to win the pennant. They had not played to their potential in the playoffs. Ozark was blamed for uninspiring leadership and Schmidt for driving in just one run during the playoffs.

That winter the Phillies decided on drastic action. They signed free agent Pete Rose, who they believed was the missing piece that could put them over the hump. Vice president Bill Giles arranged a complicated deal using revenue from a TV contract to lure Rose to play first for the Phillies with a four-year contract worth $3.8 million. To strengthen the Phillies at second base Owens negotiated a major deal with the Cubs, who got five Phillies players for second baseman Manny Trillo and outfielder Greg Gross, a lifetime .290 hitter.

These actions made the Phillies the prohibitive favorite to repeat as NL East champs in 1979. Everything fell into place as the Phillies streaked off to a 24–10 record and four-game lead by May 8, but then went 5–15 to drop to third place. The season turned into a nightmare. In the space of 24 hours in July the Phillies lost three starters: Christenson, Randy Lerch, and Ruthven. The bullpen was a disaster, especially McGraw, who recorded the highest ERA of his career, 5.14, and also tied a major-league record by serving four grand-slam homers.

Offensively, Schmidt's 45 homers led the Phillies. Rose did all that was asked of him, hitting .331 and leading the NL in hits with 208, but Trillo broke his arm and missed 46 games. Luzinski was plagued by leg problems and finished with his lowest batting average, .252, and only 18 homers.

On August 31 Owens fired Ozark, replacing him with farm director Dallas Green. Under Green the Phillies went 17–11 and finished the season in fourth place, 84–78, the team's poorest record since 1974.

Owens and Green believed the Phillies had been complacent under Ozark. The core of the team, together since 1973, had lost its aggressiveness. Green's job was to reignite the spark under the Phillies or, if he couldn't, begin reshaping the team.

WORLD CHAMPIONS FINALLY

In 1980 the Phillies finally won their first and only world championship in one of the most difficult and painful seasons in team history. Green was an irascible individual who decided to challenge his underperforming players. He was confrontational and at times at war with most of his players. In spring training Green told them this was their last chance: succeed, or the team would be broken up. He had Owens and owner Ruly Carpenter's support, and the players soon found out that they couldn't go to the boss behind Green's back.

Green surprised many by adding five rookies, including outfielder Lonnie Smith, who hit .339 and set a Phillies rookie record for stolen bases, and Keith Moreland, who platooned behind Bob Boone. The Phillies spun their wheels for the first three months of the season. By early July they were in second place, two games out of first but seemingly going nowhere. They hit their nadir in early August, six games out of first. Between games of a doubleheader loss in Pittsburgh Green lashed out at the team for their lifeless play and questioned their courage, and almost came to blows with pitcher Ron Reed in the dugout. This incident somehow got the Phillies on the right track. They finished the season 36–19, good for a 91–71 record and the divisional title. The success was primarily due to Carlton, Schmidt, and McGraw. Carlton won 24 games. McGraw, injured early in the season, was almost perfect when he came off the disabled list on July 17, allowing three runs in 52 1/3 innings for a 0.52 ERA. Schmidt broke the major-league record for homers by a third baseman by hitting 48, while leading the league with 121 RBIs. He also drove in the winning runs in the two late-season games in Montreal that won the pennant. Other Phillies who had good years included Rose, who led the NL in doubles; Trillo, who hit a career high .292; McBride, who hit .309; and Ruthven, who won 17 games.

The playoff between the Phillies and Houston is often regarded as the best in NL history. The Phillies split two games at home and then lost to Houston 1–0 in 10 innings. Things looked grim in game four as the Phillies went to bat in the top of the eighth inning behind 2–0. The Phillies rallied to go ahead 3–2, only to have Houston tie the score. The Phillies won the game in the 10th on a clutch double by Luzinski when Rose scored from first, knocking the ball from the catcher's hand.

In the final game, the Phillies fell behind 5–2 to Nolan Ryan but scored five runs in the eighth inning to take the lead. Houston tied the score. The Phillies won in the 10th on a hit by Maddox. The Phillies had finally gotten over the hump.

The World Series against Kansas City was somewhat anticlimactic. The Phillies won the first two games at home and then lost two in Kansas City. In game five, with Kansas City leading 3–2 in the ninth inning and their great closer Dan Quisenberry on the mound, the Phillies staged another desperate rally. Schmidt singled and scored when pinch hitter Del Unser doubled past first. Trillo lined a single off Quisenberry's glove to give the Phillies the lead. McGraw came in, loaded the bases, and then struck out Jose Cardenal to end the game. The Phillies returned home with a rested Carlton to close out the series. He won 4–1, with McGraw again getting the save.

The Phillies had finally won it all, and the city went crazy. The next day, a beautiful sunny autumn afternoon, over 1 million fans gathered to watch a victory parade down Broad Street to JFK Stadium, where another 80,000 awaited their heroes. McGraw captured the mood of the crowd best. He held up the cover of the *Daily News* with its huge headline: "WE WIN." Every long-suffering Phillies fan felt part of the "WE."

The years 1981–84 constituted the end of the successful Phillies team that Owens built. The Phillies were getting old at key positions, and the infusion of talent from the minor-league system ceased after 1980. When Green took over as manager, his successors in the farm system overestimated the value of their farmhands. Owens had also dipped into the team's minor-league system for trade material, which kept the Phillies in contention for a couple of more years.

The 1981 campaign started well, and the Phillies were leading the NL East with a 34–21 record when the season was interrupted by baseball's first major strike. The strike hurt the Phillies, who lost their spirit when the season resumed after 50 days. Their record for the second half was 25–27. In a complicated formula drawn up by MLB, the Phillies played the Montreal Expos, winner of the second half, in a five-game division playoff. Scoring just two runs, the Phillies lost the first two games in Montreal despite solid pitching from Carlton and Ruthven. Christenson won game three and the Phillies evened the series with a dramatic walk-off home run by reserve outfielder George Vukovich in game four. The next day Steve Rogers outdueled Carlton to win the NL East title for the Expos.

The 1981 season was the beginning of the end of the great Phillies teams of the past decade. The basis of a good team was still there, and the Phillies would be competitive for two more years, even winning another pennant. Green left to take over the Chicago Cubs as general manager, and the Phillies brought in Pat Corrales to manage. Corrales was no Green—he lacked his influence with Owens and was an unknown to the veterans.

Even more shocking than Green's departure was Carpenter's decision in March to sell the Phillies because the game "wasn't fun anymore." He did not like the business aspects of the game, in which mediocre players were signing million-dollar contracts. Bill Giles, executive vice president of the Phillies, put together a partnership of leading Philadelphians that bought the team for $30 million, quite an appreciation from the $400,000 that the Carpenter family had paid 37 years earlier.

Owens made three poor trades at the end of the 1981 season that cost the Phillies dearly. He sent Lonnie Smith to the Cardinals as part of a three-team trade whereby the Phillies got catcher Bo Diaz from Cleveland. Owens also traded Keith Moreland to the Cubs for pitcher Mike Krukow, and sent Larry Bowa, who wanted a contract extension, to the Cubs for shortstop Ivan DeJesus, along with a throw-in that Green wanted, the lowly regarded minor leaguer Ryne Sandberg, who became a Hall of Fame second baseman.

THE WHEEZE KIDS

The 1982–84 Phillies were a solid, professional team. Despite their poor play during the second half of the 1981 season, Owens believed that the Phillies were still pennant contenders. The season started badly when the Phillies lost Schmidt to a nagging rib injury for 14 games. After Schmidt's return the team jelled, briefly taking over first place on June 30. The catalysts for this success were Schmidt's hitting plus dominating pitching by Carlton. After beginning the season 0–4, Carlton won 10 of his next 13 games.

From the end of June the Phillies stayed on the heels of the red-hot St. Louis Cardinals. In late August the Phillies put on a spurt, and on September 13, behind a 2–0 Carlton shutout of the Cardinals, took over first place by half a game. But the next night the Cardinals won, and from that point the Phillies dropped out of the race. The Cardinals won the division by three games.

It was a commendable season, with attendance averaging slightly over 30,000 fans per game. The team hit .260, but only managed 112 homers. Schmidt hit 36 homers, second in the NL. Carlton had his last dominant season, winning the Cy Young Award for the fourth time, with 23 victories, 286 strikeouts, and a 3.10 ERA.

Owens made a series of aggressive moves in the off-season in an effort to give the team better left-handed hitting. He traded Krukow to the Giants for second baseman Joe Morgan and reliever Al Holland. Then Owens sent five players, including Trillo and rookie prospect Julio Franco, to Cleveland for left-handed-hitting outfielder Von Hayes, which caused consternation among Phillies fans, who felt that five for one was too much. Corrales was heavily criticized because he did not rest his key players for the September run.

In 1983, the Phillies started sluggishly, but then so did every other team in the NL East. The club was often called "the Wheeze Kids" because of the ages of many of its players. Owens pulled off a major trade in late May when he sent Ruthven to the Cubs for reliever Willie Hernandez, who won 8 games and saved 7 more in 63 games. On July 18, with the Phillies in first place with a 43–42 record, Owens removed Corrales and took over as manager. Suddenly the Phillies got hot, going 47–30 the rest of the way to win the division by a comfortable six games.

The Phillies' turnabout was remarkable. John Denny, who had come over to the Phillies the previous September, went 19–6 with a 2.37 ERA to win the Cy Young Award. Carlton was 15–16, but led the league in innings pitched and strikeouts. He won the 300th game of his career in September, only the fourth left-hander to reach that level. Schmidt had another good power year, leading the league in homers with 40 and finishing third with 109 RBIs. Morgan, who had struggled all season, got hot in September and helped fuel a stretch run where the Phillies won 14 of their last 16 games. Holland saved 25 games. The Phillies basically won the pennant on pitching, because their offense averaged just .249, the lowest of an NL division winner since the 1973 Mets.

The Phillies got some revenge against the Dodgers in the playoffs, winning three of four games. But their luck didn't hold out in the World Series, where they met the Baltimore Orioles in the so-called I-95 Series. The Phillies won game one but then were swept by the Orioles in four straight. The Phillies hit just .195, with Schmidt leading the futility, going 1 for 20.

The Phillies were at a crossroads. They had won five division titles, two pennants, and one World Series in eight years, but the 1983 team was old and difficult to build upon. Rose, Morgan, and Tony Perez were let go and Owens began a major restructuring with younger players, but the farm system was thin. Owens also made a couple of foolish trades, sending outfielders Gary Matthews and Bob Dernier to the Cubs for reliever Bill Campbell, 35, and coming off a mediocre season, and Hernandez to the Tigers for two nonproductive players. These trades helped the Cubs and Tigers make the playoffs in 1984, while the Phillies struggled all season, finishing in fourth place with a .500 record. The team led the NL in hitting, but the pitching collapsed. The Phillies' future didn't look bright.

The Phillies also were undergoing a breakdown at the organizational level. Owens did not have the influence with Giles that he had had with Carpenter, and director Jim Baumer of the farm system was a flop. By the mid-1980s the Phillies system, once regarded as one of the best in baseball, was a disaster. None of the Phillies' top 50 prospects in 1987 became impact players, and only a few reached the majors. From the mid-1980s on, the Phillies were an organization in free fall. Giles tried to be his own general manager, but, like Carpenter, failed. Experienced scouts were let go and important judgments were made not by professional baseball people like Owens but by Giles.

Between 1985 and 2002, the Phillies finished better than .500 just three times. In 1993, they came out of nowhere to win the NL pennant, but otherwise the Phillies were an underperforming, directionless team.

Mike Schmidt waves to the crowd after receiving his National League Most Valuable Player award, 1986. © AP / Wide World Photos

Beginning in 1985 the cadre of talent that had made the Phillies such a powerhouse in baseball began to fade. Carlton was finished for all practical purposes after a disastrous 1–8 1985 season. Schmidt led the league in homers, RBIs, and slugging percentage in 1986 and hit 35 homers with 113 RBIs the next season. But injuries shortened his 1988 season, and he retired early in 1989.

After Owens stepped down following the 1984 season, the Phillies went through five managers in seven years (John Felske, Lee Elia, John Vukovich, Nick Leyva, and Jim Fregosi). Only Fregosi managed in the majors after leaving the Phillies.

The late 1980s and early 1990s were a nightmare for Philadelphia baseball. A franchise whose city had embraced its team with enthusiasm and had set attendance records now fell upon hard times. In the decade after 1984 the Phillies topped the 2 million mark only twice. The Phillies found themselves bypassed as the city's favorite sports franchise by the Eagles. Phillies fans were bored with a dull team that was 100 games under .500 from 1985 to 1992.

SEARCHING FOR A NEW DIRECTION

The Phillies gradually hit bottom in the late 1980s, finishing in the cellar in both 1988 and 1989. Before that happened, Giles had finally begun an overhaul of the organization in 1987, hiring as general manager Woody Woodward, who had run the Cincinnati Reds' minor-league operation before moving on to the New York Yankees as general manager in 1986. However, Giles and Woodward could not work together, largely because Giles would not stop interfering in baseball operations.

Giles's next general manager was Lee Thomas, the St. Louis Cardinals' director of player development. Thomas began dismantling an awful club through a series of key trades, a process that so completely revamped the Phillies that only Darren Daulton remained with the squad four years later. It was the Phillies' biggest housecleaning since the days of John Quinn.

In mid-June 1989, Thomas began building a new team. Steve Bedrosian, an effective reliever with the Phillies who won the Cy Young Award in 1987, was sent to San Francisco for third baseman Charlie Hayes and pitchers Terry Mulholland and Dennis Cook. Thomas then traded outfielder Chris James to San Diego for infielder Randy Ready and first baseman John Kruk. In one of his best deals, Juan Samuel went to the Mets for Lenny Dykstra and relief pitcher Roger McDowell. Toward the end of the 1990 season Thomas acquired Dale Murphy from Atlanta along with pitcher Tommy Greene. These moves upgraded the Phillies, who improved by 10 games in 1990. Thomas fired Nick Leyva in mid-1991 and brought in Jim Fregosi to take over a team that needed a more experienced manager, and he led them to third place, their highest finish since 1986. The team then was worth about $115 million.

The 1992 season was a deceptive one. After showing promise of improvement, they fell back to the cellar, largely due to injuries to key players. At one point they had 17 players on the disabled list. On the positive side, catcher Darren Daulton finally matured as a player, hitting 27 homers and leading the NL in RBIs. John Kruk hit .323, and Dave Hollins, whom Thomas had drafted from San Diego in 1989, had a breakout year, hitting 27 homers while driving in 93 runs. Curt Schilling, who came over from Houston, surprised the Phillies by winning 14 games and finishing fourth in ERA.

When the 1993 season opened the Phillies sprinted off to an 8–1 record, their best start since 1915. By June they were in first place with a 34–14 record, a .708 pace. The team won 97 games and came in first by three games. The league-leading offense was led by Dykstra, who batted first and hit .305 while scoring 143 runs, the highest in the NL in 61 years. Kruk hit .316 and drove in 85 runs. Daulton hit 24 homers and drove home 104 runs. The pitching staff was less dominant, but Schilling and Greene both won 16 games. The bullpen was anchored by the exciting, but often nerve-racking, Mitch "Wild Thing" Williams, who set a Phillies record of 43 saves.

In the playoffs the Phillies were underdogs against a powerful Braves team led by one of the best pitching staffs in baseball, with a team ERA a full one run lower than the Phillies'. The playoffs were tied, but in the critical fifth game, the Phillies pulled out a 10th-inning win when Dykstra hit a dramatic homer off Braves closer Mark Wohlers. Then, in game six in Philadelphia, Greene beat Greg Maddux 6–3, giving the Phillies their first pennant in 10 years.

The 1993 Phillies earned a special place in the hearts of Philadelphia fans. The players were perceived as a group of blue-collar, hard-nosed types. The team had come out of nowhere to win the pennant and beat "America's Team" with its awful Tomahawk Chop. The fans responded to the season as never before in team history, with attendance setting a new record of 3.1 million.

Alas, the Phillies couldn't sustain their success in the World Series against a Toronto Blue Jays team that was at the peak of its success, with John Olerud, Paul Molitor, and Roberto Alomar, the top three hitters in the AL, and a pitching staff led by 19-game winner Pat Hentgen and closer Duane Ward, with 45 saves. The teams split the first two games in Toronto, but in game three in Philadelphia, Toronto battered Jackson and Rivera for 10 runs. Game four was the wildest contest in World Series history, setting a record for the most runs scored. In the bottom of the fifth the Phillies took an apparently commanding 12–7 lead. Toronto got two runs in the top of the sixth, but the Phillies added runs in the sixth and seventh innings. Then, in the top of the eighth, Toronto scored six times to take a 15–14 lead.

Schilling got the Phillies back to 3–2 in games with a shutout in game five, but the terrible thumping in game four had taken a toll on their pitching. In the climactic sixth game the Phillies fell behind 5–1, but came back in the top of the seventh when Dykstra hit a three-run homer and two more runs scored on a single by Hollins and a sacrifice fly by Pete Incaviglia. In the ninth Fregosi brought in Williams to save the game, but he walked a batter, and after one out, gave up a single and then Joe Carter's walk-off homer to win the World Series. The Phillies were outhit by the Blue Jays, and the staff ERA was a ghastly 7.57. Williams was a major factor in the Phillies' defeat, losing twice.

No one, including the players and the organization, expected the Phillies to repeat in 1994. Thomas believed that many Phillies had had their career years, and the team had benefited from being virtually injury free. Right after the season Kruk was diagnosed with testicular cancer while Dykstra began to experience back problems that eventually ended his career. Two key players were traded after the season—Mulholland and the vilified Mitch Williams.

The 1994 season turned out to be a disaster, with multiple injuries and subpar performances. Only Danny Jackson topped his 1993 season, going 14–6 before the season came to an abrupt end with the worst strike in baseball history. The team took over control of the ballpark from the city, which had allowed the edifice to fall into disrepair.

The Phillies did not reach the .500 mark over the next five years, finishing about 30 games out of first place each year. The key players of 1993 were all gone within a few years, either traded, like Daulton, or retired, like Kruk, Greene, and Dykstra. Only Schilling bounced back strongly, becoming one of the most dominant pitchers in baseball in the late 1990s, when he had two consecutive seasons of 300 strikeouts. After campaigning for a trade, he was sent to the Arizona Diamondbacks in 2000.

Fregosi was fired after the 1996 season, replaced by young Terry Francona, and Thomas followed shortly as the Phillies began another rebuilding effort. The Phillies were hindered by the reluctance of ownership to spend to keep the team in contention. The Phillies had a high payroll during the 1970s, when the team was consistently a pennant contender. But after Carpenter left, succeeding owners failed to keep pace with the big spenders. As the Phillies dropped from contention, so did their payroll. Despite being in the fifth-largest market in the nation, the Phillies' payroll in 2001 of $49 million was ranked 23rd, led by catcher Mike Lieberthal, a product of the farm system, at $6.3 million. The team that year was worth an estimated $156 million, ranking it 24th of 30 teams. According to *Forbes*, it lost $2.6 million. The team brought in $30.4 million in box-office receipts (ranking 22nd), $18.9 million in media revenue (a low $3.06 per person in its large market), and a lowly $7.7 million in concessions, parking, and luxury seating (San Francisco, by contrast, made $61.5 million). The Phillies also failed to develop their television market. Once one of the leaders in television revenue, the Phillies ranked 13th in local media income, behind smaller markets such as Cleveland and Seattle. Overall its total local revenue was $57 million, compared to the MLB average of $94 million.

Thomas at least had left the minor-league system in good shape. Mike Arbuckle was brought in from Atlanta to upgrade player development. As a result, the Phillies began to promote new blood into the team in the late 1990s. Their premier player, third baseman Scott Rolen, arrived in 1997 and hit .289 with 21 homers and 92 RBIs to win the Rookie of the Year Award. Rolen also won Gold Gloves in 1998 and 2000–2.

The Phillies also made a series of trades to strengthen the lineup, most notably getting outfielder Bobby Abreu for shortstop Kevin Stocker. Abreu became one of the best right fielders in the NL. A lifetime .300 hitter, in 2001 he hit 31 homers, drove in 110 runs, and stole 36 bases, becoming the first Phillies player to reach the 30-30 club in homers and stolen bases. However, the Phillies lacked the depth to compete with the best teams. Under Francona the Phillies made some progress, winning 77 games in 1999 for their best showing since 1993. But a disastrous 2000 season saw the Phillies slump to fifth place, with their worst record (67–95) since 1972. Francona was fired and local favorite Larry Bowa was named manager.

The 2001 Phillies surprised the baseball world. On June 18, they were in first place with a 35–18 record. Led by Abreu, Jimmy Rollins, Rolen, and reliever Jose Mesa, who saved 42 games, the Phillies remained in the pennant race all season, but finished second to Atlanta.

Having been burned badly in the past, Philadelphia fans responded warily to the Phillies' revival in 2001. The choice of Bowa as manager was a popular one, reminding the fans of the great Phillies teams of the late 1970s and early 1980s. With their farm teams productive for the first time in years, the Phillies appear to have a future. But things quickly turned sour. In 2002 the Phillies slipped below .500 (80–82) amid rumblings of discontent with Bowa's irascible managerial style. In July strained relations between Bowa and Scott Rolen led to the latter's trade to the Cardinals.

The 2003 season would be the Phillies' last in the Vet. They were picked to contend for the NL pennant, especially after they signed Cleveland's slugging first baseman Jim Thome as a free agent for $11.2 million. His hardworking qualities appealed to the Phillies' blue-collar fans. They also got the Braves' 18-game winner Kevin Millwood in a trade for minor-league catcher Johnny Estrada. Thome delivered, leading the NL in home runs with 47 while driving in 100 runs. Millwood hurled a no-hitter early in the season against the Giants, but then faltered after the All-Star break. Four pitchers won 14 or more games, but the bullpen collapsed late in the season. The team's offense, led by .300 hitters Abreu and Mike Lieberthal, was inconsistent. The Phillies finished with an 86–76 record. Largely because of Thome and the excitement over the last days of the Vet, the Phillies drew 2.2 million fans, the team's largest attendance since 1994.

Going into 2004 the Phillies, reportedly worth $281 million, 15th in MLB, surprised the baseball world by spending lavishly in the free-agent market. The team's player payroll of $93 million was the second highest in the NL. They brought back Millwood at $11 million and traded for Houston's $9 million All-Star closer Billy Wagner. The Phillies were counting on increased revenue from their new ballpark, the 43,500-seat Citizens Bank Park (the naming went for $95 million over 20 years), which opened in April 2004 at a cost of over $450 million, divided between public and private financing. The site is just east of Veterans Stadium and features a view of the downtown skyline. The seating is in a bowl style, reminiscent of the city's early ballparks, and includes 72 luxury suites. The site is very accessible, directly connected to the Broad Street subway, and there are 20,000 parking spaces in the area.

The Phillies opened the 2004 campaign as favorites to win the pennant. Expectations for a successful season plus a new ballpark led to a record attendance of 3.25 million. But on the field things quickly turned sour. The team got off to a slow start, losing six of their first seven games. They recovered to take the lead in the NL East by the All-Star break, but collapsed in the second half to finish 10 games back of the Braves. There were a lot of pitching injuries, and woeful hitting with men on base.

The Phillies were led by Abreu, who hit 30 homers and 47 doubles and stole 40 bases while batting .300, and Rollins, who scored 119 runs. In an injury-plagued season Thome managed to hit 42 homers and drive in 100 runs. The team's failure cost Bowa his job.

In late October 2004 the Phillies chose Charlie Manuel, former Indians skipper and a former member of the Phillies organization, as their new manager. He was selected because he was temperamentally the polar opposite of the intense Bowa and a close friend of the Phillies' team leader, Jim Thome. The 2005 season was a heartbreaking one for the Phillies. They compiled their best record, 88–74, since the pennant-winning 1993 squad. They finished in second place in the NL East just two games behind the Atlanta Braves. They missed out on the Wild Card on the last day of the season one game back of the Houston Astros. There were outstanding performances by younger players that bode well for the future. Second baseman Chase Utley hit 28 homers and drove in 105 runs, a team record for a player at that position. Shortstop Rollins played brilliantly in the field, and veteran left fielder Pat Burrell hit 32 homers and drove in 117 runs. Philadelphia's long-suffering and fickle baseball fans finally seemed to embrace the Phillies, whose attendance was 2.6 million, and seemed to have rekindled the enthusiasm fans had for the team in the 1970s and early 1980s. Only time will tell.

NOTABLE ACHIEVEMENTS

Most Valuable Players

Year	Name	Position
1932	Chuck Klein	OF
1950	Jim Konstanty	P
1980	Mike Schmidt	3B
1981	Mike Schmidt	3B
1986	Mike Schmidt	3B

Cy Young Winners

Year	Name	Position
1972	Steve Carlton	LHP
1977	Steve Carlton	LHP
1980	Steve Carlton	LHP
1982	Steve Carlton	LHP
1983	John Denny	RHP
1987	Steve Bedrosian	RHP

Rookies of the Year

Year	Name	Position
1957	Jack Sanford	P
1964	Dick Allen	3B
1997	Scott Rolen	3B
2005	Ryan Howard	2B

Batting Champions

Year	Name	#
1891	Billy Hamilton	.340
1899	Ed Delahanty	.410
1910	Sherry Magee	.331
1929	Lefty O'Doul	.398
1933	Chuck Klein	.368
1947	Harry Walker	.363
1955	Richie Ashburn	.338
1958	Richie Ashburn	.350

Home-Run Champions

Year	Name	#
1889	Sam Thompson	20
1893	Ed Delahanty	19
1895	Sam Thompson	18
1896	Ed Delahanty	13
1897	Nap Lajoie	10
1913	Gavvy Cravath	19
1914	Gavvy Cravath	19
1915	Gavvy Cravath	24
1917	Gavvy Cravath	12
1918	Gavvy Cravath	8

1919	Gavvy Cravath	12
1920	Cy Williams	15
1923	Cy Williams	41
1927	Cy Williams	30
1929	Chuck Klein	43
1931	Chuck Klein	31
1932	Chuck Klein	38
1933	Chuck Klein	28
1974	Mike Schmidt	36
1975	Mike Schmidt	37
1976	Mike Schmidt	38
1980	Mike Schmidt	48
1981	Mike Schmidt	31
1983	Mike Schmidt	40
1984	Mike Schmidt	36
1986	Mike Schmidt	37
2003	Jim Thome	47

ERA Champions

Year	Name	#
1915	Grover Alexander	1.22
1916	Grover Alexander	1.55
1917	Grover Alexander	1.83
1972	Steve Carlton	1.97

Strikeout Champions

Year	Name	#
1910	Earl Moore	185
1912	Grover Alexander	195
1913	Tom Seaton	168
1914	Grover Alexander	214
1915	Grover Alexander	241
1916	Grover Alexander	167
1917	Grover Alexander	201
1940	Kirby Higbe	137
1953	Robin Roberts	198
1954	Robin Roberts	185
1957	Jack Sanford	188
1967	Jim Bunning	253
1972	Steve Carlton	310
1974	Steve Carlton	240

1980	Steve Carlton	286
1982	Steve Carlton	286
1983	Steve Carlton	275
1997	Curt Schilling	310
1999	Curt Schilling	300

No-Hitters (Italics = Perfect Game)

Name	Date
Charlie Ferguson	08/29/1885
Red Donahue	07/08/1898
Chick Fraser	09/18/1903
Johnny Lush	05/01/1906
Jim Bunning	*06/21/1964*
Rick Wise	06/23/1971
Terry Mulholland	08/15/1990
Tommy Greene	05/23/1991
Kevin Millwood	04/27/2003

POSTSEASON APPEARANCES

NL East Division Titles

Year	Record	Manager
1976	101–61	Danny Ozark
1977	101–61	Danny Ozark
1978	90–72	Danny Ozark
1980	91–71	Dallas Green
1981	59–48	Dallas Green
1983	90–72	Pat Corrales
		Paul Owens
1993	97–65	Jim Fregosi

NL Pennants

Year	Record	Manager
1915	90–62	Pat Moran
1950	91–63	Eddie Sawyer
1980	91–71	Dallas Green
1983	90–72	Pat Corrales
		Paul Owens
1993	97–65	Jim Fregosi

World Championships

Year	Opponent	MVP
1980	Kansas City	Mike Schmidt

MANAGERS

2005–	Charlie Manuel
2004	Gary Varsho
2001–2004	Larry Bowa
1997–2000	Terry Francona
1991–1996	Jim Fregosi
1989–1991	Nick Leyva
1988	John Vukovich
1987–1988	Lee Elia
1985–1987	John Felske
1983–1984	Paul Owens
1982–1983	Pat Corrales
1979–1981	Dallas Green
1973–1979	Danny Ozark
1972	Paul Owens
1970–1972	Frank Lucchesi
1969	George Myatt
1968–1969	Bob Skinner
1969	George Myatt
1960–1968	Gene Mauch
1960	Andy Cohen
1958–1960	Eddie Sawyer
1955–1958	Mayo Smith
1954	Terry Moore
1952–1954	Steve O'Neill
1948–1952	Eddie Sawyer
1948	Dusty Cook
1945–1948	Ben Chapman
1943–1945	Freddie Fitzsimmons
1943	Bucky Harris
1942	Hans Lobert
1939–1941	Doc Prothro
1938	Hans Lobert
1934–1938	Jimmy Wilson
1928–1933	Burt Shotton
1927	Stuffy McInnis
1923–1926	Art Fletcher

1921–1922	Kaiser Wilhelm
1921	Bill Donovan
1919–1920	Gavvy Cravath
1919	Jack Coombs
1915–1918	Pat Moran
1910–1914	Red Dooin
1907–1909	Bill Murray
1904–1906	Hugh Duffy
1903	Chief Zimmer
1898–1902	Bill Shettsline
1897–1898	George Stallings
1896	Billy Nash
1894–1895	Arthur Irwin
1891–1893	Harry Wright
1890	Bob Allen
1890	Al Reach
1890	Jack Clements
1884–1890	Harry Wright
1883	Blondie Purcell
1883	Bob Ferguson

Team Records by Individual Players

Batting Leaders

	Single Season			Career		
	Name		Year	Name		Plate Appearances
Batting average	Ed Delahanty	.410	1899	Billy Hamilton	.361	3,606
On-base %	Billy Hamilton	.523	1894	Billy Hamilton	.468	3,606
Slugging %	Chuck Klein	.687	1930	Chuck Klein	.553	6,770
OPS	Chuck Klein	1.123	1930	Chuck Klein	.935	6,770
Games	Pete Rose	163	1979	Mike Schmidt	2,404	10,062
At bats	Juan Samuel	701	1989	Mike Schmidt	8,352	10,062
Runs	Billy Hamilton	192	1894	Mike Schmidt	1,506	10,062
Hits	Lefty O'Doul	254	1929	Mike Schmidt	2,234	10,062
Total bases	Chuck Klein	445	1930	Mike Schmidt	4,404	10,062
Doubles	Chuck Klein	59	1930	Ed Delahanty	442	7,130
Triples	Sam Thompson	27	1894	Ed Delahanty	157	7,130
Home runs	Mike Schmidt	48	1980	Mike Schmidt	548	10,062
RBIs	Chuck Klein	170	1930	Mike Schmidt	1,595	10,062
Walks	Lenny Dykstra	129	1993	Mike Schmidt	1,507	10,062
Strikeouts	Jim Thome	182	2003	Mike Schmidt	1,883	10,062
Stolen bases	Billy Hamilton	111	1891	Billy Hamilton	508	3,606
Extra-base hits	Richie Ashburn	181	1951	Richie Ashburn	1,811	8,223
Times on base	Billy Hamilton	355	1894	Mike Schmidt	3,820	10,062

(Continued)

Pitching Leaders (Continued)

	Single Season			Career		
	Name		Year	Name		Innings Pitched
ERA	Grover C. Alexander	1.22	1915	George McQuillan	1.79	926.3
Wins	Kid Gleason	38	1890	Steve Carlton	241	3,697.3
Won-loss %	Al Orth	.824	1899	Grover C. Alexander	.676	2,513.7
Hits/9 IP	Grover C. Alexander	6.05	1915	George McQuillan	6.93	926.3
Walks/9 IP	John Coleman	0.80	1883	John Coleman	0.91	692.7
Strikeouts	Curt Schilling	319	1997	Steve Carlton	3,031	3,697.3
Strikeouts/9 IP	Curt Schilling	11.29	1997	Curt Schilling	8.43	1,659.3
Games	Kent Tekulve	90	1987	Robin Roberts	529	3,739.3
Saves	Jose Mesa	45	2002	Jose Mesa	111	203.0
Innings	John Coleman	538.3	1883	Robin Roberts	3,739.3	3,739.3
Starts	John Coleman	61	1883	Steve Carlton	499	3,697.3
Complete games	John Coleman	59	1883	Robin Roberts	272	3,739.3
Shutouts	Grover C. Alexander	16	1916	Grover C. Alexander	61	2,513.7

Source: Drawn from data in "Philadelphia Phillies Batting Leaders (seasonal and career) http://baseball-reference.com/teams/PHI/leaders_bat.shtml; "Philadelphia Phillies Pitching Leaders (seasonal and career)." http://baseball-reference.com/teams/PHI/leaders_pitch.shtml.

BIBLIOGRAPHY

Allen, Dick, and Tim Whitaker. *Crash: The Life and Times of Dick Allen.* New York: Ticknor and Fields, 1989.

Bartell, Dick, with Norman Macht. *Rowdy Richard: A Firsthand Account of the National League Baseball Wars of the 1930s and the Men Who Fought Them.* Ukiah, CA: North Atlantic Books, 1987.

Bodley, Hal. *The Philadelphia Phillies: The Team That Wouldn't Die.* Wilmington, DE: Serendipity Press, 1981.

Burk, Robert F. *Much More than a Game: Players, Owners, and American Baseball Since 1921.* Chapel Hill: University of North Carolina Press, 2001.

———. *Never Just a Game: Players, Owners, and American Baseball to 1920.* Chapel Hill, NC: University of North Carolina Press, 1994.

Callison, John, with Austin Sletten. *The Johnny Callison Story.* New York: Vantage, 1991.

Fitzpatrick, Frank. *You Can't Lose Them All: The Year the Phillies Finally Won the Pennant.* Dallas: Taylor Trade, 2001.

Honig, Donald. *The Philadelphia Phillies: An Illustrated History.* New York: Simon and Schuster, 1992.

Jordan, David M. *Occasional Glory: The History of the Philadelphia Phillies.* Jefferson, NC: McFarland, 2002.

Jordan, David M., Larry R. Gerlach, and John P. Rossi. "A Baseball Myth Exploded: Bill Veeck and the 1943 Sale of the Philadelphia Phillies." *The National Pastime* 18 (1998): 3–13.

Koppett, Leonard. *The Man in the Dugout: Baseball's Top Managers and How They Got That Way.* Expanded ed. Philadelphia: Temple University Press, 2000.

Kuklick, Bruce. *To Every Thing a Season: Shibe Park and Urban Philadelphia, 1909–1976.* Princeton, NJ: Princeton University Press, 1991.

Lewis, Allen. *The Philadelphia Phillies: A Pictorial History.* Virginia Beach, VA: JCP Corp. of Virginia, 1983.

Orodenker, Richard. *The Phillies Reader.* Philadelphia: Temple University Press, 2005.

Richter, Ed. *The View from the Dugout: A Season with Baseball's Amazing Gene Mauch.* Philadelphia: Chilton Books, 1964.

Roberts, Robin, and C. Paul Rogers III. *The Whiz Kids and the 1950 Pennant.* Philadelphia: Temple University Press, 1996.

Rossi, John P. *The 1964 Phillies: The Story of Baseball's Most Memorable Collapse.* Jefferson, NC: McFarland, 2005.

Veeck, William, and Ed Linn. *Veeck—as in Wreck: The Autobiography of Bill Veeck.* New York: Putnam, 1962.

Westcott, Rich. *Philadelphia's Old Ballparks.* Philadelphia: Temple University Press, 1996.

Westcott, Rich, and Frank Bilovsky. *The New Phillies Encyclopedia.* Philadelphia: Temple University Press, 1993.

12

Pittsburgh Pirates

Richard Peterson

THE ORIGINS

On February 22, 1876, just 20 days after Pittsburgh lost its bid for a team in the newly formed National League, local organizers formed the independent Allegheny Base Ball Club. The beginning of professional baseball in Pittsburgh coincided with the city's dramatic transformation from a center for trade and commerce into a manufacturing and industrial giant. Pittsburgh, known since the American Revolution as the Gateway to the West because of the confluence of the Monongahela and Allegheny Rivers into the Ohio River, was now regarded as the Birmingham of America because of its production of iron and steel. By the end of the Civil War, Pittsburgh's blast furnaces were producing nearly half of the country's iron. By 1880, after Andrew Carnegie declared, "The day of iron has past! Steel is king!" the city's mills were providing America with two-thirds of its crucible steel.

Once a river town, Pittsburgh emerged in the late nineteenth century as one of America's largest and most important cities, but at a cost to its population. So much soot and smoke billowed from its mills that English novelist Anthony Trollope, stopping at Pittsburgh on his tour of America, described the city as "the blackest place . . . I ever saw." At night, the fires from blast furnaces lit the skies so dramatically that biographer James Parton called Pittsburgh "Hell with the lid taken off." Beneath the dark, billowing clouds that often turned day into night, Pittsburgh, badly divided by the incredible wealth of its steel, coal, and banking barons and the desperate poverty of its largely immigrant working class, struggled for an identity beyond its "Smoky City" reputation and its capacity for work and production.

Though baseball was on its way to becoming the national pastime, the Allegheny Base Ball Club did little to divert attention away from Pittsburgh's class divisions and labor struggles in its first year of sporadic independent play. A year later, however, the Alleghenies paid a $25 entrance fee and joined the newly formed International Association, a 15-team league set up as a rival to the NL. Though the league had a law banning the practice of revolving—"a person leaving one club and joining another without a proper release"—the Alleghenies were hit hard by player defections and disbanded a year later, on June 8, 1878, after winning only 3 of 26 games.

After a three-year absence, professional baseball returned to Pittsburgh in 1882, when the Alleghenies were reorganized by popular local business leader H.D. "Denny" McKnight, one of the founders of the American Association and the league's first president. The Pittsburgh Alleghenies, under McKnight's leadership, became a charter member of the AA, which quickly gained notoriety as a "two-bit" and "beer ball" league for charging only 25 cents for admission, selling beer at its games, and playing on Sunday. These practices made attending a baseball game more attractive for Pittsburgh's hardworking, hard-drinking population, though mill laborers, working 12-hour shifts and making 15 cents an hour, hardly had the leisure time or the money for a ticket. Workers who had the Sabbath off were further stymied by Pennsylvania's blue laws, which prohibited Sunday baseball. Even among the city's white-collar community, the Alleghenies lacked solid fan support because of the constant flooding of its home field, Exposition Park, which was located near the north shore of the Allegheny River, and the team's consistently poor play. After finishing 1882 with a 39–39 record, the Alleghenies fell to 31–67 in 1883, and in 1884 finished 11th in a 12-team league with a 30–78 record.

In 1885, the Alleghenies moved into Recreation Park, a 2,000-seat ballpark located on higher ground on the north side of the Allegheny. For the first time in a decade of professional baseball, Pittsburgh fans flocked to the ballpark to attend games as an infusion of new talent from the disbanded Columbus team enabled the Alleghenies improve to third place in 1885 and finish a strong second in 1886 to Chris Von der Ahe's St. Louis Browns, who went on to defeat the NL's Chicago White Stockings in a postseason championship series. The local fandom had even more reason to be excited about baseball in 1887. After Kansas City lost its NL franchise at the end of the 1886 season, Alleghenies president William N. Nimmick, upset by the ouster of his good friend Denny McKnight as president of the AA, applied for membership in the more established league. When Pittsburgh was voted into the NL for 1887, the city, once regarded as the Gateway to the West, now became the gateway city for the NL. McKnight, however, left baseball behind and returned to his business interests.

NATIONAL LEAGUE ENTRY

Pittsburgh began its NL tradition in grand style on April 30, 1887, with a stunning 6–2 victory at Recreation Park against the defending champion Chicago White Stockings, led by Adrian "Cap" Anson. The opposing pitchers, John Clarkson for Chicago and James "Pud" Galvin for Pittsburgh, were future members of the Hall of Fame. Over 9,000 fans watched the game, and gate receipts totaled about $4,500. The *Pittsburgh Post* indicated that "gamblers of the city lost heavily on the Chicagos Saturday" and reported that the *Cincinnati Inquirer* "thinks that many of the 'League blowhards' will strike a snag before they are through with the Smoky City boys."

Despite the excitement of Pittsburgh's debut in the NL and brash predictions that the team, after a second-place finish in the AA, would win a pennant, the Alleghenies ended the 1887 season with a losing record. With the exception of its climb to second place in 1893, the team would finish no higher than fifth place for the rest of the century. Their losing ways included a disastrous record of 23–113 in 1890, the year of the Great Player Revolt. In late 1889, John Montgomery Ward's Brotherhood of Professional Base Ball Players, organized four years earlier to aid indigent ex-players, formed its own Players' League after the NL's magnates imposed a new salary scale based on "conduct on and off the field." Many of the NL's best players signed on with the Players' League, but Pittsburgh was especially decimated when Ned Hanlon convinced most of his teammates to join the Pittsburgh Burghers of the new league. The NL team barely survived the year, by filling its roster with local amateurs. The team was so inexperienced and inept that it was disparagingly called the Pittsburgh Innocents. Their record of futility would stand as the worst ever until the hapless Cleveland Spiders finished at 20–134 in 1899.

The Players' League collapsed after only one year of play, but the upstart league forever changed the face, if not the fortune, of the Pittsburgh franchise in the NL. All of the players from the AA and NL were to return to their original teams for the 1891 season, but the AA's Philadelphia Athletics, ready to resume play after not fielding a team in 1890, accidentally omitted the names of Louis Bierbauer and Harry Stovey from their reserve list. After Pittsburgh signed Bierbauer to a new contract, Philadelphia protested, but an interleague committee ruled in favor of Pittsburgh. Bierbauer earned a special place in Pittsburgh's baseball history after the Philadelphia papers started calling Pittsburgh "the Pirates" for stealing Bierbauer from the Athletics. The name stuck and eventually replaced "the Alleghenies" as the team name. The newly christened Pirates also had a new home field in 1891, when they moved into the 16,000-seat Exposition Park, remodeled by the Burghers but vacated after the collapse of the Players' League.

Even with a new team name and home field, the Pittsburgh franchise continued its struggles. Under the mercurial ownership of local coffee magnate William K. Kerr, who took over the ball club when the AA collapsed after the 1891 season and was absorbed into an expanded 12-team NL, the team hired and fired a half dozen managers in the 1890s, including player-manager Connie Mack. Kerr's interference with his managers did little to change the team's losing record, but Pittsburgh's fortune as a baseball town would finally undergo a dramatic change when the NL, after the 1899 season, decided to reduce its teams from 12 to 8. When Louisville owner Barney Dreyfuss realized that he was about to lose his NL franchise, he hurriedly bought a 50 percent interest in the Pittsburgh operation with the understanding by Pirate and league officials that he would bring his best players with him. Almost overnight Dreyfuss converted the dismal Pirates into a baseball dynasty.

THE DREYFUSS DYNASTY

Before the public announcement that Louisville was being dropped by the NL, Dreyfuss, with a major interest in both the Pittsburgh and Louisville ball clubs, "traded" 14 players to Pittsburgh, including Tommy Leach, Rube Waddell, Deacon Phillippe, player-manager Fred Clarke, and the great Honus Wagner, for four players and $25,000. Fred Clarke played 21 years in the majors with a lifetime .312 batting average. He managed 19 seasons for Dreyfuss, retiring after the 1915 season. He compiled a brilliant .595 record in his 16 years in Pittsburgh.

When the Louisville franchise officially disbanded, Jack Chesbro, one of the four traded Pirates, returned to Pittsburgh along with two other Louisville players. After the wholesale movement of Louisville's best players to Pittsburgh produced a second-place finish in 1900, the Pirates went on to win three straight NL pennants. The 1901 team (90–49) led the NL in pitching (2.58 ERA), led by Deacon Phillippe, Jack Chesbro, and Jess Tannehill, who won 61 games be-

Honus Wagner, 1900. Courtesy of the Baseball Hall of Fame

tween them, and was second in hitting (.286), led by shortstop Honus Wagner's .353 and 126 RBIs. The next season the Pirates did even better, with a record-shattering 103–36 season in 1902. It remains the second-best winning percentage, .741, next to the 1906 Cubs' mark of .763. The team led the NL in virtually every batting and pitching category, as the big three starters won 68 games. Dreyfuss, who gained control of the Pirates at the end of the 1900 season by buying out Kerr after a power struggle between the two men, was helped by another dramatic shift in baseball politics when Ban Johnson's American League declared war on the NL in 1901. While many NL teams were hard-hit by defections, the Pirates, with rumors circulating that the upstart AL wanted a strong team in Pittsburgh to upset the NL's competitive balance, managed to hold on to its key players for its 1901 and 1902 pennant-winning seasons.

A German Jew who made his fortune in the whiskey-distillery business after he came to America at the age of 17, Dreyfuss was the perfect owner for a baseball franchise in the Smoky City. A staunch Republican, he was a comfortable fit in a city run by Christopher Magee and William Flinn, corrupt Republican bosses who learned their politics by studying the Tweed machine in New York. Dreyfuss, however, also identified with the immigrant character of the city and its stubborn determination and pride in hard work. His proudest boast about his adopted city was that "we are a first-division town and I'm a first-division club owner. I just couldn't—I wouldn't—stand for a second-division team." In Dreyfuss's 32 years as the Pirates' owner, his teams won six pennants and two World Series championships. The Pirates, during Dreyfuss's long tenure, finished in the second division only six times.

Dreyfuss was also one of baseball's visionaries, and, while not as colorful as some of the game's more storied owners, probably deserves a place in the Baseball Hall of Fame for his contributions to baseball history. After the NL and AL signed a peace agreement in early 1903, effectively ending two years of open warfare, it was Barney Dreyfuss who challenged the AL's pennant-winning Boston team to a postseason series against his own pennant winners for the "championship of the United States" despite the defections of 28-game winner Jack Chesbro and 20-game winner Jesse Tannehill to the AL that year. Dreyfuss still had great confidence in his team's strong lineup, led by Honus Wagner, who led the league in hitting (.355), and Clarke, who was second, and the pitching of Phillippe and Sam Leever, who both won 25 games, along with Ed Doheny. Dreyfuss bet several thousand dollars on the series outcome, but the nine-game championship series turned into a professional and personal disaster. Effectively down to one starting pitcher after the mental breakdown of Ed Doheny and a shoulder injury to Sam Leever, the Pirates, after taking a 3–1 lead on the strong pitching of Deacon Phillippe, went on to lose the next four games and the series, 5–3. Despite his heavy gambling losses, Dreyfuss, in appreciation of his team's effort and the city's loyalty, turn over his owner's share of the gate receipts to his players, whose individual share was $1,316, compared to $1,182 for Boston's champions.

A NEW BALLPARK AND A WORLD CHAMPIONSHIP

After a year's delay, the championship series between the two leagues evolved into one of America's greatest sporting traditions and earned Dreyfuss the title of "the Father of the First World Series." It would, however, take five frustrating years of near misses before Dreyfuss had a chance to overcome his disappointment in losing baseball's first modern world championship. After dropping to fourth in 1904, the Pirates climbed into second place in 1905 behind John McGraw's New York Giants. They won 93 games in 1906, but finished in third place, 23 1/2 games behind the Chicago Cubs, who had an amazing 116–36 record. The Pirates were 91–63 in 1907 and 98–56 in 1908, but ended each season in second place. In 1908, the year of the Merkle Boner, they could have won the pennant on the last day of the regular season, but lost 5–2 to the Cubs in Chicago.

In 1909, the Pirates finally won another NL pennant by dethroning the powerful Chicago Cubs, then went on to defeat Ty Cobb's Detroit Tigers in the World Series. The timing of Pittsburgh's first world-championship season was perfect for Dreyfuss because the Pirates had begun play in a magnificent steel and concrete ballpark that cost $1 million for the land and the construction. Since 1891, the Pirates had played their home games at Exposition Park, located only about 50 yards from the Allegheny River's north shore. Dreyfuss was determined to get his team out of Exposition Park because of its shabby nineteenth century conditions, its industrial surroundings, and its constant flooding in the spring. Noting that "many of the better class of citizens, especially when accompanied by their womenfolk, were loathe to go there," he decided to build a new ballpark that would stand as a symbol of civic pride and as a monument to baseball's growing status as the national pastime.

With a strong conviction that Pittsburgh's development as a "first-class city" was to its east, Dreyfuss looked at the Oakland area in the East End and its 100-acre Schenley Park. By 1908, Oakland, under the influence of Andrew Carnegie, had become a cultural center, with its two major colleges (Pitt and Carnegie Tech), massive new library and museum, and large concert hall and amusement park. When Carnegie alerted Dreyfuss to a seven-acre parcel of land one block south of Forbes Avenue, the main artery connecting Oakland and downtown Pittsburgh, Dreyfuss jumped at the opportunity and made the purchase on October 18, 1908. Once news of the purchase became public, many in Pittsburgh laughed at the decision. Even Dreyfuss admitted that "there was nothing there but a livery stable and a hothouse, while a few cows roamed the countryside," but "the more I looked over the property, the better I liked it."

The decision to build a new ballpark in Oakland was dubbed "Dreyfuss's Folly," but Dreyfuss forged ahead with his plans and hired New York architect Charles W. Leavitt Jr., best known for designing steel and concrete racetracks, including Belmont Park. Dreyfuss, who hoped that his new ballpark would attract a better class of fans, insisted that the majority of seats be in the higher-priced grandstand. The result was a magnificent three-tiered, fire-resistant structure with inclined ramps between decks and an elevator leading up to the third tier's box seats. While the bleachers along the left-field foul line were left exposed, Leavitt included a spacious promenade inside the main entrance for protection from the rain for the grandstand patrons. Because of a problem with an unsettled landfill, there were no right-field stands constructed until 1925, when the ballpark's seating capacity was expanded from 25,000 to 33,500.

After ground-breaking on January 1, 1909, local contractor Franklin Nicola began the construction of the new ballpark, to be called Forbes Field after British general John Forbes, "the Father of Pittsburgh," who drove the French out of Fort Duquesne and renamed it Fort Pitt in honor of British prime minister William Pitt. Working double shifts and blessed with unusually good weather, Nicola was able to complete his work by early summer and in time for an inaugural game on June 30 against the defending world champion Chicago Cubs. The Pirates lost the first game at Forbes Field to the Cubs 3–2, but the ballpark, filled with an overflow crowd of 30,338, the largest in Pittsburgh history, was a resounding success. The *Pittsburgh Post* praised the ballpark for being "planned by Pittsburghers, erected with Pittsburgh money, and completed in record time with the city's customary 'hustle.'" In his homage to Forbes Field, the *Post* reporter claimed "no trace of smoke blurred the sun-bathed lawns, woodlands, and drives of Schenley Park . . . It was a scene to make participants forget the business cares of a manufacturing city." He also reported that Pittsburgh's high society "played a prominent part in the gala event," but "interest in the event was confined to no class or creed. Millionaire shouted with mechanic, and office boy with bank president."

When the Pirates followed up their grand opening of Forbes Field with their fourth NL pennant and a World Series victory over the Detroit Tigers, Republican mayor William A. Magee proclaimed Monday, October 18, 1909, a public holiday. The highlight of the celebration was a parade that snaked its way from the Fort Pitt Hotel in downtown Pittsburgh to Forbes Field in Schenley Park. At Forbes Field, the loudest ovation went to rookie pitcher Babe Adams, winner of three games against Detroit, including an 8–0 shutout in the seventh and deciding game. The celebration, however, was especially gratifying for Dreyfuss as he stood on the victory platform at his new million-dollar baseball palace. The World Series victory was also a personal triumph for Honus Wagner, winner of eight NL batting titles and arguably the greatest player in Pirates history. Born in Carnegie, Pennsylvania, just south of Pittsburgh, to German immigrant parents, the barrel-chested Wagner, who grew up working in the coal mines and steel mills of western Pennsylvania, was Pittsburgh's first baseball hero. When, however, he performed poorly in the 1903 World Series, many fans and writers questioned his character and wondered if he had a "yellow streak." In the 1909 World Series, Wagner redeemed himself and clearly outplayed Ty Cobb, outhitting him .333

to .231 and stealing six bases to Cobb's two. He also proved his courage in a legendary confrontation on the basepaths when Cobb threatened Wagner on an attempted steal and ended up with three stitches in his lip from Wagner's hard tag.

A SECOND-DIVISION DECADE

At the beginning of the 1910 season, Dreyfuss had every reason to believe in a bright financial future for his Pirates franchise. The home season attendance figure had jumped from 382,444 in 1908 to a record-breaking 534,950 in 1909. The 82,885 fans who attended the three World Series games at Forbes Field, a figure that far exceeded the entire attendance for the 1908 World Series, boosted the gate receipts for the seven-game series to $188,302. Dreyfuss, who kept his owner's share this time, collected $51,273, and the players' share for each Pirate was $1,825.22. Dreyfuss also believed his veteran ball club, after its first world championship, was in a strong position to dominate the NL as it had at the beginning of the century. Unfortunately, key players, including player-manager Fred Clarke and Honus Wagner, were moving toward the end of their careers, and Dreyfuss, the "first-division" owner, was about to face his worst decade.

After finishing a disappointing third in 1910 and 1911, the Pirates climbed to second place in 1912 before dropping to fourth in 1913 and seventh in 1914, the Pirates' first second-division finish under Dreyfuss's ownership. After two more second-division finishes, the Pirates sank to eighth in 1917, their first season in last place since the early 1890s, before climbing back into the first division by the end of the decade. Attendance, after its record-breaking 534,950 in 1909, fell to 436,586 in 1910 and dropped every year until it fell to a record low for Forbes Field of 139,620 in 1914. It was also the first of two seasons that the Pirates faced serious competition from the Pittsburgh Rebels in the rival Federal League, the last serious challenge to the major-league monopoly held by the AL and NL.

Dreyfuss, who had become one of the most prominent and respectable figures in a city dominated by industrial and banking giants, began to hear the first serious criticism of his ownership of the Pirates. By the middle of the decade, after developing an early reputation for generosity, Dreyfuss was also attacked for cutting the salaries of Fred Clarke and Honus Wagner just before their retirements and for being too cheap in his efforts to acquire new ballplayers, especially when Tris Speaker, after a contract dispute with the Boston Red Sox, was sold to the Cleveland Indians for $55,000. In a June 22, 1916, article in the *Sporting News*, Dreyfuss angrily declared, "It's not a question of money. I would spend $50,000 in a minute for a player of the proper caliber."

Dreyfuss's cheapness was hardly on display when the Pirates were still capable of battling Frank Chance's Cubs and John McGraw's Giants for NL supremacy earlier in the decade. On July 20, 1911, he shocked the baseball world by paying a record $22,500 for rookie minor-league phenom Marty O'Toole, twice the NL record of $11,000 the Giants paid for Rube Marquard in 1908. Dreyfuss also purchased the contract of high-school sensation George Sisler, after Sisler had signed with a minor-league team just before he enrolled at the University of Michigan. O'Toole, unfortunately, flopped badly, and Sisler, after graduating from Michigan in 1915, won his long-standing appeal to the National Commission to release him from Pittsburgh's claim of a prior contract. When Sisler won his appeal and signed a new contract with Branch Rickey's St. Louis Browns, Dreyfuss was furious and vowed revenge on commission chairman August "Garry" Herrmann, president of the Cincinnati Reds and a good friend of AL president Ban Johnson. Dreyfuss did everything in his power to undermine Herrmann and the commission, which collapsed after the Black Sox scandal and was replaced by a baseball commissioner.

Once the Pirates sank into the second division, Pittsburgh's sportswriters began to question Dreyfuss's leadership, and by 1917 were calling on him to sell the ball club. The *Pittsburgh Press* demanded, in a front-page headline, that "Dreyfuss Must Go." Its criticism was highly unusual because Dreyfuss had cultivated a close relationship with Pittsburgh's leading newspaper, whose president and business manager were stockholders in the Pirates. Sports editor Will Locke was club secretary until he left the Pirates in 1913 to become president and part owner of the cross-state rival Phillies. For years, the *Press* had such close ties with Dreyfuss that its sports section was regarded as little more than the ball club's media guide. But with the Pirates' last-place finish in 1917, Dreyfuss faced a mounting opposition, also fueled by fired manager Jimmy Callahan, who, exploiting anti-German feelings in a war year, claimed that the worst thing he could wish on the Kaiser was to manage the Pirates under Barney Dreyfuss.

THE CHAMPIONSHIP TWENTIES

Dreyfuss managed to survive his first serious crisis with the Pirates franchise when his ball club returned to the first division, finishing in fourth place in 1918, 1919, and 1920. This was a harbinger of things to come in the new decade. The Pirates would finish in the first division every year in the 1920s, winning two more NL pennants (in 1925 and 1927) and their second World Series championship (in 1925), this time against Walter Johnson's Washington Senators. The Pirates also added to their claims on baseball history when pioneering radio station KDKA, after becoming the first to broadcast the presidential-election returns on November 2, 1920, aired the first baseball broadcast, on August 5, 1921, of a game played at Forbes Field, won by the Pirates 8–5 over the Phillies. Harold Arlin, a *Post-Gazette* sportswriter, hampered by crowd noise and an erratic transmitter, announce the game from a box seat just behind the home-plate screen. The broadcast, then, was little more than a crude experiment, but a year later the first live broadcast of the World Series was aired in the

New York area, and in 1924 WMAQ in Chicago was broadcasting Cubs and White Sox home games.

The Pirates' success in the 1920s returned Pittsburgh to its status as a first-division town, but the city also went through its own boom as its industrial and financial barons continued to build downtown skyscrapers and other monuments to their own magnificence. The Oakland area, as Dreyfuss had anticipated, also flourished. On September 26, 1925, less than two weeks before the Pirates played the opening game of the 1925 World Series at Forbes Field, 60,000-seat Pitt Stadium opened with a 28–0 Panther victory over Washington and Lee. A year later, almost to the day, the University of Pittsburgh broke ground for the Cathedral of Learning, a 42-story gothic tower that, barely a baseball throw away from Forbes Field, appeared to loom over the left-field bleachers to fans sitting along the first-base line.

The 1925 championship season was in many ways as gratifying for Barney Dreyfuss as the 1909 season. To get into the World Series, the Pirates had to overcome John McGraw's New York Giants, winners of four consecutive NL pennants. Since 1905, when McGraw had publicly taunted Dreyfuss for allegedly welshing on gambling debts, Dreyfuss saw McGraw as his archenemy and the Giants as his team's chief rival. The feud had reached a new level of intensity in 1924 when a bribe was offered to Heine Sand, the Philadelphia shortstop, in a crucial late-season series between the Giants and the Phillies. Several Giants were implicated in the bribe, including stars Frankie Frisch, Ross Youngs, and George Kelly, but Commissioner Kenesaw Mountain Landis banned only rookie Jimmy O'Connell, who admitted offering the bribe, and coach Cozy Dolan, who instructed O'Connell to make the bribe. When Dreyfuss demanded the cancellation of the World Series and asked for a full-scale investigation of the attempted bribe, Landis ignored him.

Dreyfuss got his revenge when the Pirates dethroned McGraw's Giants in 1925 and went on to defeat the defending champion Washington Senators in one of the most dramatic World Series in baseball history. The Pirates were led by Kiki Cuyler, who batted .357. The entire team hit .307 and led the NL in nearly every batting category. The 1925 World Series had a wonderful cast of characters, including Pirates Cuyler, Pie Traynor, Max Carey, and several other future members of the Hall of Fame. It also had a great plot line. The Pirates fell behind three games to one and were vilified by the press and fans for their lack of skill and courage. No team had ever come back from a 3–1 deficit to win a best-of-seven World Series, but the Pirates rallied to win the next two games against the Senators and set the stage for a seventh and deciding game, played in the rain and fog at Forbes Field on October 15. When the Pirates won 9–7 on Cuyler's dramatic two-out, bases-loaded, two-run double in the bottom of the eighth against the great Walter Johnson, the *Sporting News* headline read, "Sweet Part of Pirate Victory Is Answer to 'Lack of Courage.'"

After the seventh game ended, a rain-soaked, red-coated band made its way onto the muddy infield and played "There'll Be a Hot Time in the Old Town

Tonight." Pittsburghers, living in "the drinkiest town in the West" before Prohibition, had no trouble celebrating because most of the bars and saloons had been converted into speakeasies and cabarets. Sixth Street, in downtown Pittsburgh, was popularly known as "the Great Wet Way." Many Pittsburghers also collected the winnings from their World Series bets. The city was notorious for its gambling rings and numbers barons, and it was not uncommon for gamblers to circulate freely at Pirate games. There were reports of heavy wagering on the 1925 World Series. Joe Vila, in the *Sporting News,* claimed that while there was no serious evidence of attempted bribes, a gambler who had "cleaned up" in the notorious 1919 World Series lost $80,000 in bets after the Pirates came back to win the last three games.

The Pirates' championship season in 1925 was a great success. Each victorious Pirate earned a World Series share of $5,332. Dreyfuss also saw home attendance, after a decade-long slump, reach a record high of 804,254 in 1925. Once the 171,753 figure for the four World Series games played at Forbes Field was added in, home attendance had climbed to nearly 1 million for the year. Dreyfuss declared a dividend of $166,445, and overall the team made $341,365, a league record. With his new financial windfall, Dreyfuss, criticized in the past for being too cheap, purchased Paul Waner from San Francisco of the Pacific Coast League for $100,000 after Waner had hit .401 for the 1925 season. The addition of Waner raised expectations that the Pirates, with their balance of young players and veterans (including four future Hall of Famers), would repeat their championship season in 1926.

Waner lived up to expectations and hit .336 in 1926. He also led the NL in doubles and triples and scored 101 runs. The defending champion Pirates, however, struggled throughout the season and finished a disappointing third. The ball club was riddled by dissension in 1926, including a near player revolt involving former manager Fred Clarke, who, at Dreyfuss's request, had returned as a coach and supervisor in 1925. The blowup began when veteran Max Carey, openly ridiculed by Clarke, called a team meeting to decide if Clarke should be removed from the bench. After the vote went against Carey by a margin of 18–6, the Pirates, on the orders of Dreyfuss, who was on a European vacation, sold Carey to Brooklyn and released veterans Carson Bigbee and Babe Adams for their support of Carey's action. The affair, because of the names of the three released players, became known as the A-B-C mutiny and cost manager Bill McKechnie his job.

After the fiasco of the previous season, Dreyfuss was determined to return to glory in 1927. He first hired disciplinarian Donie Bush as his new manager. The former Detroit shortstop had starred against the Pirates in the 1909 World Series. Dreyfuss also made several key player moves, but the most important was the signing of Lloyd Waner, at the recommendation of brother Paul, who hit .380, with Lloyd at .355. Paul led the NL in batting, RBIs (131), hits (237), triples (18), and total bases (342). With the Waner brothers flanking Kiki Cuyler, the Pirates had three future Hall of Fame outfielders until Cuyler was benched in midseason for insubordination. The Pirates, even with their strong lineup, which batted a league-leading .305, and excellent starting pitchers, all of whom won at least 15 games, had to fight off strong challenges from the Cardinals, Giants, and Cubs. They did not clinch the NL pennant until the next-to-last day of the season, compiling a 94–60 record. The exciting pennant race resulted in a record NL profit of $467,046. While they were in a desperate pennant race, the New York Yankees, with Ruth hitting 60 home runs, were coasting to the AL pennant.

The 1927 World Series would become one of the most lopsided in baseball history and turn Dreyfuss's last pennant-winning season into a bitter disappointment. After the Yankees swept the Pirates in four games, the story circulated in the press that the Pirates, after watching Ruth, Gehrig, and the rest of Murderers' Row in batting practice, were so intimidated that they gave up before playing the first game. Just two years earlier, the Pirates had won the praise of the baseball world for their thrilling comeback in the World Series, but they now were regarded as one of the worst teams in the history of the Fall Classic.

While bitterly disappointed, Dreyfuss expected to win another pennant in 1928 and a return trip to the World Series. But his Pirates, despite Burleigh Grimes's 25-win season and a team batting average of .309, including six .300 hitters in the lineup, fell back into fourth place. One year later the Pirates moved up to second place behind the Cubs, with six .300 hitters. Pie Traynor led the team with a .356 average and 108 RBIs, while Lloyd and Paul Waner hit .353 and .336, respectively. Both scored over 130 runs, while Lloyd led the NL with 20 triples. The double-play combination of Dick Bartell and George Grantham also hit over .300, as did outfielder Adam Comorsky, at .321. The season, however, marked Dreyfuss's last first-division finish. During the 1920s, when the Pirates were never out of the first division, the team averaged $230,000 a year in profit. However, Dreyfuss was about to begin a period of personal tragedy and franchise turbulence that coincided with the city's own struggles during the Great Depression.

DEPRESSION BASEBALL

Pittsburgh, like the rest of the country, was devastated by the Great Depression. By 1930, its factories had dramatically cut back production and workers were being dismissed in droves. In 1931, relief agencies in Pittsburgh warned that without immediate additional funds, 47,750 Pittsburgh residents would begin starving to death. Armies of the unemployed roamed Pittsburgh's streets and thousands joined in a hunger march on Washington, led by Father James Cox, who ran for president in 1932 on the "Jobless Party" ticket. Despite massive relief efforts, one-third of Pittsburgh's employable population was out of work. In 1934, out of 544,187 employable workers, 176,156 were still desperately seeking jobs.

The impact of the depression on baseball was not felt immediately, thanks to an explosive offensive season in 1930. For a time, the national pastime seemed invulnerable to the country's economic hardships. *Baseball Magazine* claimed that organized baseball was "an impregnable industry . . . vitally necessary to the public welfare." In 1931, however, baseball owners, faced with sharply declining attendance, began a series of cost-cutting moves, including major salary cuts and roster reductions. In 1932, after a 45 percent drop in attendance, baseball owners, despite the cuts, collectively lost over $1 million. Only the pennant-winning Chicago Cubs and the Philadelphia teams made a profit in 1932, though the Cubs' major-league-leading attendance figure of 990,000 was down 500,000 from 1930. The second-place Pirates' attendance was 287,262, resulting in an $86,960 deficit.

In Pittsburgh, Dreyfuss had already seen a major decline in attendance before the impact of the depression on baseball. After a record-breaking 869,720 fans came out to Forbes Field in the pennant-winning 1927 season, attendance dropped off dramatically in 1928 to 495,070, and even with a second-place finish fell slightly, to 491,377, in 1929. In 1930, the first full year of the depression, the Pirates, plagued by poor trades and injuries, ended the season in fifth place, their first second-division finish since 1917, and attendance dropped to 357,795, the worst full-season figure since 1917, when the Pirates sank into last place. After another fifth-place finish in 1931, attendance fell to a dismal 260,392. The Pirates averaged about $92,000 in profits those years.

For Dreyfuss, personal tragedy overshadowed the 1931 season. For years, he had been grooming his son, Sammy, a Princeton graduate, to take over the operations of the ball club. By 1931, Sammy Dreyfuss, just 36 years old, had held the positions of vice president, treasurer, and business manager in the Pirates front office. On February 19, 1931, however, Sammy died of pneumonia, just four days before his father's 65th birthday. The grief-stricken Dreyfuss never recovered from his son's death. On February 5, 1932, only a year after losing Sammy, Dreyfuss himself died of pneumonia after a glandular operation.

After Sammy's death, Dreyfuss turned to his son-in-law, Bill Benswanger, for help with the operations of the ball club. After Dreyfuss's own death a year later, his widow asked her son-in-law to become president of the organization. William E. Benswanger, an insurance executive and patron of the arts, never wanted to be involved with the Pittsburgh baseball club, though he was an avid fan in his youth. But he agreed to succeed his father-in-law and run the Pirates organization, as long as Mrs. Dreyfuss remained the controlling stockholder. He would serve effectively and stay on as president until 1946, when the Dreyfuss family sold the Pirates.

In 1932, Benswanger's first year as president, the Pirates, after second-division finishes in 1930 and 1931, climbed into second place with the help of the strong hitting of the Waner brothers, Pie Traynor, and rookie Arky Vaughn. They repeated their second-place finish in 1933, but Pirate fans were also energized by the return of the legendary Honus Wagner. After learning that Wagner had become nearly destitute because of several business failures, Benswanger, who had fought against the decision to reduce league rosters, hired Wagner as a coach, a move that proved immensely popular in Pittsburgh and around the NL. Benswanger, in another popular move, gave free admission to 25 unemployed fans and their wives to any game except those played on Saturday or a holiday. He was also helped in his efforts to improve attendance when, on November 7, 1933, Pennsylvanians voted out the blue laws that had banned Sunday baseball.

After their consecutive second-place finishes, the Pirates were expected to contend for the NL pennant in 1934, but when the team slumped badly in June, Benswanger made his first major personnel change, firing George Gibson, in his second stint as Pirates manager after running the ball club from 1920 to midseason 1922, and convincing Pie Traynor, who along with Paul Waner had played in the first All-Star Game the previous year, to take over the struggling ball club. The soft-spoken Traynor had another All-Star year, but he couldn't turn the Pirates franchise around. Plagued by injuries and poor pitching, the team played under .500 for the rest of the season and finished in fifth place.

With the struggling Pittsburgh economy beginning to show signs of a recovery and with the popular Traynor and Wagner on board, the Pirates front office saw a steady increase in attendance, from 352,885 in 1935 to 641,033 in 1938. The Pirates climbed back into the first division in 1935 with a fourth-place finish and repeated its performance in 1936. Pirate fans also saw two remarkable home-run performances at Forbes Field, a ballpark notoriously unfriendly to home-run hitters. On May 25, 1935, Babe Ruth, now 40 years old and days away from his final game as a player, thrilled 10,000 fans by hitting three home runs, the last clearing the right-field roof, a feat never before done at Forbes Field. A little more than a year later, on July 10, 1936, Chuck Klein of the Phillies hit four home runs in a 10-inning game at Forbes Field and joined Lou Gehrig, the only other player to have accomplished the feat in the modern era.

In 1937, the Pirates, led once more by the strong hitting of the Waner brothers and Arky Vaughn, moved up into third place. Fans who couldn't afford to go out to Forbes Field that year now had the wonderful voice and colorful expressions of Rosey Rowswell to entertain them on the radio. Sixteen years after Harold Arlin's historic first broadcast of a major-league game on KDKA, Rowswell began the first complete season broadcast of Pirate games, including away games that he re-created in the studio from a Western Union ticker tape. Immensely popular in Pittsburgh, especially with women fans, who loved his folksy style and listened to afternoon games in the parlor and kitchen, Rowswell, who called a Pirates extra-base hit a "doozie marooney" and told Aunt Minnie "to get upstairs and raise the window" every time a Pirate hit a home run, continued as the voice of the Pirates until his death in 1955.

Rowswell and Pirate fans had plenty to cheer about in 1938, though the season would become the most heartbreaking in Pirates history. Led by strong hitting and the remarkable relief pitching of Mace Brown, the Pirates dominated the NL that summer. By September, Bill Benswanger was so certain the Pirates were going to win the pennant that he had a World Series press box added on to the third tier of Forbes Field. The Pirates' pennant drive cooled, however, when a hurricane swept along the East Coast in mid-September, forcing the cancellation of four Pirate games against second-division Philadelphia and Boston that were never rescheduled. In late September, the Pirates arrived in Chicago for a three-game series with the second-place Cubs with only a one-and-a-half-game lead. On September 28, after losing the first game in the series to Dizzy Dean, the Pirates and Cubs battled to a 5–5 tie going into the bottom of the ninth. With darkness moving into Wrigley Field, and players, umpires, and fans barely able to see the play, Gabby Hartnett hit his famous two-out, two-strike "homer in the gloaming" off a disconsolate Mace Brown and put the Cubs into first place, where they would remain for the rest of the season.

After the devastating loss of the pennant, Benswanger hoped the Pirates would bounce back in 1939, but the ball club struggled and finished in sixth place. Hurt by the team's poor play and the effects of a business recession, attendance dropped from a decade-high 641,033 in 1938 to 376,734 in 1939. At the end of the season, a frustrated Benswanger demoted Pie Traynor to scout and farm director. He replaced Traynor with another future Hall of Famer, Frankie Frisch, who had managed the St. Louis Cardinals from 1933 to 1938, but was fired after a sixth-place finish. Frisch, a disciple of John McGraw, managed the Pirates to five first-division finishes in his first six years, but was replaced near the end of the 1946 season when his ball club, riddled with dissension, fell into seventh place.

THE WAR YEARS AND NEW OWNERSHIP

The war years produced an economic boom in Pittsburgh. As early as the closing months of 1940, business activity equaled that of 1929, and the steel mills were operating at 100 percent capacity. The steel industry set a new production record in 1941, and in 1942, for the first time in Pittsburgh's history, the steel mills remained in operation on Christmas Day. By 1943, Pittsburgh was recognized at the nation's top steel center as employment in the city climbed another 10 percent. In 1944, a survey revealed that war contracts to Pittsburgh plants totaled $322 million. The only drawback was that the more the mills produced the darker the skies became over Pittsburgh. On January 18, 1944, the pollution in the city was so bad that it prevented workers from reaching their jobs and their homes.

The war years were a period of transition for the Pirates, as the team traded or released their Hall of Fame ballplayers and brought in new talent mixed with aging veterans. In 1940, after a fourth-place season that featured the first night game at Forbes Field on June 4, 1940, the Pirates released Paul Waner. On May 7, 1941, on their way to another fourth-place finish, they traded Lloyd

Waner to Boston. Five days after Pearl Harbor, the Pirates sent Arky Vaughn, the last of their future Hall of Famers, to the Brooklyn Dodgers. Before the 1942 season, the team suffered its first serious loss to the war effort when Billy Cox, projected as Vaughn's replacement at shortstop, was drafted into the service. Yet the Pirates were fortunate in losing fewer players in the draft than most major-league teams, and didn't lose an everyday starter until Elbie Fletcher left for the service in 1944.

After dropping to fifth in 1942, the Pirates returned to fourth place in 1943 on the strong hitting of Bob Elliott and Vince DiMaggio and Rip Sewell's 21-game-winning season. With Rip Sewell throwing his famous "eephus" or blooper pitch and winning another 21 games, the Pirates climbed into second place in 1944, their best finish in the war years, before falling back to fourth in 1945. When so many ball clubs got their best players back for the 1946 season, the Pirates, getting no similar boost in talent, were vulnerable to a drop in the standings despite their fans' hope that the team's first-division finishes during the war years would continue into the first postwar season.

While Pirate fans dreamed of a postwar pennant, Pittsburgh's business and civic leaders had their own postwar vision. They decided to use Pittsburgh's major industrial role in winning the war and the country's postwar economic boom to rescue what they believed had become a dying city. The Democratic machine, the dominant political force in Pittsburgh since the depression and now headed by recently elected mayor and future governor David L. Lawrence, put aside its animosity with wealthy Republican industrialists and financiers like Richard King Mellon and joined forces with its traditional enemies to forge a Pittsburgh renaissance. It would take years for Pittsburgh to shed its national image as "the Smoky City," but by the late 1940s, after a citywide campaign that included slogans ("Smoke must go") painted on streetcars and women shoppers in the downtown area wearing surgical masks in protest, county and state governments finally passed smoke-control legislation and brought the beginning of the end to Pittsburgh's gloomy, soot-filled skies.

The Pirates' first postwar season also produced a major change, but only after the team was plagued by controversy in the clubhouse and front office. The Pirates ended the 1946 season in seventh place, its worst finish since 1918, but team morale had already reached a low point by early June when Boston lawyer Robert Murphy, after organizing the American Baseball Guild, decided to concentrate on Pittsburgh, a strong union city, as a test case for a strike over player grievances. The strike vote barely failed, but only after Bill Benswanger came into the clubhouse and made a personal appeal to his players. A few weeks later, the Pirates front office had to deal with another public-relations nightmare when it refused admission to 500 Pittsburgh Post-Gazette newsboys the day after a rainout forced the cancellation of a special game in their honor.

Faced with poor play, clubhouse dissension, and a hostile press, the Dreyfuss family decided that it had had enough and instructed Benswanger to sell the franchise. On August 8, 1946, Benswanger announced that the Pirates had been purchased for a price "not exceeding $2,500,000" by a syndicate comprised of Frank McKinney, an Indianapolis banker; John Galbreath, a Columbus, Ohio, real-estate agent; Tom Johnson, vice president of Standard Steel and the only Pittsburgher among the new owners; and popular Hollywood singer and actor Bing Crosby. McKinney, the major stockholder, became the new president of the franchise, and Roy Hamey, president of the American Association in 1946, was appointed the team's general manager.

The new owners moved quickly to win the confidence of Pirate fans, though some moves, like hiring manager Babe Herman, would turn into major blunders. Herman, acquired from the Boston Braves for the popular Bob Elliott, was unable to control the drinking, gambling, and womanizing on a team that ringleader Kirby Higbe called "the traveling casino" and was fired at the end of the season. The troublemaking Higbe had been acquired in a trade with the Brooklyn Dodgers after he told Branch Rickey he didn't want to play on the same team with Jackie Robinson. Pittsburgh also acquired other players through trades or waivers, including Detroit Tigers slugger Hank Greenberg, the first great Jewish American player in the major leagues. The Pirates made several concessions to sign Greenberg, including the construction of a fenced-off double bullpen, dubbed "Greenberg Gardens," that shortened left field from 365 to 335 feet.

Though Greenberg hit only 25 home runs in 1947 and the Pirates finished in a tie for seventh place, Pittsburgh's baseball fans, excited by new ownership and so many new players, set an attendance record of 1,283,531. While fans complained that everyone was hitting home runs into Greenberg Gardens except Greenberg, they also had another slugger to root for at Forbes Field. In 1946, rookie Ralph Kiner led the NL in home runs with 23 and tied Johnny Rizzo's all-time Pirates record. Under Greenberg's tutelage, Kiner hit 51 home runs in 1947 and tied Johnny Mize for the NL lead. Kiner would go on to win or tie for the NL home-run title in each of his seven full seasons with the Pirates, a record that still stands. He became so proficient at hitting home runs that his ratio of 7.1 per 100 times at bat is second only to Babe Ruth among players in the Hall of Fame.

After the Pirates replaced Babe Herman with Bill Meyer, who had won four minor-league pennants with Kansas City and Newark, two Yankee farm teams, the Pirates nearly won the NL pennant in 1948. They were in first place on June 16, and in September, after winning seven straight games, were in second place, only two and a half games out of first. But they went 9–13 the rest of the season and finished in fourth place. While the popular Meyer was named the *Sporting News* Manager of the Year, the Pirates were sparked by Ralph Kiner's 40 home runs and the strong play of several new players, including future manager Danny Murtaugh and Dixie Walker, another former Dodger who resented playing on the same team with Jackie Robinson. Excited by the pennant race, Pirate fans set another attendance record, but the 1,517,021 fans who came out to Forbes Field in 1948 were watching their ball club's last winning season until 1958.

THE RICKEY YEARS

Despite Ralph Kiner's 54 home runs, the Pirates began a team-record-breaking streak of nine consecutive losing seasons in 1949, when they finished the season at 71–83 and fell into sixth place. The Pirates decided to go with younger players in 1950, but the team continued its slide and ended up in last place for the first time since 1917. Nearly 1.5 million Pirate fans came out to Forbes Field, primarily to watch Kiner's heroics, but president Frank McKinney became disillusioned by midseason and sold his stock to his fellow owners. John Galbreath, who now owned a controlling interest in the franchise, took over the presidency, and at the end of a dismal season, highlighted only by Kiner's selection as the *Sporting News* NL Player of the Year, began negotiations with Branch Rickey, ousted by the Dodgers organization, to take over the operations of the Pirates.

When Rickey arrived in Pittsburgh, he loudly proclaimed a five-year plan for the Pirates: "We're pointing toward 1955. That's when the bells will start ringing as the red wagon comes down the street." Unfortunately for Pirate fans, Rickey, despite his Hall of Fame achievements in St. Louis and Brooklyn, became a dismal failure in Pittsburgh. The Pirates finished next to last in 1951 and dead last for the next four years. Attendance fell steadily, from 980,590 in 1951 to 469,397 in 1955. In 1951, the team even became the subject of a Hollywood movie called *Angels in the Outfield*, in which a hapless Pirates team becomes a pennant winner only when the angelic spirits of baseball greats descend upon Forbes Field. To make matters even worse, the legendary Honus Wagner died in December, just a few months after the unveiling of his statue in Schenley Park, just next to Forbes Field.

Rickey's 1952 Pirates were so bad, finishing with a record of 42–112, the worst in modern team history, that they became the joke of the NL. Joe Garagiola, who had the misfortune of playing on the 1952 team, called the Pirates a ninth-place ball club in an eight-team league. They had the worst hitting (.231) and pitching (4.65 ERA) in the NL. At the end of the season, Rickey replaced Bill Meyer with Fred Haney, but the Pirates still lost over 100 games in 1953. In early June of that year, Rickey, after a salary dispute with Ralph Kiner in the off-season, made the most unpopular trade in the team's history when he sent Kiner, with Garagiola and two other players, to the Chicago Cubs for six players, including five ex-Dodger farmhands, and $150,000.

The Pirates lost over 100 games in 1954 for the third consecutive year, but the season had one historic moment. Even with the presence of Branch Rickey in the front office, the Pirates, well aware of their white working-class fan base, had been very reluctant to sign minorities. Pittsburgh's working class was largely defined by its ethnic enclaves, its steel-mill mentality, and its fear and distrust of minorities. The very geography of Pittsburgh seemed to reinforce the city's racial segregation. The business district or downtown area, undergoing a postwar renaissance in the 1950s, was at the apex of a "Golden Triangle" formed by the confluence of the Monongahela and Allegheny into the Ohio River. The north side and south side formed white working-class barriers across the rivers from downtown Pittsburgh, in effect isolating much of the black population of the city between the rivers and at the base of the Golden Triangle in a ghetto called the Hill District. The many bridges in Pittsburgh were avenues for commerce, not for integration.

In 1954, seven seasons after Jackie Robinson crossed baseball's color line, Curt Roberts became the first African American to play for the Pittsburgh Pirates. After Roberts had an outstanding season with the Pirates' minor-league Denver Bears, Rickey signed him to a major league contract. He also warned Roberts that because he was the first black Pittsburgh Pirate, he would face the same fan abuse as had Jackie Robinson. Despite Rickey's warning, fan hostility and teammate indifference had a devastating effect on Roberts. He slumped badly in his first year with the Pirates and, after appearing in only six games in 1955, was sent back to the minor leagues. The only major off-season news for the Pirates going into the 1955 season was the death in February of popular broadcaster Rosey Rowswell. He was replaced as lead announcer by the colorful and controversial Bob Prince, who had teamed up with Rowswell in 1948.

BUILDING A CHAMPIONSHIP TEAM

In 1955, the Pirates finished in last place for the fourth consecutive year. At the end of the season, Rickey replaced manager Fred Haney with the brash Bobby Bragan, but a few months later Rickey himself was replaced as general manager by his assistant and protégé Joe L. Brown, the son of famous comedian Joe E. Brown. The Rickey years in Pittsburgh were plagued by bad player decisions, but by the time Rickey departed, several of the players that would lead the Pirates to a world championship in 1960 were already in uniform, including future NL MVP Dick Groat and future Cy Young Award winner Vernon Law. No Rickey acquisition, however, was more important to the future of the Pirates than Roberto Clemente. Originally signed as a bonus baby by the Brooklyn Dodgers but assigned to the minor leagues, Clemente was drafted by the Pirates on November 22, 1954, and made his major-league debut at Forbes Field on April 17, 1955.

Clemente struggled in his first year with the Pirates, but in 1956 he hit .311 and finished third in the NL batting race. With rookie Bill Mazeroski playing second base and 1955 NL Rookie of the Year Bill Virdon, acquired from St. Louis, joining Clemente in the outfield, the Pirates had unexpectedly surged into first place by early June. The highlight of their early-season success came in late May when first baseman Dale Long homered in eight consecutive games, something that had never been done before in baseball

Roberto Clemente, 1955. Courtesy of the Baseball Hall of Fame

history. Long's heroics so captured the imagination of America that he was invited to appear on *The Ed Sullivan Show*. The Pirates eventually fell back into their losing ways and finished in seventh place, but attendance, sparked by the early-season excitement, increased to 949,878, more than double the 1955 figure of 469,397.

The Pirates seemed on the verge of a return to the first division, but not until the next year. The franchise suffered through its ninth consecutive losing season in 1957 and finished in seventh place. At a congressional hearing, baseball commissioner Ford Frick, reporting on the financial risks of club owners, cited the Pirates, who had spent large sums of money on signing bonus babies and acquiring veteran players, as the worst-run franchise in baseball. Frick told congressmen that the Pirates had spent $1,537,303 and had nothing but last-place finishes to show for it. Frustrated by another losing season, Pirates ownership fired Bobby Bragan in midseason after he served orange drinks to a team of umpires that had ejected him the day before, and hired coach Danny Murtaugh to manage for the last two months of the season. When the Pirates played over-.500 baseball for Murtaugh, he was rehired for 1958, amid rumors that the Galbreath family was interested in moving the Pirates to New York now that the Dodgers and Giants had moved to the West Coast.

John Galbreath announced that the Pirates were staying in Pittsburgh, but he also asked for assistance from the city, county, and state for the building of a new stadium to replace the now-decaying Forbes Field. Galbreath's request took on greater urgency on September 9, 1958, when Chancellor Edward Litchfield announced that the University of Pittsburgh's planned multimillion-dollar expansion in the Oakland area would require the eventual buyout of the Pirates from Forbes Field. In late November, Pitt purchased Forbes Field for $3 million, but agreed to lease the ballpark to the Pirates for five years or until the new stadium, planned for the north side, was constructed and ready for occupancy. The off-field activity had little effect on the Pirates in 1958, as the team soared to its first winning season since 1948 and its first second-place finish since 1944. Joe

L. Brown was named General Manager of the Year by the *Sporting News*, and Danny Murtaugh the NL Manager of the Year. Attendance climbed to 1,311,988, third highest in franchise history.

During the off-season, Brown made the most controversial Pirates trade since Branch Rickey sent Ralph Kiner to the Chicago Cubs when he dealt popular Pittsburgh native Frank Thomas with three other players to Cincinnati for third baseman Don Hoak, catcher Smoky Burgess, and pitcher Harvey Haddix. Thomas had been an All-Star through the Pirates' losing seasons and had led them to their second-place finish in 1958. Pirate fans were infuriated by the trade and felt that Brown was responsible when the Pirates dropped to fourth place in 1959. The only dividend from the trade came in late May at Milwaukee County Stadium when Harvey Haddix made baseball history by pitching 12 perfect innings against the Braves, only to lose the game in the 13th.

Whatever disappointment Pirate fans experienced in 1959 was erased in 1960 when the Pirates won their first NL pennant since 1927 and their first World Series since 1925 with a mark of 95–59. A then team record 1,705,828 flocked to Forbes Field to watch a scrappy, come-from-behind ball club that seemed to match the working-class spirit of the city and its pride in the postwar renaissance. Led by the clutch hitting of All-Stars Dick Groat (.325), Don Hoak, Bob Skinner, Smoky Burgess, and Roberto Clemente (.314) and the strong pitching of Vernon Law (20–9), Bob Friend (18–12), and reliever Roy Face, the Pirates, after a midseason trade with the Cardinals for pitcher "Vinegar Bend" Mizell, moved into first place on July 26, where they remained until they clinched the pennant on September 25.

The crowds at Forbes Field, stirred by "Beat 'em Bucs" slogans and songs, became so large and rowdy that, in August, the Pirates organization banned fans from bringing their own beer into the ballpark, a practice previously allowed because Pennsylvania law prevented the selling of beer at public events. After the Pirates clinched the pennant and were honored with a victory parade in downtown Pittsburgh, fans became even more excited because their Bucs were to face another powerful Yankees team in the World Series, this time led by Mickey Mantle, Yogi Berra, and Whitey Ford.

The 1960 World Series opened in Pittsburgh on October 5 with a 6–4 Pirates victory, sparked by the strong pitching of Vernon Law and a two-run homer by Bill Mazeroski. The Yankees tied the series the next day with a lopsided 16–3 win and took a 2–1 lead when they walloped the Pirates at Yankee Stadium 10–0 on the shutout pitching of Whitey Ford. After the Pirates won the next two games at Yankee Stadium by the close scores of 3–2 and 5–2, the Yankees bounced back at Forbes Field, winning 12–0 behind another shutout performance by Ford. With the series tied at 3–3, the Pirates and the Yankees battled back and forth in the seventh game until Hal Smith's dramatic two-out, three-run homer gave the Pirates a 9–7 lead going into the top of the ninth inning. After the Yankees tied the score on Mickey Mantle's brilliant baserunning, Bill

Mazeroski led off the bottom of the ninth against Ralph Terry and, on a 1–0 count, hit the most famous home run in World Series history over the 406 mark in left center field.

When Mazeroski's home run ended an exciting and improbable World Series of lopsided Yankee wins and close Pirate victories, Pittsburgh erupted into a frenzy comparable, according to the *Pittsburgh Press*, "to V-J Day, New York Times Square on New Year's Eve and New Orleans in the Mardi Gras." Pittsburgh's safety director estimated the crowd in downtown Pittsburgh at 300,000. Fearing a riot, he ordered a shutdown of traffic into the downtown area and appealed on radio and television for people to stay home. His fears, however, proved unfounded when only 28 people were arrested, and most for public drunkenness. A handful of Pittsburghers did stay home to watch the second Kennedy-Nixon debate, but most participated in a celebration that lasted until the early-morning hours. Pittsburghers also celebrated during the off-season when Dick Groat was named the NL MVP, Vernon Law the Cy Young Award winner, and Danny Murtaugh the NL Manager of the Year.

THE CLEMENTE DECADE

The hope in Pittsburgh that the magic of 1960 would carry over into the next season was quickly dashed when the Pirates struggled in 1961 and ended up in sixth place. The key to the Pirates' decline was Vernon Law's shoulder injury, but several other Pirates were also injured, including Bob Skinner, while Dick Groat, Hal Smith, Rocky Nelson, and Roy Face had poor seasons. After a fourth-place finish in 1962, the team returned to the second division for the next two years, including an eighth-place finish in 1963. Attendance dropped steadily each year until it had sunk to 759,496 in 1964, nearly a million fewer fans than the record-breaking 1,705,828 who attended games at Forbes Field in 1960. As the Pirates struggled in the early 1960s, Joe L. Brown, in a desperate attempt to improve the team, traded most of the heroes of the 1960 season, including Dick Groat, Don Hoak, and Dick Stuart. At the end of the 1964 season, Danny Murtaugh, citing poor health, resigned as manager and was replaced by Harry Walker.

While the Pirates, as a team, failed to live up to the miracle 1960 season, Roberto Clemente, spurned in the balloting for the NL MVP Award despite an outstanding year, played like a champion in the 1960s and had a Hall of Fame decade. Since his rookie season in 1955, Clemente had become a controversial figure in Pittsburgh because of his flamboyant play and his constant complaints about injuries and ailments. Pittsburgh sportswriters often portrayed him as a "Puerto Rican hot dog" and criticized him for a being a whining hypochondriac, only interested in "numero uno." Believing that he was denigrated by the press and fans because of his skin and his heritage, Clemente refused to wear his 1960 world-championship ring. Carrying his anger and bitterness into the 1961 season, he won his first NL batting title with a .351 average and his first Gold Glove award. By the end of the decade, Clemente had won four batting titles and nine Gold Gloves, and in 1966, though the Pirates failed to win the pennant after contending all season, was finally named the NL MVP.

Slow to integrate in the 1950s, the Pirates, thanks to more aggressive scouting, finally began to change the racial makeup of their team in 1960s by signing and bringing up more African American and Latin American players. Playing inspired baseball and speaking out against racial prejudice, Clemente became a team leader and spokesman for younger black players like Willie Stargell, Bob Veale, and Donn Clendenon. In a decade characterized by racial change and political turmoil, Clemente became the most visible and provocative sports figure in Pittsburgh. When Martin Luther King Jr. was assassinated on April 4, 1968, Clemente played a pivotal role in the decision by the Pirates, who had 11 black players, more than any other team in the major leagues, to postpone its season opener in Houston.

While the integrated Pirates of the 1960s were a reflection of the civil rights movement of the decade, there were Pittsburgh fans who saw the presence of so many black players as the reason for the team's failure to repeat the success of the 1960 season. The team's struggles on the field and declining attendance were often linked to the Pirates' growing number of black athletes. Despite the racial controversy, the Pirates, under the leadership of Harry Walker, improved to a third-place finish in 1965 and, after challenging the Dodgers for first place all season, finished in third again in 1966. Attendance, which had steadily fallen since 1960, increased to 1,196,618 in 1966.

Joe L. Brown acquired stolen-base king Maury Wills during the off-season, but when the Pirates, preseason favorites to win the NL pennant, struggled through the first half of 1967, Brown fired Harry Walker. He convinced Danny Murtaugh to return as manager for the rest of the season, but the ball club failed to improve and finished in sixth place. Brown added future Hall of Famer Jim Bunning to his pitching staff in 1968, but under manager Larry Shepard, the Pirates finished sixth again with a record of 80–82. In 1969, the first year of division play in the major leagues, the Pirates, with an infusion of young talent led by rookies Al Oliver, Richie Hebner, and Manny Sanguillen, improved their record by eight games and finished in third place. Brown, however, fired Shepard with five games remaining in the season and replaced him with coach Alex Grammas.

SEASONS OF TRIUMPH AND TRAGEDY

When Joe L. Brown again convinced Danny Murtaugh to come out of retirement, the Pirates began the 1970s with the manager who had led them to a world championship at the beginning of the last decade. The ball club also began play in a new home when Three Rivers Stadium, after years of delay, finally was completed and opened on July 16, 1970, to a record crowd of 48,846. The city needed a new ballpark because Forbes Field had become decrepit and there was a need for greater capacity, especially for football. The city hoped to use a new multipurpose field to help revive the downtown in a declining rust-belt city, as was being done in Philadelphia, Cincinnati, and St. Louis. Political wrangling over city and county financing had stalled the project until the end of 1968, when the Pittsburgh Stadium Authority approved final plans for a 52,000-seat multisport stadium, to be built near the point of the Golden Triangle, on the northern shore of the convergence of the Monongahela and Allegheny rivers into the Ohio, close to the site of old Exposition Park. The main access to the stadium was to be over the Fort Pitt Bridge linking the north and south shores of the point. The original estimate for building the stadium was $28 million, but unexpected labor disputes caused delays and drove up costs. The stadium was finally completed in 1970, but with a price tag of $40 million for the construction and $15 million for other improvements.

The stadium, designed by the Pittsburgh architectural firm of Deeter and Richey, was a six-level, bowl-shaped configuration similar to those constructed in St. Louis, Cincinnati, and Philadelphia. With its artificial turf, electronic scoreboard, and glass-enclosed Allegheny Club, Three Rivers was a state-of-the-art facility, but it drew immediate criticism from Pittsburgh fans because of the high construction costs and the traffic bottlenecks created before and after games. Pirate fans were also unhappy with the distance and arrangement of the seating, which seemed more suited for football than for baseball; the high cost of concessions; and the uniform look of the stadium, often described as "a concrete doughnut." The new stadium did have an initial positive impact on attendance, which rose from 769,369 in 1969 to 1,341,947 in 1970, but it would take 18 years for Three Rivers to break the attendance record set at Forbes Field in 1960.

When the Pirates won their first Eastern Division title in 1970 (89–73), with Clemente batting .352, it appeared that the ball club was going to repeat the championship magic of its first season at Forbes Field. The Pirates, however, fell short of the World Series when they were swept in three games by the Cincinnati Reds in the NL Championship Series. In 1971, the Pirates won the East again (97–65), thanks to their league-leading offense and strong defense. Playing at Three Rivers, with its shorter fences, the 1971 team led the NL in home runs for the first time since 1903 and led the majors in runs scored. Veterans Clemente (.342) and Willie Stargell (who belted 48 homers to lead the league, and drove in 125 runs) helped carry the club. The team's most distinguishing feature, however, was the appearance of seven African American and six Latin American ballplayers on its roster. On September 1, 1971, the Pirates made history when they fielded the first all-black lineup in the history of baseball. The Pirates then defeated the San Francisco Giants in the playoffs three games to one to earn their first trip back to the World Series since 1960.

Roberto Clemente, finally honored with a fan appreciation night in 1970, was still the driving force behind the Pirates, and promised his teammates that if they made it to the postseason, he would lead them to the world championship. However, it looked dark after the Pirates dropped the first two games in Baltimore. Clemente then carried the Pirates to victory on his back. He played so brilliantly that the 1971 World Series became his personal showcase. He fielded perfectly, batted .414, and homered in the seventh and deciding game, won by the Pirates 2–1. When he received the Series MVP award, Clemente believed that, after 17 years, he had finally proven his greatness. In the weeks after the World Series, the outspoken Clemente used his public appearances to support Curt Flood's court case against baseball's reserve clause and to criticize baseball for failing to hire black managers. He also announced plans to build a sports center for children in his native Puerto Rico.

The only blemish on the 1971 season was a planned party in downtown Pittsburgh that, unlike the spontaneous 1960 celebration, was marred by violence and forced an early end to the Pirates' motorcade after the team returned from Baltimore. As the city recovered from its embarrassment, Pirate fans looked forward to 1972, even though Danny Murtaugh, once again, had announced his retirement. With Bill Virdon as manager, the Pirates repeated as Eastern Division champions in 1972, highlighted by Clemente's 3,000th hit in his last regular-season at bat. But the year turned into a bitter disappointment when the ball club lost a heartbreaking fifth and deciding game to the Cincinnati Reds in the NL playoffs on a wild pitch. The Reds scored twice in the bottom of the ninth to win 4–3.

The worst, however, was still to come for Pirate fans. Less than three months later, on December 31, 1972, at 9:22 P.M., a DC-7 cargo plane filled with supplies for the victims of a devastating earthquake in Managua crashed into the Atlantic minutes after takeoff, killing everyone on board, including Roberto Clemente, who had personally taken charge of relief efforts in Puerto Rico to help in Nicaragua's recovery. Clemente's tragic death shocked the baseball world and devastated the city of Pittsburgh and the Pirates organization. Though Clemente's teammates tried to rally back in 1973, the Pirates, finishing below .500, failed to win the Eastern Division title for the first time in four years, and Bill Virdon was replaced by Danny Murtaugh near the end of the season. The season was a bitter disappointment for Pirate fans, who had cheered in March after the Baseball Writers Association of America waived the five-year waiting rule and elected Clemente into the Baseball Hall of Fame. When Clemente was inducted that summer, he became the first Latin American player to enter baseball's shrine.

Under Murtaugh's leadership, the Pirates, with breakout years by young players like Richie Zisk, Rennie Stennett, and Dave Parker and the hitting of veterans Willie Stargell, Al Oliver, and Manny Sanguillen, bounced back to win division titles in 1974 and 1975, but they lost in the playoffs to the Dodgers in 1974 three games to one and were swept by the Reds in 1975. After a second-place finish in 1976, Murtaugh, still struggling with poor health, stepped down as manager. On December 2, 1976, the most popular manager in Pirates history died at the age of 59. Murtaugh's passing was just the latest baseball tragedy for the Pirates in a turbulent decade that began so promisingly with a World Series victory. In 1973, Steve Blass, a World Series hero in 1971, suddenly lost the ability to throw strikes, and retired two years later. At the end of the 1975 season, the Pirates organization, to the dismay of many fans, fired the colorful and controversial Bob Prince, who had been the voice of the Pirates for four decades. In 1976, shortly before the death of Danny Murtaugh, pitcher Bob Moose, whose wild pitch ended the 1972 playoffs, was killed in an automobile accident on his 29th birthday.

Besides the tragic losses, the Pirates also had to contend with a struggling Pittsburgh economy, baseball free agency, and frustrated fans who were becoming increasingly unhappy with the cost of attending a game at Three Rivers. With the retirement and death of so many postwar renaissance leaders, the city had also lost much of its spirit of civic cooperation. The decade was characterized by constant political strife between Mayor Peter Flaherty's administration and county and business leaders. Adding to the turmoil was an inflationary rise in prices and increasing job losses. By 1975, Jones and Laughlin, after expanding its operations in the past two decades, had laid off 2,600 Pittsburgh steelworkers. The effect on the Pirates was a steady drop in attendance from 1,705,828 in 1971 to 964,106 in 1978, the first year attendance fell under 1 million at Three Rivers.

Before the beginning of the 1977 season, Joe L. Brown added to the losses in the Pirates organization by announcing his retirement as general manager. He was replaced by Harding Peterson, the organization's minor-league director and head of scouting. Peterson's first major decision was to hire Chuck Tanner, a native of New Castle, Pennsylvania, just 45 miles from Pittsburgh. Peterson had to trade popular catcher Manny Sanguillen to the Oakland A's to get Tanner, who was under contract to Charlie O. Finley. To replace free agent Richie Hebner, another popular player from the 1971 world-championship team, Peterson traded once again with Oakland, this time giving up six more players for Phil Garner.

Though the Pirates were going through a period of transition in which they traded Richie Zisk and Al Oliver before losing them to free agency, the club finished a strong second to the Phillies in 1977 and 1978. Important to the team's success was the emergence of Dave Parker, who won the NL batting title in 1977 and earned NL MVP honors the following year. Even more critical was the leadership and performance of veteran Willie Stargell, who was awarded the NL's Comeback Player of the Year Award in 1978. Going into the 1979 season, the Pirates, determined to field a championship team, signed Dave Parker to a five-year, $7 million contract, the largest in team history. The organization failed in its bid to sign free agent Pete Rose, but Peterson made early-season trades for Tim Foli and Bill Madlock that paved the way for a return to the World Series.

In 1979, the Pirates closed out the decade by winning the division (98–64) and going on to capture their second world championship of the 1970s. The team, as usual, relied on strong offense and decent pitching—six hurlers had from 10 to 14 wins. As was the case in 1971, the season and the postseason became the personal showcase for a Pirate superstar. Willie Stargell, affectionately known as "Pops," was the emotional leader and driving force for a ball club that adopted Sister Sledge's "We Are Family" for its theme song. He was named the cowinner of the NL MVP Award with Keith Hernandez of the St. Louis Cardinals and went on to win the MVP in both the playoff sweep over the Cincinnati Reds and the World Series victory over the Baltimore Orioles. The 1979 World Series was also noteworthy because, for the second time in club history, the Pirates rallied from a three-games-to-one deficit to win the championship, including the last two games in Baltimore. Strong pitching performances by Jim Rooker, Bert Blyleven, and John Candelaria helped the Pirates tie the series, and Willie Stargell's two-run homer sparked a 4–1 win in the seventh game in Baltimore. Kent Tekulve, the all-time Pirates save leader, got off to a rocky start, but he saved three games in the World Series, including game seven. With the Pirates victory, the franchise finished the decade with six division titles, two NL pennants, and two World Series crowns.

THE TROUBLED EIGHTIES

Buoyed by a bounce in attendance to 1,435,454 in 1979 (only 10th best in the NL) and the spirit of family, the Pirates' promotion for 1980 was an optimistic "Two in a Row and Two Million Fans," but with an aging Stargell struggling with injuries, the ball club fell short on both counts. Attendance increased to 1,646,757, but the team finished a disappointing third. With Stargell playing very little and a pitching staff depleted by injuries and trades, the Pirates continued to struggle in 1981 and the strike-shortened 1982 season, finishing fourth both years. With Bill Madlock winning his fourth batting title and second-year players Tony Pena and Johnny Ray having solid years, the team did bounce back to second place in 1983, but fell into last place for the next three years. With the Pirates playing so poorly, attendance also suffered, dropping, by 1985, to 735,900, the lowest full-season figure since 1955. Facing a financial crisis, the Galbreath family, after nearly 40 years of ownership, finally decided to sell the Pirates. For the past decade they had been subsidizing the franchise with profits from their real-estate development firm and thoroughbred racing stable. When there were no local buyers, they threatened to move the franchise, on the verge of its centennial year in the NL, to another city.

The declining attendance was tied to the prevailing economic slump in the region and to the declining quality of the team, which could not afford to compete in the free-agency market. A national recession turned into a rust-belt depression in Pittsburgh. The city, with more than 40 major steel mills and industrial plants closing, lost over 130,000 jobs. An estimated 176,000 people left the area, including 14 percent of its young. The city itself suffered a population decrease of 10 percent. The Pirates also faced continuing financial problems with Three Rivers and had to sue the city to take over its maintenance because they were losing so much money. Pirate fans, never happy with Three Rivers, were even more reluctant to spend their money attending games because of their growing perception, fueled by million-dollar free-agent signings and a drug scandal involving several players, including Dave Parker, that the current generation of ballplayers were spoiled and corrupt. Matters reached a low point when the employee hired to dress as the Pirate mascot was charged with distributing drugs in the Pirate locker room.

Pittsburgh's baseball franchise was saved from becoming the New Orleans Pirates by the Pittsburgh Associates, a group of nine corporations, including Fortune 500 firms Alcoa and PPG; one educational institution, Carnegie Mellon; and three private investors. With strong leadership from popular mayor Richard Caliguiri, who also provided $20 million in loans, the new ownership coalition purchased the franchise from the Galbreath family for $21.8 million. The most prominent business partners included Malcolm Prine, CEO of Ryan Homes; Carl Barger, managing partner of a Pittsburgh law firm; Douglas Danforth, CEO of Westinghouse Electric; and Vincent Sarni, retired CEO of PPG. Prine was elected the new president of the franchise, but stepped down in 1988. Carl Barger became the new president, with Danforth replacing Barger as chairman of the board. When Barger left in 1991 to head the new Florida Marlins franchise, Mark Sauer, a former St. Louis Cardinals executive, was appointed president, with Vincent Sarni taking over as board chairman.

The Pittsburgh Associates' first challenge was to find a replacement for Joe L. Brown, who had agreed to serve as temporary general manager in 1985 after Harding Peterson was fired, but was now a member of the new ownership group. They selected Syd Thrift, who was best known as the founding director of the Kansas City Royals' Baseball Academy. Thrift's first task was to find a replacement for Chuck Tanner as Pirates manager. He hired Jim Leyland, a highly successful minor-league manager and a coach for Tony LaRussa and the Chicago White Sox. With new owners and a new management team, attendance increased slightly to over 1 million fans in 1986, despite another sixth-place finish. After climbing into a tie for fourth in 1987, the Pirates, sparked by the hitting of outfielders Bobby Bonilla, Andy Van Slyke, and Barry Bonds and the pitching of Doug Drabek, surged into second place in 1988 as a record-breaking 1,866,713 fans came out to Three Rivers Stadium, a remarkable attendance increase of over 1 million in just three years. This occurred despite the team's salary of just $7,627,500, 22nd out of 26 teams.

Jim Leyland was named NL Manager of the Year in 1988, but much of the Pirates' success was attributed to Syd Thrift's trades for future All-Stars Drabek, Van Slyke, and Bonilla and the development of young talent like Barry Bonds and John Smiley. Despite Thrift's success as general manager, he was constantly embroiled in disputes with ownership over control of the ball club. A power struggle led to the resignation of Pirates president Malcolm Prine in 1988, but Thrift himself was fired at the end of the season and replaced by assistant general manager Larry Doughty, a former director of scouting for the Cincinnati Reds.

THE UNCERTAIN NINETIES

After the Pirates dropped back into fifth place in 1989, they went on to win the NL East in 1990 (95–67) with pretty much the same cast. Doug Drabek's 22–6 record and 2.72 ERA earned him the Cy Young Award. Barry Bonds won the MVP Award with 33 homers, 114 RBIs, and a league-leading .565 slugging percentage. Bobby Bonilla had 32 homers and 120 RBIs. Jim Leyland collected his second NL Manager of the Year Award. Attendance, for the first time in franchise history, went over 2 million. The Pirates, however, ended the year in disappointment, losing the playoffs in six games to the Cincinnati Reds. Despite the success on the field, the Pirates were valued at just $82 million, 20th of all major-league teams, and fell to the bottom in 1994 at $70 million.

In 1991, after a much-publicized spring-training confrontation between Jim Leyland and Barry Bonds, the Pirates went on to win their second straight division title, but lost again in the playoffs, this time in seven games to the Atlanta Braves. In 1992, after new president Mark Sauer appointed ex-Cardinal Ted Simmons to replace Larry Doughty as general manager, the Pirates, despite the loss of Bobby Bonilla to free agency, won their third consecutive division title, but suffered a devastating loss in the playoffs when the Atlanta Braves scored three runs in the bottom of the ninth to defeat the Pirates 3–2 in the seventh and deciding game. The Braves scored the tying and winning runs on Francisco Cabrera's two out, bases loaded single. For Pirate fans, watching ex-Pirate Sid Bream scoring the winning run was a bitter moment, rivaling Gabby Hartnett's infamous "homer in the gloaming."

In 1993, with the loss of Barry Bonds and Doug Drabek to free agency, the Pirates suffered their first losing season of the 1990s after averaging better than 96 wins from 1990 to 1992. It was the beginning of a record string of consecutive losing seasons that would last through the rest of the decade and into the new century. The Pirates also lost their general manager when Ted Simmons, after a suffering a mild heart attack, resigned in June and was replaced by his assistant, Cam Bonifay. The only highlights of the 1994 season were the All-Star Game played at Three Rivers Stadium before a record 59,568 fans and the unveiling of a $300,000 statue a few days earlier honoring the great Roberto Clemente. The Pirates continued to struggle during a season that ended prematurely on August 12 with a baseball strike, the third work stoppage since 1972, that eventually led to the cancellation of the World Series.

After threatening to use replacements, baseball's owners accepted the players' offer to play the 1995 season without a collective bargaining agreement. The delayed 1995 season finally began on April 26. Playing in the newly formed Central Division, the Pirates opened the season at Three Rivers to protests and disruptions from the fans, unhappy with the players' strike. By the end of the season, the Pirates were mired in last place, attendance had dropped below 1 million for the first time since 1985, and the Pirates, for the second time in 10 years, were up for sale. The Pittsburgh Associates had lost more than $22 million and, after a decade of mounting debt, were ready to rid themselves of the franchise. When John Rigas, owner of Adelphia Cable, failed in a bid to purchase the team and keep it in Pittsburgh, the Pirates were, once again, on the brink of moving to another city. At the Pirates' last home game of the season, many of the 11,190 fans in attendance believed that, after 109 years of NL baseball, the ball club had played its final game in Pittsburgh.

On February 14, 1996, the franchise was rescued at the final deadline for keeping the team in Pittsburgh by California-based Kevin McClatchy, whose family had founded the *Sacramento Bee* in 1857. The 34-year-old McClatchy, after failing in a bid for the Oakland A's, forged a limited partnership of about 30 business leaders and individuals, ranging from Heinz CEO Anthony O'Reilly to Indy car team owner Chip Garnassi, and convinced many of the members of the Pittsburgh Associates to stay on as limited partners. Though McClatchy's own investment was only $8 million of the nearly $90 million needed to purchase the franchise, he became the CEO and youngest owner of a major-league team.

Though first hailed as a baseball savior, McClatchy ran into criticism in his initial season when, faced with increasing debt and a losing ball club, he started trading his major-league veterans for minor-league prospects to cut the franchise's payroll. When he agreed to release popular manager Jim Leyland from his contract at the end of the season, Pirate fans and sportswriters suspected that McClatchy was deliberately ruining the team so that he could move it to another city, despite McClatchy's claims to the contrary. Leyland had managed 11 years in Pittsburgh, compiling a .496 record. In his last season, the Pirates finished in last place, with a payroll barely over $9 million, $1 million less than the salary of Cleveland Indians star Albert Belle. In 1997 they finished the season under .500 at 79–83, but improved to second place in the Central Division standings. Former White Sox manager Gene Lamont, hired to replace Jim Leyland, finished second in the balloting for NL Manager of the Year Award, and general manager Cam Bonifay was named NL Executive of the Year. *Baseball America* selected Pittsburgh's minor-league system as the best in baseball, and *USA Today* named the front office as baseball's best organization.

After the heady performance of 1997, the Pirates fell back into last place in 1998, but the year, while disappointing on the field, proved exciting off the field. When McClatchy and his partners bought the team, McClatchy had promised to keep the franchise in Pittsburgh if financing for a new ballpark was in place in three years and the ballpark constructed by 2001. Mayor Tom Murphy established the Forbes Field II Task Force to consider the project and recommended a north-side site one block from Three Rivers as the best location. It would be part of an $803 million package that also funded a new Steelers Stadium, retired the debt on Three Rivers and demolished the stadium, expanded the Convention Center, and constructed a new Pittsburgh Development Center. But when voters in Allegheny and the 10 counties surrounding Pittsburgh rejected a referendum in November 1997 to fund a new facility for the Pirates with a 0.5 percent sales-tax increase, local politicians and civic leaders, concerned about the loss to Pittsburgh and the surrounding area in revenue, jobs, and prestige, initiated "Plan B" in March 1998 to save the project. Four months later, the Regional Asset District Board committed $13.4 million a year for the next 30 years for the new ballpark, and state legislators provided $150 million in funding. The board had originally opposed the plan, but a Republican county commissioner replaced a foe of the park with a supporter and rammed it through. The Pirates agreed to put up $14 million, and were expected to cover operating costs as long as they received the revenues from concessions and advertising. Additional funding came from PNC Bank Corporation, which paid $30 million for naming rights through 2020. Pittsburgh fans were disappointed. Some wanted to name the field "Jammed Down the Taxpayers' Throat Park," although most were hoping to name it for Roberto Clemente.

After rejecting several locations around the city, the Pirates organization, wanting to keep the new ballpark accessible from downtown Pittsburgh, selected a site on the north shore of the Allegheny River, just across the downtown's Sixth Street Bridge and near Three Rivers Stadium. Ground-breaking ceremonies, with Governor Tom Ridge, Mayor Tom Murphy, and Commissioner Bud Selig participating, were held on April 7, 1999. They also attended a ceremony renaming the Sixth Street Bridge in honor of Roberto Clemente.

The contract for building PNC Park was awarded to HOK Sport of Kansas City, Missouri, at a projected cost of $216 million. The actual cost was $237 million for construction plus $25 million for the site. HOK Sport had already designed several new ballparks, including Camden Yards in Baltimore and Jacobs Field in Cleveland. After meeting with Pirate officials, David Greusel, the lead designer for the project, came up with a concept that combined the traditional look of Forbes Field, the coziness of Wrigley Field, and the innovations of Camden Yards. The result was a two-tiered, opened-ended design that would bring fans closer to the playing field (two-thirds of the seats are at field level, and as close as 45 feet to the baselines) and at the same time yield a panoramic view of the downtown Pittsburgh skyline. The ballpark itself would be constructed out of yellow limestone and blue steel and feature light standards similar to those at Forbes Field. The playing field would be asymmetrical and feature natural grass. It promised, with its spectacular design and setting, to be one of the most beautiful ballparks in baseball.

As construction began on PNC Park, the Pirates suffered through another losing season in 1999, but climbed in the standings to third place. In 2000, the Pirates began the new century with their eighth consecutive losing season and dropped to fifth place, but because it was the team's last year in Three Rivers Stadium, attendance increased to 1,748,908. On October 1, 2000, at the last game played at Three Rivers, Pirate fans set a regular-season attendance record of 55,532 as the Pirates lost to the Cubs 10–9. After the game, a seriously ill Willie Stargell walked to the mound and threw the last pitch at Three Rivers. A few days earlier, plans had been announced for a statue of Stargell, to be unveiled on Opening Day at PNC Park. After the season was over, the Pirates front office also announced the firing of Gene Lamont and replaced him with Lloyd McClendon, the Pirates' hitting coach. The team's value that year reached $211 million, a one-third increase over the prior year, probably in anticipation of the new park.

The grand opening of PNC Park on April 9, 2001, became a bittersweet moment for Pittsburgh fans when Willie Stargell died just hours before the opening game. Stargell's death and the Pirates' 8–2 loss to the Cincinnati Reds were harbingers for a season in which the ball club would lose 100 games for the first time since 1985 and fall into last place. By midseason general manager Cam Bonifay was fired and replaced by Marlins assistant general manager Dave Littlefield. Despite the Pirates' struggles, fans flocked to the 38,000-seat PNC Park, second smallest in the majors after Fenway Park. The Pirates had 19 sellouts during the season and set an attendance record of 2,436,139. During the 2001 season, Pirate fans were also thrilled by the induction of Bill Mazeroski into the Hall of Fame, after years of delay.

The construction of PNC Park, regarded by many as one of the most beautiful ballparks in America, brought a secure future to major-league baseball in Pittsburgh, but not necessarily a winning future. The team has not had a winning season since 1992. The Pirates' ninth consecutive losing season in 2001 tied a team record dating back to the 1950s, and losing seasons from 2002 through 2005 broke and extended that record. Since PNC opened, attendance consistently declined until 2005, when it rose to 1,817,245. There were, however, reminders of the franchise's winning tradition beyond the team uniforms modeled after the 1960 Pirates. On June 25, 2002, the Pirates won their 9,000th game in franchise history, becoming only the fourth major-league team to reach that figure. In June 2003, the Pirates played an interleague series with the Boston Red Sox, marking the centennial of the first World Series played between the two teams. At the start of the 2005 season, *Forbes* reported the team was worth $218 million, 23rd in major league baseball, and that the team was 28th in salaries at $38.1 million, down from $54.8 million in 2003.

THE FUTURE

The challenge for the Pirates franchise 100 years after the team played in the first World Series is as much about economics as it is about talent. To become successful once again, the Pirates have to overcome the reality of being a small-market ball club in an unbalanced economic system that, with free agency, without a salary cap, and with only modest revenue sharing, favors large-market teams. It also has to market itself in a city that, while becoming one of the most attractive and livable in America, has lost many of its industries and suffered a major decline in population. Once one of the largest American cities because of its thriving steel industry, Pittsburgh suffered a population loss from 676,806 in 1950 to 334,563 in 2000. From 1990 to 2003, Pittsburgh's population fell 12 percent. Pittsburgh dropped to 54th place among America's major cities. This combined with the poor quality of the team resulted in an attendance of only 1.58 million in 2004, the lowest of any NL team other than the hapless Montreal Expos.

The situation for the Pirates, however, is far from hopeless. To overcome its small-market handicap and take advantage of its attractive new ballpark, the franchise has stressed the development of its farm system, especially its young pitching. It has also traded veterans, as they approach free agency, for younger talent and used their own modest free-agent signings to fill gaps until the best of their minor-league prospects are ready to play in the majors. Without a major change in baseball economics, the Pirates, like other small-market franchises, will have to work at a disadvantage to field a competitive team, but as the success of other small-market teams has shown, the Pirates, with an influx of young talent and judicious use of resources, can once again become a first-division team in Barney Dreyfuss's "first-division city."

NOTABLE ACHIEVEMENTS

Most Valuable Players

Year	Name	Position
1960	Dick Groat	SS
1966	Roberto Clemente	OF
1978	Dave Parker	OF
1979	Willie Stargell	1B
1990	Barry Bonds	OF
1992	Barry Bonds	OF

Cy Young Winners

Year	Name	Position
1960	Vern Law	RHP
1990	Doug Drabek	RHP

Rookies of the Year

Year	Name	Position
2004	Jason Bay	OF

Batting Champions

Year	Name	#
1900	Honus Wagner	.381
1902	Ginger Beaumont	.357
1903	Honus Wagner	.355
1904	Honus Wagner	.349
1906	Honus Wagner	.339
1907	Honus Wagner	.350
1908	Honus Wagner	.354
1909	Honus Wagner	.339
1911	Honus Wagner	.334
1927	Paul Waner	.380
1934	Paul Waner	.362
1935	Arky Vaughan	.385
1936	Paul Waner	.373
1940	Debs Garms	.355
1960	Dick Groat	.325
1961	Roberto Clemente	.351
1964	Roberto Clemente	.339
1965	Roberto Clemente	.329
1966	Matty Alou	.342
1967	Roberto Clemente	.357
1977	Dave Parker	.338
1978	Dave Parker	.334
1981	Bill Madlock	.341
1983	Bill Madlock	.323

Home-Run Champions

Year	Name	#
1902	Tommy Leach	6
1946	Ralph Kiner	23
1947	Ralph Kiner	51
1948	Ralph Kiner	40
1949	Ralph Kiner	54
1950	Ralph Kiner	47
1951	Ralph Kiner	42
1952	Ralph Kiner	37
1971	Willie Stargell	48
1973	Willie Stargell	44

ERA Champions

Year	Name	#
1900	Rube Waddell	2.37
1901	Jesse Tannehill	2.18
1903	Sam Leever	2.06
1926	Ray Kremer	2.61
1927	Ray Kremer	2.47
1935	Cy Blanton	2.59
1955	Bob Friend	2.84
1977	John Candelaria	2.34

Strikeout Champions

Year	Name	#
1900	Rube Waddell	130
1945	Preacher Roe	148
1964	Bob Veale	250

No-Hitters

Name	Date
Nick Maddox	09/20/1907
Cliff Chambers	05/06/1951
Bob Moose	09/20/1969
Dock Ellis	06/12/1970
John Candelaria	08/09/1976

POSTSEASON APPEARANCES

NL East Division Titles

Year	Record	Manager
1970	89–73	Danny Murtaugh
1971	97–65	Danny Murtaugh
1972	96–59	Bill Virdon
1974	88–74	Danny Murtaugh
1975	92–69	Danny Murtaugh
1979	98–63	Chuck Tanner
1990	95–67	Jim Leyland
1991	98–64	Jim Leyland
1992	96–66	Jim Leyland

NL Pennants

Year	Record	Manager
1901	90–49	Fred Clarke
1902	103–36	Fred Clarke
1903	91–49	Fred Clarke
1909	110–42	Fred Clarke
1925	95–58	Bill McKechnie
1927	94–60	Donie Bush
1960	95–59	Danny Murtaugh
1971	97–65	Danny Murtaugh
1979	98–64	Chuck Tanner

World Championships

Year	Opponent	MVP
1909	Detroit	
1925	Washington	
1960	New York	
1971	Baltimore	Roberto Clemente
1979	Baltimore	Willie Stargell

MANAGERS

2006–	Jim Tracy
2001–2005	Lloyd McClendon
1997–2000	Gene Lamont
1986–1996	Jim Leyland
1977–1985	Chuck Tanner
1973–1976	Danny Murtaugh
1972–1973	Bill Virdon
1970–1971	Danny Murtaugh
1969	Alex Grammas
1968–1969	Larry Shepard
1967	Danny Murtaugh
1965–1967	Harry Walker
1957–1964	Danny Murtaugh
1956–1957	Bobby Bragan
1953–1955	Fred Haney
1948–1952	Billy Meyer
1947	Bill Burwell
1947	Billy Herman
1946	Spud Davis
1940–1946	Frankie Frisch
1934–1939	Pie Traynor

1932–1934	George Gibson
1929–1931	Jewel Ens
1927–1929	Donie Bush
1922–1926	Bill McKechnie
1920–1922	George Gibson
1917–1919	Hugo Bezdek
1917	Honus Wagner
1916–1917	Nixey Callahan
1900–1915	Fred Clarke
1899	Patsy Donovan
1898–1899	Bill Watkins
1897	Patsy Donovan
1894–1896	Connie Mack
1892–1894	Al Buckenberger
1892	Tom Burns
1891	Bill McGunnigle
1891	Ned Hanlon
1890	Guy Hecker
1889	Fred Dunlap
1884–1889	Horace Phillips
1884	George Creamer
1884	Joe Battin
1884	Bob Ferguson
1884	Denny McNight
1883	Joe Battin
1883	Ormond Butler
1882–1883	Al Pratt

Team Records by Individual Players

Batting Leaders

	Single Season			Career		
	Name		Year	Name		Plate Appearances
Batting average	Arky Vaughn	.385	1935	Paul Waner	.340	9,532
On-base %	Aarky Vaughn	.491	1935	Brian Giles	.426	3,114
Slugging %	Ralph Kiner	.658	1949	Brian Giles	.592	3,114
OPS	Arky Vaughn	1.098	1935	Brian Giles	1.018	3,114
Games	Bill Mazeroski	163	1967	Honus Wagner	2,433	10,220
At bats	Matty Alou	698	1969	Roberto Clemente	9,454	10,212
Runs	Jake Stenzel	148	1894	Honus Wagner	1,521	10,220

(Continued)

Batting Leaders (Continued)

	Single Season			**Career**		
	Name		Year	Name		Plate Appearances
Hits	Paul Waner	237	1927	Roberto Clemente	3,000	10,212
Total bases	Kiki Cuyler	369	1925	Roberto Clemente	4,492	10,212
Doubles	Paul Waner	62	1932	Paul Waner	558	9,532
Triples	Chief Wilson	36	1912	Honus Wagner	232	10,220
Home runs	Ralph Kiner	54	1949	Willie Stargell	475	9,026
RbIs	Ralph Waner	131	1927	Willie Stargell	1,540	9,026
Walks	Ralph Kiner	137	1951	Willie Stargell	937	9,026
Strikeouts	Craig Wilson	169	2004	Willie Stargell	1,936	9,026
Stolen bases	Omar Moreno	96	1980	Max Carey	688	9,654
Extra-base hits	Willie Stargell	90	1973	Willie Stargell	953	9,026
Times on base	Arky Vaughn	313	1936	Honus Wagner	3,951	10,220

Pitching Leaders

	Single Season			**Career**		
	Name		Year	Name		Innings pitched
ERA	Denny Driscoll	1.21	1882	Vic Willis	2.08	1,209
Wins	Ed Morris	41	1886	Wilbur Cooper	202	3,199
Won-loss %	Elroy Face	.947	1959	Jesse Tennehill	.667	1,499
Hits/9 IP	Al Mamaux	6.51	1915	Nick Maddox	7.24	605.3
Walks/9 IP	Denny Driscoll	0.54	1882	Denny Driscoll	0.85	537.3
Strikeouts	Ed Morris	326	1886	Bob Friend	1,682	3,480.3
Strikeouts/9 IP	Oliver Perez	10.97	2004	Bob Veale	7.96	1,868.7
Games	Kent Tekulve	94	1979	Elroy Face	802	1,314.7
Saves	Matt Williams	46	2002	Elroy Face	188	1,314.7
Innings	Ed Morris	581	1885	Bob Friend	3,480.3	3,480.3
Starts	Ed Morris	63	1885	Bob Friend	4,77	3,480.3
Complete games	Ed Morris	63	1885	Ed Morris	297	2,678
Shutouts	Ed Morris	12	1886	Babe Adams	44	2,991.3

Source: Drawn from data in "Pittsburgh Pirates Batting Leaders (seasonal and career)." http://baseball-reference.com/ teams/PIT/leaders_bat.shtml; "Pittsburgh Pirates Pitching Leaders (seasonal and career)." http://baseball-reference. com/teams/PIT/leaders_pitch.shtml.

BIBLIOGRAPHY

Alexander, Charles C. *Breaking the Slump: Baseball in the Depression Era.* New York: Columbia University Press, 2002.

DeValaria, Dennis, and Jeanne Burke DeValaria. *Honus Wagner: A Biography.* New York: Henry Holt, 1995.

Finoli, David, and Bill Ranier. *The Pittsburgh Pirates Encyclopedia.* Urbana, IL: Sports Publishing, 2003.

Goldstein, Warren. *Playing for Keeps: A History of Early Baseball.* Ithaca, NY: Cornell University Press 1989.

Graham, Laurie. *Singing the City.* Pittsburgh: University of Pittsburgh Press, 1998.

Kiner, Ralph, with Danny Peary. *Baseball Forever: Reflections on Sixty Years in the Game.* Chicago: Triumph Books, 2004.

Lieb, Frederick J. *The Pittsburgh Pirates.* New York: G. P. Putnam's Sons, 1948.

Lorant, Stefan. *Pittsburgh: The Story of an American City.* Lenox, MA: Authors Edition, 1975.

Masur, Louis P. *Autumn's Glory: Baseball's First World Series.* New York: Hill and Wang, 2003.

McCollister, John. *The Bucs! The Story of the Pittsburgh Pirates.* Lenexa, KS: Addax Publishing, 1998.

O'Toole, Andrew. *Branch Rickey in Pittsburgh.* Jefferson, NC: McFarland, 2000.

Peterson, Richard. *The Pirates Reader.* Pittsburgh: University of Pittsburgh Press, 2003.

Riess, Steven A. *Touching Base: Professional Baseball and American Culture in the Progressive Era.* Rev. ed. Urbana, IL: University of Illinois Press, 1999.

Roberts, Randy, ed. *Pittsburgh Sports: Stories from the Steel City.* Pittsburgh: University of Pittsburgh Press, 2000.

Spink, Alfred H. *The National Game.* St. Louis: National Game Publishing Company, 1911.

Toker, Franklin. *Pittsburgh: An Urban Portrait.* University Park: Pennsylvania State University Press, 1986.

Wagenheim, Kal. *Clemente!* New York: Praeger, 1973.

White, G. Edward. *Creating the National Pastime: Baseball Transforms Itself, 1900–1953.* Princeton, NJ: Princeton University Press, 1996.

13

San Diego Padres

Sarah Trembanis

The San Diego Padres began their existence as a minor-league team in the Triple-A Pacific Coast League. Previously the Hollywood Stars, the team was purchased by Bill Lane in 1936 and moved to San Diego. He renamed the club in honor of Junipero Sera, who had founded the first California mission in the sixteenth century. The minor-league Padres competed downtown at WPA-funded Lane Field until 1957, when they moved to 8,200-seat Westgate Park.

San Diego's population growth to nearly 700,000 residents in 1970 (making it the second-largest Californian city), coupled with the increasing on-the-field success of the Padres, who won PCL pennants in 1962, 1964, and 1967, inspired owner C. Arnholt Smith to petition the National League to grant him franchise rights in San Diego. Smith, a bank and business owner, had purchased the Padres in 1955. Fully aware that San Diego required a major-league-capacity stadium in order to win over NL officials, Smith began to court civic support for a bond to cover construction costs. Smith found assistance from sportswriter Jack Murphy, who conducted a large public campaign to establish civic support for a new ballpark. In 1965, as a result of Murphy's efforts, 72 percent of San Diego voters passed a bond issue guaranteeing $27.75 million for the stadium construction fund. This money was used to construct 50,000-seat San Diego Stadium, which hosted the San Diego Chargers during the football season and was the home field for the Padres' last minor-league season in 1968.

The stadium's location reflected the shifting population growth of San Diego and a general trend within baseball. San Diego Stadium was built in Mission Valley, a largely undeveloped area of San Diego that the Padres obtained cheaply, yet had excellent potential as a sports facility because it was conve nient to three interstate highways that made it very accessible to fans. Moreover, construction reflected the contemporary emphasis on progress with little concern for environmental consequences, as engineers rerouted the San Diego River to build on the 166-acre site.

Smith was not wealthy enough to secure a major-league franchise and had to borrow 90 percent of the $10.2 million franchise fee from outside sources. His new partner in seeking a franchise was Emil J. "Buzzie" Bavasi, a former Dodgers official with more than 25 years' major-league experience. Bavasi, with the assistance of Dodgers owner Walter O'Malley, purchased a one-third share in the Padres and became club president. The fee entitled the club to select 30 mediocre players in the expansion draft.

San Diego in the late 1960s was a strong candidate for a major-league franchise. The metropolis had a growing population and a supportive minor-league fan base as well as ideal weather conditions for baseball. Land values boomed in San Diego County in the 1960s and 1970s as residents pushed the boundaries of the metropolitan area, establishing strapping suburbs. Additionally, the Padres had secured a stadium that neither Seattle nor Montreal, the two other franchise candidates, could match. Moreover, the city had a strong partnership bidding for the franchise, with the backing of the powerful Dodgers magnate. Other team owners believed Smith was financially stable, having secured the franchise fee, and knew Bavasi as a savvy baseball man. *Sports Illustrated* described Bavasi as "one of the few men in the world tricky enough to enter a revolving door behind you and come out ahead." On May 27, 1968, the Padres and the Montreal Expos were awarded franchises.

Despite the faith of the NL owners, Smith's debt placed the fledgling franchise on the brink of bankruptcy from the beginning. The Padres were immediately faced with a large payment on their debt, making it almost impossible for the management to assemble a competitive team. Additionally, the Padres would not share national television revenue for three years as part of the franchise agreement. Without a large pool of capital, the Padres could not pursue high-salaried veterans.

Adding greatly to the franchise's underlying financial problems were bureaucratic mishaps and weak first-year attendance. The Padres suffered myriad difficulties establishing themselves, enduring two months without a mail slot because of city paperwork, waiting a full month to get a phone number, and losing their only copy of home-ticket proofs in a delivery-truck accident. The beginning of the season revealed a more fundamental problem. Despite an opening three-game sweep of the Houston Astros, the Padres failed to attract many fans, drawing only about 613,000—well below the projected attendance of 800,000. The paltry attendance was a result of several factors. First, San Diego is geographically constricted, with an ocean to the west, a desert to the east, Mexico to the south, and Los Angeles, home of the Dodgers, to the north. Moreover, most residents had already adopted the Dodgers as their unofficial hometown team and were unwilling to switch allegiance. The Padres also suffered from competition with the many leisure-time activities available to its residents. Local citizens had their choice of outdoor recreations and had to be drawn into the baseball stadium. Adding to attendance woes was an imbalanced schedule with many home games at the end of the season to take advantage of the warm fall weather. The strategy initially seemed beneficial, but with the Padres firmly entrenched in last place in the NL's Western Division, few fans attended.

The Padres attempted to take advantage of the heavy local Dodgers interest through Bavasi's connections. Many of the main team officials had strong Dodger ties. Preston Gomez, a Dodgers coach, was appointed as manager, and former Dodgers superstar Duke Snider broadcast Padres games. These hirings failed to bring about strong attendance numbers or a competitive team. Due to their poor performance, the Padres failed to attract crowds even for home games against the beloved Dodgers. During their first five years, the Padres finished last in their division, averaging over 100 losses a season and never drawing more than 645,000 fans, the lowest in the NL.

In May 1973, the public finally became aware of the Padres' perilous finances when the *San Diego Union* exposed the team's financial woes and Smith's intent to sell the team, as he was deeply in debt. While Smith was paying $700,000 in annual loan interest, the Padres were earning approximately $50,000 each year, leaving a substantial shortfall. The Padres' economic situation was so dire that by June, Smith was authorizing trades just to acquire enough money to satisfy his payroll.

At this point, the Padres were in dire need of an owner with deep pockets. The first offer came from an investment group desperate to return baseball to Washington, DC. Their spokesman, Joseph Danzansky, offered Smith a down payment of $100,000 and pledged to negotiate a lease with RFK Stadium within 45 days, and Smith agreed to consult Danzansky on all personnel decisions. At this point, the Padres' relocation seemed inevitable, merely requiring NL approval. Topps Baseball Cards even released the 1974 series with the Padres identified as the Washington, DC, club.

Two unforeseen complications arose, namely O'Malley's opposition to the move and lawsuits filed by the city of San Diego. O'Malley wanted to keep a franchise in San Diego because it benefited his club in nearby Los Angeles. This position was directly opposite Commissioner Bowie Kuhn's, who had strong Washington ties and favored a move to the capital. San Diego's attorney initiated lawsuits claiming breach of contract, declaring the move would prematurely break the 20-year lease between the team and the city-owned stadium, and sought $84 million in damages. The city's suits were unsuccessful in court, but city attorney John Witt pursued $12 million in damages for breach of contract. Because of O'Malley's opposition and potential legal action, NL owners encouraged Smith to find a buyer willing to keep the Padres in San Diego.

In October 1973, Smith faced even more substantial problems. One of his major holdings, the U.S. National Bank of San Diego, was found to be insolvent, and the Internal Revenue Service demanded $22.8 million in back taxes. Then the Securities and Exchange Commission investigated Smith on charges of fraud.

Fortunately for the Padres and Smith, a new buyer came to the forefront. Ray Kroc, the majority shareholder in McDonald's and a longtime Cubs fan, offered to purchase the team. Kroc, worth $500 million, offered Smith $12 million for the Padres and agreed to keep the team in San Diego. City officials offered Kroc certain concessions that gave the Padres a greater share of the parking and concessions revenues, plus a subsidy for stadium maintenance. In return, the new owner agreed to pay a substantial relocation fee if the Padres left. Kroc signed a lease ensuring the Padres would remain in San Diego until at least 1980, and maintained continuity by retaining Bavasi as co-owner and general manager. League owners quickly approved the deal.

The close call with relocation and Kroc's professed enthusiasm reinvigorated local fans, and attendance quickly improved. The Padres attracted 39,000 fans for their 1974 home opener and drew over a million fans during the season. Immediately, Kroc went after well-known veteran players to improve the quality of play and offered more fan promotions to increase attendance. Morale sharply improved among players, who appreciated such upgrades as a new airplane for road trips and a lounge for use by the Padres and their families. Kroc also managed to cross-promote his primary business, making McDonald's the new sponsor for Bat Night. Moreover, Kroc's enthusiasm for his team endeared him to San Diego fans.

However, Kroc soon committed a blunder that would briefly alienate the players. During Kroc's first game, the Padres trailed the Astros 9–2 due to sloppy playing. Kroc addressed the crowd of more than 39,000 in the eighth inning, saying, "Ladies and gentlemen, I suffer with you." After being briefly interrupted by a streaker, Kroc then remarked, "I've never seen such stupid ball playing in my life."

During his tenure as club owner, Kroc won over his players as well as the fans through various strategic improvements. Trading on the success of his commercial mascot, Ronald McDonald, Kroc encouraged the antics of one of the more notorious mascots in baseball, the San Diego Chicken, who enthralled fans and created a more family-friendly atmosphere at San Diego Stadium. Having developed carefully coordinating uniforms for his McDonald's employees, Kroc also improved the aesthetics of the Padres uniforms, replacing the garish yellow home uniform with a more traditional white one. Kroc also increased the number of promotions the club staged, drawing fans to the stadium and to their radios. Players made appearances at local McDonald's to bring further publicity to the club and Kroc's fast-food empire. These changes had financial and competitive benefits. In 1974, the Padres registered their first profitable season. On-the-field success took longer. Even with newly acquired veterans Matty Alou and Willie McCovey, the Padres did not achieve a winning season until 1978.

During the latter half of the 1970s, the Padres registered a greater number of victories and also witnessed the emergence of their first superstar, Dave Winfield, a San Diego outfielder from 1973 to 1980, a hot prospect when drafted in 1973 out of the University of Minnesota. Bypassing the minor leagues, Winfield joined the club in June and quickly made his presence known, batting .277 as a rookie. As a Padre, he annually was one of the club's top offensive players. In 1976, despite a stint on the disabled list, Winfield led the team in five offensive categories. Winfield also brought increased national attention to the Padres, contending for MVP in 1979, receiving the second-most votes for the All-Star Game, and receiving a Gold Glove Award. In 2001, Winfield became the first player to enter the Hall of Fame as a Padre.

In many ways, Kroc proved to be the right owner at the right time. An inherently conservative public figure and financial booster for Nixon in 1972, Kroc fit the political climate of the 1970s and 1980s. Kroc and his Padres took advantage of the increased connection of society and baseball after 1975. With Vietnam and most student protests at an end, baseball seemed less frivolous and more acceptable. In addition, the continual shifting of baseball franchises had abated by the mid-1970s, and fans felt more committed to their hometown teams. Locally, San Diego's population continued to rise, increasing almost 40 percent during the 1970s, while highway development in the San Diego area also expanded, which helped the Padres' attendance climb.

In 1977 Buzzie Bavasi, co-owner and general manager since their inception as a major-league franchise, left his positions as a result of his contentious relationship with Ray's wife, Joan Kroc. His replacement, Bob Fontaine, used an increased budget to acquire new players. Fontaine added veteran pitcher Gaylord Perry and rookie sensation Ozzie Smith, and hired Roger Craig as manager to replace Alvin Dark. Despite a losing April, the Padres launched a comeback in late June that continued throughout the 1978 campaign. The Padres finished fourth, recorded their first winning season (84–78), and set an attendance record of more than 1.67 million.

Kroc's willingness to bid on high-priced veteran players to bring a championship to San Diego fit in well with the local economic emphasis on speculation and trade. Unfortunately, Kroc was insufficiently experienced in the rules of free agency and trade. In 1979, after a post–All-Star Game slump, Kroc publicly announced his intention to devote $5–10 million toward acquiring free agents Joe Morgan and Graig Nettles. Commissioner Kuhn found Kroc guilty of tampering and levied a $100,000 fine. Consequently, Kroc removed himself as club president and named executive vice president Ballard Smith Jr., his son-in-law, as his replacement.

As the 1970s drew to a close, the major leagues, including the Padres, entered an era of big spending, labor problems, and well-publicized scandals. In 1979 Jerry Coleman was brought in from the TV booth to manage the club. The 1980 season was difficult for Coleman, the Padres, and San Diego fans. Early in the year, it became evident that the franchise's star player, Winfield, would pursue free agency at the conclusion of the season. As Winfield's departure became a foregone conclusion, local fans vented their frustration toward him. The fans' anger increased as the Padres slumped, culminating in the termination of general manager Fontaine in early July.

Kroc hired a new general manager who thrived in the competition of the 1980s, "Trader Jack" McKeon, whose intent was to rebuild through acquiring new young talent and discarding older, less productive veterans. McKeon, under this rubric, presciently remarked that he could bring a pennant to San Diego within four or five years. While the team finished last in 1980, a late-season improvement seemed to reenergize the team for the future. Three players stole over 50 bases for the first time in NL history. Near the end of the season, the ballpark was renamed for the late Jack Murphy, who had been so instrumental in bringing major-league ball to San Diego. Shortly after the end of the season, Smith fired manager Jerry Coleman, who returned to broadcasting, and replaced him with former slugger Frank Howard.

McKeon engineered an off-season 11-player trade with St. Louis in line with his plan to unload high-salaried veterans. Four Padres, including Hall of Famer Rollie Fingers, moved to St. Louis in exchange for seven young Cardinals. McKeon followed this up with several more trades. Winfield, as expected, left San Diego, signing a multiyear contract with the New York Yankees. McKeon, in just four months, orchestrated a massive transformation of the team roster, trading away or adding 28 players. McKeon's dealings produced a young, inexperienced, moderately paid team.

The Padres began 1981 dismally, and ended it equally poorly. The players' strike split the season into two parts, and the Padres came in last in the NL West in both the first and second halves. Their 41–69 record was the low point of Ray Kroc's ownership. The Padres fired manager Frank Howard after just one year and brought in experienced manager Dick Williams. Williams compiled an 81–81 record in 1982, which was the rookie season of future Hall of Famer Tony Gwynn, the Padres' best player ever. In 20 seasons with the Padres Gwynn batted .338 and had 3,141 hits. He won five Gold Gloves and eight batting championships, and appeared in 15 All-Star Games. After the season the Padres made a huge error, trading Ozzie Smith in a multiplayer deal to the Cardinals. The Padres were also 81–81 in 1983, when the team welcomed free-agent Dodgers star first baseman Steve Garvey, who set an NL record that year of playing in 1,207 consecutive games. His signing sent a message that San Diego was serious about winning.

With two consecutive .500 seasons behind them, increased attendance, and two superstar players, the Padres had great hopes for 1984. In a devastating blow to the team, Ray Kroc died on January 14. Kroc's wife, Joan, became owner and chairwoman of the board.

McKeon continued to engineer trades that would help the Padres establish a well-rounded roster. Before the 1984 season, McKeon added free-agent reliever Goose Gossage and traded for Graig Nettles from the Yankees, adding experience and leadership to the roster. The Padres had a strong April, ending the month in first place in the NL West. After a short May slump, the Padres reasserted themselves as division contenders, virtually wrapping up the division title by the end of July. They finished with a record of 92–70, taking the West by 10 games.

In the postseason, the Padres faced the Chicago Cubs in the NL Championship Series. The Padres appeared to have little chance of success, losing the first two games of the series in Chicago. After moving to San Diego for game three, San Diego launched a comeback. Playing in front of an unprecedented 58,000 fans, the Padres capitalized on their home-field advantage and prevailed over the Cubs, winning three games to two to take the NL pennant. Garvey was named NLCS MVP. But in the World Series against the Tigers, the Padres only scored 15 runs in five games, and lost four games to one. Nonetheless, the excellent season in 1984 seemed to foreshadow future success for the Padres.

The next three years were marred by drug problems and club politics. The club went through three managers (Williams, Steve Boros, and Larry Bowa) and dropped successively from third to fourth to sixth (65–97 in 1987). Numerous key players suffered injuries at the start of the 1985 season. Alan Wiggins added to the Padres' difficulties, abandoning the team in April and checking into a rehabilitation center for a recurrent drug problem. Wiggins was traded to Baltimore shortly after he completed treatment. Drugs also hurt the career of pitcher La Marr Hoyt. He was twice arrested in February 1986 for drug possession. He went into drug-rehabilitation program and missed most of spring training. After the season he was arrested at the Mexican border for illegal drugs and sentenced to 45 days in jail. Commissioner Peter Ueberroth ordered a season-long suspension, but in June an arbitrator ordered him reinstated.

Steve Wulf, in a 1989 *Sports Illustrated* article, compared the Padres under Joan Kroc's leadership to a soap opera. Disputes had erupted between Kroc and son-in-law Ballard Smith Jr. After the disappointing 1985 season, when the Padres finished in third place, Smith and McKeon wanted to fire Dick Williams. Kroc, however, vetoed the decision, and kept Williams on as club manager. But Williams found the situation too strained, and decided to quit at the beginning of the next spring training. As a result of the increased tension, Smith resigned in 1987.

The Padres also were unable to escape the sex scandals that plagued baseball in the 1980s. Revelations about the private life of beloved Padre Steve Garvey came to light in a tell-all book by ex-wife Cyndy. Then, two years after retirement, he admitted having fathered children by different women. Garvey suffered a dramatic loss in status and was shunned by the organization that had retired his number.

In 1988, McKeon's power in the organization significantly expanded. Frustrated with the annual managerial switches, McKeon named himself field manager after dismissing Williams's successor, Larry Bowa. New club president

Tony Gwynn watches his two-run home run in Game 1 of the World Series against the New York Yankees, 1998. © AP / Wide World Photos

Chub Feeney had reservations about McKeon's ability to operate in the dual capacity of general and field manager and announced that McKeon would have to relinquish one of the jobs after the season. However, under great pressure from the fans and the team owners, Feeney was forced out. Tal Smith was named executive in charge of daily operations, while Dick Freeman became club president. McKeon retained both his positions but yielded draft duties to another Padres employee. The team's salaries came to $9,878,168, 19th of 26 teams.

In 1989 the Padres recorded the second-most wins in club history (89), while pitcher Mark Davis received the Cy Young Award and Tony Gwynn won the NL batting title. After the season, Joan Kroc sold the Padres for $90 million to a syndicate headed by TV producer Tom Werner. The new owners replaced McKeon as field manager with Greg Riddoch, who led the Padres in 1990 to a fourth-place finish and a losing record at 75–87. Following the season, McKeon was fired as general manager of the club and replaced by Joe McIlvane. The Padres compiled winning records in 1991 (83–78) and 1992 (89–73), yet finished at least 10 games behind the division leader. In 1992 Gary Sheffield led the NL in batting (.330) and Fred McGriff led in homers (35). In 1993 Randy Smith was named general manager at the age of 29, and he retained Jim Riggleman, who had taken over at the end of 1992, as manager. The season was an unmitigated disaster, as the Padres lost over 100 games for the first time since 1974.

In the strike season of 1994, the Padres compiled 70 losses under Riggleman and were on their way to a club record for futility when play was halted. Financially, the strike was a catastrophe for the Padres and the final blow for Werner's ownership group. Even though the club did not pay the players during the strike, they still had to pay the nonstriking staff while bringing in no revenue. Werner and his partners sold the Padres after the season to John Moores, the owner of a software company, for $80 million. Moores became the majority owner, while Larry Lucchino, former president of the Baltimore Orioles, became a minority owner. Bruce Bochy became the new manager.

The mid-1990s also witnessed a revolution in outreach methods for Hispanic fans. After years of ignoring their potential drawing power in Mexico, the Padres made overtures south of the border, establishing a director of Hispanic and multicultural marketing and opening a store in Tijuana to sell team merchandise and ticket packages that included transportation.

Capitalizing on the success of their outreach programs, the Padres expanded their involvement with their Mexican fans. In August 1995, the Republican Party intended to hold its convention in Jack Murphy Stadium, displacing the team. Consequently, team officials arranged to play the three home games during the convention in Monterrey, Mexico. Although the convention plans changed, the Padres kept their commitment to play the series in Mexico. To further attract Mexican fans, the Padres named native pitcher Fernando Valenzuela as the first-game starter.

Aside from their success with expanding their fan base, the Padres also experienced great success in the standings, despite having salaries ($27,133,026) that were just 20th out of 30 major-league teams. The Padres won the 1996 NL West division title with a record of 91–71, led by Gwynn's seventh batting title and Ken Caminiti's 130-RBI MVP performance, an accomplishment that was later sullied by his 2002 admission of steroid use. Unfortunately for the Padres, the division title did not result in postseason success. The St. Louis Cardinals defeated the Padres in the first round in a three-game sweep.

In 1997 the park was expanded at a cost of $78 million; $60 million was raised through city-financed bonds, and the rest came from the fee for renaming the field Qualcomm Park. This expansion added an additional 10,500 seats. A Padres' task force that year concluded that the club needed a baseball-only stadium, similar to that of other cities who were building retro ballparks downtown in hopes of benefiting from their central location and a concurrent revitalization of downtown locations. These new stadiums tended to emphasize the unique characteristics of their hometowns by integrating the architecture with the cityscape, thus more closely tying civic identity to the local baseball franchise. In San Diego, the proposed PETCO Park incorporated a historical industrial building into its design and showcased views of San Diego Bay. As they entered the 1998 season, the Padres needed to perform well and attract fans to convince San Diegans to approve a bond issue to finance the new stadium.

The Padres in 1998 again won the NL West division title (98–64), and drew over 2.5 million spectators, making a strong case for the club's ability to fill a new stadium. The team batted just .253, but were powered by Greg Vaughn's 50 homers and strong pitching from starter Kevin Brown (18–7, 2.38 ERA) and Trevor Hoffman's 53 saves. In addition, unlike 1996, the Padres advanced in the postseason, thanks to the performances of Kevin Brown, Greg Vaughn, and Tony Gwynn. After defeating Houston in the first round three games to one, the Padres faced the Atlanta Braves and won the NL pennant in a six-game series. But in the World Series the Padres were swept by the New York Yankees.

Nonetheless, the strong performances on the field and the large attendance had positive implications for the stadium bond vote. That November, San Diego voters passed Proposition C, which approved construction of a new $411 million, 46,000-seat downtown ballpark for the Padres adjacent to the San Diego Convention Center. It was planned as part of a larger Ballpark District, featuring offices, retail, hotels, and residential units with the expectation of rehabilitating a dilapidated section of downtown. Construction was delayed for two years because the city did not sell the approved bonds while defending itself against lawsuits brought by antitax activists. The project was a joint city (70%) and Padres (30%) project. The final cost came to $285 million for ballpark construction and $171.8 million for land acquisition and infrastructure, or a total of $456.8 million. This helped raise the value of the Padres at the start of the 2005 season to $329 million, 13th in MLB.

In 37 years as a major-league team, the Padres have witnessed significant ownership and leadership changes, potential relocation, the cultivation of a franchise

player in Tony Gwynn, and the extremes of competitive success and failure. They are a small-city team with revenues in the lower third of MLB. As a team, the Padres have only completed 13 winning seasons, and none from 1999 through 2003, when they were among the poorest-paying teams. The completion of PETCO Park; their 23-game improvement in 2004 to 87–75 (which reflected an increase to a midlevel pay scale), led by second baseman Mark Loretta, who batted .335; and attendance of over 3 million made San Diego fans optimistic once again. The team's financial situation has improved, although the Padres still struggle to balance team debt and payroll demands. Moores named Sandy Alderson, former president and general manager of the Oakland A's, as CEO, charging him with the responsibility of reshaping the team and its finances as the Padres move forward. The Padres made the playoffs in 2005 with a modest 82–80 record, winning the very weak NL West with the worst record of any team

Trevor Hoffman pitches in a spring training game in Peoria, Arizona, 2002. © AP / Wide World Photos to make the postseason. They were led by Jake Peavy, 13–7, with a 2.88 ERA and a league-leading 216 strikeouts, and Trevor Hoffman, with 43 saves in 46 chances. But the Padres were swept in three in the divisional playoffs by the Cardinals. Still, with two consecutive winning seasons and a popular new stadium, Padres fans are optimistic about the future.

NOTABLE ACHIEVEMENTS

Most Valuable Players

Year	Name	Position
1996	Ken Caminiti	3B

Cy Young Winners

Year	Name	Position
1976	Randy Jones	LHP
1978	Gaylord Perry	RHP
1989	Mark Davis	LHP

Rookies of the Year

Year	Name	Position
1976	Butch Metzger	P
1987	Benito Santiago	C

Batting Champions

Year	Name	#
1984	Tony Gwynn	.351
1987	Tony Gwynn	.370
1988	Tony Gwynn	.313
1989	Tony Gwynn	.336
1992	Gary Sheffield	.330
1994	Tony Gwynn	.394
1995	Tony Gwynn	.368
1996	Tony Gwynn	.353
1997	Tony Gwynn	.372

Home-Run Champions

Year	Name	#
1992	Fred McGriff	35

ERA Champions

Year	Name	#
1975	Randy Jones	2.24
2004	Jake Peavy	2.27

Strikeout Champions

Year	Name	#
1994	Andy Benes	189
2005	Jake Peavy	216

POSTSEASON APPEARANCES

NL West Division Titles

Year	Record	Manager
1984	92–70	Dick Williams
1996	91–71	Bruce Bochy
1998	98–64	Bruce Bochy
2005	82–80	Bruce Bochy

NL Pennants

Year	Record	Manager
1984	92–70	Dick Williams
1998	98–64	Bruce Bochy

MANAGERS

1995–	Bruce Bochy
1992–1994	Jim Riggleman
1990–1992	Greg Riddoch
1988–1990	Jack McKeon
1987	Larry Bowa
1986	Steve Boros
1982–1985	Dick Williams
1981	Frank Howard
1980	Jerry Coleman
1978–1980	Roger Craig
1977	Alvin Dark
1977	Bob Skinner
1974–1977	John McNamara
1973–1974	Don Zimmer
1969–1972	Preston Gomez

Team Records by Individual Players

Batting Leaders

	Single Season			Career	
	Name	Year	Name		Plate Appearances
Batting average	Tony Gwynn .394	1994	Tony Gwynn	.338	10,232
On-base %	Tony Gwynn .454	1994	Gene Tenace	.403	2,094
Slugging %	Ken Caminiti .621	1996	Ken Caminiti	.540	2,351
OPS	Ken Caminiti 1.028	1996	Ken Caminiti	.924	2,351
Games	Dave Winfield 162	1980	Tony Gwynn	2,440	10,232
At bats	Steve Finley 655	1996	Tony Gwynn	9,288	10,232
Runs	Steve Finley 126	1996	Tony Gwynn	1,383	10,232
Hits	Tony Gwynn 220	1997	Tony Gwynn	3,141	10,232
Total bases	Steve Finley 348	1996	Tony Gwynn	4,529	10,232
Doubles	Tony Gwynn 49	1997	Tony Gwynn	543	10,232
Triples	Tony Gwynn 13	1987	Tony Gwynn	85	10,232
Home runs	Greg Vaughn 50	1998	Nat Colbert	163	3,485
RBIs	Ken Caminiti 130	1996	Tony Gwynn	1,138	10,232
Walks	Jack Clark 132	1989	Tony Gwynn	790	10,232
Strikeouts	Nat Colbert 150	1970	Nat Colbert	773	3,485
Stolen bases	Alam Wiggins 70	1984	Tony Gwynn	319	10,232
Extra-base hits	Steve Finley 84	1996	Tony Gwynn	763	10,232
Times on base	Tony Gwynn 303	1987	Tony Gwynn	3,955	10,232

Pitching Leaders

	Single Season			Career	
	Name	Year	Name		Innings Pitched
ERA	Dave Roberts 2.10	1996	Trevor Hoffman 2.73		786.7
Wins	Randy Jones 22	1976	Eric Show	100	1,603.3
Won-loss %	Gaylord Perry .780	1978	Jake Peavy	.597	661.7
Hits/9 IP	Clay Kirby 7.17	1971	Trevor Hoffman 6.90		786.7
Walks/9 IP	La Marr Hoyt 0.86	1985	Randy Jones	2.11	1,766
Strikeouts	Kevin Brown 257	1998	Andy Benes	1,036	1,235
Strikeouts/9 IP	Andy Benes 9.87	1994	Trevor Hoffman 10.17		786.7
Games	Craig Lefferts 83	1986	Trevor Hoffman 728		786.7
Saves	Trevor Hoffman 53	1998	Trevor Hoffman 434		786.7
Innings	Randy Jones 315.3	1976	Randy Jones	1,766	1,766
Starts	Randy Jones 40	1976	Randy Jones	253	1,766
Complete games	Randy Jones 25	1976	Randy Jones	71	1,766
Shutouts	Randy Jones 6	1975	Randy Jones	18	1,766

Source: Drawn from data in "San Diego Padres Batting Leaders (seasonal and career)." http://baseball-reference.com/ teams/SDP/leaders_bat.shtml; "San Diego Padres Pitching Leaders (seasonal and career)." http://baseball-reference. com/teams/SDP/leaders_pitch.shtml.

BIBLIOGRAPHY

Bjarkman, Peter C. *Baseball with a Latin Beat: A History of the Latin American Game*. Jefferson, NC: McFarland, 1994.

"Caminiti Comes Clean." CNNSI, May 28, 2002, http://sportsillustrated.cnn.com/si_online/special_report/steroids/.

Danielson, Michael N. *Home Team: Professional Sports and the American Metropolis*. Princeton, NJ: Princeton University Press, 1997.

Fishwick, Marshall. *Ronald Revisited: The World of Ronald McDonald*. Bowling Green, OH: Bowling Green State University Popular Press, 1983.

Helyar, John. *Lords of the Realm: The Real History of Baseball*. New York: Villard Books, 1994.

Hofmann, Dale, and Martin J. Greenberg. *Sport$biz: An Irreverent Look at Big Business in Pro Sports*. Champaign, IL: Leisure Press, 1989.

Hogan, Richard. *The Failure of Planning: Permitting Sprawl in San Diego Suburbs*. Columbus: Ohio State University Press, 2003.

Jukle, John A., and Keith A. Sculle. *Fast Food: Roadside Restaurants in the Automobile Age*. Baltimore: Johns Hopkins University Press, 1999.

Klein, Alan M. *Baseball on the Border: A Tale of Two Laredos*. Princeton, NJ: Princeton University Press, 1997.

Koppett, Leonard. *Koppett's Concise History of Major League Baseball*. Philadelphia: Temple University Press, 1998.

Kroc, Ray, with Robert Anderson. *Grinding It Out: The Making of McDonald's*. Chicago: Contemporary Books, 1977.

Leggett, William. "One Hundred and One." *Sports Illustrated,* April 14, 1969, 44–47.

Love, John F. *McDonald's: Behind the Arches*. Toronto: Bantam Books, 1986.

Miller, Marvin. *A Whole Different Ball Game: The Sport and Business of Baseball*. Secaucus, NJ: Carol Publishing Group, 1991.

"Old Saws Over a New Mays." *Sports Illustrated*, April 14, 1969, 86–89.

Papucci, Nelson. *The San Diego Padres, 1969–2002: A Complete History*. San Diego: Big League Press, 2002.

Porter, David L. "San Diego Padres: The Saga of Big Mac and Trader Jack." In *Encyclopedia of Major League Baseball Team Histories: National League*, ed. Peter C. Bjarkman, 465–512. Westport, CT: Meckler, 1991.

Porter, David, and Joe Naiman. *The Padres Encyclopedia*. Champaign, IL: Sports Publishing, 2002.

San Diego Padres official Web site. "History." http://sandiego.padres.mlb.com/NASApp/mlb/sd/history/sd_history_timeline.jsp.

Tygiel, Jules. *Past Time: Baseball as History*. New York: Oxford University Press, 2000.

Winfield, Dave, and Tom Parker. *A Player's Life*. New York: Avon Books, 1989.

Wulf, Steve. "All My Padres." *Sports Illustrated,* April 1989, special baseball issue, 42–44.

———. "You've Got to Hand It to the Padres." *Sports Illustrated,* October 15, 1984, 28–35.

San Francisco Giants

Andrew Goldblatt

BIRTH OF THE GIANTS

The pitcher wore a frilled shirt, mauve pants, silk socks, and crimson-laced tennis shoes. But that wasn't why his teammates threw him off the field. They threw him off because he gave up 12 runs in the first inning and, jauntily drying his brow with an embroidered handkerchief, assured them he *usually* did better over the rest of the game.

From that unpromising moment grew the New York, later San Francisco, Giants. Through the first quarter of the twentieth century the Giants were the wealthiest, winningest, most obnoxious team in baseball. To put it another way, they were the Yankees before the Yankees were the Yankees. But with every success came a setback, and eventually their fortunes declined. Only at the beginning of the twenty-first century did they rejoin the top rank of major-league franchises.

The popinjay pitcher was John B. Day, a prosperous Manhattan tobacco merchant with dreams of diamond glory. But he had more money than talent, as proved by that abbreviated 1880 stint for the Washington Nationals at Brooklyn's Union Grounds. While he sat in the stands and nursed his humiliation, he was approached by James Mutrie, who had walked to New York from Fall River, Massachusetts, as part of a race that he lost. The enterprising Mutrie explained that he had recently organized a ball club back home, and with Day's support could assemble a fresh team in New York that would put the haughty Nationals to shame. Soon after, Day and Mutrie formed the Metropolitan Base Ball Club.

The Mets, as the new team was called, started as an independent outfit. A Wall Street bootblack asked Day why the team played at the Union Grounds in Brooklyn when a Manhattan polo field owned by *New York Herald* scion James Gordon Bennett Jr. sat idle. Day followed up on the tip and leased the original Polo Grounds at Sixth Avenue and 110th Street, just above Central Park. The Mets drew sizable crowds, leading Day and Mutrie to schedule exhibitions against opponents from the National League. They had more than attendance in mind. They were seeking exposure for their team when neither the NL nor a brand-new circuit, the American Association, had a franchise in New York.

The AA offered the Mets membership for its inaugural season in 1882. But as a son of the age of monopoly, Day wanted to corner New York's professional baseball market. He conceived of a scheme that depended on a bid from the more established NL, and declined the AA's offer.

Class also factored into his decision. The AA proposed to charge only half as much (25 cents) for admission as the NL, guaranteeing a large blue-collar turnout. It planned to sell alcohol in the stands, earning itself the epithet "Beer Ball League," and scheduled games for Sundays. The dandified Day, who shuttled from his elegant brownstone to his Lower East Side factory to Wall Street to the Polo Grounds in his own coach, didn't want himself or his team branded lower class, especially when more money could be made appealing to the middle class.

In 1882 the still-independent Mets averaged nearly 1,500 fans a game, impressive for those times. The NL came courting, and Day put his plan in action. He accepted membership, then placed the Mets in the AA and demanded that the NL grant him a brand-new franchise. That left the NL with three vexing choices: concede New York to the AA, recruit a different owner to compete against Day's popular Mets, or give Day what he wanted. It took the last course, and Day had his monopoly.

To fill out his new team's roster, Day purchased rights to the disbanded NL franchise in Troy, New York. It was a stroke of luck, genius, or both, for Troy had four future Hall of Famers—Buck Ewing, Roger Connor, Tim Keefe, and Mickey Welch—who would anchor Day's NL entry through decade's end. Day laid out a second diamond at the Polo Grounds so both his teams could play at once.

Day's NL franchise, originally referred to as the Gothams, played its first game on May 1, 1883, at the Polo Grounds against Boston. "When the game began it was estimated that fully 15,000 persons were in the enclosure. Among those present was Gen. [Ulysses S.] Grant. He sat in the rear of the grand stand and apparently enjoyed the game, as he at times took part in the applause given the players," said the *New York Times*. The first three batters for the home team were Ewing, Connor, and John Montgomery Ward, all future Hall of Famers. They paced the club to a 7–5 victory.

Although Day had assigned Mutrie to manage the Mets and given him Tim Keefe to handle the pitching, the NL Gothams were his pride and joy.

After the Mets won the AA pennant in 1884 and participated in professional baseball's first meaningful postseason tournament, a "Championship of the United States" against the Providence Grays, Day transferred Mutrie, Keefe, and third baseman Dude Esterbrook to the Gothams. Keefe and Esterbrook were tall for that era, reaching nearly six feet. They joined other imposing figures like Roger Connor, the six-foot-three 220-pounder whose career record for home runs (138) stood until Babe Ruth broke it. In his jubilation over an 11-inning win at Philadelphia on June 3, 1885, the effusive Mutrie proclaimed his players "My big fellows! My *giants!*" The name stuck.

As the NL increased its dominance and the Giants became a force within it, Day let the Mets wither, selling the franchise to the AA's Brooklyn team for $15,000 in October 1887. Under Mutrie's "We are the people!" battle cry, the Giants won their first pennant in 1888 with an 84–47 record. Keefe led the league with 35 wins and a 1.74 ERA. The Giants prevailed in a championship series against the AA's St. Louis Browns, six games to four.

Despite cordial relations with Manhattan's notoriously corrupt Tammany Hall political machine, Day was evicted from the Polo Grounds so the land could be used for a majestic entrance to the north end of Central Park (Douglass Circle). In 1889 the world champions had to play in Jersey City and Staten Island until July 8, when a fresh grandstand, christened the new Polo Grounds, opened at the base of Coogan's Bluff, a craggy hill abutting the Hudson River between 155th and 157th Streets in upper Manhattan. In their first game there the Giants beat Pud Galvin and the Pittsburgh Pirates 7–5 in front of more than 10,000 fans. The site remained the Giants' home for the next 68 years.

The Giants won the NL crown again in 1889 with an 83–43 record. Along with balanced pitching, they had the best hitting in the NL, averaging nearly a run more per game than any other team. Their postseason opponents were the AA's Brooklyn Bridegrooms, who later became the Dodgers. It was the first time the two teams, archrivals to this day, played for something more than pride. In a series sullied by poor umpiring, the Giants won their second consecutive world championship "as easily as a negro would beat a carpet," said the *Sporting News*.

Day and Mutrie had succeeded beyond their wildest dreams. Their team was the toast of New York. It even had female fans, having introduced Ladies' Days on June 16, 1883. DeWolf Hopper, the actor who popularized the poem "Casey at the Bat," helped organize an October 20, 1889, benefit at the Broadway Theatre to present the Giants with the NL pennant. According to the *Times*, "hundreds of people were turned away, and outside the building, both on Broadway and Forty-First Street, there was such a jam that the police had to interfere to make a passage way on the sidewalks." James J. Coogan, owner of the land on which the new Polo Grounds had been built, offered to buy the Giants for the stupendous sum of $200,000.

DOUBLE WHAMMY: THE PLAYERS' LEAGUE AND ANDREW FREEDMAN

Day should have taken Coogan's offer, for disaster loomed. He had been antagonizing ballplayers since 1883, when he successfully proposed rules barring teams from signing players deemed to have violated the reserve clause. In response to further attempts by Day and his fellow owners to restrict the salary and movement of players, Giants shortstop John Montgomery Ward organized the Brotherhood of Professional Base Ball Players. Ward's teammates formed the core of the union's support.

Ward was one of the most remarkable figures in baseball history, a star shortstop and labor leader combined. In the summer of 1887 he published an impassioned diatribe in *Lippincott's Magazine* arguing that the reserve clause "inaugurated a species of serfdom which gave one set of men a life-estate in the labor of another, and withheld from the latter any corresponding claim . . . Its justification, if any, lay only in its expediency." Day responded to this and other incitements by replacing Ward as team captain (the equivalent of field manager) with Buck Ewing.

After the 1887 season the owners formally recognized the Brotherhood and made a few minor concessions. By that point, however, little could make Day and Ward friends. In 1888 Ward successfully held out for a $4,000 salary. He led the Giants to their first championship, then joined Chicago owner Albert Spalding and several players on a world tour, staging baseball exhibitions from New Zealand to France. While he was away, Day sold him to the Washington Senators for the unprecedented sum of $12,000. Ward refused to report to Washington unless he received at least half the sale price, forcing cancellation of the deal. The incident fueled Ward's dream of a league controlled by the players.

In the summer of 1889 he laid plans for just such a venture, and on November 4, six days after leading the Giants to their second straight championship, he published the Brotherhood Manifesto, declaring the players' intention to form their own league. Day and two other owners, Chicago's Spalding and Boston's John Rogers, issued a puffed-up rebuttal that further enraged the Brotherhood. The players gathered in New York in December 1889, and a dozen Giants (every frontliner except pitcher Mickey Welch and outfielder Mike Tiernan, the latter of whom was enticed into staying by a three-year, $12,000 contract, well above the $2,500 he earned in 1889) announced their defection to the new Players' League.

Just like that, John B. Day's valuable asset vanished. He sued Ward for violating the reserve clause, but Ward, a Columbia law-school product, argued his own case, and on January 29, 1890, emerged from court victorious. Day next sued Buck Ewing amid rumors he had offered Ewing a three-year, $33,000 contract to stay with the Giants. On March 26, 1890, a U.S. circuit court granted Ewing's freedom.

All the Giants defectors except Ward (who played for and managed Brooklyn) moved to the Players' League's New York team, which built Brotherhood Park just north of the new Polo Grounds. Naturally the fans went to see the championship-caliber players, not Day's hastily assembled replacements. Averaging fewer than a thousand fans a game, Day warned his fellow NL owners in July that without a cash infusion of $80,000 he would have to sell his franchise to the Players' League. Led by John T. Brush, who had earlier dissolved his Indianapolis team and sold his players to Day, NL owners rescued the Giants from bankruptcy.

The Players' League folded after a year. Day lasted only a little longer. He commandeered Brotherhood Park (which soon reverted to the name Polo Grounds) and found a new ace in future Hall of Famer Amos Rusie, whose blazing fastball was one of the main reasons pitchers were pushed to 60 feet, 6 inches from home plate in 1893. The reconstituted Giants finished third and drew well in 1891, setting a single-game attendance record of 22,289 for a June match against Chicago. But after the season Day's stockholders demanded (and received) the removal of Mutrie, who had spent an unheard-of $55,000 on payroll. A year later the financially strapped Day himself was ousted when Edward Talcott, an attorney and investor credited by the *Times* as the only Giants owner other than Day to "know the difference between a base hit and a foul flag," joined with Brush to gain a controlling block of stock.

Talcott stayed just long enough to win another world championship in 1894, when the Giants beat the first-place Baltimore Orioles in the Temple Cup, a postseason series between the NL's first- and second-place teams. Rusie led the NL with 36 wins, a 2.78 ERA, and 195 strikeouts. Talcott sold out to Andrew Freedman for an estimated $53,000.

If the Giants were the Yankees before the Yankees were the Yankees, then Andrew Freedman was George Steinbrenner before Steinbrenner was Steinbrenner. A real-estate speculator closely tied to Richard Croker, boss of Manhattan's Tammany Hall machine, and himself a prominent figure in the Democratic Party, the overbearing Freedman irritated almost everyone he encountered. One of his first acts was to reserve grandstand seats for respectable businessmen, but under his reign Polo Grounds crowds became increasingly vulgar. In fairness, this was a problem every team faced in the 1890s, as the game on the field devolved into thuggery. Freedman inflamed the situation, however, engaging in highly publicized shouting matches with managers (he fired 12 in eight years), players, umpires, and fellow owners.

Freedman so angered his star attraction, "Hoosier Thunderbolt" Rusie, that in 1895 the pitcher gestured obscenely at Freedman, leading Freedman to assess a $200 fine that Rusie refused to pay. When Freedman deducted the money from Rusie's 1896 contract, Rusie sat out the season and filed a lawsuit challenging the reserve clause. Leery of the Giants' court record in such matters, the NL's other owners overrode Freedman's objections and raised $3,000 among themselves to settle with the star pitcher.

Paced by Rusie's 28 wins and league-leading 2.54 ERA, the Giants finished third in 1897, but after that they faded, finishing last in 1900. Attendance dropped from 390,000 in 1897 to an abysmal 121,000 (9th in the 12-team circuit) two years later. Knowing the Giants survived purely by dint of monopoly, the American League, launched in 1901 with a promise to restore the game's integrity, tried to place a franchise in New York. Freedman used his real-estate connections and Tammany Hall clout to deny AL president Ban Johnson a Manhattan ballpark site.

In August 1901 Freedman secretly proposed to the Boston, Cincinnati, and St. Louis teams that they reorganize the NL into a trust paying a seven percent annual dividend. He would receive the biggest share of the trust, at 30 percent. They would each get 12 percent. Chicago and Philadelphia would get 10 percent, Pittsburgh 8 percent, and Brooklyn 6 percent. When the scheme came to light in December 1901 it triggered a final-straw response from the other four teams, who elected Albert Spalding president of the league for the express purpose of running Freedman out of baseball. Freedman and his coconspirators boycotted the election, and then contested its validity, preventing Spalding from assuming his post. Swirls of intrigue later, the coconspirators deserted Freedman, leaving him isolated and humiliated.

Also in late 1901, reformer Seth Low was elected mayor of New York. Three years earlier Manhattan, Brooklyn, Queens, the Bronx, and Staten Island had been consolidated into New York City. An unintended consequence, at least from the perspective of Freedman and his Tammany Hall cronies, was an influx of Republican votes from Brooklyn sufficient to topple their crooked machine. With another nemesis, former Manhattan police commissioner Theodore Roosevelt, ensconced in the White House, many Tammany types thought it best to go underground until the good-government fad blew over. Freedman did so literally, becoming a director of the subway-digging Interborough Rapid Transit Construction Company.

MCGRAW ARRIVES

But first Freedman had to sell the Giants. Knowing he would not get much for them as is, he made what turned out to be a lasting improvement to the team's value by hiring John J. McGraw to manage.

The 29 year-old McGraw had been a star with the NL Orioles, the most innovative, and lawless, team in baseball history. After the NL shut down the Orioles in 1900, McGraw spent a year with the Cardinals, and then returned to Baltimore as player, manager, and part owner of the new AL Orioles. The team drew poorly, and was likely to move to New York as soon as Ban Johnson could find space for a ballpark. McGraw yearned to prove himself in the city he called "the cornerstone of baseball." But he still had the old, cheating Oriole in him, which Johnson despised. Concluding that Johnson would never let him be the AL's point man in New York, McGraw leaped when Freedman invited him to manage the Giants.

McGraw sold his half of the Diamond Café, a Baltimore saloon, to business partner and former Orioles teammate Wilbert Robinson in exchange for Robinson's share of the Orioles. McGraw then sold his and Robinson's stock to a group fronting for Freedman. Even before the group took over the Orioles, Freedman signed McGraw to a lucrative four-year contract. Once Freedman's ownership became official, he followed McGraw's advice and brought several other Orioles to New York, including future Hall of Famers Roger Bresnahan and Joe McGinnity.

As one of the biggest names in baseball (his single-season NL record for on-base percentage, .547 in 1899, lasted until the Giants' Barry Bonds broke it in 2002), McGraw attracted almost 10,000 fans to his first game on July 19, 1902. It was the Giants' biggest crowd since the season opener. The Giants played .397 ball under the fiery young manager, unimpressive until compared to the .299 they had been playing before he arrived. That September Freedman sold his interest in the team for $100,000 to Cincinnati Reds owner John T. Brush.

The cadaverous Brush had repeatedly figured in Giants history. His 1888 plan to rank players by skill level and pay everyone at the same level the same amount of money (the Brush Classification Plan) expedited formation of the Players' League, which hit the Giants harder than any other team. Brush profited from the Giants' duress by selling his Indianapolis players to John B. Day in 1890, and accepted a chunk of Giants stock in exchange for helping to rescue Day later that summer. As owner of the Reds, he supported Freedman's plan to turn the NL into a trust. In December 1900, he traded Christy Mathewson to the Giants for the worn-out Amos Rusie; since he was too astute to believe the trade fair, he probably knew he would soon be running the Giants. When Freedman and McGraw launched their takeover of the Orioles, Brush was there again, buying shares of the Baltimore franchise on Freedman's behalf.

Brush had the good sense to let McGraw run the team. McGraw was born in 1873 in Truxton, New York (some 50 miles west of Cooperstown), and was shaped by a miserable childhood. A diphtheria epidemic killed his mother, three siblings, and stepsister, and by 12 he was on his own, selling snacks and newspapers to survive. Practicing baseball every spare moment, he turned pro six days shy of his 17th birthday. He reached the majors at 18 and began his managerial career at 26.

McGraw combined a brilliant baseball mind with a keen eye for talent, an iron hand, and a vicious tongue. He controlled his team's every move, telling his players, "Do what I tell you, and I'll take the blame if it goes wrong." He was ready to fight anyone who stood in the way of a Giants victory, and also got in trouble for gambling and drinking. But he had a benevolent side, doling out cash and jobs to destitute alumni like Mickey Welch, Amos Rusie, and even John B. Day. His legion of detractors called him "Muggsy," a nickname he reviled. His admirers dubbed him "the Little Napoleon."

Together, Brush and McGraw built the Giants into baseball's richest and most glamorous franchise. And not a moment too soon, for after the 1902 season the AL announced it had found the backers and stadium site to transfer its Baltimore team to New York. If nothing else united Brush and McGraw, it was hatred of Ban Johnson's AL and its interloping Highlanders (later the Yankees). The NL and AL declared peace in January 1903, but it was over the Giants' objections.

In 1903 McGraw's Giants finished an amazing 34 1/2 games better than the year before, going from last place to second. That October, Pittsburgh and Boston played the first modern World Series. But when the Giants won the NL pennant in 1904, Brush and McGraw refused to participate in the Series. "There is nothing in the constitution or playing rules of the National League which requires its victorious club to submit its championship honors to a contest with a victorious club in a minor league," said Brush dismissively.

Brush and McGraw had fielded what is still the winningest team in Giants history (106 victories in 153 decisions). "Iron Man" McGinnity led the league with 35 wins, 408 innings pitched, and a 1.61 ERA. Mathewson had 33 wins and led the NL with 212 strikeouts. The hitters scored nearly a run more per game than the league average. The team attracted a league record 610,000 fans and made an estimated $100,000 profit. But for refusing to play in the World Series, Brush and McGraw were branded losers, cowards, and worse. Their own players were so peeved over the missed opportunity for a postseason paycheck that Brush felt compelled to dole out $5,000 in bonuses. When the leagues soon signed an agreement to play the World Series every fall, Brush and McGraw stifled their disapproval.

The Giants won 105 games and another pennant in 1905 with what McGraw considered his best team. Christy Mathewson won the triple crown of pitching with 31 wins, a 1.28 ERA, and 206 strikeouts. In the World Series, Mathewson shut out the Philadelphia Athletics three times, further heralding his arrival as the NL's greatest pitcher. The American idea of the role-model athlete largely originated with Mathewson, a tall, blond, blue-eyed Pennsylvanian nicknamed "Big Six," ostensibly because Manhattan's Big Six Fire Company responded fastest to fires. He refused to play on Sundays (not the sacrifice it sounds, since most cities banned athletic events on the Sabbath), spoke humbly despite a college education, and pursued his craft with a tenacity equal to McGraw's. Before Babe Ruth, he was the game's most popular figure. His 373 lifetime wins tie him with Grover Cleveland Alexander for most among NL pitchers and third best all-time.

McGraw's reputation moved in the opposite direction. Although New Yorkers loved him, in other NL cities his arrogance and combativeness provoked jeers and sometimes violence. He relished his role as the embodiment of everything people hated about New York, saving his most outrageous behavior for Pittsburgh and Chicago, homes to the only teams capable of beating his.

On May 19, 1905, McGraw violated etiquette by crassly calling, "Hey, Barney!" to Pittsburgh's gentleman owner, Barney Dreyfuss. He accused Dreyfuss of controlling the umpires through league president Harry Pulliam, a former Pirates executive, and offered to bet Dreyfuss $10,000 the Giants would win that day. (McGraw and Brush detested Pulliam for cooperating with the AL and leading the drive to reinstitute the World Series.) Dreyfuss reported the incident to Pulliam, who fined McGraw $150 and suspended him for 15 days. Giants fans rallied to McGraw's defense, filing a 12,000-name petition that decried Pulliam's actions. A defensive Dreyfuss complained that this wasn't the first time he and McGraw had argued over bets, an indiscretion that so alarmed the other NL owners that they exonerated McGraw and censured Dreyfuss.

McGraw was not as successful against the Cubs, whose infield trio of Tinker, Evers, and Chance owes much of its fame to the doggerel of Giants fan Franklin P. Adams ("These are the saddest of possible words: Tinker to Evers to Chance"). Frank Chance loved trading insults with McGraw. From 1905 to 1912, when Chance managed the Cubs, the Giants were only 75–101 (.426) against Chicago while compiling a winning record against every other NL team.

The rivalry with the Cubs culminated in 1908, a year that saw the Giants attract a record 910,000 fans, more than a quarter of the NL's attendance. The peak moment was Merkle's Boner, still one of the most controversial plays in baseball history. On September 23, with only two weeks remaining in the season and the Giants leading the Cubs by one game, the teams went to the bottom of the ninth at the Polo Grounds tied 1–1. With two outs, Giants rookie Fred Merkle singled to right, sending base runner Moose McCormick to third. Al Bridwell followed with a solid liner over second base, scoring McCormick with the winning run. Players poured out of the dugouts and 20,000 elated Giants fans spilled onto the field.

But was it really the winning run? Evers insisted to umpires Bob Emslie and Hank O'Day (a star pitcher for the Giants in the championship series of 1889) that Merkle never touched second base. If Evers got the ball and stepped on second, Merkle would become the third out and the run would not count. Cubs center fielder Solly Hofman threw the ball in, but Giants pitcher Joe McGinnity yanked it from Evers's hands and heaved it into left field. An unidentified Cub returned a ball, perhaps the game ball, perhaps not. Evers stepped on the bag, but didn't get the call he wanted; desperate to escape the masses of volatile fans, neither Emslie nor O'Day watched him make the play. From the safety of his hotel room that night, however, O'Day ruled that Merkle had failed to touch second and that the game had ended in a 1–1 tie.

New York talked of nothing else. The story ran on the front page of newspapers, rare prominence for baseball in those days. McGraw protested the decision, but league president Pulliam upheld O'Day. The ruling "sort of took the heart out of the gang," McGraw conceded years later. The Giants and Cubs ended the regular season with identical 98–55 records, and had to replay the tie game to determine the league champion.

The Cubs were jeered by thousands of New Yorkers on their ride from Penn Station to the Polo Grounds. "I never heard anybody or any set of men called as many foul names as the Giants fans called us that day from the time we showed up till it was over," Cubs pitcher Mordecai Brown recalled. After the

Cubs won 4–2 over Mathewson to clinch the pennant, one Giants fan injured Frank Chance with a punch to the neck, and another stabbed pitcher Jack Pfiester. The Cubs got out of the park only with the protection of revolver-brandishing policemen.

After the game umpires Bill Klem and James Johnstone alleged that Giants team physician Joseph Creamer offered them $2,500 apiece to throw the game. Creamer was banned from baseball. McGraw, in whose name Creamer claimed to act, got off scot-free. Over the next 15 years McGraw figured in several more bribery allegations, but never had to pay a price for them.

THE LAST POLO GROUNDS

The Giants set a major-league record of 347 stolen bases while beating the Cubs for the pennant in 1911. To win they had to overcome a huge early setback: just after midnight on April 14, fire destroyed the Polo Grounds. Only the left-field bleachers remained of what had been baseball's largest wooden grandstand, a double decker seating almost 30,000. An ailing John T. Brush decided to erect

Christopher Mathewson's baseball card, 1911. Courtesy of the Library of Congress

a steel and concrete stadium so long as the Coogan family gave him a long-term lease to make the investment worthwhile. On May 3, James Coogan's widow Harriet granted Brush a 35-year lease, and Brush's architects hastily designed the fourth (and final) Polo Grounds.

Although the Giants had done nothing but undercut the Yankees since 1903, Yankees owner Frank Farrell offered the Giants temporary shelter at Hilltop Park, less than a mile north of the Polo Grounds. Anxious not to wear out his welcome, Brush expedited construction of the new park by paying contractors their cost plus a set profit to work around the clock. On June 28, just 75 days after the fire, the Polo Grounds reopened. The weather was fiendishly hot—"many persons were fearful that the big fire was still burning," said the *Times*—and only 6,000 fans turned out to watch Mathewson shut out Boston. But 38,281 fans turned out for the first game of the World Series that October, a record crowd that guaranteed the then-astonishing sum of $1,000 per man to the series victor (the Philadelphia Athletics, in six games).

One of Brush's last acts as Giants owner was to invite the Yankees to play in his new stadium starting in 1913. In repaying a kindness and providing the Yankees with a truly big-league home, he also secured a rental income of up to $65,000 a year to repay construction loans.

The Polo Grounds wasn't finished until 1923. In its final form it seated nearly 56,000 fans. Its elongated, bathtub-like design featured boundless foul territory and a deep, narrow outfield (the center-field fence was 483 feet away), favoring pitchers. But the left-field line ended just 277 feet from home plate (an overhanging upper deck made the home-run distance even shorter) and the right-field line was just 257, so it was also a pull hitter's paradise. Players and fans alike left the park through center field, the players to a tower housing the clubhouses, the fans to the Eighth Avenue subway.

Brush didn't have much chance to enjoy his creation. On November 26, 1912, he passed away at age 67. He had lived to see the park built, and drew no small pleasure in hearing it called Brush Stadium. He had also seen his team win its second straight pennant, although it blew the World Series in spectacular fashion. Mathewson took a one-run lead over Boston into the bottom of the 10th of the final game. Center fielder Fred Snodgrass dropped a routine fly ball (later called "the $30,000 Muff" for how much it cost the players in World Series shares) to put the tying run on second. After Mathewson walked weak-hitting Steve Yerkes, Tris Speaker lofted a pop foul over the first-base coaches' box. Merkle inexplicably let it fall untouched. Given fresh life, Speaker rapped a game-tying single and Yerkes scored on a sacrifice fly to clinch the world championship for the Red Sox.

But Brush accomplished even more with the Giants than four pennants and a fabled ballpark would suggest. He turned them into the game's cornerstone franchise, stabilizing the NL (and, by extension, all of professional baseball) after a quarter century of uncertainty. Under him, the Giants' fame spread beyond Broadway, where John McGraw could earn $3,000 a week in the off-season telling baseball stories. The Giants became ambassadors for the game, holding spring training in Texas and Cuba and staging exhibitions against all comers, including African American teams. A year after Brush's death, the Giants embarked on a worldwide tour with the Chicago White Sox, playing in Japan, China, the Philippines, Australia, Ceylon, Egypt, France, and England. Such ubiquity made their name the most recognized in professional sports, and is the reason so many barnstorming African American teams (and Japan's first professional baseball team) took it for their own. (Some African American teams were using the name as far back as the 1880s.) Even New York's new football team called itself the Giants.

TURBULENT TEENS

Brush bequeathed the Giants to son-in-law Harry Hempstead. Like most family men who inherit a fortune, Hempstead was cautious. Whereas Brush let McGraw buy and sell players freely, Hempstead instituted restraints. But he placated McGraw by signing him to a five-year contract at the princely sum of $30,000 per annum. The Giants won their third consecutive pennant in 1913 with 101 victories, relying primarily on pitching: Mathewson, Rube Marquard, and Jeff Tesreau won 70 games combined. The Giants lost the World Series to the Philadelphia Athletics four games to one, however, leading Mathewson to publicly lament that "with a few exceptions the [Giants] are not of championship caliber."

Once again an upstart league spoiled the Giants' success. The Federal League, which competed as a rival major league from 1914 to 1915, barely affected the Giants personnel-wise; their players were well paid and loath to leave a three-time champion. Attendance, however, was sapped by Federal League franchises in Brooklyn and (in 1915) Newark, New Jersey. Although the NL and AL experienced a 25 percent decline in attendance from 1912–13 to 1914–15, business at the Polo Grounds was down 40 percent. It didn't help that the Giants struggled on the field, finishing a distant second in 1914 and last, for the only time in McGraw's career, in 1915. Team profits dipped from $150,000 per year before the Federal League to $50,000 in 1915.

When a July 4, 1916, doubleheader loss to the Dodgers left the Giants three games under .500, Hempstead and McGraw overhauled the team. Among those traded was Christy Mathewson. New Yorkers still loved Mathewson, but he had lost his skills (he would win only one more game), so McGraw sent him to Cincinnati to fill the managerial vacancy there. The reconstructed Giants set a still-standing major-league record of 26 consecutive wins, but finished fourth.

In March 1917 Hempstead gave McGraw another five-year contract, this one for $40,000 annually (the highest salary in baseball) plus a share of team profits. The Giants won the pennant by 10 games, posting the best on-base percentage and lowest ERA in the league. They also led the league in attendance, their draw of 500,264 topping the next-highest NL team by 140,000. But even with things going right, McGraw's combativeness got the better of him. After a game in Cincinnati on June 8, 1917, he punched umpire Bill Byron in the face for taunting him with the mild "you were run out of Baltimore." League president John Tener suspended McGraw for two weeks and fined him an unprecedented $500. McGraw dug an even deeper hole for himself by impugning Tener's integrity and pronouncing league umpires the worst he had seen. Called to account, McGraw denied his remarks, whereupon New York sportswriters, their own integrity at stake, insisted to Tener that McGraw had been correctly quoted. Tener fined McGraw another $1,000. Despite a cooling toward the Giants in some papers, New York fans continued to worship McGraw, giving him a huge ovation after the punishment was announced.

The Giants lost the 1917 World Series in six games to the White Sox. They were on their way to returning to the Fall Classic in 1918 when military callups for World War I deprived them of several frontline players. On October 5, reserve infielder Eddie Grant became the first major leaguer killed in battle, falling in the Argonne Forest five weeks before the armistice. The Giants placed a monument to Grant in deepest center field in 1921.

After the war, Harry Hempstead decided to sell. His family had endured seven years of ups and downs, and to his thinking, the federal government's war-related decision to shut down the 1918 season on Labor Day presaged an extended downturn. The Giants were the most valuable commodity in professional sports, having returned at least a 13 percent dividend to stockholders every year since 1912, and they attracted a swarm of interested buyers. With John McGraw as the go-between, on January 14, 1919, Hempstead sold 58 percent of the team to Charles Stoneham and two partners: Francis X. McQuade, a local judge and Sunday-baseball advocate, and McGraw. The price, variously cited as between $1,030,000 and $1,350,000, was the most ever paid for a ball club and was at least 10 times what Brush paid in 1902.

THE STONEHAM ERA BEGINS

Jersey City native Stoneham was a professional swindler who made his fortune running a bucket shop, a brokerage peddling investments without connection to a stock exchange. He also owned a stable of race horses. His gambling, his call to increase rosters from 21 to 25 (ostensibly to encourage the development of local players), and his willingness to spend, spend, spend panicked NL owners. Led by Brooklyn's Charles Ebbets, they passed baseball's first salary cap, limiting roster payrolls to $11,000 per month ($57,000 for a five-month, one-week season).

Stoneham was livid. Five Giants—outfielders George Burns and Benny Kauff and pitchers Pol Perritt, Slim Sallee, and Ferdie Schupp—made $30,000 by themselves, meaning he would have to pay his other 16 players about $1,700 apiece, less than players earned back in the 1890s. "It is the worst move made by the National League in its 43 years' history. It is so radical, silly and utterly impossible that we hardly can believe that the club owners mean to go through with it," fumed New York sportswriter Dan Daniel.

The players talked of a strike, and the AL rejected a similar salary cap. The latter development particularly troubled the NL owners, who feared that a new era of contract jumping might begin if one league paid better than another. A day after approving the cap, they rescinded it.

Free to spend as he pleased, Stoneham brought back the old days of the Brush regime, when McGraw could buy and sell players regardless of price. The Giants paid at least $40,000 for pitcher Art Nehf, at least $50,000 for third baseman Heinie Groh, $75,000 for minor leaguer Jimmy O'Connell, and $100,000 for pitcher Hugh McQuillan. The Giants also signed Fordham University infielder Frankie Frisch. After a couple years' apprenticeship, the Bronx-born Frisch became the driving force behind a Giants juggernaut that won four consecutive pennants from 1921 to 1924.

For McGraw, that made 10 pennants in 22 full seasons. No NL team or manager has ever won so consistently. But McGraw's clubs fared poorly in World Series play. When the Giants beat the Yankees in 1921, it was their first world championship in five tries. They swept the Yankees in 1922, giving McGraw his third postseason triumph, but he never won another Fall Classic. Despite the heroics of outfielder Casey Stengel, who won two games with homers, the Giants lost to the Yankees in six games in 1923. In 1924, despite beating Walter Johnson twice, they fell to the Senators in a memorably tight seven-game series, losing the finale in the bottom of the 12th inning.

Regardless of how they fared in the postseason (or whether they even made it that far), the Giants earned a fortune in the Roaring Twenties. The New York state legislature's legalization of Sabbath-day baseball in 1919 led to regular Sunday draws of 30,000 at the Polo Grounds. Most of those fans were working-class people who could not take time from their jobs to see games during the week. The Giants led the league in attendance five times over the decade, allowing Stoneham's club to average an annual profit of $183,193. Shareholder dividends crested at an amazing $625,000 in 1926, a year in which the Giants finished third in league attendance.

As successful as the Giants were, the period was not without scandals or seeds of doom. The nefarious Black Sox affair forced the major leagues to end their wink-and-nod tolerance of professional gambling. The Polo Grounds was a mecca for gamblers, and when Judge Kenesaw Mountain Landis was named commissioner and given a mandate to clean up the game, John McGraw and the Giants received close scrutiny. McGraw had owned a Herald Square pool hall with Arnold Rothstein, an alleged orchestrator of the Black Sox scandal, and the Giants had been periodically accused of throwing games, once (in October 1916, after the Dodgers clinched a pennant against them) by McGraw himself.

Particularly fishy was McGraw's eagerness to hire first baseman Hal Chase in 1919 after close friend Christy Mathewson, a paragon of integrity, had accused Chase of throwing games in Cincinnati. In September 1920 McGraw acknowledged to a grand jury that Chase and third baseman Heinie Zimmerman threw games in 1919, possibly costing the Giants a pennant. Landis imposed a lifetime ban on Zimmerman, but not Chase. He also banned star outfielder Benny Kauff, indicted for (but never convicted of) participating in a brother's car thievery. In a final flourish, Landis ordered Stoneham and McGraw to sell a Cuban racetrack they had recently bought.

You would expect a team watched that closely to play it extra straight, but no. During a drinking binge in August 1922, pitcher Phil Douglas wrote St. Louis Cardinal outfielder Les Mann offering to throw games for a price. Landis banned Douglas for life. Then in October 1924, with the Giants fighting for their fourth straight pennant, outfielder Jimmy O'Connell offered Philadelphia shortstop Heinie Sand $500 to go easy. Brought before Landis, O'Connell fingered teammates Frankie Frisch, George Kelly, and Ross Youngs and coach

Cozy Dolan as accomplices. Landis banned O'Connell and Dolan, but let the rest off.

THE DOWNWARD SLIDE BEGINS

The Giants survived the sleaze only to fall prey to the Yankees. In 1920 New York's AL team turned the Polo Grounds into the birthplace of the lively-ball era as Babe Ruth blasted 54 homers, forever changing the way baseball was played. The reason for Ruth's surge was the short right-field fence at the Polo Grounds. When he set the record for homers in a season in 1919, he hit 20 on the road, 9 at home in Fenway Park. In that first memorable season with the Yankees, he hit just 5 more homers in road games than the year before, but 20 more in home games.

Fans loved the new power game. Although the Giants drew an NL record 929,609 customers and made a hefty $296,803 profit, Ruth's Yankees brought in 1,289,422 fans (the first million-plus attendance for anyone) and cleared a record $373,862. A jealous Charles Stoneham sent the Yankees an eviction notice. Though he soon withdrew it (their lease entitled them to stay through 1922), the Yankees took the hint and arranged for construction of their own stadium across the Harlem River in the Bronx.

Not only did Ruth's exploits captivate the baseball world, not only did the Yankees build a magnificent park for themselves within walking distance of the Polo Grounds, and not only did the Yankees face the Giants in the World Series three of the four consecutive seasons the Giants won pennants, but in 1925 New Yorker Lou Gehrig, very much in the mold of Christy Mathewson and soon to become as popular, joined the Yankees lineup. The fears Brush and McGraw had about the AL 20 years earlier finally came true: the Yankees made the Giants number two in New York.

McGraw despised the home-run craze: "I think the game far more interesting when the art of making scores lies in scientific work on the bases." But knowing the Giants needed a slugger to compete at the turnstiles, in 1926 he brought up shy teenager Mel Ott. In time the high-kicking, dead-pulling lefty learned to feast off the Polo Grounds' short right-field fence; of his 511 lifetime homers, 323 were hit at home. After the 1926 campaign McGraw dealt Frankie Frisch to the Cardinals for Rogers Hornsby, one of the first NL players to emulate Ruth's uppercut swing and aim for the fences. But Hornsby ruined clubhouse morale with his fractious personality and was traded after just one season in New York.

McGraw further sought to enhance the Giants' appeal by finding a good Jewish player. By 1920 Jews comprised nearly 30 percent of New York's population. Moses Solomon and Harry Rosenberg looked promising in the minors, but collected only 13 big-league at bats between them. Andy Cohen was given two years to nail down the job at second base, but couldn't shake off mediocrity. The Giants scouted a strapping kid from the Bronx named Hank Greenberg, but passed.

Keeping up with the Yankees required more energy than the aging McGraw could muster. In the late 1920s he often wore street clothes to games, disqualifying himself from taking the field to argue with umpires. He occasionally skipped road trips. Treacherous front-office politics sapped him further. He sniped at Charles Stoneham for favoring team secretary James Tierney, then joined Stoneham in ousting Francis McQuade from the partnership, which led to years of lawsuits and embarrassing court testimony. McGraw had to protect his 10 percent stake in the Giants, which in 1928 was worth about $500,000 and returned more ($75,000) than he earned as manager ($50,000). He especially needed the money after a sizable Florida real-estate venture went bust, costing him $100,000.

On June 3, 1932, with his team in last place and his health declining, McGraw retired. He had managed the Giants for 30 of their 50 years and had become the name most associated with them. As Philadelphia Phillies manager Burt Shotton said, "They won't seem like the Giants without McGraw." The Little Napoleon made one last diamond appearance on July 6, 1933, as manager of the NL team in the first-ever All-Star Game. He died of prostate cancer on February 25, 1934.

McGraw's job went to first baseman Bill Terry. An acerbic personality doing well enough in private business to say and do as he pleased within baseball, Terry gave the players more freedom than McGraw, and they responded as if set free from jail. They won a pennant in 1933, led by screwballing pitcher Carl Hubbell, nicknamed "the Meal Ticket" for his dependability. Hubbell led the league in wins, shutouts, innings pitched, and ERA. The Giants then mauled the Washington Senators in the World Series, four games to one. Terry had the Giants in a first-place tie with two games to go in 1934, but the rival Brooklyn Dodgers came to the Polo Grounds mindful of Terry's wintertime crack, "Are they still in the league?" It was a comment on the Dodgers' failure to make trades, not their long-standing ineptitude. But the vengeful Bums beat the Giants in their last two games while St. Louis's Gas House Gang beat Cincinnati to take the flag.

Terry, Ott, and Hubbell were immensely popular. Terry was the last NL player to hit .400 (.401 in 1930), Ott became the first in the league to hit more than 500 lifetime homers, and Hubbell shocked the baseball world in 1934 when he struck out Babe Ruth, Lou Gehrig, Jimmie Foxx, Al Simmons, and Joe Cronin consecutively during the second annual All-Star Game. But as the Great Depression set in, the Giants' attendance tumbled, falling below 500,000 in 1932. The Giants had revived their Ladies' Day tradition in 1930, and on September 24, 1931, they played a three-way exhibition against the Yankees and Dodgers at the Polo Grounds to support the Mayor's Committee on Unemployment, raising $59,000. The sympathetic gestures helped, but attendance continued to lag until 1936, when Ott and Hubbell again led the Giants to a pennant. It rose above 900,000 in 1937, yet another pennant-winning season. The Giants cleared more than $300,000 in both years. But disappointing losses to the Yankees in the 1936 and 1937 World Series and deteriorating play in subsequent regular seasons caused attendance to sink below 800,000 in 1938 and remain lackluster through World War II.

HORACE STONEHAM TAKES OVER

The Giants might have fared better with firm guidance from the front office, but Charles Stoneham died of nephritis on January 6, 1936. His mild-mannered son Horace, 32, took over. The younger Stoneham had been involved with the team since his father bought it, and he had a basic understanding of the baseball business. But he was an alcoholic who lacked vision. He owned the Giants longer than anyone and fielded many exciting teams, yet presided over a gradual decline that left the Giants in shambles. His attitude toward the two biggest developments of the 1930s, night games and radio broadcasts, helps explain why.

As the Great Depression dragged on, fans were increasingly unwilling to take days off from precious jobs to see games. Playing at night would remove the obstacle. But when Larry MacPhail of the Cincinnati Reds asked for permission to play night games in 1935, the Giants were among three teams to vote no. Charles Stoneham flatly refused to play at night, arguing that night ball would increase injuries to players and fans and cost a fortune in installation and utility bills. What's more, the owner of baseball's most urban team claimed, nocturnal play flouted the sport's mythic, bucolic origins.

Night ball in Cincinnati was a huge success. But when MacPhail took over the Dodgers in 1938 and asked each NL opponent to play one night game a year at Ebbets Field, the younger Stoneham was the only owner to say no. Dodgers attendance shot up by 180,000, due mostly to night contests, while the Giants' slid by 127,000. A year later the Dodgers, fielding a competitive team for the first time in years, outdrew the Giants by a whopping 250,000. Belatedly, Stoneham installed lights at the Polo Grounds at a cost of nearly $150,000.

On May 24, 1940, the Giants became the last team in the NL to play after dark. The Cubs, famed for their refusal to play night games at home until 1988, were playing night games on the road by the late 1930s. Mayor Fiorello LaGuardia threw out the first ball, and the Giants trounced Casey Stengel's Boston Braves, 8–1. "Night baseball stinks," manager Terry, a purist, insisted afterward. Reminded how much revenue the change would bring, he responded dryly, "Nevertheless."

The story with radio was a little different, because the Giants were one of the first teams to experiment with the medium: Grantland Rice called the initial game of the 1922 World Series against the Yankees over Newark's WJZ. But Charles Stoneham, afraid fans wouldn't pay to see a game if they could hear it for free, joined the Yankees and Dodgers in a 1934 handshake deal barring baseball broadcasts from New York ballparks for at least the next five years.

When an outfit called Tele-Flash equipped an employee overlooking the Polo Grounds with a telegraph and used his messages to re-create home games, the Giants sued.

The Giants lost the suit, but continued to forbid radio broadcasts from their home park. By 1939 the Giants, Yankees, and Dodgers were the only teams holding out against radio. Larry MacPhail changed that too, arranging to broadcast Dodger games over 50,000-watt WOR. After waffling, Stoneham joined the Yankees in a deal to broadcast weekday and Saturday home games over WABC, another 50,000-watt clear channel. Arch McDonald and Mel Allen did the announcing, sponsored by General Mills, Procter and Gamble, and Mobil.

Horace Stoneham's archaic thinking extended to the makeup of his team. His baseball aesthetic hardened around the time Ruth and Gehrig captured the imagination of baseball fans, so for the rest of his life he believed that if two or three sluggers were good, five or six were better. Between 1936 and 1950 the Giants led the league in homers nine times, but the rest of their game suffered. And though Stoneham heeded Bill Terry's entreaties to build a farm system, placing the Giants' top affiliate in his father's hometown of Jersey City, he moved too slowly to keep up with the competition. When Terry, Ott, and Hubbell passed their prime, there was no one to replace them, and the 1940s became the first decade in which the Giants did not win a pennant. They slid to third (and last) in New York.

THE WAR YEARS

Then came World War II. No sooner had Stoneham bolted lights atop the Polo Grounds than they were deemed a security risk and he was forbidden to use them; the 200-million-candlepower system illuminated ships in New York Harbor. His team played as if in the dark, finishing at least 19 games out every year from 1942 to 1945.

The Giants were firmly patriotic. Even before Pearl Harbor—on May 27, 1941—management halted a night game for 45 minutes so fans could listen to President Roosevelt's radio address declaring a national emergency. Before 1942's first game at the Polo Grounds, Mayor LaGuardia ceremoniously handed new Giants manager Mel Ott and Dodgers skipper Leo Durocher war bonds they had purchased. That year every major-league team pledged to donate the proceeds from one home game to a defense-related cause. On August 3 the Giants hosted the Dodgers in a benefit for the Army Emergency Relief fund that drew 57,305 fans and netted nearly $80,000.

But the response from Giants fans wasn't always ideal. When umpire George Magerkurth, observing the wartime curfew, halted that fund-raising game in the bottom of the ninth with the tying run at the plate, the fans nearly rioted. Shining a light on the American flag failed to appease them, so a band struck up "The Star-Spangled Banner." Eventually singing drowned out the jeers and the crowd thinned. Another betrayal of national unity marred the end of a September 26, 1942, doubleheader. The Giants let in free any kid bringing scrap metal for the war effort, but with the Giants ahead 5–2 in the eighth inning of the second game, the kids poured onto the field and ran wild, causing the umpires to declare a forfeit.

On June 25, 1944, with the Normandy invasion well underway, the Giants played the Dodgers and Yankees in a three-way exhibition at the Polo Grounds. Over 50,000 fans bought a $25 (or more) war bond to attend. The teams rotated six times between batting, fielding, and resting, and the Dodgers won, 5–1–0, over the Yankees and Giants. After the war in Europe ended, General Dwight Eisenhower was driven around the Polo Grounds in triumph. The Giants lost that afternoon's game, their 18th setback in 23 tries, leading manager Mel Ott to ask, "Tell me, General, just how does one go about bringing up reinforcements quickly?"

BASEBALL'S BIGGEST MOMENT

Ott really needed an answer to that question in 1946, when seven players, including promising hurler Sal Maglie, defected to the Mexican League, which was trying to become a third major league. The Giants were hurt by the rebel circuit more than any other team. On July 5 of that year, Dodgers manager Leo Durocher pointed to Ott from the visiting dugout at the Polo Grounds and said, "Being a nice guy gets you nowhere. Absolutely nowhere. Look over there. There's one of the nicest guys in the world. Is it doing him any good? He's in last place. That's where nice guys finish. Last." Conflated to "Nice guys finish last," the gibe is one of baseball's most notorious contributions to the American argot. That year it was also true, as the Giants did finish last.

When the Mexican League failed, the ex-Giants were eager to return, but MLB imposed a five-year ban on them for contract jumping. In October 1947 blacklisted outfielder Danny Gardella sued for $300,000, alleging the ban amounted to restraint of trade. At bottom was the legality of the reserve clause. Gardella settled two years later for an estimated $60,000 and a release from the Giants, which gave him an opportunity to try out for the Cardinals. According to the *New York Sun*, ownership "heaved a tremendous sigh of relief" that the reserve clause survived this latest threat from a Giants player.

Meanwhile, over in Brooklyn, another of baseball's injustices fell. Until 1947, both major leagues had excluded African Americans. John McGraw in 1902 had tried (albeit halfheartedly) to break the color line by claiming that African American Charley Grant was an American Indian, but Charles Comiskey sniffed out the truth, and Grant's major-league career was aborted. Forty-five years later, Horace Stoneham allegedly warned his fellow owners that if the Brooklyn Dodgers brought up Jackie Robinson, blacks in Harlem would burn down the Polo Grounds.

It didn't turn out that way, of course, and two years later, on July 5, 1949, the Giants became the second NL team to integrate, bringing up Hank Thompson and Monte Irvin. On July 8, Thompson and the Dodgers' Don Newcombe became the first African American batter and pitcher to face each other in a major-league game.

Giants fans might have been forgiven for overlooking that milestone. They were still coming to grips with the fact that Leo Durocher, for years the skipper of the detested Dodgers, was now *their* manager. In July 1948, Horace Stoneham decided to fire Mel Ott and replace him with elderly Burt Shotton, who had guided the Dodgers to a pennant in 1947 but been put out to pasture when Durocher returned from a yearlong suspension. When Stoneham asked Dodgers general manager Branch Rickey for permission to speak to Shotton, Rickey answered, "No, I may need him at any moment myself." Stoneham asked if that meant Durocher was available. When Rickey said yes, Stoneham, in one of his sharpest moments, engineered Durocher's overnight transfer from the Dodgers to the Giants. New York responded with the kind of shock reserved for assassinations. Hilda Chester, the Dodgers' most famous fan and a Durocher diehard, announced she was switching allegiance. As for Giants fans: "It took them two years to learn to barely tolerate me," Durocher rued.

Though perceived as the ultimate repudiation of John McGraw's legacy, Durocher actually restored it. Like the Little Napoleon, Leo the Lip grew up in the Northeast (West Springfield, Massachusetts), the son of poor immigrants. He too had ready fists, a love of gambling, and contempt for umpires. On the field, McGraw and Durocher shared a fondness for the one-run tactics nearly forgotten in the lively-ball era. And both would do anything (cheating included) to succeed.

Durocher told Stoneham that if the Giants were to win, the power hitters had to go in favor of pitching, speed, and defense. Stoneham hesitated, in part because the long ball was good business: when the Giants set a major-league record with 221 homers in 1947, they drew over 1.6 million fans, their best in New York. He relented, though, and by the end of 1950 Durocher had turned the Giants into contenders. In May 1951 they got an added boost with the arrival of 20-year-old Willie Mays. But on July 18, 1951, the Giants were a disappointing eight games behind the first-place Dodgers. A desperate Durocher decided to cheat.

He had the Polo Grounds electrician install a buzzer in the clubhouse behind center field and connect it to the phone in the Giants bullpen. A spy in the clubhouse peered through a telescope, stole the opposing catcher's signs, and buzzed once for a fastball, twice for anything else. Then someone in the bullpen clued in the batter by a prearranged sign.

The Giants fell 13 1/2 games behind the Dodgers on August 11. But then they went on one of the most amazing tears in baseball history, winning 37 of their last 44 games to tie the flat-footed Dodgers for first. The pennant had to be decided by a three-game playoff. The Giants won the first game, 3–1. The Dodgers took the second game, 10–0. Everything came down to the final contest, played at the Polo Grounds on October 3.

Through seven innings the score was tied, 1–1. In the top of the eighth Giants workhorse Sal Maglie, 23–6 for the year and an amazing 41–10 since

Commissioner Chandler pardoned him for joining the Mexican League, yielded three runs, putting the Giants behind, 4–1. Dodgers ace Don Newcombe mowed down the Giants in the bottom of the eighth. After Larry Jansen, who replaced Maglie, retired the Dodgers in the top of the ninth, the stage was set for the most dramatic moment in baseball history.

Giants leadoff batter Alvin Dark hit a grounder to the right side that deflected off first baseman Gil Hodges's mitt for a single. Don Mueller followed with a grounder between Hodges and second baseman Jackie Robinson for another single. Monte Irvin, the league's leading RBI man, came to the plate as the tying run but popped out. That brought up Whitey Lockman. He lashed a double down the left-field line, scoring Dark to make it 4–2.

Dodgers manager Charlie Dressen replaced Newcombe with Ralph Branca. The Giants had already beaten Branca five times in 1951, and the next batter, Bobby Thomson, had homered off him in the first playoff game. With first base open, Dressen had to decide whether to pitch to Thomson or intentionally walk him to set up the force at any base and bring up the inexperienced Mays. Dressen decided that putting the winning run on base was too risky, and pitched to Thomson.

On the second pitch of the at bat, Branca threw a fastball up and in. Thomson swung. Giants announcer Russ Hodges's immortal radio call told all: "There's a long fly . . . It's gonna be, I believe . . . *The Giants win the pennant! The Giants win the pennant! The Giants win the pennant! The Giants win the pennant!* Bobby Thomson hits into the lower deck of the left field stands! The Giants win the pennant and they're going crazy! They're going crazy! *Waaah-hoe!*"

For 50 years there were rumors that the Giants' miracle comeback and playoff victory weren't on the level. Not until January 2001, however, did surviving Giants players admit that they stole signs at the Polo Grounds. The revelation tarnished not only Thomson's "Shot Heard 'Round the World," as the momentous homer came to be known, but the Giants' whole season.

But should it have? There is no evidence that the Giants' sign stealing, technically legal back then, actually helped. If Giants hitters had gained an advantage by knowing the next pitch, it would have shown as an increase in runs scored at home. Before the sign stealing, they scored an average of 5.46 runs per game at the Polo Grounds. After the sign stealing, they scored an average of 4.57 runs per game at home, almost nine-tenths of a run per game *less*. The real secret of the Giants comeback was pitching. Through games of July 18, the Giants allowed an average of 4.69 runs per game. From July 20 on they allowed an average of 3.30 per game, a decrease of 1.39.

THE MOVE

Exhausted by the playoff with the Dodgers, the Giants lost the World Series to the Yankees. Then Durocher's hopes of repeating in 1952 were thwarted when Willie Mays was drafted into the army. Attendance fell below a million for the first time since World War II, and dropped further in 1953 as the Giants finished 35 games out. With Mays back in 1954 the Giants won the pennant, compiling their best record (97–57) since 1917. The pitching staff logged the NL's lowest ERA thanks largely to Johnny Antonelli, received from the Braves at the start of the year in a trade for Bobby Thomson. The Giants went on to sweep the heavily favored Indians in a World Series best known for Mays's brilliant, over-the-head snare of Vic Wertz's drive to the deepest part of the Polo Grounds. The championship performance raised attendance back over a million, but when the Giants collapsed in 1955, prompting Durocher's departure, the turnstile count swooned by more than 300,000, leaving Horace Stoneham to face hard facts.

The Giants had conclusively lost the battle of New York, beating the Yankees' attendance only once since 1935 and the Dodgers' only three times since 1939. The Yankees drew the front-runners (they had taken Wall Street from the Giants) and the Dodgers the catharsis seekers, leaving the Giants with a vestigial following on Broadway (including Tallulah Bankhead, who said, "There have been only two authentic geniuses in the world, Willie Mays and Willie Shakespeare") and a dwindling core that either went back to the McGraw days or dutifully carried on the family loyalty.

Willie Mays, 1958. Courtesy of the Baseball Hall of Fame

The neighborhood surrounding the Polo Grounds had been prosperous during the Giants' heyday, but by the 1950s it had turned into a dangerous African American ghetto that most white New Yorkers considered the ultimate forbidden zone. The railroad yard next door had been replaced by a crime-riddled public housing project, and on July 4, 1950, a fan watching a Giants-Dodgers doubleheader was killed when a 14-year-old boy fired a pistol from a nearby tenement roof.

The Polo Grounds itself, built in haste four decades earlier, was dilapidated. Cars had become the preferred means of transportation, but there was little proximate parking, and in 1955 Stoneham lost a battle with the city to prevent conversion of a 400-car lot into a playground. With the lease on

Coogan's Hollow set to expire in 1962, the ball club's days in upper Manhattan appeared numbered.

Yet the Giants remained profitable. In 1956 they received $730,000 for radio and television rights, second in the league to the Dodgers. Tattered as it was, the Polo Grounds remained the largest public venue in Manhattan, allowing Stoneham to rent it for football games, boxing matches, religious revivals, and even baseball, most notably to the New York Cubans Negro League team. Many tenants were irked by Stoneham's terms, which included up to 25 percent of net receipts. In October 1947 Reverend Robert Gannon, president of Fordham University, labeled the Giants "extortionists" for collecting $1.5 million in rental fees over 25 years' worth of university football games.

Even so, Stoneham's financial well-being depended heavily on the Dodgers' 11 annual visits to the Polo Grounds. In some years Dodger games accounted for 40 percent of the Giants' attendance. Now Brooklyn owner Walter O'Malley was talking about leaving town, and without the Dodgers, Stoneham saw little hope for the Giants' survival in New York. On August 18, 1955, a day before O'Malley was to meet with Mayor Robert Wagner and Construction Coordinator Robert Moses about a new ballpark in Brooklyn, Stoneham announced that he wanted a new stadium too, proposing that the city build one for the Giants and Yankees in the eastern Bronx, near the Whitestone Bridge.

New York officials were in a jam. An exodus of middle-class whites to suburbia, combined with an influx of poor African Americans and Puerto Ricans, was driving up social welfare costs while eroding the tax base. Construction of municipally owned ballparks would not only require huge capital outlays, but would take acres of private property off the tax rolls. There was also the prospect of litigation to determine whether building ballparks for private owners was a public interest that entitled the city to condemn and take over land. In the Giants' case, the question quickly became moot. Yankees general manager George Weiss dashed the Whitestone idea by saying, "We're very happy with Yankee Stadium."

Noting the success of other clubs that had moved out of multiple-team markets, Stoneham briefly considered going to Minneapolis, where the Giants had transferred their top farm club after major-league broadcasts killed interest in the Jersey City affiliate. Instead he fruitlessly pursued an agreement with the Yankees and Dodgers to stop televising home night games and encouraged Manhattan borough president Hulan Jack's far-fetched scheme to build a 110,000-seat stadium on stilts above a West Side railroad yard. He rebuffed a September 1955 overture from Bill Terry to buy the team and move it to Yankee Stadium.

The need for a new ballpark grew more urgent in 1956, when the football Giants gave notice they were leaving the Polo Grounds, depriving Stoneham of rental income, and the baseball Giants' sixth-place finish caused an attendance dip to 629,000, the lowest total since 1943. As 1957 rolled around, Stoneham was desperate for good news.

He got it on May 10 from George Christopher, mayor of San Francisco. Christopher had met with Los Angeles mayor Norris Poulson and Dodgers owner Walter O'Malley a week before. Poulson and O'Malley had agreed in principle that the Dodgers would move to Los Angeles for 1958, but worried that the NL wouldn't approve unless a second team transferred to the West Coast and made the long road trips worthwhile. Would Christopher hook up with Stoneham, who fondly remembered San Francisco from his footloose youth, and try to lure the Giants to northern California?

While sitting in Stoneham's Polo Grounds office and watching the Giants beat the Dodgers on the field, Christopher made his offer. In exchange for the Giants' commitment to a 35-year lease, San Francisco would build them a new stadium with 40,000 seats and 10,000 parking spaces; the city had already passed a bond measure authorizing $5 million for construction. Stoneham would receive concession rights and free office space as well as other perks. His annual rent would be the higher of either $125,000 or five percent of gross receipts adjusted for taxes and other expenses. There would be no rental charge for World Series games. If the new park wasn't ready by Opening Day 1958, San Francisco would rent minor-league Seals Stadium to the Giants under the same conditions as the new facility.

It was all Stoneham needed to hear. The Giants were going to San Francisco.

At the end of May, NL owners unanimously approved the move to California as long as Stoneham and O'Malley formally committed themselves by October 1, 1957. But Emanuel Celler, the Brooklyn congressman whose House Anti-trust Subcommittee had been looking into the baseball business for years, was not about to let his local teams leave so easily. He subpoenaed Stoneham and O'Malley for June 26. O'Malley's testimony took all day, forcing Stoneham to come back in July.

The subcommittee expressed only minor indignation at Stoneham's claim that New York could no longer support three teams. The committee's own data showed the Giants averaging less than $70,000 a year in profit since 1952, seventh among the major leagues' 16 teams. According to Stoneham, after-tax profits had shrunk from 29 percent in 1954 to less than 6 percent in 1956. He denied that he and O'Malley were working in concert, and insisted that he intended to move to San Francisco even if the Dodgers remained in Brooklyn. In addition to lining up a municipal ballpark with plenty of parking, he had reached agreement with Skiatron, a cable-television operator, to broadcast games via closed circuit for an estimated $125,000 per game, of which he would keep a hefty share.

True to his word, Stoneham assembled his board of directors on August 19, 1957, nearly two months before the Dodgers moved to Los Angeles, and asked for permission to notify the NL that the team would play in San Francisco in 1958. He estimated annual profits in California at over $200,000 before broadcast revenue. The board, consisting almost entirely of relatives and cronies, backed him by a vote of eight to one.

New Yorkers were forlorn but resigned to the Giants' departure. The *Herald Tribune* editorialized, "The Giants brought New York too many thrills and too much pride for anyone here to wish them anything but good as they prepare to leave for their new home." John McGraw's widow, Blanche, a mainstay at the Polo Grounds for decades, lamented, "I can't conceive that I'll never again watch the Giants play at the Polo Grounds. I don't know what I will do with myself." Flanked by a host of former Giants, including Jack Doyle, who had managed the team under Andrew Freedman in 1895, she watched the Giants lose their final game in New York to the Pirates on September 27, 1957. The crowd size of 11,606 was disappointing until compared with the season average of 8,452. Officially designated the last fan to leave, she watched thousands of ruffians tear up the grounds and demand to see Horace Stoneham "with a rope around his neck!"

SAN FRANCISCO, HERE WE COME

In San Francisco, Mayor Christopher was jubilant. The city needed $275,000 a year to amortize its ballpark debt, and he expected Giants games to bring in $518,000. Boosters believed the Giants would add at least $25 million a year to the local tourist economy.

But not every San Franciscan celebrated. Some thought the Giants got too good a deal. "When the mayor signs that lease he ought to wear white whiskers and a red suit," griped one. There would also be financing problems, because a new stadium would cost more than the $5 million raised by the bond measure. And the city would lose its beloved Pacific Coast League Seals, who had been around since 1904 and had sent many local stars to the majors.

In October 1957 Stoneham secured baseball rights to San Francisco by trading his Minneapolis minor-league team to the Red Sox for the Seals. Boston could have ransomed the Seals for a fortune, but general manager Joe Cronin was a San Francisco native eager to see a major-league team in his hometown. The PCL was less accommodating. Fearing serious harm to their circuit, the PCL owners made Stoneham pay a $300,000 indemnity over three years. They also got him to purchase the Class A minor-league team in Phoenix, Arizona, to replace the Seals.

The new ballpark wasn't ready in time, so the Giants used Seals Stadium, nestled between the Mission District and Potrero Hill. Opened in 1931, it seated just 22,900. "It had a warmth and a sense of community not unlike Wrigley Field or Fenway Park," said Orlando Cepeda, whose popularity in San Francisco owed much to his accessibility to fans sitting near first base.

Manager Bill Rigney used the move to give the team a fresh identity, putting three rookies in the Opening Day lineup: Cepeda, Jim Davenport, and Willie Kirkland. Bob Schmidt debuted the next day, and Felipe Alou, first of the famous brothers, arrived in early June. Willie McCovey came up in 1959, Juan Marichal in 1960. "It seemed that a new young player was joining the club all the time," Rigney recalled.

Most of the talent came from Latin America. Horace Stoneham's one great innovation was to recruit in Puerto Rico, the Dominican Republic, and Cuba while most other teams were still coming to terms with having African Americans on the roster. After the New York Cubans went out of business in 1951, director of scouting Jack Schwarz suggested that Stoneham hire Cubans owner Alex Pompez to scout the Caribbean. Pompez was soon funneling a stream of Spanish-speaking athletes into the Giants farm system.

In the first major-league baseball game played on the West Coast, on April 15, 1958, the Giants shut out the Dodgers behind Ruben Gomez, 8–0. Giants infielder Daryl Spencer hit the first West Coast home run. "It's like the World Series," said Mays of the atmosphere.

But Mays couldn't have been happy. Regarded as royalty in New York, in San Francisco he was received coolly. "It was as if I had done something wrong by doing well in New York," he said later. Mays was well on his way to establishing himself as the most complete player in the game's history. Not only could he hit for average, hit for power, run, field, and throw, but he could do them all at a Hall of Fame level. He retired with 660 home runs, trailing only Hank Aaron and Babe Ruth. But even though he hit .347 and led the league in runs scored and stolen bases during the Giants' first year in San Francisco, the natives considered Cepeda the more valuable player. Worse still, Mays faced discrimination. When he tried to buy a house in the wealthy Sherwood Forest district, neighbors pressured the seller into refusing his bid. An appalled Mayor Christopher offered Mays space in his own house. The seller eventually made the deal, but a week after Mays moved in, someone threw a brick through his living-room window.

Meanwhile, the scent of boondoggle began wafting from the Giants' new ballpark. Candlestick Cove, at the city's southeast edge, was too far from downtown to benefit other businesses. Contractor Charles Harney had offered the city the 80-acre tract at a bargain price of $2.7 million on condition that his construction firm build the stadium, a deal too good to pass up. Harney boasted he would finish construction in eight months, but when a naming contest didn't go as expected (how could they not call it Harney Park?) his zeal for the project flagged. The Giants spent two years in Seals Stadium, and didn't play their first game in horseshoe-shaped Candlestick Park until April 12, 1960.

Candlestick Park was a whopping mistake. It was notorious for howling wind, fierce cold, and impenetrable fog. On all but the most unseasonably warm days, sweaters and winter jackets were de rigueur for fans. Hot water passing through 35,000 feet of pipe in the concrete was supposed to warm the high-priced sections (for those sitting in general admission or the bleachers, it was bring your own blankets), but the system never worked. A wind baffle curling over the top of the stadium never worked either. The entire country learned of Candlestick's forbidding environment on July 11, 1961, when the 30th All-Star Game was held there. Trying to save the game for the NL, pitcher Stu Miller was blown off the mound by the wind, earning a balk call that advanced the tying run to third. A subsequent groundout tied the game. The NL pulled it out in the 10th when the wind rendered AL pitcher Hoyt Wilhelm's knuckleball ineffective.

The Giants drew well at Candlestick despite the weather. A team record 1,795,356 customers turned out in 1960, and the Giants averaged more than 1.4 million fans per year over their first decade there, as opposed to 980,000 over their last decade at the Polo Grounds. Even though the Skiatron deal never panned out, Horace Stoneham had every reason to think he had made a terrific business decision, even better than the one made by Walter O'Malley, who had financed his own ballpark and assumed an enormous debt.

ROCK BOTTOM

But Stoneham was operating under ideal conditions. The Giants were the only big-league team for 400 miles. They had five future Hall of Famers in Mays, Cepeda, McCovey, Marichal, and Gaylord Perry. They posted a winning record each of their first 14 years out west, a streak even John McGraw could not match. And last, but most important, they were wholeheartedly embraced by San Franciscans. When the Giants clinched their first West Coast pennant on October 3, 1962, in a three-game playoff with the Dodgers that nearly matched the 1951 cliffhanger for drama, an estimated 50,000 fans clogged the airport in hopes of welcoming the players, forcing the team plane to land in a maintenance area. To avoid the mob, Cepeda found a back exit, walked to the freeway, and hitchhiked home. Mays heard shouts of "We want Mays!" and ducked into a taxi. Once fans found the team bus, they rocked it back and forth. "That was about as scared as I've ever been," recalled catcher Ed Bailey. In the World Series, the Giants lost to the Yankees in the seventh game when New York second baseman Bobby Richardson speared Willie McCovey's scorching line drive with the tying run on third and two out in the last of the ninth.

The rivalry with the Dodgers flourished as never before, drawing more fans (805,172) to 18 games in 1966 than the Chicago Cubs or Cincinnati Reds drew for *all* their home games that year. Leonard Koppett, the eminent New York sportswriter who moved to the Bay Area shortly after the Giants did, deemed the rivalry "the richest in American sports." It was also the most intense, culminating in the worst act of on-field player-on-player violence in history. On August 22, 1965, Giants pitcher Juan Marichal raised his bat and brought it down full force on the head of Dodgers catcher John Roseboro. Fortunately Roseboro wasn't seriously injured, but Marichal was suspended for eight days and fined a then NL record $1,750. So much did the incident overshadow the high-kicking Marichal's other achievements—more wins and innings pitched than Dodger greats Sandy Koufax and Don Drysdale, with a 2.89 ERA, 244 complete games, and nine All-Star Games—that it delayed his election to the Hall of Fame by several years.

Despite all their talent, the Giants of the 1960s failed to win another pennant, finishing second five times in a row from 1965 to 1969. (Many fans believed that Marichal's 1965 suspension, which cost him two starts, was the reason the Giants fell short by two games that year.) In 1971, after the NL had expanded to 12 teams and split into divisions, the Giants won the Western Division title, but lost to Pittsburgh in a playoff. With that, the team's Hall of Fame core dispersed, and the Giants lost their fan appeal.

Stoneham also lost his Bay Area monopoly. The Kansas City Athletics moved to Oakland in 1968, causing Giants attendance to sink below 1 million for the first time in San Francisco. After a rebound in the division-winning 1971 season, attendance plummeted even further in 1972 to 648,000, less than the last year at the Polo Grounds.

Horace Stoneham had seldom been innovative, but he had been adaptable. As he approached 70, however, he found it harder to move with the times. In an increasingly media-driven age he continued to rely heavily on gate receipts, televising just a few road games a year, mostly against the Dodgers. It took a riot (literally) to get him to televise more often. On September 27, 1966, San Francisco erupted in violence after a white police officer fatally shot an unarmed African American teenager who had stolen a car. The Giants, battling the Dodgers and Pirates for the pennant, were in Atlanta. The city's Human Relations Commission asked Stoneham to televise that night's game as a way of getting people off the streets. The Giants owner consented, and shortly after the broadcast began, the violence abated.

By 1971, out-of-town buyers had noticed Stoneham's distress and made inquiries. "We couldn't leave the area if we wanted to. We signed a 35-year contract with the city of San Francisco when we moved here in 1958. It still has 22 years to run," he replied. That winter the city began a major renovation of Candlestick, closing the horseshoe to blunt the wind and to seat more fans for football's 49ers. Stoneham felt betrayed. Not only were the Giants inconvenienced by the construction, but their fans had to fork over an extra 50 cents per ticket to pay off the bond, a hefty surcharge at a time when seats behind the dugout cost just three dollars. As the turnstile count shrank even further, to a low of 520,000 in 1974, Stoneham traded one exciting young player after another (Bobby Bonds, George Foster, Dave Kingman, Garry Maddox) for lesser players and the cash to stay afloat.

In May 1975 he exhausted his $1 million credit line, all but forcing him to sell. Offers poured in, including one from Japan's Fukuoka Lions for $18 million. The Giants had been the first team to bring a native Japanese player to the big leagues, pitcher Masanori Murakami in 1964. But in September Fukuoka rescinded its offer, citing fears that San Franciscans would resent foreign ownership. Galloping inflation in the world economy also contributed to the deal's collapse.

While waiting for his dream buyer (he wanted $17 million for the team and its properties, which included a hotel in Arizona, an industrial park in Minnesota, and a condominium development in Florida), Stoneham took out a $500,000 loan from the NL, repayable by December 1. He also withheld payment of the Giants' $125,000 Candlestick rental fee. Even so, he had to declare a loss for the year of $1.8 million. The franchise hit its nadir in December 1975 when Stoneham defaulted on his loan and the NL took over day-to-day administration of the team.

Two Bay Area engineers and their attorney formed a grassroots group called Giant Owners Inc. that hoped to sell 100,000 shares at $150 apiece to buy the team. It never had a chance. On January 9, 1976, Stoneham agreed to an offer from Labatt, a Toronto brewery, for $13.25 million, $8 million for the team plus $5.25 million to pay off the Candlestick lease and any litigation.

A stunned George Moscone, freshly inaugurated as San Francisco's mayor, declared, "The San Francisco Giants will remain the San Francisco Giants if I have anything to do about it." He had the city attorney prepare a restraining order to prevent the sale, and flew to the NL owners meeting a few days later to serve the order personally. The owners assured Moscone that if the city made a viable offer, they would let the team stay in San Francisco. On February 11, 1976, the day the restraining order expired, Moscone brought together potential buyers Bob Short and Bob Lurie. The trio rushed into court to announce that San Francisco had an ownership group to rival Labatt. Judge John Benson told a gallery packed with Giants fans, "The court considers the equities to be overwhelming on the side of the city and the court will issue a preliminary injunction." Moscone triumphantly shouted, "Bobby Thomson still lives!"

The joy was premature. Stoneham and the NL bosses still had to approve the sale, and though Stoneham assented, the owners balked at Short, who had infuriated their AL brethren by moving, then abandoning, the Washington Senators–Texas Rangers. They decided that Short could own a piece of the Giants, but could not be the managing partner. Short refused to invest unless he was in charge, so the deal dissolved.

But on March 2, Arizona cattleman Bud Herseth called Moscone out of the blue and volunteered $4 million to keep the Giants in San Francisco. Moscone connected Herseth and Lurie, who worked out a partnership. Secretly, Moscone also wrote a letter to NL owners assuring them that if the Giants averaged fewer than a million fans a season over the next three years, he would not oppose a subsequent sale and move, but would "agree to such transfer upon the payment of $2,500,000 damages to San Francisco." With that understanding the league owners approved the deal, and on March 4, 1976, Horace Stoneham sold the Giants (not including the other properties) for $8 million, ending his family's 57-year ownership.

THE LURIE YEARS

Lurie bought out Herseth in 1978. Son of colorful real-estate magnate Louis Lurie, the new Giants owner was a small, unassuming man, but as his father bragged to *San Francisco Chronicle* sports editor Art Rosenbaum after the pennant celebration of 1962, "See that kid over there? That kid is worth $26 million in his own name." Despite serving on the Giants' board of directors, Lurie knew little about the baseball business. "I firmly believe that it can be profitable but I would say I got involved mainly not to let the club leave town, and because of the challenge involved," he said.

Lurie retained general manager Spec Richardson, assigned by the NL when it took over the team. Richardson lived up to his reputation for recklessness, trading seven players to the Athletics for pitcher Vida Blue and signing broken-down infielder Rennie Stennett to a munificent free-agent contract. Except for 1978, Richardson's teams never contended. That was also the Giants' best year for attendance since 1960, as they capitalized on an expiring TV contract to advertise at cut rates on three Bay Area stations hoping to pick up local broadcast rights. Two years later attendance was back below 1,100,000, 23rd out of 26 teams.

Lurie named Frank Robinson the NL's first African American manager in 1981, and later that year hired Tom Haller as his new general manager. Haller did even worse than Richardson. He assembled a surprise contender in 1982, but in 1984 the Giants lost 96 games, their most since 1943, and in 1985 they lost 100 games for the only time in franchise history. Attendance fell below a million. A disenchanted Lurie announced he was putting the Giants up for sale with the proviso that the buyer keep the team in San Francisco. He blamed Candlestick Park for the franchise's misfortunes and called for the city to build a new stadium.

Candlestick was indeed a handicap, but Lurie's ownership coincided with an across-the-board plunge in San Francisco's fortunes. In 1978 the city was traumatized by the murder-suicide in Guyana of 912 people from the Tenderloin-based People's Temple and, just eight days later, by the assassination of Mayor Moscone and County Supervisor Harvey Milk, the first openly gay elected official in America. Then in the early 1980s the city was overwhelmed by epidemics of homelessness and AIDS. Locals could be excused if supporting a losing baseball team ranked low on their list of priorities.

The turning point came on September 18, 1985, when Lurie dumped general manager Haller in favor of Al Rosen, an experienced executive in and out of baseball and a member of the 1954 Cleveland Indians team the Giants had beaten to win their last world championship. Rosen's first act was to name Roger Craig manager. The following spring Craig brought up a couple of promising rookies in Will Clark and Robby Thompson, taught the pitching staff to throw the split-fingered fastball, and banished negativity with the corny phrase "humm baby." In 1986 the Giants improved by 21 games. The next year they won the division title, but lost the NL Championship Series to St. Louis in seven games. In 1989, led by sluggers Kevin Mitchell and Will Clark, they beat the Chicago Cubs in the playoffs and went to their first World Series in 27 years.

The Bay Area's fortunes improved at the same time, as upstart companies in the so-called Silicon Valley south of San Francisco virtually cornered the market in computers and other emerging technologies. The boom soon spread throughout the region, and the Giants shared in the wealth. Attendance rose to a franchise record 1,917,168 in 1987 and crossed the 2 million mark in 1989.

Lurie sought to take advantage of the good times. Announcing that the Giants would not play in Candlestick beyond the 1994 expiration of their lease, in 1987 he sponsored Proposition W, a nonbinding referendum that would make it city policy to build a new stadium at Seventh and Townsend Streets, an area south of Market Street that was run-down but convenient to the city's major freeways (101 and 280). Most local politicians backed the initiative, and the *San Francisco Chronicle* said, "Along with museums, opera, theater and ballet, baseball constitutes an important part of entertainment in a sophisticated metropolis. The voters should say 'yes' to remaining a big-league city in all senses of the term."

But voters said no by a margin of 53 to 47 percent. Burned by the siting of Candlestick Park 30 years earlier, they were reluctant to locate a new stadium in an undesirable neighborhood. They also resented Lurie's veiled threats that unless the ballot measure was approved, the Giants would leave San Francisco.

Though bitter, Lurie bounced back in 1989 with Proposition P, which called for the city to build a stadium in China Basin, an industrial zone along the waterfront. Sponsored by Mayor Art Agnos, the measure would have cost the city upward of $60 million. Even so, it appeared headed for passage until disaster struck. The Loma Prieta earthquake of October 17 not only destroyed parts of San Francisco's Marina District, but halted the Giants' first home World Series game since 1962 minutes before it was to begin. Candlestick Park weathered the quake with minimal damage, which gave voters second thoughts, and the Giants lost to the Athletics in four straight, which took some of the luster off the team. A leaflet mailed to San Francisco voters by a group interested in moving the franchise to Sacramento spread further doubt by claiming that ballpark funding would come at the expense of earthquake victims. On November 7, 1989, Proposition P lost by 51 to 49 percent, fewer than 2,000 votes overall.

With that, Lurie gave up on San Francisco. But noting the high proportion of Giants fans coming from the South Bay (and all that money in Silicon Valley), in 1990 he put a trio of ballot initiatives before Santa Clara County voters. County Measure G would finance a new park via a one percent utility tax. Measure H, for San Jose only, would let that city use tax money to build a park. Measure N, for the city of Santa Clara only, would permit the Giants to build the new stadium on 96 acres near an amusement park. Although the first two narrowly lost, the third passed.

That encouraged Lurie to work with San Jose mayor Susan Hammer on a June 1992 ballot measure that would increase utility taxes by two percent, raising $265 million to build a stadium and fund education and public safety. But

the economy was mired in recession, and the ballpark proposal was expected to result in an annual tax increase of $35 per household. Liberals viewed
it as a corporate subsidy. Moderates worried about additional traffic on the
area's overcrowded freeways. Conservatives just hated the tax. On June 2,
1992, Measure G garnered less than 46 percent of the vote.

Forsaking the Bay Area once and for all, Lurie obtained approval from baseball commissioner Fay Vincent to shop the team elsewhere.

THE TAMPA GIANTS?

San Francisco still wanted the Giants. Mayor Frank Jordan enlisted
76-year-old real-estate mogul (and nationally prominent Democratic fund-
raiser) Walter Shorenstein to drum up local buyers. A native Long Islander and
a Giants fan in his youth, Shorenstein started by putting a few million of his
own dollars toward a partnership. But on August 7, 1992, Lurie sold the Giants
to a group from Tampa, Florida, for $115 million.

While Jordan tried to foment popular opposition, Shorenstein tried to raise a
competitive bid. George Shinn, owner of the NBA's Charlotte Hornets, pledged
$20 million of his own and promised to take out a loan for $30 million more to
bring San Francisco halfway to its goal of $100 million. Shorenstein rounded
up a group of local investors to provide the rest of the money. But the hurried
arrangement was unlikely to trump Tampa's solid package at the September 9
owners meeting.

San Francisco got a huge break when Peter O'Malley, owner of the Dodgers,
announced he would vote against moving the Giants. If the leagues expanded
and realigned into three divisions, as was expected, O'Malley wanted teams
familiar to Dodger fans in the NL West. One day later, the owners committee
looking into the sale ruled that two key Tampa investors represented too much
out-of-town money and needed to reduce their stakes in the partnership.

Wonderful news for San Francisco, but if the owners were concerned about
out-of-town money in the Tampa bid, what about North Carolinian George
Shinn's role in San Francisco's counteroffer? Shorenstein went back to his
Bay Area investors. Led by Safeway stores CEO Peter Magowan, on October 5
they squeezed out Shinn and cobbled together their own $95 million bid. That
wasn't enough for league owners, so on October 28 the bid was raised to $100
million. Mayor Jordan sweetened the pot further by promising to reduce the
Giants' rent to a dollar a year and to use municipal funds to pay for ballpark
maintenance and security.

That satisfied the NL magnates, but not Lurie. The bid was $15 million short
of Tampa's, and the city's concessions did nothing for him. The owners sympathized with Lurie's desire to maximize the value of his asset, but professed
dismay that he would sell the team to another city without notice. As one anonymous owner put it, "He [Lurie] had to get approval before making a deal and
he didn't."

But the prior-notification issue was a smokescreen. With the contracts for national TV broadcasts expiring after 1993, NL owners were not about to trade down from the 5th-largest media market (the Bay Area) to the 20th (Tampa–St. Petersburg). Also, the expansion Florida Marlins' owner, Wayne Huizenga, made it clear he wanted exclusive rights to the Sunshine State. So the NL chieftains voted nine to four against the move (only four nays were needed), leaving Lurie with the Shorenstein-Magowan group's lower offer of 12 times the price he had paid for the franchise 16 years earlier. He grumbled, but accepted.

NEW ENERGY

Managing partner Peter Magowan became a Giants fan while growing up in New York. Grandson of Safeway's founder, he moved with his family to the Bay Area a year before the team. After graduating from Stanford, he obtained a master's degree in politics, philosophy, and economics from Oxford. While running the family business he also found time to serve on the Giants' board of directors. Even before he and Lurie formalized the sale in January 1993, Magowan made two moves to show Giants fans his ownership group cared about winning.

On December 5, 1992, Magowan signed Barry Bonds to a six-year, $43.75 million contract, at the time the highest in baseball. Son of former Giants out-fielder Bobby Bonds and godson of Willie Mays, Bonds had won two MVP Awards and shown signs of becoming the greatest player since Mays himself, a fact that might have been acknowledged more readily had he possessed more of his godfather's charm. For the first time since Mays and McCovey departed, the Giants had a Hall of Fame slugger anchoring their lineup.

Eleven days later, Magowan appointed Dusty Baker manager. Baker brought desperately needed stability to the clubhouse, managing the team longer than anyone since John McGraw. Baker was a true players' manager, sticking with slumping or injured regulars, showing his emotions so every-one knew where he stood, and remaining calm through losing streaks. He instilled an ethic of inclusiveness, keeping at least one white, one black, and one Hispanic coach on his staff. He assured new players that whatever un-favorable reputation they might have had elsewhere, they started fresh with him. He also allowed the players' children (and his own) to sit in the dugout and serve as batboys.

Under Magowan, the Giants hired the first female ballpark announcer, Sherry Davis, in March 1993. In 1994 they sponsored the first major-league benefit for AIDS victims, Until There's a Cure Day, which donated one dollar from each ticket to vaccine research and care for the afflicted. It became an annual event. The Magowan group also encouraged each player to become "a Giant in the community," giving time and money to favored causes. Bonds led a campaign to register African Americans as bone-marrow donors for leukemia

Undated photo of Barry Bonds. Courtesy of the Baseball Hall of Fame

victims, sponsored computer-based learning programs for disadvantaged children, and sat on the board of the San Francisco United Way.

The Giants did spectacularly well in 1993. Bonds won another MVP Award, Baker won the Manager of the Year Award, and the team won 103 games, the most since 1962. They had nothing to show for it, however, finishing a game behind Atlanta in the NL West. Attendance skyrocketed to 2,606,354, a new San Francisco record. But in time-honored fashion, disaster followed success: a bitter strike ruined the 1994 season and spilled into 1995. Attendance was down 30 percent league-wide in 1994, but dropped even more in San Francisco. In 1995, attendance at Candlestick fell to less than half of what it had been before the strike. The team's revenues sank from $69.1 million in 1993 to $46.4 million in 1995.

The Giants turned things around on the field in 1997, when they won 90 games and the Western Division title. (They were swept in the NL Division Series by the wild-card Florida Marlins.) From a business perspective, though, they were still in trouble, as attendance remained fourth lowest in the league. To succeed in both spheres, they needed something more. But what?

A HOME OF THEIR OWN

Rather than descend into a Lurie-esque funk, in 1995 the new owners proposed construction of a stadium at China Basin. Why would the idea work this time? Because the Giants would pay for the project themselves, becoming the first team since the Dodgers to finance their own park.

The odds were long. San Franciscans had twice voted down ballpark projects. The board of supervisors had overridden Mayor Jordan's rent reduction, requiring the team to pay $800,000 a year for Candlestick and to absorb its own maintenance, utility, and security expenses (although the board did grant the Giants a two-year exemption from the city ticket tax). The 13 acres Magowan wanted to build on were owned by the city's Port Commission and Cal-Trans, the state transportation agency, meaning every step would require both municipal and state approval. Last but not least, the team needed millions of dollars to make a down payment.

The plan had detractors, too. Other major-league owners, in the midst of the biggest stadium-building frenzy in 80 years, didn't want it known that they could build facilities without hundreds of millions of dollars in taxpayer subsidies. They muted their objections out of professional courtesy. Neighborhood activists feared the project would cause everything from traffic tie-ups to sewage overflows and would require the city to spend $100 million improving nearby infrastructure, but they received little financial support or media exposure.

Measure B appeared on the March 26, 1996, ballot. Among other things, it asked that San Franciscans approve a zoning variance that would allow the stadium to rise more than 40 feet above the waterfront. A carefully assembled campaign was chaired by State Senator Quentin Kopp, a prickly conservative; Roberta Achtenberg, the first open lesbian approved by the U.S. Senate for a post in the executive branch; and Reverend Cecil Williams, the city's best-known advocate for the poor. With that broad a coalition behind it and no public money at stake, Measure B succeeded where four previous stadium measures had failed, garnering 66 percent of the vote. Even the precincts closest to the construction site voted in favor. "Dreams do come true!" began the Giants' full-page ad thanking voters the next day.

Chief operating officer Larry Baer was put in charge of building and financing the stadium. Baer blazed through the environmental-impact process, getting the state to evict 40 small businesses on the CalTrans land before the process was finished so the Giants could break ground three months early. On July 22, 1997, he concluded lease negotiations with the Port Commission. The Giants would pay $1.2 million per year in rent for 25 years, with inflation-adjusted options for another 41 years. They could use the entire stadium for non-baseball events 14 times a year, including three rock concerts, but had to allow union representation for most of their workers. And, putting to rest two decades of anxiety about the team's future, they agreed not to leave the stadium before December 2022.

Now all the ownership group had to do was pay for the park. Baer worked out a deal with Chase Securities for a $170 million mortgage, provided the Giants' down payment at least matched that amount. The largest single piece of the Giants' share came from the Pacific Bell telephone company, which paid $50 million to name the stadium. (A corporate merger prompted the change to SBC Park and AT&T in 2006.) Another 14 corporate sponsors shelled out about $75 million for a decade's worth of prominent placement for their advertisements. Coca-Cola paid a reported $25 million over 12 years to erect an 80-foot replica of a Coke bottle behind the left-field bleachers.

Another $40 million came from the sale of charter-seat licenses. From $7,500 for a choice location in the lower deck to $1,500 for an upper box, fans could secure the right to buy season tickets for a particular seat. Though widely disparaged as a form of blackmail, the charter-seat licenses sold well. To cover the remainder of their $187 million down payment, the Giants took advantage of the park's status as a redevelopment project to arrange for tax-increment financing, under which the Redevelopment Agency issued a $15 million bond to be paid off through the Giants' property taxes over the next 30 years.

The Giants broke ground for Pacific Bell Park on December 11, 1997. Between January 1, 1996, and June 1998 the China Basin neighborhood experienced more than $270 million in land sales. The 215 real-estate transactions over that period equaled the number over the previous 25 years. In all, 44 percent of the land around Pacific Bell Park changed hands from about the time Measure B was approved to the time aboveground construction began. (It took a year to pound more than two thousand concrete piles into bedrock and create a foundation that would support the structure in earthquakes.) Improvements to the land, chiefly condominium complexes just north of the ballpark, added hundreds of millions of dollars to the area's assessed value.

By the time Pacific Bell Park opened in 2000, China Basin was completely revitalized. Thousands of fans a game, knowing the new stadium had less than half as many parking spaces as Candlestick, walked down the Embarcadero from nearby BART and Muni stations, stopping at restaurants and sports bars along the way. More fans came from a CalTrain depot a block west of the ballpark, and still others from a nearby ferry terminal built by the Port Commission.

The Giants sold a record 31,000 season tickets their first year, 75 percent of the stadium's capacity. Attendance for 2000 was 3,318,800, an increase of almost 60 percent over the final year at Candlestick. In 2001 the Giants led the NL in attendance for the first time in 57 years. Their revenue nearly doubled, from $71.9 million in 1999 to $142 million in 2001. *Forbes* estimated their 2001 profit at $16.8 million.

They soared on the field, too, led by Barry Bonds, who matured into the greatest hitter since Babe Ruth, although an investigation by the *San Francisco Chronicle* suggested that performance-enhancing substances may have helped to account for his eye-popping achievements. In 2001 Bonds set a new record for home runs in a season with 73. In 2002 he became only the fourth Giant to win a batting title since 1900 (after Larry Doyle in 1915, Bill Terry in 1930, and Willie Mays in 1954). In 2003 he became the first player to attain 500 career homers and 500 stolen bases. In 2004 he set the all-time single-season records for bases on balls (232) and on-base percentage (.609) while cracking his 700th career homer. Despite alienating fans and the media with his standoffish personality, he was widely acclaimed as the greatest player of his era. He won his seventh MVP award in 2004; no other player has won more than three.

Propelled by Bonds, the Giants became perpetual contenders. They won the NL West in 2000, but lost in the first round of the playoffs to the New York Mets in five games. After missing the playoffs by just two games in 2001, they returned as the NL's wild-card entry in 2002 and beat the Atlanta Braves and St. Louis Cardinals to reach the World Series. They nearly became world champions for the first time in San Francisco, but blew a five-run lead over the Anaheim Angels late in game six and lost convincingly in game seven. In 2003 the Giants won the NL West easily, but suffered a quick exit from the playoffs at the hands of the Florida Marlins. In 2004 they fought for the wild-card berth until the season's next-to-last day, when the Dodgers overcame a three-run deficit in the ninth to knock them out of contention.

A key reason for the Giants' success was a brilliant home record. The Giants were immediately comfortable in their waterfront stadium, which played like a pitchers' park for everyone except Bonds, who blasted the first "splash hit" homer into San Francisco Bay on May 1, 2000. They also benefited from superior field managers. After the revered Dusty Baker left at the end of 2002, the Giants replaced him with Felipe Alou, a star outfielder for the team in the early 1960s. Alou had demonstrated his managerial acumen by overachieving with poorly supported Montreal Expo teams from 1992 to 2001. In Alou's first year with the Giants, they won 100 games for only the third time in San Francisco.

FUTURE PROSPECTS

Although a severe recession in the early years of the new century hit the Bay Area hard, the Giants were able to keep attendance over 3 million and field a contending club. In 2004 *Forbes* rated the Giants the seventh-most-valuable franchise in the major leagues, at $368 million.

But it is too early to declare the privately financed park a success and the Giants a new force in baseball. Unlike other big-league teams, the Giants have to pay a mortgage on top of their other expenses. They increased their average ticket price by 75 percent when they moved from Candlestick to Pac Bell, and in 2002 they introduced variable pricing, charging non-season-ticket holders extra for weekend games and contests against popular opponents (like the Dodgers, still the archrival after all these years). They also rent out the park for various events, from football games to corporate meetings. Yet after the 2003 season, the Giants announced they had lost money and needed to reduce payroll.

Whether this was actually true was doubtful; *Forbes* estimated that in 2003 the Giants made a slim profit of $700,000. Judging from their history, however, the Giants need to prepare for a misfortune of some sort—perhaps nothing more than Bonds's retirement, perhaps something as devastating as a decision by the major-league owners to override the Giants' territorial rights and allow the Athletics to move to fan-rich San Jose. The Giants got a foretaste of life without Bonds in 2005, when a knee injury kept him out of the lineup until September and the team finished below .500 for the first time in nine years. Even so, they drew over 3 million fans. When the seemingly inevitable setback occurs, paying off their gleaming new stadium may yet interfere with a promising trend toward returning the franchise to its former glory.

NOTABLE ACHIEVEMENTS

Most Valuable Players

Year	Name	Position
1933	Carl Hubbell	P
1936	Carl Hubbell	P
1954	Willie Mays	OF
1965	Willie Mays	OF
1969	Willie McCovey	1B
1989	Kevin Mitchell	OF
1993	Barry Bonds	OF
2000	Jeff Kent	2B
2001	Barry Bonds	OF
2002	Barry Bonds	OF
2003	Barry Bonds	OF
2004	Barry Bonds	OF

Cy Young Winners

Year	Name	Position
1967	Mike McCormick	LHP

Rookies of the Year

Year	Name	Position
1951	Willie Mays	OF
1958	Orlando Cepeda	1B
1959	Willie McCovey	1B
1973	Gary Matthews	OF
1975	John Montefusco	P

Batting Champions

Year	Name	#
1885	Roger Connor	.371
1890	Jack Glasscock	.336
1915	Larry Doyle	.320
1930	Bill Terry	.401
1954	Willie Mays	.345
2002	Barry Bonds	.370
2004	Barry Bonds	.362

Home-Run Champions

Year	Name	#
1883	Buck Ewing	10
1890	Mike Tiernan	13
1891	Mike Tiernan	16
1909	Red Murray	12
1916	Dave Robertson	12
1917	Dave Robertson	12
1921	George Kelly	23
1932	Mel Ott	38
1934	Mel Ott	35
1936	Mel Ott	33
1937	Mel Ott	31
1938	Mel Ott	36
1942	Mel Ott	30
1947	Johnny Mize	51
1948	Johnny Mize	40
1955	Willie Mays	51
1961	Orlando Cepeda	46
1962	Willie Mays	49
1963	Willie McCovey	44
1964	Willie Mays	47
1965	Willie Mays	52
1968	Willie McCovey	36
1969	Willie McCovey	45
1989	Kevin Mitchell	47
1993	Barry Bonds	46
1994	Matt Williams	43
2001	Barry Bonds	73

ERA Champions

Year	Name	#
1904	Joe McGinnity	1.61
1905	Christy Mathewson	1.28
1908	Christy Mathewson	1.43
1909	Christy Mathewson	1.14
1911	Christy Mathewson	1.99
1912	Jeff Tesreau	1.96
1913	Christy Mathewson	2.06
1922	Phil Douglas	2.63

1929	Bill Walker	3.09
1931	Bill Walker	2.26
1933	Carl Hubbell	1.66
1934	Carl Hubbell	2.30
1936	Carl Hubbell	2.31
1949	Dave Koslo	2.50
1950	Sal Maglie	2.71
1952	Hoyt Wilhelm	2.43
1954	Johnny Antonelli	2.30
1958	Stu Miller	2.47
1959	Sam Jones	2.83
1960	Mike McCormick	2.70
1969	Juan Marichal	2.10
1983	Atlee Hammaker	2.25
1989	Scott Garrelts	2.28
1992	Bill Swift	2.08
2003	Jason Schmidt	2.34

Strikeout Champions

Year	Name	Strikeouts
1888	Tim Keefe	335
1890	Amos Rusie	341
1891	Amos Rusie	337
1893	Amos Rusie	208
1894	Amos Rusie	195
1895	Amos Rusie	201
1898	Cy Seymour	239
1903	Christy Mathewson	267
1904	Christy Mathewson	212
1905	Christy Mathewson	206
1907	Christy Mathewson	259
1908	Christy Mathewson	237
1937	Carl Hubbell	159
1944	Bill Voiselle	161

No-Hitters

Name	Date
Amos Rusie	07/31/1891
Christy Mathewson	07/15/1901
Christy Mathewson	06/13/1905
Hooks Wiltse	07/04/1908
Jeff Tesreau	09/06/1912

Rube Marquard	04/15/1915
Jesse Barnes	05/07/1922
Carl Hubbell	05/08/1929
Juan Marichal	06/15/1963
Gaylord Perry	09/17/1968
Ed Halicki	08/24/1975
John Montefusco	09/29/1976

POSTSEASON APPEARANCES

NL West Division Titles

Year	Record	Manager
1971	90–72	Charlie Fox
1987	90–72	Roger Craig
1989	92–70	Roger Craig
1997	90–72	Dusty Baker
2000	97–65	Dusty Baker
2003	100–61	Felipe Alou

NL Wild Cards

Year	Record	Manager
2002	95–66	Dusty Baker

NL Pennants

Year	Record	Manager
1888	84–47	Jim Mutrie
1889	83–43	Jim Mutrie
1904	106–47	John McGraw
1905	105–48	John McGraw
1911	99–54	John McGraw
1912	103–48	John McGraw
1913	101–51	John McGraw
1917	98–56	John McGraw
1921	94–59	John McGraw
1922	93–61	John McGraw
1923	95–58	John McGraw
1924	93–60	John McGraw
1933	91–61	Bill Terry
1936	92–62	Bill Terry
1937	95–57	Bill Terry
1951	98–58	Leo Durocher

1954	97–57	Leo Durocher
1962	103–62	Alvin Dark
1989	92–70	Roger Craig
2002	95–66	Dusty Baker

World Championships

Year	Opponent
1888	St. Louis
1889	Brooklyn
1894	Baltimore
1905	Philadelphia
1921	New York
1922	New York
1933	Washington
1954	Cleveland

MANAGERS

2003–	Felipe Alou
1993–2002	Dusty Baker
1985–1992	Roger Craig
1985	Jim Davenport
1984	Danny Ozark
1981–1984	Frank Robinson
1979–1980	Dave Bristol
1977–1979	Joe Altobelli
1976	Bill Rigney
1974–1975	Wes Westrum
1970–1974	Charlie Fox
1969	Clyde King
1965–1968	Herman Franks
1961–1964	Alvin Dark
1960	Tom Sheehan
1956–1960	Bill Rigney
1948–1955	Leo Durocher
1942–1948	Mel Ott
1932–1941	Bill Terry
1902–1932	John McGraw

1902	Heinie Smith
1902	Horace Fogel
1900–1901	George Davis
1900	Buck Ewing
1899	Fred Hoey
1899	John Day
1898	Cap Anson
1896–1898	Bill Joyce
1896	Arthur Irwin
1895	Harvey Watkins
1895	Jack Doyle
1895	George Davis
1893–1894	John M. Ward
1892	Pat Powers
1885–1891	Jim Mutrie
1883–1884	John B. Day

Team Records by Individual Players

Batting Leaders

	Single Season			Career		
	Name		Year	Name		Plate Appearances
Batting average	Bill Terry	.401	1930	Bill Terry	.341	7,111
On-base %	Barry Bonds	.609	2004	Barry Bonds	.478	7,381
Slugging %	Barry Bonds	.863	2001	Barry Bonds	.680	7,381
OPS	Barry Bonds	1.422	2004	Barry Bonds	1.159	7,381
Games	Josse Pagan	164	1962	Willie Mays	2,857	12,012
At bats	Jo-Jo Moore	681	1935	Willie Mays	10,477	12,012
Runs	Mike Tiernan	147	1889	Willie Mays	2,011	12,012
Hits	Bill Terry	254	1930	Willie Mays	3,187	12,012
Total bases	Barry Bonds	411	2001	Willie Mays	5,907	12,012
Doubles	Jeff Kent	49	2001	Willie Mays	504	12,012
Triples	George Davis	27	1893	Mike Tiernan	162	6,716
Home runs	Bobby Bonds	73	2001	Willie Mays	646	12,012
RBIs	Mel Ott	151	1929	Mel Ott	1,860	11,337
Walks	Barry Bonds	232	2004	Mel Ott	1,708	11,337

(Continued)

Batting Leaders   (Continued)

| | Single Season | | | Career | |
	Name	Year	Name		Plate Appearances
Strikeouts	Bobby Bonds	189	1970	Willie Mays	1,436	12,012
Stolen bases	John M. Ward	111	1887	Mike Tiernan	428	6,716
Extra-base hits	Barry Bonds	107	2001	Willie Mays	1,289	12,012
Times on base	Barry Bonds	376	2004	Mel Ott	4,648	11,337

Pitching Leaders

| | Single Season | | | Career | |
	Name	Year	Name		Innings Pitched
ERA	Christy Mathewson	1.14	1909	Christy Mathewson	2.12	4,771.7
Wins	Mickey Welch	44	1885	Christy Mathewson	372	4,771.7
Won-loss %	Hoyt Wilhelm	.833	1952	Jason Schmidt	.705	856.3
Hits/9 IP	Christy Mathewson	6.28	1909	R. Schupp	7.07	561.3
Walks/9 IP	Christy Mathewson	0.62	1909	Slim Sallee	1.10	572.7
Strikeouts	Mickey Welch	345	1884	Christy Mathewson	2,499	4,771.7
Strikeouts/ 9 IP	Jason Schmidt	10.04	2004	Jason Schmidt	9.30	856.3
Games	Julian Taverez	89	1997	Gary Lavelle	647	980.3
Saves	Rod Beck	48	1993	Rob Nen	206	378.3
Innings	Mickey Welch	557.3	1884	Christy Mathewson	4,771.7	4,771.7
Starts	Mickey Welch	65	1884	Christy Mathewson	550	4,771.7
Complete games	Mickey Welch	62	1884	Christy Mathewson	433	4,771.7
Shutouts	Christy Mathewson	11	1908	Christy Mathewson	79	4,771.7

Source: Drawn from data in "San Francisco Giants Batting Leaders (seasonal and career)." http://baseball-reference.com/teams/SFG/leaders_bat.shtml; "San Franciso Giants Pitching Leaders (seasonal and career)." http://baseball-reference.com/teams/SFG/leaders_pitch.shtml.

BIBLIOGRAPHY

Alexander, Charles C. *John McGraw.* New York: Penguin, 1988.

Durocher, Leo, with Ed Linn. *Nice Guys Finish Last.* New York: Simon and Schuster, 1975.

Giants Media Guide. Walnut Creek, CA: Diablo Publications, 2002.

Graham, Frank. *The New York Giants: An Informal History of a Great Baseball Club.* Carbondale: Southern Illinois University Press, 2002.

James, Bill. *The New Bill James Historical Baseball Abstract.* New York: Free Press, 2001.

Mandel, Mike. *SF Giants: An Oral History.* N.p.: self-published, 1979.

Mays, Willie, with Lou Sahadi. *Say Hey: The Autobiography of Willie Mays.* New York: Simon and Schuster, 1988.

McGraw, John J. *My Thirty Years in Baseball.* Lincoln: University of Nebraska Press, 1995.

Plaut, David. *Chasing October: The Dodgers-Giants Pennant Race of 1962.* South Bend, IN: Diamond, 1994.

Riess, Steven A. *Touching Base: Professional Baseball and American Culture in the Progressive Era.* Westport, CT: Greenwood Press, 1980.

Rosenbaum, Art, and Bob Stevens. *The Giants of San Francisco.* New York: Coward-McCann, 1963.

Schott, Tom, and Nick Peters. *The Giants Encyclopedia.* Champaign, IL: Sports Publishing, 1999.

Stein, Fred, and Nick Peters. *Giants Diary: A Century of Giants Baseball in New York and San Francisco.* Berkeley, CA: North Atlantic Books, 1987.

Sullivan, Dean A., ed. *Early Innings: A Documentary History of Baseball, 1825–1908.* Lincoln: University of Nebraska Press, 1995.

Thomson, Bobby, with Lee Heiman and Bill Gutman. *The Giants Win the Pennant! The Giants Win the Pennant!* New York: Kensington, 1991.

Thorn, John, et al., eds. *Total Baseball.* 6th ed. New York: Total Sports, 1999.

Thornley, Stew. *Land of the Giants: New York's Polo Grounds.* Philadelphia: Temple University Press, 2000.

White, G. Edward. *Creating the National Pastime: Baseball Transforms Itself, 1903–1953.* Princeton, NJ: Princeton University Press, 1996.

St. Louis Cardinals

Jon David Cash

The epic history of the St. Louis Cardinals, winners of more World Series championships than any other National League club, started with another nickname in another league. On May 2, 1882, the franchise, then known as the Brown Stockings and a charter member of the American Association (AA), made its major-league debut with a 9–7 victory over the Louisville Eclipse at the original Sportsman's Park. For over 80 years, the destiny of this baseball team would be intertwined with the ballpark on Grand Avenue, located on the northwestern outskirts of St. Louis.

WHEN CARDINALS WERE BROWNS

Chris Von der Ahe, a German immigrant and proprietor of the Golden Lion Saloon, owned these forerunners of the Cardinals. His saloon, a block away from Grand Avenue Park, relied on the support of customers on their way to and from amateur and early professional baseball games. St. Louis amateurs had endured repeated drubbings from the professional Chicago White Stockings. Local businessmen, already frustrated over losing midwestern trade supremacy to Chicago, assembled St. Louis's first professional team to restore civic pride. The original St. Louis Brown Stockings took the field in 1875, the final season of the National Association of Professional Base Ball Players. They led the league in attendance and, in the following year, were influential in forming the National League. The new league doubled ticket prices to 50 cents, causing a decline in public support. In December 1877, plagued by deficits and a gambling scandal, the Brown Stockings resigned from the NL.

For the next three seasons, they survived only as an impoverished semiprofessional club. In October 1880, when deteriorating Grand Avenue Park faced demolition, Von der Ahe took over a five-year lease for $6,500. He also supplied most of the $5,000 expended to refurbish the ballpark, now renamed Sportsman's Park.

The 1881 grand opening of Sportsman's Park sparked a resurgence of St. Louis baseball. Sportsman's Park, with its new double-decked covered grandstand and renovated playing grounds, lured better competitors from larger cities. The Brown Stockings met the challenge of stiffer competition, and crowds packed the ballpark. Attendance peaked on Sundays, when most men were off from work and could enjoy a bustling beer garden in the right-field corner.

On the first Sunday that year, with the Brown Stockings opposing the Cincinnati Red Stockings, 4,000 spectators overflowed the grandstand of Sportsman's Park and swarmed across the outfield. Von der Ahe built additional seating to meet public demand, adding bleachers down the first-base line. Six thousand seats were filled for Sunday games against the Philadelphia Athletics and Louisville Eclipse.

This baseball rejuvenation fueled interest in forming a league. Von der Ahe spent another $1,800 to acquire a controlling interest in the Brown Stockings, and his team joined five others in creating the AA. Its appeal differed from that of the older NL, mirroring contemporary cultural and political divisions. The NL charged 50 cents for tickets and prohibited beer sales and Sunday games. In the eyes of William Hulbert of the Chicago White Stockings, these policies enabled the NL to gain the "support and respect of the best class of people" and avoid "the patronage of the degraded." Von der Ahe, the German-born Democratic saloon owner, convinced the AA to cater to the ethnic working classes with quarter tickets, beer sales, and Sunday games.

AA attendance outpaced the NL for five years, and in three of those seasons the St. Louis Browns led the majors in total attendance. Von der Ahe possessed a flair for showmanship, and his promotional instincts enhanced his team's popularity. He built ladies' rooms to encourage female attendance, hired bands as pregame entertainment, and scheduled doubleheaders featuring the Browns and Buffalo Bill's Wild West Show. A profitable afternoon often ended with the spectacle of Von der Ahe, surrounded by armed guards, hauling away the day's take with a wheelbarrow.

While Von der Ahe possessed promotional genius, his intrusions into baseball operations, despite a limited grasp of the game, hampered his team. This paradox caused tension between Von der Ahe and a parade of managers. Von der Ahe twice fired his manager in midseason and appointed first baseman Charles Comiskey as interim replacement. In 1885, Von der Ahe gave Comiskey a chance to manage a full season, and Comiskey responded by winning the pennant. The Browns established a still-existing major-league record with 27 straight wins at home and outdistanced second-place Cincinnati by 16 games. Then they took on the White Stockings, the NL pennant winners, in the first postseason "World Series" (a phrase coined by St. Louis sportswriter Al Spink, who a year later founded the influential *Sporting News*).

The opening game in Chicago resulted in a darkness-shortened tie, and the second game concluded in such chaos that the outcome of the World Series was thrown into dispute. In the sixth inning, 200 furious St. Louis fans stormed onto the field and chased NL umpire Dave Sullivan out of Sportsman's Park. Sullivan retreated to his hotel room and awarded a forfeit to Chicago. The Browns protested, because the rules stated that a forfeit could only be declared on the field of play. Each team won two of the next four contests. Immediately before the final game, umpire John Kelly issued a public announcement at the request of Comiskey and White Stockings player-manager Cap Anson. This well-respected umpire, nicknamed "Honest John," explained that the forfeit no longer counted, and thus the upcoming seventh game would decide the championship. The Browns prevailed, 13–4, and staked their claim to the title of world champions. However, A. G. Spalding, successor to the late Hulbert as White Stockings owner, objected that he had never agreed to relinquish the forfeited game. Contemporary opinion divided bitterly along league lines, but modern accounts tend to accept Spalding's depiction of the 1885 World Series as a tie.

In the long run, though, the 1885 World Series merely served as a prelude to the rematch of the following year. Anson, pouring fuel onto the flames of the rivalry, bragged in July 1886 that the Browns would finish no better than "fifth or sixth" in the NL. Once the Browns and White Stockings clinched their respective pennants, Spalding insisted his club would only play the Browns on a winner-take-all basis. When Von der Ahe accepted, this daring format captured the public's imagination, and daily attendance tripled over the previous year.

After losing two of three games in Chicago, the Browns returned home to Sportsman's Park and swept three straight to take the World Series. In the bottom of the 10th inning of the sixth game, Browns' center fielder Curt Welch scored the winning run on a wild pitch, a play later known as "the $15,000 Slide." It gave the Browns the entire $13,920 in gate receipts. Von der Ahe pocketed half of the proceeds and divided the other half between his 12 players. Their winners' share of $580 exceeded the yearly income of a typical manufacturing worker.

The 1887 season would be a tumultuous one for Von der Ahe and St. Louis baseball. When acts passed by the Missouri legislature threatened Sunday baseball in St. Louis, Von der Ahe pondered whether to accept an offer of $25,000 to transfer the Browns to the NL. However, his political connections saved Sunday baseball. Von der Ahe chaired the Democratic Party's Eighth Congressional District Committee, which helped elect John O'Neill, the Browns' vice president, to five terms in Congress. When Von der Ahe defied the Sunday closing laws of the Missouri legislature, his case went before the Court of Criminal Correction, and Congressman O'Neill testified on Von der Ahe's behalf.

Judge Edward Noonan, a rising Irish Democratic politician, was influenced by O'Neill and Von der Ahe, but he also genuinely opposed Sabbatarianism and ruled in favor of Sunday games.

Nevertheless, as the Browns wrapped up their third consecutive runaway pennant, the AA's lack of competitive balance caused attendance to dwindle at Sportsman's Park. After losing the 1887 World Series to the Detroit Wolverines, Von der Ahe devised a plan. He sold five of his best players to AA rivals in Brooklyn and Philadelphia for $26,750, compensating for the decline in profits. These player sales also attempted to address two underlying causes of the Browns' economic downturn. First, by replacing well-paid veterans with less heralded youngsters, Von der Ahe slashed his payroll. Second, the transactions weakened the Browns and strengthened both Brooklyn and Philadelphia, bolstering parity among AA teams.

Yet the sales created unforeseen problems. In St. Louis, resentment smoldered over the loss of five popular Browns, and many fans stayed away from Sportsman's Park. Furthermore, closer competition unleashed a fierce rivalry between the Browns and the Brooklyn Bridegrooms that tore the AA apart. Despite the transactions, Comiskey and the Browns captured their fourth straight pennant. However, in a controversial finish to the 1889 season, Brooklyn dethroned the Browns as AA champions. In a crucial September contest in Brooklyn, the Browns took a 4–2 lead into the ninth, but Comiskey pulled his team off the field when umpire Fred Goldsmith refused to call the game on account of darkness. Although Goldsmith forfeited the game to the Bridegrooms, Brooklyn fans attacked the departing Browns. Citing security concerns, the Browns refused to play the next day, so the Bridegrooms were awarded another forfeit. Two weeks later, the AA reversed the original forfeit and declared the Browns the victors, but still upheld the second forfeit. The Bridegrooms ultimately won the pennant by two games over the Browns. If the AA had ordered the second disputed contest to be decided on the field, the Browns could have surpassed the Bridegrooms (by percentage points) with a win.

One month later, with animosities running high, the AA convened to elect a new president. When the convention deadlocked between candidates supported by Von der Ahe and Bridegrooms owner Charles Byrne, the AA self-destructed. All four teams in the pro-Bridegrooms faction (Brooklyn, Cincinnati, Baltimore, and Kansas City) resigned from the league, with Brooklyn and Cincinnati jumping to the NL.

Von der Ahe by then had earned approximately $500,000 from the Browns and beer sales at Sportsman's Park. Much of this windfall was invested in the predominately German American community that then surrounded Sportsman's Park, where Von der Ahe built entire city blocks and placed neighborhood bars on every corner. His financial empire soon crumbled.

At the dawn of the 1890s, Von der Ahe struggled to keep the AA alive, a mission complicated by two years of baseball warfare. In 1890, the new Players' League formed as a result of a labor dispute between the NL and the Brotherhood of Professional Base Ball Players. Before the formation of the Players' League, no AA players were affiliated with the Brotherhood, and the AA had rejected the NL's Salary Classification Plan, which had provoked the Brotherhood. However, despite the AA's desire to avoid this war, 28 AA players showed sympathy for the Brotherhood and joined the Players' League. The 1890 season turned into a fiscal disaster for all three leagues, and after only one year, the Players' League folded.

Another squabble soon erupted over the rights to returning Brotherhood players. When the NL claimed two former AA standouts, the AA withdrew from the National Agreement, which had prevented either organization from raiding the player rosters of the other. Without the National Agreement, pandemonium ensued. In October and November 1891, the AA signed 13 players off NL squads, while the NL reached agreement with 15 from the AA's ranks.

The Browns, more than anybody in the AA, bore the brunt of these baseball wars. Their roster, "the Four-Time Winners," presented an inviting target. Furthermore, the Browns were ripe for plucking. Von der Ahe, always a volatile personality, frequently issued unreasonable fines to his players. Comiskey would usually wait for Von der Ahe's anger to subside, then intervene and resolve the disputes, normally persuading Von der Ahe to reward a fined player with a bonus for some extraordinary performance of recent vintage. In 1889, though, Von der Ahe had installed his teenage son, Edward, as a club official. Eddie Von der Ahe neutralized the influence of Comiskey, and a flurry of fines and suspensions followed. Without Comiskey as a restraint, Von der Ahe alienated most of his players, leaving them receptive to offers from the Brotherhood. In 1890, the Browns lost seven players to the new league, including Comiskey, making them the hardest-hit AA team.

When the Players' League collapsed, Comiskey returned to St. Louis, reunited with five of his old players, and again ran the Browns for Von der Ahe. In August 1891, while the Von der Ahes administered more fines and suspensions, the Browns fell out of pennant contention. After finishing second, Comiskey and six other Browns bolted for NL offers. The 1891 raids and counterraids hurt the Browns more than any major-league club.

Seven departing Browns escaped the eccentricities of Von der Ahe for salary increases. Once the signing frenzy ended, escalating salaries concerned owners. The lack of a National Agreement had given marketplace freedom to the players, and to eliminate this privilege, the NL offered Von der Ahe the same terms of consolidation that he had sought since 1887. A three-man delegation of NL owners met with Von der Ahe in St. Louis, and in December 1891, they hammered out a preliminary agreement. Four AA clubs would merge with four NL clubs and four clubs that the NL had previously raided from the AA. All 12 clubs in the new "big league" would be granted local option regarding Sunday games, beer sales, and quarter tickets.

The consolidation of the NL and the AA marked the last significant victory of the baseball career of Chris Von der Ahe. His 1891 St. Louis squad, thanks to the return of Comiskey and other old Browns, once again topped the majors in total attendance. NL owners had sought Von der Ahe to discuss peace terms and had surrendered on the key issues of Sunday games, beer sales, and quarter tickets. Von der Ahe accepted the terms of consolidation that he had wanted for four years, rather than warring with the NL and providing financial support for the poorest AA clubs.

If the consolidation had taken place in 1887, Von der Ahe might have thrived in the NL. By the end of 1891, though, the Browns could no longer count on Comiskey, their sole source of stability throughout Von der Ahe's ownership. The task of rebuilding the Browns' roster fell upon Von der Ahe, and he lacked sufficient expertise, capital, or patience.

Von der Ahe's worst mistake judging talent occurred when he disregarded the advice of his former shortstop Bill Gleason to purchase a minor-league prospect from the Cedar Rapids Canaries. Following a brief tryout, Von der Ahe dismissed the diminutive teenager as better suited to becoming a jockey than a baseball player. Gleason eventually secured the lad a major-league contract with the Baltimore Orioles, and the fiery play of young John McGraw sparked the Orioles to three consecutive NL pennants. The failure to sign McGraw illustrated Von der Ahe's inability to distinguish greatness from mediocrity and demonstrated that Von der Ahe had developed an unwillingness to listen to expert advice.

In his 1880s heyday, Von der Ahe had heeded the recommendations of baseball insiders such as Comiskey and other trusted scouts, sparing no expense and simply outbidding rivals to acquire highly touted players. He also compensated players well and, as late as 1887, boasted about the Browns being baseball's best-paid club. Unfortunately, after joining the NL, Von der Ahe could no longer afford the free-spending tactics that had built the Browns into champions. His economic downfall was due to several factors. Von der Ahe was overextended by purchasing property near Sportsman's Park when real estate values in the late 1880s plummeted, and he still owed a considerable sum to the Northwestern Savings Bank of St. Louis. These money woes were complicated by excessive drinking, lavish expenditures, and constant womanizing.

Von der Ahe's deteriorating finances forced him to stock the Browns with an ineffective collection of over-the-hill veterans and unproven youngsters. For seven successive seasons, the Browns suffered losing records, while Von der Ahe restlessly changed managers. Eighteen different men, including Von der Ahe himself, tried to reverse their declining fortunes. However, Von der Ahe hindered the efforts of his managers, often selling the best Browns for funds that temporarily alleviated his economic woes. From 1892 to 1898, the Browns were always rebuilding, but lacked a long-range vision because of the procession of managers and Von der Ahe's proclivity to yank away every cornerstone that had been laid. The same St. Louis newspapers that had hailed Von der Ahe for the success of "the Four-Time Winners" now deserted him and served up relentless criticism.

Meanwhile, Von der Ahe pursued the short-term solution of building another ballpark. In April 1893, he opened the new Sportsman's Park at Vandeventer Avenue and Natural Bridge Road, a few blocks from the original Sportsman's Park. Both sites were selected for proximity to streetcar lines. A different ballpark, however, could not mask a losing team. While disappointing seasons mounted, the Browns dropped from the top of baseball attendance figures for 1891–92 to near the bottom. By 1896, Von der Ahe had desperately transformed the new Sportsman's Park into "the Coney Island of the West," complete with amusement-park rides and horse racing. Yet one year later, the Browns plunged to last place, and outdrew only the hapless Cleveland Spiders.

In 1898, the amusement park and horse track were scrapped, and Von der Ahe intended to restore baseball as the center of attention at Sportsman's Park. During the second game of the season, though, a devastating blaze engulfed the ballpark. Although nobody perished, hundreds of lawsuits were filed for injuries suffered from the fire or the fleeing crowds. Sportsman's Park was nearly destroyed, and on top of that, Von der Ahe's financial distress had prevented him from securing sufficient insurance. Von de Ahe spent his entire settlement of $35,000 to rebuild the ballpark with an 8,000-seat capacity, but could not fend off the creditors. He lost a foreclosure case brought by the Mississippi Valley Trust Company, and his Browns were sold on March 14, 1899, in a public auction.

Von der Ahe had played a pivotal role in popularizing major-league baseball. When he arrived on the baseball scene, public support for the game had been withering away. The NL, determined to appeal solely to the middle class, had lost six of its original eight members. Von der Ahe and his partners in the AA took major-league baseball into cities that the NL had either abandoned or neglected, and they appealed to the working class with quarter tickets, Sunday games, and beer sales. Ironically, after reviving major-league baseball in St. Louis and propelling the game to an unprecedented height of prosperity, Von der Ahe nearly undermined all that he had accomplished. Once he had been the savior of St. Louis baseball, but by 1899, St. Louis baseball would have to be saved from him. Von der Ahe's legacy now depended on his successors.

BIRTH OF THE CARDINALS

Frank and Stanley Robison, brothers who operated a streetcar line and the Spiders baseball team in Cleveland, took over ownership of the St. Louis baseball franchise. Economics dictated their baseball policy. Their Spiders had strung together seven successive winning seasons, but attendance lagged behind the Browns. Embittered over their hometown's lack of support, the Robisons reasoned that a winning team would return St. Louis to the ranks of the best-drawing cities in baseball. Therefore, for the 1899 season, they transferred their best Spiders to St. Louis.

On Opening Day, the changing of the guard took place in St. Louis with a mismatch between the Robisons' teams. The entire St. Louis starting nine had played the preceding season for the Cleveland Spiders, while eight of the Cleveland starters had belonged to Von der Ahe's last-place Browns of 1898. The new St. Louis club trounced the former St. Louis squad 10–1. The former Browns bumbled their way to the worst record in major-league history, 20–134, and Cleveland left the NL. But the arrival of the old Spider players rescued NL baseball for St. Louis.

Besides better players, the new owners also gave the St. Louis club a new identity, altering its traditional brown trim on caps and stockings to cardinal red. A season-opening string of seven victories lent some support to the new nickname of "Perfectos," though as the team slipped, this name sounded pretentious. By midseason, the use of "Perfectos" faded away, and the name of "Cardinals" eventually won out over "Red Caps." The 1899 Cardinals delivered a record of 84–67, finished 5th in the 12-team NL, and thrilled St. Louis with its first winning season since the AA folded. Trailing only Philadelphia in attendance, they drew a franchise record 373,909 fans to the remodeled (and renamed) League Park located on the same site as the 1898 fire, Vandeventer Avenue and Natural Bridge Road.

The Robisons, determined to win the 1900 pennant, paid $15,000 to purchase three players from the disbanded Baltimore Orioles. Two of the former Orioles, catcher Wilbert Robinson and third baseman John McGraw, were future Cooperstown enshrinees who joined three other future Hall of Famers already on the Cardinals' roster (shortstop Bobby Wallace, left fielder Jesse Burkett, and pitcher Cy Young). Yet despite all this talent, the 1900 Cardinals ended 10 games below the .500 mark and dropped to the second division of the NL. Their experiment of mixing the volatile commodities of old Spiders and old Orioles, formerly bitter rivals, adversely affected team chemistry. Manager Patsy Tebeau, previously a fiery leader, failed to bridge the gap between the feuding factions and quit in mid-August. The holdout of McGraw and Robinson did not help matters. Neither joined the Cardinals for the first month of the season. In order to bring them to terms, the Cardinals were forced to pay the duo a $6,000 signing bonus, give McGraw a $10,000 salary to make him the highest-paid player in the game, and waive the reserve clause in their contracts to allow them to sign elsewhere for the following season.

In 1901, both McGraw and Robinson departed to the newly organized American League. This new league also lured away Cy Young, the Cardinals' best pitcher. Yet under new manager Pat Donovan, the Cardinals still improved dramatically. They climbed back into the NL's first division, finished fourth with a record of 76–64, and topped major-league baseball in attendance. The club averaged 5,000 for each home game and attracting a franchise record 379,988, one-fifth of the total NL attendance.

The Robison brothers had revitalized St. Louis baseball. In 1902, taking notice of their success, the rival AL transferred the Milwaukee Brewers to

St. Louis. These newcomers staked a claim to both the past and present of St. Louis baseball. Appealing to tradition, they took residence at the original Sportsman's Park on Grand Avenue and adopted the nickname of Browns. Capturing as much as they could of current St. Louis baseball, the new Browns signed seven players off the Cardinals' roster. Over the next 52 years, the Cardinals and Browns fought for the hearts of the baseball fans of St. Louis.

THE BATTLE FOR ST. LOUIS

For almost a quarter century, neither side gained a clear-cut advantage, although the Browns were usually more popular and successful. This early preference for the Browns surfaced in 1902, following their raid of the Cardinals. The decimated Cardinals dropped to sixth place in the NL, and their record of 56–78 marked the start of nine straight losing seasons. Meanwhile, the new Browns were bolstered by former Cardinals, such as Burkett and Wallace. They finished second in the AL with a record of 78–58, only five games behind the Philadelphia Athletics. The 1902 season established them as local favorites, and in seven of eight seasons from 1902 to 1909, the Browns drew more fans than the Cardinals. In 1907 the Cards drew just 185,377, their third lowest attendance ever.

The Browns' superiority peaked in 1908, led by their new acquisition, Rube Waddell, the most flamboyant pitcher in the game. This eccentric left-hander had worn out his welcome with the Athletics despite leading AL pitchers in strikeouts for six consecutive seasons. Waddell won 19 games, keeping the Browns in the thick of a four-team pennant race. They faded in September, but their fourth-place finish and 83–69 record were still the best results for a St. Louis club since their 1902 debut. Waddell's magnetism enabled the Browns to welcome 618,947 customers to Sportsman's Park, triple the crowds of the last-place Cardinals at League Park, and shatter the St. Louis attendance record.

Sportsman's Park, built by beer sales from Chris Von der Ahe's saloon, was renovated by ticket sales from Rube Waddell's left arm. Robert Lee Hedges, the Browns' absentee owner from Cincinnati, utilized profits from the 1908 season to modernize the ballpark. At the forefront of a movement away from hazardous wooden parks, he constructed a double-decked concrete and steel grandstand. His poverty-stricken rivals, the Cardinals, defied warnings from the building commissioner about the dangers of their wooden ballpark, which in 1916 became the last all-wooden major-league facility.

Although the Browns played in a superior park, their on-field performance faltered and permitted the Cardinals to present a local challenge. After contending in 1908, the Browns finished either last or next to last for five consecutive years. The Cardinals took advantage of the Browns' collapse, and in five of six seasons from 1910 to 1915 outshined their neighborhood rivals on the diamond and at the box office, especially in 1911. While the Browns languished in the AL cellar for a second successive season, the Cardinals enjoyed a winning record for the first time in a decade. This enabled the Cardinals to pull in a franchise record 447,768 fans, double the Browns' attendance.

Cardinals manager Roger Bresnahan, acquired in 1908 from the New York Giants for pitcher Bugs Raymond and outfielder Red Murray, was credited with the turnaround. Stanley Robison, completely in charge of the Cardinals after the death of his brother Frank three years earlier, gave Bresnahan a free hand. Bresnahan transformed the Cardinals, retaining only first baseman Ed Konetchy and left-handed pitcher Slim Sallee while obtaining many newcomers through trades. Bresnahan shared catching responsibilities and brought over his old Giants teammate Steve Evans to play right field. From the Cincinnati Reds, he secured second baseman Miller Huggins, center fielder Rebel Oakes, and third baseman Mike Mowrey. These additions kept the Cardinals in a five-team pennant race until August. The Cardinals' subsequent swoon dropped them to fifth, and they barely finished with a winning record of 75–74.

Nevertheless, by arousing local support, Bresnahan's 1911 team turned a profit of $165,000. Helene Robison Britton, the daughter of Frank Robison and the first female owner of a major-league club, had inherited the Cardinals upon the death of her uncle Stanley in March 1911. After the season, she utilized the team's unexpected earnings to pare down their outstanding debts. Britton rewarded Bresnahan with a new five-year contract for $10,000 a year and 10 percent of profits.

This agreement lasted only one season, due to constant bickering between Bresnahan and Britton, dubbed "Lady Bee" by the press corps. First, Bresnahan persistently tried to buy the Cardinals, long after Britton explained that she had no intention of selling. Second, suspicious that Huggins might be angling for his job, Bresnahan attempted to trade the popular second baseman. Lady Bee intervened to block the trade of her favorite player. Then, with the Cardinals' record slipping toward their final mark of 63–90, Britton questioned her manager's strategy. Bresnahan, exploding into an outburst of expletives, expressed his belief that women were incapable of sharing baseball insights.

At the end of her second season as a baseball owner, Britton fired one future Hall of Famer as manager and replaced him with another, Miller Huggins. While Huggins would gain greater acclaim for guiding the New York Yankees to six pennants in eight years from 1921 to 1928, he might have done a better job of managing the Cardinals. The Yankees had wealthy owners who used their pocketbooks to purchase 15 players from the Boston Red Sox alone, while the Cardinals were too poor to even renovate their archaic ballpark.

In Huggins's first year, the Cardinals continued on their downward spiral, falling from sixth in 1912 to last in 1913. Future prospects seemed equally bleak, especially after starting outfielders Evans and Oakes jumped to the rival Federal League. Huggins filled these holes in the "three-for-five deal" with Pittsburgh. This trade cost the Cardinals three significant players (Konetchy, Mowrey, and pitcher Bob Harmon) in return for two-thirds of their 1914 outfield, half of their infield, and a pitcher, which helped the Cardinals finish in third place.

During the next two seasons, though, the team failed to sustain any momentum. Their record plummeted to sub-.500 again, and they fell back to the second division. By 1917, when Huggins restored a winning ledger and returned the Cardinals to third place, the culmination of the Federal League war had changed St. Louis baseball.

The rival Feds had tried for two years to establish a third major league, but after two years of dwindling attendance and mounting debts, most of its investors accepted a $600,000 buyout offer from the two older leagues. As part of this peace agreement, the owners of the Chicago and St. Louis Federal League teams acquired major-league clubs. Phil Ball, owner of the St. Louis team, paid $425,000 to Robert Lee Hedges for the Browns and Sportsman's Park.

This connection between Ball and the Browns reshaped the fight for local baseball supremacy. Britton had moved to St. Louis in 1913 and, as a hometown owner with a better ball club than the Browns, had swung public opinion toward the Cardinals. But now she faced a more dangerous adversary. Ball, a wealthy St. Louis businessman who earned millions from his ice-manufacturing plants, stalemated her hometown advantage and could draw from deeper reservoirs of capital.

In 1916, Ball combined his holdovers from the St. Louis Federal League team with the old Browns to finish 79–75, snapping the Browns' seven-year losing skid. Attendance had declined to a franchise low of 150,358 in the last year of Hedges's ownership, but doubled under Ball. Meanwhile, the inconsistent Cardinals dropped to the bottom of the NL. Their attendance had surpassed the Browns for five of the previous six seasons, but fell 33 percent short of the 1916 Browns.

Besides these professional setbacks, Britton endured the disintegration of her marriage. A single mother of two, she longed for financial security, and decided to sell the Cardinals and their ballpark for $375,000. She offered them to Huggins and her attorney, James Jones, and the latter reached an agreement with her. Jones had encouraged civic leaders to purchase stock. His sales campaign gave birth to "the Knothole Gang," a promotional idea linking support for the Cardinals with battling juvenile delinquency. Businessmen, for each share purchased, received a season pass that they could dispense to a local youth. The Knothole Gang also benefited the Cardinals by developing future generations of loyal fans.

Sam Breadon, an affluent automobile dealer who introduced the Model T to St. Louis, emerged as the leading figure of the syndicate. He started out in 1917 with a $200 purchase, but continued to add shares. He became team president in 1920, and controlled 78 percent of the club's stock by 1923. Breadon demoted Cardinals president Branch Rickey to vice president. Rickey, a former Browns catcher, had graduated from law school in 1911, and took a front-office job with the Browns two years later. He was named manager of the last-place Browns late in the 1913 season, and then led the Browns to fifth in 1914 and sixth in 1915. He was supplanted when Ball purchased the Browns and brought his old Feds manager with him. Rickey remained in a front-office capacity, but felt unappreciated and disenchanted. In January 1917, when Jones offered to double Rickey's salary and make him team president, he moved into the Cardinals organization.

Huggins, much like Rickey with the 1916 Browns, felt like the odd man out. After failing to buy the Cardinals, he had seen Jones bring in Rickey to run them. Huggins took the Cardinals back to third place in 1917 and then departed to become the Yankees' manager. In the World War I–shortened season of 1918, Rickey went into military service, and the Cardinals sank to last. In 1919, Rickey undertook the dual role of field manager and Cardinals president, but the team barely improved to seventh. However, the following season laid the foundation for future greatness. By 1920, the Cardinals had a pair of executives who would take them to the top of the NL. The Breadon-Rickey tandem paid immediate dividends. Their first big step came after Breadon convinced Ball to rent Sportsman's Park to the Cardinals for an annual rent of $35,000 and half of maintenance expenses. Then they sold the site of the Cardinals' old ballpark to the Board of Education to build Beaumont High School. Finally, rather than using the $275,000 proceeds as a nest egg, Breadon invested the money to develop Rickey's notion of a farm system.

Various major-league clubs had previously arranged to farm out a few of their promising prospects to gain seasoning in the minors, but Rickey and the Cardinals created the modern concept of a farm system. The Cardinals were unique in concentrating on scouting and developing young, unproven players. They assigned recruits to a low-classification minor-league team, such as Fort Smith of the Western Association. If a youngster showed promise there, the Cardinals advanced him to a higher-classification minor-league team, like Houston in the Texas League. The Cardinals owned 50 percent of the Fort Smith club and, after starting with 18 percent, eventually acquired full ownership of the Houston club. As their farm system grew, the Cardinals continued to purchase minor-league teams, but they also developed working agreements with others. Under a working agreement, the Cardinals provided financial support to the minor-league team and received an option on their players.

This approach marked a radical break with the past, when independent minor-league teams auctioned off their best players to the highest-bidding major-league club. The Cardinals could not compete against wealthier major-league clubs for top minor leaguers. Since 1902, their infrequent winning seasons had relied on managers pulling off shrewd trades for major-league veterans. After 1920, the Cardinals' fate changed for the better, as they were soon harvesting their own crop of minor leaguers. Sunny Jim Bottomley, a future Hall of Fame first baseman, was the farm system's first graduate. In August 1922, with Bottomley batting .348 for Syracuse of the International League, the Cardinals promoted him to the majors. He proceeded to hit .325 and drive home 35 runs in 37 games. Over the next three years, Bottomley would be joined by many former farmhands.

Despite an influx of talent, the Cardinals still trailed their landlords at currying local favor. Entering the 1926 season, the Browns had outdrawn the Cardinals for 8 of the last 10 years. However, this changed when the Cardinals brought St. Louis a pennant after a drought of 38 years and established themselves as the city's favorite ball club.

GLORY YEARS

On Memorial Day 1925, with the Cardinals mired in last place, Breadon fired Rickey as field manager. Under Rickey's guidance, the Cardinals had risen as high as back-to-back third-place finishes in 1921–22, but they had fallen to fifth in 1923 and sixth a year later. Breadon believed his club would be better off with Rickey focusing on front-office responsibilities and presiding over the farm system.

The managerial reins were handed to Cardinals second baseman Rogers Hornsby, then on his way to a sixth consecutive NL batting championship. Hornsby enjoyed quick success. While Rickey, verbose and theoretical, had bored ballplayers by diagramming strategy on a blackboard, Hornsby, profane and earthy, threw the blackboard out of the clubhouse. After changing leaders, the 1925 Cardinals climbed from the NL cellar to the first division. They finished fourth with a record of 77–76 (13–25 under Rickey and 64–51 with Hornsby).

For the Cardinals and their fans, this recovery renewed hope. The Cardinals had reaped a bounty of homegrown talent from their farm system and only needed to shore up a few positions. A week before Hornsby became manager, Breadon and Rickey had acquired catcher Bob O'Farrell from the Chicago Cubs. O'Farrell hit .293 in 1926, led NL catchers in putouts, and earned the league's MVP Award. Shortly after Hornsby took over, he demanded the Cardinals call up shortstop Tommy Thevenow from Syracuse, and in 1926, he topped NL shortstops in putouts and assists. Their presence solidified the middle defense.

In June the Cardinals made two critical moves to push them over the top. First, on June 14, the Cardinals obtained 33-year-old outfielder Billy Southworth in a trade with the New York Giants, adding an experienced and powerful bat to the lineup. He hit .317 in 99 games with the Cardinals, drove across 69 runs, and slugged 11 homers. Eight days later, the Cardinals claimed future Hall of Famer Grover Cleveland Alexander for the $4,000 waiver price. The 39-year-old 318-game winner had been released by the Chicago Cubs. In his Cardinals debut, Alexander thrilled a capacity crowd of 37,000 at Sportsman's Park with a 10-inning 3–2 victory over Joe McCarthy and the Cubs. He pitched three months for the Cardinals, notched nine wins, and posted a staff best 2.91 ERA.

The Cardinals moved into first place on their last regularly scheduled home stand, which ended on September 1. They completed their season with a monthlong road trip, ending with a record of 89–65, two games ahead of the

Cincinnati Reds. They clinched the pennant on the final weekend of the season when Southworth slammed a home run in a 6–4 triumph over the Giants. The Yankees won the AL championship, and since the World Series opened in New York, the Cardinals waited there a week.

The Yankees, in their fourth World Series appearance in six years, were heavily favored to defeat the Cardinals, whose .578 winning percentage was the worst of any pennant winner in the NL's first half century. The Cardinals' small chance for victory hinged on off-speed pitching to neutralize Yankee firepower. The Yankees, paced by their Murderers' Row batting order, had led the major leagues in runs and home runs. However, in the World Series, they were frustrated by changeups from Bill Sherdel, curves from Alexander, and knucklers from Jesse Haines.

Sherdel lost a pitching duel in the opener, 2–1, but in game two, Alexander retired the last 21 Yankees to even matters with a 6–2 victory. The Cardinals returned to St. Louis, received exuberant greetings from a million fans in a downtown parade, and took the series advantage when Haines hurled a shutout in a 4–0 win. In game four, Yankee hitters feasted on the fastballs of Flint Rhem, pounding out 14 hits for a 10–5 rout. Hornsby then returned the Yankees to a diet of off-speed pitching, but Sherdel again lost a hard-luck decision, 3–2, in 10 innings. The Cardinals then staved off elimination at Yankee Stadium, 10–2, behind the pitching of Alexander.

In the seventh and deciding game, Haines carried the Cardinals to the seventh inning, clinging to a 3–2 lead. With two on, two out, and two strikes against Lou Gehrig, his control wavered. He threw four straight balls to load the bases. The veteran knuckleballer, bleeding profusely, had developed blisters on the knuckles of his throwing hand, rendering his trademark pitch ineffective. Hornsby summoned Alexander from the bullpen.

According to legend, Alexander had been dozing, either sleeping off a hangover from an all-night binge, or perhaps still inebriated. The myth borrows a cloak of plausibility from Alexander's personal problems. Alexander, a sergeant in the 89th Infantry Division, had served in the trenches of the western front during World War I, emerging shell-shocked, deaf in one ear, and prone to epileptic seizures. At a time when alcoholism seemed more socially acceptable than epilepsy, then stigmatized as akin to demonic possession, Alexander masked his symptoms of epilepsy with his fondness for booze.

After Hornsby called for him, Alexander ambled to the mound and confronted Tony Lazzeri, a 22-year-old rookie who had driven home 114 runs. The old pitching master carved up the youngster with the precision of a surgeon, striking him out. In the eighth inning, he retired the Yankees on a grounder and two pop-ups and faced the top of their vaunted batting order in the ninth. Earle Combs and Mark Koenig both grounded out, but then Alexander went to a full count with Babe Ruth, and walked him. Ruth promptly attempted to steal second to get into scoring position, but O'Farrell gunned him down, giving the World Series championship to the Cardinals.

The 1926 season signified a turning point for the Cardinals. After trailing the Browns in attendance for seven of the previous eight years, the Cardinals doubled the crowds of their local rivals. Apart from short-term benefits, though, this banner year marked the beginning of the long-term triumph of the Cardinals' strategy of player development. The farm system quickly matured into a self-sustaining bonanza, producing a surplus of players, permitting the Cardinals to choose the cream of the crop and sell their leftovers to other major-league clubs. The Cardinals plowed back proceeds from player sales into further expansion of the farm system. Between 1926 and 1946, their farm system peaked at 32 teams and turned the Cardinals into perennial contenders, producing nine pennants and six World Series titles.

However, since the Cardinals relied on farms as renewable sources of player development, they parted with old heroes to make way for new prospects. Breadon even traded Hornsby in December 1926, withstood local furor over the deal—irate fans threatened to boycott the season—and honed his ability to view popular players as dispensable cogs. Breadon dealt Hornsby because of a confrontation during the September stretch drive, when Breadon had scheduled an exhibition game on a rare off-day. Hornsby thought the team needed a day to rest, and in front of his team branded Breadon as a penny-pincher, consumed more with pocketing spare change from a meaningless exhibition than with winning the pennant. Breadon refused to tolerate this insubordination and, just five days before Christmas, shipped off the manager and star second baseman of the defending world champions.

The Cardinals and New York Giants swapped future Hall of Fame second sackers. In exchange for Hornsby, who had hit .359 in 12 years with the Cardinals, Breadon acquired Frankie Frisch, the Giants' veteran second baseman and captain, who had undergone his own falling-out with manager John McGraw. In 1927, Frisch batted .337, led the majors in stolen bases with 48, and played second base better than anybody. He topped all major-league second basemen in fielding percentage, double plays, and assists (setting an all-time single-season record for assists by a second baseman that still stands). Breadon always considered Frisch's season to be the best individual performance of any Cardinals player. Breadon saw 1927 as an epiphany: "I knew than that it was the ball club that counted. I never again feared trading a player."

Breadon was just as willing to fire managers. O'Farrell replaced Hornsby as manager and piloted the Cardinals to 92 wins, 3 more than their championship season. However, the 1927 Cardinals fell a game and a half short and wound up second. Yet Breadon, dissatisfied with a near miss, dismissed O'Farrell and appointed Cardinals coach Bill McKechnie as manager. Under McKechnie's guidance, the Cardinals improved to 95 wins, gained another pennant by two games over the Giants, and established a St. Louis attendance record of 761,574. Jim Bottomley was MVP, and led the league in homers (31), RBIs (136), and total bases (362). However, unlike 1926, the Yankees swept the Cardinals in the World Series. Breadon reacted by demoting McKechnie to his minor-league team in Rochester, and promoted that team's former skipper, Billy Southworth, a Series hero in 1926. Southworth, later one of the Cardinals' best managers, was not yet ready for big-league managerial responsibilities. He had to manage veterans who had been his teammates, and in trying too hard to exert his authority, alienated his former friends. By July, with the Cardinals floundering at 43–45, Breadon recalled McKechnie to St. Louis and sent Southworth back to Rochester. After McKechnie's return, the Cardinals pulled themselves above .500, finishing fourth at 78–74. Breadon intended to retain McKechnie for the next season, but he hopped off the Cardinals' managerial merry-go-round, opting for the job security of a five-year contract from the Boston Braves. Breadon then turned to another Cardinals coach, Gabby Street, as his sixth manager in six years.

Street took the Cardinals to consecutive World Series appearances. In 1930, his Cardinals outlasted three other NL contenders, winning 39 of their final 49 contests and capturing the pennant by two games over the Chicago Cubs. The team batted .314, third best in the league, and an NL leading 1004 runs. They fell in the World Series, though, to the Philadelphia Athletics in six games. A year later, the Cardinals avenged their World Series loss, defeating Philadelphia in seven games and derailing the A's quest to become the first team to win three straight World Series titles.

Over a six-year span, the Cardinals had claimed four pennants and two world championships. By 1931, only center fielder Taylor Douthit, left fielder Chick Hafey, and first baseman Bottomley remained from the everyday lineup of the 1926 champions, and younger farm products soon replaced them. Douthit had set single-season and career fielding records that still stand. In nine years with the Cardinals, he had batted an even .300, and as the mid-June trading deadline approached in 1931, he pounded out eight consecutive hits to boost his season average to .331. Nevertheless, Rickey believed that the 30-year-old center fielder had lost a step, and dealt him to the Cincinnati Reds. This cleared center field for 27-year-old Pepper Martin, coming off a year of batting .363 for Rochester, who earned $10,000 less than Douthit, an important consideration during the depression. Martin hit .300 in the regular season and turned the 1931 World Series into a personal showcase. He batted .500, stole five bases, and set a Series record with 12 hits that stood for 33 years.

Hafey, who had hit .326 for his eight-year career, went next. From 1927 to 1931 he had batted .337, averaging 23 home runs and 100 RBIs per season, and in 1931 he won the NL batting championship with a .349 average. However, he had skipped spring training while holding out for more money, and when he held out again in 1932, the Cardinals shipped him to the Reds. Later that year, the Cardinals brought up 20-year-old Ducky Medwick, who had been playing on their Houston farm club, tearing apart the Texas League. In 26 games with the Cardinals, Medwick hit .349. He manned left field for the Cardinals until June 1940 and, like Hafey, blazed his way to the Hall of Fame.

Bottomley was the last to leave. From 1923 to 1930 Bottomley batted .324, averaging 20 homers and 118 RBIs per season. Beginning in 1931, though, the 31-year-old shared first base with 27-year-old Rip Collins, who had batted .376 the preceding season for Rochester and socked 40 home runs. After a two-year battle, in which Bottomley hit for a higher average, .325 to .286, but Collins compiled more home runs (25 to 20) and RBIs (150 to 123), the Cardinals chose Collins's youth, smaller salary, and versatility to play the outfield. They traded Bottomley in December 1932 to the Reds.

The Cardinals' revamped lineup in 1932 resulted in a losing record and a sixth-place finish, and in July 1933, Breadon replaced Street as manager with Frisch. The team ended with a winning record, but just fifth place. Attendance declined 58 percent over a two-year span. In 1934, the Redbirds trailed the defending world champion Giants by seven games as late as September 4, and rumors were rampant that Frisch would be fired and that Breadon, after losing $200,000 from 1932 to 1933, would sell the Cardinals, who might move elsewhere. However, with 20 wins in their final 25 games, the Cardinals silenced these rumors and overtook the Giants on the last weekend of the season. The team led the NL in batting (.288), Collins led in homers (35) and total bases (369), and Martin led in stolen bases (23). Then, in a thrilling seven-game World Series, they came from behind to defeat the Detroit Tigers.

Following St. Louis's 8–3 victory in the series opener, *New York World-Telegram* sports columnist Joe Williams described the Cardinals as looking "like a bunch of boys from the gas house district who had crossed the railroad tracks for a game of ball with the nice kids." Less than a week later, after the Cardinals went into Detroit to take the sixth and seventh games, his colleague Dan Daniel summarized the series as a triumph of the "gas house gang" over "nice boys from the right side of the tracks." The term "gas house gang" conveyed connotations of the working-class neighborhoods of major cities. Gene Karst, hired by the Cardinals in 1931 as the first major-league public-relations director, had widely distributed background information about the Cardinals' second generation of farm products. Perceptive writers were well aware of the working-class origins of many Cardinals. Eventually, Karst influenced enough stories written about individual players that their collective working-class affiliations coalesced into the team identity of "the Gas House Gang."

The 1934 Cardinals blended rural and urban players from coast to coast and truly resembled a cross-section of the American working class. Collins, a coal miner from Pennsylvania, only pursued a baseball career when his union went on strike. Martin, who transferred to third base for the Cardinals from 1933 to 1935, had been a jack-of-all-trades in his native Oklahoma, where he worked as a farmer, ranch hand, well digger, posthole digger, and garage mechanic. His Italian American replacement in center field, Ernie "Showboat" Orsatti, had worked in Hollywood setting up props and occasionally as a stunt man. Medwick, the son of Hungarian immigrants, had grown up in Carteret, New Jersey, where his father labored at a sawmill. The top pitchers were a pair of Arkansas-born brothers, Dizzy and Paul Dean, who had toiled throughout their youth as migratory cotton pickers across the Southwest.

Dizzy Dean, after winning 20 games in 1933, startled reporters the following spring with his prediction that he and his younger brother would win 45 games for the 1934 Cardinals. He was wrong. Paul Dean earned 19 victories in his rookie season, while Dizzy garnered 30, and they combined for 12 shutouts. Then the Dean brothers pitched St. Louis to all four wins in the World Series.

The Cards drew one-fourth of their total of 325,056 spectators during the final frantic week of the pennant race. The Gas House Gang's stretch drive symbolized the survival of America's common man against all odds. The proceeds from the World Series enabled Sam Breadon to turn a profit of $80,000, when just a month earlier he had had another $100,000 shortfall staring him in the face. Breadon believed MLB had turned the corner toward recovery and decided not to sell the Cardinals. Folklore quickly embraced the never-say-die spirit of the 1934 Cardinals, and in the process elevated the Gas House Gang into one of the most famous teams of baseball history, despite its lack of sustained success.

The Cardinals would not deliver another pennant for eight years, although they were runners-up in four seasons. The Gas House Gang lacked pitching depth and depended too much on the Deans. In 1935, the Dean brothers combined for 47 of the Cardinals' 96 wins. But the Cubs' 21-game winning streak overtook the front-running Cardinals. Paul Dean tore cartilage in his right shoulder in June 1936, and he never recovered. That year the Cardinals tied for second, although Dizzy won 24 and led the league in games pitched, innings, complete games, and saves. Dean averaged 24 wins a year from 1932 to 1936, and in 1937 had 12 wins at midseason. He started the 1937 All-Star Game, and in the third inning, Earl Averill of the Cleveland Indians smashed a liner off the big toe of Dean's left foot. Diz limped back into action two weeks later, and placed an unnatural strain on his throwing arm. He suffered a shoulder injury that abruptly halted his brilliant career. The Cardinals tumbled to fourth place and wasted Medwick's Triple Crown performance, with 31 homers, 154 RBIs, and a .374 batting average. A year later, without either Dean for a full season, they fell back to sixth, which cost Frisch his managerial job.

The Cards weathered the depression well on the field and off. They lost money only in three seasons, while in 1930 and 1931, they made a combined $576,181. Overall in the 1930s, the Redbirds made an average annual profit of about $78,000.

The farm system yielded abundant harvests in the late 1930s and early 1940s, supplying a far deeper pitching staff than the Gas House Gang had enjoyed. Under Ray Blades, the club finished second in 1939, led by slugger Johnny Mize, who led the league in batting (.349) and homers (28) and was third in RBIs (108). This third generation of farm products broke the pennant drought in 1942. Nicknamed "the St. Louis Swifties" for their speed on the base paths, this may have been the best Cardinals team ever. Every player except pitcher Harry "Gunboat" Gumbert was a farm product. Manager Billy Southworth, sent to the minors for seasoning in 1929, returned in 1940, and led the Cards to third- and second-place finishes.

The 1942 championship club was one of the youngest ever, averaging just 26 years old. Six were in their first full major-league season, most notably Stan Musial, who had joined the Cardinals as a 20-year-old in September 1941 and hit .426 over a 12-game stint. In 1942, as the starting left fielder, he teamed with center fielder Terry Moore and right fielder Enos "Country" Slaughter to form a stellar trio. Slaughter and Musial finished second and third in the NL batting race, and the team led the NL in offense. Mort Cooper was MVP, leading the league in wins (22) and ERA (1.78). Taking 41 of their final 48 games, the Swifties erased the 10-game lead of the defending NL champion Dodgers. They ended up nipping the Dodgers by two games and finishing with a franchise record 106 wins. Despite dethroning the Dodgers in one of the most torrid of pennant races, the Cardinals entered the World Series as heavy underdogs to the Yankees, defending champions who had won five of the last six World Series.

When the World Series opened at Sportsman's Park, the veteran Yankees appeared invincible, taking a 7–0 lead into the ninth, winning 7–4. However, the next day, Musial singled home Slaughter with the winning run of a 4–3 victory. The Cardinals then swept three straight contests at Yankee Stadium. Ernie White pitched a 2–0 shutout, and the Cardinals took the next game 9–6. The Cards clinched the series after rookie third baseman Whitey Kurowski clouted a two-run homer in the top of the ninth to break a 2–2 tie.

World War II prevented the Cardinals from performing at their peak again. After the 1942 season, the draft depleted major-league rosters. Before Opening Day 1943, the war deprived the Cardinals of Johnny Beazley, a 21-game winner in 1942, along with Slaughter and Moore. Then, during the 1943 season, military service summoned second baseman Jimmy Brown and pitcher Howie Pollett. Even so, the Cardinals were not as hard-hit as most clubs. Thanks to draft deferments, they retained eight top players from their championship squad, including Musial, the MVP in 1943, who hit .357, and Mort Cooper, who won 21, both league-leading performances. Shortstop Marty Marion was MVP in 1944. Given the available talent, nobody was stunned when the Cardinals won 105 games each year and coasted to the NL title.

The World Series provided a surprising climax to 1943 and 1944. In 1943, the Cardinals were favored to repeat their prior victory over the Yankees. Despite having fewer holdovers than the Cardinals, the Yankees reversed the outcome and won the series in five games. On the final day of the 1944 regular season, the St. Louis Browns captured their only pennant, allowing Sportsman's Park to host the first World Series played entirely west of the Mississippi River. Local opinion tended to support the underdog Browns, who won two of the opening three games. In the first inning of the fourth game, Musial walloped a two-run homer over the right-field pavilion, which turned the tide of "the Streetcar Series." The Cardinals proceeded to take game four, 5–1, and reclaimed the world championship with wins in the next two contests.

In 1945, the Cardinals lost Musial, Max Lanier, and Walker Cooper to the military and finished second. After the season, when Southworth departed for a lucrative offer to run the Boston Braves, Breadon turned to Eddie Dyer, a veteran minor-league manager in his farm system. Dyer had managed many Cardinals on their way to the majors, and made a smooth transition to the big leagues.

The Cardinals and Dodgers revived their rivalry after the war, abetted by returning veterans. They were again battling with the same ferocity as their tussle of 1942. The saga of Branch Rickey further spiced up the competition. He and Breadon, effective partners for more than two decades, were polar opposites. Rickey, a Republican teetotaler from rural Ohio, avoided the ballpark on Sundays and advocated Prohibition. Breadon, a New York Irish Democrat, toasted special occasions with his whiskey glass and manipulated weekday sprinkles to schedule Sunday doubleheaders. Breadon did not renew Rickey's contract after the 1942 World Series, and one month later, Rickey became president and general manager of the Dodgers. Throughout 1946, Breadon's Cardinals and Rickey's Dodgers waged a seesaw struggle, and finished deadlocked at 96–58, the first tie in major-league history. The Cards had the top offensive team in the NL, backed by the lowest ERA. Musial led the NL in batting at .365, and was first or second in virtually every other category. A best-of-three playoff would determine the NL championship. In the opener, at Sportsman's Park, 21-game winner Howie Pollett pitched the Cardinals to a 4–2 triumph. Needing only one win at Ebbets Field to wrap up another crown, the Cardinals built an 8–1 advantage after eight innings. The Dodgers tallied three times in the bottom of the ninth and loaded the bases with only one out. Harry "the Cat" Brecheen, beckoned from the bullpen, struck out successive Brooklyn batters to nail down the pennant.

The Cardinals entered the 1946 World Series in the underdog role that they relished. They faced the Boston Red Sox, triumphant in 104 contests and AL champions by 12 games. For six games of the World Series, the clubs traded victories. The Red Sox gained the upper hand three times; the Cardinals evened the series three times.

The series came down to game seven at Sportsman's Park, where 36,143 spectators witnessed one of the most exciting games of baseball history. The teams were tied, 3–3, with two out in the bottom of the eighth. Slaughter, aboard on a leadoff single, took off on a pitch to Harry "the Hat" Walker, who dropped a hit into left center. Slaughter sped around the bases without ever stopping. As the relay throw reached Red Sox shortstop Johnny Pesky, Slaughter headed for home, gambling on the element of surprise. Pesky, with his back to the infield, could not see Slaughter turning third, and the crowd drowned out the directions of second baseman Bobby Doerr. Pesky sensed that Walker was trying for second, and initially turned to throw there. When he spotted Slaughter halfway home, he hastily heaved the ball to the plate, off line and too late. Walker was officially received credited with a double, although he actually took second on the throw home. In the top of the ninth, the Red Sox put runners on first and third with one out, but Brecheen wiggled out of the jam and won his third game of the 1946 World Series. "Slaughter's Mad Dash" stood up as the deciding run of the Cardinals' 4–3 seventh-game victory, and it would become known as the most famous baserunning exploit in World Series history. Dyer became only the second skipper to win a World Series without any previous major-league experience.

By the slimmest of margins, the 1946 Cardinals had given Sam Breadon his ninth pennant and sixth world championship. Americans, after 16 years scarred with either economic depression or wartime anxiety, were flocking to major-league ballparks and making the turnstiles click like never before. The increased availability of night games, introduced in St. Louis in 1940, made baseball more accessible. The Cardinals surpassed the million mark in attendance for the first time, and earned nearly $700,000.

Breadon, as owner for more than a quarter century, had overseen the fortunes of the Cardinals through good times and hard times. His club had flourished during the Roaring Twenties, survived the hardships of the Great Depression and World War II, and prospered again in the postwar renaissance. In Breadon's 28 years as president, the Cardinals earned over $4 million.

FROM BREADON TO BUSCH

In the late 1940s, the Cardinals were extremely competitive, finishing second to the Dodgers in 1947 and 1949 and to Southworth's Braves in 1948. Breadon, suffering from the onset of cancer, reluctantly sold his beloved team in November 1947 to Robert Hannegan and Fred Saigh. Hannegan, a fellow Irishman, was U.S. postmaster general under longtime friend Harry Truman, but resigned to preside over the Cardinals. Unfortunately, ill health forced him to sell his shares in January 1949 to Saigh.

Saigh presided over the Cardinals for four years, including the 1949 season when attendance peaked to over 1.4 million spectators, establishing the all-time attendance record for Sportsman's Park and a record $857,553 profit. Yet on the field, the exciting season was a disappointment, when the Cardinals, famed for their stretch drives, saw themselves collapse. They dropped four of their last five contests and allowed a two-game lead to evaporate to the Dodgers, who won the pennant by a single game.

Despite this sad end to the 1940s, the Cardinals had enjoyed a brilliant decade. For nine successive seasons (1941–49), they had finished either first or second and, along with the Dodgers, dominated the NL. Excluding the three wartime years of severe manpower shortages, these teams ran one-two for five of the six years from 1941 to 1942 and 1946 to 1949. Then, while the Cardinals declined in the 1950s, the Dodgers became the premier NL club. The turnaround of this rivalry was attributed to the Cardinals finally suffering from their practice of selling veteran players and the Dodgers breaking the color line.

In the late 1940s and early 1950s, the Cardinals fielded three perennial All-Stars and future Hall of Famers: Musial, Slaughter, and Red Schoendienst. However, their farm system failed to produce a fourth-generation crop of players as talented as their predecessors. Only second baseman Schoendienst, arriving in 1945, could be compared to earlier generations of farm products. With Rickey no longer presiding over the once-fertile farm system, the Cardinals lacked substitutes as strong as shortstop Marion, third baseman Kurowski, or center fielder Moore when injuries shortened their careers.

During Saigh's tenure, the Cardinals signed no African American or Latino players. Saigh defended his segregation policy, claiming the Cardinals were "a team for the South." Multitudes of southern fans attended Cardinals home games, and their roster included numerous southerners. Yet after the Cardinals integrated, their southern fan base still traveled to St. Louis, where team chemistry became a model of racial harmony.

Saigh, an attorney of Syrian descent, had attained wealth from wheeling and dealing in real estate. His financial practices ran afoul of the IRS, and he eventually served 15 months for income-tax evasion. On February 20, 1953, before his incarceration, he sold the Cardinals to the Anheuser-Busch Brewing Association for $3.75 million. August "Gussie" Busch, president and chief operating officer of Anheuser-Busch, took over the reins of the Cardinals and did not relinquish them until his death.

ANHEUSER-BUSCH, GUSSIE BUSCH, AND THE CARDINALS

After Anheuser-Busch acquired the Cardinals, the landscape of St. Louis baseball changed again. The rival Browns, following the 1933 death of Phil Ball, had passed through several owners, ending up in 1951 with Bill Veeck, who arrived "knowing perfectly well that the city could only support one team." In the previous quarter century, only the 1944 champion Browns had outdrawn the Cardinals. Nevertheless, Veeck believed that he could run the Cardinals out of St. Louis.

Until the Anheuser-Busch purchase of the Cardinals, Veeck had been pleased with his progress. Afterward, unwilling to battle the vast financial reserves of Anheuser-Busch, Veeck looked to move the Browns, but was thwarted by the other owners. Veeck had no choice except to spend the 1953 season in St. Louis, where his popularity had plummeted. Angry fans hung him in effigy at Sportsman's Park, and hundreds canceled their season tickets. Desperate for revenue, Veeck sold Sportsman's Park to Anheuser-Busch for $1.1 million on the eve of the 1953 season. The St. Louis Browns finished last in their lame-duck year, and the franchise moved to Baltimore before the 1954 season.

Gussie Busch turned the tables on Veeck. He pumped in $1.5 million of corporate funds to redesign the ballpark. He wanted to dub the field Budweiser Stadium in honor of his brewery's best-selling product. The name change raised howls of protest. Busch relented, renaming Sportsman's Park as Busch Stadium, and then introducing a new beverage, Busch Bavarian Beer. However, St. Louisans continued calling their old ballpark Sportsman's Park.

The financial infusion enhanced the attractiveness of Sportsman's Park, but it was harder to improve the team. When Gussie Busch took control, the Cardinals were still a winning club, but had fallen from pennant contention. In his initial year, the Cardinals finished third for the third successive season, behind the integrated Dodgers and Giants.

Seating at Sportsman's Park had been integrated since 1944, and Anheuser-Busch marketed to all races. Gussie Busch saw no reason to maintain a segregated ball club, and integrated the Cardinals with first baseman Tom Alston in 1954. A decade later, when the Cardinals returned to the World Series, they tranquilly blended southern whites with African Americans and Latinos. Alston came to St. Louis along with other rookies, part of the Cardinals' "force-feeding" plan of 1954–55. The Cardinals management decided the team had taken too long to promote minor-league prospects. Now they threw youngsters into the fire to see if they withstood the heat.

On April 11, 1954, the Cardinals dealt Slaughter to the New York Yankees for three minor-league prospects, including center fielder Bill Virdon, signaling the end of one era and the start of the youth movement. Slaughter, a 10-time All-Star outfielder, had worked his way through the farm system and joined the Cardinals in 1938. Over 13 seasons, he batted .305 for the Cardinals and topped the NL in several hitting and fielding categories.

The force-feeding plan resulted in a losing record, the first since 1938, and the team was even worse the next year (68–86), coming in seventh. But despite these growing pains, many talented rookies emerged. In 1954 and 1955, six future All-Stars made their major-league debut: first baseman and outfielder Wally Moon, third baseman Ken Boyer, first baseman and outfielder Joe Cunningham, and pitchers Larry Jackson, Luis Arroyo, and Brooks Lawrence. Moon was NL Rookie of the Year in 1954, and Virdon won the award in 1955.

The rebuilding project never ran its course. In 1956, Busch hired Frank Lane as general manager. Lane brought a new field manager, Fred Hutchinson, and under Hutchinson's leadership, the youthful Cardinals seemed on the verge of maturing. During spring training, the Cardinals boasted the best record in baseball, and once the regular season started, they seized the lead in the NL. However, Lane tore this promising team apart with deals that defied baseball logic. In mid-May, he traded away both of his shortstops and received two players, neither a natural shortstop, who combined to hit just .172 for the 1956 Cardinals. The next day, he sent Virdon to the Pirates for Bobby Del Greco. Virdon, one of the best defensive center fielders in the game, hit .334 the rest of the year, while Del Greco batted .215.

These transactions decimated the Cardinals' middle defense and forced Hutchinson to play rookie second baseman Don Blasingame out of position at shortstop. Finally, desperate to acquire veteran shortstop Alvin Dark from the Giants, Lane resorted to trading nine-time All-Star second baseman Red Schoendienst. Schoendienst, in his 12th year with the Cardinals, had hit .289 and led NL second basemen in fielding percentage four times, putouts and assists three times, and double plays twice. Schoendienst and Musial were the Cardinals' last links to the 1946 Series champions. Shortly afterward, word leaked out that Lane intended to swap Musial for Phillies pitcher Robin Roberts. Musial, a three-time MVP, threatened to retire rather than report to Philadelphia. Busch stepped in, blocked the trade, and revoked Lane's right to trade without his authorization, ending Lane's reign of terror. The Cardinals fell from first to fifth and finished 76–78, their third consecutive losing record. The potential of force-feeding went unrealized. However, in 1957, the Cardinals gave a glimpse of what might have been, finishing second (87–67), eight games behind the Milwaukee Braves, who had added Schoendienst as their second baseman. Lane, forewarned by Busch that his job depended on winning the 1957 pennant, moved on to the Cleveland Indians.

Stan Musial, 1957. Courtesy of the Baseball Hall of Fame

Busch replaced Lane as general manager with Bing Devine, a longtime Cardinals farm-system executive. Devine sought to overhaul the Cardinals as thoroughly as Lane, but with a more coherent vision. His plan called for a faster club, and made the entire pitching staff expendable to achieve that goal. Devine believed that since scouts searched harder for pitchers and farm systems produced more pitchers, pitchers were plentiful. The farm system provided quality starters Ray Sadecki and future Hall of Famer Bob Gibson, and in 1960 Devine added veteran pitcher Curt Simmons.

The Cardinals completed three significant transactions between 1957 and 1960. Devine parted with five pitchers for center fielder Curt Flood, first baseman Bill White, and second baseman Julian Javier, who all played vital roles in reviving the Cardinals. However, the Cardinals again struggled at the start of another rebuilding project, closing the 1950s with back-to-back losing seasons. In 1958, after a fifth-place finish, Busch dismissed Hutchinson and appointed Solly Hemus manager. By July 1961, with the Cardinals mired in sixth place, Busch lost patience with Hemus and his mediocre record, and replaced him with Johnny Keane, the Cardinals' seventh manager since Anheuser-Busch had bought the team.

Keane had been a Cardinals' coach since 1959 and had previously managed for 20 years in their farm system. His first step as manager was to bridge the gulf between his predecessor and African Americans Flood and Gibson, who considered him a racist. Hemus had frequently benched Flood, and never gave Gibson a regular spot in the starting rotation. Keane soothed their discontent by providing them with a shot. Keane turned center field over to Flood, who won seven successive Gold Gloves and topped NL outfielders in putouts four times. A former career .250 hitter, Flood transformed himself into a legitimate batting threat, averaging .302 from 1961 to 1969. Gibson, placed in the starting rotation, won 11 games in the second half of the 1961 season. From 1962 to 1972, he pitched the Cardinals to another 206 victories, establishing a new club record for career wins.

The 1961 Cardinals, only 33–41 under Hemus, improved to 47–33 with Keane. A year later, Keane led the Cardinals to an 84–78 record, the first manager to put together consecutive winning seasons since Anheuser-Busch had purchased the club. Keane and Devine, both St. Louis natives who honed their organizational skills in the Cardinals' farm system, shared similar backgrounds and philosophies. They collaborated closely to fortify the Cardinals' roster. In November 1962, the Redbirds swapped shortstops with the Pirates, giving up Julio Gotay for veteran All-Star Dick Groat.

Entering the 1963 season, the Cardinals still needed a starting catcher and some outfielding help. Twenty-one-year-old Tim McCarver, a future All-Star, emerged from the farm system in the spring of 1963 and filled the catching void. The entire infield of Boyer, Groat, Javier, and White started the 1963 All-Star Game, and led the team to 93 wins and a second-place finish.

Devine sought outfielders to flank Flood, particularly with the retirement of seven-time batting champion Musial, who had bashed out 3,630 hits and a .331 average over 22 years of service. In June 1964, Devine and Keane traded to the Cubs pitchers Ernie Broglio, a 20-game winner, and Bobby Shantz, and received Lou Brock, a speedy 24-year-old outfielder with only modest major-league credentials. Brock immediately displayed a surprising combination of power and speed that took him to the Hall of Fame. Over the final 103 games of the season, Brock hit .348, slugged 12 homers, and stole 33 bases. He scored 81 runs and served as a spark plug at the top of the Cardinals' batting order.

Right field remained a persistent dilemma until early July, when the Cardinals called up Mike Shannon from their Jacksonville farm club. Shannon, another St. Louis native, had given up a football scholarship at the University of Missouri to sign with the Cardinals. In the second half of the 1964 season, the hometown hero added power and punch to the middle of the Cardinals' lineup, clouting nine homers and driving in 43 runs. Jacksonville also supplied 37-year-old veteran knuckleballer Barney Schultz., who in the last third of the season appeared in 30 games and saved 14.

These midseason additions invigorated the Cardinals, who were only 39–40 before the All-Star Game, but 54–29 afterward. Yet with two weeks left in the season, the Cardinals still lagged six and a half games behind the first-place Phillies. Then the Phillies faltered, and with a week to play they trailed the Reds by a game and were only half a game ahead of the Cardinals. The Cardinals took three contests from Philadelphia, extending the Phillies' losing streak to 10, while the Reds lost two of three games, putting the Cardinals into first place. Entering the final weekend of the regular season, the Cardinals held a half-game advantage over the Reds. The Phillies, apparently all but eliminated, trailed by two and a half games.

The final weekend brought a bizarre conclusion to one of the strangest stretch drives of baseball history. After winning eight in a row, the Cardinals appeared hexed by the last-place New York Mets, losing to them on both Friday and Saturday. The floundering Phillies snapped their losing streak and defeated the Reds twice. By late Sunday afternoon, as the Phillies finished a 10–0 pounding of the Reds, the eyes of the baseball world focused on St. Louis and Sportsman's Park. Another Mets upset, and the NL race would end in an unprecedented three-way tie; if the Cardinals won, they would claim their first pennant in 18 years. The Mets took a 3–2 lead into the bottom of the fifth, but the Cardinals responded with three runs in the bottom of the frame, and tacked on three more in the sixth. The Cardinals cruised to an 11–5 victory and the pennant, setting the stage for the fifth Cardinals-Yankees matchup. Boyer was MVP, batting .295 and leading the NL with 119 RBIs.

In 1964 the Yankees were making their fifth consecutive World Series appearance and were favored over the inexperienced Cardinals. The Yankees led the series two games to one, and in the third game held a 3–0 lead in the sixth inning. But then the Cardinals loaded the bases and team captain Boyer deposited a grand slam into the left-field stands of Yankee Stadium. The Cardinals went on to hold the lead and even the series. Boyer's shot was the key blow of the series.

Bob Gibson then pitched the Cardinals to the championship, and was Series MVP. In game five, he defeated the Yankees 5–2 in 10 innings, striking out 13. Then, working the decisive seventh game on two days' rest, Gibson fanned nine batters and pitched another complete game. The Cardinals prevailed, 7–5, in the last World Series contest at Sportsman's Park.

Bing Devine, the primary architect of the champion Cardinals, did not share in their clubhouse celebration, having been fired on August 17, when the Cardinals trailed the Phillies by nine games. Moreover, the impulsive Gussie Busch also intended to discard Keane in favor of Leo Durocher after the season. But after Keane piloted the Cardinals to the Series title, Busch reconsidered and decided the Cardinals should reward Keane with a contract extension and a hefty raise. Keane resented Busch's plotting and harbored a grudge toward him for firing Devine, his friend and collaborator. Busch arranged a press conference, prepared his announcement of signing Keane to a new contract, and awaited Keane's arrival. Keane showed up late with a letter of resignation, and soon accepted an offer to manage the Yankees.

Busch recognized he had alienated local fans by firing Devine and was blamed for driving out Keane, the local boy and World Series skipper. Busch tried to repair the damage by hiring the popular Red Schoendienst, a 10-time All-Star and future Hall of Famer, as manager. Schoendienst had returned to the Cardinals in 1961, and two years later, following the end of his playing career, joined Keane's coaching staff. He was similar to Keane as a low-key manager who believed in putting the best performers on the field and letting them play.

Less popular was the new general manager, Bob Howsam, who claimed inordinate credit for the 1964 championship and seemed like an interloper. He antagonized players with petty memorandums directing them to keep their hair trimmed short, wear the legs of their pants high, and avoid slouching on the bench. Howsam inherited a world-championship club, but in 1965 they nose-dived to seventh place (80–81), despite a 20-win season for Gibson. After the season, Howsam unloaded Boyer, White, and Groat, the club's oldest and highest-paid veterans. The absence of Boyer and White, who had led the Cardinals in the early 1960s in home runs and RBIs, forced Howsam to deal for other proven run producers. In 1966, Howsam acquired Orlando Cepeda from the San Francisco Giants and Roger Maris from the Yankees. The Cardinals had winning record (83–79) but still finished sixth. The Cardinals then were the type of team that thrived on clubhouse camaraderie, and Howsam's senseless front-office regulations chipped away at their treasured team harmony. Then, after Howsam departed, the 1967–68 Cardinals claimed consecutive pennants.

The 1966 squad played at a new ballpark. The Civic Center Redevelopment Corporation, a coalition of businessmen committed to the restoration of downtown St. Louis, raised over $50 million and built the city owned new stadium. On May 12, 1966, Busch Stadium opened and, along with the nearby Gateway Arch, became a centerpiece of the revitalized St. Louis riverfront. It was one of the first multipurpose stadiums of the era. The structure was named for Gussie Busch, who donated $5 million from the coffers of Anheuser-Busch to get the project rolling. He bought the field from the city in the mid-1960s. In 1966, despite a sixth-place finish, the Cardinals capitalized on the novelty of the new stadium's appeal and its increased seating capacity to draw over 1.7 million spectators, a club record for attendance.

One year later, led by MVP Cepeda, with 111 RBIs; Flood, who hit .335; and Brock, who stole 52 bases, the Cardinals captured the pennant with 101 victories and eclipsed the 2 million mark in attendance. They played the Red Sox in the World Series and took a commanding 3–1 game lead. The Sox won the next two, but the Redbirds prevailed in game seven by a 7–2 score. The

Cards were led by Bob Gibson, who won three games, including the decisive contest, while Brock averaged .414 and set an all-time Series record with seven stolen bases. The Cardinals repeated as NL champions the next year with 96 wins. The season was dominated by pitching, Gibson was MVP and won the Cy Young Award with 22 wins, leading the NL with 268 strikeouts and a scintillating 1.12 ERA. The club batted just .249, fourth best in the league, and no one drove in more than 79 runs. In the World Series the Cards, with two victories by Gibson, led the Tigers by three games to one, but the Tigers roared back to win the next three and take the championship.

In both 1967 and 1968, they far outdistanced the second-place Giants, who might have had better talent but were divided along racial and ethnic lines, while the Cardinals tore down these barriers. The Cardinals' cocaptains were Flood, an African American who had grown up in the poverty of an Oakland ghetto, and McCarver, a white southerner and son of a Memphis policeman, and they credited Gibson for prodding the Cardinals toward a heightened awareness of racial cooperation. Cepeda, a future Hall of Fame first baseman and son of a Puerto Rican baseball legend, emerged as another team leader.

This unity extended to the relationship between the players and the Cardinals' front office. When Howsam departed to take over as general manager of the Reds, Busch appointed local icon Stan Musial as general manager. Musial did not make any major personnel moves, but was a vast improvement in terms of personnel management. Many of the 1967 Cardinals remembered Musial as an affable teammate and valued his friendship. Musial treated players with respect and, unlike Howsam, did not deluge the Cardinals with memorandums on appropriate behavior.

Following the examples of Musial and Schoendienst, even Gussie Busch developed a paternalistic bond with his players. After winning the 1967 World Series, the Cardinals received relatively prodigious salaries by the standards of the time. The payroll of their starting nine, including ace pitcher Gibson, totaled $565,000. In addition, the Cardinals gained perks that other clubs lacked. All starters had private rooms on road trips, and the Cardinals flew exclusively on a charter jet. The players believed they worked for the most benevolent of baseball organizations.

Busch destroyed this goodwill in spring training of 1969, his disposition soured by off-season negotiations with the MLB Players Association. The owners had tried to reduce the percentage of television and radio revenue allocated to the players' pension fund, and the Players Association responded with a strike threat. Players refused to sign contracts until a compromise resolved this acrimonious dispute. Then, once negotiations commenced, several pennant-winning Cardinals demanded raises. Busch reluctantly complied, but he now viewed ballplayers as ingrates. On March 22, at the Cardinals' St. Petersburg training site, Busch gathered together the Cardinals, sportswriters, and

Anheuser-Busch executives and lashed out at the team, accusing them of being more concerned with money than about their fans or the image of the game.

Busch had crossed a line of no return, and his team could not recover from their public humiliation. In 1967 and 1968, "El Birdos" had drawn strength from their pride in the organization. However, once the players felt the front office no longer appreciated them, they played like other talented teams that fell short of their potential. The Cardinals dropped from 97 wins in 1968 to 87 in 1969, and finished fourth in the new six-team division of the NL East.

Over the ensuing three years, all of the champion Cardinals either retired or were auctioned away, except for Brock and Gibson. Musial had resigned as general manager after the 1967 World Series to devote more time to his business interests, and Devine was brought back. He worked side by side with Busch to dismantle the championship club. In March 1969 they dealt Cepeda, and seven months later traded cocaptains Flood and McCarver. Flood was despondent over leaving St. Louis and refused to report to Philadelphia, which had a racist reputation. He sued MLB for the freedom to negotiate with a team of his own choosing, and although the Supreme Court ruled against him in 1972, the Flood case paved the way for free agency four years later.

In 1970, the Cardinals dipped to a record of 76–86, but Schoendienst rallied them the next year to 90 wins and a second-place finish. Joe Torre, acquired from the Atlanta Braves for Cepeda, earned the MVP award. The three top pitchers were an aging Gibson and a pair of young left-handed Cardinal farm products, Steve Carlton and Jerry Reuss. Carlton had joined the Cardinals as a 20-year-old in 1965 and, after being rarely used for two seasons, blossomed with a 14–9 record in 1967. For the following four seasons, he averaged 15 victories per year, capped with 20 in 1971. Reuss, a 22-year-old hometown product, won 14 games that year.

The two young hurlers requested raises, but Busch proved "as immovable as a Clydesdale with a mule's disposition." After negotiations broke down, Busch ordered Devine to trade both pitchers. In the next dozen years, Carlton compiled 223 more victories, pitched the Phillies to five divisional titles, and became a 300-game winner. Reuss won over 200 games in his career and pitched for five divisional champions with the Pirates and Dodgers. From 1974 to 1978, the best pitcher on the NL East champions was either Reuss or Carlton.

The Cardinals paid a heavy price for Busch's stubbornness. After another losing record in 1972, Schoendienst and the Cardinals fell a game and a half short of the divisional crowns in 1973 and 1974. Their runner-up finish in 1974, the third in four years, was especially poignant because Reuss was the star pitcher for the victorious Pirates. Thereafter, the Cardinals slipped to the status of also-rans, finishing a distant third in 1975 with an 82–80 record. In 1976, they lost 90 games, prompting Busch to make Schoendienst the fall guy for his own mistakes.

New manager Vern Rapp tried to reinstate Howsam's rules and regulations. Rapp raised a ruckus, but was cashiered 17 games into his second season. The Cardinals' former All-Star third baseman, Ken Boyer, replaced Rapp and returned to the relaxed managerial style of Schoendienst, even bringing him back as a coach. But while Boyer restored individual freedom to the Cardinals, he could not make them contenders.

Fortunately, Busch provided one last positive legacy for St. Louis baseball. In June 1980, he replaced Boyer as manager with Whitey Herzog, and within three months hired Herzog as general manager as well. Herzog had a proven track record, having guided the 1976–78 Kansas City Royals to three straight division titles. Unlike Rapp, he did not impose rules on hair length, facial hair, or uniform attire. However, Herzog believed the players had taken advantage of Boyer, and demanded all-out effort. After Herzog's arrival, the Cardinals played over .500 baseball and escaped the NL East cellar.

The 1980 Cardinals had some obvious deficiencies, particularly a weak bullpen. Herzog also realized the Cardinals were ill suited for spacious Busch Stadium and similarly dimensioned NL ballparks because of a lack of speed and inability to stop their opponents' running game. Herzog used every means of player development, plus wheeling and dealing like a whirlwind for nearly two years. He promoted farmhands second baseman Tommy Herr and starting pitcher John Stuper, and signed his former Royals catcher Darrell Porter as a free agent. Most of all, Herzog traded, even sending away popular catcher Ted Simmons, whom he regarded as a defensive liability. The Cardinals acquired in nine different deals shortstop Ozzie Smith, left fielder Lonnie Smith, center fielder Willie McGee, three-fifths of their starting rotation (Joaquin Andujar, Dave Lapoint, and Steve Mura), and three-quarters of their top relief pitchers (Bruce Sutter, Doug Bair, and Jeff Lahti).

The team performed well in the split season of 1981, finishing second in each half, and missing the playoffs despite an overall record of 59–43, best in the NL East. The 1982 team had just seven holdovers, including George Hendrick in right field, Keith Hernandez at first base, and Ken Oberkfell, who moved to third base. Herzog's 1982 squad relied on a recipe of speed, defense, and a strong bullpen. In 1982, his "Runnin' Redbirds" hit fewer home runs than any NL team, but stole the most bases. Ozzie Smith, arguably the greatest defensive shortstop ever, anchored one of the slickest-fielding infields in the history of baseball while the speedy outfielders ranged far and wide to chase down fly balls or prevent extra-base hits. Herzog had braced up the entire bullpen, and Sutter topped all major-league relievers with 36 saves, earning the Rolaids Relief Award.

The 1982 Cardinals, with a 12-game winning streak in April, went quickly to the front of the NL East. They set the pace nearly all season, but the Phillies nosed a half a game ahead on September 13. A day later, Stuper and Sutter combined to shut out the Phillies 2–0, and the Cardinals reclaimed first place. That crucial victory launched the Cardinals on an eight-game winning streak, and they outdueled their Philadelphia pursuers by three games for the Eastern

Division title. In the best-of-five NL Championship Series, the Cardinals swept the Western Division champion Braves.

The World Series offered a study in contrasts, with Herzog's Runnin' Redbirds facing Harvey Kuenn's Milwaukee Brewers. "Harvey's Wallbangers" had topped the major leagues with 216 home runs, while Herzog's speedsters had stolen 200 bases. The so-called Suds Series, waged between the two biggest beer-producing cities in the country, opened in St. Louis with Harvey's Wallbangers smashing 17 hits in a 10–0 rout. But the next night, the resilient Runnin' Redbirds struck back, using their speed to erase a 3–0 deficit. Relievers Jim Kaat, Bair, and Sutter shut down the Brewers for five innings, enabling the Cardinals to rally for a 5–4 victory.

Up in Milwaukee, Andujar pitched a shutout into the seventh inning, when a line drive caromed off his knee and knocked him out of the game. He won 6–2, with McGee hitting two home runs and making a pair of spectacular catches. However, the Brewers took the last two Milwaukee contests, and, as the World Series returned to St. Louis, the Cardinals faced elimination. For game six, Herzog handed the ball to rookie Stuper, who faced future Hall of Famer and 17-year veteran Don Sutton. The Cardinals shelled Sutton in the fifth inning and clobbered the Brewers 13–1, while Stuper pitched a complete game.

Andujar, despite his injured knee, started the seventh game. He trailed 3–1 until the Cardinals staged a sixth-inning comeback. With the bases loaded, Hernandez lined a single to center, scoring Ozzie and Lonnie Smith. Hendrick then grounded a single to right, driving home pinch runner Mike Ramsey and giving the Cardinals a 4–3 advantage. Andujar and Sutter clamped down the Brewers the rest of the way, allowing the Cardinals to salt away a 6–3 triumph and the World Series championship.

The Cardinals fell to fourth and third the next two years, but regained the pennant in 1985 with 101 wins, based on the NL's leading offense, 314 stolen bases, and very strong pitching. Willie McGee, who batted .353 to lead the league, was MVP; Vince Coleman, who stole 110 bases, was Rookie of the Year; and Herzog was Manager of the Year. The team defeated the Dodgers in the NLCS, four games to two, but lost the World Series to the Royals, in a controversial seven game affair.

Two years later, the Redbirds won 95 games and took the NL East. The team had a lot of timely hitting, with over 100 RBIs from McGee and Jack Clark, and Coleman stole 109 bases and scored 121 runs. They captured the NLCS over the Giants, four games to three, but, once again, faltered in the World Series, this time to the Minnesota Twins. Herzog preserved the Cardinals' emphasis on speed, defense, and a superior bullpen, but often changed personnel. Only Ozzie Smith, Herr, McGee, and Bob Forsch played on all three pennant winners. During the 1980s, the Runnin' Redbirds topped the NL in steals seven consecutive years and aroused St. Louis with an exciting brand of baseball. The Cardinals broke their season attendance record five times in the decade, and in 1987 and 1989 drew over 3 million and exceeded every NL team in attendance.

The relationship between Herzog and Anheuser-Busch executives frayed over time. August Busch III, the eldest son of Gussie Busch, had forced his father out as the head of the company in 1975, and, although Gussie remained president of the Cardinals, the brewery owned the ball club. Herzog had a close friendship with Gussie, and originally answered only to him. However, after the Cardinals won the 1982 World Series, the brewery insisted on governing the Cardinals with a three-man executive committee, comprised of Gussie Busch and two company attorneys.

Herzog, a model of efficiency, resented needless bureaucracy. He had taken over a last-place team with the second-highest payroll in the NL, slashed payroll 30 percent, and won the World Series. Company attorneys on the new executive committee delayed and complicated salary negotiations, and Herzog blamed them for sabotaging salary discussions and the loss of Sutter in 1984 to free agency. Four years later power hitter Jack Clark also was gone for a higher contract. In 1988 the team did rank sixth in salaries ($14 million), but got little bang for the bucks.

As long as Gussie Busch lived, Herzog had leverage with the Cardinals' front office, but late in the 1989 season, he passed away at 90, leaving Herzog without power at corporate headquarters. Fred Kuhlman, one of the Anheuser-Busch attorneys with whom Herzog feuded, became president of the Cardinals.

BEYOND ANHEUSER-BUSCH

The 1990 Cardinals, unlike their recent predecessors, were a demoralized club. Ten players were in their option year, and Kuhlman refused to negotiate. Team spirit dissolved, and in July Herzog resigned as manager. Ironically, he left the Cardinals in last place, where they had been when he took over. Joe Torre, who had first joined the Cardinals in March 1969 at a low ebb in team morale, now became manager under similar circumstances. He could not lift the gloom surrounding the Cardinals, and for the first time since 1918 they finished last. Over the next three years, the farm system produced talented outfielders (Ray Lankford, Bernard Gilkey, and Brian Jordan), and Torre put together winning teams that finished either second or third in the NL East. Attendance in St. Louis declined from 1990 to 1992, but rebounded beyond 2.8 million in 1993.

The 1994 season looked like a potential breakthrough year. Divisional realignment and expanded playoffs had transferred the Cardinals into the newly created NL Central, where they were favored. But the pitchers' ERA ballooned to 5.14, next to last in the NL and the worst pitching performance for the franchise since 1897. By August 12, when the players went on a strike that ultimately canceled the rest of the season and playoffs, the Cardinals were floundering at 53–61.

Skyrocketing salaries caused the clash between players and owners. In 1969, when the Cardinals traded Flood and unwittingly started the game down the road of a salary revolution, major-league players had earned an average of $24,909. A quarter century later, the average major leaguer made $1.2 million, and the minimum salary had reached $100,000. Horrified owners called for a salary cap while players refused to accept restraints on their marketplace freedom and argued that the owners bore responsibility for the parameters of the salary structure.

The dispute lingered through spring training, and owners planned to start the 1995 season with replacement players. Two days before the season opened, U.S. District Judge Sonia Sotomayor intervened and ruled that, until a new collective bargaining agreement could be reached, MLB would operate under the old collective bargaining agreement. Many embittered fans avoided big-league ballparks in 1995, and crowds decreased 20 percent per game from the preceding year.

Attendance plunged precipitously at Busch Stadium. Torre had improved his pitching staff, but the Cardinals had the least productive offense in the NL, and finished 62–81. Torre was dismissed after 47 games and replaced by Mike Jorgenson. August Busch III, who had never shown interest in baseball even at the height of the Runnin' Redbirds mania, was irate at the poststrike fan support. In December 1995, Anheuser-Busch sold the Cardinals for $150 million to a group of investors, including local banker Andrew Baur and William DeWitt Jr. (whose father and uncle had once co-owned the Browns and Sportsman's Park).

These new owners adopted "Baseball Like It Oughta Be" as the Cardinals' slogan for the 1996 season. They replaced the artificial turf, which had carpeted Busch Stadium since 1970, with natural grass. The blue backdrop of Busch Stadium was repainted green to match the hue of the grass, and upper-level outfield seats were eliminated to add an old-time scoreboard and flags commemorating Cardinals championships and retired players' numbers. Tony LaRussa, who had won three consecutive AL pennants with the Oakland Athletics from 1988 to 1990, was brought in as manager, and he got more financial support than Torre had received. Team salaries that year rose from $31 million to $38 million.

LaRussa guided the 1996 Cardinals to 88 wins and victory in the NL Central by six games over the Houston Astros. Yet he did not endear himself to St. Louis fans because of his treatment of local hero Ozzie Smith, whom they felt the manager forced into retirement. LaRussa acquired 26-year-old shortstop Royce Clayton from the Giants and turned the 41-year-old star into a part-timer. Clayton started more than two-thirds of the games, even though the Cardinals' winning percentage was barely above .500 in his starts and over .600 in Smith's.

LaRussa's consistent success calmed local critics, although some still grumbled over the team's postseason problems. In ten seasons as Cardinals manager, LaRussa has taken his club to the playoffs six times (1996, 2000–2, and 2004–5). The Cardinals have lost only one opening-round series, an agonizing five-game setback in 2001 to the eventual world champion Arizona Diamondbacks. On four occasions (1996, 2000, 2002, and 2005), they swept the NL Division Series but fell short in the NLCS. In 2004 the club made a shambles of the Central Division, with 105 victories and a 13-game margin. The Cards led the league in batting and were second in pitching. After dispatching the Dodgers in the NLDS, the Cardinals finally surmounted the obstacle of the NLCS, defeating the Astros in seven games, claiming the franchise's 16th NL pennant and first since 1987. But giddiness over their triumph evaporated quickly when the Red Sox embarrassed the Cards with a Series sweep.

One of LaRussa's most important accomplishments as manager was giving the team a chance to sign slugger Mark McGwire, who would bring fans back to Busch Stadium in record-setting numbers. Attendance had partially recovered in the divisional-championship year of 1996, surpassing 2.6 million, but was still seven percent behind the last prestrike year of 1993, and then attendance dipped in the losing 1997 season. On July 31, the Cardinals acquired McGwire, the Oakland first baseman who had played for LaRussa from 1986 to 1995. McGwire, scheduled to become a free agent after the 1997 season, wanted to sign with a team from his native Southern California. The Athletics, reconciled to losing McGwire to free agency, were willing to trade him for established players. The Cardinals gambled on the trade, banking that LaRussa could sell McGwire on the virtues of St. Louis.

The strategy paid off. Energetic Busch Stadium crowds inspired McGwire, who hit 24 home runs in the final two months of the season, and he signed with the Cardinals. His late-season heroics fueled speculation that McGwire might break Roger Maris's single-season home-run record of 61 in 1998, especially after he opened the season with four homers in four games. He reached 27 by the end of May. The Cardinals began allowing crowds inside the gates two hours before game time just to watch McGwire's batting practice. When the season ended, the club had drawn nearly 3.2 million fans, breaking the attendance record of the 1989 Cardinals.

McGwire clubbed 10 more homers in June, but Sammy Sosa of the Cubs slammed 20 and emerged as a challenger. Heading into July, McGwire held a 37-to-33 edge, and the Great (and friendly) Home-Run Chase was on. On Labor Day, September 7, the Cubs arrived in St. Louis for a pair of games, with McGwire up 60–58. That afternoon, McGwire tied Maris's record, and he surpassed it the next night. Within a week, Sosa also surpassed Maris, and on September 25 he went ahead of McGwire. But 46 minutes later, McGwire knotted the count at 66. McGwire snapped the deadlock on the final two days with four more homers. He had finished with 5 homers in his final 11 at bats and the major-league record over Sosa, 70 to 66.

Three years later, Barry Bonds broke McGwire's record, while McGwire, hobbled with a knee injury, retired. Many fans credit the Great Home-Run Chase of 1998 with saving major-league baseball. MLB attendance exceeded 1993 for the first time. McGwire and Sosa, filling ballparks at home and on the road, had provided "a glorious season of redemption."

St. Louis Cardinals slugger Mark McGwire watches his record-setting 70th home run of the season, 1998. © AP / Wide World Photos

Beyond his on-field presence and box-office appeal, McGwire rejuvenated the Cardinals' front office. The successful courting of McGwire emboldened general manager Walt Jocketty to continue the strategy that had attracted Mc-Gwire to St. Louis. By 2004, when the Cardinals won the NL championship, their lineup included seven starters added by trades or free agency, including Larry Walker, who earned $12.7 million. The entire team's salary was $83.2 million, ninth highest in MLB.

The only homegrown regular on the 2004 Cardinals, Albert Pujols, has succeeded McGwire as the symbolic face of the ball club. After Pujols homered in his Busch Stadium debut on April 9, 2001, the late Jack Buck, in his 48th and last year of Cardinals radio broadcasts, prophetically anointed the 21-year-old rookie as a new hero in town. A unanimous choice as the league's Rookie of the Year, Pujols pounded 114 homers from 2001 to 2003, tying Hall of Famer Ralph Kiner's record for the most home runs in a player's initial three major-league seasons. He won the 2003 batting championship with a .359 average, and in 2004 joined the immortals Ted Williams and Joe DiMaggio as the only players to drive in over 500 runs in their first four major-league seasons. He was runner-up to Bonds in the MVP balloting in 2002 and 2003. Pujols hit .500 against Houston in the 2004 NLCS and was named MVP of that series.

The Cardinals broke ground on a new $387 million stadium at a January 2004 ceremony. Stan Musial serenaded fans with "Take Me Out to the Ballgame" on his harmonica, and other former Cardinal stars also attended. The Cardinals insisted that, as the only major-league franchise in the lower third of market size and the upper third of salary expenditures, they need additional revenue from a new ballpark to maintain a competitive team. Yet in 2001, a year for which there are detailed records, the Cards behaved more like a large-market city. They drew over 3 million spectators for a gate of $67 million, sixth in all of MLB and $15 million more than anyone in their division. The team overall generated $109 million in total local revenue, well above the average for MLB, and $50 million more than the Phillies in their much larger city of Philadelphia. On the other hand, the Cards were only 17th in revenue from parking, concessions, stadium advertising, and luxury boxes, which supported the team's call for a new park. In 2001 the team finished in the black, but because it gave up $8.2 million in revenue sharing, the team (according to MLB) actually lost $6 million.

The Cards will move into a new, $344.8 million, 46,000-seat Busch Stadium, adjacent to and somewhat overlapping the present field on Opening Day of 2006. The Cardinals planned on sharing construction costs with the state, county, and city governments, but many politicians and taxpayers opposed public funding. Eventually, a compromise was crafted with the state and local governments that required the Cardinals to shoulder more of the financial burden than originally envisioned. The negotiations also called for the Cardinals to spearhead a $300 million Ballpark Village, a commercial-residential-entertainment neighborhood to be built on the site of the current stadium. The Cardinals turned to private investors as a source of revenue to alleviate their obligations, selling naming rights to the new park to Anheuser-Busch.

In 2005, the Cardinals, worth an estimated $370 million, won 100 games for the second straight year in their farewell season at current Busch Park. Pujols hit .330 with 41 homers and 117 RBIs and was elected MVP, and the team received terrific pitching, led by Chris Carpenter at 21–5. The Cards swept the Padres in the first round of the playoffs and moved on to the NLCS against Houston. In game five, with the team one out from elimination, Pujols hit a dramatic three-run homer to prolong the series; however, the Cards lost in game six to end their season.

The future appears bright. Since the new owners bought the Cardinals in 1995, the value of the ball club has more than doubled. *Forbes* has described St. Louis as "the best baseball town in America," and for seven of the last eight seasons the Cardinals have drawn more than 3 million spectators. The 2005 Cards set a new record at 3.5 million, second highest in the NL.

If Chris Von der Ahe visited the twenty-first-century Cardinals, he would recognize the baseball business. Von der Ahe would be amused that Anheuser-Busch had obtained beer concession rights at the new ballpark, just like he had done in 1881. Applauding the development of the Ballpark Village, he would compare this project to his nineteenth-century investments in the neighborhood surrounding Sportsman's Park. Above all, Von der Ahe would derive pride from having formed a major-league franchise considered a revered component of the traditions and history of St. Louis.

NOTABLE ACHIEVEMENTS

Most Valuable Players

Year	Name	Position
1931	Frankie Frisch	2B
1934	Dizzy Dean	P
1937	Joe Medwick	OF
1942	Mort Cooper	P
1943	Stan Musial	OF
1944	Marty Marion	SS
1946	Stan Musial	1B
1948	Stan Musial	OF
1964	Ken Boyer	3B
1967	Orlando Cepeda	1B
1968	Bob Gibson	P
1971	Joe Torre	3B
1979	Keith Hernandez	1B
1985	Willie McGee	OF
2005	Albert Pujols	1B

Cy Young Winners

Year	Name	Position
1968	Bob Gibson	RHP
1970	Bob Gibson	RHP
2005	Chris Carpenter	RHP

Rookies of the Year

Year	Name	Position
1954	Wally Moon	OF
1955	Bill Virdon	OF
1974	Bake McBride	OF
1985	Vince Coleman	OF
1986	Todd Worrell	P
2001	Albert Pujols	1B

Batting Champions

Year	Name	#
1901	Jesse Burkett	.376
1920	Rogers Hornsby	.370
1921	Rogers Hornsby	.397
1922	Rogers Hornsby	.401
1923	Rogers Hornsby	.384
1924	Rogers Hornsby	.424
1925	Rogers Hornsby	.403
1931	Chick Hafey	.349
1937	Joe Medwick	.374
1939	Johnny Mize	.349
1943	Stan Musial	.357
1946	Stan Musial	.365
1948	Stan Musial	.376
1950	Stan Musial	.346
1951	Stan Musial	.355
1952	Stan Musial	.336
1957	Stan Musial	.351
1971	Joe Torre	.363
1979	Keith Hernandez	.344
1985	Willie McGee	.353
1990	Willie McGee	.335
2003	Albert Pujols	.359

Home-Run Champions

Year	Name	#
1922	Rogers Hornsby	42
1925	Rogers Hornsby	39
1928	Jim Bottomley	31
1934	Rip Collins	35
1937	Joe Medwick	31
1939	Johnny Mize	28
1940	Johnny Mize	43
1998	Mark McGwire	70
1999	Mark McGwire	65

ERA Champions

Year	Name	#
1914	Bill Doak	1.72
1921	Bill Doak	2.59

1942	Mort Cooper	1.78
1943	Howie Pollet	1.75
1946	Howie Pollet	2.10
1948	Harry Brecheen	2.24
1968	Bob Gibson	1.12
1976	John Denny	2.52
1988	Joe Magrane	2.18

Strikeout Champions

Year	Name	#
1906	Fred Beebe	171
1930	Bill Hallahan	177
1931	Bill Hallahan	159
1932	Dizzy Dean	191
1933	Dizzy Dean	199
1934	Dizzy Dean	195
1935	Dizzy Dean	182
1948	Harry Brecheen	149
1958	Sam Jones	225
1968	Bob Gibson	268
1989	Jose DeLeon	201

No-Hitters

Name	Date
Jesse Haines	07/17/1924
Paul Dean	09/21/1934
Lon Warneke	08/30/1941
Ray Washburn	09/18/1968
Bob Gibson	08/14/1971
Bob Forsch	04/16/1978
Bob Forsch	09/26/1983
Jose Jimenez	06/25/1999
Bud Smith	09/03/2001

POSTSEASON APPEARANCES

AA Pennants

Year	Record	Manager
1885	79–33	Charles Comiskey
1886	93–46	Charles Comiskey

| 1887 | 95–40 | Charles Comiskey |
| 1888 | 92–43 | Charles Comiskey |

NL East Division Titles

Year	Record	Manager
1982	92–70	Whitey Herzog
1985	101–61	Whitey Herzog
1987	95–67	Whitey Herzog

NL Central Division Titles

Year	Record	Manager
1996	88–74	Tony La Russa
2000	95–67	Tony La Russa
2002	97–65	Tony La Russa
2004	105–57	Tony La Russa
2005	100–62	Tony La Russa

NL Wild Cards

Year	Record	Manager
2001	93–69	Tony LaRussa

NL Pennants

Year	Record	Manager
1926	89–65	Rogers Hornsby
1928	95–59	Bill McKechnie
1930	92–62	Gabby Street
1931	101–53	Gabby Street
1934	95–58	Frankie Frisch
1942	106–48	Billy Southworth
1943	105–49	Billy Southworth
1944	105–49	Billy Southworth
1946	98–58	Eddie Dyer
1964	93–69	Johnny Keane
1967	101–60	Red Schoendienst
1968	97–65	Red Schoendienst

1982	92–70	Whitey Herzog
1985	101–61	Whitey Herzog
1987	95–67	Whitey Herzog
2004	105–57	Tony LaRussa

World Championships

Year	Opponent	MVP
1926	New York	
1931	Philadelphia	
1934	Detroit	
1942	New York	
1944	St. Louis	
1946	Boston	
1964	New York	Bob Gibson
1967	Boston	Bob Gibson
1982	Milwaukee	Darrell Porter

MANAGERS

1996	Tony LaRussa
1995	Mike Jorgensen
1990–1995	Joe Torre
1990	Red Schoendienst
1981–1990	Whitey Herzog
1980	Red Schoendienst
1980	Whitey Herzog
1980	Jack Krol
1978–1980	Ken Boyer
1978	Jack Krol
1977–1978	Vern Rapp
1965–1976	Red Schoendienst
1961–1964	Johnny Keane
1959–1961	Solly Hemus
1958	Stan Hack
1956–1958	Fred Hutchinson
1955	Harry Walker
1952–1955	Eddie Stanky
1951	Marty Marion
1946–1950	Eddie Dyer
1940–1945	Billy Southworth

1940	Mike Gonzalez
1939–1940	Ray Blades
1938	Mike Gonzalez
1933–1938	Frankie Frisch
1930–1933	Gabby Street
1929	Bill McKechnie
1929	Gabby Street
1929	Billy Southworth
1928	Bill McKechnie
1927	Bob O'Farrell
1925–1926	Rogers Hornsby
1919–1925	Branch Rickey
1918	Jack Hendricks
1913–1917	Miller Huggins
1909–1912	Roger Bresnahan
1906–1909	John McCloskey
1905	Stanley Robison
1905	Jimmy Burke
1904–1905	Kid Nichols
1901–1903	Patsy Donovan
1900	Louis Heilbroner
1899–1900	Patsy Tebeau
1898	Tim Hurst
1897	Chris Von der Ahe
1897	Bill Hallman
1897	Hugh Nicol
1896–1897	Tommy Dowd
1896	Roger Connor
1896	Chris Von der Ahe
1896	Arlie Latham
1896	Harry Diddlebock
1895	Lew Phelan
1895	Joe Quinn
1895	Chris Von der Ahe
1895	Al Buckenberger
1894	Doggie Miller
1893	Bill Watkins
1892	Bob Caruthers
1892	George Gore
1892	Jack Crooks
1892	Cub Stricker
1892	Jack Glasscock
1891	Charles Comiskey

1890	Joe Gerhardt
1890	Count Campau
1890	Chief Roseman
1890	John Kerins
1890	Tom Gerhardt
1884–1889	Charles Comiskey
1884	Jimmy Williams
1883	Charles Comiskey
1883	Ted Sullivan
1882	Ned Cuthbert

Team Records by Individual Players

Batting Leaders

	Single Season			Career		
	Name		Year	Name		Plate Appearances
Batting average	Tip O'Neill	.435	1887	Rogers Hornsby	.359	6,714
On-base %	Rogers Hornsby	.507	1924	Mark McGwire	.427	2,251
Slugging %	Rogers Hornsby	.756	1925	Mark McGwire	.683	2,251
OPS	Rogers Hornsby	1.245	1925	Mark McGwire	1.111	2,251
Games	Jose Oquendo	163	1989	Stan Musial	3,026	12,712
At bats	Lou Brock	689	1967	Stan Musial	10,972	12,712
Runs	Tip O'Neill	167	1887	Stan Musial	1,949	12,712
Hits	Rogers Hornsby	250	1922	Stan Musial	3,630	12,712
Total bases	Rogers Hornsby	450	1922	Stan Musial	6,134	12,712
Doubles	Ducky Medwick	64	1936	Stan Musial	725	12,712
Triples	Werden	29	1893	Stan Musial	177	12,712
Home runs	Mark McGwire	70	1998	Stan Musial	475	12,712
RBIs	Ducky Medwick	154	1937	Stan Musial	1,951	12,712
Walks	Mark McGwire	162	1998	Stan Musial	1,599	12,712
Strikeouts	Jim Edmonds	167	2000	Lou Brock	1,469	9,927
Stolen bases	Arlie Latham	129	1887	Lou Brock	888	9,927
Extra-base hits	Stan Musial	103	1948	Stan Musial	1,377	12,712
Times on base	McGwire	320	1998	Stan Musial	5,282	12,712

Pitching Leaders

	Single Season			Career		
	Name		Year	Name		Innings Pitched
Era	Bob Gibson	1.12	1968	Ed Karger	2.46	647
Wins	Silver King	45	1888	Bob Gibson	251	3,884.3
Won-loss %	Howie Krist	.812	1942	John Tudor	.705	881.7
Hits/9 IP	Bob Gibson	5.85	1968	Fred Beebe	7.29	8,610
Walks/9 IP	Bob Tewksbury	0.77	1992	Cy Young	1.04	690.7
Strikeouts	Jack Stivetts	289	1890	Bob Gibson	3,117	3,884.3
Strikeouts/9 IP	Rick Ankiel	9.98	2000	Todd Stottlemyre	7.97	565.7
Games	Steve Kline	89	2001	Jesse Haines	554	3,203.7
Saves	Lee Smith	47	1991	Lee Smith	160	266.7
Innings	Silver King	585.7	1888	Bob Gibson	3,884.3	3,884.3
Starts	Silver King	65	1888	Bob Gibson	482	3,884.3
Complete games	Silver King	64	1888	Bob Gibson	255	3,884.3
Shutouts	Bob Gibson	13	1968	Bob Gibson	56	3,884.3

Source: Drawn from data in "St. Louis Cardinals Batting Leaders (seasonal and career)." http://baseball-reference.com/teams/STL/leaders_bat.shtml; "St. Louis Cardinals Pitching Leaders (seasonal and career)." http://baseball-reference.com/teams/STL/leaders_pitch.shtml.

BIBLIOGRAPHY

Borst, Bill. *Baseball through a Knothole: A St. Louis History.* St. Louis: Krank Press, 1980.

Broeg, Bob. *Redbirds: A Century of Cardinals' Baseball.* St. Louis: River City, 1984.

Cash, Jon David. *Before They Were Cardinals: Major League Baseball in Nineteenth-Century St. Louis.* Columbia: University of Missouri Press, 2002.

Flood, Curt, with Richard Carter. *The Way It Is.* New York: Pocket Books, 1972.

Gibson, Bob, with Phil Pepe. *From Ghetto to Glory: The Story of Bob Gibson.* New York: Popular Library, 1968.

Gregory, Robert. *Diz: The Story of Dizzy Dean and Baseball during the Great Depression.* New York: Viking, 1992.

Halberstam, David. *October 1964.* New York: Fawcett Columbine, 1995.

Herzog, Whitey, and Kevin Horrigan. *White Rat: A Life in Baseball.* New York: Perennial Library, 1988.

Herzog, Whitey, and Jonathan Pitts. *You're Missin' a Great Game: From Casey to Ozzie, the Magic of Baseball and How to Get It Back.* New York: Simon and Schuster, 1999.

Honig, Donald. *Baseball's 10 Greatest Teams.* New York: Macmillan, 1982.

Kaplan, David A., and Brad Stone. "Going . . . Going . . ." *Newsweek,* September 14, 1998, 54–60.

Mead, William B. *Even the Browns: The Zany, True Story of Baseball in the Early Forties.* Chicago: Contemporary Books, 1978.

Pietrusza, David. *Major Leagues: The Formation, Sometimes Absorption, and Mostly Inevitable Demise of Eighteen Professional Baseball Organizations, 1871 to Present.* Jefferson, NC: McFarland, 1991.

Primm, James Neal. *Lion of the Valley: St. Louis, Missouri, 1764–1980.* 3rd ed. St. Louis: Missouri Historical Society Press, 1998.

Slaughter, Enos, with Kevin Reid. *Country Hardball: The Autobiography of Enos "Country" Slaughter.* Greensboro, NC: Tudor Publishers, 1991.

Stockton, J. Roy. "The St. Louis Cardinals." In *The National League,* ed. Ed Fitzgerald. New York: Grosset and Dunlap, 1959, 170–209.

Tygiel, Jules. *Baseball's Great Experiment: Jackie Robinson and His Legacy.* New York: Vintage Books, 1984.

Veeck, Bill, with Ed Linn. *Veeck—as in Wreck: The Autobiography of Bill Veeck.* New York: Putnam, 1962.

Washington Nationals

Michel Vigneault

In 2004, the first franchise shift in over 30 years took place when the Montreal Expos moved to Washington, DC, the city deserted by the Senators after the 1971 season. The Expos had been created in 1969 as the first expansion team located outside of the United States. For 35 years, baseball was played in a city where French was the primary language and that had a distinctly different culture than the rest of North America. But baseball was a game played in the city as long as ice hockey.

Professional baseball was not new to the city. From 1898 to 1961, there was a professional team located in Montreal known as the Royals. They played in the Triple-A International League and became a Dodgers farm team in 1939. In 1946, the Royals became a focal point for baseball when Jackie Robinson was signed by the Dodgers and assigned to their Canadian minor-league team. Robinson was the first African American to play in a white league in the twentieth century. He helped the Royals beat Louisville in the Little World Series, and after the final game, the crowd hailed Robinson as a hero. For some, it was the first time they had seen a white crowd cheer an African American. After the Dodgers moved to Los Angeles in 1958, many predicted the end of professional baseball in Montreal, since the Royals were located so far from the West Coast. Those predictions came true in 1961, when the Royals folded.

With the Quiet Revolution, a sociopolitical modernization movement coinciding with the 1960–66 governing reign of Quebec prime minister Jean Lesage's Liberal Party, the province announced its arrival into the modern world, though retaining its distinct French identity. One politician in the center of these changes was Mayor Jean Drapeau. By 1964, he was envisioning great things for his city. New skyscrapers were built downtown, and the sparkling new subway, the

Metro, opened in 1966. The mayor orchestrated the staging of the World Expo-sition in 1967, the same year as Canada's centennial. In 1970, Drapeau landed the Olympic Games for 1976 after being unsuccessful four years earlier.

Montreal has a strong reputation as a sporting city, with champions in many sports. The Royals were the summer team, while the Alouettes, in the Canadian Football League, and the Canadiens, in the National Hockey League, were the focal points for the rest of the year. When the Royals were disbanded, the city had no professional sport in the summer. To fill the gap, Drapeau and his col-leagues began working on bringing in a new professional baseball team, but this time in the major leagues. After all, Montreal was attracting many notable events, and as a world-class city, why shouldn't it have a major-league team as well?

MAJOR-LEAGUE BASEBALL COMES TO MONTREAL

Montreal city councillor Gerry Snyder gave Drapeau the idea of bringing such a team to the area. In 1967, when MLB announced its second expansion that decade, adding American League teams in Seattle and Kansas City for the 1969 season, Snyder and Drapeau believed the National League would soon follow suit. Snyder and fellow city councillor Lucien Saulnier met with NL president Warren Giles in 1967 and attended the MLB meetings in Mexico, New York, and Chicago to determine the potential for a new team in Montreal. They also met with expansion-committee members Walter O'Malley (Dodgers), Roy Hofheinz (Astros), and John Galbreath (Pirates), presenting plans showing how the Auto-stade, a stadium where the Alouettes played football, could be transformed to accommodate a baseball team as well. Snyder also presented a list of potential part owners, all prominent Montreal businessmen. On May 27, 1968, the NL awarded Montreal, along with San Diego, a franchise for the 1969 season.

Problems soon arose. The losing bidders complained loudly, and the U.S. Congress issued a message of condemnation for awarding a major-league fran-chise to a foreign city. Crucial deadlines came and went, and the coalition of buyers began to fall apart. Two of the seven original backers withdrew, includ-ing industrialist Jean-Louis Levesque and his considerable financial support. Seeking to keep Montreal's bid alive, Walter O'Malley conferred with liquor magnate and vice chairman of the board Charles Bronfman, who assured O'Malley he and his fellow investors would meet their financial commitments. Good on his word, a deposit of $1,112,000 on the $10 million franchise fee for the Montreal Baseball Club Ltd. was paid to the NL. Three new people joined the owners group, including John J. McHale, an experienced baseball man who worked for the baseball commissioner's office, where he had investigated the franchise's problems. McHale was hoping to become the next commissioner, but after meeting with Bronfman, the primary stockholder, accepted an offer to become team president. Bronfman was named chairman.

The team's other pressing problem was finding a site to play, pending construc-tion of a domed stadium. The Autostade was deemed inappropriate for baseball, forcing the owners to find a new site. They chose Jarry Park (Parc Jarry), a 3,000-

seat publicly owned field built for a local junior team, as an interim stadium. In October the city began renovations on Jarry Park, expanding its seating to 28,500. Jarry Park is still used today for professional tennis and other events.

The team's name, the Expos, referred to the World Exposition of 1967, billed as "Expo '67," which Montreal hosted. The name "Royals" was considered, to honor Montreal's former Triple-A Dodgers affiliate, but since the new Kansas City team had already taken the name, something else would have to be selected. McHale and Bronfman each wrote a possible name for the club on a piece of paper, and both selected Expos.

The red, white, and blue colors for the team were taken from the Canadiens hockey club, the Canadian flag, and the Quebec flag. The new team's uniform differed little from those of the other MLB team with one exception: its cap. Expo caps were tricolored, with a white section on the front. Many baseball purists were against it, but the cap became the best-selling souvenir for the Expos.

The next step was to form the team. McHale hired Jim Fanning, a former colleague in the commissioner's office, as general manager. On September 8, 1968, they selected the experienced and highly regarded Gene Mauch to manage the club, shortly after he had been fired by the Philadelphia Phillies after nine years as their skipper. Six scouts were hired to prepare for the special draft. The draft of NL players was held at the Windsor Hotel in Montreal on October 14, 1968. Every team could protect 15 players, and the new franchises drafted 30 unprotected players. The Padres went for younger players, while the Expos opted for more experienced ones. Notable Expo selectees included Manny Mota, Jesus Alou, Bill Stoneman, Maury Wills, and Jim "Mudcat" Grant. Montreal planned to use these well-known players as trade bait to strengthen its roster before the start of the inaugural season.

Right after the draft, the Houston Astros expressed interest in trading for Jesus Alou. Finalized in January 1969, the Expos sent Alou and Donn Clendenon to Houston in return for Rusty Staub. But Clendenon retired from baseball in February, seemingly voiding the trade. New MLB commissioner Bowie Kuhn declared the trade was still valid, but asked the Expos to add Jack Billingham and Skip Guinn while the Astros added Howie Reed and Steve Shea. Clendenon ended up playing briefly for the Expos that season but was eventually traded to the Mets. Born in New Orleans, the French-speaking Staub was dubbed "Le Grand Orange" because of his red hair, and became the Expos' first star.

The Expos' first official game was at New York's Shea Stadium on April 8, 1969. Many Montrealers attended, including fans, journalists, and Mayor Jean Drapeau. After more than three hours of play, the Expos won the game 11–10. Relief pitcher Dan McGinn had the honor of hitting the team's first home run.

The first home game at Jarry Park was on April 14. The Expos organized a pregame parade through the streets of Montreal. Although many American journalists had written unfavorable things in the months previous about Montreal's cold springtime temperatures, April 14, happily, turned out to be a warm, sunny day. The Expos won the game 8–7 over the St. Louis Cardinals. Left fielder Mack Jones was the game's hero, homering into the bleachers he played in front of. Thereafter, the left-field bleachers were known as "Jonesville."

In Philadelphia three days later the Expos entered the record books when Bill Stoneman pitched the first of his two career no-hitters, the second coming at Jarry Park on October 2, 1972. A local paper headline the next day was "Nos Expos, nos Amours" (Our Expos, Our Loves), a phrase that lasted as long as the Expos were in Montreal.

On August 19 the Expos made a very popular trade, acquiring native son and Montreal resident Claude Raymond from the Atlanta Braves. First pitching at Jarry Park in a Braves uniform, Raymond had dreamed of playing for the Expos ever since Montreal got the franchise. He became an instant local hero even though his career was nearing its end. He would retire after the 1971 season.

At the end of their inaugural season the Expos finished tied for the worst record with San Diego, with 52 wins and 110 losses. With a 4.33 ERA, their pitching was the worst in the NL. Expos team batting, at .240, was second worst. On the brighter side, attendance at the small park was a respectable 1.2 million, good enough to place seventh in the NL. All-Star Rusty Staub hit .302 and drove in 110 for the season. Another notable highlight was the *Sporting News* naming third baseman Jose "Coco" Laboy their NL Rookie Player of the Year.

EXPOS BALL IN THE 1970s

The 1970 season began with high hopes from the Montreal organization. They launched the slogan "70 in 70," meaning 70 wins for the 1970 season. They succeeded in winning 73 times, and were led by 18-game winner and Rookie of the Year Carl Morton.

By the end of the 1971 season, when the club moved up to fifth place after posting a 71–90 record, many new faces were wearing the Montreal uniform. Reliever Claude Raymond had retired, giving way to the young Mike Marshall. Fan favorite Rusty Staub was traded to the New York Mets a few days before Opening Day in 1972 for young and promising players Ken Singleton, Mike Jorgensen, and Tim Foli. The latter trade was big news in Montreal since Staub was the team's superstar, but the new players would have important roles in the team's future. Expos player Ron Hunt made it into the record books in 1971 after being hit by 50 pitches, the most since 1896 and still a modern record.

In 1973, the Expos improved to fourth in the NL East (79–83) and came close to contending for postseason play for the first time. One game behind New York, St. Louis, and Pittsburgh with a week to go in the regular season, the Expos faltered, finishing three and a half games behind the victorious Mets. Still, it was their best season to date.

By 1974 two promising products of the Expos' farm system had made it to Montreal, catcher Barry Foote and pitcher Steve Rogers. Over the next few years future Hall of Fame catcher Gary Carter, third baseman Larry Parrish, and outfielders Andre Dawson, Warren Cromartie, and Ellis Valentine would follow. This was known as "Phase 2" of the Expos' long-term planning. The Expos' productive farm system began to produce, due in great part to general manager Jim Fanning's baseball acumen.

However, the front office did not consider Gene Mauch the person to help these youngsters perform in the major leagues. After the 1975 season, when the club slipped to fifth place and attendance dropped under 1 million, Mauch was fired. In his seven years in Montreal, the team never had a winning record or finished higher than fourth. He was replaced by Karl Kuehl, who had managed the franchise's Triple-A minor-league team. But Kuehl did not last long. Charlie Fox, the Expos' new general manager, fired him after just 128 games and took over as manager. The Expos managed just 55 wins, their second-worst record in history. Attendance fell to 646,704 in 1976, the second lowest in franchise history and the second lowest in the NL that year. To be fair, much of the drop in attendance can be attributed to the warm reception locals gave to the 1976 Montreal Summer Olympics, which overlapped with the Expos' season and drained baseball attendance during the two-week event.

On April 15, 1977, the Montreal Expos played in a new ballpark, the Stade Olympique, built for the 1976 Summer Olympics. The cost of the Olympic facilities, including the stadium, swimming pool, velodrome, and the rest, was well above $1 billion, a tab the people of Quebec are still paying today. The playing field was revamped to make it suitable for baseball, and movable seats were installed, enabling it to double as a football field for the Alouettes. The original dimensions were 325 feet to the foul lines and 404 feet to center field. Opening attendance was 57,592, and most of the fans complained about the view because most seats were far from the field, unlike in cozy Jarry Park. Nonetheless, attendance doubled from the previous season, to 1,433,757.

The original intent was to enclose the structure as a way to deal with the cold climate. The 556-foot-high leaning tower that was going to retract the roof was half finished until the roof was completed in 1988. However, the retractable roof did not work properly. It was opened a few times in 1988, but afterward, the Régie des Installations Olympiques (RIO), a provincial government agency in charge of the stadium and other facilities, announced the roof would remain closed indefinitely. In 1998, the Expos played with an open roof the entire season because the original roof was torn down and replaced by a new one for 1999. In September 1999, a 55-ton concrete beam fell down. The authorities closed the stadium for the rest of the Expos' season, and they had to play their 13 remaining home games on the road. The roof is still a problem for the RIO, and a new one is expected for 2006 or 2007.

However, those stadium troubles lay in the future. In 1976 the Expos planned to bring a new image to the team along with a new stadium. Dick Williams was brought in to manage. Williams coached the Expos in 1970 and then departed the next year to manage the Oakland A's, where he led the team to three consecutive division titles and two World Series wins in 1972 and 1973. Veterans Tony Perez, Dave Cash, and Chris Speier were added in the off-season to help the younger players to establish themselves in the major leagues, among other more obvious reasons. In 1978 Ross Grimsley became the first Expo to win 20 games (out of a total of 78 team victories), and is the lone pitcher in team history to accomplish that feat. The Expos contended in 1979, winning 95 games that season, the club's high-water mark to date, but finished two games back of Pittsburgh. Pitching was the team's strong suit, leading the NL with a 3.14 team ERA. Winning play on the field energized fan interest, and attendance rose to 2,102,173. The club's record dropped by 5 in 1980 to 90 wins, putting them second in the NL East and finishing one game behind division-winning Philadelphia.

A popular innovation in Montreal baseball in 1979 was the creation of a mascot. Copying the San Diego Chicken (1974) and Phillie Phanatic (1978), "Youpi" ("Yippee" or "Hooray" in French) was a huge orange figure clad in an Expos uniform with an exclamation point on his back instead of a number. Youpi was very popular with children, who enjoyed him wildly running around during the games. Youpi has the distinction of being the first mascot ejected from a game. On August 23, 1999, he was tossed in the 11th inning after Dodgers manager Tom Lasorda complained about his dancing on top of the visitor's dugout.

HIGH HOPES IN THE 1980s

In 1981 there was a split season following the players' strike. The Expos finished with an overall record of 60–48, good enough for second place the NL East. They placed third in the first half (30–25) of the split season and won the second half (30–23), under the guidance of Jim Fanning, who had replaced Williams as manager. MLB decreed that the winner of each half season would meet in divisional finals before the league finals. As a result, Montreal played first-half leader and defending World Series champions Philadelphia for the divisional championship. On a complete-game shutout by ace Steve Rogers, the Expos captured their only division championship, beating the Phillies 3–0 in the decisive fifth game of the best-of-five series. Then they met the Dodgers in the NL Championship Series. After splitting the first two games in Los Angeles, the Expos took the third back in Montreal. One more win, and the Expos were in the World Series for the first time. But the Dodgers won game four 7–1 to force a fifth and final game. Expo fans remember this game as "Blue Monday." On October 19, a Monday night, the game was tied at 1–1 at the top of the ninth inning. Instead of using closer Jeff Reardon, Jim Fanning gambled by sending Steve Rogers in to relieve Ray Burris. The gambit failed when Dodgers right fielder Rick Monday hit a long solo home run off Rogers to give Los Angeles a 2–1 lead, the victory, and the NL championship, sending 36,491 Expo fans home crying that night.

Montreal was a hotbed of baseball interest in the early 1980s. Home attendance surpassed 2.3 million in 1982 and 1983. The Expos averaged 28,600 fans per game, the most in team history. On July 13, 1982, the All-Star Game was played at the Stade Olympique, the first time that spectacle had been held outside of the United States. Five Expos were named as NL All-Stars, four as starters: Gary Carter, Steve Rogers, Tim Raines, Andre Dawson, and Al Oliver. A total of 59,057 spectators saw the NL defeat the AL 4–1.

The Expos came in a disappointing third in 1982 despite a very fine offense led by first baseman Al Oliver, who led the NL in batting (.331) and RBIs (109), and excellent pitching, anchored by Steve Rogers, who was 19–8 with a league-leading 2.40 ERA. Fanning turned over the managerial reins to Bill Virdon for the 1983 season so he could return to the front office. The club again came in third but dropped to a record of 82–80. Andre Dawson was the team's star. The former Rookie of the Year (1977) had 32 homers and 113 RBIs, batted .299, and led the NL with 189 hits and 341 total bases. He also was a brilliant out-fielder who captured six straight Gold Gloves with the Expos.

The Expos went backward again in 1984, finishing fifth while compiling a losing record of 78–83 despite having one of the strongest pitching staffs in the NL. Fanning returned as manager for the last third of the season. Before the season started, the club signed Pete Rose, who reached his 4,000th hit against Philadelphia on April 13, 1984. He was traded later that season to Cincinnati.

Buck Rodgers took over as manager in 1985. The team underwent a big change before the season when Gary Carter was traded to the New York Mets for youngster pitcher Floyd Youmans, catcher Mike Fitzgerald, infielder Hubie Brooks (who drove in 100 runs in 1985 and hit .340 in 1986), and outfielder Herm Winningham. The Expos had a good season in 1985, finishing third in the East with a winning record of 84–77. Speedster outfielder Tim Raines caused much excitement that year, stealing 70 bases (and another 70 the following season), while pitcher Bryn Smith had a career year, going 18–5 with a 2.91 ERA. The club fell to fourth in 1986 with a losing record (78–83), but bounced back the following year, winning 91 games and finishing in third place, a mere three games behind the front-running St. Louis Cardinals. Third baseman Tim Wallach drove in 123, and Tim Raines hit .330 or more for the second straight year. In 1988 the Expos came in third for the third straight year (81–81). The offense struggled, but the pitching was superb, with a team ERA of 3.08, led by Pascual Perez (2.44) and Dennis Martinez (2.72). The mediocrity continued in 1989 (81–81) with a fourth-place finish, but a slight improvement the following year raised them to third (85–77), with the best pitching in the NL.

In the late 1980s the team was estimated to be worth $74 million, second lowest to Seattle in the majors, and it subsequently remained at or near the bottom. In 1991, the club foundered, and ended in sixth (71–90). Rodgers was fired a third of the way through the season and replaced by Tom Runnells. Runnells couldn't stop the bleeding, and the Expos finished last in the NL East. The only bright spot was veteran hurler Martinez, who pitched a perfect game against the Dodgers on July 28 and led the NL with a 2.39 ERA.

FELIPE ALOU AND THE EXPOS

A few weeks into the 1992 season Runnells was ousted in favor of Felipe Alou, a former star player who briefly played for the Expos in 1973. Alou had worked as a batting coach and minor-league manager for the Expos organization after his playing career was over. Under Alou, the Expos relied heavily on younger players like Larry Walker, Marquis Grissom, Pedro Martinez, and rookie Moises Alou, Felipe's son. Gary Carter returned to Montreal in 1992 after a successful stint with the New York Mets. As a sidebar, in 2003 Carter became the first Expo elected to the Baseball Hall of Fame. Alou did a great job right off the bat, bringing the club to second place (87–75), led by his excellent pitching staff, and repeating their second-place finish in 1993, despite having a weak offense. Closer John Wetteland hurled 37 saves in 1992 and 43 in 1993.

In 1994 everything came together for the Expos, but the players' strike destroyed it all. When the work stoppage began on August 12 the Expos owned the best record in the major leagues, 74–40. But there was no more baseball played that season and no World Series. Led by Alou and Walker, the team had one of the strongest lineups in the game, and the club's pitching was again the league's best. Felipe Alou was named Manager of the Year.

Just when it seemed Montreal was on the verge of greatness, management decided to cut costs for fear of losing more money after the strike-shortened 1994 season. Claude Brochu, president of the club since 1991 when he and other local investors bought the team from Bronfman, traded highly paid stars Ken Hill, John Wetteland, Marquis Grissom, and Larry Walker. The team had consistently drawn poor attendance numbers and was among the worst draws in the NL, never finishing higher than eighth starting in 1984. Even when the Expos fielded a championship-caliber team, they struggled at the gates and were 11th out of 14 NL teams by averaging just 24,543 per game. The trades marked the beginning of the end for the Expos, and in 1995 the team finished a dismal fifth (66–78). Yet they returned to respectability a year later, churning out 88 wins against 74 losses, a result of the team tapping into its excellent farm system.

Brochu suggested building a new stadium in downtown Montreal with the help of the federal and provincial governments and put forward the plans for the stadium in 1996, having secured some financial approbation from the provincial government. But the people and most politicians in Quebec did not support using public funds to help professional sports. The Canadiens had built their own arena in 1996 with their own money, and the public could not understand why the Expos felt entitled to public funding another, more storied, Canadian sports franchise did not need.

The team fell back to fourth in 1997, and another losing record. The team was bolstered by a brilliant rookie, 21-year-old Vladimir Guerrero, who hit .302, and by hurler Pedro Martinez, who went 17–9 with a sizzling 1.90 ERA and 305 strikeouts. Martinez won the Cy Young Award, but after the season was traded to the Boston Red Sox. The payroll dropped from $18.3 million in 1997 to just $8 million in 1998. That season, Alou's crew finished 41 games out of first place, with just 65 victories. The batting was the worst in the NL despite Guerrero's 109 RBIs. The Expos repeated in fourth in 1999 and 2000 (68 and

67 wins, respectively), even though Guerrero hit .316 with 42 homers and 131 RBIs in 1999, and .345 with 44 homers and 123 RBIs in 2000.

JEFFREY LORIA TAKES CHARGE OF THE EXPOS

After three years of negotiations for a new ballpark Brochu gave up trying and looked to sell out. The 11 Canadian limited partners sought an outside investor and a new managing partner. They turned to Jeffrey Loria, a New York art dealer who had previously owned the Triple-A Oklahoma City 89ers and had tried to buy the Orioles in 1993. He obtained a 24 percent share for $12 million. Stephen Bronfman and Canadian billionaire Jean Coutu also joined the team. Loria named his stepson David Samson as vice president.

Hopes ran high in Montreal with Loria's arrival. But he did business without consulting his partners, and the Expos made little forward motion—so little, in fact, that rumors spread that Loria had made a deal with Commissioner Bud Selig to disband the team or sell it later to another owner who would move it elsewhere. But these were only speculations, and no proof was ever uncovered.

When Loria and Samson took over, no agreement was reached for a TV deal, and the only media outlet in 2000 was on a French radio station. Almost no marketing was done to bring fans to Olympic Stadium. During Loria's two years in town, the Expos were almost absent from the media, both French and English. Some observers felt he had little interest in staying in Montreal. He invited Maury Wills and Jeff Torborg to work as spring-training instructors without consulting Alou. Loria stirred up a fan revolt when he fired the popular Alou midway through the 2001 season and replaced him with his friend Torborg. Alou had spent 27 seasons with the Expos as a player, minor-league manager, and Expos manager. The inexperienced team foundered in fifth place (68–94) and attendance plummeted to 642,705, the lowest in team history.

The payroll more than doubled from $15 million in 1999 to $36 million in 2000, which led to higher losses. He made initiated capital calls on his partners to meet operating expenses, which they did not meet. The partners claimed that Loria had "misrepresented important facts in an effort to destroy Major League Baseball in Montreal." The partners criticized his decisions to pull the Expos off local media and TV and to stop comping sponsors, and asserted he had undermined plans for a new stadium for which they had a site, $8 million in annual tax relief from the province, and $5 million a year from Quebec for the interest on a planned $67 million bond. Loria put up $18 million himself for the team's expenses, which set off a clause in the partnership agreement that permitted him to dilute the other owners' shares down to six percent. Consequently, he gained control of 94 percent of the team at a cost of about $30 million. On February 1, 2002, Loria sold the team to MLB for $120 million and used the money to buy the Florida Marlins for $158.5 million. No one in Montreal had expressed interest in buying the floundering team, which was a candidate for contraction until the Players Association blocked that in a grievance case. Once MLB took over the Expos, there was very little change from the Loria regime. There was no marketing and no television deals, only radio broadcasts.

THE TEAM NO ONE WANTED

Washington Nationals manager Frank Robinson tips his hat to the crowd as he is introduced during their home opener against the Arizona Diamondbacks, 2005. © AP / Wide World Photos

For three more seasons the Expos were the team nobody wanted. Almost nothing was done in Montreal to advertise the home games. Montreal continued its streak of having the lowest attendance in the NL since 1998. Under new manager Frank Robinson the Expos did surprisingly well in 2002, coming in second, but drew only 812,045 at home. The team still had some very good players, like pitchers Bartolo Colon and former Expos farmhand Javier Vazquez, along with $8 million superstar Guerrero, who hit .336 with 39 homers and 111 RBIs and led the league in hits and total bases. In 2003, splitting the season between Montreal and 22 games at San Juan's Hiram Bithorn Stadium, the club still managed to finish with a winning record. It was the only season since 1994 that attendance had surpassed 1 million. The team's payroll was $41,197,500, fifth lowest in the majors.

At the start of the 2004 season, Forbes valued the team at $145 million, half of what the average team was worth. In 2004, with Vazquez traded to the Yankees and Guerrero gone to the Angels as a free agent, the club collapsed and finished fifth with just 67 wins. Everyone in Montreal wanted to know when the team would be sold or moved. When rumors of a possible move to Washington were made public in 2003, people in Montreal were skeptical, because a new owner had not been secured. How could you move a team without any assurance of someone ready to buy it? And was there a city ready to build a new stadium for the team? It was understandable that MLB was ready to move the team, but where, and with what conditions?

Juan Rivera walks off the field before a sparse crowd at Montreal's Olympic Stadium after a game in 2004. © AP / Wide World Photos

Finally, the announcement came on September 29, 2004, that the Expos were moving to Washington, DC, right after their last home game, not giving a chance to the Montreal fans to say goodbye to the players and team. The Washington city council approved the move and the use of RFK Stadium for the new team. The suit by Canadian owners against Loria and Selig came to an end in December 2004, freeing the club to move. The new Washington Nationals had a $48,581,500 roster, and after threatening to make the playoffs, ended the season in last place, with the weakest offense in the league. Yet the squad finished with a very respectable .500 record in the very competitive NL East. Fan support was outstanding, with 2,693,123 people going to the games.

The ownership is still in the hands of MLB, seeking to sell the franchise for at least $300 million. Plans are underway for a new ballpark to open in 2008 at a cost originally pegged at $440 million, to be financed entirely by city bonds, scheduled to be paid off by in-stadium taxes on tickets, concessions, and merchandise; a new tax on businesses with over $3 million in gross receipts; and $5.5 million yearly rent from the team.

NOTABLE ACHIEVEMENTS

Cy Young Winners

Year	Name	Position
1997	Pedro Martinez	RHP

Chad Cordero pitches during the 2005 MLB All-Star Game. © AP / Wide World Photos

Rookies of the Year

Year	Name	Position
1970	Carl Morton	P
1977	Andre Dawson	OF

Batting Champions

Year	Name	#
1982	Al Oliver	.331
1986	Tim Raines	.334

ERA Champions

Year	Name	#
1982	Steve Rogers	2.40
1991	Dennis Martinez	2.39
1997	Pedro Martinez	1.90

No-Hitters (Italics = Perfect Game)

Name	Date
Bill Stoneman	04/17/1969
Bill Stoneman	10/02/1972

| Charlie Lea | 05/10/1981 |
| *Dennis Martinez* | *07/28/1991* |

POSTSEASON APPEARANCES

NL East Division Titles

Year	Record	Manager
1981	60–48	Dick Williams
		Jim Fanning
1994	74–40	Felipe Alou

MANAGERS

2002–	Frank Robinson
2001	Jeff Torborg
1992–2001	Felipe Alou
1991–1992	Tom Runnells
1985–1991	Buck Rodgers
1984	Jim Fanning
1983–1984	Bill Virdon
1981–1982	Jim Fanning
1977–1981	Dick Williams
1976	Charlie Fox
1976	Karl Kuehl
1969–1975	Gene Mauch

Team Records by Individual Players

Batting Leaders

	Single Season			Career		
	Name		Year	Name		Plate Appearances
Batting average	Vladimir Guerrero	.345	2000	Vladimir Guerrero	.323	4,220
On-base %	Mike Jorgenson	.444	1974	Rusty Staub	.402	2,163
Slugging %	Vladimir Guerrero	.664	2000	Vladimir Guerrero	.588	4,220
OPS	Vladimir Guerrero	1.074	2000	Vladimir Guerrero	.978	4,220
Games	Rusty Staub	162	1971	Tim Wallach	1,767	7,174

(Continued)

Batting Leaders   (Continued)

	Single Season			Career		Plate
	Name		Year	Name		Appearances
At bats	Cromartie	659	1979	Tim Wallach	6,529	7,174
Runs	Tim Raines	133	1983	Tim Raines	947	6,256
Hits	Vladimir Guerrero	206	2002	Tim Wallach	1,694	7,174
Total bases	Vladimir Guerrero	379	2000	Tim Wallach	2,728	7,174
Doubles	Grudzielanek	54	1997	Tim Wallach	360	7,174
Triples	Tim Raines	13	1985	Tim Raines	82	6,256
Home runs	Vladimir Guerrero	44	2000	Vladimir Guerrero	234	4,220
RBIs	Vladimir Guerrero	131	1999	Tim Wallach	905	7,174
Walks	Ken Singleton	123	1973	Tim Raines	793	6,256
Strikeouts	Andres Galarraga	169	1990	Tim Wallach	1,009	7,174
Stolen bases	Ron LeFlore	97	1980	Tim Raines	635	6,256
Extra-base hits	Vladimir Guerrero	84	1999	Tim Wallach	595	7,174
Times on base	Vladimir Guerrero	296	2002	Tim Raines	2,440	6,256

Pitching Leaders

	Single Season			Career		Innings
	Name		Year	Name		Pitched
ERA	Pedro Martinez	1.90	1997	Tim Burke	2.61	600.3
Wins	Ross Grimsley	20	1978	Steve Rogers	158	2,837.7
Won-loss %	Bryn Smith	.783	1985	Pedro Martinez	.625	797.3
Hits/9 IP	Pedro Martinez	5.89	1997	Pedro Martinez	7.00	797.3
Walks/9 IP	Bryn Smith	1.45	1988	Carlos Perez	1.92	511.3
Strikeouts	Pedro Martinez	305	1997	Steve Rogers	1621	2,837.7
Strikeouts/ 9 IP	Pedro Martinez	11.37	1997	Pedro Martinez	9.52	797.3
Games	Mike Marshall	92	1973	Tim Burke	425	600.3
Saves	C. Cordero	47	2005	Jeff Reardon	152	506.3
Innings	Steve Rogers	301.7	1977	Steve Rogers	2,837.7	2,837.7
Starts	Steve Rogers	40	1977	Steve Rogers	393	2,837.7
Complete games	Bill Stoneman	20	1971	Steve Rogers	129	2,837.7
Shutouts	Bill Stoneman	5	1969	Steve Rogers	37	2,837.7

Source: Drawn from data in "Washington Nationals Batting Leaders (seasonal and career)." http://baseball-reference. com/teams/WSN/leaders_bat.shtml; "Washington Nationals Pitching Leaders (seasonal and career)." http://baseball-reference.com/teams/WSN/leaders_pitch.shtml.

BIBLIOGRAPHY

Ballparks of Baseball. "Olympic Stadium." http://www.ballparksofbaseball. com/nl/Olympic%20Stadium.htm.

Brochu, Claude. *My Turn at Bat: The Sad Saga of the Expos*. Toronto: ECW Press, 2002.

CBC Sports. "Au Revoir, Expos: Key Dates in Expos History." CBC Sports Online, September 29, 2004. http://www.cbc.ca/sports/indepth/expos/ timeline.html.

———. "Au Revoir, Expos: Top 10 Expos Moments." CBC Sports Online, September 29, 2004. http://www.cbc.ca/sports/indepth/expos/top10.html.

Gallagher, Danny, and Bill Young. *Remembering the Montreal Expos*. Toronto: Scoop Press, 2005.

"History of the Expos." http://montreal.expos.mlb.com/NASApp/mlb/mon/ history/mon_history_feature.jsp?story=1.

"Montreal Expos." http://www.sportsencyclopedia.com/nl/mtlexpos.expos.html.

Munsey and Suppes. "RFK Stadium." Ballparks. http://www.ballparks.com/ baseball/american/rfksta.htm.

Post, Paul V. "Origins of the Montreal Expos." *Baseball Research Journal* 22 (1993): 107–10.

Sarault, Jean-Paul. *Les Expos, cinq ans après (The Expos: Five Years Later)*. Montreal: Editions de l'Homme, 1974.

Thorn, John, and Pete Palmer, eds. *Total Baseball*. New York: Warner Books, 1989.